CURRENT ABBREVIATIONS

CURRENT ABBREVIATIONS

George Earlie Shankle, Ph.D.
Head of the Department of English
Mary Washington College of the
University of Virginia

THE H . W . WILSON COMPANY
NEW YORK — NINETEEN HUNDRED FORTY-FIVE

Published January 1945
Printed in the United States of America

This complete edition is produced in full compliance with the Government's regulations for conserving paper and other essential materials.

PREFACE

The American people are in the midst of an era of abbreviations. Much of the English used both in speaking and in writing clips off so much of the essential forms of words or of sentence structure that it becomes almost unintelligible. Teachers and students of chemistry, and chemists have long used an abbreviated language; for example, they do not speak of water, but of H_2O, or of Sulphuric Acid, but of H_2SO_4. Today, however, one finds newspapers, magazines, business or trade journals, governmental agencies and bureaus, and people in general conversation using an abbreviated language almost as technical as chemical formulas. People in various trades and occupations are continually adding new combinations for brevity. They speed the day's work for the initiated, but for others they may cause hopeless confusion.

This publication lists the abbreviated forms of the names of governmental bureaus and administrative agencies; civil, political, and religious organizations; symbols for Greek letter fraternities and sororities; abbreviations of college degrees; usual commercial terms; the more common musical terms; and those of other well-known expressions. In music, medicine, science, and other fields of learning where there are special technical glossaries and dictionaries, only the more generally known and used terms are included her.

According to the English spelling of their Greek initials, the national Greek letter fraternities and sororities are alphabeted at the end of the regular list of abbreviations under the various letters of the alphabet.

There is a noticeable tendency to write abbreviations with small letters, and many of the initials are written with lower case and with capital letters, often with a different meaning for each. It will be noted that in army usage both terms and abbreviations for them are capitalized, and no period is used after the abbreviated form.

Where a word is abbreviated in more than one way, all the ways are given each time one of them appears in its proper alphabetical order. This is true also of the Latin, French, German, and abbreviations in other languages which are included in this book.

In print, the Benevolent and Protective Order of Elks is B.P.O.E.; Free and Accepted Masons is F.A.M. or F. & A.M.; absent without leave is a.w.o.l; Government Issue is G.I.; and there are hundreds of other initial forms. People often do not know what this abbreviated language means. It was to provide this needed information that the author compiled this dictionary.

The letters c and o may be combined to read CO., or C.O., co., c.o., C/O or c/o. There are about twenty-one definitions of the c and o combinations.

If Co. stands for company, so do co., Compa., compa., Compy., compy., Coy., coy. or Cia. (compania, Spanish), cie (compagnie, French), and Ges. (Gessellschaft, German).

Co stands for county, so do co., ct. and Cy. Reversing the C and O to OC (with variations in capitalization and punctuation) there are fourteen possible interpretations: office of censorship, ocean, opere citato, old crop, overcharge, o'clock, etc.

These examples from the book clearly indicate the need for a compilation of this nature, all in one alphabet. The number of possible combinations of twenty-six letters is astronomical, but the author feels that it has been approached.

For five years or more the author has collected this alphabetical assemblage from current newspapers, magazines, books, and other sources. The more recently published dictionaries and encyclopedias contain both old and newly coined abbreviations; but they are by no means complete because such books do not attempt to include all of these forms and because of the rapidity with which new forms are created.

Although the author searched through available books and other publications, had collections of abbreviations in the larger libraries photostated and sent to him, collected these forms from manuals issued by the War Department and from other military publications, likely he did not find all abbreviations in use today, for such an undertaking is like searching for a needle in a haystack; but he has assembled in one volume—allowing for possible omissions—the abbreviations used by English speaking people, which heretofore were partly available only in publications of various sorts.

Grateful acknowledgement is hereby made to the librarians of the Library of Congress in which much of the research was done; the librarians of several Carnegie libraries; the librarians of the E. Lee Trinkle Library at Mary Washington College of the University of Virginia; Vivian Henderson, Railroad Traffic Manager at Fredericksburg, Virginia; James L. Fly, Chairman of the Federal Communications Commission; Miss Alberta Worthington and others of The H. W. Wilson editorial staff who checked the manuscript, using their collection of reference books and abbreviations from major reference fields; and to all others who contributed suggestions or source material, and especially to the following persons who assisted with the clerical work and in typing or in checking the manuscript: Mrs. Levera Hume of Nashville, Tennessee, Miss Miriam Cornforth Clark of West Springfield, Massachusetts, Mrs. H. Milton Garrison, Jr., of Fredericksburg, Virginia, and Miss Jean Sherwin Bailey, also of Fredericksburg.

July 1944 G. E.S.

Current Abbreviations

A argon (Chem.)

A, A°, Å, A.U., Å.U., A.u., Å.u., a.u. or **å.u.** angstrom unit (Physics)

A. Academician; acetum; (Absolvo)(Lat.) I absolve

A. or **a.** arteria

A., a., An., an. (annus)(Lat.), **J.** (Jahr) (Ger.), **r.** (rok)(Pol.), **y.** or **yr.** year

A., a. or **an.** anode

A., a. or **ans.** answer

A., a., Art., art., artill., Arty (Mil.), **Arty.** or **arty.** artillery

A., ab., abr. (abril)(Span., Port.), **Ap., Apl., Apr., ápr.** (április)(Hung.), **av.** (avril) (Fr.) or **Kwiec.** (Kwiecień)(Pol.) April

A., Abs., abs. or **absol.** absolute

A. or **acad.** academy

A. or **Acc.** accommodation

A., Am. or **Amer.** America; American

A. (autor)(Span.), **aut.** (auteur)(Fr.), (autore)(Ital.), **Au., auth., Forf.** (Forfatter) (Dan.), **förf.** (författare, författarinna) (Swed.) or **Verf.** (Verfasser)(Ger.) author

Ā, ā, ĀĀ, āā (ana)(Greek), **p.ae., part. aeq.** or **p.e.** (partes aequales)(Lat.) in equal parts or quantities (cf. sing.)

a, a. or **@** (ad)(Lat.) at

a. amateur; are (Metric); area; assists

a., ab., abt., C., c., cir. or **circ.** (circa, circiter, circum)(Lat.) about (cf. approx.)

a. or **ac.** acre; acres

a. or **acc.** accept; accepted

a. or **act.** active

a., Actg (Mil.) or **actg.** acting

a. or **adj.** adjective

a., ae., aet. or **aetat.** (aetatis)(Lat.) aged; of age

a., aft., aftn., Em. (Eftermiddag)(Dan.), **e.m.** (eftermiddagen)(Swed.), **nachm.** or **Nm.** (Nachmittag)(Ger.) afternoon (cf. P.M.)

a., aft., P. or **p.** (post)(Lat.) after

a., Ag (Chem), **Ar., ar., arg.** (argentum) (Lat.), **s.** or **sil.** silver

a. or **alt.** alto

a. or **amp.** ampere; amperes

a., an. (anno)(Lat.), **a.d.J.** (aus dem Jahre) (Ger.) or **i.J.** (im Jahre)(Ger.) in the year

a., an., Anon. or **anon.** anonymous (cf. ign.; incog.; n.u.)

a., an. (ante)(Lat.) or **bef.** before

a., appd., approv., OK, O.K., OK'd or **O.K.'d** approved

a., as., asym. or **asymm.** asymetric; asymetrical

ā, Ā., ĀĀ, āā (ana)(Greek), **p.ae., part. aeq.** or **p.e.** (partes aequales)(Lat.) in equal parts or quantities (cf. sing.)

A1 first-class

A-1 Personnel officer (Air Forces)(cf. G-1; S-1)

A_2 aortic second sound

A-2 Intelligence officer (Air Forces)(cf. G-2; S-2)

A-3 Plans and training officer (Air Forces) (cf. G-3; S-3)

A-4 Supply officer (Air Forces)(cf. G-4; S-4)

AA (Mil.) or **A.A.** Antiaircraft

AA (autores)(Span.), (autori)(Ital.), **auths.** or **ss.** (scriptores)(Lat.) authors

A.A. achievement age; Actors' Association; American Airlines; Associate in or of Arts; (Augustiniani Assumptionis)(Lat.) Augustinians of the Assumption; Assumption Fathers; Assumptionist Fathers; Assumptioniste (cf. O.R.S.A; O.S.A.); Automobile Association

A.A. or **AA** (Mil.) Antiaircraft

ĀĀ, Ā, ā, āā (ana)(Greek), **p.ae., part. aeq** or **p.e.** (partes aequales)(Lat.) in equal parts or quantities (cf. sing.)

a.a. always afloat (Shipping)

āā, Ā, ā, ĀĀ (ana)(Greek), **p.ae., part. aeq.** or **p.e.** (partes aequales)(Lat.) in equal parts or quantities (cf. sing.)

A.A. 1, 2 or **3** Seaman qualified as 1st, 2nd or 3rd class antiaircraft gunner

AAA Antiaircraft artillery

AAA or **A.A.A.** Agricultural Adjustment Act or Administration or Agency; Amateur Athletic Association; American Athletic Association

AAA, A.A.A. or **A.A. of A.** Automobile Association of America

AAA. or **amm.** amalgama (Chem.)

A.A.A. American Anthropological Association; American Association of Anatomists

aaa. or **amal.** amalgam

AAAA or **A.A.A.A.** Amateur Athletic Association of America

A.A.A.A. American Association of Advertising Agencies

A.A.A.C.E. American Association of Agricultural College Editors

A.A.A.D.S. American Academy of Applied Dental Science

A.A.A.E. American Association for Adult Education

AAAIS Antiaircraft Artillery Intelligence Service

A.A.A.L. or **AAA & L** American Academy of Arts and Letters

A.A.& S.H. Argyll and Sutherland Highlanders

A.A.A.S. or **Am. Ass. Adv. Sci.** American Association for the Advancement of Science

A.A.A.S. or **Amer. Acad.** American Academy of Arts and Sciences

AAC or **A.A.C.** Antiaircraft Command
A.A.C. American Alpine Club; Antarctic Circle; Association of American Colleges; (anno ante Christum)(Lat.) in the [specified] year before Christ
A.A.C.B.M. American Association of Creamery Butter Manufacturers
A.A.C.C. American Association of Cereal Chemists; American Association of Commercial Colleges
A.A.C.R. American Association for Cancer Research; American Association of Clinical Research
A.A.D.C. Air aide-de-camp
A.A.E. American Association of Engineers
A.A.E.E. American Association of Economic Entomologists
AAF or **A.A.F.** Army Air Forces; Auxiliary Air Force
A.A.F.S. American Ambulance and Field Service
A.A.G. Assistant adjutant general; Assistant Attorney General; Association of American Geographers
A.A.G.O. Associate of American Guild of Organists
A.A.I. American Association of Immunologists; Associate of Auctioneers' Institute
A.A.I.C. American Association for International Conciliation
A.A. in Com. Associate of Arts in Commerce
A.A.I.P. & S. American Association of Industrial Physicians and Surgeons
AAIS Antiaircraft Intelligence Service
A.A.I.S.T.W. Amalgamated Association of Iron, Steel and Tin Workers [of America]
A.A.L.L. American Association for Labor Legislation
A.A.M. American Association of Museums
A Amb Serv Army Ambulance Service
A.A.M.C. Association of American Medical Colleges; Australian Army Medical Corps
A.A.M.M.C. American Association of Medical Milk Commissions
A. & A.S.R. or **A.A.S.R.** Ancient and Accepted Scottish Rite (Freemasonry)
A. & C.P. anchors and chains proved (Shipping)
A & F or **A.&F.** August and February (Interest)
A. & F.B.S. or **A.F.B.S.** American and Foreign Bible Society
A. & H. or **a. & h.** accident and health (Ins.)
A. & M. or **A. and M.** Agricultural and Mechanical
A. & M., A. and M. or **H.A. & M.** [Hymns] Ancient and Modern
A & O or **A. & O.** April and October (Interest)
A. & P. [Great] Atlantic & Pacific Tea Company (Chain stores)
A. & W.I. America and West Indies station (Navy)
A.A.M.P.R. American Association of Medico-Physical Research
A.A.M.S. American Air Mail Society
A.A.M.S.W. American Association of Medical Social Workers
A. and M. Apostle and Martyr
A. and M. or **A. & M.** Agricultural and Mechanical
A. and M., A. & M. or **H.A. & M.** [Hymns] Ancient and Modern
A.A.O. American Association of Orthodontists
a.a.O. (am angeführten Orte)(Ger.), **c.l.** (citato loco)(Lat.), **in loc. cit.** (in loco citato)(Lat.), **l.c.** or **loc. cit.** (loco citato) (Lat.) in the place cited (cf. loc. laud.; loc. primo cit.; op. cit.; u.s.)
A.A. of A., AAA or **A.A.A.** Automobile Association of America
A.A.O.N.M.S. Ancient Arabic Order of the Nobles of the Mystic Shrine (Freemasonry)
A.A.O.O. American Academy of Ophthalmology and Otolaryngology
A.A.P. American Academy of Periodontology; Association of American Physicians
A.A.P.B. American Association of Pathologists and Bacteriologists
A.A.P.G. American Association of Petroleum Geologists
A.A.P.S. American Association for the Promotion of Science
A.A.P.S.S. American Academy of Political and Social Science
A.A.P.S.W. American Association of Psychiatric Social Workers
A.A.P.T. American Academy of Physical Therapy
A.A.P.T.O. American Association of Passenger Traffic Officers
A.A.Q.M.G. Acting assistant quartermaster general
A.A.R. Association of American Railroads
A.A.R., A.a.r., a.a.r. or **aar** against all risks (Ins.)
Aar. Aaron
A.A.R.D. American Academy of Restorative Dentistry
A.A.R.S. American Association of Railroad Superintendents
A.A.S. (Acta Apostolicae Sedis)(Lat.) Acts of the Apostolic See; American Antiquarian Society; American Astronomical Society; Auxiliary Ambulance Service
A.A.S. (Academiae Americanae Socius) (Lat.), **F.A.A., F.A.A.A.S.** or **F.A.A.S.** Fellow of the American Academy [of Arts and Sciences]
A.A.S.A. American Association of School Administrators; Astronomical and Astrophysical Society of America [American Astronomical Society]
A.A.S.H.O. American Association of State Highway Officials
A.A.S.R. or **A. & A.S.R.** Ancient and Accepted Scottish Rite (Freemasonry)
A.A.S.S. (Americanae Antiquarianae Societatis Socius)(Lat.) Fellow of the American Antiquarian Society
A.A.T.A. American Animal Therapy Association
A.A.T.G. American Association of Teachers of German

A.A.U. Amateur Athletic Union

A.A.U.P. American Association of University Professors

A.A.U.W. or **A.U.W.** American Association of University Women (cf. A.F.C.W.)

A.A.W.C. Australian Advisory War Council

AB Air base

A.B. Aeronautical Board; Army Book; Assembly bill; axiobuccal (Med.)

A.B. or **a.b.** able-bodied [seaman]

A.B., Abp., abp., Arch., Archbp., Archieps. (Archiepiscopus)(Lat.) or **Erzb.** (Erzbishof)(Ger.) Archbishop

A.B. (Artium Baccalaureus)(Lat.), **B.A.** or **B.ès A.** (Bachelier ès Arts)(Fr.) Bachelor of Arts

A/B, a.-b. (aktiebolag, aktiebolaget)(Swed.), **A.G.** (Aktien Gesellschaft)(Ger.) **A/S** (Aktieselskab, Aktieselskapet)(Dan.) or **S.A.** (Sociedad Anómina)(Span.) joint stock company (cf. Ges., G.m.b.H.; S.en C.)

Ab alabamine (Chem.); the pure albite molecule (Petrog. and Mineral.)

Ab., Abb. or **abb.** abbot

a.B. (aug Befehl)(Ger.) by order; (auf Bestellung)(Ger.) on order (Commerce)

ab. absent

ab., a., abt., C., c., cir. or **circ.** (circa, circiter, circum)(Lat.) about (cf. approx.)

ab., abb., abbr. or **abbrev.** abbreviation

ab., abr. (abril)(Span., Port.), **A., Ap., Apl., Apr., ápr.** (április)(Hung.), **av.** (avril) (Fr.) or **Kwiec.** (Kwiecień)(Pol.) April

a.-b., A/B (aktiebolag, aktiebolaget)(Swed.), **A.G.** (Aktien Gesellschaft)(Ger.), **A/S** (Aktieselskab, Aktieselskapet)(Dan.) or **S.A.** (Sociedad Anómina)(Span.) joint stock company (cf. Ges., G.m.b.H.; S.en C.)

A.B.A. Amateur Boxing Association; American Bankers Association; American Bar Association; American Binding Association; American Booksellers Association; American Bowlers Association; American Brokers' Association; (Antoniani Benedictini Armeni)(Lat.) Mekhitarists; Mechitarists

A.B.A.J. American Bar Association Journal

abandmt. abandonment (Ins.)

Abb. or **abb.** abbess

Abb., abb. or **Ab.** abbot

Abb. (Abbildung, Abbildungen)(Ger.), **eff.** (effigies)(Lat.), **il., ill(s)., illus.** or **illust.** illustration; illustrations

abb. abbey

abb., ab., abbr. or **abbrev.** abbreviation

abbr., abbrev. or **abgk.** (abgekürzt)(Ger.) abbreviated

abbrev., ab., abb. or **abbr.** abbreviation

abbrev., abbr. or **abgk.** (abgekürst)(Ger.) abbreviated

ABC [Alphabetical] Railway Guide (Brit.)

A B C or **A.B.C.** Audit Bureau of Circulation

A.B.C. Aerial Board of Control (Brit.); American Bowling Congress; American Boxing Club; Argentina, Brazil and Chile; Australian Broadcasting Corporation; Audit Bureau of Circulations (pub.); axiobuccocervical (Med.)

A.B.C.A. Army Bureau of Current Affairs

ABCD or **A.B.C.D.** American-British-Chinese-Dutch [powers or area]

ABCFM or **A.B.C.F.M.** American Board of Commissioners for Foreign Misssions (cf. A.B.F.M.)

A.B.C.L. American Birth Control League

A.B.C.M. American Board of Catholic Missions

abd. abdicate; abdicated

A.B.D.A. American-British-Dutch-Australian [area]

Abdr. (Abdruck, Abdrücke)(Ger.), **c.** or **cop.** copy; copies

A.B.Ed., A.B. in Ed., B.A.E., B.A. in E. or **B.A. in Educa.** Bachelor of Arts in Education

ab ex. (ab extra)(Lat.) from without

A.B.F.M. American Board of Foreign Missions (cf. A.B.C.F.M.)

A.B.F.M.S. American Baptist Foreign Missionary Society

A.B.G. axiobuccogingival (Med.)

abgk. (abgekürst)(Ger.), **abbr.** or **abbrev.** abbreviated

abgk. (abgekürzt)(Ger.) or **abr.** abridged

Abh. (Abhandlung, Abhandlungen)(Ger.), **tr.** or **trans.** transaction; transactions

A.B.H.M.S. American Baptist Home Missionary Society

A.B.I. (Associazione Bibliotecari Italiani) (Ital.) Association of Italian Librarians

A.B. in Bus. and Bank. Bachelor of Arts in Business and Banking

A.B. in Ed., A.B.Ed., B.A.E., B.A. in E. or **B.A. in Educa.** Bachelor of Arts in Education

ab init. (ab initio)(Lat.) or **D.C.** (da capo) (Ital.) from the beginning (cf. ad init.)

A.B. in J., B.A. in J. or **B.A.J.** Bachelor of Arts in Journalism (cf. B.J.)

A.B. in L.S. or **A.B.L.S.** Bachelor of Arts in Library Science

A.B. in S. Sc. Bachelor of Arts in Social Sciences

A.B.I.S.W. Associated Brotherhood of Iron and Steel Workers

A.B.L. axiobuccolingual (Med.)

abl. ablative

abl. abs. ablative absolute

A.B.L.S. or **A.B. in L.S.** Bachelor of Arts in Library Science

A.B.M. Australian Board of Missions

A.B.M.A.C. American Bureau for Medical Aid to China

ABMC or **A.B.M.C.** American Battle Monuments Commission

A.B.M.U. American Baptist Missionary Union

abo. aboriginal

A.B.P. Associated Business Papers

Abp., A.B., abp., Arch., Archbp. Archieps. (Archiepiscopus)(Lat.) or **Erzb.** (Erzbishof)(Ger.) Archbishop

abp., A.B., Abp., Arch., Archbp. Archieps. (Archiepiscopus)(Lat.) or **Erzb.** (Erzbishof)(Ger.) Archbishop
A.B.P.S. American Baptist Publication Society
abr. abridger; abridgment
abr., ab. (abril)(Span., Port.), **A., Ap., Apl., Apr., ápr.** (április)(Hung.), **av.** (avril) (Fr.) or **Kwiec.** (Kwiecień)(Pol.) April
abr. or **abgk.** (abgekürzt) (Ger.) abridged
A.B.S. American Bible Society; American Bureau of Shipping
Abs., A., abs. or **absol.** absolute
Abs., Abschn. (Abschnitt)(Ger.), **Par., par.** or **pár.** (párrafo)(Span.) paragraph
Abs. (Abschnitt)(Ger.), **Abt.** (Abteilung) (Ger.), **S., s., sec.** or **sect.** section
abs. absent
abs., A., Abs. or **absol.** absolute
abs. or **absol.** absolutely
abs. or **abstr.** abstract
Abschn, Abs. (Abschnitt)(Ger.), **Par., par.** or **pár.** (párrafo)(Span.) paragraph
abs. feb. (absente febre)(Lat.) when fever is absent
A.B.S.I. Associate of the Boot and Shoe Industry
absol., A., Abs. or **abs.** absolute
absol. or **abs.** absolutely
abs. re. (absente reo)(Lat.) the defendant being absent (Law)
abstr. abstracted
abstr. or **abs.** abstract
Abt. (Abteilung)(Ger.), **Abs.** (Abschnitt) (Ger.), **S., s., sec.** or **sect.** section
Abt. (Abteilung)(Ger.), **D., Div.** or **div.** division
Abt. (Abteilung)(Ger.) **dep., Dept** (Mil.), **Dept., dept.** or **dpt.** department
Abt. (Abteilung)(Ger.), **H., Hft.** (Heft) (Ger.), **Lfg.** (Lieferung)(Ger.), **liv.** (livraison)(Fr.), **p., pt., T.** or **Th.** (Teil, Theil)(Ger.) part (cf. inst.; no.; sec.)
abt., a., ab., C., c., cir. or **circ.** (circa, circiter, circum)(Lat.) about (cf. approx.)
AB trans. airblast transformer
abut. abutment
abv., f.d. (för detta)(Swed.) or **sup.** (supra) (Lat.) above (cf. prev.; qm.)
Abyss. Abyssinia; Abyssinian
AC (Mil.) or **A.C.** Air Corps
AC (Mil.), **A.C.** or **A.K.** (Armee Korps) (Ger.) Army corps
A.C. Aero Club; air conduction (Med.); Air cooperation; Air Council; Army Cooperation; Alpine Club; Ambulance Corps; Analytical Chemist; appeal court; Arch Chancellor; Artillery College; Atlantic Charter; author's correction; axiocervical (Med.)
A.C., ac, a.c. or **a-c** alternating current (Elec.)
A.C. or **Arty. C.** Artillery Corps
A.C., Assist. Cash. or **Asst. Cash.** Assistant Cashier
A.C. (ante Christum)(Lat.), **av. C.** (avanti Cristo)(Ital.), **B.C., v.Ch.** or **v.Chr.** (vor Christo)(Ger.) before Christ
A-C or **a-c** atriocarotid (Med.); auriculocarotid (Med.)
A/C, a/c, ac., acc. or **acct.** account
A/C, a/c, C/A, Ca/c, C.C., c.c. (compte courant)(Fr.), **c/c** or **c/cte** (cuenta corriente)(Span.) account current; current account
Ac acetyl (Chem.)
Ac or **Act** actinium (Chem.)
Ac. alicyclic (Chem.)
ac, A.C., a.c. or **a-c** alternating current
ac. or **a.** acre; acres
ac., A/C, a/c, acc. or **acct.** account
ac. or **m/a/c** money of account
a.c. (ante cibum)(Lat.) before meals
a.c. (année courante)(Fr.), **d.A.** (dette Aar) (Dan.), **d. J.** (dieses Jahres)(Ger.), **f.é.** (folyó évi)(Hung.) or **h.a.** (hoc anno) (Lat.) this year; the current year
a-c, A.C., ac, or **a.c.** alternating current
a-c or **A-C** atriocarotid (Med.); auriculocarotid (Med.)
a/c, A/C, ac., acc. or **acct.** account
a/c, A/C, C/A, Ca/C, C.C., c.c. (compte courant)(Fr.,), **c/c** or **c/cte** (cuenta corriente)(Span.) account current; current account
A.C.A. Advisory Committee on Allotments; Air Conditioning Association; American Congregational Association; American Cosmeticians Association; Associate [of the Institute] of Chartered Accountants (Brit.); Association of Collegiate Alumnae
AcA, AcB, etc. actinium A; actinium B, etc.
ACAA or **A.C.A.A.** Agricultural Conservation and Adjustment Administration
acad. academic
acad. or **A.** academy
Acad. Nat. Sci. or **A.N.S.** Academy of Natural Sciences
A.C.A.S. Assistant Chief of Air Staff; Atlantic Coast Air Service
A.C.B. American Crisis Biographies
AcB actinum B
ACC or **A.C.C.** Agricultural Credit Corporation
A.C.C. American Construction Council; Anglo Catholic Congress; Army Catering Corps
A/CC or **Acft. C.** Aircraft carrier
Acc. or **A.** accomodation
acc. accompanied; accordant; according; accountant
acc. or **a.** accept; accepted
acc., ac., A/C, a/c or **acct.** account
acc., Acce., Acpt. or **acpt.** acceptance
acc. or **accomp.** accompaniment
acc. or **accus.** accusative
acc., ap. (apud)(Lat.), **if.** (ifølge)(Dan.) or **sec.** (secundum)(Lat.) according to
A.C.C.A. Aeronautical Chamber of Commerce of America
Acc.B., B.Acc. or **B. Acct.** Bachelor of Accounting
Acce., acc., Acpt. or **acpt.** acceptance
acced. (accedit)(Lat.) there follows
accel. (accelerando)(Ital.) gradually faster (Music)

ACCo or **A.C.Co.** American Can Company

accomp. or **acc.** accompaniment

accomp. d. n. (accompagné de notes)(Fr.) accompanied by notes (cf. annot.; ftnt.)

ACCP or **A.C.C.P.** American College of Chest Physicians

Accrd. Int. or **accrd. int.** accrued interest

A.C.C.S. Associate of the Corporation of Certified Secretaries (Brit.)

Acct. or **acct.** accountant

acct., ac., A/C, a/c or **acc.** account

Acct. & Aud. Accountant and Auditor

accum. accumulative

accus. or **acc.** accusative

A.C.D. absolute cardiac dullness (Med.)

A.Cdre. Air commodore

A.C.E. alcohol, chloroform and ether (Med.); Association for Childhood Education

Ac-Em or **Act-Em** actinon; actinon emanation (Chem.) (cf. An)

acet. acetone

A.C.F. American Car and Foundry [Motors Company]

Acft. C. or **A/CC** Aircraft carrier

A.C.G. Assistant chaplain general

A.C.G., Ass. Com. Gen. or **Asst. Commiss. Gen.** Assistant commissary general

A.C.G.I. Associate of the City & Guilds [of London] Institute

A.C.H. Association of California Hospitals

A. Ch. acetylcholine

ACHA or **A.C.H.A.** American College of Hospital Administrators

A.C.H.A. American Child Health Association

ACH index arm girth, chest, depth, hip width index of bodily nutrition

ACI Automobile Club d'Italia

A.C.I. Air or Army Council Instruction; American Concrete Institute

A.C.I.A. Associated Coffee Industries of America (now National Coffee Association); Associate of the Corporation of Insurance Agents

A.C.I.B. Associate of the Corporation of Insurance Brokers

A.C.I.C. Air Corps Information Circular

A.C.I.G.S. Assistant chief of the imperial general staff

A.C.I.S. Associate of the Chartered Institute of Secretaries (Brit.)

ack. acknowledge; acknowledged

ack. or **ackgt.** acknowledgment

ackgt. or **ack.** acknowledgment

A.C.L. American Constitutional League

A.C.L.S. American Council of Learned Societies

A.Cl.S. Additional Clergy Society

A.C.L.U. American Civil Liberties Union

A.C.M. Air Chief Marshal; Air Commerce Manual

A.C.M.A. Air Conditioning Manufacturers Association

A.C.M.F. Australian Commonwealth Military Forces

A.C.N. (ante Christum natus)(Lat.), **A.N.C.** (ante nativitatem Christi)(Lat.) or **v. Chr. G.** (vor Christi Geburt)(Ger.) before the birth of Christ (cf. B.C.)

A.C.N.A. Advisory Council of the National Arboretum

A.C.N.S. Assistant chief of the naval staff

AC of S (Mil.) or **A.C.of S.** Assistant chief of staff

AC of S, G-1 or **G-1** Assistant chief of staff for personnel (cf. A-1; S-1)

AC of S, G-2 or **G-2** Assistant chief of staff for military intelligence (cf. A-2; S-2)

AC of S, G-3 or **G-3** Assistant chief of staff for operations and training (cf. A-3; S-3)

AC of S, G-4 or **G-4** Assistant chief of staff for supply (cf. A-4; S-4)

AC of S,WPD Assistant chief of staff for war planning department

acoust. acoustics

A.C.P. American College of Physicians; Associate of the College of Preceptors (Brit.); Associated Collegiate Press; Association of Correctors of the Press

A.C.P.T. American Congress of Physical Therapy

Acpt., acpt., acc. or **Acce.** acceptance

A.C.R. American College of Radiology

acre-ft. acre-foot or feet

A.C.S. Additional Curates Society; American Ceramic Society; American Chemical Society; American College of Surgeons; American Colonization Society

A/CS or **a/cs** Aircraft security vessel

A.C.S.N. Association of Collegiate Schools of Nursing

A/cs Pay., a/cs pay., AP, A.P. or **A/P** accounts payable

A/cs Rec., a/cs rec., or **A.R.** accounts receivable

A.C.T. Air Council for Training; Australian College of Theology

Act or **Ac** actinium (Chem.)

Act. actuary; actuaries

act. or **a.** active

A.C.T.C. [Bureau of] Air Commerce Type Certificate

Act-Em or **Ac-Em** actinon; actinon emanation (Chem.) (cf. An)

Actg (Mil.), **Actg., actg.** or **a.** acting

Actg. Chf. Acting Chief

Actg. Sec. Acting Secretary

A.C.T.R. Air Corps Technical Report

Act S. or **A.S.** Act or Acts of Sederunt

A.C.U. American Congregational Union; Autocycle Union (Brit.)

A.Cu. alto-cumulus (Meteorol.)

ACW alternating continuous waves (Radio)

AD diphelylchlorarsine (Chem.)

A.D. Air defense; autograph document; average deviation; (auris dextra)(Lat.) right ear

A.D., A/D. or **Adrm** (Mil.) airdrome

A.D. (anno Domini)(Lat.), **A.P.C.N.** (anno post Christum natum)(Lat.), **d.C.** (dopo Cristo)(Ital.), **n.Ch.**, **n.Chr.** (nach Christo)(Ger.) or **n. Chr. G.** (nach Christi Geburt)(Ger.) after Christ; after the birth of Christ; in the year of our Lord

A.D. or **Archd.** Archduke

A/D, A.D. or **Adrm** (Mil.) airdrome

Ad Aldebaranium (Chem.)

Ad. Adam

a. D. (ausser Dienst)(Ger.)(Army), **r., Ret** (Mil.), **ret.** or **retd.** retired

ad. adapted; adaptor; (adde)(Lat.) add

ad. or **add.** (addatur)(Lat.) let there be added

ad. or **adv.** adverb

ad., adv., advert. or **advt.** advertisement

a.d. after date; (ante diem)(Lat.) before the day

ADA or **A.D.A.** Alley Dwelling Authority

A.D.A. American Dental Association (cf. N.D.A.); American Dermatological Association; American Dietetic Association

adag. or **Ad.°** (adagio)(Ital.) slow; slowly; a slow movement between largo and andante (Music)

A.D.B. or **B.D.A.** Bachelor of Domestic Arts

ADC or **A.D.C.** Alaska Defense Command

ADC (Mil.), **A.D.C., A-D-C, A.-D.-C., A.d.c.** or **a.d.c.** aide de camp

A.D.C. Amateur Dramatic Club; axiodistocervical (Med.)

a.d.c., ADC (Mil.), **A.D.C., A-D-C, A.-D.-C.,** or **A.d.c.** aide de camp

AD Comd Air Defense Command

A.D. Corps Army Dental Corps

add. additional

add. or **ad.** (addatur)(Lat.) let there be added

add., Addit. (additio)(Lat.) or **addn.** addition; addendum

add. or **Additt.** (additiones)(Lat.) addenda

add., Additt. (additiones)(Lat.) or **addns.** additions

add., adds., adr. (adress)(Swed.) or **Adrs.** (Adresse)(Ger.) address

Ad def. an. (ad defectionum animi)(Lat.) to the point of fainting (Med.) (cf. Ad deliq.)

Ad deliq. (ad deliquium)(Lat.) to fainting (cf. Ad def. an.)

Addit. (additio)(Lat.), **add.** or **addn.** addendum; addition

Additt. (additiones)(Lat.) or **add.** addenda

Additt. (additiones)(Lat.), **add.** or **addns.** additions

addn., add. or **Addit.** (additio)(Lat.) addition; addendum

addns., add. or **Additt.** (additiones)(Lat.) additions

addns., alts. & reprs. additions, alterations and repairs

Adds., add., adr. (adress)(Swed.) or **Adrs.** (Adresse)(Ger.) address

addsd. addressed

ad eund. (ad eundem [gradum])(Lat.) admitted to same standing or rank [in another college]

ad ex. (ad extremum)(Lat.) to the extreme; to the last

A.D.F. American Dairy Federation

ad fin. or **a.f.** (ad finem)(Lat.) at or to the end; finally

A.D.G. Assistant Director-General; axiodistogingival (Med.)

A.D.G.B. Air Defence of Great Britain

Ad grat. acid. (ad gratum aciditatem)(Lat.) to an agreeable sourness

ad h.l. or **a.h.l.** (ad hunc locum)(Lat.) at this place (cf. ad loc., in loc.)

A.D.I. axiodistoincisal (Med.)

ad inf. (ad infinitum)(Lat.) to infinity

ad init. (ad initium)(Lat.), **in lim.** (in limine)(Lat.), **init.** (initio)(Lat.) or **in pr.** (in principio)(Lat.) at or in the beginning

ad int. or **a.i.** (ad interim)(Lat.) in the interval; in the meantime (cf. pro tem.)

A Dist Air District

Adj. or **adj.** adjourned; adjunct; adjustment (Banking)

Adj. or **Adjt.** Adjutant

a.d.J. (aus dem Jahre)(Ger.), **a., an.** (anno)(Lat.) or **i. J.** (im Jahre)(Ger.) in the year

adj. adjudged

adj. or **a.** adjective

Adj. A. Adjunct in Arts

Adj. Gen., Adjt. Gen. or **A.G.** Adjutant general

Adj Sec Adjutant's section

adj. sp. adjustable speed

Adjt. or **Adj.** Adjutant

Adjt. Gen., Adj. Gen. or **A.G.** Adjutant general

ad l. or **ad loc.** (ad locum)(Lat.) at the place (cf. ad h.l.; in loc.)

a.d. Lat. (aus dem Lateinischen)(Ger.) from the Latin

ad lib. or **ad libit.** (ad libitum)(Lat.) at one's pleasure; freely; to the quantity or amount desired (cf. q. lib.; q. pl.; Q.s.; q.v.)

ad lit. (ad litteram)(Lat.) or **lit.** to the letter; literally (cf. a.v.)

A.D.L.M.A. American Dental Library and Museum Association

ad loc. or **ad l.** (ad locum)(Lat.) at the place (cf. a.h.l.; in loc.)

A.D.M. or **M.D.A.** Master of Domestic Arts (cf. M.D.E.)

Adm. or **adm.** administrative

Adm., adm., admor., admr., adms. or **admstr.** administrator

Adm. or **Adml.** Admiralty

Adm., Adm'l. or **Adml.** Admiral

adm. administration

A.D.M.A. American Drug Manufacturers Association

Adm.Co. or **Adm.Ct.** Admiralty Court

Adm.Ct. or **Adm.Co.** Admiralty Court

A.D.M.I. American Dry Milk Institute

admix., admrx. or **admx.** administratrix

Adml. or **Adm.** Admiralty

Adml., Adm'l. or **Adm.** Admiral
Adm O Administrative orders (Mil.)
admor., Adm., adm., admr., adms. or **admstr.** administrator
admr., Adm., adm., admor., adms. or **admstr.** administrator
admrx., admix. or **admx.** administratrix
A.D.M.S. Assistant Director of Medical Services
adms., Adm., adm., admor., admr. or **admstr.** administrator
admstr., Adm., adm., admor., admr. or **adms.** administrator
admx., admix. or **admrx.** administratrix
A.D.O. Air defense officer; axiodistocclusal (Med.)
Ad°. or **adag.** (adagio)(Ital.) slow; slowly; a slow movement between largo and andante (Music)
A.D.O.S. Assistant Director of Ordnance Services or Stores
A.D.P. or **a.d.p.** Air defense position
A. Dpo. Aircraft depot
Ad pond. om. (ad pondus omnium)(Lat.) to the weight of the whole
Adr. Adrian
adr. (adress)(Swed.), **add., adds.** or **Adrs.** (Adresse)(Dan., Ger.) address
adr. (adress)(Swed.), **Adrs.** (Adresse) (Dan.), **C/o, c/o, c.o.** or **per Adr.** (per Adresse)(Ger.) in care of
Adrm (Mil.), **adrm., A.D.** or **A/D** airdrome
Adrs. (Adresse)(Ger.), **add., adds.** or **adr.** (adress)(Swed.) address
Adrs. (Adresse)(Dan.), **adr.** (adress) (Swed.), **C/o, c.o., c/o** or **per Adr.** (per Adresse)(Ger.) in care of
A.D.S. Advanced dressing station; American Dahlia Society; American Dialect Society; American Druggists' Syndicate
A.D.S. or **a.d.s.** autograph document signed
ads. advertisements
ads., ad s. (ad sectam)(Lat.), **ats., ats.** or **at s.** at [the] suit of (Law)
a.d.s. or **A.D.S.** autograph document signed
A.D.S.A. American Dairy Science Association
A.D.S. & T. Assistant Director of Supplies and Transport
A.D.S.E. American Dental Society of Europe
a.ds.T. (an demselben Tage)(Ger.) or **s.d.** (samma dag)(Swed.) the same day
Adst. feb. (adstante febre)(Lat.) when fever is present (Med.)
ADT Active duty training
ADT. any desired thing (placebo prescription)
A.D.T. American District Telegraph or Telegrapher
A.D.T.A. American Dental Trade Association
A.D.Tn. Assistant Director of Transportation
Ad 2 vic. (ad duas vices)(Lat.) for two doses (Med.)
ad us. or **a.u.** (ad usum)(Lat.) according to custom (cf. sec. us.)
Adv (Mil.) or **adv.** advance
Adv. or **adv.** advent; advice; advise; advocate
Adv. or **advtg.** advertising
adv. adverse (cf. advs.)
adv. or **ad.** adverb
adv., ad., advert. or **advt.** advertisement
adv., advbl. or **advl.** adverbial; adverbially
adv., advs. (adversus)(Lat.), **Agst., Agt., agt., con., cont.** (contra)(Lat.), **V., v.** or **vs.** (versus)(Lat.) against
Ad val., ad val., ad v., a.v. or **A/V** (ad valorem)(Lat.) according to value
advbl., adv. or **advl.** adverbial; adverbially
Adv. Bse. Advanced base
adv. chgs. advance charges
Adv Dep (Mil.) or **Adv. Dep.** Advance depot
advert., ad., adv. or **advt.** advertisement
adv. frt. advanced freight (Shipping)
Adv Gd (Mil.) or **A.G.** Advance guard
Adv. Gen. Advocate General
advl., adv. or **advbl.** adverbial; adverbially
Adv Msg Cen Advance Message Center (Mil.)
A.D.V.S. Assistant Director of Veterinary Services
advs., adv. (adversus)(Lat.), **Agst., Agt., agt., con., cont.** (contra)(Lat.), **V., v.** or **vs.** (versus)(Lat.) against
advt., ad., adv. or **advert.** advertisement
advtg. or **Adv.** advertising
Æ or **A.E.** third-class ship in Lloyd's register
A.E. Agricultural Engineer
Ae. (aes)(Lat.), **C., c., cop., Cu** (Chem.) or **Cu.** (cuprum)(Lat.) copper
ae., aet., aetat. (aetatis)(Lat.) or **a.** aged; of age
a.e. after end (Shipping)
A.E.A. Air Efficiency Award (Brit); American Economic Association; American Export Airlines
A.E. and P. Ambassador Extraordinary and Plenipotentiary
AEB or **A.E.B.** American Ethnology Bureau
A.E.C. American Engineering Council; Army Educational Corps
A.E.E. Association of Economic Entomologists
Ae. E. or **Aero E.** Aeronautical Engineer
AEF or **A.E.F.** American Expeditionary Force or Forces
A.E.F.Sib.Vets. American Expeditionary Force Siberian Veterans
Aeg. (aeger, aegra)(Lat.) the patient (Med.)
aeg. (aeger)(Lat.) ill
aegrot. (aegrotat)(Lat.) he or she is ill
A.E.I.C. Association of Edison Illuminating Companies
A.E.L.T.C. All England Lawn Tennis Club
A-E-M plan Architect-Engineer-Manager plan
aen. (aeneus)(Lat.) made of bronze or copper
A Engr Serv Army Engineer Service
Aeol. Aeolic

A.E.O.S. Ancient Egyptian Order of Sciots
æq. (æqualis)(Lat.) or **eq.** equal
Aer., aero., Aeron. or **aeron.** aeronautics
aer., aero. or **aeron.** aeronautical
A.E.R.A. American Electric Railway Association; American Electronic Research Association
A.E.R.I. Agricultural Economics Research Institute (Oxford)
aero., Aer., Aeron. or **aeron.** aeronautics
aero., aer. or **aeron.** aeronautical
Aero E. or **Ae. E.** Aeronautical Engineer
Aeron., aeron., Aer. or **aero.** aeronautics
aeron, aer. or **aero.** aeronautical
Aero Sq. or **Aer. Sq.** Aero squadron
Aer. Sq. or **Aero Sq.** Aero squadron
A.E.S. American Electrochemical Society; American Electro-Platers Society; American Ethnological Society; American Eugenics Society
A.E.S.C. American Engineering Standards Committee
Aesth. or **aesth.** aesthetic; aesthetics
aet., ae., aetat. (aetatis)(Lat.) or **a.** aged; of age
A.E.U. Amalgamated Engineering Union (Brit.)
AF (Mil.) or **A.F.** (Brit.) Air Force
AF or **Armd F** Armored Force
AF., A.F. or **A.-Fr.** Anglo-French
A.F. Admiral of the Fleet; Agricultural Farm (Australia); Army Form or Forms
A.F., a.f. or **a-f** audio-frequency
Af. or **Afr.** Africa; African
a.f. (actum fide)(Lat.) done in faith; (anni futuri)(Lat.) of the following year; of the next year
a.f. or **ad fin.** (ad finem)(Lat.) at or to the end; finally
a.f. or **a. fir.** firkin of ale
A.F.A. Amateur Football Association; American Foundrymen's Association; American Football Association; American Forestry Association; Associate of the Faculty of Actuaries (Scot.); Auditor Freight Accounts
A.F.A.M. or **A.F. & A.M.** Ancient Free and Accepted Masons (Freemasonry)
A.F.A.S. Associate of the Faculty of Architects and Surveyors
A.F.B. American Foundation for the Blind
A.F.B.F. American Farm Bureau Federation
A.F.B.S. or **A. & F.B.S.** American and Foreign Bible Society
A.F.C. Air Force Cross (Brit.); Auditor Freight Claims
AFCC or **A.F.C.C.** Air Force Combat Command
A.F.C.U. American and Foreign Christian Union
A.F.C.W. American Federation of College Women (cf. A.A.U.W.)
A.F.D. or **D.F.A.** Doctor of Fine Arts
aff. affectionate; affirmative; affirmatively; affirming
aff. or **affly.** affectionately
AFFC or **A.F.F.C.** Air Force Ferrying Command
affly. or **aff.** affectionately
aff.^{ma}, aff.^{mo}, af.^{ma} or **af.^{mo}** (afectísima, afectísimo)(Span.) most affectionate; very truly
afft. affidavit
Afgh. Afghanistan
A.F.I. Associate of the Faculty of Insurance
a.fir. or **a.f.** firkin of ale
A.F.L. or **A. F. of L.** American Federation of Labor
A.F.L.S. American Folk-Lore Society
A.F.M. Air Force Medal (Brit.); American Federation of Musicians
af.^{ma}, af.^{mo}, aff.^{ma} or **aff.^{mo}** (afectísima, afectísimo)(Span.) most affectionate; very truly
A.F.M.R. Armed Forces Master Records
A. F. of L. or **A.F.L.** American Federation of Labor
A.F.R. Auditor Freight Receipts
Afr. or **Af.** Africa; African
AFRA American Federation of Radio Artists
A.F.R.Ae.S. Associate Fellow of Royal Aeronautical Society (London)
Afr. Miss. Soc. or **S.M.A.** (Societas Missionum ad Afros)(Lat.) African Missionary Society (cf. M.A.L.; W.F.)
A.F.S. Airline Feeder System; American Fern Society; American Field Service or Services; American Fisheries Society; Atlantic Ferry Service (R.A.F.); Auxiliary Fire Service
Afs. (Afsender)(Dan.) sender
A.F.T. Auditor Freight Traffic
aft., a., aftn., Em. (Eftermiddag)(Dan.), **e.m.** (eftermiddagen)(Swed.), **Nachm.** or **Nm.** (Nachmittag)(Ger.) afternoon (cf. P.M.)
aft., a., P. or **p.** (post)(Lat.) after
A.F.T.M. Assistant Freight Traffic Manager
aftn., a., aft., Em. (Eftermiddag)(Dan.), **e.m.** (eftermiddagen)(Swed.), **Nachm.** or **Nm.** (Nachmittag)(Ger.) afternoon (cf. P.M.)
aftwd. afterward
aftwds. afterwards
A.F.V. Armoured fighting vehicle or vehicles
A.G. Accountant General; (Adjoint du génie)(Fr.) Assistant engineer officer
A.G. (Aktien Gesellschaft)(Ger.), **A/B, a.-b.** (aktiebolag, aktiebolaget)(Swed.), **A/S** (Aktieselskab, Aktieselskapet)(Dan.) or **S.A.** (Sociedad Anómina)(Span.) joint stock company (cf. **Ges.; G.m.b.H.;** S. en C.)
A.G., Adj. Gen. or **Adjt. Gen.** Adjutant general
A.G. or **Adv Gd** (Mil.) Advance guard
A.G. or **a.g.** Anti-gas
A.G. or **Agt.-Gen.** Agent General
A.G., At.-Gen., Att. G., Att. Gen., Att.-Gen. or **Atty. Gen.** Attorney General

Ag (Chem.), **a., Ar., ar., arg.** (argentum) (Lat.), **s.** or **sil.** silver

Ag., agto. (agosto)(Span., Port.), **Aug.** or **Sierp.** (Sierpień)(Pol.) August

A.g. axiogingival (Med.)

A.G.A. American Genetic Association

A.G.A.E.M. Association of Gas Appliance and Equipment Manufacturers

A.G. & G.M.G. Adjutant general and quartermaster general

a.g.b. a or any good brand

agcy. agency

AGD (Mil.) or **A.G.D.** Adjutant General's Department

A.G.F.A. Assistant General Freight Agent

A.G.I. American Gas Institute

A.G.M.A. Associated Grocery Manufacturers of America

agn. again

AGO or **A.G.O.** Adjutant General's Office

A.G.O. Army general orders

A.G.P.P.A. American Game Protective and Propagation Association

agr., agri. or **agric.** agricultural; agriculture; agriculturist

AGRAP or **A.G.R.A.P.** American Guild of Radio Announcers and Producers

AG-Res Adjutant General's Department Reserve

agri., agr. or **agric.** agricultural; agriculture; agriculturist

agrost. agrostology

A.G.S. American Gladiolus Society; American Gynecological Society

A.G.S. or **Amer.G.S.** American Geographical Society

A.G.S.M. Associate of the Guildhall School of Music

A.G.S.S. American Geographical and Statistical Society; American Gold Star Sisters

Agt. or **agt.** agent; agreement

Agt., agt., agst., adv., advs. (adversus) (Lat.), **con., cont.** (contra)(Lat.), **V., v.** or **vs.** (versus)(Lat.) against

Agt.-Gen. or **A. G.** Agent General

agto. (agosto)(Span., Port.), **Ag., Aug.** or **Sierp.** (Sierpień)(Pol.) August

A.G.U. American Geophysical Union

A.G.V. anilin gentian violet

AGVA or **A.G.V.A.** American Guild of Variety Artists

A.G.W.I. Atlantic, Gulf, West Indies (Shipping)

A.H. after hatch (Shipping); Agricultural Homestead (Australia); (Anno Hebraico)(Lat.) in the Hebrew year; (Anno Hegirae)(Lat.) in the year of the hegira

ah hypermetropic astigmatism

a.h. or **amp.-hr.** ampere-hour; ampere-hours

AHA or **A.H.A.** American Hotel Association

A.H.A. American Historical Association; American Hospital Association; American Humane Association (cf. A.H.S.)

A.H.C. Army Hospital Corps; Associated Harvard Clubs; (ambulances et hopitaux de campagne)(Fr.) Field ambulances and hospitals

A.H.E.A. American Home Economics Association

A.H.I. American Honey Institute

a.h.l. or **ad h.l.** (ad hunc locum)(Lat.) at this place (cf. ad loc., in loc.)

A.H.M.A. American Hardware Manufacturers' Association

A.H.M.S. American Home Missionary Society

a.h.p. air horsepower

AHQ (Mil.), **A.H.Q., A.O.** (Armee Oberkommando)(Ger.) or **Q.G.A.** (Quartier général d'armée)(Fr.) Army headquarters

A.H.Q. Air headquarters

A.H.S. American Horticultural Society; American Humane Society (cf. A.H.A.)

A.H.S. (anno humanae salutis)(Lat.) or **A.S.** (anno salutis)(Lat.) in the year of human redemption; in the year of redemption or salvation

AHT Ancient Hebrew Tradition

a.h.v. (ad hanc vocem)(Lat.) at or on this word

A.H.W.C. Associate of Heriot-Watt College (Edinburgh)

A.I. American Institute; Anthropological Institute; axioincisal (Med.)

A.I. or **A.Inv.** (anno inventionis)(Lat.) in the year of the invention (add 530 years to the Christian year)

a.i. or **ad int.** (ad interim)(Lat.) in the interval, in the meantime (cf. pro tem.)

A.I.A. American Institute of Accountants; American Institute of Architects; Archaeological Institute of America; Associate of the Institute of Actuaries (Brit.)

A.I.A.A. Associate (Architect Member) of the Incorporated Association of Architects and Surveyors

A.I.A.C. Associate of the Institute of Company Accountants

A.I.A.E. Associate of the Institution of Automobile Engineers (Brit.)

A.I.A.S. Associate (Surveyor Member) of the Incorporated Association of Architects and Surveyors

A.I.B. American Institute of Banking

A.I.B.D. Associate of the Institute of British Decorators

A.I.B.N.R.M. American Institute of Bolt, Nut and Rivet Manufacturers

A.I.C. Army Industrial College; American Institute of Chemists; Associate of the Institute of Chemistry [of Great Britain and Ireland]; (Adjoint de l'intendance des troupes coloniales)(Fr.) Commissary Officer of Colonial Troops

A.I.C.A. Associate Member Commonwealth Institute of Accountants

A.I.C.E. American Institute of Chemical Engineers; American Institute of Consulting Engineers

A.I.C.E. or **A. Inst. C. E.** Associate of the Institution of Civil Engineers (Brit.)

A.I.C.L. American Institute of Child Life

A.I.C.L.L. American Institute of Comparative Law and Legislation

A.I.C.P. Association for Improving the Condition of the Poor

A.I.C.S. Associate of the Institute of Chartered Shipbrokers

A.I.D. Army Intelligence Department; Associate Interior Decorator

A.I.E.E. Associate of the Institution of Electrical Engineers (Brit.)

A.I.E.E. or **Am.Inst.E.E.** American Institute of Electrical Engineers

A.I.F. Australian Imperial Force

A.I.Fire E. Associate of the Institute of Fire Engineers

A.I.G. Adjutant inspector general; Assistant inspector general

AIGA or **A.I.G.A.** American Institute of Graphic Arts

A.I.H. American Institute of Homeopathy

A.I.H.S. American Irish Historical Society

A.I.I.A. Associate of the Institute of Industrial Administration

A.I.I.C.W. American International Institute for Child Welfare

A.I.L. Academy of International Law; Air intelligence liaison; American Institute of Laundering; Associate of the Institute of Linguists

A.I.L.O. Air intelligence liaison officer

A.I.Loco.E. Associate of the Institution of Locomotive Engineers (Brit.)

A.I.M. (Adjoint de l'intendance des troupes métropolitaines)(Fr.) Commissary Officer of Home Troops

A.I.M. & M.E. or **A.I.M.M.E.** American Institute of Mining and Metallurgical Engineers

A.I.Mar.E. or **A.I.M.E.** Associate of the Institute of Marine Engineers (Brit.)

A.I.M.E. or **A.I.Mar.E.** Associate of the Institute of Marine Engineers (Brit.)

A.I.M.E. or **A.I.Mech.E.** Associate of the Institution of Mechanical Engineers (Brit.)

A.I.M.E. or **A.I.Min.E.** Associate of the Institution of Mining Engineers (Brit.)

A.I.Mech.E. or **A.I.M.E.** Associate of the Institution of Mechanical Engineers (Brit.)

A.I. Min.E. or **A.I.M.E.** Associate of the Institution of Mining Engineers (Brit.)

A.I.M.M.E. or **A.I.M. & M.E.** American Institute of Mining and Metallurgical Engineers

A.I.M.T.A. Associate of the Institute of Municipal Treasurers and Accountants (Brit.)

A.I.M.U. American Institute of Marine Underwriters

A.I.N. American Institute of Nutrition

A.I.N.A. or **A.Inst.N.A.** Associate of the Institution of Naval Architects (Brit.)

A.Inst. C.E. or **A.I.C.E.** Associate of the Institution of Civil Engineers (Brit.)

A.Inst. N.A. or **A.I.N.A.** Associate of the Institution of Naval Architects (Brit.)

A.Inst.P. Associate of the Institute of Patentees; Associate of the Institute of Physics (Brit.)

A. Inst.P. or **A.I.P.** American Institute of Physics

A Int Air Intelligence

A Int O Air intelligence officer

A Int Sec Air intelligence section

A. Inv. or **A.I.** (anno inventionis)(Lat.) in the year of the invention (add 530 years to the Christian year)

A.I.O.B. Associate of the Institute of Builders

A.I.P. or **A.Inst.P.** American Institute of Physics

A.I.R. American Institute of Refrigeration

Aira. Airacobra (Airplane)

air hp. air horsepower

Air M. or **A.M.** Air marshal

AIS Artillery Information Service

A.I.S. American Iris Society

A.I.S.A. Associate of the Incorporated Secretaries Association; Associate of the Incorporated Society of Auctioneers

A.I.S.C. American Institute of Steel Construction

A.I.S.E. Association of Iron and Steel Engineers

A.I.S.I. American Iron and Steel Institute; Associate of the Iron and Steel Institute

A.I.S.W. Associated Iron and Steel Workers (Brit.)

A.I.T. Armour Institute of Technology

A.I.T.I. Aero Industries Technical Institute

A.I.U. American Insurance Union

A.I.W.M. American Institute of Weights and Measures

A.J. Associate Justice

A.J.H.S. American Jewish Historical Society

A.J.O.J. April, July, October and January (Interest)

A.K. (Armee Korps)(Ger.), **AC** (Mil.) or **A.C.** Army corps

AKC American Kennel Club

A.K.C. Associate of King's College (London)

A.kr. Austrian kronen

AL., **Anglo-L.** or **Anglo-Lat.** Anglo-Latin

A.L. American Legion; Annual Lease (Australia); (anno lucis)(Lat.) in the year of light (add 4000 years to the Christian year)(Freemasonry); axiolingual (Med.)

A.L. (Artillerie lourde)(Fr.), **H.A.** or **Hv. Arty.** Heavy artillery

A.L. or **a.l.** autograph letter

Al (Chem.) or **alum.** aluminum

al. alley; (alius, alia)(Lat.) other [persons or things]

a.l. (après livraison)(Fr.) after delivery

a.l. (avant la lettre)(Fr.) or **A.T.L.** (avant toute lettre)(Fr.) without lettering; first proof (that is, a print of a stamp or engraving before any inscription or legend has been placed upon it)

A.L.A. American Laryngological Association; American League of Automobilists; American Legion Auxiliary; American Library Association; Associate of the Library Association (Brit.); Automobile Legal Association

A. La. axiolabial (Med.)

Ala. Alabama

A.L.A.A. Associate of the London Association of Certified or Chartered Accountants

A.L.A.C. Abraham Lincoln Association of Connecticut

A.L.A.Jrs. American Legion Auxiliary Juniors

A. La. L. axiolabiolingual (Med.)

A.L.A.M. Association of Licensed Automobile Manufacturers

AL & D or **AL and D** Army List and Directory

AL and D or **AL&D** Army List and Directory

A.L.A.O. Association of Life Agency Officers

Alas. Alaska

A.L.A.W.F. American League Against War and Fascism

ALB or **A.L.B.** Automobile Labor Board

Alb. Albania; Albany; Albert

Alb., Alba. or **Alta.** Alberta (Can.)

Alb. or **Alban.** Albanian

Alba., Alb. or **Alta.** Alberta (Can.)

Alban. St. Albans, in signature of Bishop

Albr. Albrecht

A.L.C. American Life [Insurance] Convention; axiolinguocervical (Med.)

alc., S.V.R. or **s.v.r.** (spiritus vini rectificatus)(Lat.) rectified spirits of wine; alcohol (cf. S.V.T.)

A.L.C.A. American Leather Chemists Association

A.L.C.D. Associate of London College of Divinity

alch. or **alchem.** alchemy

A.L.C.M. Associate of the London College of Music

Alcoa Aluminum Company of America

Ald. Aldine (Bibliog., Typog.)

Ald., Aldm., Aldmn. or **Aldn.** Alderman

Alex. Alexander

Alf. Alfonso

Alf. or **Alfr.** Alfred

A.L.G. Advanced landing ground; axiolinguogingival (Med.)

Alg. Algeria; Algernon

Alg. or **alg.** algebra

A.L.G.P. (Artillerie lourde à grande puissance)(Fr.) Heavy artillery of large caliber

A.L.H. or **A.L. of H.** American Legion of Honor

A.L.I. American Library Institute; Argyll Light Infantry

alk. alkali

Al.-L. Alsace-Lorraine

al.l. (alia lectio, aliae lectiones)(Lat.), **var. lec., vl., vv.ll.** (varia lectio, variae lectiones)(Lat.) or **v.r.** other or variant reading or readings

allg. (allgemein)(Ger.), **G., g., gen.** or **genl.** general; generally

allg. (allgemein)(Ger.) or **univ.** universal; universally

all' ott. (all' ottava)(Ital.) an octave higher than written

allus. allusion; allusive; allusively

A.L.M.A. Association of Limb Manufacturers of America

Almc. almanac; almanacs

Almt (Mil.) or **almt.** allotment

A.L.O. axiolinguocclusal (Med.)

A.L.O.A. Amalgamated Lithographers of America

A.L. of H. or **A.L.H.** American Legion of Honor

Alot Allotted (Mil.)

ALP Ambulance loading post

A.L.P. American Labor Party

A.L.P.A. Air Line Pilots Association

Alph. Alphonso

A.L.R. American Law Reports

A.L.S. Associate of the Linnean Society [of London]

a.l.s. autograph letter signed

Alt. (Altesse)(Fr.) Highness

alt. alteration; alternate; alternating; alternative; alternatively

alt. or **a.** alto

alt. or **H.** (Höhe)(Ger.) altitude (cf. ht.)

Alta., Alb. or **Alba.** Alberta (Can.)

alt. dieb., dieb. alt. (alternis diebus, diebus alternis)(Lat.) or **e.o.d.** every other day

alum. or **Al** (Chem.) aluminum

Alws (Mil.) or **alws.** allowances

A.M. Air Ministry; Albert Medal (Brit.); amperemeter; amplitude modulation; (Aviation militaire)(Fr.) Army Aviation Service; Associate Member; Ave Maria; axiomesial (Med.)

A.M. or **Air M.** Air marshal

A.M. or **a.m.** (ante meridiem)(Lat.) before noon (cf. Fm.)

A.M. or **am.** meter-angle

A.M. or **a.m.** (annus mirabilis)(Lat.) the wonderful year (1666)

A.M. (anno mundi)(Lat.) or **i.J.d.W.** (im Jahre der Welt)(Ger.) in the year of the world (i.e., when the creation of the world is assumed to have been 4004 B.C.)

A.M., M.A. or **M.ès A.** (Maître ès Arts) (Fr.) Master of Arts

AM 1cl Air mechanic, first class

AM 2cl Air mechanic, second class

Am ammonium (Chem.); amyl (Chem.)

Am. Ammunition [party]

Am., A. or **Amer.** America; American

Am. or **am.** ammeter

a.M. or **a/M** (am Main)(Ger.) on the Main [River]

am. ametropia; amplitude (elliptical function); myopic astigmatism

am. or **A.M.** meter-angle

A.M.A. Airline Mechanics Association; American Management Association; American Marketing Association (cf. N.A.T.M.A.); American Medical Association; American Missionary Association; American Municipal Association

AMA or **A.M.A.** American Marketing Administration

A.M.A.C. Arlington Memorial Amphitheatre Commission

Am.Acad.A.L. or **A.A.A.L.** American Academy of Arts and Letters

Amad. Amadeus

amal. amalgamated

amal. or **aaa.** amalgam

Am.Ass.Adv.Sci. or **A.A.A.S.** American Association for the Advancement of Science

A.M.B. or **B.M.A.** Bachelor of Mechanic Arts

Amb (Mil.), **Amb.** or **amb.** ambulance

Amb. ambassador

Amb Co (Mil.) or **Amb. Co.** Ambulance company

Amb Co M Ambulance company, motor

Amb Sec Ambulance section (cf. S.A.S.)

A.M.C. Army Medical Center; Army Medical Corps (now Royal Army Medical Corps); American Mining Congress; axiomesiocervical

A.M.C.I.A. Associate Member of the Commonwealth Institute of Accountants (Australia)

Am Co Ammunition company

A.M.D. Army Medical Department; axiomesiodistal

A.M.D.G. (ad majorem Dei gloriam)(Lat.) to the greater glory of God

Am DP Ammunition distribution point

Am Dp Ammunition dump

A.M.D.S. Association of Military Dental Surgeons

amdt. or **amendt.** amendment

A.M.E. African Methodist Episcopal

AMecz Antimechanized

AMedLab Army medical laboratory

A Med Serv (Mil.) or **A.M.S.** Army Medical Service

amendt. or **amdt.** amendment

Amer., A. or **Am.** America; American

Amer. Acad. or **A.A.A.S.** American Academy of Arts and Sciences

Amer.G.S. or **A.G.S.** American Geographical Society

Amer. Hist. American history

A.M.E.S. American Mosquito Extermination Society

A.M.E.Z. African Methodist Episcopal Zion

A.M.F. American Music Foundation

AMG or **A.M.G.** Allied Military Government

A.M.G. axiomesiogingival

amg. among

A.M.G.O. Assistant Master General of Ordnance

AMGOT or **A.M.G.O.T.** Allied Military Government of Occupied Territory (now AMG)

Amh. mixed astigmatism, myopia predominating

A.M.I. axiomesioincisal

A.M.I.A.E. Associate Member of the Institution of Automobile Engineers (Brit.)

A.M.I.C.E., A.M. Inst. C.E. or **Assoc. M.I.C.E.** Associate Member of the Institution of Civil Engineers (Brit.)

A.M.I.Chem. E. Associate Member of the Institution of Chemical Engineers (Brit.)

amid. amidship

A.M.I.E.E. Associate Member of the Institution of Electrical Engineers (Brit.)

A.M.I.Fire E. Associate Member of Institute of Fire Engineers

A.M.I.Gas E. Associate Member of the Institute of Gas Engineers

A.M.I.L.E. or **A.M.I. Loco. E.** Associate Member of the Institution of Locomotive Engineers (Brit.)

A.M.I.Loco.E. or **A.M.I.L.E.** Associate Member of the Institution of Locomotive Engineers

A.M.I.Mar.E. or **A.M.I.M.E.** Associate Member of the Institute of Marine Engineers

A.M.I.M.E. or **A.M.I.Mar.E.** Associate Member of the Institute of Marine Engineers

A.M.I.M.E. or **A.M.I. Mech. E.** Associate Member of the Institution of Mechanical Engineers (Brit.)

A.M.I.N.A. Associate Member of the Institution of Naval Architects (Brit.)

A.M.I.N.E. Associate Member of the Institute of Naval Engineers (Brit.)

A.M. in Ed. or **M.A. in Ed.** Master of Arts in Education

A.M. Inst. B. E. Associate Member of the Institution of British Engineers

A.M. Inst. C.E., A.M.I.C.E. or **Assoc. M.I.C.E.** Associate Member of the Institution of Civil Engineers (Brit.)

Am. Inst. E.E. or **A.I.E.E.** American Institute of Electrical Engineers

A.M.Inst.T.E. or **A.M.I.T.E.** Associate Member of the Institute of Transport Engineers (Brit.)

A.M.I. Struct. E. Associate Member of the Institution of Structural Engineers (Brit.)

A.M.I.T.E. or **A.M.Inst.T.E.** Associate Member of the Institute of Transport Engineers (Brit.)

A.M.L. American Men of Letters

A.M.L.S. Master of Arts in Library Science

A.M.M. (Asociación Medica Mexicana) (Span.) Mexican Medical Association

A.M.M. or **M.M.A.** Master of Mechanic Arts

amm. or **AAA.** amalgama (Chem.)

amn. amunition

A.M.N.H. American Museum of Natural History

A.M.O. Air Ministry Order
amor. or **amorph.** amorphous
A.M.O.R.C. Ancient Mystical Order of Rosae Crucis (Rosicrusian Order)
AMP Army mine planter
A.M.P. Associated Music Publishers
amp. amperage
amp. or **a.** ampere; amperes
A.M.P.A. Air Mail Pilots of America
A.M.P.C. Auxiliary Military Pioneer Corps
amph. amphibian
amp.-hr. or **a.h.** ampere-hour; ampere-hours
A.M.P.S. Army Mine Planting Service
AMS or **A.M.S.** Agricultural Marketing Service; Army Medical Staff
A.M.S. American Mathematical Society; American Meteorological Society; American Metrological Society; American Microscopical Society; American Museum of Safety; American Medical Service; American Medical Staff
A.M.S. or **A Med Serv** (Mil.) Army Medical Service
AMSC American Marine Standards Committee
A.M.S.E.F. or **a.m. a.m.s.e.f.** Anti-mine-sweeping explosive float
Am. Soc. C.E. or **A.S.C.E.** American Society of Civil Engineers
Am.Soc.M.E., A.S.M.E. or **A.S.Mech.E.** American Society of Mechanical Engineers
Am.Sp. American Spanish
Amst. Amsterdam
A.M.S.U.S. Association of Military Surgeons of the United States
A.M.S.W. Master of Arts in Social Work
amt. amount
Am Tn Ammunition train
A.M.T.P.I. Associate Member of the Town Planning Institute
A.M.W.A. American Medical Women's Association (cf. M.W.N.A.)
AN., A.N. or **A.-N.** Anglo-Norman
A.N. (Artillerie navale)(Fr.) Naval artillery
A.N. or **a.n.** arrival notice (Shipping)
An actinon (Chem.) (cf. Act-Em)
An. anisometropia; Anson (Airplane)
An., an., A., a. (annus)(Lat.), **J.** (Jahr) (Ger.), **r.** (rok)(Pol.), **y.** or **yr.** year
an., A. or **a.** anode
an., A., a., An. (annus)(Lat.), J. (Jahr) (Ger.), **r.** (rok)(Pol.), **y** or **yr.** year
an., a. (anno)(Lat.), **a. d. J.** (aus dem Jahre) (Ger.) or **i.J.** (im Jahre)(Ger.) in the year
an., a., Anon. or **anon.** anonymous (cf. ign. incog.; n.u.)
an., a. (ante)(Lat.) or **bef.** before
a.n. above-named
a.n. or **A.N.** arrival notice (Shipping)
A.N.A. American Nature Association; American Negro Academy; American Neurological Association; American Nursery Association; American Nurses' Association; Association of National Advertisers; Australian Natives Association
A.N.A. or **A.N.A.D.** Associate National Academician; Associate of the National Academy of Design
ana. anastomosing
AN-AC Army-Navy Air Corps [standard]
Anac. Anacreon; Anacreontic
A.N.A.D. or **A.N.A.** Associate of the National Academy of Design; Associate National Academician
anal. analogous; analogy; analyze; analysis; analytic; analyzer
anal. or **analyt.** analytical
Anast. Anastasius
anat. anatomical; anatomist; anatomy
ANC or **A.N.C.** Army-Navy-Commerce Committee on Aircraft Requirements; Army Nurse Corps
A.N.C. (ante nativitatem Christi)(Lat.) **A.C.N.** (ante Christum natus)(Lat.) or **v. Chr. G.** (vor Christi Geburt)(Ger.) before the birth of Christ (cf. B.C.)
anc. or **anct.** ancient; anciently
A.N.C.O.A. Aerial Nurse Corps of America
anct. or **anc.** ancient; anciently
and. (andante) (Ital.) moderately slow (Music)
Anf. (Anfang)(Ger.) the beginning (cf. init.)
A.N.F.M. August, November, February, May (interest)
ANG or **A.N.G.** American Newspaper Guild
Ang. or **Angl.** (Anglice)(Lat.) in English; in the English manner; Anglia; Anglican
ang. angular (Chem.)
ang. (angaaende)(Dan.), (angående) (Swed.), **conc.** or **vedr.** (vedrørende) (Dan.) concerning (cf. abt.)
Ang. Ch. or **Angl. Ch.** Anglican Church
Ang. Ind. or **Anglo-Ind.** Anglo-Indian
Angl. or **Ang.** (Anglice)(Lat.) in English; in the English manner; Anglia; Anglican
Angl. Ch. or **Ang. Ch.** Anglican Church
Anglo-Ind. or **Ang. Ind.** Anglo-Indian
Anglo-Ir. Anglo-Irish
Anglo-Lat., AL. or **Anglo-L.** Anglo-Latin
Ang.Sax., AS., A.S. or **A-S.** Anglo-Saxon
anh. anhydrous
an.hus. animal husbandry
anim. (animato)(Ital.) animated (Music)
Anl Animal (Mil.)
Anl or **Anl-d** Animal-drawn (Mil.)
Anm. (Anmærkning)(Dan.), (Anmerkung, Anmerkungen)(Ger.), **anm.** (anmärkning)(Swed.) or **annot.** annotation; annotations (cf. ftnt.; schol.)
Anm. (Anmærkning)(Dan.), (Anmerkung, Anmerkungen)(Ger.), **anm.** (anmärkning)(Swed.), **ftnt.** or **ftnts.** footnote; footnotes (cf. annot.; schol.)

Anm. (Anmærkning)(Dan.), (Anmerkung, Anmerkungen)(Ger.), **anm.** (anmärkning)(Swed.) or **n.** note; notes (cf. annot.; ftnt.; schol.)

Anm. (Anmærkning)(Dan.), **anm.** (anmärkning)(Swed.), **Obs., obs.,** or **Obsn.** observation

Anm. (Anmærkning)(Dan.), **anm.** (anmärkning)(Swed.) or **rem.** remark

Anm. (Anmerkung, Anmerkungen)(Ger.), **app., appx.** or **apx.** appendix; appendices

ANMB Army and Navy Munitions Board

ann. annals; annual; annuities; annuity

ann. (anni)(Lat.), **y., yr.** or **yrs.** years

annot. annotated; annotator

annot., Anm. (Anmærkning)(Dan.), (Anmerkung, Anmerkungen)(Ger.) or **anm.** (anmärkning)(Swed.) annotation; annotations (cf. ftnt.; schol.)

Ann. Rep. or **ann. rep.** annual report

Annun. Annunciation

Anon., anon., a. or **an.** anonymous (cf. ign.; incog.; n.u.)

ANPA or **A.N.P.A.** American Newspaper Publishers Association

anr. another

A.N.R.C., ARC or **A.R.C.** American National Red Cross

ANS or **A.N.S.** Army Nursing Service

A.N.S. American Numismatic Society

A.N.S. or **Acad. Nat. Sci.** Academy of Natural Sciences

ans. answered

ans., A. or **a.** answer

a.n.s. autograph note signed

A.N.S.S. American Nature Study Society; Associate of the Normal School of Science

Ant. Anthony; Antigua; Antoine; Anton

ant. antonym

ant. or **antiq.** antiquarian

ant., antiq. or **antiqs.** antiquities

ant. frt. anticipated freight

Anth. or **anthol.** anthology

anthrop. or **anthropol.** anthropological; anthropology

anthropom. anthropometry

antilog antilogarithm

Antiq. or **antiq.** antiquary

antiq. or **ant.** antiquarian

antiq., ant. or **antiqs.** antiquities

ant. pit. anterior pituitary

ANZAC, Anzac or **A.N.Z.A.C.** Australian and New Zealand Army Corps

A.O. Army order or orders; (anno ordinis) (Lat.) in the year of the Order [beginning 1118 A.D.] (Knights Templar)

A.O. (Armee Oberkommando)(Ger.), **AHQ** (Mil.), **A.H.Q.** or **Q.G.A.** (Quartier général d'armée)(Fr.) Army headquarters

A.O., A/o., a.o. or **a/o** account of

A.O.A. American Orthopsychiatric Association

A.O.A.C. Association of Official Agricultural Chemists

A.O.C. Air officer commanding; Army Ordnance Corps; Auditor overcharge claims

A.O.C.A. Associated Outdoor Clubs of America

A.O.C.S. American Oil Chemists Society

A.O.D. Ancient Order of Druids (Freemasonry); Army Ordnance Department or Depot

A.O.D.R.A. American Oxford Downs Record Association

A.O.E.R. Army Officers' Emergency Reserve

A.O.F. Ancient Order of Foresters (cf. F. of A.; I.O.F.)

A.O.H. Ancient Order of Hibernians

A.O.M. or **M.O.A.** Master of Obstetric Art

aor. aorist

a/or and/or

A.O.S. American Ophthalmological Society; American Oriental Society; American Otological Society; Ancient Order of Shepherds; Army ordnance stores

A.O.S.E. American Order of Stationary Engineers

A.O.S.S. (Americanae Orientalis Societatis Socius)(Lat.) Fellow of the American Oriental Society

A.O.T.A. American Occupational Therapy Association

A.O.U. American Ornithologists Union

A.O.U.W. Ancient Order of United Workmen

AP or **A.P.** Associated Press

AP, A.P., A/P or **A/cs Pay.** accounts payable

AP or **Ap** Airplane (Mil.)

A.P. Action post; Advanced post; Ammunition point; anterior pituitary; Associate or Associated Presbyterian; automatic pistol; (Avant-poste)(Fr.) Outpost; axiopulpal

A.P. or **a.p.** armor-piercing; author's proof

A/P account paid; authority to pay; authority to purchase

A/P, AP, A.P. or **A/cs Pay.** accounts payable

Ap. Apostle; Appius

Ap., A., ab., abr. (abril)(Span., Port.), **Apl., Apr., ápr.** (április)(Hung.), **av.** (avril)(Fr.) or **Kwiec.** (Kwiecień)(Pol.) April

ap. (apud)(Lat.), **acc., if.** (ifølge)(Dan.) or **sec.** (secundum)(Lat.) according to

a.p. above proof; additional premium; after perpendicular (Shipbuilding)

a.p., Apd. or **a. pd.** assessment paid

a.p., a. pr. (anni praesentis)(Lat.) or **h.a.** (hoc anno)(Lat.) in the present year (cf. d.J.)

A.P.A. Agricultural Publishers Association; American Philological Association; American Philosophical Association; American Physiotherapy Association; American Poultry Association; American Protective Association; American Protestant Association; American Psychological Association

APB or A. P. B. Aircraft Production Board

A.P.C. Allied Purchasing Commission; Army Pay Corps

A.P.C.K. Association for Promoting Christian Knowledge (Church of Ireland)

A.P.C.N. (anno post Christum natum) (Lat.), **A.D.** (anno Domini)(Lat.), **d.C.** (dopo Cristo)(Ital.), **n. Ch., n. Chr.** (nach Christo)(Ger.) or **n. Chr. G.** (nach Christi Geburt)(Ger.) after the birth of Christ; after Christ; in the year of our Lord

A.P.D. Army Pay Department

Apd., a. pd. or **a.p.** assessment paid

A.P.E. Association of Pharmaceutic Employees

Ape. or **Aper.** (aperiens)(Lat.) aperient

A.P.F. Association for the Propagation of the Faith; (Auxiliaries des places fortes)(Fr) Fortress auxiliary troops

A.P.H. Association of Private Hospitals (New York)

A.P.H.A. American Public Health Association; American Protestant Hospital Association

A.Ph.A. American Pharmaceutical Association

A.P.I. American Petroleum Institute

A.P.I.M. Association Professionelle Internationale des Médecines

A.P.L. anterior pituitary lobe

Apl., A., ab., abr. (abril)(Span., Port.), **Ap., Apr., ápr.** (április)(Hung.), **av.** (avril)(Fr.) or **Kwiec.** (Kwiecień) (Pol.) April

A.P.M. Assistant pay master; Assistant provost marshall

A.P.M.G. Assistant Postmaster General

APO or **A.P.O.** American Post Office; Army Post Office

A.P.O. African People's Organization (So. Afr.); Association of Physical Oceanography [of the International Geodetic and Geophysical Union]

apo. or **apog.** apogee

Apoc. Apocalypse

Apoc., Apoch. or **Apocr.** Apochrypha; Apochryphal

apog. or **apo.** apogee

apos. apostrophe

App. Apostles; Appellate

app. appended

app., Anm. (Anmerkung, Anmerkungen) (Ger.), **appx.** or **apx.** appendix; appendices

app. or **appar.** apparatus; apparent; apparently

app. or **appr.** apprentice

app. or **appt.** appoint

app., appt., apptd. or **aptd.** appointed

A.P.P.A. American Paper and Pulp Association

appar. or **app.** apparatus; apparent; apparantly

appd., a., approv., OK, O.K., OK'd or **O.K.'d** approved

App. Div. Appellate Division

appl. applied; applied to; applicable

appln. application

appmt., appnt., appt., apptnt. or **apptt.** appointment

appnt. appmt., appt., apptnt. or **apptt.** appointment

appos. appositive; appositively

appr. or **app.** apprentice

appro. approbation

appro., approv., appval., OK or **O.K.** approval

approv., a., appd., OK, O.K., OK'd or **O.K.'d** approved

approv., appro., appval., OK or **O.K.** approval

approx., C., c., cir. or **circ.** (circa, circiter, circum)(Lat.) approximate; approximately (cf. abt.)

appt. or **app.** appoint

appt., app., apptd. or **aptd.** appointed

appt., appmt., appnt., apptnt. or **apptt.** appointment

apptd., app., appt. or **aptd.** appointed

apptnt., appmt., appnt., appt. or **apptt.** appointment

apptt., appmt., appnt., appt. or **apptnt.** appointment

appval., appro., approv., OK or **O.K.** approval

appx., Anm. (Anmerkung, Anmerkungen) (Ger.), **app.** or **apx.** appendix; appendices

Apr., ápr. (április)(Hung.), **A., ab., abr.** (abril)(Span., Port.), **Ap., Apl., av.** (avril)(Fr.) or **Kwiec.** (Kwiecień)(Pol.) April

ápr. (április) (Hung.), **A., ab., abr.** (abril) (Span., Port.), **Ap., Apl., Apr., av.** (avril)(Fr.) or **Kwiec.** (Kwiecień)(Pol.) April

a.pr., a.p. (anni praesentis)(Lat.) or **h.a.** (hoc anno)(Lat.) in the present year (cf. d.J.)

A.P.R.C. (anno post Roman conditam) (Lat.) in the year after the building of Rome [753 B.C.] (cf. P.R.C.)

APS, A.P.S. or **S.P.A.** (Service de la poste aux armées)(Fr.) Army Postal Service

A.P.S. Aborigines' Protection Society (Brit.); American Peace Society; American Peach Society; American Pediatric Society; American Peony Society; American Philatelic Society; American Philosophical Society; American Physical Society; American Physiological Society; American Protestant Society; Associate of the Pharmaceutical Society (Brit.)

A.P.S.A. American Political Science Association

A.P.S.L. Acting paymaster sub-lieutenant

A.P.S.S. Army Printing and Stationery Services

Apt. or **apt.** apartment

A.P.T.A. American Physical Therapy Association
A.P.T.C. Army Physical Training Corps
aptd., app., appt. or **apptd.** appointed
Apts. or **apts.** apartments
A.P.U.C. Association for Promoting the Unity of Christendom
A.P.W.A. American Public Works Association
apx., Anm. (anmerkung, Anmerkungen) (Ger.), **app.** or **appx.** appendix; appendices
A.Q. achievement quotient (Pedagogy)
Aq, aq or **aq.** (aqua)(Lat.) water
aq. aqueous
aq., Aq or **aq** (aqua)(Lat.) water
aq. astr. (aqua astricta)(Lat.) frozen water
aq. bull. (aqua bulliens)(Lat.) boiling water
aq. com. (aqua communis)(Lat.) common water
aq. dest. (aqua destillata)(Lat.) distilled water
aq. ferv. (aqua fervens)(Lat.) hot water
aq. fluv. (aqua fluvialis)(Lat.) river water
aq. font. (aqua fontana)(Lat.) spring water
A.Q.M. Assistant quartermaster
aq. mar. (aqua marina)(Lat.) sea water
A.Q.M.G. Assistant quartermaster general
aq. niv. (aqua nivialis)(Lat.) snow water
aq. pluv. (aqua pluvialis)(Lat.) rain water
aq. pur. (aqua pura)(Lat.) pure water
aq. tep. (aqua tepida)(Lat.) tepid water
AR (Mil.), **A.R.** or **H.O.** (Heeresordnung) (Ger.) Army Regulations
A.R. analyzed reagent (Chem.) (Brit.); (Artillerie Reglement)(Ger.) Artillery Regulations; autonomous republic; (Anna Regina)(Lat.) Queen Anne
A.R. or **A/cs Rec.** accounts receivable
A.R. or **a.r.** (anno regni)(Lat.) in the year of the reign
A.R., O.R.S.A. or **O.E.R.S.A.** (Ordo Recollectorum Ermemitarum Recollectorum Sancti Augustini)(Lat.) Order of Recollects of St. Augustine; Augustian Recollects; Recollect Augustinian Friars or Hermits (cf. O.S.A.; A.A.)
Ar Arrest [in quarters] (Mil.)
Ar., a., Ag (Chem.), **ar., arg.** (argentum) (Lat.), **s.** or **sil.** silver
Ar. or **Arab.** Arabia; Arabian; Arabic
Ar. or **Aram.** Aramaic
ar aromatic (Chem.)
ar., a., Ag (Chem), **Ar., arg.** (argentum) (Lat.), **s.** or **sil.** silver
ar. or **arr.** arrived
a.r. all rail
a.r., A/R or **a/r** all risks (Marine ins.)
ARA or **A.R.A.** Agricultural Research Administration
A.R.A. Air Reserve Association; American Railway Association; American Relief Administration; American Relief Association
A.R.A.A. or **A.R.A.** Associate of the Royal Academy of Arts (London)
Arab. or **Ar.** Arabia; Arabian; Arabic
arach. arachnology
Ar.Agt. Army agent
A.R.A.M. Associate of the Royal Academy of Music
Aram. or **Ar.** Aramaic
A.R.B.A. American Road Builders Association; Associate of the Royal Society of British Artists
A.R.B.B.A. American Railway Bridge and Building Association (cf. A.R.S.B.B.)
A.R.B.C. Associate of the Royal British Colonial Society of Artists
arbor. arboriculture
A.R.B.S. Associate of the Royal Society of British Sculptors
arbtrn. arbitration
arbtror. arbitrator
ARC., A.R.C. or **A.N.R.C.** American [National] Red Cross
A.R.C. Aeronautical Research Committee (Brit.); Automobile Racing Club
A.R.C.A. Arms Reference Club of America; Associate of the Royal Cambrian Academy; Associate of the Royal Canadian Academy; Associate of the Royal College of Art
ARCCTU, A.R.C.C.T.U., AUCCTU, A.U.-C.C.T.U., VTsSPS or **V.Ts.S.P.S.** (Vsesoîuznyi Tsentralnyĭ Sovet Professionalnyph Soîuzov)(Rus.) All-Russia or All-Union Central Council of Trade Unions
A.R.C.E. Academical Rank of Civil Engineer
ARCEC, A.R.C.E.C., AUCEC, A.U.C.E.C., V.Tz.I.K. (Vserossiisky Tzentralny Ispolnitelny Kommitet)(Rus.) All-Russia or All-Union Central Executive Committee (cf. CEC; Tz.I.K.; UCEC)
Arch., A.B., Abp., abp., Archbp., Archieps. (Archiepiscopus)(Lat.) or **Erzb.** (Erzbishof)(Ger.) Archbishop
Arch., arch., archit. or **Archit.** architecture
arch. archaic; archaism; archery; archipelago; architectural
arch. or **Archt.** architect
archaeol. or **archeol.** archaeology; archeology; archaeological; archeological
Archbp., A.B., Abp., abp., Arch., Archieps. (Archiepiscopus)(Lat.) or **Erzb.** (Erzbishof)(Ger.) Archbishop
Archd. Archdeacon
Archd. or **A.D.** Archduke
Arch. E. Architectural Engineer
archeol. or **archaeol.** archaeology; archeology; archaeological; archeological
Archieps. (Archiepiscopus)(Lat.), **A.B., Abp., abp., Arch., Archbp.** or **Erzb.** (Erzbishof)(Ger.) Archbishop
Archit., archit., Arch. or **arch.** architecture
Archt. or **arch.** architect
A.R.C.I. Associate of the Royal Colonial Institute (London) (now Royal Empire Society)
A.R.C.M. Associate of the Royal College of Music
A.R.C.O. Associate of the Royal College of Organists

A.R.C.S. Associate of the Royal College of Science (London) (cf. A.R.S.M.); Associate of the Royal College of Surgeons (Brit.)

A.R.D.A. American Railway Development Association

A.R.E. Associate of the Royal Society of Painter-Etchers and Engravers

A.R.E.A. American Railway Engineering Association

A.R.E.M.W.A. American Railway Engineering and Maintenance-of-Way Association

A.R.E.S. Associate of the Royal Empire Society (London) (cf. A.R.C.I.)

Arg. or **Argent.** Argentina

arg. arguments

arg., a., Ag (Chem.), **Ar., ar.** (argentum) (Lat.), **s.** or **sil.** silver

Argent. or **Arg.** Argentina

Arg. Rep. or **R.A.** (República Argentina) (Span.) Argentine Republic

Argyl. Argyllshire

A.R.H. Ammunition railhead

A.R.H.A. Associate of the Royal Hibernian Academy

A.R.I. American Refractories Institute

A.R.I.B.A. Associate of the Royal Institute of British Architects

A.R.I.C.R. American Russian Institute for Cultural Relations

Arist. Aristotle

Aristoph. Aristophanes

arith. arithmetic; arithmetical

Ariz. Arizona

Ark. Arkansas

A.R.L.N.A. Association of Record Librarians of North America

ARM or **A.R.M.** Aviation radioman

Ar.M. (Architecturae Magister) (Lat.), **M. Ar.** or **M. Arch.** Master of Architecture

Arm. or **Armen.** Armenian

Arm. or **Armor.** Armoric

arm. armature

Armd (Mil.) or **armd.** Armored

Armd Brig Armored brigade

Armd-c (Mil.) or **armd.-c.** Armored car

Armd Div Armored division

Armd F or **AF** Armored Force

Armd Regt L Armored regiment, light

Armd Regt M Armored regiment, medium

Armen. or **Arm.** Armenian

A.R.M.M.A. American Railway Master Mechanics' Association

Armor. or **Arm.** Armoric

Armr Armorer (Mil.)

A.R.M.S. Associate of the Royal Society of Miniature Painters

armt. armament

A.R.N.M.D. Association for Research in Nervous and Mental Diseases

A.R.P. Air Raid Precautions; Ammunition refilling point; Associated Reformed Presbyterian

A.R.P.A. Association for Research in Paradentosis

A.R.P.S. Associate of the Royal Photographic Society [of Great Britain]

A.R.R. (anno regni regis or reginae) (Lat.) in the year of the king's or queen's reign

arr. arrange; arranged

arr. or **ar.** arrival; arrivals; arrive; arrived; arrives

arr., arrgt. or **des.** (dessin) (Fr.) (Music) arrangement

A.R.R.C. Associate or Association of the Royal Red Cross

arrgt., arr. or **des.** (dessin) (Fr.) (Music) arrangement

A.R.R.L. American Radio Relay League

A.R.R.L.E.C. American Radio Relay League Emergency Corps

A.R.R.S. American Roentgen Ray Society

A.R.S. Airplane repair section; American Radium Society; American Rocket Society; American Rose Society

ars. arsenal

A.R.S.A. Allied Railway Supply Association; Associate of the Royal Scottish Academy; Associate of the Royal Society of Arts (London)

A.R. San. I. Associate of the Royal Sanitary Institute (London) (cf. A.San.I.)

A.R.S.B.B. Association of Railway Superintendents of Bridges and Buildings (now American Railway Bridge and Building Association)

ARSCRFC, A.R.S.C.R.F.C., AUSCRFC, A.U.S.C.R.F.C., VOKS or **V.O.K.S.** (Vsesoîuznoe obshchestvo kulturnoĭ svîazi s sagranitzeĭ) (Rus.) All-Russia or All-Union Society for Cultural Relations with Foreign Countries

A.R.S.L. Associate of the Royal Society of Literature [of the United Kingdom]

A.R.S.M. Associate of the Royal School of Mines (London) (now Royal College of Science)

A.R.S.S. (Antiquariorum Regiae Societatis Socius) (Lat.) or **F.R.S.A.** Fellow of the Royal Society of Antiquaries

A.R.S.W. Associate of the Royal Scottish Society of Painters in Water Colours

Art., art., A., a., artill., Arty (Mil.), **Arty.** or **arty.** artillery

Art. or **Arth.** Arthur

art. article; artificial; artist

art. or **Arif** (Mil.) artificer

art. or **arts.** articles

A.R.T.C. Associate of the Royal Technical College [of Glasgow]

Arth. or **Art.** Arthur

Artif (Mil.) or **art.** artificer

artill., A., a., Art., art., Arty (Mil.), **Arty.** or **arty.** artillery

arts. or **art.** articles

Arty (Mil.), **Arty., arty., A., a., Art., art.** or **artill.** artillery

Arty Brig Artillery brigade

Arty C or **A.C.** Artillery Corps

Arty H Artillery horse

Arty Ln O Artillery liaison officer

Arty R Artillery reconnaissance

A.R.U. American Railway Union

A.R.V. American [Standard] Revised Version [of the Bible]
A.R.W. Air Raid Warden; Association of Refrigerated Warehouses
A.R.W.A. Associate of the Royal West of England Academy
A.R.W.S. Associate of the Royal Society of Painters in Water Colours (Oxford)
AS., A.S., A.-S. or **Ang. Sax.** Anglo-Saxon
A.S. Academy of Science; Air Service; Air Staff; Air Station; apprentice seaman
A.S. or **Act S.** Act or Acts of Sederunt
A.S. (anno salutis)(Lat.) or **A.H.S.** (anno humanae salutis)(Lat.) in the year of redemption; in the year of human redemption or salvation
A.S., A/S or **A/s** account sales
A.S., a.s. or **asst. sec.** assistant secretary
A/S Anti-submarine
A/S (Aktieselskab, Aktieselskapet)(Dan.), **A/B, a.-b.** (aktiebolag, aktiebolaget) (Swed.), **A.G.** (Aktien Gesellschaft) (Ger.) or **S.A.** (Sociedad Anómina) (Span.) joint stock company (cf. Ges.; G.m.b.H.; S.en C.)
A/S, A.S. or **A/s** account sales
A/S, A/s or **a.s.** after sight; at sight
As arsenic (Chem.)
As. Asia; Asian; Asiatic
A/s, A.S. or **A/S** account sales
A/s, A/S or **a.s.** after sight; at sight
a.S. (andere Seite)(Ger.) the next page
as., a., asym. or **asymm.** asymetric; asymetrical
a.s., A.S. or **asst. sec.** assistant secretary
a.s., A/S or **A/s** after sight; at sight
A.S.A. Acoustical Society of America; Actuarial Society of America; Amateur Swimming Association; American Society of Agronomy; American Standards Association; American Statistical Association; American Surgical Association
A.S.A.A. Associate of the Society of [Incorporated] Accountants and Auditors (Brit.)
A.S.A.E. American Society of Agricultural Engineers
A.S.A.M. Associate of the Society of Art Masters
A.San.I. Associate of the Sanitary Institute (London) (now Royal Sanitary Institute)
A.S.B. Air Safety Board
asb. asbestos
A.S.B.C. American Society of Biological Chemists
asb-c asbestos covered
A.S.B.E. American Society of Bakery Engineers
ASC or **A.S.C.** Army Service Corps; Army Specialist Corps
A.S.C. American Society of Cinematographers
A.Sc. or **Assoc. Sc.** Associate in Science
A.S.C.A. American Speech Correction Association
ASCAP or **A.S.C.A.P.** American Society of Composers, Authors and Publishers
A.S.C.C. American Society for the Control of Cancer; American Society of Curio Collectors
A.S.C.E. or **Am. Soc. C.E.** American Society of Civil Engineers
A.S.C.E.A. American Society of Civil Engineers and Architects
A.S.C.I. American Society for Clinical Investigation
A.S.C.L.T. American Society of Clinical Laboratory Technicians
A.S.C.S. Association of Students of Christian Science
ASDIC or **Asdic** Allied Submarine-Detection Investigation Committee
A.S.D.R. American Society of Dental Radiographers
A.S.E. Amalgamated Society of Engineers (Brit.); Associate of the Society of Engineers (Brit.); Association of Engineering Societies
A.S.F. American-Scandinavian Foundation
ASG, A.S.G. or **Asst.Surg.Gen.** Assistant Surgeon General
A.S.G., Asst.Sol.Gen. or **Asst.Sol.-Gen.** Assistant Solicitor General
A.S.G.B. Aeronautical Society of Great Britain
Asgd (Mil.), **asgd., assd.** or **assnd.** assigned
Asgmt (Mil.), **asgmt.** or **assigt.** assignment
Ash (Mil.) or **ashp.** airship
A.S.H.A. American Shire Horse Association; American Social Hygiene Association; American Student Health Association
A.S.H. & V.E. or **A.S.H.V.E.** American Society of Heating and Ventilating Engineers
ashp. or **Ash** (Mil.) airship
A.S.H.S. American Society for Horticultural Science
A.S.H.V.E. or **A.S.H.& V.E.** American Society of Heating and Ventilating Engineers
A.S.I. or **a.s.i.** air speed indicator
A.S.I.C. Air Service Information Circular
A.S.I.L. American Society of International Law
ASKI or **Aski** (Ausländer-Sonderkonten für Inlands-Zahlungen)(Ger.) foreign special accounts for domestic payments
A.S.L. Acting sub-lieutenant
A.S.L.A. American Society of Landscape Architects
ASLE&F or **A. S. L. E. & F.** Associated Society of Locomotive Engineers and Firemen
assmt. or **ass't.** assessment
ASLIB or **A.S.L.I.B.** Association of Special Libraries and Information Bureau
ASLRA American Shortline Railroad Association
A.S.M. Air service mechanic
asm. assembly
asmblr. assembler
asm.doc. assembly document
A.S.M.E., Am.Soc.M.E. or **A.S.Mech.E.** American Society of Mechanical Engineers

A.S.Mech.E., **Am.Soc.M.E.** or **A.S.M.E.** American Society of Mechanical Engineers
ASMT or **A.S.M.T.** American Society of Medical Technology
asmt. assortment
A.S.N. American Society of Naturalists
A.S.O. American Society of Orthodontists
A.S.P. American Society of Parasitologists; American Society of Pediodontists; Astronomical Society of the Pacific
A.S.P.C.A. American Society for the Prevention of Cruelty to Animals
A.S.P.P. American Society of Plant Physiologists
A.S.R.E. American Society of Refrigerating Engineers
A.S.R.S. Amalgamated Society of Railway Servants
Ass. Assyria
Ass. or **Assyr.** Assyrian
ass., assist., Asst. or **asst.** assistant (cf. coad.)
ass., assn., assoc., assocn. or **Ges.** (Gesellschaft)(Ger.) association (cf. soc.; Ver.)
ass. or **assy.** assembly
A.S.S.A. American Social Science Association; American Soil Survey Association
A.S.S.C. Air Service Signal Corps
A.S.S.C. or **Av. Sec. Sig. C.** Aviation Section Signal Corps
Ass. Com. Gen., A.C.G. or **Asst. Commiss. Gen.** Assistant commissary general
assd. assessed; assured
assd., Asgd (Mil.), **asgd.** or **assnd.** assigned
A.S.S.E. American Society of Sanitary Engineering
assigt., Asgmt (Mil.) or **asgmt.** assignment
assim. assimilated; assimilative
assist., ass., Asst. or **asst.** assistant (cf. coad.)
Assist. Cash., A.C. or **Asst. Cash.** Assistant Cashier
assmt. or **ass't.** assessment
assn., ass., assoc., assocn. or **Ges.** (Gesellschaft)(Ger.) association (cf. soc; Ver.)
assnd., Asgd (Mil.), **asgd.** or **assd.** assigned
assoc. associate; associated
assoc., ass., assn., assocn. or **Ges.** (Gesellschaft)(Ger.) association (cf. soc., Ver.)
Assoc. I.S.I. Associate of the Iron and Steel Institute
Assoc.M.I.C.E., A.M.I.C.E. or A.M.Inst.C.E. Associate Member of the Institution of Civil Engineers
Assoc. Sc. or **A. Sc.** Associate in Science
assoc.w. associated with
Ass. P. assembly position
A.S.S.R. Autonomous Soviet Socialist Republic
A.S.S.R.C. Aviation Section of the Signal Reserve Corps
Asst., asst., ass. or **assist.** assistant (cf. coad.)
ass't. or **assmt.** assessment
Asst. Bus. Mgr. Assistant Business Manager
Asst. Cash., A.C. or **Assist. Cash.** Assistant Cashier
Asst. Chf. Assistant chief
Asst. Commiss. Gen., A.C.G. or **Ass. Com. Gen.** Assistant commissary general
Asst. Commr. Assistant Commissioner
asstd. assented; assorted
Asst. Lib. Assistant Librarian
asst. sec., A.S. or **a.s** assistant secretary
Asst.Sol.Gen., Asst.Sol.-Gen. or **A.S.G.** Assistant Solicitor General
Asst. Surg. assistant surgeon
Asst.Surg.Gen., ASG or **A.S.G.** Assistant Surgeon General
A.S.S.U. American Sunday School Union
assy. or **ass.** assembly
Assyr. or **Ass.** Assyrian
Assyr.-Bab. Assyro-Babylonian
A.S.T. Atlantic Standard Time (Can.)
A. St. alto-stratus (Meteorol.)
ast. astigmatism
ast., astr. or **astron.** astronomy
ASTA or **A.S.T.A.** American Steamship and Tourist Agents [Association]
asth. asthenopia
A.S.T.M. American Society for Testing Materials; American Society of Tropical Medicine
ASTP Army Special Training Program
astr., ast. or **astron.** astronomy
astr. or **astron.** astronomer; astronomical
astrol. astrologer; astrological; astrology
astron., ast. or **astr.** astronomy
astron. or **astr.** astronomer; astronomical
astrophys. astrophysical; astrophysics
A.S.W. Association of Scientific Workers (Brit.)
asym., a., as. or **asymm.** asymetric; asymetrical
A.S.Z. American Society of Zoologists
AT (Mil.), **A.T., A/T** or **A.Tk.** Antitank
A.T. or **A/T** American terms (Grain trade)
A.T. (Altes Testament)(Ger.), **Old Test., O.T.** or **V.T.** (Vetus Testamentum) (Lat.) Old Testament
A/T, AT (Mil.), **A.T.** or **A.Tk.** antitank
A/T or **A.T.** American terms (Grain trade)
at. airtight; atomic
at., atm. or **atmos.** atmosphere; atmospheres; atmospheric
at., att., atty. or **Lic.** (Licenciado)(Span.) attorney
a.t. ampere turn or turns; arch treasurer; assay ton
ATA American Touring Association; American Trucking Association
A.T.A.A. Air Transport Association of America
A.T.& T. American Telephone & Telegraph Co.
A.T.A.S. Air Transport Auxiliary Service

A.T.C. aerial tuning condenser; Airway Traffic Control; Approved Type Certificate; Associated Traffic Clubs

A.T.C.A. Air Training Corps of America

atchd (Mil.) or **att.** attached

A.T.C.L. Associate of Trinity College [of Music], London

atdt. attendant

A.T.E.A. American Transit Engineering Association

a tem. (a tempo)(Ital.) in time; return to original time (Music)

At.-Gen., A.G., Att. G., Att. Gen., Att.-Gen. or **Atty. Gen.** Attorney General

athl. athlete; athletic; athletics

athw. athwartship

A.T.I. aerial tuning inductance

A.Tk., AT (Mil.), **A.T.** or **A/T** Antitank

Atk Attack (Mil.)

A.T.L. (avant toute lettre)(Fr.) or **a.l.** (avant la lettre)(Fr.) without lettering; first proof (that is, a print of a stamp or engraving made before any inscription or legend has been placed upon it)

Atl. Atlantic

atm., at. or **atmos.** atmosphere; atmospheres; atmospheric

atmos., at. or **atm.** atmosphere; atmospheres; atmospheric

atm. pr. or **atm. press.** atmospheric pressure

At. No., at. no. or **Z** (Chem.) atomic number

at.º or **at.^{to}** (atento)(Span.) attentive; obliging

A. to O.C. attached to other correspondence

A. tps. Army troops

a.t.r.i.m.a. as their respective interests may appear

ATS or **A.T.S.** Army Transport Service

A.T.S. American Temperance Society; American Therapeutic Society; American Tract Society; antitetanic serum; Associate of Theological Study; Auxiliary Territorial Service (Brit.)

Ats., ats., at s., ads. or **ad s.** (ad sectam) (Lat.) at suit of (Law)

Att. attaché

att., at., atty. or **Lic.** (Licenciado)(Span.) attorney

att. or **atchd** (Mil.) attached

att., atten., attn. or **z. H.** (zu Händen)(Ger.) attention; to the attention

Att. G., A.G., At.-Gen., Att. Gen., Att.-Gen. or **Atty. Gen.** Attorney General

attn., att., atten. or **z. H.** (zu Händen)(Ger.) attention; to the attention

at.^{to} or **at.º** (atento)(Span.) attentive; obliging

at.^{to} y S.S. (atento y seguro servidor) (Span.), [your] attentive and faithful servant; [yours] very truly

AT Tr Antitank troop

attrib. attribute; attributive; attributively

atty., at., att. or **Lic.** (Licenciado)(Span.) attorney

Atty. Gen., A.G., At.-Gen., Att. G., Att. Gen. or **Att.-Gen.** Attorney General

at.vol. atomic volume

At. Wt., at. wt., A.W. or **a.w.** atomic weight

A.U. astronomical unit

A.U., Å.U., A.u., Å.u., a.u., å.u., A or **Å** angstrom unit (Physics)

Au (Chem.), **Au., au., aur.,** (aurum)(Lat.), **G.** or **g.** gold

Au., A., aut. (auteur)(Fr.),(autor)(Span.), (autore)(Ital.), **auth., Forf.** (Forfatter) (Dan.), **förf.** (författare, førfattarina) (Swed.) or **Verf.** (Verfasser)(Ger.) author

a.u. or **ad us.** (ad usum)(Lat.) according to custom (cf. sec.us.)

A.U.A. American Unitarian Association; American Urological Association

A.U.C. (ab urbe condita, anno urbis conditae)(Lat.) or **a.u.** (anno urbis)(Lat.) from the founding of the city [of Rome, 753 B.C.]; from the year of the founding of the city [of Rome]

AUCCTU, A.U.C.C.T.U., ARCCTU, A.R. C.C.T.U., VTsSPS or **V.Ts.S.P.S.** (Vsesoi͡uznyi Tsentralnyĭ Sovet Professionalnyph Soi͡uzov)(Rus.) All Union or All-Russia Central Council of Trade Unions

AUCEC, A.U.C.E.C., ARCEC, A.R.C.E.C. or **V.Tz.I.K.** (Vesrossiisky Tzentralny Ispolnitelny Kommitet)(Rus.) All-Union or All-Russia Central Executive Committee (cf. CEC; Tz.I.K.; UCEC)

aud. audit; auditor

Aud.-Gen. Auditor-General

a.u.d.T. (auch unter dem Titel)(Ger.) also under the title

Aufdr. (Aufdruck, Aufdrucke)(Ger.) impression; impressions

Aufdr. (Aufdruck)(Ger.) or **imp.** imprint

Aufl. (Auflage)(Ger.), **Ausg.** (Ausgabe) (Ger.), **ed., éd.** (édition)(Fr.), **edit.** or **edn.** edition

Aufl. (Auflage)(Ger.), **print., prtg., Ptg.** or **ptg.** printing

Aufs. (Aufsatz, Aufsatze)(Ger.) essay; essays

Aug. or **August.** Augustan; Augustus

Aug., Ag., agto. (agosto)(Span., Port.) or **Sierp.** (Sierpień)(Pol.) August

aug. or **augm.** augmented (cf. enl.; supl.)

aug., augm. or **augment.** augmentative

augm. or **aug.** augmented (cf. enl.; sup.)

augm., aug. or **augment.** augmentative

augment., aug. or **augm.** augmentative

a.u.n. (absque ulla nota)(Lat.) unmarked; without any marking or note

aur., Au (Chem.), **Au., au.** (aurum)(Lat.), **G.** or **g.** gold

A.U.S. Army of the United States

Aus., Aust. or **Austr.** Austria; Austrian

AUSCRFC, A.U.S.C.R.F.C., ARSCRFC, A.R.S.C.R.F.C., VOKS or **V.O.K.S.** (Vsesoi͡uznoe obshchestvo kulturnoĭ svi͡azi s sagranitzeĭ)(Rus.) All-Union or All-Russia Society for Cultural Relations with Foreign Countries

Ausg. (Ausgabe)(Ger.), **Aufl.** (Auflage) (Ger.), **ed., éd.** (édition)(Fr.), **edit.** or **edn.** edition

Ausgeb. (Ausgebessert)(Ger.), **cor.** or **corr.** corrected
Ausgew. (ausgewählt)(Ger.) or **sel.** selected
Aust. Austin
Aust., Aus. or **Austr.** Austria; Austrian
Aust. or **Aust.-Hung.** Austria-Hungary
Aust., Austl., Austr. or **Austral.** Australia; Australian; Australasia; Australasian
Aust.-Hung. or **Aust.** Austria-Hungary
Austl., Aust., Austr. or **Austral.** Australia; Australian; Australasia; Australasian
Austr., Aus. or **Aust.** Austria; Austrian
Austr., Aust., Austl. or **Austral.** Australia; Australian; Australasia; Australasian
Austral., Aust., Austl. or **Austr.** Australia; Australian; Australasia; Australasian
aut. (auteur)(Fr.), (autore)(Ital.), **A.** (autor)(Span.), **Au., auth., Forf.** (Forfatter)(Dan.), **förf.** (författare, författarinna)(Swed.) or **Verf.** (Verfasser)(Ger.) author
aut., Auto (Mil.) or **auto.,** automatic
auth. authentic; authority; authorities; authorized
auth., A. (autor)(Span.), **aut.** (auteur)(Fr.), (autore)(Ital.), **Forf.** (Forfatter)(Dan.), **förf.** (författare, författarinna)(Swed.) or **Verf.** (Verfasser)(Ger.) author
auths., AA. (autores)(Span.),(autori)(Ital.) or **s.s.** (scriptores)(Lat.) authors
Auth. Ver. or **A.V.** Authorized Version [of the Bible]
Auto (Mil.), **aut.** or **auto.** automatic
auto. automobile; automotive
A.U.W. or **A.A.U.W.** American [Association] of University Women (cf. A.F.-C.W.)
Aux (Mil.), **aux.** or **auxil.** auxiliary
Aux.F., Aux.F.I. or **Aux.F.Ind.** Auxiliary Force for India
auxil., Aux (Mil.) or **aux.** auxiliary
Aux Res Auxiliary Reserve
aux. v. auxiliary verb
AV or **A.V.** auriculoventricular
A.V. Artillery Volunteers
A.V. or **Auth. Ver.** Authorized Version [of the Bible]
A.V., a.v. (anno vixit)(Lat.) or **v.a.** (vixit anno)(Lat.) he or she lived [so many] years
A/V, a.v., ad v., Ad val. or **ad val.** (ad valorem)(Lat.) according to value
Av., av., Ave. or **ave.** avenue
av. (avril)(Fr.), **A., ab., abr.** (abril)(Span., Port.), **Ap., Apl., Apr., ápr.** (április)(Hung.) or **Kwiec.** (Kwiecień)(Pol.) April
av. or **avg.** average
av., avdp., avoir. or **P.C.** (pondus civile)(Lat.) avoirdupois
av. (avec)(Fr.) **c.** (cum)(Lat.), **m.** (mit)(Ger.) or **w.** with
a.v. (ad verbum)(Lat.) or **lit.** word for word; literal; literally (cf. ad lit.)
a.v., A.V. (anno vixit)(Lat.) or **v.a.** (vixit annos)(Lat.) he or she lived [so many] years
AVA or **A.V.A.** Administration of Veterans Affairs
A.V.C. Army Veterinary Corps
A.V.C. or **a-v-c** Automatic volume control (Radio)
av. C. (avanti Cristo)(Ital.), **A.C.** (ante Christum)(Lat.), **B.C., v.Ch.** or **v.Chr.** (vor Christo)(Ger.) before Christ
a-v-c or **A.V.C.** automatic volume control (Radio)
A.V.D. Army Veterinary Department
avdp., av., avoir. or **P.C.** (pondus civile) (Lat.) avoirdupois
Ave., ave., Av. or **av.** avenue
A.V.G. American Volunteer Group (Flying Tigers)
avg. or **av.** average
av. let. (avec lettre)(Fr.) printed with signature or title
A.V.M. Air vice marshal
A.V.M.A. American Veterinary Medical Association
Avn (Mil.) or **avn.** aviation
A.V.O. Administrative Veterinary Officer
avoir., av., avdp. or **P.C.** (pondus civile) (Lat.) avoirdupois
AVS or **A.V.S.** Army Veterinary Service
Av. Sec. Sig. C. or **A.S.S.C.** Aviation Section Signal Corps
AW Articles of War
A.W., a.w., At. Wt. or **at. wt.** atomic weight
A/W or **a.w.** all water (Transportation)
A/W or **a/w** actual weight (Transportation)
a.w., A.W., At.Wt. or **at.wt.** atomic weight
a.w. or **A/W** all water (Transportation)
a/w or **A/W** actual weight
A.W.A. American Warehouse Men's Association; American Women's Association
AWC Army War College
AWG or **A.W.G.** American wire gauge
A.W.H. Association of Western Hospitals
A.W.H.A. Australian Women's Home Army
awk. awkward
A.W.L. artesian well lease (Australia)
A.W.L. or **a.w.l.** Absent with leave
A.W.M. American War Mothers
A.W.O.L. or **a.w.o.l.** Absent without leave
A.W.P.A. American Wood Preservers Association
A.W.P.C. Aircraft War Production Council
AWS Aircraft Warning Service
A.W.S. American Welding Society
AWVS or **A.W.V.S.** American Women's Voluntary Services
A.W.W.A. American Water Works Association
Ax. or **ax.** axis (Optics)
ax. axiom
Ax Sig Com Axis or Axes of signal communication
AYC or **A.Y.C.** American Youth Congress
AYD or **A.Y.D.** American Youth for Democracy
A.Y.H. American Youth Hostels [Incorporated]

A.Y.M. Ancient York Mason; Ancient York Masonry (Freemasonry)
Az azote (Chem.)
az. azimuth; azure

A.Z.I. American Zinc Institute
ΑΑΓ (Alpha Alpha Gamma) National professional sorority (Architecture)
ΑΧ (Alpha Chi) National honor society (Scholarship)
ΑΧΑ (Alpha Chi Alpha) Honorary sorority (Journalism)
ΑΧΕ (Alpha Chi Epsilon) Professional fraternity (Fire Insurance)
ΑΧΩ (Alpha Chi Omego) National undergraduate sorority
ΑΧΡ (Alpha Chi Rho) National undergraduate fraternity
ΑΧΣ (Alpha Chi Sigma) National professional fraternity (Chemistry)
ΑΔ (Alpha Delta) Honor society (Journalism, Men and Women)
ΑΔΦ (Alpha Delta Phi) National undergraduate fraternity
ΑΔΠ (Alpha Delta Pi) National undergraduate sorority
ΑΔΣ (Alpha Delta Sigma) National professional fraternity (Advertising)
ΑΔΘ (Alpha Delta Theta) National undergraduate sorority
ΑΗΦ (Alpha Eta Phi) National undergraduate fraternity
AED (Alpha Epsilon Delta) National honor fraternity (Premedical)
ΑΕΙ (Alpha Epsilon Iota) National professional sorority (Medicine)
ΑΕΦ (Alpha Epsilon Phi) National undergraduate sorority
ΑΕΠ (Alpha Epsilon Pi) National undergraduate fraternity
ΑΓΔ (Alpha Gamma Delta) National undergraduate honor sorority
ΑΓΡ (Alpha Gamma Rho) National undergraduate fraternity (Agriculture)
ΑΚΑ (Alpha Kappa Alpha) National under graduate honorary fraternity (Philosophy)
ΑΚΔ (Alpha Kappa Delta) Professional fraternity (Sociology)
ΑΚΚ (Alpha Kappa Kappa) Professional fraternity (Medicine)
ΑΚΛ (Alpha Kappa Lambda) National undergraduate fraternity
ΑΚΠ (Alpha Kappa Pi) National undergraduate fraternity
ΑΚΨ (Alpha Kappa Psi) Professional fraternity (Commerce)
ΑΛΤ (Alpha Lambda Tau) National undergraduate fraternity
ΑΜΠΩ (Alpha Mu Pi Omega) Professional fraternity (Medicine)
ΑΜΣ (Alpha Mu Sigma) National undergraduate fraternity
ΑΩΑ (Alpha Omega Alpha) Honor society in Medicine
ΑΟΠ (Alpha Omicron Pi) National undergraduate sorority
ΑΦ (Alpha Phi) National undergraduate sorority; **Professional fraternity (Dentistry)**
ΑΦΑ (Alpha Phi Alpha) National undergraduate fraternity (Negroes)
ΑΦΔ (Alpha Phi Delta) National undergraduate fraternity
ΑΦΕ (Alpha Phi Epsilon) Honorary fraternity (Forensics)
ΑΦΓ (Alpha Phi Gamma) National undergraduate honorary fraternity (Journalism)
ΑΦΩ (Alpha Phi Omega) National service fraternity (Education and Social Service)
ΑΨ (Alpha Psi) National professional fraternity (Medical-Veterinary)
ΑΨΩ (Alpha Psi Omega) National honorary society (Dramatics)
ΑΡΧ (Alpha Rho Chi) Professional fraternity (Architecture)
ΑΣ (Alpha Sigma) Professional fraternity (Medicine—Homeopathy)
ΑΣΑ (Alpha Sigma Alpha) Professional sorority (Education)
ΑΣΦ (Alpha Sigma Phi) National undergraduate fraternity
ΑΣΤ (Alpha Sigma Tau) Professional sorority (Education)
ΑΤΩ (Alpha Tau Omega) National undergraduate fraternity
ΑΞ (Alpha Xi Delta) National undergraduate sorority
ΑΞΔ (Alpha Xi Delta) National undergraduate sorority
ΑΖ (Alpha Zeta) Professional fraternity (Agriculture)

B

B bluish (Dyeing)
B or **bor.** boron (Chem.)
B. Bacillus; Barge (Navy); Battle; bid; Bomber (Airplane)
B. or **b.** balboa; bass; basso; bat; bay; (Bancus)(Lat.) bench; bicuspid; bolivar; boliviano; brass; breadth; buccal; bug (bed bug)
B., b., bat., Batt., batt., batty., Btry (Mil.) **Btry., Bty.** or **bty.** battery
B., b., bk., L., l., lib. (liber)(Lat.), **liv.** (livre)(Fr.) or **t.** (tome)(Fr.) book
B., b., Bn. or **Frhr.** (Freiherr)(Ger.) Baron
B., b., bp. or **L.** (Läufer)(Ger.) bishop (Chess)
B., b., Br., br., bro. or **Fr.** (Frater)(Lat.) brother
B., b., f. (född)(Swed.), (født)(Dan.), **geb.** (geboren)(Ger.) or **n.** (natus)(Lat.) born
B., Bac. (baccalaureus)(Lat.), **b., ba.** or **bach.** bachelor
B., Bap. or **Bapt.** Baptist
B., Bd. (Band)(Ger.), (Bind)(Dan.), **b., bd.** (band)(Swed.), **T.** (Tome)(Ger.), **t., tom.** (tome)(Fr.), (tomo)(Span.), (tomus)(Lat.), **v., Vol.** or **vol.** volume
B. or **bd.** bond
B., Bé. or **Be.** Baumé
B. or **Bib.** Bible
B. (Beata, Beatus)(Lat.) or **Bl.** The Blessed (cf. B.B.)
B. or **bos'n.** boatswain
B., Bp., bp., Ep. or **Epus.** (Episcopus)(Lat.) bishop (Eccles.)
B., Br. or **Brit.** British

B., bul. or **bull.** bulletin
B/- or **bg.** bag
B/- or **bl.** bale
b. blue sky (Naut.); bowled (Cricket); bye
b. or **B.** balboa; bass; basso; bat; bay; (Bancus)(Lat.) bench; bicuspid; bolivar; boliviano; brass; breadth; buccal; bug (bedbug)
b., B., Bac. (Baccalaureus)(Lat.), **ba.** or **bach.** bachelor
b., B., bat., Batt., batt., batty., Btry (Mil.), **Btry., Bty.** or **bty.** battery
b., B., bk., L., l., lib. (liber)(Lat.) **liv.** (livre)(Fr.) or **t.** (tome)(Fr.) book
b., B., Bn. or **Frhr.** (Freiherr)(Ger.) Baron
b., B., bp. or **L.** (Laufer)(Ger.) bishop (Chess)
b., B., Br., br., Bro., bro. or **Fr.** (Frater) (Lat.) brother
b., B., f. (fodd)(Swed.), (fodt)(Dan.), **Geb.** (geboren)(Ger.) or **n.** (natus)(Lat.) born
b., bd. (band)(Swed.), **B., Bd.** (Band)(Ger.), (Bind)(Dan.), **T.** (Tome)(Ger.), **t., tom.** (tome)(Fr.), (tomo)(Span.), (tomus) (Lat.), **v., Vol.** or **vol.** volume
b. or **brg.** bearing
BA Branch assignment (Mil.); Bureau of Aeronautics
B.A. Board of Agriculture; British Academy; British Association [for the Advancement of Science]; Buenos Aires; (Bekleidungsamt)(Ger.) clothing depot (Mil.); (balneum arenae)(Lat.) sand bath (Med.)
B.A., A.B. (Artium Baccalaureus)(Lat.) or **B.ès A.** (Bachelier ès Arts)(Fr.) Bachelor of Arts
B.A., B.Ag., B.Agr. or **B.Agric.** (Baccalaureus Agriculturae)(Lat.) Bachelor of Agriculture
B.A. or **Br. Am.** British America
Ba barium (Chem.)
ba., b., bach., B. or **Bac.** (baccalaureus) (Lat.) bachelor
B.A. Arch. Bachelor of Art or Arts in Architecture (cf. B.Ar.)
Bab. Babylon; Babylonia
BAC or **B.A.C.** Bureau of Air Commerce; Business Advisory Council
B.A.C. British Automobile Company; buccoaxiocervical (Med.)
Bac., B. (baccalaureus)(Lat.), **b., ba.** or **bach.** bachelor
B. Acc., B. Acct. or **Acc.B.** Bachelor of Accounting
B. Acct., B. Acc. or **Acc.B.** Bachelor of Accounting
BACE or **B.A.C.E.** Bureau of Agricultural Chemistry and Engineering
B.A.Ch. Bachelor of Arts in Chemistry
bach., b., ba., B. or **Bac.** (baccalaureus) (Lat.) bachelor
back. or **bk.** backwardation
Bact. or **bact.** bacteria; bacterium
Bact., bact., Bacter., bacter. or **bacteriol.** bacteriological; bacteriologist; bacteriology
Bacter., bacter., Bact., bact. or **bacteriol.** bacteriological; bacteriologist; bacteriology
B. Adm.Eng. Bachelor of Administrative Engineering
BAE or **B.A.E.** Bureau of Agricultural Economics
B.A.E., A.B.Ed., A.B. in Ed., B.A. in E. or **B.A. in Educa.** Bachelor of Arts in Education
B.A.E. or **B.Aero. E.** Bachelor of Aeronautical Engineering
B.Aero.E. or **B.A.E.** Bachelor of Aeronautical Engineering
B.A.G. buccoaxiogingival (Med.)
B.Ag., B.A., B.Agr. (Baccalaureus Agriculturae)(Lat.) or **B. Agric.** Bachelor of Agriculture
Bag (Mil.) or **bag.** baggage
B.Agr., B.A., B.Ag. (Baccalaureus Agriculturae)(Lat.) or **B.Agric.** Bachelor of Agriculture
B. Ag. Sc., B.A.S. or **B.A.Sc.** Bachelor of Agricultural Science
BAI or **B.A.I.** Bureau of Animal Industry
B.A.I. (Baccalaureus in Arte Ingeniaria) (Lat.), **B.E., B.Eng.** or **B. of Engr.** Bachelor of Engineering
B.A. in B.A. Bachelor of Arts in Business Administration (cf. B.B.A.)
B.A. in Drama Bachelor of Arts in Drama
B.A. in E., A.B.Ed., A.B. in Ed., B.A.E. or **B.A. in Educa.** Bachelor of Arts in Education
B.A. in Ed., A.B.Ed., A.B. in Ed., B.A.E. or **B.A. in Educa.** Bachelor of Arts in Education
B.A. in J., A.B. in J. or **B.A.J.** Bachelor of Arts in Journalism (cf. B.J.)
B. A. in Nurs. Bachelor of Arts in Nursing
B.A. in P.A. Bachelor of Arts in Public Affairs
B.A. in Sp. Bachelor of Arts in Speech
B.A.J., A.B. in J. or **B.A. in J.** Bachelor of Arts in Journalism (cf. B.J.)
B.A.L. British Airways, Ltd.
Bal. or **bal.** balance
bal. balancing
Bald. Baldwin
Ball. Balliol [College]
B.A.L.P.A. British Air Line Pilots Association
Bals. or **bals.** balsam
Balt. Balthasar; Martin Baltimore (Airplane)
Balto. Baltimore
Balto-Slav. Balto-Slavic
B.A.M. (Brevet d'aptitude militaire)(Fr.) Certificate of fitness for active military service (cf. K.V.)
b. & a.r.p. bare and acid resisting paint
b. & e. beginning and ending
B. & F.B.S., BFBS or **B.F.B.S.** British and Foreign Bible Society
B. & Fl. or **Beau. & Fl.** Francis Beaumont and John Fletcher
B. & L. Assn. Building and Loan Association
b. & p. bare and painted (Shipbuilding)

B.&S., b.&s. or **B. and S.** brandy and soda
B. & S. or **B. & S. W. G.** Brown & Sharpe [wire gauge]
b. & s., B. & S. or **B. and S.** brandy and soda
B. & S. W. G. or **B. & S.** Brown & Sharpe wire gauge
B. & W. Bath and Wells, in signature of Bishop
B.A. Mus. Ed. Bachelor of Arts in Music Education
B. and S., B.&S. or **b. & s.** brandy and soda
bank. or **bkg.** banking
bank clgs. bank clearings
bank debs. bank debits
B.A.O. Bachelor of Arts in Obstetrics
Bap. Baptiste
Bap., B. or **Bapt.** Baptist
bap. or **bapt.** baptized
b.à p. (billets à payer)(Fr.), **B.P., B/P, b.p.** or **B.Pay.** bills payable (cf. A/cs Pay.)
BAPC or **B.A.P.C.** Business Advisory and Planning Council
B. App. Arts Bachelor of Applied Arts (cf. B.Sc. in App. Arts)
B.App.Sc., B.A.S. or **B.A.Sc.** Bachelor of Applied Science
Bapt., B. or **Bap.** Baptist
bapt. or **bap.** baptized
BAR Browning automatic rifle
B.Ar. or **B. Arch.** Bachelor of Architecture (cf. B.A. Arch.)
Bar. Baruch
bar. barleycorn; barometer; barometric
bar. or **barr.** barrister
bar., bbl., bl. or **brl.** barrel
b. à r. (billets à reservoir)(Fr.), **B.R., b.r., B/R, B. Rec.** or **b. rec.** bills receivable (cf. A/cs/Rec)
Barb. Barbados; Barbara
Bar Bln Barrage balloon
Bar Bln Bn Barrage balloon batalion
B. Arch. or **B. Ar.** Bachelor of Architecture
B. Arch. E. Bachelor of Architectural Engineering
barit. baritone
Barn. Barnard
barr. or **bar.** barrister
Bart. or **Bt.** Baronet
Bart's St. Bartholomew's [Hospital]
B.A.S. British Anatomical Society
B.A.S., B.Ag.Sc. or **B. A. Sc.** Bachelor of Agricultural Science
B.A.S., B.App.Sc. or **B.A.Sc.** Bachelor of Applied Science
Bas. Basilius
B.A.Sc., B.Ag.Sc. or **B.A.S.** Bachelor of Agricultural Science
B.A.Sc., B.App.Sc. or **B.A.S.** Bachelor of Applied Science
B.A.T. Boeing Air Transport
bat., B., b., Batt. batt., batty., Btry (Mil.), **btry., Bty.** or **bty.** battery
bat., batln., batn., Batt., batt., Bn (Mil.) or **bn.** battalion
bat.chg. battery charging
batln., bat., batn., Batt., batt., Bn (Mil.) or **bn.** battalion
batn., bat., batln., Batt., batt., Bn (Mil.) or **bn.** battalion
Batt., batt., B., b., bat., batty., Btry (Mil.), **btry., Bty.** or **bty.** battery
Batt., bat., batln., batn., batt., Bn (Mil.) or **bn.** battalion
batt., bat., batln., batn., Batt., Bn (Mil.) or **bn.** battalion
batty., B., b., bat., Batt., batt., Btry., Bty. or **bty.** battery
B.A.U. Baptist Adult Union; British Association Unit
Bav. Bavaria; Bavarian
Bawra or **B.A.W.R.A.** British Australian Wool Realization Association
BB double black (pencil lead)
BB, B.B. or **BOB** Bureau of the Budget
BB. (Beati)(Lat.) The Blessed [ones] (cf. Bl.)
BB., Bde. (Bände)(Ger.), **t.** (tomes)(Fr.), **v.** or **vols.** volumes
B.B. Balloon barrage; Blue Book
B.B. or **b.b.** bail bond; bank book; bill book
B.B. (billet de banque)(Fr.) or **B.N.** banknote
b.b. ball bearing; baseball; basketball; below bridges (Shipping); branch bill (Banking); break bulk
b.b. or **B.B.** bail bond; bank book; bill book
B.B.A. or **B.Bus Ad.** Bachelor of Business Administration (cf. B.A. in B.A.)
BBB treble black (pencil lead)
B.B.C. British Broadcasting Corporation; bromo-benzyl-cyanide (Gas)
B.B.C. or **b.b.c.** baseball club; basketball club
b.b.c. or **B.B.C.** baseball club; basketball club
bbl., bar., bl. or **brl.** barrel
bbls., bbl., bls. or **brls.** barrels
bbls/day, b/d, bpd or **b.p.d.** barrels per day
B.B.S. or **B.B.Sc.** Bachelor of Business Science
B.B.S.M.A. Bridge and Building Supply Men's Association
B. Bus. Ad. or **B.B.A.** Bachelor of Business Administration (cf. B.A. in B.A.)
B.B.Y.O. B'nai B'rith Youth Organization
BC bolt circle
B.C. Bachelor of Chemistry; Battle cruiser; Board of Control; Bomber Command; bone conduction; British candles (optics); British Corporation; British Council; buccocervical (Med.)
B.C. or **A.C.** (ante Christum)(Lat.), **av.C.** (avanti Cristo)(Ital.), **v.Ch.** or **v.Chr.** (vor Christo)(Ger.) before Christ
B.C. or **b.c.** bass clarinet; bad character (Brit. army); bicycle club; boat club
B.C., b.c., Btry Comdr (Mil.), **Bty Comdr** (Mil.) or **by. c.** Battery commander
B.C. or **B/Ch** Bristol Channel (Shipping)
B.C., B.Com. or **B.Comm.** Bachelor of Commerce
B.C. or **Br. Col.** British Columbia
B/C bill for collection

b.c. or **B.C.** bad character: bass clarinet; bicycle club; boat club
b.c., B.C., Btry Comdr (Mil.), **Bty Comdr** (Mil.) or **by.c.** Battery commander
B.C.E. or **B.C.Eng.** Bachelor of Civil Engineering
B.C.E., B.Ch.E. or **B.Ch. Eng.** Bachelor of Chemical Engineering
B.C.Eng. or **B.C.E.** Bachelor of Civil Engineering
B. Ch., B.C., B.Chir. (Baccalaureus Chirurgiae)(Lat.), **B.S., C.B.** or **Ch. B.** Bachelor of Surgery
B/Ch or **B.C.** Bristol Channel (Shipping)
B.Ch.D. (Baccalaureus Chirurgiae Dentium)(Lat.) or **B.D.S.** Bachelor of Dental Surgery
B.Ch.E., B.C.E. or **B.Ch.Eng.** Bachelor of Chemical Engineering
B.Chir., B.C., B. Ch. (Baccalaureus Chirurgiae)(Lat.), **B.S., C.B.** or **Ch. B.** Bachelor of Surgery
bchs. bunches
B.C.L. or **J.C.B.** (Juris Civilis Baccalaureus) (Lat.) Bachelor of Civil Law
bcl bicycle (Mil.)
bclt Bicyclist (Mil.)
B.C.M. British Consular Mail
B.C.O.G. British College of Obstetricians and Gynecologists
B.Com., B.C. or **B. Comm.** Bachelor of Commerce
B.Com.Sc. or **B.C.S.** Bachelor of Commercial Science
B.C.P., P.B. or **Pr. Bk.** Book of Common Prayer; Prayer Book
B.C.P.S. British Chess Problem Society
B.C.S. Bachelor of Chemical Science; Battle cruiser squadron; Bengal Civil Service
B. C. S. or **B. Com. Sc.** Bachelor of Commercial Science
B.D. bar draft (Grain trade); base [of prism] down; buccodistal (Med.)
B.D. or **B/D** bank draft
B.D., B/D or **b.d.** bills discounted
B.D. or **b.d.** Battle dress
B.D. or **D.B.** Bachelor of Didactics; Bachelor of Divinity
B/D or **B.D.** bank draft
B/D, B.D. or **b.d.** bills discounted
B/D, B/d or **bd.** brought down (cf. C/d)
Bd (Mil.) or **bd.** boundary
Bd., B. (Band)(Ger.), (Bind)(Dan.), **b., bd.** (band)(Swed.), **T.** (Tome)(Ger.), **t., tom.** (tome)(Fr.), (tome)(Span.), (tomus)(Lat.), **v., Vol.** or **vol.** volume
B/d, B/D or **b.d.** brought down (cf. C/d)
bd. band; board
bd., or **B.** bond
bd., b. (band)(Swed.), **B., Bd.** (Band)(Ger.), (Bind)(Dan.), **T.** (Tome)(Ger.), **t., tom.** (tome)(Fr.), (tomo)(Span.), (tomus) (Lat.), **v., Vol.** or **vol.** volume
bd., B/D or **B/d** brought down (cf. C/d)
bd. or **Bd** (Mil.) boundary
b.d. or **B.D.** battle dress
b.d., B.D. or **B/D** bills discounted
bd., bdl. or **bdle.** bundle
bd. or **bnd.** bound
b.d. back dividends
b.d. (bis die)(Lat.), **B.i.d., b.i.d.** or **bis in d.** (bis in die)(Lat.) twice a day (cf. b.d.s.)
b/d, bbls/day, bpd or **b.p.d.** barrels per day
B.D.A. British Dental Association
B.D.C. bottom dead center; British Dyestuffs Corporation
Bde., BB. (Bände)(Ger.), **t.** (tomes)(Fr.), **v.** or **vols.** volumes
Bde., Br., Brig (Mil.) or **Brig.** Brigade
Bde. Maj., B.M., b.m. or **B.Maj.** Brigade major
B.Dent.Sc., B.D.S. or **B.D.Sc.** Bachelor of Dental Science
Bde.R.O. or **B.R.O.** Brigade routine orders
B.Des. Bachelor of Design
bd.ft. board feet; board foot
bdg. or **bndg.** binding
BDI or **B.D.I.** Bureau of Dairy Industry
b.d.i. both days inclusive
bdl., bd. or **bdle.** bundle
bdle., bd. or **bdl.** bundle
Bdr., Bom., bomb. or **Br.** Bombardier
Bdr. or **Brig.** Brigadier
B. Dr. Art Bachelor of Dramatic Art
bd. rts. bond rights
B.D.S. Bomb Disposal Squad
B.D.S. or **B.Ch.D.** (Baccalaureus Chirurgiae Dentium)(Lat.) Bachelor of Dental Surgery
B.D.S., B.Dent. Sc. or **B.D.Sc.** Bachelor of Dental Science
bds. beds; boards; bonds; [bound in] boards; bundles
b.d.s. (bis die sumendum)(Lat.) to be taken twice a day (cf. b.i.d.)
B.D.Sc., B.Dent.Sc. or **B.D.S.** Bachelor of Dental Science
BE or **B.E.** Bureau of Explosives
B.E. Bachelor of Elocution; Bachelor of Expression
B.E., B.A.I. (Baccalaureus in Arte Ingeniaria)(Lat.), **B.Eng.** or **B. of Engr.** Bachelor of Engineering
B.E., b.e. or **B/E** bill of exchange
B.E., B.Ed., B.Educ. or **Ed.B.** Bachelor of Education
B.E. or **B. of E.** Bank of England; Board of Education
B.E. or **O.B.E.** [Order of the] British Empire
B/E bill of entry
B/E, B.E. or **b.e.** bill of exchange
Be beryllium (Chem.)
b.e., B.E. or **B/E** bill of exchange
Bé., Be. or **B.** Baumé
B.E.A. or **Br. E. Af.** British East Africa
B.E.A.M.A. or **B.E. & A.M.A.** British Electrical and Allied Manufacturers Association
B.E. & A.M.A. or **B.E.A.M.A.** British Electrical and Allied Manufacturers Association
bearb. (bearbeitet)(Ger.), **Comp.** or **comp.** compiled
bearb. (bearbeitet)(Ger.), **ed.** or **edit.** edited

Beau. Beaufort (Airplane)
Beau. & Fl. or **B. and Fl.** Francis Beaumont and John Fletcher
bec. because
B.E.D. Bachelor of Elementary Didactics
B.Ed., B.E., B.Educ. or **Ed.B.** Bachelor of Education
B. Ed. in Phys. Ed. Bachelor of Education in Physical Education
Beds or **Beds.** Bedfordshire
B. Educ., B.E., B.Ed. or **Ed.B.** Bachelor of Education
B.E.E. or **B.El.Eng.** Bachelor of Electrical Engineering
B.E.F. Bonus Expeditionary Force; British Expeditionary Force or Forces
bef., a. or **an.** (ante)(Lat.) before
Beibl. (Beiblatt)(Ger.), **Erg.H.** (Ergänsungsheft)(Ger.), **sup., supp.** or **suppl.** supplement
beigeb. (beigebunden)(Ger.) bound with
B.E.L. Bachelor of English Literature
Bel. Belinda
Bel. or **Belg.** Belgian; Belgic; Belgium
bel. or **inf.** (infra)(Lat.) below
B.El.Eng. or **B.E.E.** Bachelor of Electrical Engineering
Belg. or **Bel.** Belgian; Belgic; Belgium
B.E.M. British Empire Medal
Ben. or **Benj.** Benjamin
Bened. Benedict
B.Eng., B.A.I. (Baccalaureus in Arte Ingeniaria)(Lat.), **B.E.** or **B. of Engr.** Bachelor of Engineering
Beng. Bengal; Bengali
B. Eng. A. Bachelor of Agricultural Engineering
Benj. or **Ben.** Benjamin
BEO or **B.E.O.** Board of Economic Operations
BEP or **B.E.P.** Bureau of Engraving and Printing
Ber. Berlin
Berks or **Berks.** Berkshire
Bern. Bernard
Bern. or **Bernh.** Bernhard; Bernhardt
Bert. Bertram
BES or **B.E.S.** Bureau of Employment Security
B.E.S.A. British Engineering Standards Association
B.ès A. (Bachelier ès Arts)(Fr.), **A.B.** (Artium Baccalaureus)(Lat.) or **B.A.** Bachelor of Arts
beschn. (beschnitten)(Ger.) or **cond.** condensed
B.E.S.L. British Empire Service League
B. ès L. (Bachelier ès Lettres)(Fr.), **B.L., B.Litt.,** (Baccalaureus Litterarum)(Lat.), **L.B.** or **Litt. B.** (Litterarum Baccalaureus)(Lat.) Bachelor of Letters
B.E.S.L.Aux. British Empire Service League Auxiliary
B. ès S. (Bachelier ès Sciences)(Fr.), **B.S., B.Sc., S.B.** or **Sc.B.** (Scientiae Baccalaureus)(Lat.) Bachelor of Science or Sciences
Bess. Bessemer
bet., betn., betw., btwn., m- (meta-)(Greek) or **zw.** (zwischen)(Ger.) between
betw., bet., betn., btwn., m- (meta-)(Greek) or **zw.** (zwischen)(Ger.) between
BEW or **B.E.W.** Board of Economic Warfare (cf. OEW)
bez., besgw., bezw. (besiehungsweise)(Ger.) or **resp.** respectfully
B. F. Bachelor of Finance; Bachelor of Forestry
B/F, B/f, b.f. or **Brt. fwd.** brought forward (cf. C/F; C/o)
bf or **b.f.** bold face [type](cf. bklr.)
b.f. firkin of beer
b.f., B/F, B/f or **Brt.fwd.** brought forward (cf. C/F; C/o)
B.F.A. or **B. of F.A.** Bachelor of Fine Arts
B.F.A. in Ed. Bachelor of Fine Arts in Education
B.F.A. in Mus., B.F.A.Mus. or **B. of F.A. in Mus.** Bachelor of Fine Arts in Music
B.F.A. in P.S. Bachelor of Fine Arts in Painting and Sculpturing
B.F.A. in Sp. Bachelor of Fine Arts in Speech
B.F.A.Mus., B.F.A. in Mus. or **B. of F.A. in Mus.** Bachelor of Fine Arts in Music
BFBS, B.F.B.S. or **B. & F. B. S.** British and Foreign Bible Society
BFC Banks for Cooperatives
BFDC or **B.F.D.C.** Bureau of Foreign and Domestic Commerce
b15d buyer fifteen days [to take up stock]
b. fir. firkin of butter
B.G. buccogingival (Med.)
B.G., B.Gen., Brig Gen (Mil.), **Brig. Gen.** or **Brig.-Gen.** Brigadier general
B.G., BWG or **B.W.G.** Birmingham wire gauge
B/G bonded goods
bg. or **B/-** bag
b.g. bay gelding
B.G.A. British Gliding Association
bg. adj. Brigade adjutant
bg.c. brigade command
bg.c., Bg. Com. or **Brig Comdr** (Mil.) Brigade commander
Bg. Com., bg. c. or **Brig Comdr** (Mil.) Brigade commander
B.Gen., B.G., Brig Gen (Mil.), **Brig. Gen.** or **Brig.-Gen.** Brigadier general
B.G.G.S. Brigadier general, general staff
bght., bgt., bot. or **bt.** bought
Bglr (Mil.) or **Br.** bugler
BGN or **B.G.N.** Board on Geographical Names
B.G.S. Brigadier, general staff
bgs. or **B/s** bags
bg. sf. p.o. Brigade staff petty officer
bgt., bght., bot. or **bt.** bought
B.Gu. British Guiana

B.H. Bachelor of Humanics; Bachelor of Humanities
B/H bill of health (Shipping); Bordeaux to Hamburg inclusive (Shipping)
b.h. bay horse
Bhd. or **blkd.** bulkhead
BHE or **B.H.E.** Bureau of Home Economics
B'head Birkenhead
B.H.N. Brotherhood of the Holy Name [of Jesus]
B.H.N. or **Bhn.** Brinell hardness number
BHNHE Bureau of Human Nutrition and Home Economics
B.Hond. British Honduras
B.H.P., bhp, b.hp. or **b.h.p.** brake horsepower
bhp, B.H.P. b.hp. or **b.h.p.** brake horsepower
bhp-hr brake horsepower-hour or hours
bhpric. bishopric
BHQ (Mil.) or **B.H.Q.** Brigade headquarters
B.H.T. Brotherhood of the Holy Trinity (Oxford)
B.Hy. Bachelor of Hygiene
B.I. base [of prism] in; British India
Bi bismuth (Chem.)
BIA or **B.I.A.** Bureau of Insular Affairs
B.I.A.E. British Institute of Adult Education
B.I.B. or **b.i.b.** Baby incendiary bomb
Bib. or **B.** Bible
Bib. or **bib.** (bibe)(Lat.) drink
Bib., Bibl., or **bibl.** biblical
bib. or **Bib.** (bibe)(Lat.) drink
bib., bibl., biblio. or **bibliog.** bibliography
bib. or **bibliog.** bibliographer
Bibl., bibl. or **bib.** biblical
Bibl., bibl., biblio. or **bibliog.** bibliographical
Bibl., bibl., biblioth. (bibliotheca)(Lat.) or **lib.** library
bibl., bib., biblio. or **bibliog.** bibliography
biblio., Bibl., bibl. or **bibliog.** bibliographical
bibliog. or **bib.** bibliographer
bibliog., bib., bibl. or **biblio.** bibliography
bibliog., Bibl., bibl. or **biblio.** bibliographical
biblioth., Bibl., bibl. (bibliotheca)(Lat.) or **lib.** library
bicarb. bicarbonate of soda
B.i.d., b.i.d., bis in d. (bis in die)(Lat.) or **b.d.** (bis die)(Lat.) twice a day (cf. b.d.s.)
bi-m. bi-monthly
B. Ind. E. Bachelor of Industrial Engineering
bio-chem. or **biochem.** biological chemistry; biochemistry
biog. biographer; biographical; biography
biogeog. biogeography
biol. biological; biologist; biology
BIR or **B.I.R.** Bureau of Internal Revenue
B.I.S. Bank of International Settlements; British Information Services; British Interplanetary Society
bis. bis-sextile
b.i.7d. or **bis in 7d.** (bis in septem diebus) (Lat.) twice a week
bis in d., b.d., B.i.d. or **b.i.d.** (bis in die, bis die)(Lat.) twice a day (cf. b.d.s.)
bis in 7d or **b.i.7d.** (bis in septem diebus) (Lat.) twice a week
B.I.S.T. British Institute of Engineering Technology
bitum. bituminous
B.J. Bachelor of Journalism (cf. B.A. in J.; B.L. in J.)
B.K. bilge keel
bk., B., b., L., l., lib. (liber)(Lat.), **liv.** (livre)(Fr.) or **t.** (tome)(Fr.) book
bk. or **back.** backwardation
bk. or **blk.** block
bk. or **bnk.** bank
bk., bq. or **bque.** bark; barque
bkbdg. or **bkbndg.** bookbinding
bkbndr. bookbinder
bkg. or **bkpg.** bookkeeping
bkg. or **bank.** banking
bklr. or **B.L.** black letter (Printing)(cf. bf)
bkpg. or **bkg.** bookkeeping
bkpr. bookkeeper
bkpt. or **bkrpt.** bankrupt
Bkry bakery (Mil.)
Bkry Bn Bakery battalion
Bkry Co Bakery company (Mil.)
B.K.S., Bks (Mil.) or **bks.** barracks
bks. banks; books
bks., B.K.S. or **Bks** (Mil.) barracks
bkt. or **brkt.** (Drafting) bracket
bkt., bsk. or **bskt.** basket
BL or **b.l.** buttock line (Drafting)
B.L. bill lodged (Banking); buccolingual (Med.)
B.L. or **bklr.** black letter (Printing)(cf. bf)
B.L. or **b.l.** breech-loading
B.L., b.l., B/L or **b/l** bill of lading
B.L., B.Litt. (Baccalaureus Litterarum) (Lat.), **B. ès L.** (Bachelier ès Lettres) (Fr.), **L.B.** or **Litt. B.** (Litterarum Baccalaureus)(Lat.) Bachelor of Letters
B.L., B.LL. (Baccalaureus Legum)(Lat.), **J.B.** (Jurum Baccalaureus)(Lat.) or **LL.B.** (Legum Baccalaureus)(Lat.) Bachelor of Laws
Bl. Blenheim (Airplane)
Bl. or **B.** (Beata, Beatus)(Lat.) The Blessed (cf. BB.)
bl. blue
bl. or **B/-** bale
bl., bar., bbl. or **brl.** barrel
bl. or **blk.** black
b.l. base line
b.l. or **B.L.** breech-loading
b.l., B.L., B/L or **b/l** bill of lading
B.L.A. Bachelor of Liberal Arts
B.L.A. or **B.Land. Arch.** Bachelor of Landscape Architecture

bl. a. (bland andra)(Swed.), (blandt andre) (Dan.), **et al.** (et alii or aliae)(Lat.), **m. fl.** (med flera)(Swed.), (med flere) (Dan.) or **u.a.** (und andere)(Ger.) among other; and others; with others

bl. a. (bland annat)(Swed.) (blandt andet) (Dan.), **et al.** (et alii or aliae)(Lat.), **int. al.** (inter alia)(Lat.) or **u.a.m.** (und audere or anderes mehr)(Ger.) among other things; and other things

B.Land. Arch. or **B.L.A.** Bachelor of Landscape Architecture

B/L Att. bill of lading attached

bldg. or **blg.** building

bldr. builder

B.L.E. Brotherhood of Locomotive Engineers

blg. or **bldg.** building

B.L.I. Bachelor of Literary Interpretation

B.L. in J. Bachelor of Letters in Journalism (cf. B.A. in J.; B.J.)

B. Lit. (Baccalaureus Literarum) (Lat.), **L.B.** or **Lit. B.** (Literarum Baccalaureus)(Lat.) Bachelor of Literature

B.Litt. (Baccalaureus Litterarum)(Lat.), **B. ès L.** (Bachelier ès Lettres)(Fr.), **B.L., L.B.** or **Litt. B.** (Litterarum Baccalaureus)(Lat.) Bachelor of Letters

blk. bulk

blk. or **bk.** block

blk. or **bl.** black

blkd. or **Bhd.** bulkhead

blksm or **bs** Blacksmith (Mil.)

B.LL., B.L. (Baccalaureus Legum)(Lat.), **J.B.** (Jurum Baccalaureus)(Lat.) or **LL.B.** (Legum Baccalaureus)(Lat.) Bachelor of Laws

bln. balloon

Bln Gp Balloon group

Bln Sq Balloon squadron

Bln Wg Balloon wing

B.L.R. Breech-loading rifle; breech-loading rifled [gun]

BLS or **B.L.S.** Bureau of Labor Statistics

B.L.S. Bachelor of Library Science

bls., bbl., bbls. or **brls.** barrels

bls. or **B/s** bales

blt. built

Blvd., blvd., Boul. or **boul.** boulevard

BM or **B.M.** Bureau of Mines

BM (Mil.), **B.M.** or **b.m.** bench mark

B.M. Bishop and Martyr; (Beata Maria) (Lat.) Blessed Mary (cf. B.M.V.; B.V.; S.V.); buccomesial (Med.)

B.M. or **b.m.** bay mare; board measure; (beatae memoriae)(Lat.) of blessed memory (cf. sel.); (balneum marinum) (Lat.) seawater bath; (bene merenti) (Lat.) to the well deserving

B.M., b.m., B.Maj. or **Bde. Maj.** Brigade major

B.M. (Baccalaureus Medicinae)(Lat.), **B. Med.** or **M.B.** (Medicinae Baccalaureus)(Lat.) Bachelor of Medicine

B.M (Baccalaureus Musicae) (Lat), **B. Mus., M.B., Mus. B.** or **Mus. Bac.** (Musicae Baccalaureus) (Lat.) Bachelor in or of Music.

B.M., B. Mus. or **Brit. Mus.** British Museum

B/m, b/m or **B. of M.** bill of material

B.M.A. Brick Manufacturers Association; British Medical Association

B.M.A. or **A.M.B.** Bachelor of Mechanic Arts

B.Maj., Bde. Maj., B.M. or **b.m.** Brigade major

B.M.C. Bureau of Motor Carriers

B.M.E., B.Mech.E. or **B.Mech.Eng.** Bachelor of Mechanical Engineering

B.M.E. or **B. Min. E.** Bachelor of Mining Engineering

B.M.E., B. Mus. E., B. Mus. Ed. or **B. Mus. Educ.** Bachelor of Music Education

B. Mech. E., B.M.E. or **B. Mech. Eng.** Bachelor of Mechanical Engineering

B. Med., B.M. (Baccalaureus Medicinae) (Lat.) or **M.B.** (Medicinae Baccalaureus)(Lat.) Bachelor of Medicine

B.Met. Bachelor of Metallurgy

B. Met. E. Bachelor of Metallurgical Engineering

B. Min. E. or **B.M.E.** Bachelor of Mining Engineering

B.M. in P.S.M. Bachelor of Music in Public School Music

B.M. in S.M. Bachelor of Music in School Music

B.M.J. British Medical Journal

B.M.R. basal metabolic rate (Med.)

B.M.R.C. British Medical Research Council

B.M.S. Bachelor of Medical Science; British Music Society

BMU or **B.M.U.** Bureau of Manpower Utilization

B. Mus., B.M. or **Brit. Mus.** British Museum

B. Mus., B.M. (Baccalaureus Musicae) (Lat.), **M.B., Mus. B.** or **Mus. Bac.** (Musicae Baccalaureus)(Lat.) Bachelor in or of Music

B. Mus. Ed., B.M.E., B.Mus. E. or **B. Mus. Educ.** Bachelor of Music Education

B.M.V., BVM or **B.V.M.** (Beata Maria Virgo or Beata Virgo Maria)(Lat.) Blessed Mary, Virgin; Blessed Virgin Mary (cf. B.M.; B.V.; S.V.)

BN Blue Network

B.N. Bachelor of Nursing

B.N. or **B.B.** (billet de banque)(Fr.) banknote

Bn (Mil.) **bat., batln., batn., Batt., batt.** or **bn.** battalion

Bn., B., b. or **Frhr.** (Freiherr)(Ger.) Baron

bn., bat., batln., batn., Batt., batt. or **Bn** (Mil.) battalion

B.N.A. (Basle Nomina Anatomica)(Lat.) Basle anatomical nomenclature; British North America

B.N.C. Brasenose College (Oxford)

Bn Comdr (Mil.) **Bt. C.** or **bt. c.** Battalion commander

Bn C Tn Comdr Batallion combat train commander

bnd. or **bd.** bound

bndg. or **bdg.** binding
Bn.H.Q. Battalion headquarters
bnk. or **bk.** bank
B.N.O.C. British National Opera Company
Bn.R.O. Battalion routine orders
B.N.S. Bachelor of Natural Science
Bnss. or **Frhrn.** (Freiherrin)(Ger.) Baroness
B.O. Bachelor of Oratory; base [of prism] out; Board of Ordnance; body odor; buccoclusal (Med.)
B.O. or **b.o.** back order; box office; branch office
B/O, B/o or **b/o** brought over (Bookkeeping)(cf. B/F; C/o)
Bo bohemium (Chem.)
Bo. De Boeing (Flying fortress)
b.o. bad order (Transp.); broker's order; buyer's option
b.o. or **B.O.** back order; box office; branch office
b/o, B/O or **B/o** brought over (Bookkeeping) (cf. B/F; C/o)
B.O.A. British Olympic Association; British Optical Association
BOAE or **B.O.A.E.** Bureau of Agricultural Economics
B.O.A.F.G. British Order of Ancient Free Gardeners (Freemasonry)
B.O.A.S.I. Bureau of Old Age and Survivors Insurance
BOB, BB or **B.B.** Bureau of the Budget
B. of E. or **B.E.** Bank of England; Board of Education
B. of Engr., B.A.I. (Baccalaureus in Arte Ingeniaria)(Lat.), **B.E.** or **B.Eng.** Bachelor of Engineering
B. of F. A. or **B.F.A.** Bachelor of Fine Arts
B. of F.A. in Dr. Art Bachelor of Fine Arts in Dramatic Art
B. of F. A. in Mus., B.F.A. in Mus. or **B.F.A. Mus.** Bachelor of Fine Arts in Music
B. of H. Band of Hope; Board of Health
B. of M., B/m or **b/m** bill of material
B. of P.D.P.A. or **B.P.D.P.A.** Brotherhood of Painters, Decorators and Paperhangers of America
B. of Pharm., B. P. (Baccalaureus Pharmaciae)(Lat.), **Phar. B., Ph.B.** or **Phm. B.** (Pharmaciae Baccalaureus)(Lat.) Bachelor of Pharmacy
B. of S., BOS, B.O.S. or **Bur. Stds.** Bureau of Standards (cf. NBS)
B. of T., B.O.T. or **B.T.** Board of Trade
B. of Voc. Ed. Bachelor of Vocational Education
Boh. or **Bohem.** Bohemia; Bohemian
B.O.L. Bachelor of Oriental Languages or Literature
Bol. Bolivia; Bolivian
Bol. (bolus, boli)(Lat.), **Pil.** or **pil.** (pilula, pilulae)(Lat.) pill, pills
Bom., Bdr., bomb. or **Br.** Bombardier
Bomb Bombardment (Mil.)
bomb., Bdr., Bom. or **Br.** Bombardier
Bomb. C.S. Bombay Civil Service
Bomb Gp Bombardment group
Bomb H Bombardment, heavy
Bomb L Bombardment, light
Bomb M Bombardment, medium
Bomb. S.C. Bombay Staff Corps
Bomb Sq Bombardment squadron
Bomb wg Bombardment wing
B.O.P. Boy's Own Paper (Brit.)
bor. borough
bor. or **B** boron (Chem.)
BOS, B.O.S. B. of S. or **Bur. Stds.** Bureau of Standards (cf. NBS)
bos'n. or **B.** boatswain
BOT or **B.O.T.** Bureau of Transients
B.O.T. Brotherhood of Teamsters
B.O.T., B. of T. or **B.T.** Board of Trade
bot. botanical; botanist; botany; bottom
bot., bght., bgt. or **bt.** bought
bot. or **btl.** bottle
B.O.T.U. or **B.T.U.** Board of Trade Units
B.O.U. British Ornithologists' Union
Boul., boul., Blvd. or **blvd.** boulevard
B.O.W.O. Brigade ordnance warrant officer
B.P. Bachelor of Painting; (Beatus Paulus) (Lat.) Blessed Paul; (Beatus Petrus) (Lat.) Blessed Peter; blood pressure; British public (Humorous); buccopulpal (Med.)
B.P. (Baccalaureus Pharmaciae)(Lat.), **B. of Pharm., Phar. B., Ph. B.** or **Phm. B.** Bachelor of Pharmacy
B.P. or **B.-P.** Baden-Powell
B.P., B/P, b.p., b.à p. (billets à payer)(Fr.) or **B.Pay.** bills payable (cf. A/cs Pay.)
B.P., B.Ph., B.Phil. (Baccalaureus Philosophiae)(Lat.), **P.B.** or **Ph.B.** Bachelor of Philosophy
B.P., B. Ph., Brit. Pharm., P.B. or **Ph.B.** (Pharmacopoeia Britannica)(Lat.) British Pharmacopoeia
B/P, B.P. b.p. or **b. à p.** (billets à payer) (Fr.) or **B.Pay.** bills payable (cf. A/cs Pay.)
B/P or **b.p.** bill of parcels
Bp., B., bp., Ep. or **Epus.** (Episcopus)(Lat.) bishop (Eccles.)(cf. bp.)
B.p., b.p. or **bp** boiling point
bp, B.p. or **b.p.** boiling point
bp., B., b. or **L.** (Läufer)(Ger.) bishop (Chess) (cf. Bp.)
bp., b.p. or **bpl.** birthplace
b.p. below proof (spirits); brown powder; (bonum publicum)(Lat.) public good
b.p. or **B/P** bill of parcels
b.p., B.p. or **bp** boiling point
b.p., B.P., B/P, b.à p. (billets à payer)(Fr.) or **B.Pay.** bills payable (cf. A/cs Pay.)
b.p., bp. or **bpl.** birthplace
B.Pay., B.P., B/P, b.p. or **b.à p.** (billets à payer)(Fr.) bills payable (cf. A/cs Pay.)
B.P.B. or **b.p.b.** bank post bill or bills
B.P.C. British Pharmaceutical Codex; British Purchasing Commission
B.P.C.U.O.F.S.A. Benevolent and Protective and Completely Universal Order of Fred Smiths of America

B. Pd., B. Pe., B. Pg. (Baccalaureus Pedagogiae)(Lat.), **B. Py., Pd. B., Pe. B., Ped.B., Pg. B.** (Pedagogiae Baccalaureus)(Lat.) or **Py. B.** Bachelor of Pedagogy

bpd, b.p.d., bbls/day or **b/d** barrels per day

B.P.D.P.A. or **B. of P.D.P.A.** Brotherhood of Painters, Decorators and Paperhangers of America

B.P.E. Bachelor of Physical Education

B. Pe., B. Pd., B. Pg. (Baccalaureus Pedagogiae)(Lat.), **B. Py., Pd.B., Pe. B., Ped. B., Pg. B.** (Pedagogiae Baccalaureus)(Lat.) or **Py.B.** Bachelor of Pedagogy

B.Pg., B.Pd., B.Pe. (Baccalaureus Pedagogiae)(Lat.), **B.Py., Pd.B., Pe.B., Ped.B., Pg.B.** (Pedagogiae Baccalaureus)(Lat.) or **Py.B.** Bachelor of Pedagogy

B.Ph., B.P., B.Phil. (Baccalaureus Philosophiae)(Lat.), **P.B.** or **Ph.B.** (Philosophiae Baccalaureus)(Lat.) Bachelor of Philosophy

B. Ph., B.P., Brit. Pharm., P.B. or **Ph.B.** (Pharmacopoeia Britannica)(Lat.) British Pharmacopoeia

B.Phil., B. P., B.Ph. (Baccalaureus Philosophiae)(Lat.), **P.B.** or **Ph. B.** (Philosophiae Baccalaureus) Bachelor of Philosophy

BPI or **B.P.I.** Bureau of Public Inquiries

B.P.I.C. Business Publishers International Corporation

bpl., bp. or **b.p.** birthplace

B.P.O.E. Benevolent and Protective Order of Elks

BPR or **B.P.R.** Bureau of Public Roads

B.P.S.M. Bachelor of Public School Music

Bp. Suff., B. Suff. or **Suff. B.** Bishop Suffragan; Suffragan Bishop

B.P.W.C. Business and Professional Women's Club

B. Py., B. Pd., B.Pe., B.Pg. (Baccalaureus Pedagogiae)(Lat.), **Pd. B., Pe. B., Ped. B., Pg. B.** (Pedagogiae Baccalaureus)(Lat.) or **Py. B.** Bachelor of Pedagogy

B.Q. or **b.q.** (bene quiescat)(Lat.) may he or she rest well (cf. H.R.I.P.; Q.E.P.D.; R.I.P.)

bq., bk. or **bque.** barque; bark

b.q. or **B.Q.** (bene quiescat)(Lat.) may he or she rest well (cf. H.R.I.P.; Q.E.P.D.; R.I.P.)

B.Q.M.S. Battery quartermaster sergeant

bque., bk. or **bq.** barque; bark

B.R., b.à r. (billets à recevoir)(Fr.), **B/R, b.r., B.Rec.** or **b.rec.** bills receivable (cf. A/cs Rec)

B. R. or **B/R** Bill of Rights

B.R. (Banco Regis)(Lat.) or **K.B.** King's Bench

B.R. (Banco Reginae)(Lat.) or **Q.B.** Queen's Bench

B/R Bordeaux or Rouen (Grain trade)

B/R, b.à.r. (billets à recevoir)(Fr.), **B.R., b.r., B.Rec.** or **b. rec.** bills receivable (cf. A/cs Rec)

B/R or **B.R.** Bill of Rights

Br bromine (Chem.)

Br., B. or **Brit.** British

Br., B., b., br., Bro., bro. or **Fr.** (frater)(Lat.) brother

Br., bde., Brig (Mil.) or **Brig.** Brigade

Br., Bdr., Bom. or **bomb.** Bombardier

Br. or **Bglr** (Mil.) bugler

Br. or **br.** bridge; brig

Br. or **Brit.** Britain; Britannia; Britannica; Briton

br. branch; brand; brief; bronze; brown (Turf)

br. or **Br.** bridge; brig

b.r. builder's risk

b.r., b.à r (billets à reservoir)(Fr.), **B.R., B/R, B.Rec.** or **b. rec.** bills receivable (cf. A/cs Rec)

Br. Am. or **B.A.** British America

Braz. Brazil

Braz. or **Brazil.** Brazilian

B Rcn Battle reconnaissance

Br. Col. or **B.C.** British Columbia

B.R.C.S. British Red Cross Society

Br. E. Af. or **B.E.A.** British East Africa

B. Rec., b. rec., b. à r. (billets à recevoir) (Fr.), **B.R., B/R** or **b.r.** bills receivable (cf. A/cs Rec)

Brec. Breconshire

Brecon Brecknockshire

b.rend. bill rendered

Bret. Breton

Brev., brev., Bt., bt., Bvt (Mil.), **Bvt.** or **bvt.** brevet

brev. brevier

brev. or **bvt.** brevetted

brev. man. (brevis manus)(Lat.) offhand

brew. brewer; brewing

brg. or **b.** bearing

br.g. brown gelding

brh brush holder

br.h. brown horse

Brig (Mil.), **Brig., Bde.** or **Br.** Brigade

Brig. or **Bdr.** Brigadier

Brig Comdr (Mil.), **bg. c.** or **Bg. Com.** Brigade commander

Brig Gen (Mil.), **Brig. Gen., Brig.-Gen., B.G.** or **B.Gen.** Brigadier general

Brit., B. or **Br.** British

Brit. or **Br.** Britain; Britannia; Britannica; Briton

Brit. Mus., B.M. or **B. Mus.** British Museum

Brit. Pharm., B.P., B.Ph. or **P.B.** (Pharmacopoeia Britannica)(Lat.) British Pharmacopoeia

Britt. (Brit(t)an(n)iarum)(Lat.) of [all] the Britains (on coins)

brk. broken

brklyr. bricklayer

brkmn. brakeman

brkt. (Drafting) or **bkt.** bracket

BRL Battalion reserve line

brl., bar., bbl., or **bl.** barrel

brls., bbl., bbls. or **bls.** barrels

br.m. brown mare

B.R.O. or **Bde. R.O.** Brigade routine orders

Bro., bro., B., b., Br., br. or **Fr.** (Frater) (Lat.) brother
Bros., bros., FF. (fratres)(Lat.), (Frères) (Fr.), **Geb., Gbr.** (Gebrüder)(Ger.) or **Hnos.** (Hermanos)(Span.) brothers
brot., Brt. or **brt.** brought
BRP or **B.R.P.** Biblical Research in Palestine
Br.S.Af. or **B.S.A.** British South Africa
B.R.T. Brotherhood of Railroad Trainmen
Brt., brt. or **brot.** brought
Brt.fwd., B/F, B/f or **b.f.** brought forward (cf. C/F; C/o)
Brth. Berthold
Br Tn Bridge train (Mil.)
Br Tn Hv Bridge train, heavy (Mil.)
Br Tn L Bridge train, light (Mil.)
Bru. Bruno
Brun., Bruns. or **Brunsw.** Brunswick
Brux. Brussels
Bry., bry., Bryol. or **bryol.** bryological; bryology
BS Blacksmith shop (Mil.)
B.S. Blessed Sacrament; boiler survey (Shipping); bottom settlings; breath sounds (Med.); British Standard
B.S., B.C., B.Ch., B.Chir. (Baccalaureus Chirurgiae)(Lat.), **C.B.** or **Ch.B.** (Chirurgiae Baccalaureus)(Lat.) Bachelor of Surgery
B.S., B. ès S. (Bachelier ès Sciences)(Fr.), **B.Sc., S.B.** or **Sc. B.** (Scientiae Baccalaureus)(Lat.) Bachelor of Science or Sciences
B.S., B.s., bs. or **b.s.** battleship
B.S. or **b.s.** balance sheet
B/S bill of store
B/S or **b.s.** bill of sale
B/s or **bgs.** bags
B/s or **bls.** bales
Bs or **Blksm** Blacksmith (Mil.)
bs., B.S., B.s. or **b.s.** battleship
b.s. or **B.S.** balance sheet
b.s. or **B/S** bill of sale
B.S.A. Bibliographical Society of America; Botanical Society of America (cf. S.P.M.P.); Boy Scouts of America; British School at Athens
B.S.A. or **Br. S.Af.** British South Africa
B.S.A., B.S. Agr., B.S. (Agr.), B.Sc. Agr., B.Sc. in Agr., B.S. in Agr. or **B.S. in Agric.** Bachelor of Science in Agriculture
B.S.A.E., B.Sc. in Agr. Eng. or **B.S. in A.E.** Bachelor of Science in Agricultural Engineering
B.S. Agr., B.S. (Agr.), B.S.A., B.Sc. Agr., B.Sc. in Agr., B.S. in Agr. or **B.S. in Agric.** Bachelor of Science in Agriculture
b.s.&w. basic sediment and water
B.S.A.P. British South Africa Police
B.S.Arch. or **B.S. in Arch.** Bachelor of Science in Architecture
B.S.B.A., B.Sc. in Bus. Adm., B.S. in B.A. or **B.S. in Bus. Adm.** Bachelor of Science in Business Administration
B.S. Bus. or **B.S. in Bus.** Bachelor of Science in Business
B.S.C. Bengal Staff Corps; British Supply Council
B.S.C., B.S.Comm., B.S. in C., B.S. in Com. or **S.B.Com.** Bachelor of Science in Commerce
B.S.C. or **C.S.B.** Bachelor of Christian Science
B. Sc., B. ès S. (Bachelier ès Sciences)(Fr.), **B. S., S. B.** or **Sc. B.** (Scientiae Baccalaureus)(Lat.) Bachelor of Science or Sciences
Bsc Basic (Mil.)
B.Sc. Agr., B.S.A., B.S. Agr., B.S. (Agr.), B.Sc. in Agr., B.S. in Agr. or **B.S. in Agric.** Bachelor of Science in Agriculture
B. Sc. Cer. E., B.S.Cer.E. or **B.S. (Cer. E.)** Bachelor of Science in Ceramic Engineering
B.S.C.E., B.S.C. Engr., B.Sc. in C.E., B.S. in C.E. or **B.S. in Civil Engr.** Bachelor of Science in Civil Engineering
B.Sc. Econ., B.S.Econ., B.S. (Econ.), B.S. in Ec. or **B.S. in Econ.** Bachelor of Science in Economics
B.Sc.Ed., B.Sc. in Ed., B.S.E., B.S.Ed., B.S.Educ., B.S. in Ed., B.S. in Edu., B.S. in Educ., B.S. in Educa. or **S.B. in Ed.** Bachelor of Science in Education
B.S.C. Engr., B.S.C.E., B.Sc. in C.E., B.S. in C.E. or **B.S. in Civil Engr.** Bachelor of Science in Civil Engineering
B. S. Cer. E., B. Sc. Cer. E. or **B. Sc. (Cer. E.)** Bachelor of Science in Ceramic Engineering
B.Sc.F., B. Sc. For., B.S.F. or **B.S.For.** Bachelor of Science in Forestry
B.S.Ch.E., B.Sc. in Chem.E., B.Sc. in Chem. Eng., B.S. in Ch.E., B.S. in Ch. Engr. or **B.S. in Chem. Engr.** Bachelor of Science in Chemical Engineering
B.S.Chem., B.S. in Chem., S.B. in Chem. or **Sc. B. in Chem.** Bachelor of Science in Chemistry
B.Sch. Mus., B.Sch. Music, B.S.M. or **Sch. Mus. B.** Bachelor of School Music
B.Sc. in Agr., B.S.A., B.S. Agr., B.S.(Agr.), B.Sc. Agr., B.S. in Agr. or **B.S. in Agric.** Bachelor of Science in Agriculture
B.Sc. in Agr. Eng., B.S.A.E. or **B.S. in A.E.** Bachelor of Science in Agricultural Engineering
B.Sc. in Arch. Eng. or **B.S. in Arch. Engr.** Bachelor of Science in Architectural Engineering
B.Sc. in Bus. Adm., B.S.B.A., B.S. in B.A. or **B.S. in Bus.Adm.** Bachelor of Science in Business Administration
B.Sc. in C.E., B.S.C.E., B.S.C. Engr., B.S. in C.E. or **B.S. in Civil Engr.** Bachelor of Science in Civil Engineering
B.Sc. in Chem. E., B.S.Ch.E., B.Sc. in Chem.Eng., B.S. in Ch.E., B.S. in Ch. Engr. or **B.S. in Chem. Engr.** Bachelor of Science in Chemical Engineering
B.Sc. in Comm. Eng. Bachelor of Science in Commercial Engineering
B.Sc. in Dent., B.S.D. or **B.S. in Dent.** Bachelor of Science in Dentistry

B.Sc. in Ed., B.Sc.Ed., B.S.E., B.S.Ed., B.S.Educ., B.S. in Ed., B.S. in Edu., B.S. in Educ., B.S. in Educa. or **S. B. in Ed.** Bachelor of Science in Education

B.Sc.inE.E., B.S.E.E., B.S.Elec.Engr., B.S.E.Engr., B.S. in E.E., B.S. in Elec. Eng. or **B.S. in Elec. Engineer.** Bachelor of Science in Electrical Engineering

B.Sc. in General Home Econ. Bachelor of Science in General Home Economics

B.Sc. in Home Econ., B.S.H.E., B.S.H.Ec. or **B.S. in Home Econ.** Bachelor of Science in Home Economics

B.Sc. in M.E., B.S. in M.E., B.S. in Mech.E., B.S.M.E. or **B.S.Mech. Engr.** Bachelor of Science in Mechanical Engineering

B. Sc. in Med., B.S. in Med., B.S. Med. or **S.B. in Med.** Bachelor of Science in Medicine

B. Sc. in Nurs. or **B.S. in Nurs.** Bachelor of Science in Nursing

B.Sc. in Pharm., B.S. in Ph., B.S. in Pharm., B.S. in Phcy., B.S.P., B.S. Phar., B.S. Pharm. or **S.B. in Phar.** Bachelor of Science in Pharmacy

B.S. Comm., B.S.C., B.S. in C., B.S. in Com. or **S.B.Comm.** Bachelor of Science in Commerce

B.S.Comm. Educ., B.S.Commercial Educ. or **B.S. in Com. Ed.** Bachelor of Science in Commercial Education

B.Sc.Tech. Bachelor of Technical Science

B.S.D. Bachelor of Didactic Science or Scientific Didactics

B.S.D., B.Sc. in Dent. or **B.S. in Dent.** Bachelor of Science in Dentistry

B.S.E., B.Sc. Ed., B.Sc. in Ed., B.S. Ed., B.S. Educ., B.S. in Ed., B.S. in Edu., B.S. in Educ., B.S. in Educa. or **S.B. in Ed.** Bachelor of Science in Education

B.S.E., B.S. Engin., B.S. in E., B.S. in Engr., B.S. in Engrg., S.B. in Engin. or **Sc.B. in Eng.** Bachelor of Science in Engineering

B.S.Econ., B.S.(Econ.), B.Sc.Econ., B.S. in Ec. or **B.S. in Econ.** Bachelor of Science in Economics

B.S.Ed., B.Sc.Ed., B.Sc. in Ed., B.S.E., B.S. Educ., B.S. in Ed., B.S. in Edu., B.S. in Educa. or **S.B. in Ed.** Bachelor of Science in Education

B.S.E.E., B.Sc. in E.E., B.S.Elec.Engr., B.S.E. Engr., B.S. in E.E., B.S. in Elec. Eng. or **B.S. in Elec. Engineer.** Bachelor of Science in Electrical Engineering

B. S. E. M. or **B.S. in E.M.** Bachelor of Science in Engineering of Mines (cf. B.S.M.E.)

B.S. Engin., B.S.E., B.S. in E., B.S. in Engr., B.S. in Engrg., S.B. in Engin. or **Sc.B. in Eng.** Bachelor of Science in Engineering

b7d buyer seven days to take up [stocks]

B.S.F., B.Sc.F., B.Sc.For. or **B.S.For.** Bachelor of Science in Forestry

B.S.G. British Standard Gauge

BSH or **B.S.H.** Bureau of Social Hygiene

bsh., bu. or **bush.** bushel

B.S.H.E., B.Sc. in Home Econ., B.S.H.Ec. or **B.S. in Home Econ.** Bachelor of Science in Home Economics

B.S. Hyg. Bachelor of Science in Hygiene

B.S.I. British Standards Institution

B.S.I.E., B.S. Ind. Engr. or **B.S. in I.E.** Bachelor of Science in Industrial Engineering

B.S. in Accounting Bachelor of Science in Accounting

B.S. in A.E. Bachelor of Science in Administrative Engineering; Bachelor of Science in Aeronautical Engineering

B.S. in A.E., B.S.A.E. or **B.Sc. in Agr. Eng.** Bachelor of Science in Agricultural Engineering

B.S. in Aero. Adm. Bachelor of Science in Aeronautical Administration

B.S. in Agr., B.S.A., B.S.Agr., B.S.(Agr.), B.Sc. Agr., B.Sc. in Agr. or **B.S. in Agric.** Bachelor of Science in Agriculture

B.S. in Agr. Ed. Bachelor of Science in Agricultural Education

B.S. in Agric., B.S.A., B.S.Agr., B.S. (Agr.), B.Sc. Agr., B.Sc. in Agr. or **B.S. in Agr.** Bachelor of Science in Agriculture

B.S. in App. Arts Bachelor of Science in Applied Arts (cf. B.App.Arts)

B.S. in Arch. or **B.S. Arch.** Bachelor of Science in Architecture

B.S. in Arch. Engr. or **B.Sc. in Arch. Eng.** Bachelor of Science in Architectural Engineering

B. S. in Art Ed. Bachelor of Science in Art Education

B. S. in Arts Bachelor of Science in Arts

B.S. in B.A., B.S.B.A., B.Sc. in Bus. Adm. or **B.S. in Bus. Adm.** Bachelor of Science in Business Administration

B.S. in Biol. Bachelor of Science in Biology

B.S. in Bus. or **B.S.Bus.** Bachelor of Science in Business

B.S. in Bus. Adm., B.S.B.A., B.Sc. in Bus. Adm. or **B.S. in B.A.** Bachelor of Science in Business Administration

B.S. in Bus. and Public Adm. Bachelor of Science in Business and Public Administration

B.S. in Bus. Ed. Bachelor of Science in Business Education

B. S. in C., B.S.C., B.S.Comm., B.S. in Com. or **S.B.Comm.** Bachelor of Science in Commerce

B. S. in C. and E. Bachelor of Science in Commerce and Economics

B.S. in C.E., B.S.C.E., B.S.C.Engr., B.Sc. in C.E. or **B.S. in Civil Engr.** Bachelor of Science in Civil Engineering

B.S. in Ch.E., B.S.Ch.E., B.Sc. in Chem. E., B.Sc. in Chem. Eng., B.S. in Ch. Engr. or **B.S. in Chem. Engr.** Bachelor of Science in Chemical Engineering

B.S. in Chem., B.S. Chem., S.B. in Chem. or **Sc. B. in Chem.** Bachelor of Science in Chemistry

B.S. in Chem. and Chem. Eng. Bachelor of Science in Chemistry and Chemical Engineering

B.S. in Chem. Engr., B.S.Ch.E., B.Sc. in Chem. E., B.Sc. in Chem. Eng., B.S. in Ch.E. or **B.S. in Ch. Engr.** Bachelor of Science in Chemical Engineering

B.S. in Civil Engr., B.S.C.E., B.S.C.Engr., B.Sc. in C.E. or **B.S. in C.E.** Bachelor of Science in Civil Engineering

B.S. in Com., B.S.C., B.S.Comm., B.S. in C. or **S.B.Comm.** Bachelor of Science in Commerce

B.S. in Com.Ed., B.S.Comm.Educ. or **B.S. Commercial Educ.** Bachelor of Science in Commercial Education

B.S. Ind. Ed. Bachelor of Science in Industrial Education

B. S. Ind. Engr., B.S.I.E. or **B.S. in I.E.** Bachelor of Science in Industrial Engineering

B.S. in Dent., B.Sc. in Dent. or **B.S.D.** Bachelor of Science in Dentistry

B.S. in Dietetics Bachelor of Science in Dietetics

B.S. in E., B.S.E., B.E.Engin., B.S. in Engr., B.S. in Engrg., S.B. in Engin. or **Sc.B. in Eng.** Bachelor of Science in Engineering

B.S. in Ec., B.Sc. Econ., B.S.Econ., B.S. (Econ.) or **B.S. in Econ.** Bachelor of Science in Economics

B.S. in Ec. and Bus. Adm. Bachelor of Science in Economics and Business Administration

B.S. in Econ., B.Sc.Econ., B.S.Econ., B.S.(Econ.) or **B.S. in Ec.** Bachelor of Science in Economics

B.S. in Ed., B.Sc. Ed., B.Sc. in Ed., B.S.E., B.S.Ed., B.S.Educ., B.S. in Edu., B.S. in Educ., B.S. in Educa. or **S.B. in Ed.** Bachelor of Science in Education

B. S. in Ed.—Phys. Ed. Bachelor of Science in Education—Physical Education

B.S. in Edu., B.Sc.Ed., B.Sc. in Ed., B.S.E., B.S.Ed., B.S.Educ., B.S. in Ed., B.S. in Educ., B.S. in Educa. or **S. B. in Ed.** Bachelor of Science in Education

B.S. in E.E., B.Sc. in E.E., B.S.E.E., B.S. Elec. Engr., B.S.E. Engr., B.S. in Elec. Eng. or **B.S. in Elec. Engineer.** Bachelor of Science in Electrical Engineering

B.S. in Elem. Ed. Bachelor of Science in Elementary Education

B.S. in E.M. or **B.S.E.M.** Bachelor of Science in Engineering of Mines (cf. B.S.M.E.)

B.S. in Engr., B.S.E., B.S. Engin., B.S. in E., B.S. in Engrg., S.B. in Engin. or **Sc. B. in Eng.** Bachelor of Science in Engineering

B.S. in Engr. Phys. Bachelor of Science in Engineering Physics

B.S. in F.S. Bachelor of Science in Foreign Service

B.S. in Gen. Eng. Bachelor of Science in General Engineering

B.S. in Genrl. Bus. Bachelor of Science in General Business

B.S. in Geol. or **S.B. in Geol.** Bachelor of Science in Geology

B.S. in Health and Phy. Ed. Bachelor of Science in Health and Physical Education

B.S. in Health Ed. Bachelor of Science in Health Education

B.S. in Home Ec. Ed. Bachelor of Science in Home Economics Education

B.S. in Home Econ., B.Sc. in Home Econ., B.S.H.E. or **B.S.H.Ec.** Bachelor of Science in Home Economics

B.S. in I.E., B.S.I.E. or **B.S. Ind. Engr.** Bachelor of Science in Industrial Engineering

B.S. in J., B.S. in Jrnl., B.S.J. or **B.S.Jour.** Bachelor of Science in Journalism

B.S. in L. Bachelor of Science in Law

B.S. in Lab. Tech. Bachelor of Science in Laboratory Technology

B.S. in Lib. Arts Bachelor of Science in Liberal Arts

B.S. in Lib. Service Bachelor of Science in Library Service

B.S. in L.S. or **B.S.L.S.** Bachelor of Science in Library Science

B.S. in M.E., B.Sc. in M.E., B.S. in Mech. E., B.S.M.E. or **B.S.Mech. Engr.** Bachelor of Science in Mechanical Engineering

B.S. in Mech. Arts. Bachelor of Science in Mechanic Arts

B.S. in Mech. E., B.Sc. in M.E., B.S. in M.E., B.S.M.E. or **B.S.Mech.Engr.** Bachelor of Science in Mechanical Engineering

B.S. in Mech. Ind. Bachelor of Science in Mechanical Industries

B.S. in Med., B.Sc. in Med., B.S.Med. or **S.B. in Med.** Bachelor of Science in Medicine

B.S. in Med. Sc. Bachelor of Science in Medical Science

B.S. in Med. Tech. Bachelor of Science in Medical Technology

B.S. in Met. Eng. Bachelor of Science in Metallurgical Engineering

B.S. in Mining Eng., B.S. in Mining Engr., B.S.M.E. or **B.S. (Min.E.)** Bachelor of Science in Mining Engineering (cf. B.S.E.M.)

B.S. in Music or **B.S. Mus.** Bachelor of Science in Music

B.S. in N.E., B.S. in Nursing Ed. or **B. S. in Nursing Educ.** Bachelor of Science in Nursing Education

B.S. in Nurs. or **B.Sc. in Nurs.** Bachelor of Science in Nursing

B.S. in Nursing Ed., B.S. in N.E. or **B.S. in Nursing Educ.** Bachelor of Science in Nursing Education

B.S. in Optom. or **B.S. in Optometry** Bachelor of Science in Optometry

B.S. in P.A. Bachelor of Science in Practical Arts

B.S. in P.A.L. Bachelor of Science in Practical Arts and Letters

B. S. in P. E. Bachelor of Science in Petroleum Engineering

B.S. in Ph., B.Sc. in Pharm., B.S. in Pharm., B.S. in Phcy., B.S.P., B.S. Phar., B.S. Pharm. or **S.B. in Phar.** Bachelor of Science in Pharmacy

B.S. in P.H.N. Bachelor of Science in Public Health Nursing

B.S. in Phy. Ed., B.S.P.E. or **B.S. Phys. Ed.** Bachelor of Science in Physical Education

B.S. in P.S.M. Bachelor of Science in Public School Music

B.S. in Public Adm. or **B.S.P.A.** Bachelor of Science in Public Administration

B.S. in Rad. Tech. Bachelor of Science in Radiological Technology

B.S. in R. E. Bachelor of Science in Religious Education

B.S. in Ry. M.E. Bachelor of Science in Railway Mechanical Engineering

B.S. in Sc. Bachelor of Science in Science

B.S. in School L.S. or **B.S. in S.L.S.** Bachelor of Science in School Library Science

B.S. in School Mus. Bachelor of Science in School Music

B.S. in S.E. Bachelor of Science in Sanitary Engineering

B.S. in Sec. Sci. Bachelor of Science in Secretarial Science

B.S. in S.L.S. or **B.S. in School L.S.** Bachelor of Science in School Library Science

B.S. in Soc. Bachelor of Science in Sociology

B.S. in Sp. Bachelor of Science in Speech

B.S. in S.S. Bachelor of Science in Social Service

B.S. in S.Sc. Bachelor of Science in Social Science

B.S. in S.W. Bachelor of Science in Social Work

B.S. in Textile Eng. Bachelor of Science in Textile Engineering

B.S. in Voc. Ed. Bachelor of Science in Vocational Education

B.S.J., B.S. in J., B.S. in Jrnl. or **B.S. Joun.** Bachelor of Science in Journalism

B.S.J.R. Bureau of Standards Journal of Research

bsk., bskt. or **bkt.** basket

B.S.L. Bachelor of Sacred Literature; Botanical Society of London

Bs/L or **Bs/Lg** bills of lading

B.S.L.A. Bachelor of Science in Landscape Architecture

B.S. L.A. and Med. Bachelor of Science in Liberal Arts and Medicine

B.S.L.A. and Nurs. Bachelor of Science in Liberal Arts and Nursing

Bs/Lg or **Bs/L** bills of lading

B.S.L.S. or **B.S. in L.S.** Bachelor of Science in Library Science

B.S.M. Battalion or Battery sergeant major; (beso sus manos)(Span.) with great respect (lit., I kiss your hands)(cf. C.M.B.)

B.S.M., B.Sch. Mus., B.Sch. Music or **Sch. Mus. B.** Bachelor of School Music

B.S.M.E., B.Sc. in M.E., B.S. in M.E., B.S. in Mech. E. or **B.S. Mech. Engr.** Bachelor of Science in Mechanical Engineering

B.S.M.E., B.S. in Mining Eng., B.S. in Mining Engr. or **B.S. (Min. E.)** Bachelor of Science in Mining Engineering (cf. B.S.E.M.)

B.S.Mech. Engr., B.Sc. in M.E., B.S. in M.E., B.S. in Mech. E. or **B.S.M.E.** Bachelor of Science in Mechanical Engineering

B.S.Med., B.Sc. in Med., B.S. in Med. or **S.B. in Med.** Bachelor of Science in Medicine

B.S. (Min. E.), B.S. in Mining Eng., B.S. in Mining Engr. or **B.S.M.E.** Bachelor of Science in Mining Engineering (cf. B.S.E.M.)

B.S.Mus. or **B.S. in Music** Bachelor of Science in Music

bsns. or **bus.** business

B.S.P., B.Sc. in Pharm., B.S. in Ph., B.S. in Pharm., B.S. in Phcy., B.S. Phar., B.S. Pharm. or **S.B. in Phar.** Bachelor of Science in Pharmacy

B.S.P.A. or **B.S. in Public Adm.** Bachelor of Science in Public Administration

B.S.P.E., B.S. in Phy. Ed. or **B.S. Phys. Ed.** Bachelor of Science in Physical Education

B.S. Pharm., B. Sc. in Pharm., B.S. in Ph., B.S. in Pharm., B.S. in Phcy., B.S.P., B.S. Phar. or **S.B. in Phar.** Bachelor of Science in Pharmacy

B.S. Phys. Bachelor of Science in Physics

B.S. Phys. Ed., B.S. in Phy. Ed. or **B.S.P.E.** Bachelor of Science in Physical Education

B.S.R. British School at Rome

B.S.S. Biological Supply Service; British Standard Specification

B.S.S. or **B.S.Sc.** Bachelor in or of Social Science or Sciences

B.S. School Supv. Bachelor of Science in School Supervision

B.S. Sec. St. or **B.S. Sec. Stud.** Bachelor of Science in Secretarial Studies

B.S. Sec. Stud. or **B.S. Sec. St.** Bachelor of Science in Secretarial Studies

B.S.T. British Summer Time; Bulletin des Services Techniques

B.S.T. or **S.T.B.** (Sacrae Theologiae Baccalaureus) Bachelor of Sacred Theology

B/St bill of sight

BSTrk Bomb service truck

B.S.U. Baptist Student Union

B. Suff., Bp. Suff. or **Suff. B.** Bishop Suffragan; Suffragan Bishop

BT Block Template

B. T., B. of T. or **B. O. T.** Board of Trade

B.T., S.T.B. (Scientiae Theologicae Baccalaureus)(Lat.), **B.Th.** or **Th.B.** (Theologiae Baccalaureus)(Lat.) Bachelor of Theology

Bt. or **Bart.** Baronet

Bt., bt., Brev., brev., Bvt (Mil.), **Bvt.** or **bvt.** brevet

bt. boat

bt., bght., bgt. or **bot.** bought

b.t. berth terms (Shipping)

BTA or **B.T.A.** Board of Tax Appeals

B.T.C. Bachelor of Textile Chemistry

Bt. C., bt.c. or **Bn Comdr** (Mil.) Battalion commander

B.T.C. of C. Board of Transport Commissioners of Canada

B.T.E. Bachelor of Textile Engineering; British Troops in Egypt

B.T.E.A. Building Trade Employers' Association [of New York City]

b10d buyer ten days to take up [stock]

B.Th., S.T.B. (Scientiae Theologicae Baccalaureus)(Lat.), **B.T.** or **Th.B.** (Theologiae Baccalaureus)(Lat.) Bachelor of Theology
B. Th. U., B. th. u., BTU, Btu, B.T.U. or **B.t.u.** British thermal unit or units
Btk buttock
btl. or **bot.** bottle
btls. bottles
Btry (Mil.), **Btry., B., b., bat., Batt., batt., batty., Bty.** or **bty.** battery
Btry Comdr (Mil.), **B.C., b.c., Bty Comdr** (Mil.) or **by. c.** Battery commander
Btry O or **Bty O** Battery orders
BTU, B.T.U., Btu, B.t.u., B.Th.U. or **B. th. u.** British thermal unit or units
B.T.U. or **B.O.T.U.** Board of Trade Units
btwn., bet., betn., betw., m- (meta-)(Greek) or **zw.** (zwischen)(Ger.) between
B.T.W.U. Building Trade Workers Union
Bty., bty., B., b., bat., Batt., batt., batty., Btry (Mil.) or **Btry.** battery
Bty Comdr (Mil.), **B.C., b.c., Btry Comdr** (Mil.) or **by. c.** Battery commander
Bty O or **Btry O** Battery orders
B.U. base [of prism] up
Bu butyl (Chem.)
bu., bsh. or **bush.** bushel
bu. or **bur.** bureau
bu. or **bus.** bushels
buck. buckram
Bucks or **Bucks.** Buckinghamshire
Budd. Buddhism; Buddhist
B.U.F. British Union of Fascists
B.U.J. (Baccalaureus Utriusque Juris)(Lat.) Bachelor of Both [Canon and Civil] Laws
bul., B. or **bull.** bulletin
Bulg. Bulgaria; Bulgarian
Bull., bull. (bulliat, bulliant)(Lat.) or **coq.** (coque)(Lat.) boil; let boil (Pharm.)
bull., B. or **bul.** bulletin
bull. (bulliens)(Lat.), **coct.** (coctio)(Lat.) or **ferv.** (fervens)(Lat.) boiling
B.U.P. British United Press
bur. or **bu.** bureau
burl. burlesque
Bur.Stds., B. of S., BOS or **B.O.S.** Bureau of Standards (cf. NBS)
bus. omnibus
bus. or **bsns.** business
bus. or **bu.** bushels
bush. bushing (Drafting)
bush., bsh. or **bu.** bushel
butch. butcher
B.V. Bible Version [of the Psalms]; (Beata Virgo)(Lat.) Blessed Virgin (cf. B.M.; B.V.M.; S.V.); (balneum vaporis)(Lat.) vapor bath
B.V., B/V, B/v or **b.v.** book value
B.V. or **b.v.** (bene vale)(Lat.) farewell
b.v., B.V., B/V or **B/v** book value
B.V.A. Bachelor of Vocational Agriculture
BVM, B.V.M., B.M.V. (Beata Virgo Maria or Beata Maria Virgo)(Lat.) Blessed Virgin Mary; Blessed Mary, Virgin (cf. B.M.; B.V.; S.V.)
B.V.Sc. Bachelor of Veterinary Science
Bvt (Mil.), **Bvt., bvt., Brev., brev., Bt.** or **bt.** brevet
bvt. or **brev.** brevetted
B.W. Black Watch; Board of Works; bonded warehouse
Bway. Broadway
BWC or **B.W.C.** Board of War Communications
B.W.C. British War Cabinet; Bureau of Water Carriers
BWG, B.W.G. or **B.G.** Birmingham wire gauge
B.W.I. British West Indies; British Workmen's Institute
B.W.R.S. British War Relief Society
B.W.T.A. British Women's Temperance Association
Bx. Brix (Scale)
bx. box
bxd. boxed
bxs. boxes
by. c., B.C., b.c., Btry Comdr (Mil.) or **Bty Comdr** (Mil.) Battery commander
B.Y.P.U. Baptist Young People's Union
Byz. Byzantine
Bz bensoyl (Chem.)
Bz. or **bz.** benzene

ΒΑΨ (Beta Alpha Psi) National professional fraternity (Accounting)
ΒΒΒ (Beta Beta Beta) National professional fraternity (Biology)
ΒΓΣ (Beta Gamma Sigma) National honor fraternity (Commerce)
ΒΚ (Beta Kappa) National undergraduate fraternity
ΒΦΑ (Beta Phi Alpha) National undergraduate sorority
ΒΦΕ (Beta Phi Sigma) National professional fraternity (Accounting)
ΒΦΘ (Beta Phi Theta) National undergraduate fraternity
ΒΠΘ (Beta Pi Theta) National honor society (French)
ΒΨ (Beta Psi) National undergraduate fraternity
ΒΣΟ (Beta Sigma Omicron) National undergraduate sorority
ΒΣΡ (Beta Sigma Rho) National undergraduate fraternity
ΒΘΠ (Beta Theta Pi) National undergraduate fraternity

C

C, C. or **c.** carbon
C, Cir., cir. or **circfce.** circumference
C., Ae. (Aes)(Lat.), **c., cop., Cu** (Chem.) or **Cu.** (cuprum)(Lat.) copper
C. or **c.** can; canine (Teeth); cape; cervical; colt; corps; cost; cuspid (Teeth); cutter

C., c., C/-, Ca. or **ca.** case
C., c., C/- or **cp.** coupon
C., c., ¢ or **cts.** cents
C., c. or **ca.** candle
C., c., ca., cath. or **ka.** cathode; kathode
C., c., ca., cir., circ. (circa, circiter, circum) (Lat.), **a., abt.** or **abt.** about (cf. approx.)
C., c., ca., cir., circ. (circa, circiter, circum) (Lat.) or **approx.** approximate; approximately (cf. abt.)
C., c., cal., K., k. or **kal.** (kalendae)(Lat.) calends; kalends
C., c., cap. (caput)(Lat.) or **hd.** head
C., c., cap., cy. or **k.** (Elec.) capacity
C., c., cart. or **ctn.** carton
C., c., Cen (Mil.), **cen., cr.** or **ctr.** center
C., c., cen., cent., s. (siècle)(Fr.) or **w.** (wiek)(Pol.) century
C., c., Cent., cent. or **centig.** centigrade
C., c. or **cent.** centime
C., c., cent. or **cm.** centimeter; centimeters
C., c., cent., ct. (centum)(Lat.), **h** (hecto-) (Greek), **H., h., hun.** or **hund.** hundred
C., c., c^{es} or **cts.** centimes
C., c., Ch. or **ch.** child; church
C., c., Ch., ch. or **chf.** chief
C., c., Ch. or **Chanc.** chancellor; chancery
C., c., Chm., chm., Chmn., chmn. or **chn.** chairman
C., c. Ci., ci. or **cir.** cirrus (Meteorol.)
C., c. Cod. or **cod.** codex
C., c., Comp., comp. or **compn.** companion
C., c., con., cond., Condr. or **condr.** conductor
C., c., con., Cons., cons. or **cos.** consul
C., c., con., Cons., cons. or **coss.** consuls
C., c. or **conf.** confessor
C., c. or **Cong.** Congress
C., c., cong. (congius)(Lat.), **gal.** or **gall.** gallon
C., c., Cons., cons. or **conserv.** conservative
C., c., cop. or **copr.** copyright; copyrighted
C., c., Ct. or **ct.** court
C., c., ctl, cwt. or **Ztr.** (Zentner)(Ger.) cental; hundredweight
C., c., cu. or **cub.** cubic
C., c., cur, curr. or **curt.** current (of the present week, month, year)
C., c., cur., curr. or **cy.** currency
C., cap. (capitulo)(Span.), **Ch., ch., Chap., chap., chapt., Kap.** (Kapitel)(Dan.) or **kap.** (kapitel)(Swed.) chapter
C., Cath. or **Cathol.** Catholic
C., Cel. or **Cels.** Celsius (centrigrade theremometer)
C. or **Celt.** Celtic
C., Cir., cir., circfce. or **circum.** circumference
C., Ct., ct. or **Cte.** (Comte)(Fr.) Count
C/-, C., c., Ca. or **ca.** case
C/-, C., c. or **cp.** coupon
c or **sp.ht.** specific heat (Physics)
c., Abdr. (Abdruck, Abdrücke)(Ger.) or **cop.** copy; copies
c., Ae. (aes)(Lat.), **C., cop., Cu** (Chem.) or **Cu.** (cuprum)(Lat.) copper
c. (cum)(Lat.), **av.** (avec)(Fr.), **m.** (mit) (Ger). or **w.** with
c. or **C.** can; canine (Teeth); cape; cervical; colt; corps; cost; cuspid (Teeth); cutter
c., C or **C.** carbon
c., C., C/-, Ca. or **ca.** case
c., C., C/- or **cp.** coupon
c., C., ¢ or **ct.** cent
c., C., ¢ or **cts.** cents
c., C. or **ca.** candle
c., C., ca., cath. or **ka.** cathode; kathode
c., C., ca., cir., circ. (circa, circiter, circum) (Lat.), **a., ab.** or **abt.** about (cf. approx.)
c., C., ca., circ., circ. (circa, circiter, circum) (Lat.) or **approx.** approximate; approximately (cf. abt.)
c., C., cal., K., k. or **kal.** (kalendae)(Lat.) calends; kalends
c., C., cap. (caput)(Lat.) or **hd.** head
c., C., cart. or **ctn.** carton
c., C., Cen (Mil.), **cen., cr.** or **ctr.** center
c., C., cen., cent., s. (siecle)(Fr.) or **w.** (wiek)(Pol.) century
c., C. or **cent.** centime
c., C., Cent., cent. or **centig.** centigrade
c., C., cent. or **cm.** centimeter; centimeter
c., C., cent., ct. (centum)(Lat.), **h** (hecto-) (Greek), **H., h., hun.** or **hund.** hundred
c., C., c^{es} or **cts.** centimes
c., C., Ch. or **ch.** child; church
c., C., con., cond., Condr. or **condr.** conductor
c., C., con., Cons., cons. or **cos.** consul
c., C., con., Cons., cons. or **coss.** consuls
c., C., cop. or **copr.** copyright; copyrighted
c., C., cur., curr. or **cy.** currency
c., car., ct., K., k. or **kt.** carat; karat
c. or **cd.** canned; cord; could
c. or **cy.** cycle; cycles
c^3, cc., c.c., cm.^{3} or **cu.cm.** cubic centimeter
CA casehardened; chronological age; Corps Area (Mil.)
C.A. cervicoaxial (Med.); Coast Artillery; Confederate Army
C. A., C/A, or **c. a.** commercial agent
C. A. or **c.a.** chartered accountant; chartered agent; church association; claim agent; consular agent; controller of accounts; county alderman; (cor anglais)(Fr.) English horn or stops on organ giving that sound (Music);(coll' arco)(Ital.) with the bow (Music)
C.A., c.a. or **Ch.Acct.** chief accountant
C.A., c.a. or **Ct. App.** court of appeal or appeals
C.A., C. Am. or **Cen. Am.** Central America
C/A capital account; close annealed; credit account

C/A, A/C, a/c, Ca/c, C.C., c.c. (compte courant)(Fr.), **c/c** or **c/cte** (cuenta corriente)(Span.) current account; account current

Ca (Chem.) or **cal.** calcium

Ca., ca., C., c. or **C/-** case

ca. centare (Metric)

ca., C. or **c.** candle

ca., C., c., C/- or **Ca.** case

ca., C., c., cath, or ka. cathode; kathode

ca., C., c., cir., circ. (circa, circiter, circum) (Lat.), **a., ab.** or **abt.** about (cf. approx.)

ca., C., c. cir., circ. (circa, circiter, circum) (Lat.) or **approx.** approximate; approximately (cf. abt.)

c.a., C.A. or **Ct.App.** court of appeal or appeals

CAA or **C.A.A.** Civil Aeronautics Administration or Authority (cf. CAB)

CA(AA) Coast Artillery (Antiaircraft)

C.A.A.A. College Art Association of America

C.A.A.M. Civil Aeronautics Authority Manual

CAB or **C.A.B.** Civil Aeronautics Board (cf. CAA); Consumers' Advisory Board

C.A.B. Citizens Advice Bureaus; Cooperative Analysis of Broadcasting

Cab., cab., Cabt. or **cabt.** cabinet

cab. cable; cables

Cabt., cabt., Cab. or **cab.** cabinet

cabwk. cabinetwork

CAC or **C. A. C.** Coast Artillery Corps

C.A.C. Continental Advertising Association

Ca/c, A/C, a/c, C/A, C.C., or **c.c.** (compte courant)(Fr.), **c/c** or **c/cte** (cuenta corriente)(Span.) current account; account current

Cad. or **cad.** cadenza (Music)

Cad., cad. or **E.O.** (Élève officier)(Fr.) Cadet (cf. E.O.R.)

c.-à-d. (c'est-à-dire)(Fr.), **d.ä.** (det är) (Swed.), **d.h.** (das heisst)(Ger.), **d.i.** (das ist)(Ger.), **d.v.s.** (det vil sige), (Dan.),(det vill säga)(Swed.), **h.e.** (hoc or hic est)(Lat.), **i.e.** (id est)(Lat.) or **t.i.** (tudni illik)(Hung.) that is, that is to say (cf. viz.)

CA Dist Coast Artillery District

C.A.D.R. Coast Artillery Drill Regulations

caet. par. or **cet. par.** (ceteris paribus)(Lat.) other things being equal

C.A.F. Curates' Augmentation Fund (Brit.)

C.A.F. or **c.a.f.** cost, assurance and freight (cf. C.I.F.; C.F.I.)

C.A.F., c.a.f., C. and F, c. and f., C. & F., c.&f., C.F. or **c.f.** cost and freight

C.A.F.E. cartage at forwarder's expense

Cal, cal (Mil.) or **cal.** caliber

Cal. [large] calorie or calories

Cal. or **Calif.** California

Cal. or **Calv.** Calvin

cal. calcareous; calendar; [small] calorie or calories; (calando)(Ital.) gradually becoming softer and slower (Music) (cf. decres.; dimin.; perd.)

cal., C., c., K., k. or **kal.** (kalendae)(Lat.) calends; kalends

cal. or **Ca** (Chem.) calcium

cal., Cal or **cal** (Mil.) caliber

Calif. or **Cal.** California

Cal. Prin. calico printing

Calv. or **Cal.** Calvin

C. Am., C.A. or **Cen. Am.** Central America

Cam (Mil.) or **cam.** camouflage

Cam. Camillus

Cam., Camb., Cb. or **Cbr.** Cambridge (cf. Cantab.)

Camb., Cam., Cb. or **Cbr.** Cambridge (cf. Cantab.)

Cam Bn Camouflage battalion

Cambs. Cambridgeshire

c.amp., cochl.amp., coch.amp. (cochleare amplum)(Lat.), **c.mag., cochl.mag., coch. mag.** (cochleare magnum)(Lat.), **tbs.** or **tbsp.** tablespoon; tablespoonful (cochleare amplum and cochleare magnum sometimes used for large or heaping spoonful)

C & B Clothing and bath (Mil.)

C.& D., c.& d., C. and D. or **c. and d.** collected and delivered; collection and delivery

C & E or **C. & E.** Clothing and equipage (Mil.)

C.& F., c.& f., C.A.F., c.a.f., C. and F., c. and f., C.F. or **c.f** cost and freight

C&GE or **C. and G.E.** clothing and general equipment

C & GS Cor (Mil.) or **C. and G.S. Cor.** Command and general staff correspondence

C & GS Cor S (Mil.) or **C. & G.S. Cor. S.** Command and General Staff Correspondence School

C & GS Sch (Mil.) or **C. & G.S. Sch.** Command and General Staff School

C.& I., c.& i., C. and I., c. and i., C.I. or **c.i.** cost and insurance

C.& L. or **c.& l.** canal and lake

c & sc, c.& sc. or **cap.& sm.cap.** capitals and small capitals (Typography)

C. & U.D.L. College and University Departmental Librarians

Can. Canada; Canadian

Can. or **can.** canon; canto; (cantoris)(Lat.) to be sung by the cantorial, or precentor's, side in antiphonal singing (Music)

can., canc. or **cancln.** cancellation

canc. cancel; cancelled

c. and c. coal and coke

C. and D., c. and d., C.& D. or **c.& d.** collected and delivered; collection and delivery

C. and F., c. and f., C.A.F., c.a.f., C.& F., c.& f., C.F. or **c.f.** cost and freight

C. and G.S.Cor. or **C&GS Cor** (Mil.) Command and general staff correspondence

C. and I., c. and i., C.& I., c.& i., C.I. or **c.i.** cost and insurance

Can.Fr. or **Can.F.** Canadian French (cf. Fr. Can.)

Cant. Canticles; Cantonese

Cant. or **Cantuar.** (Cantuaria)(Lat.) Canterbury
Cantab. (Cantabrigiensis)(Lat.) of Cambridge [University] (cf. Camb.)
cantab. (cantabile)(Ital.) suitable for singing (Music)
Cantuar. (Cantuaria)(Lat.) or **Cant.** Canterbury
C.A.P. Civil Air Patrol
Cap., cap., cpt. (capiat)(Lat.) or **sum.** (sumat)(Lat.) let him take
cap., C., c., cy. or **k.** (Elec.) capacity
cap., C., c. (caput)(Lat.) or **hd.** head
cap. (capítulo)(Span.), **C., Ch., ch., Chap., chap., chapt., Kap.** (Kapitel)(Dan.) or **kap.** (kapitel)(Swed.) chapter
cap., Cap., cpt. (capiat)(Lat.) or **sum.** (sumat)(Lat.) let him take
cap. or **capl.** (Law) capital
cap., caps. or **u.c.** (upper case) capital [letters]; capitals
cap., Capt (Mil.), **Capt., Kap.** (Kapitän) (Ger.) or **Kpt.** (Kaptajn)(Dan.) captain
cap. or **u.c.** capital [letter]
cap.& sm.cap., c & sc or **c.& s.c.** capital or capitals and small capitals (Typography)
capl. (Law) or **cap.** capital
caps. capsule; capsules
caps., cap. or **u.c.** (upper case) capital [letters]; capitals
Capt (Mil.), **Capt., cap., Kap.** (Kapitän) (Ger.) or **Kpt.** (Kaptajn)(Dan.) Captain
Capt.-Gen., C.G., c.g. or **C.-G.** Captain-General (Brit.)
C.A.R. Children of the American Revolution; Civil Air Regulations
Car. (Carolus)(Lat.), **Ch.** or **Chas.** Charles
car., c., ct., K., k. or **kt.** carat; karat
car. or **carp.** carpentry
Card., card., cardl. or **Cdl.** cardinal
card. cardamon
Cardig. or **Cardigs.** Cardiganshire
cardl., Card., card. or **Cdl.** cardinal
ca. resp. (capias ad respondendum)(Lat.) arrest defendent and produce in court
Carib. Caribbean
Carliol. Carlisle, in the signature of a Bishop
Carm. or **Carmarths.** Carmarthenshire
Carmarths. or **Carm.** Carmarthenshire
Caro. Carolina; Caroline
carp. or **car.** carpentry
carp. or **Cptr** (Mil.) carpenter
Carr (Mil.) Carriage; Carrier
Carrd.fwd., cd.forwd., C/F or **c/f** carried forward (Bookkeeping)(cf. B/F; C/o)
cart. cartographer
cart., C., c. or **ctn.** carton
cart. or **ctge.** cartage
cartog. cartography
C.A.S. Casualty Actuarial Society; Chicago Academy of Science
cas. casual; casualty
ca. sa. (capias ad satisfaciendum)(Lat.) sieze to satisfy damages (Law)
Cash. or **cash.** cashier
Cat. or **Catal.** Catalan
cat. cataplasm; catechism
cat. or. **catal.** catalog
Catal. or **Cat.** Catalan
catal. or **cat.** catalog
Cath. (catharticus)(Lat.) cathartic (Med.); Catherine
Cath., C. or **Cathol.** Catholic
Cath. or **cath.** cathedral
cath., C., c., ca. or **ka.** cathode; kathode
Cathol., C. or **Cath.** Catholic
caus. causation; causative
C Auth, C. Auth. or **Civ. Auth.** civil authorities
cav. cavalier; cavalry; (caveat)(Lat.) let him beware (Law)(cf. cav. empt.)
c.a.v. or **cur. adv. vult** (curia advisari vult) (Lat.) the court wishes to be advised; the court wishes to consider
Cav Brig (Mil.), **C.B.** or **c.b.** Cavalry brigade
Cav C or **C.C.** Cavalry Corps
Cav DHQ (Mil.) Cavalry division headquarters
Cav Div Cavalry division
Cav Div Arty Cavalry division artillery
cav. empt. or **c.e.** (caveat emptor)(Lat.) let the buyer beware (cf. cav.)
Cav Res Cavalry Reserve
CB cast brass; (Seabee) [member of] Construction battallion (Navy)
C.B. Cape Breton; Common Bench (Brit.); Companion [of the Order] of the Bath;
C.B. or **c.b.** country bill (Banking); currency bond
C.B., c.b. or **C/B** Confined to barracks
C.B., c.b. or **Cav Brig** (Mil.) Cavalry brigade
C.B., Ch.B. (Chirurgiae Baccalaureus) (Lat.), **B.C., B. Ch., B. Chir.** (Baccalaureus Chirurgiae)(Lat.) or **B.S.** Bachelor of Surgery
C/B or **c.b.** cashbook
Cb columbium (Chem.)
Cb., Cam., Camb. or **Cbr.** Cambridge (cf. Cantab.)
c.b. center of bouyancy
c.b. or **C.B.** country bill (Banking); currency bond
c.b. or **C/B** cashbook
C.B.& H. Continent between Bordeaux and Hamburg (Shipping)
c.b.c complete blood count (Med.)
C.B.D. cash before delivery
C.B.E. Commander [of the Order] of the British Empire
C.B.I.A. or **C of BIA** (Mil.) Chief of Bureau of Insular Affairs
c.bl. (carte blanche)(Fr.) unlimited authority; full powers or discretion
C.B.M. Chief boatswain's mate
Cbr., Cam., Camb. or **Cb.** Cambridge (cf. Cantab.)
cbr. counterbore
C.B.R.A. Copper and Brass Research Association

CBS or **C.B.S.** Columbia Broadcasting Service or System
C.B.S. Church Building Society; Confraternity of the Blessed Sacrament
C.B.S.A. Clay Bird Shooting Association
cbtmkr. cabinetmaker
CC cast copper
C.C. Cape Colony; Catholic Clergyman; Catholic Curate; Corporation Commission; construction corps
C.C. or **Cav C** Cavalry Corps
C.C. or **c.c.** cash credit; cashier's check; chancery cases; chess club; city council; civil court; common councilman; consular clerk; county commissioner; county council or councilor; county court; cricket club; curate in charge; cycling club
C.C., c.c. (compte courant)(Fr.), **A/c, a/c, C/a, Ca/c, c/c** or **c/cte** (cuenta corriente)(Span.) current account; account current
C.C., c.c. or **Ch.Clk.** chief clerk
C.C., c.c. or **Circ. Ct.** circuit court
C.C., c.c. or **con. cr.** contra credit
C.C. or **Cod.Civ.** Code Civil (cf. C.C.P.)
C.C. or **C. of C.** Chamber of Commerce
cc., c.c., c³, cm.³ or **Cu. cm.** cubic centimeter
cc., chap. or **chs.** chapters
c.c. carbon copy; chief complaint (Med.); civil commotions (Insurance); compass course; continuation clause (Insurance)
c.c. or **C.C.** cash credit; cashier's check; chancery cases; chess club; city council; civil court; common councilman; consular clerk; county commissioner; county council or councilor; county court; cricket club; curate in charge; cycling club
c.c., C.C. (compte courant)(Fr.), **A/c, a/c, C/a, C/a, Ca/c, c/c** or **c/cte** (cuenta corriente)(Span.) current account; account current
c.c., C.C. or **Ch.Clk.** chief clerk
c.c., C.C. or **Circ.Ct.** circuit court
c.c., C.C. or **con.cr.** contra credit
c.c. or **c. to c.** center to center
c/c, c/cte (cuenta corriente)(Span.), **A/C, a/c, C/A, Ca/C, C.C.** or **c.c.** (compte courant)(Fr.) current account; account current
C.C.A. Canadian Chemical Association; Circuit Court of Appeals; Controlled Circulation Audit [Incorporated]; County Court of Appeals
C.C.A.R. Central Conference of American Rabbis
C Car Combat car (Mil.)
CCC or **C.C.C.** Civilian Conservation Corps; Commodity Credit Corporation
C.C.C. Central Criminal Court; Corpus Christi College
C.C.C.S. Colonial and Continental Church Society
C.C.D. Commander of Coast Defense
C.C.F. Cooperative Commonwealth Federation (Can.)
C.C.F. or **C.F.C.** (Congregatio Fratrum Charitatis)(Lat.) Congregation of the Fathers of Charity; Congregation of the Brothers of Charity; Brothers of Charity; Fathers of Charity
C.C.I.R. Catholic Council for International Relations
C.C.J. (Congregatio Charitatis Sacratissimi Cordis Jesu)(Lat.) Congregation of Charity of the Most Sacred Heart of Jesus; (Congregatio Sacredotum a Sacro Corde Jesu)(Lat.) Congregation of Priests of the Sacred Heart of Jesus
cckw. counterclockwise
C.C.L.A. Child Conservation League of America
C.Cls. or **Ct.Cls.** Court of Claims
C.C.M. Chief carpenter's mate
C.C.M.C. Committee on the Cost of Medical Care
CCMI or **C.C.M.I.** Committee on Conservation of Manpower in Industry
C.C.N.Y. Carnegie Corporation of New York; College of the City of New York
C.C.P. Code of Civil Procedure (cf. Cod. Civ.)
C.C.P. or **Ct.Com.Pleas** Court of Common Pleas
C.C.P.A. Court of Customs and Patent Appeals
C.C.R. Catholic Committee for Refugees
C.Cr.P. Code of Criminal Procedure
CCS Combined Chiefs of Staff (U.S. and Great Britain)
C.C.S. Casualty Clearing Station (Brit.); Ceylon Civil Service
c/cte, c/c (cuenta corriente)(Span.), **A/C, a/c, C/A, Ca/C, C.C.** or **c.c.** (compte courant)(Fr.) current account; account current
CD Coast defense; condemned
C.D. Chancery Division; Chief of Division; Civil defense (Brit.); Civilian defense; Colonial Dames; commercial dock; consular declaration
C.D. or **c.d.** cash discount
C.D., c.d. or **C/D** certificate of deposit
C.D. or **Conf. Doct.** Confessor and Doctor of the Church
Cd cadmium (Chem)
Cd. caudal (Anat.)
Cd. (to 1918) or **Cmd.** (since 1919) Command Paper
C/d carried down (Accounting) (cf. B/D; C/F; C/o)
cd. or **c.** cord; could
cd. or **Comd** (Mil.) command
c.d. (colla destra)(Ital.) with the right hand (Music)
c.d. or **C.D.** cash discount
c.d., C.D. or **C/D** certificate of deposit
c.d., cum d., cum d/, cum dd. or **cum div.** (cum dividendo)(Lat.) with dividend
C.D.A. Canadian Dental Association; College Diploma in Agriculture
C.D.A. or **C.D.of A.** Catholic Daughters of America
C.D.Acts Contagious Diseases Acts

CDD certificate of disability for discharge (Mil.)
CDE code (Cables)
cd.forwd., Carrd.fwd., C/F or **c/f** carried forward (Bookkeeping)(cf. B/F; C/o)
cd.ft. cord foot or feet
C.D.H. College Diploma in Horticulture
C.D.H.C. Canadian Dental Hygiene Council
Cdl., Card., card. or **cardl.** cardinal
CDLD Consumers' Division of the Labor Department
CDNRA Consumers' Division of the National Recovery Administration
C.D. of A. or **C.D.A.** Catholic Daughters of America
C.D.R.F. Canadian Dental Research Foundation
C.D.S. Chicago Dental Society
C.D.S., C.D.S.O. or **D.S.O.** Companion of the Distinguished Service [Order]
cds. cards
C.D.S.O., C.D.S. or **D.S.O.** Companion of the Distinguished Service Order
C.D.S.T. Central Daylight Saving Time
c.duob.ff.albis with two leaves blank (Book binding)
c.d.v. (carte de visite)(Fr.) visiting card
CDVO or **C.D.V.O.** Civilian Defense Volunteer Office or Officer
CE commutator end
CE or **C.E.** Corps of Engineers
C.E. Canada East; Chief Engineer; Common Era; (Service du contre-espionnage)(Fr.) Counter-Espionage Service
C.E., Ch.E., Chem.E. or **Chem. Eng.** Chemical Engineer
C.E. or **Civ. Eng.** Civil Engineer
C.E., C. of E. or **Ch. of Eng.** Church of England
C.E. or **Y.P.S.C.E.** [Young People's Society of] Christian Endeavor (cf. C.E.U.)
Ce cerium (Chem.)
c.e. or **cav. empt.** (caveat emptor)(Lat.) let the buyer beware (cf. cav.)
CEA or **C.E.A.** Commodity Exchange Administration (cf. CEC)
CEC or **C.E.C.** Commodity Exchange Commission (cf. CEA)
C.E.C. Civil Engineering Corps
C.E.C. or **Tz.I.K.** (Tzentralny Ispolnitelny Kommitet)(Rus.) [Soviet Union] Central Executive Committee (cf. U.C.E.C.; V. Tz. I.K.)
C.E.C.S.T. Committee of Experts for the Coordination of Scientific Terminology
CED or **C.E.D.** Committee for Economic Development
C.E.F. Canadian Expeditionary Force
C.E.G. Catholic Evidence Guild
C.E.I.P. Carnegie Endowment for International Peace
Cel., C. or **Cels.** Celsius (centigrade thermometer)
cel. celebrated
Cels., C. or **Cel.** Celsius (centigrade thermometer)
Celt. or **C.** Celtic
Cem Cemetery (Mil.)
cem. cement
cemf or **C.E.M.F.** counter electromotive force
C.E.M.S. Church of England Men's Society
Cen (Mil.), **cen., C., c., cr.** or **ctr.** center
Cen., cen., Cent., cent. or **Centr.** central
cen., C., c., cent., s. (siècle)(Fr.) or **w.** (wiek)(Pol.) century
Cen. Am., C. A. or **C. Am.** Central America
Cent., cent., C., c. or **centig.** centigrade
Cent., cent., Cen., cen. or **Centr.** central
cent., C. or **c.** centime
cent., C., c., cen., s. (siècle)(Fr.) or **w.** (wiek)(Pol.) century
cent., C., c. or **cm.** centimeter; centimeters
cent., C., c. ct. (centum)(Lat.), **h** (hecto-) (Greek), **H., h., hun.** or **hund.** hundred
centig., C., c., Cent. or **cent.** centigrade
Centr., Cen., cen., Cent. or **cent.** central
C.E.O. (Corps expéditionnaire d'Orient) (Fr.) Eastern Expeditionary Corps
ceram. ceramics
Cer. E. Ceramic Engineer
Cert., cert., Certc., Certif., certif. or **ctf.** certificate
cert. certiorari
cert. or **certif.** certified; certify
Certc., Cert., cert., Certif., certif. or **ctf.** certificate
Certif., certif., Cert., cert., Certc. or **ctf.** certificate
certif. certificated
certif. or **cert.** certified; certify
CES or **C.E.S.** Committee on Economic Security
C.E.S. (Corps expéditionnaire de Serbie) (Fr.) Serbian Expeditionary Corps
c^{es}, C., c. or **cts.** centimes
C.E.S.A. Canadian Engineering Standards Association
C.E.S.S.I. or **C.E.S.S. Inst.** Church of England Sunday School Institute
Cestr. Chester (in the signature of a bishop)
Cestr. or **Cicestr.** Chichester (in the signature of a bishop)
C.E.T.B.S. Church of England Temperance Benefit Society
cet. par. or **caet. par.** (ceteris paribus)(Lat.) other things being equal
C. E. T. S. Church of England Temperance Society
C.E.U. Christian Endeavour Union (cf. Y.P.S.C.E.)
C.E.W.M.S. Church of England Working Men's Society
CF Coastal frontier
C.F. carbolfushsin; center fielder; centrifugal force; Chaplain to the Forces
C.F., C.A.F., c.a.f., C.&F., c.&f., C. and F., c. and f. or **c.f.** cost and freight
C. F. or **c.f.** (cantus firmus)(Lat.) plain Gregorian chant
C/F, Carrd.fwd., cd.forwd. or **c/f** carried forward (Bookkeeping)(cf. B/F; C/o)
cf. calf (Bookbinding)

cf., **conf.** (confer)(Lat.), **comp.**, **compar.**, **cp.**, **jf.**, **jfr.** (jaevnfør)(Dan.) ,(jämför) (Swed.), **por.** (porównaj)(Pol.), **sml.** (sammenlign)(Dan.) or **vgl.** (vergleiche)(Ger.) compare
c.f. (cum figuris)(Lat.) with illustrations (cf. illus.)
c.f., **C.A.F.**, **c.a.f.**, **C.&F.**, **c.&f.**, **C. and F.**, **c. and f.** or **C.F.** cost and freight
c/f, **Carrd.fwd.**, **cd.forwd.** or **C/F** carried forward (Bookkeeping)(cf. B/F; C/o)
CFA Commission of Fine Arts
C.F.A. Canadian Freight Association; Central Freight Association; (Congregatio Fratrum Alexianorum)(Lat.) Society of Alexian Brothers; Order of St. Alexius; Alexian Brothers
C. F. & I., **c.f. & i.**, **C.F. and I.**, **c.f. and i.**, **C.F.I** or **c.f.i.** cost, freight and insurance (cf. C.A.F.; C.I.F.)
C.F.A.T. Carnegie Foundation for the Advancement of Teaching
C.F.C. Consolidated Freight Classification
C.F.C. or **C.C.F.** (Congregatio Fratrum Charitatis)(Lat.) Congregation of the Brothers of Charity
cf. ex. or **cf. ext.** calf extra (Bookbinding)
C.F.G. (Confédération Générale de Travail) (Fr.) General Confederation of Labor
C.F.I., **c.f.i.**, **C.F. and I.**, **c.f. and i.**, **C.F. & I.** or **c.f. & i.** cost, freight and insurance (cf. C.A.F.; C.I.F.)
cfm or **c.f.m.** cubic feet per minute
C.f.o. Channel for orders (Shipping); coast for orders
C.F.P. (Commandant de la force publique) (Fr.) Chief of Police; (Congregatio Fratrum Pauperum)(Lat.) Poor Brothers of St. Francis
C.F.R. Code of Federal Regulations
cfr. (Mil.) or **chauf.** chauffeur
cfs or **c.f.s.** cubic feet per second (cf. sec.-ft.)
C.F.T. complement fixation test
c.ft., **cu.ft.**, **cub.ft.** or **ft.**^{3} cubic foot or feet
C.F.T.B. Central Freight Traffic Bureau
C.F.U. Croatian Fraternal Union
C.F.X. (Congregatio Fratrum Sancti Francisci Xaverii)(Lat.) Brothers of St. Francis Xavier
CG (Mil), **C.G.** or **c.g.** Commanding general
C.G. Coast Guard; Coldstream Guards (Brit.); (Croix de guerre)(Fr.) Cross of War
C.G., **CG** (Mil.) or **c.g.** Commanding general
C.G. or **c.g.** Captain of the Guard; consul general
C.G., **c.g.**, **C.-G.** or **Capt.-Gen.** Captain-General (Brit.)
C.G., **c.g.** or **C. of G.** center of gravity
C.G., **c.g.** or **Comy.-Gen.** commissary general
C.-G., **Capt.-Gen.**, **C.G.** or **c.g.** Captain-General (Brit.)
cg. or **cgm.** centigram
c.g., **CG** (Mil.) or **C.G.** Commanding general
c.g. or **C.G.** Captain of the Guard; consul general
c.g., **C.G.**, **C.-G.** or **Capt.-Gen.** Captain-General (Brit.)
c.g., **C.G.** or **C.of G.** center of gravity
c.g., **C.G.** or **Comy.-Gen.** commissary general
c.g.a. cargo's proportion of general average (Insurance)
C.G.C. Coast Guard cutter
C.G.H. or **C. of G.H.** Cape of Good Hope
C.G.I.T. Canadian Girls in Training
C.G.L. of C. Commanding general, line of communications
C.G.M. Common gunner's mate; Conspicuous Gallantry Medal
cgm. or **cg.** centigram
cgo. contango (Brit.)
C.G.S. Chief of General Staff; Commissary General of Subsistance
C.G.S., **cgs**, **c.g.s.** or **c-g-s** centimeter-gram-second
cgse or **c.g.s.e.** centimeter-gram-second-electrostatic [system]
cgsm or **c.g.s.m.** centimeter-gram-second electromagnetic [system]
C.H. Captain of the Horse; Champion of Honor; Companion of Honour (Brit.)
C.H. or **c.h.** clearinghouse; courthouse; customhouse
Ch (Mil.), **Chap.**, **chap.** or **Chapl.** chaplain
Ch. Charlotte
Ch., **C.**, **c.** or **Chanc.** chancellor
Ch., **Car.** (Carolus)(Lat.) or **Chas.** Charles
Ch. or **ch.** check (Chess); checkered; chervonsti (Russian gold coin); chestnut; children; choir (Organ)
Ch., **ch.**, **C.** or **c.** child; church
Ch., **ch.**, **C.**, **c.** or **Chanc.** chancery
Ch., **ch.**, **C.**, **c.** or **chf.** chief
Ch., **ch.**, **C.**, **cap.** (capítulo)(Span.), **Chap.**, **chap.**, **chapt.**, **Kap.** (Kapitel)(Dan.) or **kap.** (kapitel)(Swed.) chapter
Ch., **ch.**, **chal.** or **chd.** chaldron
Ch., **ch.** (chirurgia)(Lat.) or **surg.** surgery
Ch. or **Chin.** China; Chinese
ch. chest; choice
ch. or **Ch.** check (Chess); checkered; chervonsti (Russian coin); chestnut; children; choir (Organ)
ch. or **chn.** chain
c.h. or **C.H.** clearinghouse; courthouse; customhouse
c.h. or **c-hr** candle-hour or hours
C.H.A. Colorado Hospital Association; Connecticut Hospital Association
Ch.Acct., **C.A.** or **c.a.** chief accountant
CHAL or **C.H.A.L.** Cambridge History of American Literature
Chal. or **Chald.** Chaldaic; Chaldaism; Chaldean; Chaldee
chal., **Ch.**, **ch.** or **chd.** chaldron
Chamb. Chamberlain
C.H.&H. Continent between Havre and Hamburg (Shipping)
Chanc., **C.**, **c.** or **Ch.** chancellor
Chanc., **C.**, **c.**, **Ch.** or **ch.** chancery

Chap., chap., C., cap. (capítulo)(Span.), **chapt., Kap.** (Kapitel)(Dan.) or **kap.** (kapitel)(Swed.) chapter
Chap., chap., Ch (Mil.) or **Chapl.** chaplain
chap., cc. or **chs.** chapters
Chap.-Gen. Chaplain-general (Brit.)
Chapl., Ch (Mil.), **Chap.** or **chap.** chaplain
chapt., C., cap. (capítulo)(Span.), **Ch., ch., Chap., chap., Kap.** (Kapitel)(Dan.) or **kap.** (kapitel)(Swed.) chapter
Char. or **char.** character
Char., char. or **chtr.** charter
Chart., chart. (chartula)(Lat.) (Pharm.) or **S.P.** small paper
Chas., Car. (Carolus)(Lat.) or **Ch.** Charles
chauf. of **cfr** (Mil.) chauffeur
Ch.B., C.B. (Chirurgiae Baccalaureus) (Lat.), B.C., B.Ch., B.Chir. (Baccalaureus Chirurgiae)(Lat.) or **B.S.** Bachelor of Surgery
C.H.C. Canadian Hospital Council
Ch.C. Chaplain corps
Ch.Ch. Christ Church (Oxford)
Ch. Clk., C.C. or **c.c.** chief clerk
Ch Controls Cutler hammer controls
Ch.Ct. Chancery court
Ch.D. or **Dr.Chem.** Doctor of Chemistry
chd., Ch., ch. or **chal.** chaldron
ch. de f. (chemin de fer)(Fr.), **R., r., rly., R.W., rw, Rwy.** or **Ry.** railway (cf. R.R.)
Ch.E., C.E., Chem. E. or **Chem. Eng.** Chemical Engineer
CHEL or **C.H.E.L.** Cambridge History of English Literature
Chem., chem., Cheml. or **Cml** (Mil.) chemical
chem. chemist; chemistry
Chem. E., C.E., Ch. E. or **Chem. Eng.** Chemical Engineer
Cheml., Chem., chem. or **Cml** (Mil.) chemical
Ches. or **Chesh.** Cheshire
Chev. (Chevalier)(Fr.), **K., k., knt., Kt** (Chess), **Kt.** or **R.** (Ridder)(Dan.) knight
chf., C., c., Ch. or **ch.** chief
chfd. chamfered
chg. change; charge
ch.g. chestnut gelding
chgd. changed; charged
chgs. changes; charges
Ch.Gun. Chief gunner
Ch. Hist. Church history
Chi. Chicago
Chin. or **Ch.** China; Chinese
Chino-Jap. or **Sino-Jap.** Chinese-Japanese
Chir. Doc. or **Chir. Doct.** (Chirurgiae Doctor)(Lat.) Doctor of Surgery
Ch.J. or **C.J.** Chief Judge; Chief Justice
chl chloroform
Ch. M., C.M. (Chirurgiae Magister)(Lat.), **M.C., M. Ch.** (Magister Chirurgiae) (Lat.), **M.S., M. Surg.** or **M. Surgery** Master of Surgery
Chm., chm., C., c., Chmn., chmn. or **chn.** chairman
chm. checkmate
ch.m. chestnut mare
ch.m. (charta magna)(Lat.) or **l.p.** large paper (Printing)
Chmn., chmn., C., c., Chm., chm. or **chn.** chairman
chn., C., c., Chm., chm., Chmn. or **chmn.** chairman
chn. or **ch.** chain
Ch. of Eng., C.E. or **C. of E.** Church of England
CHQ Corps headquarters
Chq., chq. or **ck.** check; cheque
Chr. or **Chris.** Christina; Christine; Christopher
Chr., X. or **Xt.** (Christos)(Greek) Christ
Chr., Xn., Xt. or **Xtian.** Christian
chr. chrestomathy
c-hr or **c.h.** candle-hour or hours
Ch-Res Chaplains' Reserve
Chris. or **Chr.** Christina; Christine; Christopher
Chris. or **Cp.** Christoph
Chron. Chronicles (Bib.)
chron. or **chronol.** chronological; chronology
Chrs. chambers
chs., cc., or **chap.** chapters
Ch Sec Chaplain section
cht. chest
chtr., Char. or **char.** charter
chtrd.frt. chartered freight (Shipping)
chtrr. charterer
CI, C.I. or **c.i.** cast iron
C.I. Channel Islands; color index; consular invoice; [Imperial Order of the] Crown of India
C.I., c.i., C.&I., c.&i., C. and I., or **c. and i.** cost and insurance
C/I certificate of insurance
Ci., ci., C., c. or **cir.** cirrus (Meteorol.)
c.i. corrguated iron (Roofing)
c.i., C.&I., c.&i., C. and I., c. and i. or **C.I.** cost and insurance
c.i., or **CI** or **C.I.** cast iron
Cía. (Compañía)(Span.), **Cie, cie** (compagnie)(Fr.), **Co., co., comp., Comp**[a], **compa., Compy., compy., Coy., coy.** or **Ges.** (Gesellschaft)(Ger.) company
C.I.&F., c.i.&f., C.I. and F., c.i. and f., C.I.F., cif or **c.i.f.** cost, insurance and freight (cf. C.F.I.; C.A.F.)
C.I. and F., c.i. and f., C.I.&F., c.i.&f., C.I.F., cif or **c.i.f.** cost, insurance and freight (cf. C.F.I.; C.A.F.)
CIC or **C.I.C.** Coordinator of Industrial Cooperation
C.I.C. (Codex Iuris Canonici)(Lat.) Code of Canon Law (cf. C. J. Can.); Chinese Industrial Cooperatives
C.I.C., C-I-C, C.-I.-C., C in C (Mil.), **C. in C., Com.-in-C., Com. in Chf.** or **Com.-in-Chf.** Commander in Chief

Cic. Cicero
c.ic. (cum iconibus)(Lat.) with engravings
Cicester. or **Cestr.** Chichester, in signature of bishop
C.I.C.M. (Congregatio Cordis Immaculati Mariae)(Lat.) Congregation of the Immaculate Heart of Mary
Ci. Cu. cirro-cumulus (Meteorol.)
C.I.D. Criminal Investigation Department; Committee of Imperial Defence
C.I.E. Companion [of the Order] of the Indian Empire
Cie, cie (compagnie)(Fr.), **Cía.** (Compañía) (Span.), **Co., co., comp., Comp**[a], **compa., Compy., compy., Coy., coy.** or **Ges.** (Gesellschaft)(Ger.) company
C.I.F., cif, c.i.f., C.I.&F., c.i.&f., C.I. and **F.** or **c.i. and f.** cost, insurance and freight (cf. C.A.F.; C.F.I.)
C.I.F.&C., c.i.f.&c., C.I.F. and C., c.i.f. and c., C.I.F.C. or **c.i.f.c.** cost, insurance, freight and charges
C.I.F.&E., c.i.f.&e., C.I.F. and E., c.i.f. and e., C.I.F.E. or **c.i.f.e.** cost, insurance, freight and exchange
C.I.F.&I., c.i.f.& i., C.I.F. and I., c.i.f. and i., C.I.F.I. or **c.i.f.i.** cost, insurance, freight and interest
C.I.F. and C., c.i.f. and c., C.I.F.&C., c.i.f.& c, C.I.F.C. or **c.i.f.c.** cost, insurance, freight and charges
C.I.F. and E., c.i.f. and e., C.I.F.&E., c.i.f.&e., C.I.F.E. or **c.i.f.e.** cost, insurance, freight and exchange
C.I.F. and I., c.i.f. and i., C.I.F.&I., c.i.f.& i., C.I.F.I. or **c.i.f.i.** cost, insurance, freight and interest
C.I.F.C., c.i.f.c., C.I.F.&C., c.i.f.&c., C.I.F. and C. or **c.i.f. and c.** cost, insurance, freight and charges
C.I.F.C.&I., c.i.f.c.&i., C.I.F.C. and I., or **c.i.f.c. and i.** cost, insurance, freight, collection and interest; cost, insurance, freight, commission and interest
CI.F.C. and I., c.i.f.c. and i., C.I.F.C.&I. or **c.i.f.c.&i.** cost, insurance, freight, collection and interest; cost, insurance, freight, commission and interest
C.I.F.E., c.i.f.e., C.I.F.&E., c.i.f.&e., C.I.F. and E. or **c.i.f. and e.** cost, insurance, freight and exchange
C.I.F.I., c.i.f.i., C.I.F.& I., c.i.f.&i. C.I.F.and I. or **c.i.f. and i.** cost, insurance, freight and interest
C.I.F.I.& E., c.i.f.i.& e., C.I.F.I. and E. or **c.i.f.i. and e.** cost, insurance, freight, interest and exchange
C.I.F.I. and E., c.i.f.i. and e., C.I.F.I.& E. or **c.i.f.i.& e.** cost, insurance, freight, interest and exchange
cif Lt or **c.i.f.L.t.** cost, insurance and freight, London terms (cf. CIF)
C.I.G.S. Chief of the Imperial General Staff
C.I. Mech. E. Companion of the Institution of Mechanical Engineers
Cin. Cincinnati
C in C. (Mil.), **C. in C., C.I.C., C-I-C, C.-I.-C., Com.-in-C., Com. in Chf.** or **Com.-in-Chf.** Commander in Chief
CINCAF Commander in Chief Asiatic Fleet
CINCLANT Commander in Chief Atlantic Fleet
CINCPAC Commander in Chief Pacific Fleet
C. Inf. Colored infantry
c. infant., coch. infant. or **cochl. infant.** (cochleare infantis)(Lat.) child's spoonful
CIO or **C.I.O.** Congress (formerly Committee) of Industrial Organizations
Cir (Mil.), **cir.** or **circ.** circular
Cir., cir., C., circfce. or **circum.** circumference
cir., C., c., ca., circ., (circa, circiter, circum) (Lat.), **a., ab.** or **abt.** about (cf. approx.)
cir., C., c., ca., circ. (circa, circiter, circum) (Lat.) or **approx.** approximate; approximately (cf. abt.)
cir., C., c., Ci. or **ci.** cirrus (Meteorol.)
cir. or **circ.** circulation
cir.bkr. circuit breaker
circ., C., c., ca., cir. (circa, circiter, circum) (Lat.), **a., ab.** or **abt.** about (cf. approx.)
circ., C., c., ca., cir. (circa, circiter, circum) (Lat.) or **approx.** approximate; approximately (cf. about)
circ. or **Cir** (Mil.). circular
circ. or **cir.** circulation
Circ.Ct., C.C. or **c.c.** circuit court
circe. circumstance
circfce., C., Cir., cir. or **circum.** circumference
Circ.J. circuit judge
circum., C., Cir., cir. or **circfce.** circumference
circumscr. (circumscriptio)(Lat.) encircling inscription (Printing)
cir.mils or **c.m.** circular mils (wire measure
CISS or **C.I.S.S.** Canadian Institute of Sewage and Sanitation
Ci. St. cirro-stratus (Meteorol.)
C.I.T. California Institute of Technology; Carnegie Institute of Technology; Commercial Investment Trust
cit. citation; cited; citizen
c.i.t. compression in transit
C.I.T.E.J.A. (Comité International Technique D'Experts Juridiques Aériens) (Fr.) International Technical Committee of Legal Experts on Air Questions
citr. citron
C.I.U.S.S. Catholic International Union for Social Service
C.I.V. City Imperial Volunteers; Colonial Imperial Volunteers
Civ. or **civ.** civil; civilian
Civ. Auth., C.Auth., or **C Auth** civil authorities or authority
Civ. Eng. or **C.E.** Civil Engineer
C.I.W. Carnegie Institution of Washington
C.J. Congregation of Josephites; Sons of St. Joseph; Josephites
C.J. or **Ch. J.** Chief Judge; Chief Justice
cj. conjectural

C.J.Can., Corp. Jur. Can. or **Corpus Jur. Can.** (Corpus Juris Canonici)(Lat.) the body of canon law (cf. C.I.C.)
C.J.Civ. or **Corp.Jur.Civ.** (Corpus Juris Civilis)(Lat.) the body of civil law
C.J.F. Council of Jewish Federations
C.J.M. (Congregatio Jesu et Mariae)(Lat.) Congregation of Jesus and Mary; Eudist Fathers
Ck (Mil.) or **ck.** cook
ck., Chq. or **chq.** check; cheque
ck. or **csk.** cask
cks. casks; checks
ckw. clockwise
CL or **c.l.** center line
C.L. Canadian Legion; Commander [of the Order] of Leopold
C.L. or **c.l.** carload; carload lots
C.L., c.l. or **Com. Law** common law
C/L cash letter
Cl chlorine (Chem.); clay (Mil.)
Cl. closure [of an electric unit]
Cl., cl. or **clo.** cloth
cl. centiliter; claim; clause; clearance
cl. or **class.** classification; classified; classify
cl., clerg. or **clk.** (clericus)(Lat.) clergyman
cl. or **clk.** clerk
cl or **Kl.** (Klasse)(Dan.) class
c.l. civil law; craft loss (Insurance)
c.l. (citato loco)(Lat.), **a.a.O.** (am angeführten Orte)(Ger.), **in loc. cit.** (in loco citato)(Lat.), **l.c.** or **loc.cit.** (loco citato)(Lat.) in the place cited (cf. loc. laud.; loc. primo cit.; op. cit.; u.s.)
c.l. or **CL** center line
c.l. or **C.L.** carload; carload lots
c/l. (curso legal)(Span.) legal procedure
CLAB or **C.L.A.B.** College Library Advisory Board
C.L.& R. or **c.l.& r.** canal, lake and rail
Clar. Clarence; Clarendon (Typog.)
clar. clarinet
C.L.A.S. Catholic Ladies' Aid Society
Class. or **class.** classic; classical; classics (cf. Lit.Hum.)
class. or **cl.** classification; classified; classify
Class. Myth. Classical Mythology
C.L.B. Church Lads' Brigade
cl.bds. cloth boards (Bookbinding)
C.L.D., D.C.L. or **J.C.D.** (Juris Civilis Doctor)(Lat.) Doctor of Civil Law
Cld (Mil.), **cld., col.** or **kol.** (koloriert)(Ger.) colored
cld. called (Bonds); cleared
cld., Cld (Mil.), **col.** or **kol.** (koloriert) (Ger.) colored
c.l.d. cost laid down
Clem. Clemens; Clement
cler. clerical
clerg., cl. or **clk.** (clericus)(Lat.) clergyman
cl. gt. cloth gilt (Bookbinding)
climatol. climatological; climatology
clin. clinic; clinical
Cl I Sup Class one supplies (Mil.)
clk. clock
clk. or **cl.** clerk
clk. (clericus)(Lat.), **cl.** or **clerg.** clergyman
Clk.O. Clerk in Orders
cl. L. classical Latin
cl. lp. cloth limp (Bookbinding)
Clm (Mil.) or **col.** column
Clo clothing (Mil.)
clo., Cl. or **cl.** cloth
C.L.P.A. Common Law Procedure Act (Brit.)
Clr Clearing (Mil.)
Clr (Mil.), **clr.** or **col.** color
Clr Co Clearing company (Mil.)
Cls. Claudius
C.L.S.C. Chautauqua Literary and Scientific Circle
clt. collateral trust (Bonds)
C.L.T.S. Chicago Leisure Time Service
C.L.U. Chartered Life Underwriter
C.M. Certificated Master or Mistress; common meter; (Congregatio Mariæ) (Lat.) Congregation of Mary; Fathers of the Company of Mary; (Congregatio Missionis)(Lat.) Congregation of the Mission; Lazarist Fathers or Vincentian Fathers; court-martial
C.M., Ch. M. (Chirurgiae Magister)(Lat.), **M.C., M. Ch.** (Magister Chirurgiae) (Lat.), **M.S., M. Surg.** or **M. Surgery** Master of Surgery
C.M. or **c.m.** church missionary
C.M., c.m., Cor. Mem. or **Corr. Mem.** Corresponding Member
C/m call of more [stocks]
cm., C., c. or **cent.** centimeter; centimeters
cm.^{2}, **cmr.**^{2} or **sq. cm.** square centimeter(s)
cm.^{3}, **c**^{3}, **cc,** or **cu.cm.** cubic centimeter(s)
c.m. (causa mortis)(Lat.) by reason of death; (cras mane)(Lat.) tomorrow morning (Pharm.)
c.m. or **cir.mils** circular mils (wire measure)
c.m. (carat métrique)(Fr.) or **M.C.** metric carat
C.M.A. California Medical Association
Cma. Camilla
C.M.A.A. Chief Master-at-Arms
c.mag., cochl.mag., coch.mag. (cochleare magnum)(Lat.), **c.amp., cochl.amp., coch.amp.** (cochleare amplum)(Lat.), **tbs.** or **tbsp.** tablespoon; tablespoonful (cochleare amplum and cochleare magnum often used for large or heaping spoonful)
C.M.A.S. Clergy Mutual Assurance Society (Brit.)
C.M.B. carbolic methylene blue; China Medical Board
C. M. B. or **c.m.b.** (cuyas manos beso) (Span.) very respectfully (lit., whose hands I kiss)(cf. B.S.M.)
CMCM Changes, Manual for Courts-Martial (Mil.)

C.M.D. or **c.m.d.** common meter double
Cmd. (since 1919) or **Cd.** (to 1918) Command Paper
c.m.d. or **C.M.D.** common meter double
cmdg., Comdg. or **comdg.** commanding
c.med., coch.med., cochl.med. (cochleare medium)(Lat.), **c. mod., cochl. mod.** or **coch. mod.** (cochleare modicum)(Lat.) dessertspoonful
C.M.F. (Congregatio Missioniorum Filiorum Immaculati Cordis Beatae Mariae Virginis)(Lat.) Congregation of Missionary Sons of the Immaculate Heart of Mary; Missionaries of the Immaculate Heart of Mary; Claretian Missionaries; Claretians
C.M.G. central machine gun; Companion [of the Order] of St. Michael and St. George
C.M.I.A. Coal Mining Institute of America
C.M.I.U.A. Cigar Manufacturers International Union of America
Cml (Mil.), **Chem., chem.** or **Cheml.** chemical
cml., com., Coml., coml. Comm., comm., Comml. or **comml.** commercial
Cml Am Tn Chemical ammunition train (Mil.)
Cml Bn Chemical battalion (Mil.)
Cml Co Chemical company (Mil.)
Cml Mort Chemical mortar (Mil.)
Cml O Chemical officer (Mil.)
Cml Regt Chemical regiment (Mil.)
Cml Sec Chemical section (Mil.)
C.M.M. Chief machinist's mate
cmm., cu.mm. or **mm^3** cubic millimeter
C.M.Mh. (Congregatio Missioniorum de Mariannhill)(Lat.) or **R.M.M.** Congregation of Missionaries of Mariannhill; Religious Missionaries of Mariannhill; Mariannhill Fathers
c. mod., cochl.mod., coch.mod. (cochleare modicum)(Lat.), **c.med., cochl.med.** or **coch.med.** (cochleare medium)(Lat.) dessertspoonful
cmp. compromise
cm.pf. cumulative preferred [stocks]
Cmpn (Mil.) or **comp.** compilation
CMR Committee on Medical Research
C.M.R. Cape mounted rifles
$cmr.^2$, $cm.^2$ or **sq.cm.** square centimeter or centimeters
C.M.S. Church Missionary Society
c.m.s. (cras mane sumendus)(Lat.) to be taken tomorrow morning (Pharm.)
c.m.tab. aeri incisis (cum multis tabulis aeri incisis)(Lat.) with many ingravings in copperplate
CMTC or **C.M.T.C.** Citizens' Military Training Camp
C.M.U.A. Commercial Motor Users' Association
C.M.Z.S. Corresponding Member of the Zoological Society
CN compass north
C.N. Code Napoléon
C.N. or **c.n.** (cras nocte)(Lat.) tomorrow night (cf. c.v.)
C/N circular note (Banking); consignment note; cover note; credit note
Cn. Canon (Law); Cnaeus
cn cosine of the amplitude
cn. (Bonds), **con., cons.** or **consol.** consolidated
c.n. or **C.N.** (cras nocte)(Lat.) tomorrow night (cf. c.v.)
C.N.A. Central Neuropsychiatric Association
C.N.A.C. China National Aviation Corporation
C.N.D. Council of National Defense
C.N.L.P. Committee on National Land Problems
CNO or **C.N.O.** Chief of Naval Operations
C.N.S. central nervous system (Med.)
c.n.s. (cras nocte sumendus)(Lat.) to be taken tomorrow night
CO (Mil.) or **C.O.** Commanding Officer
C.O. (Canonnier observateur)(Fr.) Artillery observer; Colonial Office; conscientious objector; Criminal Office; Crown Office
C/O certificate of origin (Commerce)
C/O, C.O. or **c/o** cash order
Co (Chem.) or **Co.** cobalt
Co., Cía. (Compañía)(Span.), **Cie, cie** (compagnie)(Fr.), **co., comp., Comp^a, compa., Compy., compy., Coy., coy.** or **Ges.** (Gesellschaft)(Ger.) company
Co., co., ct. or **Cy.** county
C/o, adr. (adress)(Swed.), **Adrs.** (Adresse) (Dan.), **c.o., c/o** or **per Adr.** (per Adresse)(Ger.) in care of
C/o, c.o. or **c/o** carried over (Bookkeeping) (cf. B/F;C/F)
co. colon
co., Cía. (Compañía)(Span.), **Cie, cie** (compagnie)(Fr.), **Co., comp., Comp^a, compa., Compy., compy., Coy., coy.** or **Ges.** (Gesellschaft)(Ger.) company
c.o. (compte ouvert)(Fr.) open account (cf. A/C)
c.o., C/o or **c/o** carried over (Bookkeeping) (cf. B.F.; C.F.)
c/o, adr. (adress)(Swed.), **Adrs.** (Adresse) (Dan.), **c/o, c.o.** or **per Adr.** (per Adresse)(Ger.) in care of
c/o, C.O. or **C/O** cash order
c/o, C/o or **c.o.** carried over (Bookkeeping) (cf. B.F.; C.F.)
C.O.A. (Commis et ouvriers d'administration)(Fr.) Clerks and workmen [enlisted as such for military service]
Coad. or **coad.** coadjutor (cf. asst.)
Coal. L. or **Co. L.** Coalition Liberal
Coal. U. or **Co. U.** Coalition Unionist
coam. coaming
Cobl. Coblenz
coch. or **cochl.** (cochleare)(Lat.) a spoonful
coch.amp., c.amp., cochl.amp. (cochleare amplum)(Lat.), **c.mag., cochl.mag., coch.mag.** (cochleare magnum)(Lat.), **tbs.** or **tbsp.** tablespoon; tablespoonful (cochleare amplum and cochleare magnum sometimes used for large of heaping spoonful)

coch.infant., c.infant. or **cochl.infant.** (cochleare infantis)(Lat.) child's spoonful

cochl. amp., c. amp., coch. amp. (cochleare amplum)(Lat.), **c. mag., cochl. mag., coch.mag.** (cochleare magnum)(Lat.), **tbs.** or **tbsp.** tablespoon; tablespoonful (cochleare amplum and cochleare magnum sometimes used for large or heaping spoonful)

cochl.infant., c.infant. or **coch.infant.** (cochleare infantis)(Lat.) child's spoonful

cochl.mag., c.mag., coch.mag. (cochleare magnum)(Lat.), **c. amp., coch.amp., cochl.amp.** (cochleare amplum)(Lat.), **tbs.** or **tbsp.** tablespoon; tablespoonful (cochleare amplum and cochleare magnum sometimes used for large or heaping spoonful)

cochl. med., c. med., coch.med. (cochleare medium)(Lat.), **coch.mod., c. mod.** or **cochl. mod.** (cochleare modicum)(Lat.) dessertspoonful

cochl.mod., c. mod., coch.mod. (cochleare modicum)(Lat.), **c. med., cochl.med.** or **coch.med.** (cochleare medium)(Lat.) dessertspoonful

cochl.parv., coch.parv., c.par., c.parv. (cochleare parvum)(Lat.), **ts.** or **tsp.** teaspoon; teaspoonful

coch.mag., c.mag., cochl.mag. (cochleare magnum)(Lat.), **c. amp., coch. amp., cochl. amp.** (cochleare amplum)(Lat.), **tbs.** or **tbsp.** tablespoon; tablespoonful (cochleare amplum and cochleare magnum sometimes used for large or heaping spoonful)

coch. med., c. med., cochl. med., (cochleare medium)(Lat.), **coch. mod., cochl. mod.** or **c.mod.** (cochleare modicum)(Lat.) dessertspoonful

coch.mod., c.mod., cochl.mod. (cochleare modicum)(Lat.), **c. med., cochl.med.** or **coch.med.** (cochleare medium)(Lat.) dessertspoonful

coch.parv., cochl.parv., c.par., c.parv. (cochleare parvum)(Lat.), **ts.** or **tsp.** teaspoon; teaspoonful

Co Comdr Company commander (Mil.)

coct. (coctio)(Lat.), **bull.** (bulliens)(Lat.) or **ferv.** (fervens)(Lat.) boiling

C.O.D. Concise Oxford Dictionary

C.O.D. or **c.o.d.** cash on delivery; collect on delivery

Cod., cod., C. or **c.** codex

Cod.Civ. or **C.C.** Code Civil

codd. codices

coef. or **coeff.** coefficient

C.O.F. Catholic Order of Foresters

C of A (Mil.) or **C. of A.** Chief of Artillery

C of AC (Mil.) or **C. of A.C.** Chief of Air Corps

C of AS (Mil.) or **C. of A.S.** Chief of Air Service

C of Avn (Mil.) or **C. of Avn.** Chief of Aviation

C. of B. confirmation of balance (Banking)

C of BIA (Mil.) or **C.B.I.A.** Chief of Bureau of Insular Affairs

C. of C. or **C.C.** Chamber of Commerce

C of CA (Mil.) or **C. of C.A.** Chief of Coast Artillery

C of Cav (Mil.) or **C. of Cav.** Chief of Cavalry

C of Chap (Mil.) or **C. of Chap.** Chief of Chaplains

C of CWS (Mil.) or **C. of C.W.S.** Chief of the Chemical Warfare Service

C. of E. Chief of Engineers

C. of E., C.E. or **Ch. of Eng.** Church of England

C. of F. Companions of the Forest

C. of F. or **C of Fin** (Mil.) Chief of Finance

C. of F. A. Chief of Field Artillery

coff. cofferdam

C of Fin (Mil.) or **C. of F.** Chief of Finance

C. of F. of A. Companions of the Forest of America

C. of G., C.G. or **c.g.** center of gravity

C. of G.H. or **C.G.H.** Cape of Good Hope

C of Inf (Mil.) or **C. of Inf.** Chief of Infantry

C. of M. Certificate of Merit

C of MB Chief of Militia Bureau

C of Ord (Mil.) or **C. of Ord.** Chief of Ordnance

C. of R. Community of the Resurrection

C of S (Mil.), **C. of S.** or **C.O.S.** Chief of Staff; Chief of section

cog. or **cogn.** cognate

COGSIS Committee on Government Statistics and Information Service

Co Hq (Mil.) or **Co.Hq.** Company headquarters

COI or **C.O.I.** Coordinator of Information (functions transferred to OWI and OSS)

coins.cl. coinsurance clause

Co. L. or **Coal. L.** Coalition Liberal

Col (Mil.), **Col.** or **col.** Colonel

Col. Columbia

Col., col., Colg (Mil.), **Coll.** or **coll.** college

Col. or **Colo.** Colorado

Col. or **Coloss.** Colossians (Bible)

col. coliander (Pharm.); collected; colonial; colony; (cola)(Lat.) strain (Pharm.)

col., Cld (Mil.), **cld.,** or **kol.** (koloriert) (Ger.) colored

col. or **Clm** (Mil.) column

col., Clr (Mil.) or **clr.** color

col. or **coll.** collect; collection; collections; collegiate

col., coll. or **collr.** collector

col. or **cols.** columns

Col. Eng. College English

Colg (Mil.), **Col., col., Coll.** or **coll.** college

Coll., coll., Col., col. or **Colg** (Mil.) college

coll. colleague

coll. or **col.** collect; collection; collections; collegiate
coll., col. or **collr.** collector
coll. or **collat.** collateral; collaterally
coll. or **collect.** collective; collectively
coll. or **colloq.** colloquial; colloquialism; colloquially
collab. collaboration; collaborator
collat. or **coll.** collateral; collaterally
coll.cl. collision clause (Insurance)
Coll Co Collecting company (Mil.)
collect. or **coll.** collective; collectively
Coll/L collection letter
colloq. or **coll.** colloquial; colloquialism; colloquially
Coll Pt Collecting point (Mil.)
collr., col. or **coll.** collector
Coll Sta Collecting station (Mil.)
coll.tr. collateral trust (Bonds)
Coln. Cologne
Colo. or **Col.** Colorado
colog cologarithm
Colom. Colombia
Colon. Agrip (Colonia Agrippina) Cologne imprint
colorl. colorless
Coloss. or **Col.** Collossians
cols. or **col.** columns
Col. Sergt. or **Col. Sgt.** Color sergeant
Co. Ltd., G.m.b.H. (Gesellschaft mit beschränkter Haftung)(Ger.), **n.v.** (naamloose vennootschap)(Dutch), **S. en C.** (Sociedad en Comandita)(Span.) or **Soc. an^e** (Société anonyme)(Fr.) limited company (cf. A. G.; cie; S. A.)
Com (Mil.), **com.** or **comm.** communication; communications
Com. Communist
Com., com., Comdr (Mil.), **Comdr., comdr.** or **comm.** commander
Com., com., Comm., comm., Commn. or **commn.** commission
Com., com., Comm. or **Commo.** commodore
Com. or **comm.** commonwealth
Com., Commisr., commissr., Commr. or **Comr.** commissioner
com. comedy; comic; comma; commoner; commonly; commune; communicate; communicated; community
com., cml., Coml., coml., Comm., comm., Comml. or **comml.** commercial
com., Com (Mil.) or **comm.** communication; communications
com., Com., Comm. or **Commo.** commodore
com., comd. or **comd.** commissioned
com., Comdr (Mil.), **Comdr., comdr.** or **comm.** commander
com. or **comm.** commerce; committee
com., comm. or **comment.** commentary
com. or **cs.** (communis)(Lat.) common
COMAIRLANT Commander Air Force, Atlantic
Com. Arr. Committee of Arrangements
comb. combination
Com Car or **Comd Car** Command car (Mil.)
com. carr. common carrier
COMCRULANT Commander Cruisers, Atlantic
comd., com. or **commd.** commissioned
Comd (Mil.) or **cd.** command
Comd Car or **Com Car** Command car (Mil.)
Comdg., comdg. or **cmdg.** commanding
Comdr (Mil.), **Comdr., comdr., com.** or **comm.** Commander
Comdt (Mil.), **comdt.** or **Komdt.** (Kommandant)(Ger.) Commandant
Com. E. Commercial Engineer
Com.-in-C., Com. in Chf., Com.-in-Chf., C.I.C., C-I-C, C.-I.-C., C in C (Mil.) or **C. in C.** Commander in Chief
COMINCH Commander in Chief, U.S. Fleet
Coml., coml., cml., com., Comm., comm., Comml. or **comml.** commercial
Com. Law, C.L. or **c.l.** common law
com'l ppr. commercial paper
Comm (Mil.), **Commy.** or **Comsry.** commissary
Comm., Com., com. or **Commo.** commodore
Comm., comm., cml., com., Coml., coml., Comml. or **comml.** commercial
Comm., comm., Com., com., Commn. or **commn.** commission
comm. commutator
comm., Com (Mil.) or **com.** communication; communications
comm. or **Com.** commonwealth
comm. or **com.** commerce; committee
comm., com., Comdr (Mil.), **Comdr.** or **comdr.** Commander
comm., com. or **comment.** commentary
comm. or **Comtn** (Mil.) commutation
commd., com. or **comd.** commissioned
comment., com. or **comm.** commentary
Commisr., Commisar., Com., Commr. or **Comr.** commissioner
Comml., comml., cml., com., Coml., coml., Comm. or **comm.** commercial
Commn., commn., Com., com., Comm. or **comm.** commission
Commo., Com., com. or **Comm.** commodore
commod. commodity
Commr., Com., Commisr., commissr. or **Comr.** commissioner
commt. commencement
Commy., Comm (Mil.) or **Comsry.** commissary
Com O Communication officer
Com. Off. or **com. off.** commissioned officer
Comp., bearb. (bearbeitet)(Ger.) or **comp.** compiled
Comp., C., c., comp. or **compn.** companion
Comp. or **comp.** compensation; compile; compiler; compose; composer; composite; composition; compositor; compounded; comprising

Comp., comp. or **compar.** comparison
Comp., comp., compl. or **cplt.** complete
Comp., comp. or **cpd.** compound
Comp., Compt. or **Comp't.** Comptroller (cf. contr.)
comp., C., c., Comp. or **compn.** companion
comp., Cía. (compañía)(Span.), **Cie, cie** (compagnie)(Fr.), **Co., co., Comp**[a], **compa., Compy., compy., Coy., coy.,** or **Ges.** (Gesellschaft)(Ger.) company
comp. or **Cmpn** (Mil.) compilation
comp., Comp., compl. or **cplt.** complete
comp. or **compar.** comparative
comp., compar., cf., conf. (confer)(Lat.), **cp., jf., jfr.** (jaevnfør)(Dan), (jämför) (Swed.), **por.** (porównaj)(Pol.), **sml.** (sammenlign)(Dan.) or **vgl.** (vergleiche)(Ger.) compare
Comp[a], **compa., Cía.** (Compañía)(Span.), **Cie, cie** (compagnie)(Fr.), **Co., co., comp., Compy., compy., Coy., coy.** or **Ges.** (Gesellschaft)(Ger.) company
compar., cf., conf. (confer)(Lat.), **comp., cp., jf., jfr.** (jaevnfør)(Dan.), (jämför) (Swed.), **por.** (porównaj)(Pol.), **sml.** (sammenlign)(Dan.) or **vgl.** (vergleiche)(Ger.) compare
compar., Comp. or **comp.** comparison
compar. or **comp.** comparative
Comp Dec (Mil.) or **Compt. Dec.** Comptroller's Decisions
comp.g. compressed gas
Comp.Gen. or **Compt.Gen.** Comptroller General
Comp Gen Dec Comptroller General's Decisions
compl., Comp., comp. or **cplt.** complete
Com Plat Communication platoon (Mil.)
compn., C., c., Comp. or **comp.** companion
Compt., Comp't. or **Comp.** Comptroller (cf. contr.)
compt. compartment; comptometer
Compt. Dec. or **Comp Dec** (Mil.) Comptroller's Decisions
Compt.Gen. or **Comp.Gen.** Comptroller General
Compy., compy., Cía. (Compañía)(Span.), **Cie, cie** (compagnie)(Fr.), **Co., co., comp., Comp**[a], **compa., Coy., coy.** or **Ges.** (Gesellschaft)(Ger.) company
Comr., Com., Commisr., commissr. or **Commr.** commissioner
Com Sec Communication section
Com. Serg., C.S., Com. Serj. or **Com. Serjt.** Common Sergeant or Serjeant (Brit.)
Com Sq Communication squadron
Comsry., Comm (Mil.) or **Commy.** commissary
Com.Sub., Comsy.Sub., C.S. or **c.s.** commissary of subsistence
Comsy.Sub., Com.Sub., C.S. or **c.s.** commissary of subsistence
comt. commentator
Comtn (Mil.) or **comm.** commutation
Com. Ver., Com. Vers. or **C.V.** Common Version [of the Bible]
Comy.-Gen., C.G. or **c.g.** commissary general
Com Z Communications zone (Mil.)
Con (Mil.) concrete
con. conform; conformist; conics; consol; conundrum
con., C., c., cond., Condr. or **condr.** conductor
con., C., c., Cons. cons. or **cos.** consul
con., C., c., Cons., cons. or **coss.** (consules) (Lat.) consuls
con., cn. (Bonds), **cons.** or **consol.** consolidated
con., concl. or **conclu.** conclusion
con. or **cond.** condense; condenser; conduct; conducted; conductivity
con. or **conn.** connection
con., cont. (contra)(Lat.), **adv., advs.** (adversus)(Lat.), **Agt., agt., agst., V., v.** or **vs.** (versus)(Lat.) against
con. or **conv.** conversation
con. or **cto.** concerto
con. (conjunx)(Lat.), **Fr.** (Frau)(Ger), **ux.** (uxor)(Lat.) or **w.** wife
conc. concentrate; (concilium)(Lat.) council (Eccl.)
conc., ang. (angaaende)(Dan.), (angående) (Swed.) or **vedr.** (vedrørende)(Dan.) concerning
conc. or **concd.** concentrated
conc. or **concn.** concentration
concd. or **conc.** concentrated
Conch. or **conch.** conchology
concl., con. or **conclu.** conclusion
conclu., con. or **concl.** conclusion
concn. or **conc.** concentration
con. cr., C.C. or **c.c.** contra credit
Cond., G. or **g.** conductance (Elec.)
cond. or **beschn.** (beschnitten)(Ger.) condensed
cond., C., c., con., Condr. or **condr.** conductor
cond. or **con.** condense; condenser; conduct; conducted; conductivity
Condr., C., c., con., cond. or **condr.** conductor
Conf (Mil.) or **conf.** confined; confinement
Conf., C., c. or **conf.** confessor
Conf. or **conf.** conference
Conf. or **Confed.** Confederation
conf (Mil.) or **confd.** conferred
conf. (confectio)(Lat.)(Pharm.) confection; confer
conf., C., c. or **Conf.** confessor
conf., cf. (confer)(Lat.), **comp., compar., cp., jf. jfr.** (jaevnfør)(Dan.), (jämför) (Swed.), **por.** (porównaj)(Pol.), **sml.** (sammenlign)(Dan.) or **vgl.** (vergleiche)(Ger.) compare
conf. or **Conf.** conference
confd. or **conf** (Mil.) conferred
Conf. Doct. or **C.D.** Confessor and Doctor of the Church
Confed. Confederate
Confed. or **Conf.** Confederation
Cong. Congress; Congressional
Cong. or **cong.** congregation

Cong. or **Congl.** Congregational
Cong., Congl. or **Conglist.** Congregationalist
cong., C., c. (congius)(Lat.), **gal.** or **gall.** gallon
cong. or **Cong.** congregation
Congl. or **Cong.** Congregational
Congl., Cong. or **Conglist.** Congregationalist
Conglist., Cong. or **Congl.** Congregationalist
Cong. Orat., C. Orat., Congr.Orat. (Congregatio Oratorii)(Lat.) or **P.O.** (Presbyteri Oratorii)(Lat.) Congregation of the Oratory of St Philip Neri; Fathers of the Oratory; Oratorians
Cong. Rec. Congressional Record
conj. conjugation; conjunction; conjunctive
Conn. or **Ct.** Connecticut
conn. connected
conn. or **con.** connection
conn.w. connected with
Con Py Contact party (Mil.)
conq. conquest
Conr. Conrad
Cons. (conserva)(Lat.) keep (Pharm.)
Cons., C., c., con., cons. or **cos.** (consul) (Lat.) consul
Cons., C., c., con., cons. or **coss.** (consules) (Lat.) consuls
Cons., cons., C., c. or **conserv.** conservative
Cons., cons., Const., const. or **conston.** constitution
cons. consecrated; conserve; consigned; consignment; consonant; constitutional; consult; consulting
cons., C., c., con., Cons. or **cos.** consul
cons., C., c., con., Cons. or **coss.** (consules) (Lat.) consuls
cons., cn. (Bonds), **con.** or **consol.** consolidated
cons., Const. or **const.** constable
cons., constr. or **constron.** construction
Cons Co Construction company (Mil.)
consec.ds. consecutive days
con. sect. conic section or sections
conserv., C., c., Cons. or **cons.** conservative
consol., cn. (Bonds), **con.** or **cons.** consolidated
Consols. Consolidated Bank Annuities; Consolidated Funds (Government stock)
Cons Plat Construction platoon (Mil.)
Cons Sec Construction section (Mil.)
cons. sp. constant speed
Const., const., Cons., cons. or **Conston.** constitution
Const., const. or **cons.** constable
Const., const., K or **k.** constant
Conston., Cons., cons., Const. or **const.** constitution
constr. constructing; construed
constr., cons. or **constron.** construction
constron., cons. or **constr.** construction
const.w. construed with
Cont. (contusus)(Lat.) bruise
Cont. or **cont.** contents; continent; continuation; continue
Cont., cont. or **contl.** continental
cont., contd., contin. or **contind.** continued
cont. or **contg.** containing
cont. or **contr.** contracted; contraction; contractions; contrary; control
cont., contr. or **contt.** contract
contbg. or **contrib.** contributing
cont.bon.mor. or **contr.bon.mor.** (contra bonos mores)(Lat.) contrary to good manners
contd., cont., contin. or **contind.** continued
contemp. contemporary; contemporaries
contg. or **cont.** containing
cont hp continental horsepower
contin. continuer; (continuetur)(Lat.) let it be continued
contin., cont., contd. or **contind.** continued
contl., Cont. or **cont.** continental
contr. contralto; controller (cf. Comp.)
contr. or **cont.** contracted; contraction; contractions; contrary; control
contr., cont. or **contt.** contract
contr. or **contra.** contradict; contradiction
contra. or **contr.** contradict; contradiction
contrbn. or **contrib.** contribution
contr.bon.mor. or **cont.bon.mor.** (contra bonos mores)(Lat.) contrary to good manners
contrib. contributed
contrib. or **contbg.** contributing
contrib. or **contrbn.** contribution
contrib. or **contribor.** contributor
contrib.val. contributory value (Insurance)
contt., cont. or **contr.** contract
Cont.U.S.&C. Continental United States and Canada
Conv (Mil.) or **conv.** convenience
Conv. or **conv.** convent; conversion; converter
conv. convention; conversation
conv., cv. or **cvt.** convert; convertible
Conv Hosp Convalescent hospital (Mil.)
C.O.O. Chief Ordnance Officer
cook. cookery
coop. or **co-op.** cooperative
co-ops. or **coops.** cooperatives
Cop. Copernican
Cop. or **Copt.** Coptic
cop., Abdr. (Abruck, Abdrücke)(Ger.) or **c.** copy; copies
cop., Ae. (Aes)(Lat.), **C., c., Cu** (Chem.) or **Cu.** (cuprum)(Lat.) copper
cop., C., c. or **copr.** copyright; copyrighted
Copec or **C.O.P.E.C.** Conference on Politics, Economics and Christianity (Church of Eng.)
copr., C., c. or **cop.** copyright; copyrighted
Copt. or **Cop.** Coptic

coq. (coque)(Lat.) or **bull.** (bulliat, bulliant)(Lat.) boil, let boil (Pharm.)

Cor. Corinthians; Cornelia; Cornelius

Cor. or **cor.** coroner

cor. (corpus)(Lat.) body; corner; cornet

cor., Ausgeb. (ausgebessert)(Ger.) or **corr.** corrected

cor. or **Cor.** coroner

cor. or **corr.** correction; corrupt; corrupted; corruption

cor., corr. or **corresp.** correspondence; corresponding

cor., corr., corresp. or **corspdt.** correspondent

cor. or **correl.** correlative

cor., OK or **O.K.** correct

C. Orat., Cong Orat., Congr.Orat. (Congregatio Oratorii)(Lat.) or **P.O.** (Presbyteri Oratorii)(Lat.) Congregation of the Oratory of St. Philip Neri; Fathers of the Oratory; Oratorians

Cord. Cordelia

Cor. Mem., Corr. Mem., or **c.m.** Corresponding Member

Corn. Cornish

Corn. or **Cornw.** Cornwall

corol. or **coroll.** corollary

Corp (Mil.), **Corp., corp.** or **Cpl** (Mil.) Corporal

Corp., corp. or **corpn.** corporation

Corp. Jur. Can., Corpus Jur.Can. or **C.J. Can.** (Corpus Juris Canonici)(Lat.) the body of canon law (cf. C.I.C.)

Corp.Jur.Civ. or **C.J.Civ.** (Corpus Juris Civilis)(Lat.) body of civil law

corpn. or **corp.** corporation

Corpus Jur. Can., C.J. Can. or **Corp. Jur. Can.** (Corpus Juris Canonici)(Lat.) the body of the canon law (cf. C.I.C.)

corr. correspond

corr., Ausgeb. (Ausgebessert)(Ger.) or **cor.** corrected

corr. or **cor.** correction; corrupt; corrupted; corruption

corr., cor. or **corresp.** correspondence; corresponding

corr., cor., corresp. or **corspdt.** correspondent

correl. or **cor.** correlative

corresp., cor. or **corr.** correspondence; corresponding

corresp., cor., corr. or **corspdt.** correspondent

Corr. Fell. Corresponding Fellow

Corr. Mem., c.m. or **Cor. Mem.** Corresponding Member

Corr. Sec. or **Cor.Sec.** corresponding secretary

Cor.Sec. or **Corr.Sec.** corresponding secretary

corspdt., cor., corr. or **corresp.** correspondent

Cort. or **cort.** (cortex)(Lat.) bark; cortex; cortical (Anat.)

C.O.S. Charity Organisation Society (Brit.); Clinical Orthopedic Society

C.O.S. or **c.o.s.**. cash on shipment

C.O.S. or **C of S** (Mil.) Chief of section

Cos. Cossack

cos cosine

cos. companies; counties; countries

cos., C., c., con., Cons. or **cons.** consul

c.o.s. or **C.O.S.** cash on shipment

cosec or **csc** cosecant

cosh hyperbolic cosine

cosmog. cosmography

co.so. (come sopra)(Ital.), **u.s., ut sup.** (ut supra)(Lat.) or **w.o.** (wie oben)(Ger.) as above

coss. (consules)(Lat.) **C., c., con., Cons.** or **cons.** consuls

cot cotangent

coth hyperbolic cotangent

C.O.T.S. Central Officers Training School

Co. U. or **Coal. U.** Coalition Unionist

Cov Covered (Mil.)

Cox., cox or **coxen.** coxswain

coxen., Cox. or **cox** coxswain

Coy., coy., Cía. (Compañía)(Span.), **Cie, cie** (compagnie)(Fr.), **Co., co., comp., Comp[a], compa., Compy., compy.** or **Ges.** (Gesellschaft)(Ger.) company

CP Command post (Mil.)

CP or **C.P.** Canadian Press; Central Press

C.P. Cape Province; carriage paid; Central Provinces (India); Common Prayer; Conditional Purchase (Australia); (Congregatio Passionis)(Lat.) Congregation of the Passion; Passionist Fathers; Passionists

C.P., C.p. or **c.p** candlepower

C.P. or **c.p.** center of pressure; chemically pure; civil power; clerk of the peace; code of procedure; common pleas; court of probate

C.P., C.S.P. (Congregatio Sancti Pauli) (Lat.) or **P.P.** Congregation of of St. Paul the Apostle; Missionary Society of St. Paul the Apostle; Society of St. Paul; Paulist Fathers; Paulists

C/P charter party

Cp cassiopeium (Chem.); [molecular heat at] constant pressure

Cp. or **Chris.** Christoph

cp., C., c. or **C/-** coupon

cp., comp., compar., cf., conf. (confer) (Lat.), **jf., jfr.** (jaevnfør)(Dan.), (jämför)(Swed.), **por.** (porównaj)(Pol.), **sml.** (sammenlign)(Dan.) or **vgl.** (vergleiche)(Ger.) compare

c.p. circular pitch

c/p custom of port (Grain trade)

CPA Council of Personnel Administration

C.P.A. or **c.p.a.** Certified Public Accountant; Chartered Public Accountant

C.P.A.I. Coal Producers Association of Illinois

c. par., c. parv., coch. parv., cochl. parv. (cochleare parvum)(Lat.) **ts.** or **tsp.** teaspoon; teaspoonful

C.P.A.S. Church Pastoral Air Society

C.P.C. Clerk of the Privy Council; Cotton Production Chart

C.P.C.& N. certificate of public convenience and necessity

C.P.D. charterers pay dues (Shipping)
cpd., Comp. or **comp.** compound
c.p.f.f. cost plus fixed fee
c.p.g. cotton piece goods
C.P.H. Certificate in Public Health
C.P.H.A. Canadian Public Health Association
C.P.I. Commitee on Public Information; Crop Protection Institute
C.P.I.A. Contracting Plasterers' International Association
C.P.L. Conditional Purchase Lease (Australia)
Cpl, Corp (Mil.), **Corp.** or **corp.** Corporal
cplt., Comp., comp. or **compl.** complete
CPM Chief of Procurement and Material (Navy)
C.P.M. common particular meter (Hmynol.)
C.P.O. or **c.p.o.** chief petty officer
cp.off coupon off (Bonds)
cp.on coupon on (Bonds)
C.PP.S. (Congregatio Pretiosissimi Sanguinis)(Lat.) Society of the Most Precious Blood; Fathers of the Most Precious Blood; Sanguinist Fathers
C.P.R.E. Council for the Preservation of Rural England
C.P.S. Church Patronage Society; Clerk of Petty Sessions; Congregational Publishing Society; (Custos Privati Sigilli) (Lat.) Keeper of the Privy Seal
C.P.S. (Congregatio Presbyterorum Sanctissimi Stigmati)(Lat.) or **C.S.F.** Congregation of Priests of the Most Holy Stigmati; Congregation of Stigmatine Fathers; Stigmatine Fathers
cps. coupons
c.p.s. cycles per second
C.P.T. Civilian Pilot Training
cpt. counterpoint
cpt., Cap., cap. (capiat)(Lat.) or **sum.** (sumat)(Lat.) let him take
Cptr (Mil.) or **carp.** carpenter
CPX Command post exercise (Mil.)
C.Q.M. Chief Quartermaster
C.Q.M.S. Company Quartermaster Sergeant
CR (Mil.) or **X rds.** crossroads
C.R. Camping Reserve [Lands](Australia); Chief Ranger (Foresters); (Congregatio Resurrectionis)(Lat.) Congregation of the Resurrection; Recurrectionist Fathers; Costa Rica; (Custos Rotulorum)(Lat.) Custodian of the Rolls; (Carolus Rex)(Lat.) King Charles; (Civis Romanus)(Lat.) Roman citizen
C.R. or **c.r.** carrier's risk; center of resistance; class rate; company rate; company's risk; current rate
C.R. or **C.R.T.** (Clereci Regulares Theatini)(Lat.) Clerks Regular, Theatine: Theatine Fathers
Cr chromium (Chem.)
Cr (Mil.) or **cr.** creek
Cr. or **cr.** credit; creditor
Cr. or **cr. 8vo** crown octavo
cr. created
cr., C., c., Cen (Mil.), **cen.** or **ctr.** center
cr. or **Cr** (Mil.) creek
cr. of **Cr.** credit; creditor
cr., cres. or **cresc.** (crescendo)(Ital.) with gradually increasing volume (Music)
cr. of **crt.** crate
cr., K., k., kn., Kr., kr. or **krn.** crown; crowns; korona; krona; kronar; krone; kronen; kroner (Coins)
c.r. or **C.R.** carrier's risk; center of resistance; class rate; company rate; company's risk; current rate
C.R.A. Commander of the Royal Artillery
craniol. craniology
craniom. craniometry
C.R.B. Commission for Relief in Belgium
C.R.C. Canadian Railway Commission
C.R.C.S. or **C.R.S.** (Clerici Regulares Congregationis Somaschae)(Lat.) Clerks Regular of the Society of Somaschi; Somaschi Fathers
C.R.E. Commander of the Royal Engineers
C.R.E.A. Committee on the Relation of Electricity to Agriculture
cres. crescent
cres., cr. or **cresc.** (crescendo)(Ital.) with gradually increasing volume (Music)
C.R.I.C. (Canonici Regulares Immaculatae Conceptionis)(Lat.) Canons Regular of the Immaculate Conception; Augustinians
crim. criminal
crim. con. criminal conversation
criminol. criminology
crit. critic; critical; criticism; criticized
C.R.L. (Canonici Regulares Lateranensis [Sanctissimi Salvatoris])(Lat.) Canons Regular of the Lateran; Canons Regular of the Lateran of Our Most Holy Redeemer; Lateran Canons; Augustinians
c.r.l. cotton rubber lined (firehose)
CRM chief radioman
C.R.M. (Clerici Regulares Minores)(Lat.) Clerks Regular Minor, Mariani
C.R.M.D. (Clerici Regulares Matris Dei) (Lat.) Clerks Regular of the Mother of God
C.R.M.I. (Clerici Regulares Ministrantes Infirmis)(Lat.), **M.I., Min. Inf.** or **O.S.Cam.** (Ordo Sancti Camilli)(Lat.) Clerks Regular Ministering to the Infirm; Clerks Regular Attendant on the Sick; Ministers of the Sick; Order of St. Camillus; Camillian Fathers; Camillians
C.R.O.M. (Confederación Regional Obrera Mexicana)(Span.) Mexican Sectional Labor Federation
cross. crossing
C.R.P. (Calendarium Rotulorum Patentium) (Lat.) Calendar of Patent Rolls (Law); (Congregatio Reformatorum Praemonstratensium)(Lat.) Society of the Reformed Praemonstratensians; Praemonstratensians; (Cononici Regu-

lares Praemonstratensis)(Lat.) Canons Regular of Premonmarté or Premontre; Premonstratensian Canons Regular (cf. Ord. Praem.)

cr. ref. or **x-ref.** cross reference

CRS cold-rolled steel

C.R.S. Catholic Record Society

C.R.S. or **C.R.C.S.** (Clerici Regulares Congregationis Somaschae)(Lat.) Clerks Regular of the Society of Somaschi; Somaschi Fathers

crs. creditors; credits

C.R.S.P. (Clerici Regulares Sancti Pauli) (Lat.) Clerks Regular of St. Paul; Barnabites

C.R.S.P. (Clerici Regulares Pauperum Matris Dei Scholarum Piarum)(Lat.), **Sch.P.** or **P.S.P.** (Patres Scholarum Piarum)(Lat.) Clerks Regular of the Poor Men of the Mother of God for Pious Schools; Fathers of the Religious Schools; Piarists; Scolopii

Crsp. Crispian, Crispin; Crispus

C.R.T. or **C.R.** (Clerici Regulares Theatini) (Lat.) Clerks Regular, Theatine; Theatine Fathers

crt. or **cr.** crate

crtkr. caretaker

crts. crates

cry., crys. or **cryst.** crystals

cry. or **cryst.** crystalline; crystallized

crys., cry. or **cryst.** crystals

cryst. or **cry.** crystalline; crystallized

cryst., cry. or **crys.** crystals

cryst. or **crystal.** crystallography

CS or **c.s.** cast steel

C.S. Christian Science; Christian Scientist; current strength

C.S., Com. Serg., Com. Serj. or **Com. Serjt.** Common Sergeant or Serjeant (Brit.)

C.S., Com.Sub. Comsy.Sub. or **c.s.** commissary of subsistence

C.S. or **c.s.** capital stock; chemical society; civil service; clerk of sessions; clerk to the signet; court of sessions; (Custos Sigilli)(Lat.) Keeper of the Seal

C.S. or **C.S.A.** Confederate States [of America]

C/S colliery screened (Coal trade)

Cs cesium (Chem.)

Cs. Caesar

C/s or **cs.** cases

cs. centistere; commanders; current series

cs. (Communis)(Lat.) or **com.** common

cs. or **C/s** cases

c.s. (colla sinistra)(Ital.) with the left hand (Music)

c.s., Com.Sub., Comsy.Sub. or **C.S.** commissary of subsistence

c.s. or **CS** cast steel

CSA or **C.S.A.** Civilian Supply Administration

C.S.A. Confederate States Army

C.S.A. or **C.S.** Confederate States of America

C.S.A.A. Child Study Association of America

C.S.B. Central Statistical Board; (Congregatio Sancti Basilii)(Lat.) Congregation of St. Basil; Congretation of the Priests of St. Basil; Basilian Fathers (cf. O.S.B.M.)

C.S.B. or **B.S.C.** Bachelor of Christian Science

CSC or **C.S.C.** Civil Service Commission

C.S.C. Civil Service Club; Conspicuous Service Cross

C.S.C. (Congregatio Sanctae Crucis)(Lat.) or **O.S.Cr.** (Ordo Sanctae Crucis)(Lat.) Congregation of the Holy Cross; Order of the Holy Cross; Crozier Fathers; Croziers (cf. O.S.C.R.)

csc or **cosec** cosecant

C.S.C.B. (Congregatio Missionarii Sancti Caroli Borromeo)(Lat.), **M.S.C.** (Missionarii Sancti Caroli)(Lat.) or **P.S.S.C.** Society of Missionaries of St. Charles Borromeo; Missionaries of St. Charles; Pious Society of St. Charles; Pious Society of Missionaries of St. Charles Borromeo

C.S.C.R. Central Society for Chemical Research

C.S.D., D.C.S. or **D.S.C.** Doctor of Christian Science

C.S.F. cerebrospinal fluid

C.S.F. or **C.P.S.** (Congregatio Presbyterorum Sanctissimi Stigmati)(Lat.) Congregation of Priests of the Most Holy Stigmati; Stigmatine Fathers

C.S.I. Chartered Surveyors' Institution (Brit.); Companion of [the Order of] the Star of India

C Sig O (Mil.) or **C.S.O.** Chief Signal Officer

C.S.I.R. Council of Scientific and Industrial Research

C.S.K. Chief storekeeper

csk. countersink

csk. or **ck.** cask

C.S.M. cerebrospinal meningitis; Company sergeant-major

C.S.M.M.G. Chartered Society of Massage and Medical Gymnastics (Brit.)

C.S.N. Confederate States Navy

C.S.O. Chief staff officer

C.S.O. or **C Sig O** (Mil.) Chief Signal Officer

Cs.o.S. Chiefs of Section

C.S.P. (Congregatio Sancti Pauli)(Lat.), **C.P.** or **P.P.** Congregation of St. Paul the Apostle; Society of St. Paul; Missionary Society of St. Paul the Apostle; Paulist Fathers; Paulists

C.S.P.H.A.N.A. Conference of State and Provincial Health Authorities of North America

C.S.R. Certified Shorthand Reporter

C.S.S.A. Civil Service Supply Association

C.SS.CC. (Congregatio Sacratissimorum Cordium (Lat.), (Congregatio Sacrorum Cordium Jesu et Mariae)(Lat.) Congregation of the Sacred Hearts of Jesus and Mary; Missionaries of the Sacred Hearts of Jesus and Mary

C.S.Sp. (Congregatio Sancti Spiritus) (Lat.) Society of the Holy Ghost; Fathers of the Holy Ghost; Holy Ghost Fathers

C.SS.R. or **C. Ss. R.** (Congregatio Sanctissimi Redemptoris) (Lat.) Society of the Most Holy Redeemer; Redemptorist Fathers; Redemptorists (cf. O.SS.T.; M. S. SS.T.)

C. SS. S. (Congregatio Sanctissimi Salvatoris) (Lat.) Congregation of the Most Holy Savior; Bridgettines

C.S.T. Central Standard Time

C. Surg. Chief Surgeon

C.S.V. (Clerici Sancti Viatoris) (Lat.) Clerks or Clerics of St. Viateur or Viator; Viatorians; Congregation of St. Viator

C.T. Candidate in Theology; Central Time

C.T. or **C/T** cable transfer

C.T. or **c.t.** certificated teacher (Brit.); certified teacher; commercial traveler

C/T Californian terms (Grain trade)

C/T or **C.T.** cable transfer

Ct celtium (Chem.)

Ct. or **Conn.** Connecticut

Ct., ct., C. or **c.** court

Ct., ct., C. or **Cte** (Comte) (Fr.) Count

ct. caught

ct., C., c. or **¢** cent

ct., C., c., cent. (centum) (Lat.), **h** (hecto-) (Greek), **H., h., hun.** or **hund.** hundred

ct., c., car., K., k. or **kt.** carat; karat

ct., Co., co. or **Cy.** county

c.t. communication trenches

c.t. or **C.T.** certificated teacher (Brit.); certified teacher; commercial traveler

c.t.a. (cum testamento annexo) (Lat.) with the will attached

Ct.App., C.A. or **c.a.** court of appeal or appeals

C.T.A.U. Catholic Total Abstinence Union (Brit.)

C.T.B. Chief of Tariff Bureau

CTC or **C.T.C.** Citizens' Training Camp or Corps

C.T.C. Canadian Transport Commission; Chief turret captain; Civilian Technical Corps (Brit.)

c.t.c. corn trade clauses

Ct.Cls. or **C.Cls.** Court of Claims

Ct.Com.Pleas or **C.C.P.** Court of Common Pleas

Cte (Comte) (Fr.), **C., Ct.** or **ct.** count

cte. (corriente) (Span.), **d.M.** (denne Maaned) (Dan.), **Inst.** or **inst.** instant; this month; the present month

Ctesse (Comtesse) (Fr.) or **Ctss.** Countess

ctf., Cert., cert., Certc., Certif. or **certif.** certificate

ctfs. of **cts.** certificates

ctge. or **cart.** cartage

C. Theod. (Codex Theodocian) (Lat.) code of laws of Theodocius II

ctl., C., c., cwt., or **Ztr.** (Zentner) (Ger.) cental; hundredweight

c.t.l. constructive total loss (Insurance)

c.t.l.o. constructive total loss only (Insurance)

C.T.M. (Confederation de Trajabadores Mexicanos) Confederation of Mexican Workers

ctmo. centesimo; centimo

C.Tn. Combat train

ctn cotangent

ctn., C., c. or **cart.** carton

cto. or **con.** concerto

c. to c. or **c.c.** center to center

C. to S. or **c. to s.** carting to shipside

C.T.P.S. Chicago Tribune Press Service

C.T.R. (court tiré rapide) (Fr.) short rapid fire

ctr., C., c., Cen (Mil.), **cen.,** or **cr.** center

ctrsgd. countersigned

ctrsig. countersignature

C.T.S. Catholic Truth Society (Brit.)

cts., C., c. or **¢** cents

cts., C., c. or **c^es^** centimes

cts. or **ctfs.** certificates

Ctss. or **Ctsse** (Comtesse) (Fr.) Countess

ct.stp. certificate stamped (Securities)

CTU centigrade thermal unit; Citizens' Training Unit (cf.CTC)

ctvo. centavo

C.U. Cambridge University

Cu (Chem), **Cu.** (cuprum) (Lat.), **Ae.** (aes) (Lat.) **C., c.** or **cop.** copper

Cu., cu. or **k.** cumulus (Meteorol.)

cu., C., c. or **cub.** cubic

C.U.A.C. Cambridge University Athletic Club

C.U.A.F.C. Cambridge University Association of Football Clubs

cub., C., c. or **cu.** cubic

C.U.B.C. Cambridge University Boat Club

cub.ft., c.ft., cu.ft. or **ft.^{3}** cubic foot or feet

cu. cm., cc, c.c., c^3 or **cm.^{3}** cubic centimeter

C.U.C.P. Columbia University College of Pharmacy

cu.ft., c.ft., cub.ft. or **ft.^{3}** cubic foot or feet

C.U.G.C. Cambridge University Golf Club

C.U.H.C. Cambridge University Hockey Club

cu. in. or **in.^{3}** cubic inch or inches

cuj. (cujus) (Lat.) of which

cu.km. or **km.^{3}** cubic kilometer

Cul culvert (Mil.)

cum. cumulated; cumulative

cu.m. or **m^3** cubic meter

cu.μ, cu.mu or **μ^3** cubic micron

Cumb. Cumberland

cum d., c.d., cum d/, cum dd. or **cum div.** (cum dividendo) (Lat.) with dividend

cum int. with interest

cu.mm., cmm. or **mm^3** cubic millimeter

Cum.Pref., cum. pref. or **cu.pf.** cumulative preferred (Stocks)

C.U.M.S. Cambridge University Musical Society

cum. tabb. aen. (cum tabulis aeneis) (Lat.) with copperplates

cu.mu, cu.μ or**μ^3** cubic micron
C.U.N.A. Credit Union National Association
Cu. Nb. cumulo-nimbus (Meteorol.)
cu.pf., Cum.Pref. or **cum.pref.** cumulative preferred (Stocks)
cur., C., c., curr. or **curt.** current (of the present week, month, year)
cur., C., c. or **cy.** currency
cur. adv. vult or **c.a.v.** (curia advisari vult) (Lat.) the court wishes to be advised; the court wishes to consider
curr., C., c., cur. or **curt.** current (of the present week, month, year)
curr., C., c., cur. or **cy.** currency
curt., C., c., cur. or **curr.** current (of the present week, month, year)
cus. or **cust.** (custos, custodes)(Lat.) guide words (Biblio.)
Custod. or **custod.** custodian
cu. yd. or **yd.**^{3} cubic yard or yards
C.V. caloric volume
C.V., Com.Ver. or **Com. Vers.** Common Version [of the Bible]
C.V. or **c.v.** (cras vespere)(Lat.) tomorrow evening (cf. c.n.)
Cv [molecular heat at] constant volume
cv., conv. or **cvt.** convert; convertible
c.v. chief value
c.v. or **C.V.** (cras vespere)(Lat.) tomorrow evening (cf. c.n.)
C.V.A. California Vineyardists Association
cv.db. convertible debentures (Securities)
C.V.O. Commander or Companion of the [Royal] Victorian Order
cv.pf. convertible preferred (Securities)
cvt., conv. or **cv.** convert; convertible
CW, C.W. or **cw** continuous waves (Radio)
c.w. commercial weight
CWA or **C.W.A.** Civil Works Administration
CWAC or **C.W.A.C.** Canadian Women's Army Corps
CWES or **C.W.E.S.** Civil Works Educational Service
CWI or **C.W.I.** Coordinator of War Information
C.W.I. Catholic Workers' International
C.W.L. Catholic Women's League
C.W.L.A. Child Welfare League of America
CWO or **C.W.O.** Chief Warrant Officer
C.w.o. or **c.w.o.** cash with order
CWS or **C.W.S.** Chemical Warfare Service; Civil Works Service
CWS-Res Chemical Warfare Service Reserve
C.W.T. Central War Time; Chief water tender
cwt., C., c., ctl. or **Ztr.** (Zentner)(Ger.) hundredweight; cental
C.W.Y. Christian Working Youth
Cx. convex
Cy cyanogen
Cy., Co., co. or **ct.** county
cy., C., c., cap. or **k.**(Elec.) capacity
cy., C., c., cur. or **curr.** currency
cy. or **c.** cycle; cycles
cyath. (cyathus)(Lat.) glassful
cyath.vinos. (cyathus vinosus)(Lat.) wineglassful
cyc. cycling
cyc. or **cyclo.** cyclopedia; cyclopedic
Cyl. or **cyl.** cylindrical
cyl. cylinder
Cym. Cymric
C.Y.M.S. Catholic Young Men's Societies of Great Britain
CYO or **C.Y.O.** Catholic Youth Organization
CZ Combat zone (Mil.)
C.Z. or **I.C.Z.** [Isthmian or Panama] Canal Zone
Czech. Czechoslovakia
Czerw. (Czerwiec)(Pol.), **Je, Ju., Jun.** or **jun.** (junio)(Span.) June
Cz.kr. Czechoslovakian kronen

ΧΒΦ (Chi Beta Phi) National professional society (Science)
ΧΔΦ (Chi Delta Phi) National honor sorority (Literature)
ΧΕ (Chi Epsilon) Professional fraternity (Civil Engineering)
ΧΩ (Chi Omega) National undergraduate sorority
ΧΦ (Chi Phi) National undergraduate fraternity
ΧΨ (Chi Psi) National undergraduate fraternity

D

D deuterium (Chem.); didymium
D (Mil.), **D.** or **d.** deserted
D (Math.), **der.** or **deriv.** derivation
D. distal; dorsal; duration; (Deus)(Lat.) God
D., Abt. (Abteilung)(Ger.), **Div.** or **div.** division
D. or **d.** dam (in pedigrees); date; deserter; dime; dinar; diopter; diopters; door (Theat.); double (Hymnol.)
D., d. or **d-** dextro-
D. (dona)(Port.), **d.** (donna)(Ital.), **D.ª** or **Dña.** (Doña)(Span.) title of courtesy prefixed to Christian name of lady; mistress; lady (cf. L.; Mrs.)
D., d. or **da.** day
D., d., da. or **dau.** daughter
D., d., da. or **ds.** days
D., d., dec., déc. (décédé, décédée)(Fr.) **decd., gest.** (gestorben)(Ger.) or **ś.p.** (świętej pamięci) (Pol.) deceased (cf. B.M.; L.; ob.; Q.E.P.D.; R.I.P.; sel.)
D., d. or **decid.** deciduous
D., d. or **deg.** degree; degrees
D., d., del., dele. or **delt.** (deleatur)(Lat.) delete (Printing)
D., d. or **Dem.** democrat; democratic
D., d., den. or **dens.** density

D., d., Dep., dep., dept. or **depty.** deputy
D., d., det. (detur)(Lat.), **Exhib.** or **exhib.** (exhibeatur)(Lat.) let it be given (cf. cap.; d.t.d.; sum.)
D., d., di. or **dia.** diameter
D., d., Dir. or **dir.** director
D., d. or **div.** dividend
D., d., dlr., dol. or **doll.** dollar
D., d., Dow. or **dow.** dowager
D., d., dy, dy. (denarius, denarii)(Lat.) or **p.** penny; pence
D., d. (dux)(Lat.) or **ldr.** leader
D., d. (decretum, decreta)(Lat.) or **ord.** ordinance; ordinances
D., d., pl. or **pla.** (placitum, placita)(Lat.) decision; decisions; decree; decrees (Law)
D., dbre. (diciembre)(Span.), **Dec., déc.** (décembre)(Fr.), **des.** (desember)(Norw.), **Dez.** (Dezember)(Ger., Hung.), **dez.** (dezembro)(Port.), **dic.** (dicembre)(Ital.) or **Grudz.** (Grudzień)(Pol.) December
D., Dnus. or **Dom.** (Dominus)(Lat.) Lord; Master
D., Doc., Doct., Dr, Dr., dr or **d:r** (doktor)(Swed.) doctor
D. or **dos.** (dosis)(Lat.) dose
D., Du. or **holl.** (hollandais, hollandaise)(Fr.) Dutch; Hollander
D., Du. or **Hzg.** (Herzog)(Ger.) Duke
D., duo., 12°, 12mo or **12mo.** duodecimo
D. or **Hzgin.** (Herzogin)(Ger.) Duchess
D. (Dom.)(Port.), (Don)(Span.) or **Sr.** Sir
d differentiation (Math.); dyne (Elec.)
d (deci-)(Lat.), **dk** or **dk.** (deka-, deca-)(Greek) ten
d. angular deformation (Mech.)
d., D (Mil.) or **D.** deserted
d. or **D.** dam (in pedigrees); date; deserter; dime; dinar; diopter; diopters; door (Theat.); double (Hymnol.)
d., D. or **d-** dextro
d. (donna)(Ital.), **D.** (Dona)(Port.), **D.ª** or **Dña** (Doña)(Span.)(title of courtesy) lady; madam (cf. Mrs.; L.; Mme.)
d., D. or **da.** day
d., D., da. or **dau.** daughter
d., D., da. or **ds.** days
d., D., dec., déc. (décédé, décédée)(Fr.), **decd., gest.** (gestorben)(Ger.) or **s.p.** (swieitej)(Pol.) deceased
d., D. or **decid.** deciduous
d., D. or **deg.** degree; degrees
d., D., del., dele. or **delt.** (deleatur)(Lat.) delete
d., D. or **Dem.** democrat; democratic
d., D., den. or **dens.** density
d., D., Dep., dep., dept. or **dpty.** deputy
d., D., det. (detur)(Lat.), **Exhib.** or **exhib.** (exhibeatur)(Lat.) let it be given (cf. cap.; d.t.d.; sum.)
d., D., di. or **dia.** diameter
d., D., Dir. or **dir.** director
d., D. or **div.** dividend
d., D., dlr., dol. or **doll.** dollar
d., D., Dow. or **dow.** dowager
d., D., dy, dy. (denarius, denarii)(Lat.) or **p.** penny; pence
d., D. (dux)(Lat.) or **ldr.** leader
d., D. (decretum, decreta)(Lat.) or **ord.** ordinance; ordinances
d., D., pl. or **pla.** (placitum, placita)(Lat.) decision; decisions; decree; decrees
d. (droite)(Fr.), **dcha.** (derecha)(Span.), **D.M.** (destra mano)(Ital.), **M.D.** (main droite)(Fr.), **m.d.** (mano destra)(Ital.), **R.H.**, or **r.h.** right hand
d., dis., dist., DX or **D.X.** (Radio) distance
d., ob. or **obt.** (obiit)(Lat.) died (cf. dec.)
d. (destra)(Ital.), (droit)(Fr.), **R., r.** or **rt.** right
DA directional antenna
D.A. Diploma in Anaesthesia
D.A. or **D/A** documentary bills for acceptance; documents against (for, or on) acceptance
D.A. or **d.a.** direct action (Elec.)
D.A. or **Dist. Atty.** District Attorney
D/A deposit account; discharge afloat (Chartering)
D/A or **D.A.** documentary bills for acceptance; documents against (for, or on) acceptance
D/A or **d/a** days after acceptance
Da. or **Dan.** Danish
D.ª, Dña (Doña)(Span.), **D.** (dona)(Port.) or **d.** (donna)(Ital.) title of courtesy prefixed to Christian name of lady; madam; mistress; lady (cf. L.; Mrs.)
d. A. (dette Aar)(Dan.), **a.c.** (année courante)(Fr.), **d.J.** (dieses Jahres)(Ger.), **f.é.** (folyó évi)(Hung.) or **h.a.** (hoc anno)(Lat.) this year; the current year
d. A. (der Ältere)(Ger.), **d.ä.** (den äldre)(Swed.) or **er.** elder (cf. Sr.)
d. A. (der Ältere)(Ger.), **d.ä.** (den äldre)(Swed.), **Sen., sen., Senr., senr., Sr.** or **sr.** senior
da., D. or d. day
da., D., d. or **dau.** daughter
da., D., d. or ds. days
d.a. (dicti anni)(Lat.) of the said year
d.ä. (det är)(Swed.), **c.-à-d.** (c'est-à-dire)(Fr.), **d.h.** (das Heisst)(Ger.), **d.i.** (das ist)(Ger.), **d.v.s.** (det vil sige)(Dan.), (det vill saga)(Swed.), **h.e.** (hoc or hic **est)(Lat.), i.e.** (id est)(Lat.) or **t.i.** (tudni illik)(Hung.) that is; that is to say (cf. viz.)
d.ä. (den äldre)(Swed.), **d.A.** (der Ältere)(Ger.) or **er.** elder (cf. Sr.)
d.ä. (den äldre)(Swed.), **d.A.** (der Ältere)(Ger.), **Sen., sen., Senr., senr., Sr.** or **sr.** senior
d/a or **D/A** days after acceptance
D.A.A. Deputy Assistant Adjutant (Brit.)
D.A.A.G. Deputy Assistant Adjutant-General (Brit.)
DAB or **D.A.B.** Dictionary of American Biography
d.a.c. deductible average clause (Insurance)
D.A.C.G. Deputy Assistant Commissary-General (Brit.)

D.A.D.G. Deputy Assistant Director-General (Brit.)
D.A.D.M.S. Deputy Assistant Director of Medical Services (Brit.)
D.A.D.O.S. Deputy Assistant Director of Ordnance Services (Brit.)
D.A.G. Deputy Adjutant-General (Brit.); Deputy Advocate-General (Brit.)
dag. or **dkg.** decagram; dekagram
D. Agr. Doctor of Agriculture
D.A.H. disordered action of the heart (Med.)
DAI or **D.A.I.** Division of Applications and Information
Dak. Dakota
dal., dkl. or **dl.** decaliter; dekaliter
dal s., D.S. or **d.s.** (dal segno)(Ital.) repeat from the sign (Music)
dam., dkm. or **dm.** decameter or dekameter
D.&B. Dunn & Bradstreet
D. & d. drunk and disorderly
D & FS Discharge and final statement (Mil.)
D. & J. December and June (Interest)
D.& S., d.& s. or **d. and s.** demand and supply
Dan. or **Da.** Danish
Dan. or **Danl.** Daniel
D. and C. Dean and Chapter
d. and s., d.&s. or **D.& S.** demand and supply
Danl. or **Dan.** Daniel
Danz. Danzig
D.A.Q.M.G. Deputy Assistant Quartermaster-Gerenal (Brit.)
D.A.R. or **D.R.** Daughters of the American Revolution
D. Arch. Doctor of Architecture
dat. dative
dau., D., d. or **da.** daughter
D.A.V. Disabled American Veterans
Dav. David
D.A.V.Aux. Disabled American Veterans Auxiliary
D.B. Domesday Book; deals and battens (Lumber)
D.B. or **B.D.** Bachelor of Didactics; Bachelor of Divinity
D.B. or **d.b.** day book
db decibel; decibels
db., Deb., deb., Deben. or **deben.** debenture
d.b. double-breasted; doubly biased
d.b. or **D.B.** day book
D.B.A. Doctor of Business Administration
d.b.a. doing business as
DBB or **D.B.B.** Director of the Bureau of the Budget
D.B.B. deals, battens and boards (Lumber)
D.B.E. Dame [Commander of the Order] of the British Empire
D.B.G. Disciplinary barracks guard
d.b.h diameter breast high or at breast height
D. Bib. or **D. Bible** Douay Bible
dbk. drawback
dbl., or **dble.** double; doubled
d.b.n. (de bonis non)(Lat.) of the goods not [yet administered]
dbre. (diciembre)(Span.), **D., Dec., déc.** (décembre)(Fr.), **des.** (desember) (Norw.), **Dez.** (Dezember)(Ger., Hung.), **dez.** (dezembro)(Port.), **dic.** (dicembre)(Ital.) or **Grudz.** (**Grudzień**) (Pol.) December
db.rts. debenture rights
DC (Mil.) or **D.C.** Dental Corps
D.C. Deputy Captain (Brit.); Deputy Consul (Brit.); Doctor of Chiropractic
D.C. (da capo)(Ital.) or **ab init.** (ab initio) (Lat.) from the beginning (cf. ad init.)
D.C. or **DC** (Mil.) Dental Corps
D.C., d.c., D.-C. or **d.-c.** direct current
D.C. or **Dist.Ct.** District Court
D.-C., D.C., d.c. or **d.-c.** direct current
d.C. (dopo Cristo)(Ital.), **A.D.** (anno Domini)(Lat.), **A.P.C.N.** (anno post Christum natum)(Lat.), **n.Ch., n. Chr.** (nach Christo)(Ger.) or **n. Chr. G.** (nach Christi Geburt)(Ger.) after Christ; after the birth of Christ; in the year of our Lord
d.c. double column (Bookkeeping)
d.c., D.C., D.-C. or **d.-c.** direct current
d.c. or **dev.cl.** deviation clause (Insurance)
DCB or **D.C.B.** Defense Communications Board
D. C. C. double cotton covered [wire] (Elec.)
D.Cc. double concave
D.C.E. Doctor of Civil Engineering
D.C.G. Deputy Commissary-General (Brit.)
D.C.H. Diploma in Child Health
dcha. (derecha)(Span.), **d.** (droite)(Fr.), **D.M.** (destra mano)(Ital.), **M.D.** (main droite)(Fr.), **m.d.** (mano destra)(Ital.), **R.H.** or **r.h.** right hand
D.C.L., C.L.D. or **J.C.D.** (Juris Civilis Doctor)(Lat.) Doctor of Civil Law
D.C.L., D.Cn.L. or **J.C.D.** Doctor of Canon Law
D.C.L.I. Duke of Cornwall's Light Infantry
D.C.M. Distinguished Conduct Medal (Brit.); District Court Martial
D.Cn.L., D.C.L. or **J.C.D.** Doctor of Canon Law
DC of S or **D.C. of S** Deputy Chief of Staff
D.C.O.G. Diploma of the College of Obstetrics (Brit.)
DCS or **D.C.S.** Deputy Clerk of Session or Sessions
D.C.S., C.S.D. or **D.S.C.** Doctor of Christian Science
D.C.S. or **S.C.D.** Doctor of Commercial Science
D.C.T. Doctor of Christian Theology (cf. D.S.T.)
D.C.V.O. Dame Commander of the Royal Victorian Order
D.Cx. double convex
DD or **D.D.** Dishonorable discharge (Mil.)
DD. or **Ded.** (dedicavit)(Lat.) dedicated

D.D. (Divinitatis Doctor)(Lat.) Doctor of Divinity

D.D., D/D or **d.d.** demand draft

D.D. (Dags Dato)(Dan.), **D/D, D/d** or **d/d** day's date

D.D. or **d.d.** (dono dedit)(Lat.) he or she gave as a gift

D/D, D.D. (Dags Dato)(Dan.), **D/d** or **d/d** day's date

D/D, D.D. or **d.d.** demand draft

D/D or **D/d** days after date; days after delivery

D.d. (Deo dedit)(Lat.) he or she gave to God

D/d, D.D. (Dags dato)(Dan.), **D/D** or **d/d** day's date

D/d or **D/D** days after date; days after delivery

dd., d/d, deld. or **dld.** delivered

d.d. delayed delivery; double deck

d.d. or **D.D.** (dono dedit)(Lat.) he or she gave as a gift

d.d., D.D. or **D/D** demand draft

d/d delivered at docks

d/d, D.D. (Dags Dato)(Dan.), **D/D** or **D/d** day's date

d/d, D/D or **D/d** days after date; days after delivery

d/d, dd., deld. or **dld.** delivered

D.D.D. (dono dedit, dedicavit)(Lat.) he or she gave and consecrated as a gift; (dat, dicat, dedicat)(Lat.) he or she gives, devotes, dedicates

D.D.H.C. Division of Defense Housing Coordination

d. d. in d. or **de d. in d.** (de die in diem) (Lat.) from day to day (Pharm.)

D.D.M. or **D.M.D.** (Dentariae Medicinae Doctor)(Lat.) Doctor of Dental Medicine

D.D.M.S. Deputy Director of Medical Services (Brit.)

D.D.S. Doctor of Dental Surgery

D.D.S. or **D.D.Sc.** Doctor of Dental Science

dd/s delivered sound (Grain trade)

D.E. Doctor of Entomology; Dynamic Engineer

D.E., D. Eng., Doc.Eng., Dr.Eng., E.D. or **Eng.D.** Doctor of Engineering

d.e. double entry (Bookkeeping)

Dea. Deacon

Deb. Deborah

Deb., db., deb., Deben. or **deben.** debenture

deb., db., Deb., Deben. or **deben.** debenture

Deben., db., Deb., deb. or **deben.** debenture

deben., db., Deb., deb. or **Deben.** debenture

Dec. decorated; (decanta)(Lat.) pour off (Pharm.)

Dec., D., dbre. (diciembre)(Span.), **déc.** (décembre)(Fr.), **des.** (desember)(Norw.), **Dez.** (Dezember)(Ger., Hung.), **dez.** (dezembro)(Port.), **dic.** (dicembre) (Ital.) or **Grudz.** (Grudzień)(Pol.) December

Dec., dec. or **decor.** decoration

dec. declaration; declination; decorative; decrease; (decani)(Lat.) to be sung by the decanal

dec., D., d., déc. (décédé, décédée)(Fr.), **decd., gest.** (gestorben)(Ger.) or **ś.p.** (świętej pamięci)(Pol.) deceased (cf. B.M.; L.; ob.; Q.E.P.D.; R.I.P.; sel.)

déc. (décembre)(Fr.), **D., dbre.** (diciembre) (Span.), **Dec., des.** (desember)(Norw.), **Dez.** (Dezember)(Ger., Hung.), **dez.** (dezembro)(Port.), **dic.** (dicembre) (Ital.) or **Grudz.** (Grudzień)(Pol.) December

dec. or **decd.** decreased

dec., decim., dim. or **dm.** decimeter

dec. or **decl.** declension

dec., decres. or **decresc.** (decrescendo) (Ital.) with a gradual decrease in volume (Music)(cf. cal.; dimin.)

decd. D., d., dec., déc. (décédé, décédée) (Fr.), **gest.** (gestorben)(Ger.), or **ś.p.** (świętej pamięci)(Pol.) deceased (cf. B.M., L.; ob.; Q.E.P.D.; R.I.P.; sel.)

decd. or **dec.** decreased

decid., D. or **d.** deciduous

decim., dec., dim. or **dm.** decimeter

decl. declensional

decl. or **dec.** declension

decoct. (decoctum)(Lat.) a decoction (Pharm.)

Decon Decontamination (Mil.)

decor., Dec. or **dec.** decoration

decres., dec. or **decresc.** (decrescendo) (Ital.) with a gradual decrease in volume (Music) (cf. cal.; dimin.)

D.Ed. or **Ed. D.** Doctor of Education

Ded. or **DD.** (dedicavit)(Lat.) dedicated

Ded., ded. or **dedic.** dedication

dedic., Ded. or **ded.** dedication

de d. in d. or **d.d. in d.** (de die in diem) (Lat.) from day to day (cf. P.D.)

Def. or **def.** deferred (Stock); defined

Def., def., deft. or **dft.** defendant

def. defense; definite; definition

def. or **Def.** deferred (Stock); defined

def., Def., deft. or **dft.** defendant

deft., Def., def. or **dft.** defendant

deg., D. or **d.** degree; degrees

Del. Delaware

del. delegate; deliver

del., D., d., dele. or **delt.** (deleatur)(Lat.) delete (Printing)

del. or **delt.** (delineavit)(Lat.) he or she drew it (cf. des.; exc.; fec.; inv.)

del acct Delinquent account (Mil.)

deld., dd., d/d or **dld.** delivered

dele., D., d., del. or **delt.** (deleatur)(Lat.) delete (Printing)

deliq. deliquescent

delt., D., d., del. or **dele.** (deleatur)(Lat.) delete (Printing)

delt. or **del.** (delineavit)(Lat.) he or she drew it (cf. des.; exc.; fec.; inv.)

Dely., dely., dlvy., Dly., dly., D/y or **dy.** delivery

Dem., D. or **d.** democrat; democratic

dem. demurrage

DEML (Mil.) or **D.E.M.L.** Detached Enlisted Men's List

Demon., demon., Demons. or **demons.** demonstration; demonstrative

Den. Denmark

den., D., d. or **dens.** density

D.Eng., D.E., Doc.Eng., Dr.Eng., E.D. or **Eng.D.** Doctor of Engineering

D. Eng. S. Doctor of Engineering Science

denom. denomination

dens., D., d. or **den.** density

dent. dental; dentist; dentistry

Dent. Hyg. Dental Hygienist

Dent. Sec. Dental section

Dep (Mil.) or **dep.** depot

Dep. dependency; (depuratus)(Lat.) purified

Dep., D., d., dep., dept. or **dpty.** deputy

Dep. or **dep.** deposit

dep. departs; departure (Naut.); deposed

dep., Abt. (Abteilung)(Ger.), **Dept** (Mil.) **Dept., dept.** or **dpt.** department

dep., D., d., Dep., dept. or **dpty.** deputy

dep. or **Dep** (Mil.) depot

dep., dept. or **dpt.** deponent

Dep Bn Depot battalion (Mil.)

Dep. Commr. Deputy Commissioner

dep.ctf. deposit certificate

depr. depreciation

Dept (Mil.), **Abt.** (Abteilung)(Ger.), **dep., Dept., dept.** or **dpt.** department

dept., Abt. (Abteilung)(Ger.), **dep., Dept** (Mil.), **Dept.,** or **dpt.** department

dept., D., d., Dep., dep. or **dpty.** deputy

dept., dep. or **dpt.** deponent

De R., DR, Ea.R. (Entartungs-Reaktion) (Ger.) or **R.D.** reaction of degeneration

der., D (Math.) or **deriv.** derivation

der. or **deriv.** derivative; derive; derived

derg. (dergleichen)(Ger.) the like; such

deriv., D (Math.) or **der.** derivation

deriv. or **der.** derivative; derive; derived

dermatol. dermatological; dermatologist; dermatology

des. design; designed (cf. inv.)

des. (dessin)(Fr.)(Music), **arr.** or **arrgt.** arrangement

des. (desember)(Norw.), **D., dbre.** (diciembre)(Span.), **Dec., déc.** (décembre) (Fr.), **Dez.** (Dezember)(Ger., Hung.), **dez.** (dezembre)(Port.), **dic.** (dicembre) (Ital.) or **Grudz.** (Grudzień)(Pol.) December

des. (dessin)(Fr.), **dr., Drg., drg., dwg.** or **Entw.** (Entwerf)(Ger.) drawing

desc. or **Descdt.** descendant

descr. descriptive

desid. (desideratum, desiderata)(Lat.) anything desired or needed

D. ès L. (Docteur ès Lettres)(Fr.), **D. Litt.** (Doctor Litterarum)(Lat.), **L.D.** or **Litt. D.** (Litterarum Doctor)(Lat.) Doctor of Letters (cf. D.Lit.)

desp. despatch

D. ès S. (Docteur ès Sciences)(Fr.) Doctor of Sciences (cf. D.Sc.)

destn. or **dstn.** destination

Det (Mil.) or **det.** detached; detachment

Det. detector

det. detach; detail

det., D., d. (detur)(Lat.), **Exhib.** or **exhib.** (exhibeatur)(Lat.) let it be given (cf. cap.; d.t.d.; sum.)

det. or **Det** (Mil.) detached; detachment

Det. in dup. or **Det. in 2 plo.** (detur in duplo)(Lat.) let twice as much be given

D. et s. (detur et signetur)(Lat.) let it be given and labeled

Deut. or **Dt.** Deuteronomy

Dev. Devonshire

dev. deviation

dev.cl. or **d.c.** deviation clause

devel. development

dev.lgth. developed length

Dez. (Dezember)(Ger., Hung.), **dez.** (dezembro)(Port.), **D., dbre.** (diciembre) (Span.), **Dec., déc.** (décembre)(Fr.), **des.** (desember)(Norw.), **dic.** (decembre)(Ital.) or **Grudz.** (Grudzień)(Pol.) December

D.F. Dean of the Faculty; Doctor of Forestry; (Distrito Federal)(Span.),(Districto Federal)(Port.) Federal District

D.F. or **D/F** direction-finding (Radio)

D.F. (Defensor Fidei)(Lat.), **F.D., Fid. Def.** or **fid. def.** (Fidei Defensor)(Lat.) Defender of the Faith (Brit.)

D/F or **D.F.** direction-finding (Radio)

d.f. dead freight (Shipping)

d.-f. double-fronted

D.F.A. Division Freight Agent

D.F.A. or **A.F.D.** Doctor of Fine Arts

D.F.C. Distinguished Flying Cross (Brit.)

D.F.M. Distinguished Flying Medal

D.F.M.S. Domestic and Foreign Missionary Society

D.F.P.A. Daughters of Founders and Patriots of America

Dft., dft. or **haust.** (haustus)(Lat.)(Pharm.) draft

dft., Def., def. or **deft.** defendant

dft., Dft. or **haust.** (haustus)(Lat.)(Pharm.) draft

dftsmn., Drftm (Mil.) or **drftsmn.** draftsman

D.G. (Dei gratia)(Lat.) by the grace of God; (Deo gratias)(Lat.) thanks to God; Director-General (Brit.); Dragoon Guards

Dg. or **dg.** decigram

D.G.I.A.B. Durable Goods Industries Advisory Board

DGID or **D.G.I.D.** Division of Grazing of the Interior Department

D.G.M.W. Diréctor-General of Military Works
D.H. or **d.h.** deadhead (Freight)
d.h. (das heisst)(Ger.), **c.-à-d.** (c'est-à-dire) (Fr.), **d.ä.** (det är)(Swed.), **d.i.** (das ist) (Ger.), **d.v.s.** (det vil sige)(Dan.),(det vill säga)(Swed.), **h.e.** (hoc or hic est) (Lat.), **i.e.** (id est)(Lat.) or **t.i.** (tudni illik)(Hung.) that is; that is to say (cf. viz.)
DHC or **D.H.C.** Defense Homes Corporation
D.H.I.A. Dairy Herd Improvement Association
D.H.L. Doctor of Hebrew Literature
DHQ (Mil.), **D.H.Q., Div Hq** (Mil.) or **Q.G.D.** (Quartier général de division) (Fr.) Division headquarters
D. Hy. or **Dr. Hy.** Doctor of Hygiene
Di didymium (Chem.)
di., D., d., dia. or **diam.** diameter
d.i. (das ist)(Ger.), **c.-à-d.** (c'est-à-dire) (Fr.), **d.ä.** (det är)(Swed.), **d.h.** (das heisst)(Ger.), **d.v.s.** (det vil sige)(Dan.), (det vill säga)(Swed.), **h.e.** (hoc or hic est)(Lat.), **i.e.** (id est)(Lat.) or **t.i.** (tudni illik)(Hung.) that is; that is to say (cf. viz.)
D.I.A. Design and Industries Association (Brit.)
dia., D., d., di. or **diam.** diameter
diag. or **diagr.** diagram
dial. dialect; dialectic; dialectical
diam.. D., d., di. or **dia.** diameter
D.I.C. Diploma of the Imperial College [of Science and Technology] (Brit.)
dic. (dicembre)(Ital.), **D., dbre.** (diciembre) (Span.), **Dec., déc.** (décembre)(Fr.), **des.** (desember)(Norw.), **Dez.** (Dezember)(Ger., Hung.), **dez.** (dezembro) (Port.) or **Grudz.** (Grudzień)(Pol.) December
dict. dictation; dictator; dictionary
dicta. dictaphone
dieb. alt., alt. dieb. (diebus alternis, alternis diebus)(Lat.) or **e.o.d.** every other day
dieb.tert. (diebus tertius)(Lat.) every third day
diet. dietetics
dif. or **diff.** differ; difference; different; differential; differs
difclt. difficult
difclty. difficulty
diff. or **dif.** differ; difference; different; differential; differs
Dig. (digeratur)(Lat.) let it be disgested
dig. digest
dil. or **Dilut.** (dilutus)(Lat.) dilute
Dilut. (dilutus)(Lat.) or **dil.** dilute
Dim. or **dim.** (dimidium)(Lat.) one half (cf. hf.)
dim. dimension
dim., dec., decim. or **dm.** decimeter
dim. or **Dim.** (dimidium)(Lat.) one half (cf. hf.)
dim. or **dimin.** diminutive; (diminuendo) (Ital.) with gradually diminishing power (Music)(cf. cal.; decres.)

D. in p. aeq. (divide in partes aequales) (Lat.) divide in equal parts (cf. āā)
dioc. diocesan; diocese
dioc.conf. diocesan conference
dioc.syn. diocesan synod
Dipl. diploma; diplomat
Dipl., dipl., Diplo. or **Diplom.** diplomatic
dipl. diplomatist
Dipl. Ing. (Diplomingeniör)(Ger.) Certificated Engineer
Diplo., Dipl., dipl. or **Diplom.** diplomatic
Dir., D., d. or **dir.** director
dir. (direxit)(Lat.) he or she directed; he or she guided (cf. exc.)
dir., D., d., or **Dir.** director
dir-conn direct-connected
Dir. prop. (directione propria)(Lat.) with the proper direction
dis. disciplinary; discipline
dis., d., dist., DX or **D.X.** (Radio) distance
dis., disc., disct. or **dist.** discount
dis., disch. or **Dische.** discharge; discharged
dis. or **dist.** distant
dis. or **distr.** distribute
disbs. disbursements
disbs.&/or ant.earns. disbursements and/or anticipated earnings (Insurance)
disc. discover; discovered (cf. inv.); discoverer
disc., dis., disct. or **dist.** discount
disch., dis. or **Dische.** discharge; discharged
dis. ch. discovered check (Chess)
Dische., dis. or **disch.** discharge; discharged
disct. discounted
disct., dis., disc. or **dist.** discount
Dishon. dishonorable; dishonorably
dismd. dismissed
Disp. or **disp.** dispensary; dispensatory
diss. dissertation; dissipation
dissd. or **solut.** (solutus)(Lat.) dissolved (cf. sol.; solv.)
Dist. (distilla)(Lat.) distil
Dist. or **dist.** district
dist. distinguish; distinguished
dist., d., dis., DX or **D.X.** (Radio) distance
dist. or **dis.** distant
dist., dis., disc. or **disct.** discount
dist. or **Dist.** district
Dist. Atty. or **D.A.** District Attorney
Dist.Chf. District Chief
Dist.Comdr. District Commander
Dist.Ct. or **D.C.** District Court
Dist.Eng. District Engineer
disting. distinguishing
Dist.J. or **D.J.** District Judge
Dist.Mgr. District Manager
distr. distributed; distribution; distributive; distributor
distr. or **dis.** distribute
Div. Divinity
Div., Abt. (Abteilund)(Ger.), **D.** or **div.** division

div. divergence; diversion; divide; divided; divine; divisor; divorced
div., Abt. (Abteilung)(Ger.), **D.** or **Div.** division
div., D. or **d.** dividend
Div Adj Division adjutant
Div Avn Division aviation
Div Comdr Division commander
Div.Eng. or **Div Engr** (Mil.) Division engineer
Div Engr (Mil.) or **Div.Eng.** Division engineer
Div Hq, DHQ (Mil.) **D.H.Q.** or **Q.G.D.** (Quartier général de division)(Fr.) Division headquarters
Div Hq Comdt & PM Division headquarters commandant and provost marshal
Div JA Division judge advocate
Div Mun O Division munitions officer
Div OO Division ordinance officer
Div QM Division quartermaster
Div Sig O Division signal officer
Div Surg Division surgeon
D.J. or **Dist.J.** District Judge
D.J., Dr.Jur. (Doctor Juris)(Lat.), **D.L., J.D.** or **Jur.D.** (Juris Doctor)(Lat.) Doctor of Law (cf. LL.D.; D.J.S.)
d.J. (dieses Jahr)(Ger.), **a.c.** (année courante)(Fr.), **d.A.** (dette Aar)(Dan.), **f.é.** (folyó évi)(Hung.) or **h.a.** (hoc anno) (Lat.) this year; the current year (cf. a.pr.; curr.)
d.J. (der Jungere)(Ger.), **d.y.** (den yngre) (Swed.), **Jnr., jnr., Jr., jr., Jun., jun., Junr.** or **junr.** junior
d.J. (dieses Jahres)(Ger.) or **h.a.** (huius anno)(Lat.) of this year; this year's
D.J.S. or **S.J.D.** (Scientiae Juridicae Doctor) (Lat.) Doctor of Juridical Science
dk, dk. (deca-, deka-)(Greek) or **d** (deci-) (Lat.) ten
dk. dark; deck; dock; duck (Fabric)
dkg. or **dag.** dekagram; decagram
dkl., dal. or **dl.** decaliter; dekaliter
dkm., dam. or **dm.** decameter; dekameter
dkm.^{2} square dekameter
dkm.^{3} cubic dekameter
dks. dekastere
DL day letter
D.L. Deputy-Lieutenant (Brit.); descriptive list
D.L., D.J., Dr.Jur. (Doctor Juris)(Lat.), **J.D.** or **Jur.D.** (Juris Doctor)(Lat.) Doctor of Law (cf. LL.D.; D.J.S.)
D/L or **d.l.** demand loan
dl, d-l or **d+ l** dextro-levo (Chem.)
dl. deciliter
dl., dal. or **dkl.** decaliter; dekaliter
d.l. or **D/L** demand loan
d-l, dl or **dtl** dextro-levo (Chem.)
DLB or **D.L.B.** Deposit Liquidation Board
D.L.B. (Dienstvorschrift für das Luftschiffer-Batallion)(Ger.) Balloon battalion instructions
DLC or **D.L.C.** Disaster Loan Corporation
D.L.C. Doctor of Celtic Literature
dld., dd., d/d or **deld.** delivered
D.L.I. Durham Light Infantry
D. Lit. (Doctor Literarum)(Lat.) or **Lit. D.** (Literarum Doctor)(Lat.) Doctor of Literature (cf D.Litt.)
D. Litt. (Doctor Litterarum)(Lat.), **D. ès L.** (Docteur ès Lettres)(Fr.), **Litt. D.** (Litterarum Doctor)(Lat.) or **L.D.** Doctor of Letters (cf. D.Lit.)
D.L.O. Dead Letter Office (now R.L.O.) (Brit.)
d.l.o. dispatch loading only (Shipping)
D.L.R. Dominion Law Reports
dlr. dealer
dlr., D., d., dol. or **doll.** dollar
dlrs., dls., dols. or **dolls.** dollars
D.L.S. Doctor of Library Science
dls., dlrs., dols. or **dolls.** dollars
dls/shr dollars per share
dlvy., Dely., dely., Dly., dly., D/y or **dy.** delivery
Dly., Dely., dely., dlvy., dly., D/y or **dy.** delivery
dly., Dely., dely., dlvy., Dly., D/y or **dy.** delivery
D.M. (Corps militaire des douanes)(Fr.) Army Customs Service; Deputy Master (Freemasonry); Doctor of Mathematics
D.M. (destra mano)(Ital.), **d.** (droite)(Fr.), **dcha.** (derecha)(Span.), **M.D.** (main droite)(Fr.), **m.d.** (mano destra)(Ital.), **R.H.** or **r.h.** right hand
D.M., D. Mus., Mus. D., Mus.Doc., Mus. Doct. or **Mus. Dr.** (Musicae Doctor) (Lat.) Doctor of Music
D.M., Dr. Med. (Doctor Medicinae)(Lat.) or **M.D.** (Medicinae Doctor)(Lat.) Doctor of Medicine (cf. D.M.S.)
d.M. (denne Maaned)(Dan.), **cte.** (corriente) (Span.), **Inst.** or **inst.** instant; this month; the present month (cf. curr.)
dm., dam. or **dkm.** decameter; dekameter
dm., dec., decim. or **dim.** decimeter
dm.^{2} square decimeter
dm.^{3} cubic decimeter
DMA or **D.M.A.** Department of Military Aeronautics
D.M.A.A. Direct Mail Advertising Association
D.M.A.P. (Direction de matériel automobile et de personnel)(Fr.) Bureau of Automobile Material and Personnel
DMC or **D.M.C.** Dairy Marketing Corporation
D.M.D. Doctor of Mathematics and Didactics
D.M.D. (Dentariae Medicinae Doctor)(Lat.) or **D.D.M.** Doctor of Dental Medicine
D. Met. Doctor of Metallurgy
D.M.J.S. December, March, June and September (Interest)
D.M.L. Doctor of Modern Languages
dmnstr. demonstrator
D.M.R.E. Diploma in Medical Radiology and Electrology
D.M.S. Director of Medical Services (Brit.)

D.M.S., Med.Sc.D., M.Sc.D. or **Sc.D.Med.** Doctor of Medical Science (cf. M.D.)
D. Mus., D. M., Mus. D., Mus. Doc., Mus. Doct. or **Mus. Dr.** (Musicae Doctor) (Lat.) Doctor of Music
D.N. (Dominus Noster)(Lat.), **N.S.** or **N.-S.** (Notre-Seigneur)(Fr.) Our Lord
D/N debit note
dn delta amplitude (elliptic function)
dn. down
Dña, D.ª (doña)(Span.), **D.** (dona)(Port.) or **d.** (donna)(Ital.) title of courtesy prefixed to Christian name of lady; madam; mistress; lady (cf. L.; Mrs.)
DNB or **D.N.B.** Dictionary of National Biography (Brit.)
D.N.B. Diploma of the National Board of Medical Examiners
D.N.J.C. (Dominus Noster Jesus Christus) (Lat.) Our Lord Jesus Christ
D.N.Ph. or **N.Ph.D.** Doctor of Natural Philosophy
D.N.P.P. (Dominus Noster Papa Pontifex) (Lat.) Our Lord, the Pope
DNT or **D.N.T.** dinitrotoluene
Dnus., D., or **Dom.** (Dominus)(Lat.) Lord; Master
D.O. Diploma in Ophthalmology; District officer; Doctor of Optometry; Doctor of Oratory; Doctor of Osteopathy
D/O or **d.o.** delivery order
do. (ditto)(Ital.), **d:o** (dito)(Swed.), **ead.** (eadem)(Lat.), **Id., id.** (idem)(Lat.) or **íd.** (ídem)(Span) the same; ditto
D.O.A. dead on arrival
D.O.C. District officer commanding
Doc., D., Doct., Dr, Dr., dr or **d:r** (doktor) (Swed.) doctor
doc. document
Doc.Eng., D.E., D.Eng., Dr.Eng., E.D. or **Eng.D.** Doctor of Engineering
Doct., D., Doc., Dr, Dr., dr or **d:r** (doktor) (Swed.) doctor
D.Oec. (Doctor Oeconomiae)(Lat.) Doctor of Economics
D. of A. Daughters of America
D. of C. Daughters of the Confederacy
D. of '98 Daughters of '98
D. of P. Degree of Pocahontas
D. of S. Daughters of Scotia
DOL (Mil.) or **D.O.L.** Detached Officers' List
D.O.L. Doctor of Oriental Languages
dol. (dolce)(Ital.) sweet (Music)
dol., D., d., dlr. or **doll.** dollar
doll., D., d., dlr. or **dol.** dollar
dolls., dlrs., dls. or **dols.** dollars
dols., dlrs., dls. or **dolls.** dollars
D.O.M. (Deo, Optimo, Maximo)(Lat.) to God, the Best, the Greatest
Dom. Dominicus
Dom., D. or **Dnus.** (Dominus)(Lat.) Lord; Master
dom. or **Dom.** domestic; dominion
D.O.M.C. Diploma in Ophthalmology, Medicine and Surgery (cf. D.O.M.S.)
Dom. Can. Dominion of Canada
dom. econ. domestic economy
dom. ex. or **Dom.Ex.** domestic exchange (Banking)
Dom. Prel. Domestic Prelate (Eccl.)
Dom. Proc., D.P. (Domus Procerum)(Lat.) or **H.L.** House of Lords
D.O.M.S. Diploma in Ophthalmic Medicine and Surgery (cf. D.O.M.C.)
D.O.P. developing-out paper (Photog.)
Dor. Doric
D.O.R.A. Defense of the Realm Act
D.O.R.C. Dental Officers' Reserve Corps
D.O.S. Director of Ordnance Services; Doctor of Optical Science
dos. or **D.** (dosis)(Lat.) dose
Dow., dow., D. or **d.** dowager
Doz. (Dozent)(Ger.), **L., L.ᵈᵒ** or **l.ᵈᵒ** (licenciado)(Span.) licenciate
doz., dz., dzn. or **dzne.** (douzaine)(Fr.) dozen
DP Distributing point (Mil.)
D.P. (directione propria)(Lat.) with proper directions
D.P., Dom. Proc. (Domus Procerum)(Lat.) or **H.L.** House of Lords
D.P. or **d.p.** double pole
D.P., D.Ph., D. Phil., Dr. Phil. (Doctor Philosophiae)(Lat.), **P.D.** or **Ph.D.** (Philosophiae Doctor)(Lat.) Doctor of Philosophy
D.P., Ph.D., Phar.D. or **Pharm.D.** (Pharmaciae Doctor)(Lat.) Doctor of Pharmacy
D/P documents against payment (Com.)
Dp Dump (Mil.)
d.p. diametral pitch; direct port (Shipping); documents (that is documentary bills) for payment (Com.)
d.p. or **D.P.** double pole
d.p., P.D. or **p.d.** potential difference (Elec.)
D.P.A. Discharged Prisoners' Aid
D.P.A.S. Discharged Prisoners' Aid Society
D.P.B. deposit pass book (Banking)
DPC or **D.P.C.** Defense Plant Corporation
DPCLD or **D.P.C.L.D.** Division of Public Contracts of the Labor Department
D.Pd., D.Pe., D.Ped., D.Pg. (Doctor Pedagogiae)(Lat.), **D.Py., Pd.D., Pe.D., Ped.D., Pg.D.** (Pedagogiae Doctor) (Lat.) or **Py.D.** Doctor of Pedagogy
D.Pe., D.Pd., D.Ped., D.Pg. (Doctor Pedagogiae)(Lat.), **D.Py., Pd.D., Pe.D., Ped.D., Pg.D.** (Pedagogiae Doctor) (Lat.) or **Py.D.** Doctor of Pedagogy
D.Ped., D.Pd., D.Pe., D.Pg. (Doctor Pedagogiae)(Lat.), **D.Py., Pd.D., Pe.D., Ped.D., Pg.D.** (Pedagogiae Doctor) (Lat.), or **Py.D.** Doctor of Pedagogy
D.Pg., D.Pd., D.Pe., D.Ped. (Doctor Pedagogiae)(Lat.), **D.Py., Pd.D., Pe.D., Ped.D., Pg.D.** (Pedagogiae Doctor) (Lat.) or **Py.D.** Doctor of Pedagogy
D.P.H. Diploma in Public Health
D.P.H. or **Dr. P.H.** Doctor of Public Hygiene
D.P.H., Dr. P.H. or **P.H.D.** Doctor of Public Health
D.Ph., D.P., D.Phil., Dr. Phil. (Doctor Philosophiae)(Lat.), **P.D.** or **Ph.D.** (Philosophiae Doctor)(Lat.) Doctor of Philosophy

D. Phil., D.P., D.Ph., Dr. Phil. (Doctor Philosophiae)(Lat.), **P.D.** or **Ph.D.** (Philosophiae Doctor)(Lat.) Doctor of Philosophy

D.P.I. Director of Public Instruction

dpl. diploma

D.P.O. or **d.p.o.** distributing post office

d.p.o. or **D.P.O.** distributing post office

dpt., Abt. (Abteilung)(Ger.), **dep., Dept** (Mil.), **Dept.** or **dept.** department

dpt., dep. or **dept.** deponent

Dp Trk Dump truck (Mil.)

dpty., D., d., Dep., dep. or **dept.** deputy

D.P.W. Department of Public Works

D.Py., D.Pd., D.Pe., D.Ped., D.Pg. (Doctor Pedagogiae)(Lat.), **Pd.D., Pe.D., Ped.D., Pg.D.** (Pedagogiae Doctor) (Lat.) or **Py.D.** Doctor of Pedagogy

D.Q. direct question

D.Q.M.G. Deputy Quartermaster-General (Brit.)

d. q. s. (de quo supra)(Lat.) concerning the above

DR, De R., Ea.R. (Entartungs-Reaktion) (Ger.) or **R.D.** reaction of degeneration

D.R. Dutch Reformed; (Division de réserve)(Fr.) Reserve division

D.R. or **D.A.R.** Daughters of the [American] Revolution; Daughters of the American Revolution

D.R. or **d.r.** dead reckoning; deposit receipt (Banking)

Dr, D., Doc., Doct., Dr., dr or **d:r** (doktor) (Swed.) doctor

Dr (Mil.), **dr.** or **drn.** drawn

Dr., D., Doc., Doct., Dr, dr or **d:r** (doktor) (Swed.) doctor

Dr. or **dr.** debtor

dr, d:r (doktor)(Swed.), **D., Doc., Doct., Dr** or **Dr.** doctor

dr. debit; dram; drams; drawer; drum

dr., des. (dessin)(Fr.), **Drg., drg., dwg.** or **Entw.** (Entwerf)(Ger.) drawing

dr., Dr (Mil.) or **drn.** drawn

dr. or **Dr.** debtor

dr. or **drch.** drachma

d.r. differential rate; district registry; dock receipt; drill regulations

d.r. or **D.R.** dead reckoning; deposit receipt (Banking)

d:r, dr (doktor)(Swed.), **D., Doc., Doct., Dr** or **Dr.** doctor

Dra. (doutora)(Port.),(doctora)(Span.) doctress

dr.a. or **dr. ap.** apothecaries' dram

dram. pers. (dramatis personae)(Lat.) characters in a play; cast

dr. ap. or **dr.a.** apothecaries' dram

dr. av. dram, avoirdupois

Dr.Bot. Doctor of Botany

drch. or **dr.** drachma

Dr.Chem. or **Ch.D.** Doctor of Chemistry

D.R.E. Doctor of Religious Education

Dr.Eng., D.E., D.Eng., Doc.Eng., E.D. or **Eng.D.** Doctor of Engineering

drftm (Mil.), **dftsmn.** or **drftsmn.** draftsman

drftsmn., dftsmn. or **drftm** (Mil.) draftsman

Drg., des. (dessin)(Fr.), **dr., drg., dwg.** or **Entw.** (Entwerf)(Ger.) drawing

drg., des. (dessin)(Fr.), **dr., Drg., dwg.** or **Entw.** (Entwerf)(Ger.) drawing

Dr. Hy. or **D. Hy.** Doctor of Hygiene

Dr.Jur., D.J. (Doctor Juris)(Lat.), **D.L., J.D.** or **Jur.D.** (Juris Doctor)(Lat.) Doctor of Law (cf. LL.D.; D.J.S.)

Dr. Med., D.M. (Doctor Medicinae)(Lat.) or **M.D.** (Medicinae Doctor)(Lat.) Doctor of Medicine

drn., Dr (Mil.) or **dr.** drawn

Dr.Nat.Hist. Doctor of Natural History

Dr.Nat.Phil. Doctory of Natural Philosophy

Dr.Nat.Sc. Doctor of Natural Science

D.R.P. (Deutsches Reichspatent)(Ger.) German Patent

Dr. P.H. or **D.P.H.** Doctor of Public Hygiene

Dr.P.H., D.P.H. or **P.H.D.** Doctor of Public Health

Dr. Phil., D.P., D. Ph., D. Phil. (Doctor Philosophiae)(Lat.), **P.D.** or **Ph.D.** (Philosophiae Doctor)(Lat.) Doctor of Philosophy

Dr.Phys.Sc. Doctor of Physical Science

drs. drawers

Dr.Sci., D.S., D.Sc., Sc.D. or **S.D.** (Scientiae Doctor)(Lat.) Doctor of Science (cf. D.ès S.)

drsmkr. dressmaker

Dr.Univ.Par. Doctor of the University of Paris

Dr.u.Vrl. (Druck und Verlag)(Ger.) printed and published by

DS (Mil.) Distant surveillance; drugstore

DS (Mil.) or **D.s.** Detached service; On detached service

D.S., dal s. or **d.s.** (dal segno)(Ital.) repeat from the sign (Music)

D.S., Dr. Sci., D. Sc., Sc.D. or **S.D.** (Scientiae Doctor)(Lat.) Doctor of Science (cf. D.ès S.)

D.S. or **d.s.** document signed

D/S or **d/s** double screened (Coal)

Ds or **Dy** dysprosium (Chem.)

D.s. or **DS** (Mil.) Detached service; On detached service

ds. decistere; decisteres

ds., D., d. or **da.** days

d.s. (de suo)(Lat.) from his own

d.s., dal s. or **D.S.** (dal segno)(Ital.) repeat from the sign (Music)

d.s. or **D.S.** document signed

d.s. or **d/s** days after sight

d.s., d/s or **d/v** (días vista)(Span.) day's sight; days' sight

d/s delivery service (Express)

d/s or **D/S** double screened (Coal)

d/s, d.s. or **d/v** (días vista)(Span.) day's sight; days' sight

D.S.A. Dairy Science Association

DSC or **D.S.C.** Defense Supplies Corporation

D.S.C. Distintuished Service Cross (U.S., Brit.); Doctor of Surgical Chiropody; double silk covered [wire] (Elec.)

D.S.C., C.S.D. or **D.C.S.** Doctor of Christian Science

D.Sc., Dr. Sci., D.S., Sc.D. or **S.D.** (Scientiae Doctor) (Lat.) Doctor of Science (cf. D.ès S.)

D.Sc.Hyg. Doctor of Science in Hygiene

DSL Direct Selling Legion

D.S.M. Distinguished Service Medal (U.S., Brit.)

D.S.O. District Staff Officer

D.S.O., C.D.S. or **C.D.S.O.** [Companion of the] Distinguished Service Order

d.s.p. (decessit sine prole) (Lat.), **ob.s.p.** or **o.s.p.** (obiit sine prole) (Lat.) he or she died without issue (cf. s.l.p.; s.m.p.; s.p.; s.p.s.)

D.Spec. design specifications

d.s.q. Discharged to sick quarters (Mil.)

D.S.S. (Doctor Sacrae Scripturae) (Lat.) or **S.S.D.** (Sacrae Scripturae Doctor) (Lat.) Doctor of Sacred Scripture (cf. D.S.T.)

D.S.Sc. or **S.Sc.D.** Doctor of Social Science

DS Sec Distant surveillance section

D.S.T. Daylight Saving Time

D.S.T. or **S.T.D.** (Sacrae Theologiae Doctor) (Lat.) Doctor of Sacred Theology (cf. **D.C.T; D.Th.**)

dstn. or **destn.** destination

D.Surg. Dental Surgeon (cf. D.D.S.)

D.T. daylight time; Director of Transport; distance test (Optometry)

D.T. or **d.t.** delirium tremens

D.T., D. Th., D. Theol., S.T.D. (Scientiae Theologiae Doctor) (Lat.) or **Th.D.** (Theologiae Doctor) (Lat.) Doctor of Theology

Dt. or **Deut.** Deuteronomy

d.t double-throw [switch] (Elec.); double time (Mil.)

D.T.D. or **d.t.d.** (detur talis dosis) (Lat.) give of such a dose (cf. det.)

D.T.H. Diploma in Tropical Hygiene

D. Th., D.T., D. Theol., S.T.D. (Scientiae Theologicae Doctor) (Lat.) or **Th.D.** (Theologiae Doctor) (Lat.) Doctor of Theology

D.T.I. (Dépôt de transition des isolés) (Fr.) Depot for soldiers traveling alone

D.T.M. Diploma in Tropical Medicine; Doctor of Tropical Medicine

D.T.V.M. Diploma in Tropical Veterinary Medicine

Du., D. or **holl.** (hollandais, hollandaise) (Fr.) Dutch; Hollander

Du., D. or **Hzg.** (Herzog) (Ger.) Duke

Dub. Dublin

dub. (dubitans) (Lat.) doubting; (dubitatur) (Lat.) it is doubted; dubious

dun. dunnage

Dunelm. Durham, in the signature of bishop

duo., D., 12°, 12mo or **12mo.** duodecimo

dup. or **dupl.** duplicate; duplicated

dupl. or **dup.** duplicate; duplicated

D.U.V.C.W. Daughters of Union Veterans of the Civil War

D.V. (Deo volente) (Lat.) God willing

d.v. double vibrations

d/v (días vista) (Span.), **d.s.** or **d/s** day's sight; days' sight

D.V.H. Diploma in Veterinary Hygiene

D.V.M., M.V.D. or **V.M.D.** (Veterinariae Medicinae Doctor) (Lat.) Doctor of Veterinary Medicine

D.V.M.S. Doctor of Veterinary Medicine and Surgery

d.v.p. (decessit vita patris) (Lat.) he died during the lifetime of his father

D.V.S. Doctor of Veterinary Surgery

D.V.S. or **d.v.s.** double vibrations per second

D.V.S. or **D.V.Sc.** Doctor of Veterinary Science

d.v.s. (det vil sige) (Dan.), (det vill säga) (Swed.), **c.-à-d.** (c'est-à-dire) (Fr.), **d.ä.** (det är) (Swed.), **d.h.** (das heisst) (Ger.), **d.i.** (das ist) (Ger.), **h.e.** (hoc or hic est) (Lat.), **i.e.** (id est) or **t.i.** (tudni illik) (Hung.) that is; that is to say (cf. viz.)

d.v.s. or **D.V.S.** double vibrations per second

D.V.S.C. Diploma in Veterinary State Surgery (Chirurgia)

D. V. Sc. or **D. V. S.** Doctor of Veterinary Science

D.V.S.M. Diploma in Veterinary State Medicine

D/W dock warrant

d.w. dead weight; dust wrappers

d.w.c. dead weight capacity

dwg. dwelling

dwg., des. (dessin) (Fr.), **dr., Drg., drg.** or **Entw.** (Entwerf) (Ger.) drawing

dwt. or **pwt.** pennyweight (denarius weight)

d.w.t.f. daily and weekly till forbidden

DX, D.X. (Radio), **d., dis.** or **dist.** distance

Dy or **Ds** dysprosium (Chem.)

D/y, Dely., dely., dlvy., Dly., dly. or **dy.** delivery

dy, dy., D., d. (denarius, denarii) (Lat.) or **p.** penny; pence

dy., Dely., dely., dlvy., Dly., dly. or **D/y** delivery

d.y. (den yngre) (Swed.), **d.J.** (der Jungere) (Ger.), **Jnr., jnr., Jr. jr., Jun., jun., Junr.** or **junr.** junior

dyn. or **dynam.** dynamics

D.Z. Doctor of Zoology

D.-Z. (Durchgangszug) (Ger.) Through train; corridor train

dz., doz., dzn. or **dzne.** (douzaine) (Fr.) dozen

ΔΑΠ (Delta Alpha Pi) National undergraduate fraternity

ΔΒΦ (Delta Beta Phi) National undergraduate fraternity

ΔΧ (Delta Chi) National undergraduate fraternity

ΔΔΔ (Delta Delta Delta) National undergraduate sorority

ΔΕ (Delta Epsilon) National undergraduate fraternity (Art)

ΔΕΣ (Delta Epsilon Sigma) Honor society (Scholarship)

ΔΓ (Delta Gamma) National undergraduate sorority

ΔΚΕ (Delta Kappa Epsilon) National undergraduate fraternity

ΔΚΓ (Delta Kappa Gamma) National graduate honorary sorority

ΔΚΦ (Delta Kappa Phi) National undergraduate fraternity

ΔΜΔ (Delta Mu Delta) National honorary society (Commerce)

ΔΩ (Delta Omega) National professional sorority (Osteopathathy)

ΔΟ (Delta Omicron) National professional sorority (Music)

ΔΦ (Delta Phi) National undergraduate fraternity

ΔΦΔ (Delta Phi Delta) National professional society (Art) (Men and Women)

ΔΦΕ (Delta Phi Epsilon) National undergraduate sorority; National professional fraternity (Foreign Service)

ΔΦΥ (Delta Phi Upsilon) National honor sorority (Kindergarten-primary)

ΔΨ (Delta Psi) National undergraduate fraternity

ΔΨΚ (Delta Psi Kappa) National professional sorority (Physical Education)

ΔΣΔ (Delta Sigma Delta) National professional fraternity (Dentistry)

ΔΣΕ (Delta Sigma Epsilon) National professional sorority (Education)

ΔΣΛ (Delta Sigma Lambda) National undergraduate fraternity

ΔΣΦ (Delta Sigma Phi) National undergraduate fraternity

ΔΣΠ (Delta Sigma Pi) National professional fraternity (Commerce)

ΔΣΡ (Delta Sigma Rho) National honor society (Forensics)

ΔΣΘ (Delta Sigma Theta) National undergraduate fraternity (Negroes)

ΔΤΔ (Delta Tau Delta) National undergraduate fraternity

ΔΘΦ (Delta Theta Phi) National undergraduate fraternity; National professional fraternity (Law)

ΔΥ (Delta Upsilon) National undergraduate fraternity

ΔΖ (Delta Zeta) National undergraduate sorority

E

E eccentricity [of a curve] (Math.); a Fraunhofer line caused by iron (Astrophysics)

E or **E.** [Young's modulus of] elasticity

E, E., e., EMF, emf, E.M.F., e.m.f. or **f.e.m.** (fuerza electromotriz)(Span.) electromotive force

E, E., e. or **O.** (Osten)(Ger.) east

E, Eb or **Er** erbium (Chem.)

E (Mil.) or **eff.** efficiency

E (Mil.), **Ex.** or **exc.** excellence; excellent

E., e. or **east.** eastern

E. or **e.** earth

E., e. or **Em.** emmetropia (Optics)

E., e., Eng., eng., Engin., engin., Engr (Mil.) or **engr.** engineer

E., East., E.T., P., Pas. (Pasch)(Lat.) or **Pas. T.** (Terminus Paschae)(Lat.) Easter or Paschal Term

E., East., P. or **Pas.** (Pasch)(Lat.) Easter

E., Eng. or **Engl.** English

e [coefficient of] elasticity; [the numerical value of the] electric charge of an electron or proton (Psysics); erg

e. early; entrance (Theat.); longitudinal strain per unit length (Mech.)

e., E, E., EMF, emf, E.M.F., e.m.f. or **f.e.m.** (fuerza electromotriz)(Span.) electromotive force

e., E, E., or **O.** (Osten)(Ger.) east

e. or **E.** earth

e., E. or **east.** eastern

e., E. or **Em.** emmetropia (Optics)

e., E., Eng., eng., Engin., engin., Engr (Mil.) or **engr.** engineer

e., el. or **eld.** eldest (cf. Sr.)

e., eng., engg. or **engin.** engineering

E.A. educational age

ea. each

EAD Extended active duty (Mil.)

ead. (eadem)(Lat.), **do.** (ditto)(Ital.), **d:o** (dito)(Swed.), **Id., id.** (idem)(Lat.) or **íd.** (ídem)(Span.) the same

EAD/CCC Extended active duty, Civilian Conservation Corps

E. & O.E., S.E.e.O. or **s.e.e.o** (salvo errore et omissione)(Lat) error and omission excepted; (also used in the plural) errors and omissions excepted (cf ee; e.o.o.e.)

E. and P. Extraordinary and Plenipotentiary

e.a.o.n. or **E.A.O.N.** except as otherwise noted (cf. e.o.h.p.)

Ea.R. (Entartungs-Reaktion)(Ger.), **De R., DR** or **R.D.** reaction of degeneration

East., E., E.T., P., Pas. (Pasch)(Lat.) or **Pas. T.** (Terminus Paschae)(Lat.) Easter or Paschal Term

East., E., P. or **Pas.** (Pasch)(Lat.) Easter

east., E., or **e.** eastern

EB or **e.b.** east bound

E.B. or **E. Bi.** Encyclopedia Biblica

E.B., E. Br., Ency. Brit. or **Encyc. Brit.** Encyclopaedia Britannica

Eb, E or **Er** erbium (Chem)

Eb. Ebenezer

e.b. or **EB** east bound

E.B.A. Education Buyers' Association

E.Bi. or **E.B.** Encyclopedia Biblica

EbN east by north

Ebor. (Eboracensis)(Lat.) of York; (Eboracum)(Lat.) York

E. Br., E.B., Ency. Brit. or **Encyc. Brit.** Encyclopaedia Britannica

E.B.S. electric bond and share

EbS east by south

E.C. Eastern Central [Postal District, London]; Engineering Corps; Established Church; expansive system [of cataloging]

E.C. or **e.c.** enamel-covered [wire] (Elec.)

E.C. or **Exec. C.** Executive Council (cf. TEC)

e.c. earth closet

e.c. or **E.C.** enamel covered

e.c. (exempli causa)(Lat.), **e.g., ex. gr.** (exempli gratia)(Lat.), **f.e., f. Eks.** (for Eksempel)(Dan.), **f.i., n.p.** (na przykład)(Polish), **p. ex.** (par exemple) (Fr.), **t. ex.** (till exempel)(Swed.), **v.g.** (verbi gratia)(Lat.) or **z. B.** (zum Beispiel)(Ger.) for example; for instance

ECC or **E.C.C.** Employees Compensation Commission

Eccl., Eccles. or **Eccls.** Ecclesiastes

eccl. or **eccles.** ecclesiastic; ecclesistical

eccl., eccles. or **ecclesiol.** ecclesiology

Eccles., Eccl. or **Eccls.** Ecclesiastes

eccles. or **eccl.** ecclesiastic; ecclesiastical

eccles., eccl. or **ecclesiol.** ecclesiology

ecclesiol., eccl. or **eccles.** ecclesiology

Eccls., Eccl. or **Eccles.** Ecclesiastes

Ecclus. Ecclesiasticus

ECCP or **E.C.C.P.** Executive Committee on Commercial Policy

E.C.C.P. East Coast coal port

e.c.e. extended coverage endorsement (Insurance)

ECFL or **E.C.F.L.** Emergency Crop and Feed Loans

ecg. electrocardiogram

E.C.G.B. East Coast of Great Britain

Ech (Mil.) or **ech.** echelon

E.C.I. East Coast of Ireland

ecl or **eclec.** eclectic

ecol. ecological; ecology

econ. economic; economics; economy

E.C.P.D. Engineers' Council for Professional Development

E.C.U. English Church Union

Ecua. Ecuador

E.C.U.K. East Coast of United Kingdom

ECW or **E.C.W.** Emergency Conservation Work

ECWA or **E.C.W.A.** Emergency Conservation Works Administration

ED Existence doubtful

ED, E.D. or **e.d.** Extra duty (Mil.)

E.D. Eastern Department (U.S.A.); Efficiency Decoration (Brit); erythema dose (Med.)

E.D., D.E., D.Eng., Doc.Eng., Dr.Eng. or **Eng.D.** Doctor of Engineering

E.D., ED or **e.d.** extra duty

Ed., Edin. or **Edinb.** Edinburgh

Ed. or **Edg.** Edgar

Ed., Edn. or **Edw.** Edwin

Ed., Edw. or **Edwd.** Edward

éd. (édition)(Fr.), **Aufl.** (Auflage)(Ger.), **Ausg.** (Ausgabe)(Ger.), **ed., edit.** or **edn.** edition

ed., bearb. (bearbeitet)(Ger.) or **edit.** edited

ed., éd. (édition)(Fr.), **Aufl.** (Auflage) (Ger.), **Ausg.** (Ausgabe)(Ger.), **edit.** or **edn.** edition

ed., edit., R., r., réd. (rédacteur)(Fr.), **Red.** (Redaktør)(Dan.) or **red.** (redaktör) (Swed.) editor; redactor

ed. or **educ.** educated

ed. (editus)(Lat.), **hrsg.** (herausgegeben) (Ger.), **pub., pubd.** or **publ.** published

éd. (éditeur)(Fr.), **pub., publ., V.A.** (Verlagsanstalt)(Ger.) or **V.B.** (Verlagsbuchhandlung)(Ger.) publisher

e.d., ED or **E.D.** extra duty

e.d., ex d., ex div., X.D., xd, x.d., x-d, xdiv or **x-div.** ex dividend; without dividend (Stocks)

EDB or **E.D.B.** Economic Defense Board

Ed.B., B.E., B.Ed. or **B.Educ.** Bachelor of Education

Ed. D. or **D.Ed.** Doctor of Education

edd. or **eds.** editions; editors

Edg. or **Ed.** Edgar

Edin., Ed. or **Edinb.** Edinburgh

Ed. in Ch. Editor in Chief

edit., bearb. (bearbeitet)(Ger.) or **ed.** edited

edit., ed. éd. (édition)(Fr.), **edn., Aufl.** (Auflage)(Ger.) or **Ausg.** (Ausgabe) (Ger.) edition

edit., ed., R., r., Red. (Redaktør)(Dan.), **red.** (redaktör)(Swed.) or **réd.** (rédacteur)(Fr.) editor; redactor

e.d.l. Edition de Luxe

Ed. M., M. Ed., M. in Ed. or **M. of Ed.** Master in or of Education

Edm. Edmund

Edn., Ed. or **Edw.** Edwin

Edn., edn. or **educ.** education

edn., ed., éd. (édition)(Fr.), **edit., Aufl.** (Auflage)(Ger.) or **Ausg.** (Ausgabe) (Ger.) edition

edn., Edn. or **educ.** education

ednl. or **educ.** educational

ed. opt. (editio optima)(Lat.) best edition

E.D.S. English Dialect Society

eds. or **edd.** editions; editors

E.D.S.T. Eastern Daylight Saving Time

ed. ster. (editio stereotypa)(Lat.) stereotyped edition

E.D.T. Eastern daylight time (cf. E.D.S.T.)

educ. or **ed.** educated

educ., Edn. or **edn.** education
educ. or **ednl.** educational
ed ult. (editio ultima)(Lat.) last edition
Edw., Ed. or **Edn.** Edwin
Edw., Ed. or **Edwd.** Edward
Edwd., Ed. or **Edw.** Edward
EE or **E.E.** Early English
E.E. Electrical Engineer
E.E. or **EE** Early English
E.E., E.Eng. or **Eng.E.** English ells
E.E. or **e.e.** errors expected (cf. E.& O.E.; e.o.o.e.)
Edw., Ed. or **Edn.** Edwin
E.E., Env. Ext. or **Env. Extr.** Envoy Extraordinary
e.e. or **E.E.** errors expected (cf. E.& O.E.; e.o.o.e.)
E.E. & M.P. Envoy Extraordinary and Minister Plenipotentiary
E.E.D.S. Early English Dialect Society
E.E.F. Egyptian Expeditionary Force
E.E.I. Edison Electric Institute (cf N.E.L.A.)
E. Eng., E.E. or **Eng. E.** English ells
E.E.P. Educational Emergency Program
E.E.T.S. Early English Text Society
EE. UU., E. U. (Estados Unidos)(Port., (Span.), **U.S.** or **Ver.St.** (Vereinigte Staaten)(Ger.) United States (cf. U.S.A.)
EE.UU.da A., E.U.A. (Estados Unidos da América)(Port.), **EE.UU.de A., E.U.A.** (Estados Unidos de América)(Span.), **ÉU.A.** (États-Unis-Amérique)(Fr.) or **U.S.A.** United States of America (cf. U.S.)
E.F. Expeditionary Force or Forces
E.F., E.Fl., F.E. or **Fl.E.** Flemish ells
E.F., E.Fr., F.E. or **Fr.E.** French ells
e.F. (erforderlichen Falls)(Ger.), **si op.sit, S.op.S., S.O.S.** or **s.o.s.** (si opus sit) (Lat.) in case of need; if nesessary (Pharm.)
EFC or **E.F.C.** Emergency Fleet Corporation
E.F.D.S. English Folk Dance Society
eff. (effigies)(Lat.), **Abb.** (Abbildung, Abbildungen)(Ger.), **il., ill(s)., illus.** or **illust.** illustration; illustrations
eff. or **E** (Mil.) efficiency
eff. (effigies)(Lat.), **por.** or **port.** portrait
efflor. efflorescent
E.F.I.B. Eastern Freight Inspection Bureau
E.Fl., E.F., F.E. or **Fl.E.** Flemish ells
E.Fr., E.F., F.E. or **Fr.E.** French ells
E.F.S.C. European Federation of Soroptimist Clubs
EG Expert gunner
Eg. Egypt
Eg., Egp., Egy. or **Egypt.** Egyptian
Eg. or **Egyptol.** Egyptology
e.g. all edges gilt (cf. g.e.); (ejusdem generis)(Lat.) of a like kind (cf. ej.)
e.g., ex g. or **ex gr.** (ex grege)(Lat.) among the rest; from the flock
e.g., ex. gr. (exempli gratia)(Lat.), **e.c.** (exempli causa)(Lat.), **f.e., f. Eks.** (for Eksempel)(Dan.), **f.i., n.p.** (na przykład) (Polish), **p. ex.** (par exemple)(Fr.), **t. ex.** (till exempel)(Swed.), **v.g.** (verbi gratia)(Lat.) or **z. B.** (zum Biespiel (Ger.) for example; for instance
Egb. Egbert
E.G.M. (État-major général)(Fr.), **GS** (Mil.), **G.S.** or **g.s.** General Staff
Egp., Eg., Egy. or **Egypt.** Egyptian
EGT or **E.G.T.** Expositor's Greek Testament
Egy., Eg., Egp. or **Egypt.** Egyptian
Egyptol. Egyptological
Egyptol. or **Eg.** Egyptology
EHC or **E.H.C.** Emergency Housing Corporation
EHFA or **E.H.F.A.** Electric Home and Farm Authority
e.h.p. effective horsepower; electric horsepower
E.I. East India; East Indian; East Indies
E/I endorsement irregular (Banking)
EIB or **E.I.B.** Export-Import Banks
EIBW The Export-Import Bank of Washington
E.I.C. Engineering Institute of Canada
E.I.C. or **E.I.Co.** East India Company
E.I.C.S. East India Civil Service; East India Company's Service
E.I.D. East India Docks
8vo., 8vo, O., o. or **oct.** octavo
E.I.O. Economic Intelligence Office
E.I.S. East India Service; Engineers Information Service
E.I.T. Electrical Insurance Trustees
ej., Ejusd. or **ejusd.** (ejusdem)(Lat.) of the same (Pharm.)
ejusd., ej. or **Ejusd.** (ejusdem)(Lat.) of the same (Pharm.)
Eks. (Eksempel)(Dan.) or **ex.** example
E.L. Eastern Lines; elastic limit; Epworth League
El. or **Eli.** Elias
el. elect; elected
el., e. or **eld.** eldest (cf. Sr.)
el. or **elev.** elevated; elevation
eld., e. or **el.** eldest (cf. Sr.)
Elec (Mil.), **elec., Electn** (Mil.) or **electrn.** electrician
elec., Elec (Mil.), **Electn** (Mil.) or **electrn.** electrician
elec. or **elect.** electric; electrical; electricity; electuary
elect. or **elec.** electric; electrical; electricity; electuary
Electn (Mil.), **Elec** (Mil.), **elec.** or **electrn.** electrician
electrn., Elec (Mil.), **elec.** or **Electn** (Mil.) electrician
electrochem. electrochemical; electrochemistry
electrophys. electrophysical; electrophysics
elem. elementary; elements
elem. or **Elm** (Mil.) element
elev. or **el.** elevated; elevation

el.fo. elephant folio
Eli. or **El.** Elias
Elij. Elijah
Elim Eliminate (Mil.)
Elis. Elisabeth
Eliz. Elizabeth; Elizabethan
ellipt. elliptical
Elm (Mil.) or **elem.** element
E.Long. or **E.long.** east longitude
elong. elongation
Elz. Elzevir
EM Enlisted man or men
E.M. Earl Marshall (Brit.); (Equitum Magister)(Lat.) Master of the Horse; Engineer of Mines; Mining Engineer
Em (Chem), **Em.** or **eman.** emanation
Em. Emanuel; Emily; Emma
Em. (Eftermiddag)(Dan.), **a., aft., aftn., e.m.** (eftermiddagen)(Swed.), **Nachm.** or **Nm.** (Nachmittag)(Ger.) afternoon (cf. P.M.)
Em., E. or **e.** emmetropia
Em., Em (Chem.) or **eman.** emanation
Em. or **em.** eminence
e.m. (eftermiddagen)(Swed.), **a., aft., aftn., Em.** (Eftermiddag)(Dan.), **Nachm.** or Nm. (Nachmittag)(Ger.) afternoon (cf. P.M.)
E.M.A. (État-major d'armée)(Fr.) Staff of an army
eman., Em (Chem.) or **Em.** emanation
Emb Embarkation (Mil.)
Emb. or **embryol.** embryology
emb. embargo; embossed
embryol. or **Emb.** embryology
E.M.D.P. or **e.m.d.p.** Electromotive difference of potential
emerg. emergency
E. Met. Engineer of Metallurgy
EMF, emf, E, E., e., E.M.F., e.m.f. or **f.e.m.** (fuerza electromotriz)(Span.) electromotive force
e.m.f. electromagnetic force
EMIC Emergency Maternity and Infant Care (New York)
Emk. estmark (Estonia)
E.M.P. (ex modo praescripto)(Lat.), **Mod. praesc., M.P.** (modo praescripto)(Lat.) or **mor. dict.** (more dictor)(Lat.) in the manner or way prescribed or directed (Pharm.)(cf. **ut dict.**)
Emp. (emplastrum)(Lat.) plaster (Med.)
Emp., emp., i. or **imp.** (imperium)(Lat.) empire
Emp., I., i. or **Imp.** (Imperator)(Lat.) Emperor
Emp., I., i., Imp. or **Impx.** (Imperatrix) (Lat.) Empress
emp.agcy. employment agency
emph. emphasis; emphatic
Emp. vesic. (emplastrum vesicatorium) (Lat.) plaster blister
E.M.S. Emergency Medical Service (Brit.)
E.M.U., e.m.u., or **emu** electromagnetic units
emul. emulsion
E.M.V. e.m.v. or **emv** electromagnetic volume
enc., encd., encld. or **enclod.** enclosed
enc., encl. or **enclo.** enclosure
enc., ency., encyc. or **encycl.** encyclopedia
encd., enc., encld. or **enclod.** enclosed
encl., enc. or **enclo.** enclosure
encld., enc., encd. or **enclod.** enclosed
enclo., enc. or **encl.** enclosure
enclod., enc., encd. or **encld.** enclosed
ency., enc., encyc. or **encycl.** encyclopedia
Ency. Amer. Encyclopedia Americana
Ency. Brit., E.B., E. Br. or **Encyc. Brit.** Encyclopaedia Britannica
encyc., enc., ency. or **encycl.** encyclopedia
Encyc. Brit., E.B., E. Br. or **Ency. Brit.** Encyclopaedia Britannica
encycl., enc., ency. or **encyc.** encyclopedia
end. endorse; endorsed; endorsement
end.guar. endorsement guaranteed (Banking)
ENE, E.N.E., or **e.n.e.** east-northeast
Eng. England
Eng., E., e., eng., Engin., engin., Engr (Mil.) or **engr.** engineer
Eng., E. or **Engl.** English
eng. engine
eng., E., e., Eng., Engin., engin., Engr (Mil.) or **engr.** engineer
eng., e., engg. or **engin.** engineering
eng. or **engr.** engraver; engraving (cf. **etch.; ic.**)
eng., engr. or **engs.** engravings
eng., engr., inc., incis. (incisus)(Lat.) or **sculpt.** (sculptus)(Lat.) engraved
Eng Bn (Mil.) or **Engr Bn** (Mil.) Engineers battalion
Eng.D., D.E., D.Eng., Doc.Eng., Dr.Eng. or **E.D.** Doctor of Engineering
Eng.E. E.E. or **E. Eng.** English ells
engg., e., eng. or **engin.** engineering
Engin., E., e., Eng., eng., engin., Engr (Mil.) or **engr.** engineer
engin., E., e., Eng., eng., Engin., Engr (Mil.) or **engr.** engineer
engin., e., eng. or **engg.** engineering
Engl., E. or **Eng.** English
Eng.law & us. English law and usage
Eng.O.R.C., E.O.R.C. or **Engr. O.R.C.** Engineer Officers Reserve Corps
Engr (Mil.), **E., e., Eng., eng., Engin., engin.** or **engr.** engineer
engr., E., e., Eng., eng., Engin., engin. or **Engr** (Mil.) engineer
engr. or **eng.** engraver; engraving (cf. etch., ic.)
engr., eng. or **engs.** engravings
Engr Bn (Mil.) or **Eng Bn** (Mil.) Engineers battalion
Engr Bn Armd Engineers batallion armored
Engr Bn Tr Engineers battalion train (Mil.)
Eng.R.C. or **E.R.C.** Engineers Reserve Corps
Engr Co Engineer company

Engr. O Engineer officer
Engr.O.R.C., E.O.R.C. or **Eng.O.R.C.** Engineer Officers Reserve Corps
Engr Regt Engineers Regiment (Mil.)
engrs. or **Engrs.** engineers
Engrs C Engineers combat
Engrs Gen Serv Engineers general service
Engr Sq Engineer squadron
engs., eng. or **engr.** engravings
enl. enlisted
enl. or **verm.** (vermehrte)(Ger.) enlarged (cf. augm.; sup.)
Enlmt Enlistment (Mil.)
eno. (enero)(Span.), **genn.** (gennaio)(Ital.), **Ja., Jan., janv.** (janvier)(Fr.) or **Stycz.** (Styczeń)(Pol.) January
Ens. Ensign
E.N.S.A. Entertainments National Service Association (Brit.)
ent., Entom., entom. or **entomol.** entomology
entd. entered
Entom., entom., ent. or **entomol.** entomology
entom. entomological
entomol., ent., Entom. or **entom.** entomology
Ent. Sta. Hall Entered at Stationers' Hall (Brit.)
Entw. (Entwerf)(Ger.), **des.** (dessin)(Fr.), **dr., Drg., drg.** or **dwg.** drawing
Env. Ext., E.E. or **Env. Extr.** Envoy Extraordinary
E.O. (Élève officier)(Fr.), **Cad.** or **cad.** Cadet (cf. E.O.R.)
e.o. or **ex off.** (ex officio)(Lat.) by virtue of office
e.o.d., alt. dieb. or **dieb., alt.** (alternis diebus, diebus alternis)(Lat.) every other day
eod. loc. (eodem loco)(Lat.), **ib., ibid.** (ibidem)(Lat.) or **id. loc.** (idem loco) (Lat.) in the same place (cf. ad loc.; in loc.; loc. cit.)
e.o.h.p. except as otherwise herein provided (cf. E.A.O.N.)
E.O.M., E.o.m. or **e.o.m.** end of the month (Payments)
e.o.m. every other month
e.o.m., E.O.M. or **E.o.m.** end of the month (Payments)
E.O.O.E., e.o.o.e. (erreurs ou omissions exceptées)(Fr.), **s.e.o.o., S.E. ou O.** (sauf erreur ou omission)(Fr.) or **S.E.u o.** (salvo error u omisión)(Span.) errors or omissions excepted (singular and plural) (cf. E. & O.E.; e.e.)
E.O.R. (Élève officier du reserve)(Fr.) Cadet in the reserves
E.O.R.C., Eng.O.R.C. or **Engr.O.R.C.** Engineer Officers Reserve Corps
EP Entrucking point (Mil.)
E.P. English Patent
Ep., Epis., or **Epist.** Epistle; Epistles (Bib.)
Ep., Epus. (Episcopus)(Lat.), **B., Bp.** or **bp.** bishop (Eccles.)
ep. (epistola)(Lat.), **Ltr** or **ltr.** letter
e.p. electric primer; electrically polarized; electroplate (Australia); end point
e.p. (en passant)(Fr.) or **ob.** (obiter)(Lat.) by the way; incidentally
E.P.A.A. Employing Printers Association of America
E.P.C. Educational Policies Commission
e.p.c. editor's presentation copy
E.P.D. Excess Profits Duty (Brit.)(cf. e.p.t.)
E.P.D. (en paz descanse)(Span.), **Q.E.P.D.** (que en paz descanse)(Span.) or **R.I.P.** may he rest in peace (cf. B.Q.; H.R.I.P.; Q.D.D.G.; Q.D.G.; Q.E.G.E.)
Eph. Ephriam
Eph. or **Ephes.** Ephesians
epil. epilogue
Epiph. Epiphany
Epis., Ep. or **Epist.** Epistle; Epistles (Bib.)
Episc., episc., Epis. or **epis.** episcopal
Epist., Ep. or **Epis.** Epistle; Epistles (Bib.)
epit. epitaph; epitome
epp. (epistolae)(Lat.) or **lett.** epistles; letters
épr. (épreuve)(Fr.) proof-sheet
e.p.t. excess profits tax (cf. E.P.D.)
EPTE Existed prior to enlistment
Epus., Ep. (Episcopus)(Lat.), **B., Bp.** or **bp.** bishop (Eccles.)
E.Q. educational quotient (Pedogagy and Psychology)
Eq. Equity
eq. equalize; equalizer; equalizing; equation
eq. or **æq.** (æqualis)(Lat.) equal (cf. āā)
eq. or **equip.** equipment
eq. or **equiv.** equivalent
eq.tr. equipment trust (Bonds)
equip. or **eq.** equipment
ER Expert rifleman
E.R. East Riding, Yorkshire; engine room; external resistance; (Eduardus Rex) (Lat.) King Edward
Er, E or **Eb** erbium (Chem.)
Er. Eric; Erich
er., d. A. (der Ältere)(Ger.) or **d.ä.** (den äldre)(Swed.) elder (cf. Sr.)
e.r. (en route)(Fr.), **i.t.** or **in trans.** (in transitu)(Lat.) en route; in transit
ERA or **E.R.A.** Emergency Relief Administration
E.R.A. Educational Research Association; electronic reactions of Abrahms; Eugenics Research Association
E.R. & I. or **E.R. et I.** (Eduardus Rex et Imperator)(Lat.) Edward, King and Emperor
E.R.C. Enlisted Reserve Corps
E.R.C. or **Eng.R.C.** Engineers Reserve Corps
E.S.E. electrostatic units
E.R. et I. or **E. R. & I.** (Eduardus Rex et Imperator)(Lat.) Edward, King and Emperor

erg. (ergänzt)(Ger.) completed; supplemented (cf. sup.)

Erg.H. (Ergänzungsheft)(Ger.), **Beibl.** (Beiblatt)(Ger.), **sup., supp.** or **suppl.** supplement

erkl. (erklärt)(Ger.) or **expl.** explained

erm. ermine; (ermässigter Preis)(Ger.) reduced price

Ern. Ernest; Ernst

E.R.P. Employees Representative Plan

err. (errata)(Lat.) errors

erron. erroneous; erroneously

E.R.V. English Revised Version [of the Bible]

Erzb. (Erzbishof)(Ger.), **A.B., Abp., abp., Arch., Archbp.** or **Archieps.** (Archiepiscopus)(Lat.) Archbishop

E.S. ells Scotch

e.s. eldest son

E.S.A. Entomological Society of America; Ethnological Society of America

ESB or **E.S.B.** Economic Stabilization Board

esc. escadrille

eschat. eschatology

Esd. Esdras

ESE, E.S.E., or **e.s.e.** east-southeast

E.S.F. Eastern sea frontier

Esk. Eskimo

E.S.P. extra-sensory perception

Esp. Esperanto

esp. (espressivo) (Ital.) expressive; with expression (Music)

esp. or **espec.** especially

Esq. or **Esqr.** Esquire

Ess. Essex

Ess. or **ess.** essence; essences

EST or **E.S.T.** Eastern standard time

Est (Mil.) or **est.** estuary

est. estimate; estimated

est. or **Est** (Mil.) estuary

est., estab. or **establ.** established

est. or **Este.** estate

estab., est. or **establ.** established

Este. or **est.** estate

Esth. Esther; Esthonia

est.wt. estimated weight

E.S.U. electrostatic units; English Speaking Union

ET or **E.T.** Eastern time

E.T. English Translation

E.T., E., East., P., Pas. (Pasch)(Lat.) or **Pas. T.** (Terminus Paschae)(Lat.) Easter or Paschal Term

E.T. or **e.t.** electric telegraph

Et or **et** ethyl (Chem.)

e.t. or **E.T.** electric telegraph

e.t.a. estimated time of arrival

et al. (et alii or aliae)(Lat.), **bl. a.** (bland annat)(Swed.), (blandt andet)(Dan.), **int.al.** (inter alia)(Lat.) or **u.a.m.** (und andere or anderes mehr)(Ger.) among other things; and other things

et al. (et alii or aliae)(Lat.), **bl. a.** (bland andra)(Swed.), (blandt andre)(Dan.), **m. fl.** (med flera)(Swed.), (med flere) (Dan.) or **u.a.** (und andere)(Ger.) and others; among others; with others

et al. (et alibi)(Lat.) or **u.a.a.O.** (und an andern Ort)(Ger.) and elsewhere

E.T.C. Eastern Telegraph Company

etc. (et cetera)(Lat.), **i t.d.** (i tak dalej), (Pol), **k.t.l.** (kai ta loipa)(Greek), **m.m.** (med mer)(Swed.), (med mere)(Dan.), **o.d.** (ock dylikt or dylika)(Swed.), **o.s.v.** (och så vidare)(Swed.), (og saa videre)(Dan.), **u.drgl.** (und dergrelchen) (Ger.), **u.s.f.** (und so fort)(Ger.), **usw.** or **u.s.w.** (und so weiter)(Ger.) and so forth; and the like; and others [of like kind] (cf. et al.)

etch. etcher; etching (cf. engr.)

etch. or **fec. aq. fort.** (fecit aqua forte) (Lat.) etched

Eth. Ethel

Eth. or **Ethiop.** Ethiopia; Ethiopian; Ethiopic

eth. ether; ethical; ethics

eth. acet. ethyl acetate

Ethiop. or **Eth.** Ethiopia; Ethiopian; Ethiopic

ethnog. ethnographical; ethnography

ethnol. ethnological; ethnology

ETO or **E.T.O.** European theatre of operations

ETS Expiration of term of service

et seq., et seqq., et sq., et sqq. (et sequens, et sequentes, et sequntia)(Lat.) or **ff.** and what follows; and the following

E.T.U. Electrical Trades Union (Brit.)

et ux. (et uxor)(Lat.) and wife (Law)

etym. or **etymol.** etymological; etymology

E.U. Evangelical Union

E.U., EE.UU. (Estados Unidos)(Port., Span.), **U.S.** or **Ver.St.** (Verteinigte Staaten)(Ger.) United States (cf. E.U.A.)

Eu europium (Chem.)

E.U.A., É.U.A. (États-Unis-Amérique) (Fr.), **E.E.U.U.da A.** (Estados Unidos da América)(Port.), **E.E.U.U.de A.** (Estados Unidos de América)(Span) or **U.S.A.** United States of America (cf. U.S.)

Eug. Eugen; Eugene

euphem. euphemism; euphemistic; euphemistical; enphemistically

Eur. Europe; European

Eus. Eusebius

Eust. Eustace; Eustachius

E.V. (Eingang vorbehalten)(Ger.) rights reserved; English Version (Bible)

Ev., Evang. or **evang.** evangelical; evangelist

Evac (Mil.) or **evac.** evacuation

evac. or **Evac** (Mil.) evacuation

Evac Hosp Evacuation hospital

Evang., evang. or **Ev.** evangelical; evangelist

evap. evaporation

eve., even. or **evg.** evening
Evel. Evelina; Evelyn
even., eve. or **evg.** evening
evg., eve. or **even.** evening
Evid (Mil.) or **evid.** evidence
evy., om. or **omn.** (omni)(Lat.) every
EWB or **E.W.B.** Emergency Work Bureau
E.W.I. Educational Workers' International
E.W.T. Eastern War Time
Ex., E (Mil.) or **exc.** excellence; excellent
Ex. or **Exod.** Exodus
ex from (cf. frm.); out of (as: ex steamer, ex warehouse); without (as: ex coupon; ex rights (cf. w.o.)
ex. excursion; executed
ex. or **Eks.** (Eksempel)(Dan.) example
ex., exam. or **exd.** examined
ex. or **exc.** except; excepted
ex., exc. or **exch.** exchange
ex., exc. or **und.** (undantag)(Swed.) exception
ex. or **exec.** executive
ex. of **exp.** export
ex. or **ext.** extra; extract
exam. examination; examine; examining
exam., ex. or **exd.** examined
Ex B/L or **Ex B.L.** exchange bill of lading
Exc., exc., Exmo. (Excel(l)entíssimo) (Port.) or **Exz.** (Excellenz)(Ger.) Excellency
exc. excite; exciter; excuse; (excudit) (Lat.) he or she fashioned it (cf. del.; des.; fec.; inv)
exc., E (Mil.) or **Ex.** excellence; excellent
exc. or **ex.** except; excepted
exc., ex. or **exch.** exchange
exc., ex. or **und.** (undantag)(Swed.) exception
exch. exchequer
exch., ex. or **exc.** exchange
excl. exclusive
excl. or **exclam.** exclamation
Excma., Exc.[ma] (Excelentísima)(Span.), **Excmo., Exc.**[mo] (Excelentísimo)(Span.) or **M.E.** Most Excellent (cf. Hon.)
Ex.Com. or **Exec.Com.** Executive Committee
ex coup., ex cp., ex cu., X.C., xc, x-c., xcp, xcp., x/cp. or **x-cp.** ex coupon; without coupon (Bonds)
ex cp., ex coup., ex cu., X.C., xc, x-c., xcp, xcp., x/cp. or **x-cp.** ex coupon; without coupon (Bonds)
ex cu., ex coup., ex cp., X.C., xc, x-c., xcp, xcp., x/cp. or **x-cp.** ex coupon; without coupon (Bonds)
exd., ex. or **exam.** examined
ex d., e.d., ex div., X.D., xd, x.d., x-d, xdiv or **x-div.** ex dividend; without dividend (Stocks)
ex div., e.d., ex d., X.D., xd, x.d., x-d, xdiv or **x-div.** ex dividend; without dividend (Stocks)
Ex. Doc. Executive Document
exec. or **ex.** executive
exec., exor. or **exr.** executor
Exec. C. or **E.C.** Executive Council (cf. TEC)
exec.clk. executive clerk
Exec.Com. or **Ex.Com.** Executive Committee
exec.off. executive office
execx., exrx. or **exx.** executrix
ex.fcy. extra fancy
ex g., e.g. or **ex gr.** (ex grege)(Lat.) among the rest; from the flock
ex.g., e.g., ex.gr. (exempli gratia)(Lat.), **e.c.** (exempli causa)(Lat.), **f.e., f. Eks.** (for Eksempel)(Dan.), **f.i., n.p.** (na przyklad)(Polish), **p.ex.** (par example) (Fr.), **t.ex.** (till exempel)(Swed.), **v.g.** (verbi gratia)(Lat.) or **z.B.** (zum Beispiel)(Ger.) for example; for instance
ex gr., e.g. or **ex g.** (ex grege)(Lat.) from the flock; among the rest
ex. gr., e.g., ex.g. (exempli gratia)(Lat.), **e.c.** (exempli causa)(Lat.), **f.e., f. Eks.** (for Eksempel)(Dan.), **f.i., n.p.** (na przyklad)(Polish), **p. ex.** (par exemple) (Fr.), **t. ex.** (till exempel)(Swed.), **v.g.** (verbi gratia)(Lat.) or **z. B.** (zum Beispiel)(Ger.) for example; for instance
exh. exhaust
Exhbn. or **exhbn.** exhibition
exhbn. or **Exhbn.** exhibition
Exhib., exhib. (exhibeatur)(Lat.), **D., d.** or **det.** (detur)(Lat.) let it be given (cf. cap.; d.t.d.; sum.)
exhib. exhibit
ex int., X.i., x.i., x-i., X. in., x in., x. int. or **x-int.** ex interest; without interest (Stock exchange)
ex lib. or **ex-lib.** (ex libris)(Lat.) from the books[of]; bookplate
Exmo. (Excel(l)entíssimo)(Port.), **Exc., exc.** or **Exz.** (Exzellenz)(Ger.) Excellency
exmr. examiner
ex n., X-N., X-n., x-n. or **X-new** ex new; without the right to new shares (Stock exchange)
Ex O Executive officer (Mil.)
Ex.O. Executive order
Exod. or **Ex.** Exodus
ex. off. or **e.o.** (ex officio)(Lat.) by virtue of office
Exon. (Exonia)(Lat.) Exeter; (Exoniensis) (Lat.) of Exeter (in the signature of a bishop)
exor., exec. or **exr.** executor
exp expotential [function]
exp. expense; expenses; expotential; exportation; exported; express
exp. or **ex.** export
exp., ex p. or **ex pte.** (ex parte)(Lat.) from one party; in the interests of one side only (Law)
exp., exper., expt. or **exptl.** experimental
exp. or **expn.** expiration

exp. or **exptr.** exporter
expdn. or **exped.** expedition
exped. or **expdn.** expedition
exper., exp., expt. or **exptl.** experimental
expl. explanatory
expl. or **erkl.** (erklärt)(Ger.) explained
expl., explic. (explicit)(Lat.) or **fin.** (fine) (Ital.),(finis)(Lat.) the end
explos. explosives
expn. exposition
expn. or **exp.** expiration
exp.o. experimental order
ex pr., xpr or **x pr.** ex privileges; without privileges (Securities)
expt. experiment
expt., exp., exper. or **exptl.** experimental
ex pte., exp. or **ex p.** (ex parte)(Lat.) in the interests of one side only; from one party (Law)
exptl., exp., exper. or **expt.** experimental
exptr. or **exp.** exporter
Ex. R. f. d. I. (Exerzier-Reglement für die Infantrie)(Ger.) **I.D.R.** or **I.E.R.** (Infantrie-Exerzier-Reglement)(Ger.) Infantry Drill Regulations
exr., exec. or **exor.** executor
ex r., xr, X-rts. or **x rts.** ex-rights; without rights (Stock exchange)
Ex Rel. or **ex rel.** (ex relatione)(Lat.) by or on the relation, or information [of] (Law)
exrx., execx. or **exx.** executrix
ex ship delivered from the ship
ext. extend; extension; exterior; external; externally; extinct
ext. or **ex.** extra; extract
ex w. or **xw** ex warrants; without warrants (Stock exchange)
exx. examples
exx., execx. or **exrx.** executrix
Exz. (Exzellenz)(Ger.), **Exc., exc.** or **Exmo.** (Excel(l)entíssimo)(Port.) Excellency
Ez. or **Ezr.** Ezra
Ezek. Ezekiel
Ezr. or **Ez.** Ezra

ΕΠΤ (Epsilon Pi Tau) National undergraduate fraternity (Practical Arts and Vocational Education)
ΗΚΝ (Eta Kappa Nu) National honor fraternity (Electrical Engineering)
ΗΣΦ (Eta Sigma Phi) Professional society (Classics) (Men and women)
ΗΥΓ (Eta Upsilon Gamma) National undergraduate sorority

F

F firm (Pencils); Fixed [lights] (Naut.); a Fraunhofer line caused by hydrogen (Astrophysics); free energy (Physics); [degree of] freedom (Physics); function (Math.)
F, F., f. or **far.** farad
F (Mil.), **F., Fd** (Mil.), **Fld** (Mil.) or **fld.** field
F or **Fl** fluorine (Chem.)
F. Falsifier (formerly branded on the guilty person); ([dies] fastus)(Lat.) a day of fast (Roman calendar); Felon
F., F (Mil.), **Fd** (Mil.), **Fld** (Mil.) or **fld.** field
F. or **f.** feast (Eccl.); (forte)(Ital.) loud (Music); filly; fine; for (in Mss.); form; formed; formula; formulas
F., f., far., q., quar or **qr.** (quadrans)(Lat.) farthing
F., f., fath., fm., fth. or **fthm.** fathom; fathoms
F., f., fc. or **fr.** franc
F., f., fcs. or **frs.** francs
F., f., or **fem.** female; feminine
F., f., ff., fol., foll., seq., seqq., sq., sqq. (sequens, sequentes, sequentia)(Lat.) or **subseq.** (subsequens)(Lat.) the following (cf. et seq.)
F., f. or **Fi** (Mil.) fighter
F., f. or **fl.** flower
F., f., fl. or **flr.** florin; florins
F., f. or **fl. oz.** fluid ounce
F., f., fo., f°, fol. or **in-f°** (in-folio)(Fr.) folio (cf. ff.; ll.)
F., f., Fr., P. or **p.** (padre)(Span.), (pater) (Lat.), (père)(Fr.) father
F., f., Ft. or **ft.** (fiat, fiant)(Lat.) let there be made or done
F., f. or **ft.** feet; flat (Theat.); foot
F., f. or **fur.** furlong; furlongs
F., f. (filius)(Lat.) or **s.** son
F., Fah. or **Fahr.** Fahrenheit
F. or **fam.** family
F., Fb., fbro. (febrero)(Span.), **Feb., febb.** (febbraio)(Ital.), **fev.** (fevereiro)(Port.) or **fév.** (févier)(Fr.) February
F. or **Fr.** France; French
F., Fr. or **Fri.** Friday
F., S. or **s.** (socius, sodalis)(Lat.) Fellow
F., V.F. or **V.f.** field of vision; visual field
f focal length; fordable (Mil.); fugacity [of gases]
f. Fog (Naut.); (fillér)(Hung.) halfpenny
f. (född)(Swed.), (født)(Dan.), **B., b., geb.** (geboren)(Ger.) or **n.** (natus) (Lat.) born
f., F, F. or **far.** farad
f. or **F.** feast; forte (Music); filly; fine; for (Mss.); form; formed; formula; formulas
f., F., far., q., quar. or **qr.** (quadrans)(Lat.) farthing
f., F., fath., fm., fth. or **fthm.** fathom; fathoms
f., F., fc. or **fr.** franc
f., F., fcs. or **frs.** francs
f., F. or **fem.** female; feminine
f., F., ff., fol., foll., seq., seqq., sq., sqq. (sequens, sequentes, sequentia)(Lat.) or **subseq.** (subsequens)(Lat.) the following (cf. et.seq.)

f., F. or **fi.** fighter
f., F. or **fl.** flower
f., F., fl. or **flr.** florin; forins
f., F. or **fl.oz.** fluid ounce
f., F., fo., f°, fol. or **in-f°** (in-folio)(Fr.) folio (cf. ff.; ll.)
f., F., Fr., P. or **p.** (padre)(Span.), (pater)(Lat.), (père)(Fr.) father
f., F., Ft. or **ft.** (fiat, fiant)(Lat.) let there be made, or done
f., F. or **ft.** feet; flat (Theat.); foot
f., F. or **furl.** furlong; furlongs
f., F. (filius)(Lat.) or **s.** son
f. or **fec.** (fecit)(Lat.) he or she made it (cf. del.; des.; exc.; inv.)
f., Ft. or **ft.** fort
FA fatty acid
FA or **F.A.** Field Artillery; Food Administration; Fuel Administration
F.A. or **f.a.** football association; freight agent; freight association
f.A. (forrige Aar)(Dan.) last year
f.a. fire alarm; free alongside (Shipping) (cf. f.a.s.; f.f.a.; f.o.); freight auditor
f.a. or **F.A.** football association; freight agent; freight association
FAA or **F.A.A.** Federal Alcohol Administration
F.A.A. Fleet Air Arm
F.A.A., A.A.S. (Academiae Americanae Socius) (Lat.), **F.A.A.A.S.** or **F.A.A.S.** Fellow of the American Academy [of Arts and Sciences]
F.A.A. or **f.a.a.** free of all average (cf. f.f.a.)
f.a.a. or **F.A.A.** free of all average (cf. f.f.a.)
F.A.A.A.S. Fellow of the American Association for the Advancement of Science
F.A.A.A.S., A.A.S. (Academiae Americanae Socius)(Lat.), **F.A.A.** or **F.A.A.S.** Fellow of the American Academy of Arts and Sciences
F. A. A. R. Fellow of the American Academy in Rome
FA Armd Field artillery armored
F.A.A.S., A.A.S. (Academiae Americanae Socius)(Lat.), **F.A.A.** or **F.A.A.A.S.** Fellow of [the American] Academy of Arts and Sciences
FA Bn Field artillery battalion
FA Bn Armd Field artillery battalion armored
FA Brig Field artillery brigade
FAC or **F. A. C.** Federal Advisory Council; Federal Aviation Commission
fac., facs., facsim. or **fs.** facsimile; facsimiles
f.a.c. fast as can
FACA or **F.A.C.A.** Federal Alcohol Control Administration
F.A.C.D. Fellow of the American College of Dentists
facet. facetious
F.A.C.I. Fellow of the Australian Chemical Institute
F.A.C.P. Fellow of the American College of Physicians
F.A.C.S. Fellow of the American College of Surgeons
facs., fac., facsim. or **fs.** facsimile; facsimiles
facsim., fac., facs. or **fs.** facsimile; facsimiles
F.A.E.S. Federated American Engineering Society
F.A.G.S. Fellow of the American Geographical Society
Fahr., F. or **Far.** Fahrenheit
F.A.I. Fellow of the Auctioneers' Institute
F.A.I.A. Fellow of the American Institute of Architects
F.A.L.P.A. Fellow [of the Incorporated Society] of Auctioneers and Landed Property Agents
F.A.M. Federal Air Mail; Foreign Air Mail
F.A.M. or **F. and A.M.** Free and Accepted Masons
fam. familiar
fam. or **F.** family
F.A.M.A. Fellow of the American Medical Association
F. Amb. or **Fd Amb** Field ambulance
F & A or **F. & A.** February and August (Interest)
f.& a. fore and aft
f.& d. or **f. and d.** freight and demurrage (Shipping)
F. & F. furniture and fixtures
f. & w.chg. feeding and watering charge (Transp.)
F. & W.L.S. or **FWS** Fish and Wild Life Service
F. and A.M. or **F.A.M.** Free and Accepted Masons
f. and d. or **f.& d.** freight and demurrage (Shipping)
F. and R. force and rhythm (Pulse)
FANY or **F.A.N.Y.** First Aid Nursing Yeomanry
F.A.O. Fleet accountant officer
FA Obsn Bn Field artillery observation battalion
F.A.P. first-aid post
F.A.P.S. Fellow of the American Physical Society
F.A.P.S. or **S.P.A.S.** (Societatis Philosophiae Americanae Socius)(Lat.) Fellow of the American Philosophical Society
F.A.Q., F.a.q. or **f.a.q.** free at quay (cf. f.d.; f.o.q.)
F.A.Q. or **f.a.q.** fair average quality
f.a.q. or **F.A.Q.** fair average quality
f.a.q., F.A.Q. or **F.a.q.** free at quay (cf. f.d.; f.o.q.)
f.a.q.s. or **F.A.Q.S.** fair average quality of season
far. farrier; farriery
far., F, F. or **f.** farad
far., F., f., q., qua. or **qr.** (quadrans)(Lat.) farthing
FARC Field Artillery Reserve Corps
FA Regt Field Artillery Regiment
FA-Res Field Artillery Reserve
F.A.S. Fellow of the Anthropological Society

F.A.S. or **f.a.s.** free alongside ship (cf. f.a.; f.f.a.; f.o.)

F.A.S. or **F.S.A.** Fellow of the Society of Arts (London) (now Royal Society of Arts)

F.A.S. or **S.A.E.** (Societatis Antiquariorum Socius)(Lat.) Fellow of the Society of Antiquaries; Fellow of the Antiquarian Society

f.a.s. firsts and seconds (Lumber)

f.a.s. or **F.A.S.** free alongside ship (cf. f.a.; f.f.a.; f.o.)

F.A.S.A. Fellow of the Acoustical Society of America

F.A.S.B. Fellow of the Asiatic Society of Bengal (now Royal Asiatic Society of Bengal)

Fasc., fasc. (fasciculus)(Lat.) or **Lfg.** Lieferung)(Ger.) fascicle

F.A.S.E. Fellow of the Antiquarian Society, Edinburgh (cf. F.S.A.E.; F.S.A.S.)

F.A.S.L. Fellow of the Anthropological Society of London (now Royal Anthropological Institute of Great Britain and Ireland) (cf F.E.S.; F.R.A.I.)

fath., F., f., fm., fth. or **fthm.** fathom; fathoms

F.A.V.O. Fleet aviation officer

FB fog bell

F.B. Fenian Brotherhood; fire brigade; Flying boat; Free Baptist (cf. F.W.B.)

F.B. or **f.b.** freight bill

Fb., F., fbro. (febrero)(Span.), **Feb., febb.** (febbraio)(Ital.), **fev.** (fevereiro) (Port.) or **fév.** (févier)(Fr.) February

f.b. or **F.B.** freight bill

F.B.A. Fellow of the British Academy

F.B.A.A. Fellow of the British [Association of] Accountants and Auditors

f.b.c. fallen building clause (Insurance)

f.b.c.w. fallen building clause waiver (Insurance)

FBG or **F.B.G.** Federation of British Growers

FBH or **F.B.H.** Federal Board of Hospitalization

F.B.H. fire brigade hydrant

FBI or **F.B.I.** Federal Bureau of Investigation

F.B.I. Federation of British Industries

F.B.I.S. Foreign Broadcast Monitoring Service

fbm, f.b.m. or **ft.b.m.** feet board measure (cf. bd. ft.)

F.B.O.A. Fellow of the British Optical Association

F.B.O.U. Fellow of the British Ornithologists' Union

fbro. (febrero)(Span.), **F., Fb., Feb., febb.** (febbraio)(Ital.), **fev.** (fevereiro) (Port.) or **fév.** (févier)(Fr.) February

F.B.S. Fellow of the Botanical Society

F.B.S.E. Fellow of the Botanical Society, Edinburgh

F.B.S.I. Fellow of the Boot and Shoe Industry

FBSM or **F.B.S.M.** Federal Board of Surveys and Maps

F.B.S.M. Fellow of the Birmingham School of Music

F.C. Federal Cabinet (Australia); Ferry Command; Food Controller; football club; Free Church (Scotland)

F/C Flying cadet

fc., F., f. or **fr.** franc

f.c. follow copy (Printing)

FCA or **F.C.A.** Farm Credit Administration (cf. FFCA)

F.C.A. or **F.I.C.A.** Fellow of the [Institute of] Chartered Accountants

F.C.A.B. Fire Companies' Adjustment Bureau

F.C.& S., f.c.& s., F.C. and S., f.c. and s., F.C.S. or **f.c.s.** free of capture and seizure (Insurance)

F.C. and S., F.C.& S., f.c.& s., f.c.and s., F.C.S. or **f.c.s.** free of capture and seizure (Insurance)

f.c.and s., F.C.& S., f.c.& s., F.C.and S., F.C.S. or **f.c.s.** free of capture and seizure (Insurance)

Fcap., fcap., fcp. or **fp.** foolscap

fcap., Fcap., fcp. or **fp.** foolscap

FCAT or **F.C.A.T.** Federal Committee on Apprentice Training

F.C.B. Freight Container Bureau

FCC or **F.C.C.** Federal Communications Commission

F.C.C. Federal Council of Churches (cf. F.C.C.C.; F.C.C.C.A.); First Class Certificate; Food Control Committee

F.C.C.C. Federal Council of Churches of Christ (cf. F.C.C.; F.C.C.C.A.)

F.C.C.C.A. Federal Council of Churches of Christ in America (cf F.C.C.; F.C.C.C.)

F.C.C.S. Fellow of the Corporation of Certified Secretaries (Brit.)

F.C.G.I. Fellow of the City and Guilds [of London] Institute

F.C.H. Fellow of Coopers Hill College

F.C.I.A. Fellow of Corporation of Insurance Agents

F.C.I.B. Fellow of Corporation of Insurance Brokers

FCIC or **F.C.I.C.** Farm Crop Insurance Corporation; Federal Crop Insurance Corporation

F.C.I.I. Fellow of the Chartered Insurance Institute (Brit.)

F.C.I.S. Fellow of the Chartered Institute of Secretaries (Brit.)

F.C.O. Fellow of the College of Organists (now Royal College of Organists); Fleet construction officer

fco., fr. (franco)(Ital.),(franko)(Ger.), **P.P., p.p.** or **ppd.** postpaid

f.co. fair copy

F.C. of T., FCT or **F.C.T.** Federal Coordinator of Transportation

F.C.O.G. Fellow of the College of Obstetrics and Gynaecology

F.C.P. Fellow of the College of Preceptors (Brit.)

fcp., Fcap., fcap. or **fp.** foolscap

F.C.R.A. Fellow of the Corporation of Accountants (Glasgow)

F.C.S. Fellow of the Chemical Society

F.C.S., F.C.& S., f.c.& s., F.C. and S., f.c.and s. or **f.c.s.** free of capture and seizure (Insurance)

Fcs. Frances (cf. Fs.)

fcs., F., f. or **frs.** francs

f.c.s., F.C.& S., f.c.& s., F.C.and S., f.c.and s. or **F.C.S.** free of capture and seizure (Insurance)

F.C.S.I. Fellow of the Chartered Surveyors' Institution (Brit.) (cf. F.S.I.)

FCT, F.C.of T. or **F.C.T.** Federal Coordinator of Transportation

F.C.T., F.C.of T. or **FCT** Federal Coordinator of Transportation

F.C.T.B. Fellow of the College of Teachers of the Blind

FCUS or **F.C.U.S.** Federal Credit Union System

F.C.W.A. Fellow of the Institute of Cost and Works Accountants (Brit.)

fcy. pks. fancy packs

FD Fog diaphone (Mil.)

FD or **Fin Dept** Finance Department (Mil.)

F.D. fire department; focal distance

F.D. or **Fest. Dev.** (Festum devotionis) (Lat.) Feast of Devotion

F.D., Fid. Def., fid. def. (Fidei Defensor) (Lat.) or **D.F.** (Defensor Fidei)(Lat.) Defender of the Faith (Brit.)

Fd (Mil.), **F** (Mil.), **F., Fld** (Mil.) or **fld.** field

Fd., fd. or **fdg.** funding

Fd., Fer. or **Ferd.** Ferdinand

fd. fund

fd., Fd. or **fdg.** funding

f.d. free at dock (cf. f.a.q.) free delivery; free discharge; free dispatch

f.d. (för detta)(Swed.), **abv.** or **sup.** (supra) (Lat.) above (cf. prev.; qm.)

f.d. or **f/d.** free dock

f.d. (för detta)(Swed.) or **qm.** (quondam) (Lat.) formerly (cf. prev.; sup.)

f/d or **f.d.** free dock

FDA or **F.D.A.** Food and Drug Act; Food and Drug Administration; Food Distribution Administration

Fd Amb or **F. Amb.** Field ambulance

F.D.B. Fighter dive bomber

Fd Bde Field brigade

Fd Bty Field battery

FDCB or **F.D.C.B.** Foreign and Domestic Commerce Bureau

Fd Coy Field company

fdg., Fd. or **fd.** funding

F.D.I. (Fédération Dentaire Internationale) (Fr.) International Dental Federation

FDIC or **F.D.I.C.** Federal Deposit Insurance Corporation

fd ldg forced landing

fdn., fndn. or **found.** foundation

F.D.P. (Filii Divinae Providentiae)(Lat.) or **O.D.P.** Sons of Divine Providence; Order of Divine Providence

FDPA or **F.D.P.A.** Florida Dairy Products Association

Fd P.O. or **F.P.O.** Field Post Office

f. dr. or **fl. dr.** fluid dram

FDRB or **F.D.R.B.** Federal District Recovery Board

fdry. foundry

F.E. Far East; Far Eastern

F.E., E.F., E.Fl. or **Fl.E.** Flemish ells

F.E., E.F., E.Fr. or **Fr.E.** French ells

F.E. or **F. Eng.** Forest Engineer

Fe (Chem.), **fe.** (ferrum)(Lat.) or **i.** iron

f.é. (folyó évi)(Hung.), **a.c.** (année courante)(Fr.), **d.A.** (dette Aar)(Dan.), **d.J.** (dieses Jahres)(Ger.) or **h.a.** (hoc anno)(Lat.) this year; the current year

f.e., e.c. (exempli causa)(Lat.), **e.g., ex gr.** (exempli gratia)(Lat.), **f. Eks.** (for Eksempel)(Dan.), **f.i., n.p.** (na przykład)(Polish), **p.ex.** (par exemple)(Fr.), **t.ex.** (till exempel)(Swed.), **v.g.** (verbi gratia) (Lat.) or **z. B.** (zum Beispiel) (Ger.) for example; for instance

FEAPW or **F.E.A.P.W.** Federal Emergency Administration of Public Work (superseded by PWA)

feath. feathery

F.E.A.T.M. Far Eastern Association of Tropical Medicine (Brit.)

Feb., F., Fb., fbro. (febrero)(Span.), **febb.** (febbraio)(Ital.), **fev.** (fevereiro)(Port) or **fév.** (févier)(Fr.) February

feb. dur. (febre durante)(Lat.) while the fever continues

fec. or **f.** (fecit)(Lat.) he or she made it (cf. del.; des.; exc.; inv.)

fec. aq.fort. (fecit aqua forte)(Lat.) or **etch.** etched

Fed. Federal; Federalist

Fed. or **fed.** federation

fed. federated

fed. or **Fed.** federation

Fed. Rep. Federal Reporter

Fed.Res.Bd., FRB, F.R.B. or **F.R.Bd.** Federal Reserve Board

Fed.Res.Bk., FRB, F.R.B. or **F.R.Bk.** Federal Reserve Bank

FEHC or **F.E.H.C.** Federal Emergency Housing Corporation

F.E.I.S. Fellow of the Educational Institute of Scotland

f.Eks. (for Eksempel)(Dan.), **e.c.** (exempli causa)(Lat.), **e.g., ex. gr.** (exempli gratia)(Lat.), **f.e., f.i., n.p.** (na przykład) (Polish), **p.ex.** (par exemple)(Fr.), **t. ex.** (till exempel)(Swed.), **v.g.** (verbi gratia)(Lat.) or **z.B.** (zum Beispiel)(Ger.) for example; for instance

Fel. Felix

fem., F. or **f.** female; feminine

f.e.m. (fuerza electromotriz)(Span.), **E, E., e., EMF, emf, E.M.F.** or **e.m.f.** electromotive force

Fem. intern. (femoribus internus)(Lat.) inner side of the thighs

fenc. fencing

F. Eng. or **F. E.** Forest Engineer

F.E.O. Fleet engineer officer

FEPC or **F.E.P.C.** Fair Employment Practices Committee

Fer., Fd. or **Ferd.** Ferdinand

FERA or **F.E.R.A.** Federal Emergency Relief Administration

Ferd., Fd. or **Fer.** Ferdinand
ferv. (fervens)(Lat.), **bull.** (bulliens)(Lat.) or **coct.** (coctio)(Lat.) boiling
F.E.S. Fellow of the Entomological Society; Fellow of the Ethnological Society (now Royal Anthropological Institute of Great Britain and Ireland) (cf. F.R.A.I.)
FESB or **F.E.S.B.** Federal Emergency Stabilization Board
FESO or **F.E.S.O.** Federal Employment Stabilization Office
Fest. Dev. or **F.D.** (Festum devotionis) (Lat.) Feast of Devotion
feud. feudal
feud. or **feudm.** feudalism
fev. (fevereiro)(Port.) **F., Fb., fbro.** (febrero)(Span.), **Feb., febb.** (febbraio) (Ital) or **fév.** (février)(Fr.) February
FF. (Felicissimus)(Lat.) Most Fortunate
FF. (fratres)(Lat.), (Frères)(Fr.), **Bros., bros., Geb., Gbr.** (Gebrüder)(Ger.) or **Hnos.** (Hermanos)(Span.) brothers
F.F. Fleet fighter; Folklore Fellows; (Felicissimi Fratres)(Lat.) Most Fortunate Brothers; thick fog (Naut.)
Ff. or **F.f.** (Forsetzung folgt)(Ger.) to be continued (cf. cont.)
Ff. or **ff.** (fecerunt)(Lat.) they made it (cf. del.; des.; exc.; inv.)
F.f. or **Ff.** (Forsetzung folgt)(Ger.) to be continued (cf. cont.)
ff. (fortissimo, forte forte)(Ital.) very loud (Music)
ff., et seq., et seqq., et sq. or **et sqq.** (et sequens, et sequentes, et sequentia) (Lat.) and what follows
ff., F., f., fol., foll., seq., seqq., sq., sqq. (sequens, sequentes, sequentia)(Lat.) or **subseq.** (subsequens)(Lat.) the following (cf. et seq.)
ff. or **Ff.** (fecerunt)(Lat.) they made it (cf. del.; des.; exc.; inv.)
ff. or **foll.** folios (cf. fo.; ll.)
f.f. fixed focus (Photog.); folded flat
F.F.A. Fellow of the Faculty of Actuaries [in Scotland]
F.F.A., F.f.a. or **f.f.a.** free foreign agency; free foreign agent; free from alongside (cf. f.a.; f.a.s.; f.o.)
F.F.A. or **f.f.a.** foreign freight agent; free from average (cf. f.a.a.)
F.f.a., F.F.A. or **f.f.a.** free foreign agency; free foreign agent; free from alongside (cf. f.a.s.; f.a.; f.o.)
f.f.a. or **F.F.A.** foreign freight agent; free from average (cf. f.a.a.)
f.f.a., F.F.A. or **F.f.a.** free foreign agency; free foreign agent; free from alongside (cf. f.a.; f.a.s.; f.o)
F.F.A.S. Fellow of the Faculty of Architects and Surveyors
FFC or **F.F.C.** Federal Fire Council
FFCA or **F.F.C.A.** Federal Farm Credit Administration (cf FCA)
fff. or **F.F.F.** (fortississimo)(Ital.) as loud as possible (Music)
FFMC or **F.F.M.C.** Federal Farm Mortgage Corporation (cf FMC)
F.F.P.S. Fellow of the Faculty of Physicians and Surgeons
F.F.P.S.G. Fellow of the Faculty of Physicians and Surgeons, Glasgow
F.F.R. Fellow of the Faculty of Radiologists; Fleet fighter reconnaissance
F.Fr. Free French
F.Fr.H.Q. Free French Headquarters
F.F.Sc. Fellow of the Faculty of Sciences
F.F.V. First Families of Virginia
ffy. faithfully
FG fog gun
F.G. (Brit.) or **f.g.** footguards
f.g. field gun; fine grain; friction glaze; fully good
f.g. or **F.G.** footguards
F.G.A. or **f.g.a.** foreign general average; free of general average
f.g.f. fully good, fair
F.G.H.S. Fellow of the Genealogical and Historical Society
F.G.I. Fellow of the Institute of [Certified] Grocers; Fellow of the Grocers' Institution
F.G.O. Fleet gunnery officer
F.G.S. Fellow of the Geological Society; Friends of the Golden State
F.G.S.A. Fellow of the Geological Society of America
F.G.S.M. Fellow of the Guildhall School of Music
fgt., frgt. or **frt.** freight
FH fog horn
F.H. fire hydrant; fore hatch
F.h., f.h. or **ft. haust.** (fiat haustus)(Lat.) let a draft be made (Pharm.)
FHA or **F.H.A.** Federal Housing Administration (cf. N.H.A.)
F.H.A.S. Fellow of the Highland and the Agricultural Society [of Scotland]
F.H.C. Farmers Home Corporation
F.Hist.S., F.H.S., H.S.S. (Historiae Societatis Socius)(Lat.) or **S.H.S.** (Societatis Historiae Socius)(Lat.) Fellow of the Historical Society
FHLB or **F.H.L.B.** Federal Home Loan Bank
FHLBA or **F.H.L.B.A.** Federal Home Loan Bank Administration
FHLBB or **F.H.L.B.B.** Federal Home Loan Bank Board
F.Hort.S. or **F.H.S.** Fellow of the Horticultural Society
f. hosp. or **FL** (Feldlazarett)(Ger.) Field hospital
f.h.p. friction horsepower
F.H.S., F.Hist.S., H.S.S. (Historiae Societatis Socius)(Lat.) of **S.H.S.** (Societatis Historiae Socius)(Lat.) Fellow of the Historical Society
F.H.S. or **F.Hort.S.** Fellow of the Horticultural Society
fhv. (forhenvaerende)(Dan.) or **qm.** (quondam)(Lat.) former; late (cf. dec.)
F.I. Falkland Islands
Fi (Mil.), **F.** or **f.** fighter

f.i., e.c. (exempli causa)(Lat.), **e.g., ex.gr.** (exempli gratia)(Lat.), **f.e., f.Eks.** (for Eksempel)(Dan.), **n.p.** (na przyład) (Pol.), **p.ex.** (par exemple)(Fr.) **t. ex.** (till exempel)(Swed.), **v.g.** (verbi gratia)(Lat.) or **z.B.** (zum Beispiel) (Ger.) for instance; for example

F.I.A. Fellow of the Institute of Actuaries (Brit.)

F.I.A. or **f.i.a.** full interest admitted

f.i.a. or **F.I.A.** full interest admitted

F.I.A.A. Fellow Architect Member of the Incorporated Association of Architects and Surveyors

F.I. Arb. Fellow of the Institute of Arbitrators (Brit.)

F.I.A.S. Fellow Surveyor Member of the Incorporated Association of Architects and Surveyors; Fellow of the Institute of Aeronautical Sciences

F.I.B. Fellow of the Institute of Bankers (Brit.)

F.I.B. or **f.i.b.** free into barge (Shipping); free into bunker (Coal)

f.i.b. or **F.I.B.** free into barge (Shipping); free into bunker (Coal)

F.I.B.D. Fellow of the Institute of British Decorators

F.I.B.P. Fellow of the Institute of British Photographers

F.I.C. Fellow of the Institute of Chemistry [of Great Britain and Ireland]

F.I.C.A. or **F.C.A.** Fellow of the Institute of Chartered Accountants

FICB or **F.I.C.B.** Federal Intermediate Credit Banks

F.I.C.D. Fellow of the Institute of Chartered Dealers

F.I.C.I. Fellow of the International Colonial Institute

F.I.C.S. Fellow of the Institute of Chartered Shipbrokers; Fellow of the International College of Surgeons

fict. fiction; fictioned; fictitious; (fictilis) (Lat.) made of clay (cf. pot.)

F.I.D. Fellow of the Institute of Directors; Field Intelligence Department

fid. fidelity; fiduciary

F.I.D.A.C. (Fédération Interalliée des Anciens Combattants)(Fr.) Interallied Federation of [World War I] Veterans

Fid. Def., fid. def., F.D. (Fidei Defensor) (Lat.) or **D.F.** (Defensor Fidei)(Lat.) Defender of the Faith (Brit.)

fi.fa. (fieri facias)(Lat.) cause it to be done

fig. figurative; figuratively; figure (cf. ic.; il.)

fig. or **figs.** figures

F.I.G.C.M. Fellow of the Incorporated Guild of Church Musicians

figs. or **fig.** figures

F.I.H. Fellow of the Institute of Hygiene (Brit.)

F.I.I. or **F.I. Inst.** Fellow of the Imperial Institute (Brit.)

F.I.I.A. Fellow of the Institute of Industrial Administration

F.I. Inst. or **F.I.I.** Fellow of the Imperial Institute (Brit.)

F.I.J. or **F.J.I.** Fellow of the Institute of Journalists

F.I.L. Fellow of the Institute of Linguists

Fil. filament

filt. filter

F.I.M.T.A. Fellow of the Institute of Municipal Treasurers and Accountants (Brit.)

Fin. Finland

Fin. or **Finn.** Finnish

fin. finance; financial; finish

fin. (fine)(Ital.), (finis)(Lat.), **expl.** or **explic.** (explicit)(Lat.) the end

fin. or **find.** finished

Fin Dept or **FD** Finance Department (Mil.)

Finn. or **Fin.** Finnish

Fin O, FO (Mil.) or **F.O.** Finance officer

Fin-Res Finance [Department] Reserve (Mil.)

Fin. Sec. or **F. S.** Financial Secretary

F. Inst. F. Fellow of the Institute of Fuel (Brit.)

F. Inst. P. or **F.I.P.** Fellow of the Institute of Physics (Brit.)

F.I.O. Fellow of the Institute of Ophthalmic Opticians (Brit.)

f.i.o. free in and out (Shipping)

F.I.O.B. Fellow of the Institute of Builders

F.I.P. or **F. Inst. P.** Fellow of the Institute of Physics

F.I.P.I. Fellow of the Institute of Patentees, Incorporated

F.I.P.S. Fellow of the Institute of Private Secretaries

fir. firkin; firkins

f.i.r. floating-in rates (Shipping)

F.I.S.A. Fellow of the Incorporated Secretaries Association

F.I.S.E. Fellow of the Institute of Structural Engineers (Brit.)

F.I.S.P. Franklin Institute of the State of Pennsylvania

F.I.T. or **f.i.t.** free in truck; free of income tax

f.i.w. free in wagon (Shipping)

F.I.W.T. Fellow of the Institute of Wireless Technology (Brit.)

F.J.I. or **F.I.J.** Fellow of the Institute of Journalists (Brit.)

f.k. flat keel (Shipbuilding)

F.K.C. or **F.K.C.L.** Fellow of King's College [London]

FL (Feldlazarett)(Ger.) or **f. hosp.** Field hospital

Fl Flashing [lights] (Naut.)

Fl or **F** fluorine (Chem.)

Fl. Flanders

Fl., Fla. or **Flor.** Florida

Fl. or **Flav.** Flavius

Fl. or **Flem.** Flemish

fl. floor; flour; fluid; flute

fl., F. or **f.** flower

fl., F., f. or **flr.** florin; florins

fl., flo. or **flor.** (floruit)(Lat.) flourished

f.l. (falsa lectio)(Lat.) a false reading

FLA or **F.L.A.** Federal Loan Agency

F.L.A. Fellow of the Library Association (Brit.)
Fla., Fl. or **Flor.** Florida
F.l.a. (fiat lege artis)(Lat.) let it be done according to rule (cf. sec. reg.)
F.L.A.A. Fellow of the London Association of [Certified] Accountants
F Lab Field laboratory (Mil.)
Flak. or **flak** (Flugabwehrkanone)(Ger.) Antiaircraft gun (cf. AA)
F.L.A.S. Fellow of the Land Agents' Society (Brit.)
Flav. or **Fl.** Flavius
FLB or **F.L.B.** Federal Land Banks
F.L.C.M. Fellow of the London College of Music
Fld (Mil.), **F** (Mil.), **F.**, **Fd** (Mil.) or **fld.** field
fld., **F** (Mil.), **F.**, **Fd** (Mil.) or **Fld** (Mil.) field
fl.dr. or **f.dr.** fluid dram
Fl.E., E.F., E.Fl. or **F.E.** Flemish ells
Flem. or **Fl.** Flemish
flex. flexible
flg. flange
F.L.G.A. Fellow of the Local Government Association
flgd. flanged
f.l.n. following landing numbers (Shipping)
Flo. Florence
flo., fl. or **flor.** (floruit)(Lat.) flourished
Flor., Fl. or **Fla.** Florida
flor., fl. or **flo.** (floruit)(Lat.) flourished
fl. oz., F. or **f.** fluid ounce
fl. pl. (flore pleno)(Lat.) in full bloom
flr., F., f. or **fl.** florin; florins
F.L.S. Fellow of the Linnæan Society
F.L.S.A. Fair Labor Standards Acts
Flt (Mil.), **Flt.** or **flt.** flight
flt., Flt (Mil.) or **Flt.** flight
Flt Cmdr (Mil.) or **Flt. Cmdr.** Flight Commander
Flt Lt (Mil.) or **Flt.Lt.** Flight Lieutenant
Fltr. floater (Insurance)
Flt Sgt (Mil.), **F.S.** or **F.Sgt.** Flight sergeant
fluores. fluorescent
fly. flinty
FM Field manual (Mil.)
FM or **F.M.** frequency modulation (Radio)
F.M. Field marshal; Foreign Mission or Missions; (Fraternitas Medicorum) (Lat.) Fraternity of Physicians; (front de mer)(Fr.) sea front
F.M., f.m., ft.mist. (fiat mistura)(Lat.), **M.ft.** or **m.ft.** (mistura fiat)(Lat.) make a mixture
F.M. or **F.M.S.** (Fratrum Maristarum Scholarum)(Lat.) Marist Brothers of the Schools (cf. S.M.)
Fm Fireman (Mil.)
Fm. (Formiddag)(Dan.), **f.m.** (förmiddagen) (Swed.), **v.m.** or **Vorm.** (Vormittags) (Ger.) forenoon (cf. A.M.)
fm., F., f., fath., fth. or **fthm.** fathom; fathoms
fm., fr., frm. or **v.** (van)(Dutch), (von) (Ger.) from (cf. ex)
f.m., F.M., ft.mist. (fiat mistura)(Lat.), **M.ft.** or **m.ft.** (mistura fiat)(Lat.) make a mixture
f.m. (förmiddagen)(Swed.), **Fm.** (Formiddag)(Dan.), **v.m.** or **Vorm.** (Vormittags)(Ger.) forenoon (cf. A.M.)
F.M.A.N. February, May, August and November (Interest)
FMC or **F.M.C.** Farm Mortgage Corporation (cf. FFMC)
F.M.D. or **f.m.d.** foot-and-mouth disease
f.m.d. or **F.M.D.** foot and mouth disease
F.M.F. Fleet Marine Forces
FMk Finnish marks
F.M.Lt. (Feldmarschall-Leutnant)(Ger.) or **L.F.M.** Lieutenant field marshal
F.M.M. (Frater Misericordia)(Lat.) Brothers of Mercy
fmn. or **formn.** formation
F.M.N.H. Field Museum of Natural History
F.M.O. Fleet medical officer
F.M.R.A. Furniture Manufacturers Representatives Association
F.M.S. Federated Malay States; Fellow of the Medical Society
F.M.S. or **F.M.** (Fratrum Maristarum Scholarum)(Lat.) Marist Brothers of the Schools (cf. S.M.)
f.n., Anm. (Anmerkung)(Ger.) or **ftnt.** footnote (cf. annot.; schol.)
f.n., Anm. (Anmerkungen)(Ger.), **ftnt.** or **ftnts.** footnotes (cf. annot.; schol.)
fnd. found
fndd. funded
fndd. or **found.** founded
fndg. founding
fndn., fdn. or **found.** foundation
fndr. founder
F.N.I. Fellow of the National Institute [of Sciences in India]
FNMA or **F.N.M.A.** Federal National Mortgage Association
fnp, fn.p. or **fu.p.** fusion point
fn.p., fnp or **fu.p.** fusion point
FO (Mil.), **F.O.** or **Fin O** (Mil.) Finance officer
FO (Mil.) **F.O.** or **f.o.** Field orders
F.O. Flag officer; Flying officer; Foreign Office
F.O. or **f.o.** firm offer; free overside (cf. f.a.s.); fuel oil; full organ (Music)
F.O., f.o. or **F. Offr.** Field officer
F/o, f.o. or **f/o** for orders
f°, F., f., fo., fol. or **in-f°** (in-folio)(Fr.) folio (cf. ff.; ll.)
fo., F., f., f°, fol. or **in-f°** (in-folio)(Fr.) folio (cf. ff.; ll.)
f. ö. (för övrigt)(Swed.) besides
f.o., FO (Mil.) or **F.O.** Field orders
f.o. or **F.O.** firm offer; free overside (cf. f.a.; f.a.s.); fuel oil; full organ (Music)
f.o., F.O. or **F.Offr.** Field officer
f.o., F/o or **f/o** for orders

f.o. or **f/o** full out terms
f/o or **f.o.** full out terms
f/o, f.o. or **F/o** for orders
F.O.B., F.o.b. or **f.o.b.** free on board
f.o.b., F.O.B. or **F.o.b.** free on board
F.O.C. or **f.o.c.** free of charge; free on car
f.o.c. or **F.O.C.** free of charge; free on car
FOCB or **F.O.C.B.** Federal Oil Conservation Board
F.O.D. or **f.o.d.** free of damage
f.o.d. or **F.O.D.** free of damage
F.O.E. Fraternal Order of Eagles
F. of A. Foresters of America (cf. A.O.F.; I.O.F.)
F. Offr., F.O. or **f.o.** Field officer
Fol. (Folia)(Ital., Lat.), **hh.** (hojas)(Span.), **L., l., LL. or ll.** leaves (cf. ff.; f°)
fol., F., f., ff., foll., seq., seqq., sq., sqq. (sequens, sequentes, sequentia)(Lat.) or **subseq.** (subsequens)(Lat.) the following (cf. et seq.)
fol., F., f., fo., f° or **in-f°** (in-folio)(Fr.) folio (cf. ff.; ll.)
foll., F., f., ff., fol., seq., seqq., sq., sqq. (sequens, sequentes, sequentia)(Lat.) or **subseq.** (subsequens)(Lat.) the following (cf. et seq.)
foll. or **ff.** folios (cf. fo.; ll.)
fo. max. (folium maximum)(Lat.) great folio
F.O.Q. or **f.o.q.** free on quay (Shipping) (cf. f.a.q.)
F.O.R. Fellowship of Reconciliation
F.O.R., F.o.r. or **f.o.r.** free on rail; free on road
For. Forester
For. or **for.** forestry
F.o.r., F.O.R. or **f.o.r.** free on rail; free on road
for. foreign
f.o.r., F.O.R. or **F.o.r.** free on rail; free on road
for'd. or **fwd.** forward
Forf Forfeit (Mil.)
Forf. (Forfatter)(Dan.), **A.** (autor)(Span.), **aut.** (auteur)(Fr.), (autore)(Ital.), **Au., auth., förf.** (författare, författarinna)(Swed.) or **Verf.** (Verfasser) (Ger.) author
förf. (författare, författarinna)(Swed.), **A., Au., aut.** (auteur)(Fr.), (autor)(Span.), (autore)(Ital.), **auth., Forf.** (Forfatter) (Dan.) or **Verf.** (Verfasser)(Ger.) author
Forg. or **forg.** forgery
forg. forge; forged; forging
For. Min. Minister for Foreign Affairs
formn. foreman
formn. or **fmn.** formation
fo.ro., f.r. (folio recto)(Lat.), **R., r., Ro.,** or **ro.** (recto)(Lat.) right-hand page
fort. or **ft.** fortification; fortified
f.o.r.t. full out rye terms (Grain)
forwn. forewoman
F.O.S. or **f.o.s.** free on station; free on steamer
f.o.s. or **F.O.S.** free on station; free on steamer
F.O.T. or **f.o.t.** free on truck
f.o.t. or **F.O.T.** free on truck
found., fdn. or **fndn.** foundation
found. or **fndd.** founded
4 max great quarto
4°, 4to., 4to, Q., q., Q° or **qto.** quarto
4-P four-pole (Elec.)
f.o.w or **F.O.W.** first open water (Shipping)
F.P. or **f.p.** fire plug; fire policy; floating policy (Insurance); **(forte piano) (Ital.)** loud and then soft (Music)
F.p., f.p., f.pd. or **fy.pd.** fully paid
fp., Fcap., fcap. or **fcp.** foolscap
fp., F.P., f.p., Ft. lb. or **ft-lb** foot-pound or pounds
fp. or **f.p.** freezing point
f.p. fine paper; forward perpendicular (Shipbuilding)
f.p. or **F.P.** fire plug; fire policy; floating policy (Insurance); **(forte piano) (Ital.)** loud and then soft **(Music)**
f.p., F.p., f.pd. or **fy.pd.** fully paid
f.p. or **fp** freezing point
FPA or **F.P.A.** Food Production Administration
F.P.A. Foreign Press Association [in London]
F.P.A. or **f.p.a.** free of particular average
f.p.a. or **F.P.A.** free of particular average
F.P.A.A.C. or **f.p.a.A.c.** free of particular average, American conditions
F.P.A.E.C. or **f.p.a.E.c.** free of particular average, English conditions
FPC or **F.P.C.** Federal Power Commission
f.pd., F.p., f.p. or **fy.pd.** fully paid
FPEA or **F.P.E.A.** Federal Postal Employees Association
FPHA or **F.P.H.A.** Federal Public Housing Administration or Authority
F.Ph.S., F.Phys.S., F.P.S. or **F.P.S.L.** Fellow of the Physical Society, London
F.Phys.S., F.Ph.S., F.P.S. or **F.P.S.L.** Fellow of the Physical Society, London
F.P.I. Inc. Federal Prisons Industries, Incorporated
f. pil. or **Ft. pil.** **(fiat pilula)(Lat.)** let a pill be made (Pharm.)
f.p.i.l. full premium if [vessel] lost (Insurance)
FPL or **F.P.L.** Forest Products Laboratory
F.Pl. face plate
fpm or **f.p.m.** foot (feet) per minute
f.p.m. or **fpm** foot (feet) per minute
F.P.O. or **Fd P.O.** Field Post Office
F.P.S. Fellow of the Pathological Society [of Great Britain and Ireland]; Fellow of the Philharmonic Society; Fellow of the Philological Society (Brit.); Fellow of the Philosophical Society
F.P.S., F.Ph.S., F.Phys.S. or **F.P.S.L.** Fellow of the Physical Society, London
F.P.S., fps, f.p.s. or **f-p-s** feet-per-second system
fps, F.P.S. or **f.p.s.** foot-pound-second

fps, F.P.S., f.p.s. or **f-p-s** feet-per-second system
fps, f.p.s. or **ft/s** feet per second
f.p.s., F.P.S., fps, or **f-p-s** feet-per-second system
f.p.s., fps or **ft/s** feet per second
f-p-s, fps, F.P.S. or **f.p.s** feet-per-second system
fpse foot-pound-second electrostatic [system]
F.P.S.L., F.Ph.S., F. Phys.S. or **F.P.S.** Fellow of the Physical Society, London
F. P. V. P. C. Federation of Paint and Varnish Production Clubs
FR Flash ranging (Mil.)
F.R. Forest Reserve (Australia); (Forum Romanum)(Lat.) Roman forum; freight release
F/R Fighter reconnaissance
Fr. Friar
Fr. (Frater)(Lat.), **B., b., Br., br.** or **bro.** brother (cf. FF.)
Fr. (Frau)(Ger.), **con.** (conjunx)(Lat.), **ux.** (uxor)(Lat.) or **w.** wife (cf. Mrs.)
Fr. or **F.** France; French
Fr., F., f., P. or **p.** (padre)(Span.),(pater)(Lat.),(père)(Fr.) father
Fr., F. or **Fri.** Friday
Fr. or **Fs.** Francis (cf. Fcs.)
fr. fragment; fragments
fr., F., f. or **fc.** franc
fr., fco. (franco)(Ital.), (franko)(Ger.), **P.P., p.p.** or **ppd.** postpaid
fr., fm., frm. or **v.** (van)(Dutch), (von)(Ger.) from (cf. er)
fr. or **freq.** frequent
f.r., fo.ro. (folio recto)(Lat.), **R., r., Ro.,** or **ro.** (recto)(Lat.) right-hand page
FRA or **F.R.A.** Federal Re-employment Administration
F.R.A. Fellow of the Royal Academy of Arts, London
F.R.A.C.P. Fellow of the Royal Australasian College of Physicians
F.R.A.C.S. Fellow of the Royal Australasian College of Surgeons
F.R.Ae.S. Fellow of the Royal Aeronautical Society (London)
F.R.A.H.S. Fellow of the Royal Australian Historical Society
F.R.A.I. Fellow of the Royal Anthropological Institute of Great Britain and Ireland (cf. F.A.S.L.; F.E.S.)
F.R.A.M. Fellow of the Royal Academy of Music
Fr. Am. French American
f.r.& c.c. free of riots and civil commotions (Insurance)
F.R.A.S. Fellow of the Royal Asiatic Society [of Great Britain and Ireland]; Fellow of the Royal Astronomical Society
F.R.A.S.B. Fellow of the Royal Asiatic Society of Bengal (cf. F.A.S.B.)
F.R.Assn. Fleet Reserve Association
F.R.Assn.Aux. Fleet Reserve Association Auxiliary
Frat. or **frat.** fraternity
frat. or **Frat.** fraternity
FRB, Fed.Res.Bd., F.R.B. or **F.R.Bd.** Federal Reserve Board
FRB, Fed.Res.Bk., F.R.B. or **F.R.Bk.** Federal Reserve Bank
F.R.B., Fed.Res.Bd., FRB or **F.R.Bd.** Federal Reserve Board
F.R.B., Fed.Res.Bk., FRB or **F.R.Bk.** Federal Reserve Bank
F.R.Bd., Fed.Res.Bd., FRB or **F.R.B.** Federal Reserve Board
F.R.Bk., Fed.Res.Bk., FRB or **F.R.B.** Federal Reserve Bank
F.R.B.S. Fellow of the Royal Botanic Society [of London]; Fellow of the Royal [Society of] British Sculptors
FRC or **F.R.C.** Federal Radio Commission; Federal Relief Commission
Fr. Can. French Canadian
F.R.C.I. Fellow of the Royal Colonial Institute (now Royal Empire Society)
F.R.C.M. Fellow of the Royal College of Music
F.R.C.O. Fellow of the Royal College of Organists (cf. F.C.O.)
F.R.C.O.G. Fellow of the Royal College of Obstetricians and Gynaecologists
F.R.C.P. or **F.R.C.P.L.** Fellow of the Royal College of Physicians, London
F.R.C.P.E. or **F.R.C.P.Ed.** Fellow of the Royal College of Physicians of Edinburgh
F.R.C.P.I. Fellow of the Royal College of Physicians of Ireland
F.R.C.P.L. or **F.R.C.P.** Fellow of the Royal College of Physicians, London
F.R.C.S. or **F.R.C.S.L.** Fellow of the Royal College of Surgeons, London
F.R.C.Sc. Fellow of the Royal College of Science (London)
F.R.C.S.E. or **F.R.C.S.Ed.** Fellow of the Royal College of Surgeons of Edinburgh
F.R.C.S.I. Fellow of the Royal College of Surgeons of Ireland
F.R.C.S.L. or **F.R.C.S.** Fellow of the Royal College of Surgeons, London
Fr. Cu. fracto-cumulus (Meteorol.)
F.R.C.V.S. Fellow of the Royal College of Veterinary Surgeons
F.R.Dist. Federal Reserve District
Fr.E., E.F., E.Fr. or **F.E.** French ells
FREB or **F.R.E.B.** Federal Real Estate Board
FREC or **F.R.E.C.** Federal Radio Education Committee
F.R.Ec.S., F.R.Econ.S., F.R.Econ.Soc. or **F.R.E.S** Fellow of the Royal Economic Society, London
Fred. Frederic; Frederick
Freem. Freemasonry
F Remt Dep or **F Rmt Dep** Field remount depot
freq. or **fr.** frequent; frequently
freq. or **frequent.** frequentative
freq. m. frequency meter
F.R.E.S. Fellow of the Royal Empire Society, London (cf. F.R.C.I.); Fellow of the Royal Entomological Society; Fellow of the Royal Ethnological Society

F.R.E.S., F.R.Econ. S., F.R.Econ. Soc. or **F.R.Ec. S.** Fellow of the Royal Economic Society (London)

F.R.F.P.S. Fellow of the Royal Faculty of Physicians and Surgeons

F.R.F.P.S.G. Fellow of the Royal Faculty of Physicians and Surgeons of Glasgow

F.R.G.S. Fellow of the Royal Geographical Society (London)

frgt., fgt. or **frt.** freight

F.R.Hist.S., F.R.Hist.Soc. or **F.R.H.S.** Fellow of the Royal Historical Society (London)

F.R.Hort.S., F.R.Hort.Soc. or **F.R.H.S.** Fellow of the Royal Horticultural Society (London)

Frhr. (Freiherr)(Ger.), **B., b.** or **Bn.** Baron

Frhrn. (Freiherrin)(Ger.) or **Bnss.** Baroness

F.R.H.S., F.R.Hist.S. or **F.R.Hist.Soc.** Fellow of the Royal Historical Society (London)

F.R.H.S., F.R.Hort.S. or **F.R.Hort.Soc.** Fellow of the Royal Horticultural Society

F.R.I. Fellow of the Royal Institution; Food Research Institute

Fri., F. or **Fr.** Friday

F.R.I.A. Fellow of the Royal Irish Academy

F.R.I.B.A. Fellow of the Royal Institute of British Architects

Fries. or **Frs.** Friesic

Fris. Frisia

Fris. or **Frs.** Frisian

Frk. (Frøken)(Dan.), **frk.** (fröken)(Swed.), **Frl.** (Fraulein)(Ger.), **Mdlle, Mlle.** (Mademoiselle)(Fr.), **Snrta., Srta.** (senhorita)(Port.), **Srita., Srta.** or **Sta.** (Señorita)(Span.) Miss; unmarried woman or girl

Frl. (Fraulein)(Ger.), **Frk.** (Frøken)(Dan.), **frk.** (fröken)(Swed.), **Mdlle., Mlle.** (Mademoiselle)(Fr.), **Snrta., Srta.** (senhorita)(Port.), **Srita., Srta.** or **Sta.** (Señorita)(Span.) Miss; unmarried woman or girl

frl. fractional

frm., fm., fr. or **v.** (van)(Dutch), (von)(Ger.) from (cf. ex)

F.R.Met. Soc. Fellow of the Royal Meteorological Society (London)

F.R.M.S. Fellow of the Royal Microscopical Society (London)

F Rmt Dep or **F Remt Dep** Field remount depot

Fr. Nb. fracto-nimbus (Meteorol.)

F.R.N.S. Fellow of the Royal Numismatic Society (London)

F.R.N.S.A. Fellow of the Royal Navy School of Architects (cf. F.R.S.N.A.)

front. frontispiece

F.R.P.S. Fellow of the Royal Photographic Society [of Great Britain]

F.R.P.S.L. Fellow of the Royal Philatelic Society, London

FRR, F.R.R., OFRR, O.F.R.R., OFRRO or **O.F.R.R.O.** [Office of] Foreign Relief and Rehabilitation [Operations] (cf. UNRRA)

FRS or **F.R.S.** Federal Reserve System

F.R.S., R.S.S. (Regiae Societatis Sodalis) (Lat.) or **S.R.S.** (Societatis Regiae Socius)(Lat.) Fellow of the Royal Society [of London]

Frs. or **Fries.** Friesic

Frs. or **Fris.** Frisian

frs., F., f. or **fcs.** francs

F.R.S.A. Fellow of the Royal Society of Arts (London)(cf. F.S.A.)

F.R.S.A. or **A.R.S.S.** (Antiquariorum Regiae Societatis Socius)(Lat.) Fellow of the Royal Society of Antiquaries

F.R.S.A.I. or **F.R.S.A. Irel.** Fellow of the Royal Society of Antiquaries of Ireland

F.R.San.I. or **F.R.S.I.** Fellow of the Royal Sanitary Institute (London)(cf. F.S.I.)

F.R.S.C. Fellow of the Royal Society of Canada

F.R.S.E. Fellow of the Royal Society of Edinburgh

F.R.S.G.S. Fellow of the Royal Scottish Geographical Society

F.R.S.I. or **F.R.San.I.** Fellow of the Royal Sanitary Institute (London) (cf. F.S.I.)

F.R.S.L. Fellow of the Royal Society of Literature [of the United Kingdom]

F.R.S.M. Fellow of the Royal Society of Medicine (London)

F.R.S.N.A. Fellow of the Royal School of Naval Architecture (cf. F.R.N.S.A.)

F.R.S.N.Z. Fellow of the Royal Society of New Zealand

F.R.S.S. Fellow of the Royal Statistical Society (London)(cf. F.S.S.)

F.R.S.S.A. Fellow of the Royal Scottish Society of Arts; Fellow of the Royal Society of South Africa

F.R.S.S.I. Fellow of the Royal Statistical Society of Ireland

F.R.S.S.S. Fellow of the Royal Statistical Society of Scotland

Fr. St. fracto-stratus (Meteorol.)

frt., fgt. or **frgt.** freight

F.R.U.I. Fellow of the Royal University of Ireland

frust. (frustillatim)(Lat.) in small pieces (Pharm.)

F.R.V.A. Fellow [of the Royal Society of the Incorporated Association] of Rating and Valuation Officers

F.R.V.I.A. Fellow of the Royal Victorian Institute of Architects (Melbourne)

FS Film strip (Mil.); Fog siren (Mil.)

F.S. factor of safety; Federal Specifications; Field Security; Field Service (Mil.); Fleet surgeon; Forest Service

F.S. or **Fin. Sec.** Financial Secretary

F.S., Flt Sgt or **F.Sgt.** Flight sergeant

F.S., fs., f.s. or **ft-sec** foot-second or seconds

Fs. or **Fr.** Francis (cf. Fcs.)

fs., fac., facs. or **facsim.** facsimile; facsimiles

fs., F.S., f.s. or **ft-sec** foot-second or seconds

f.s. (faire suivre)(Fr.) to be forwarded

f.s., F.S., fs. or **ft-sec** foot-second or seconds

FSA or **F.S.A.** Farm Security Administration; Federal Security Agency

F.S.A. Fellow of the Society of Antiquaries [of London]

F.S.A. or **F.A.S.** Fellow of the Society of Arts (London) (now Royal Society of Arts)

F.s.a. (fiat secundum artem)(Lat.) let it be made skillfully

F.S.A.A. Fellow of the Society of [Incorporated] Accountants and Auditors (Brit.)

F.S.A.E. Fellow of the Society of Antiquaries, Edinburgh (cf. F.A.S.E.; F.S.A.S.)

F.S.A.I. Fellow of the Society of Antiquaries of Ireland

F.S.Arch. Fellow of the Society of Architects (Brit.)

F.S.A.S. or **F.S.A. Scot.** Fellow of the Society of Antiquaries of Scotland (cf. F.A.S.E.; F.S.A.E.)

F.S.A. Scot. or **F.S.A.S.** Fellow of the Society of Antiquaries of Scotland (cf. F.A.S.E.; F.S.A.E.)

F.S.B.C. Foreign Service Buildings Commission

F.S.C. (Institutum Fratrum Scholarum Christianarum)(Lat.) Brothers of the Christian Schools; Christian Brothers; De La Salle Brothers

F.S.C. or **S.F.S.C.** (Societas Fratrum Sacri Cordis)(Lat.) Society of Brothers of the Sacred Heart; Brothers of the Sacred Heart

FSCC or **F.S.C.C.** Federal Surplus Commodities Corporation

F.S.C.J. Congregation of the Sons of the Sacred Heart of Jesus

F.S.E. Fellow of the Society of Engineers (Brit.)

F.S.G.T. Fellow of the Society of Glass Technology (Brit.)

F.Sgt., Flt Sgt or **F.S.** Flight sergeant

F.S.H. follicle stimulating hormone

FSHC or **F.S.H.C.** Federal Subsistence Homestead Corporation

F.S.I. Fellow of the Sanitary Institute [of Great Britain] (now Royal Sanitary Institute); Fellow of the Surveyors' Institution (Brit.)(now Chartered Surveyors' Institution); Free Sons of Israel

FSLA or **F.S.L.A.** Federal Savings and Loan Association

FSLIC or **F.S.L.I.C.** Federal Savings and Loan Insurance Corporation

F.S.M.B.U.S. Federation of State Medical Boards of the United States

F.S.O. Field security officer; Fleet signals officer

F.S.O.T.R. Foreign Service Officers' Training School

F.Sp. Flash spotting

FSR or **F.S.R.** Field Service Regulations

FSRC or **F.S.R.C.** Federal Surplus Relief Corporation

F.S.S. Fellow of the Statistical Society [of London] (now Royal Statistical Society)

F.S.Sc.A. Fellow of the Society of Science and Art

F.S.S.I. Fellow of the Statistical Society of Ireland

FT Fog trumpet (Mil.)

Ft., F., f. or **ft.** (fiat, fiant)(Lat.) let there be done, or made

Ft., f. or **ft.** fort

ft. faint

ft., F. or **f.** feet; flat (Theat.); foot

ft., F., f. or **Ft.** (fiat, fiant)(Lat.) let there be made, or done

ft., f. or **Ft.** fort

ft. or **fort.** fortification; fortified

ft.^{2} or **sq.ft.** square foot or feet

ft.^{3}, **c.ft., cub.ft.** or **cu.ft.** cubic foot or feet

f.t. full terms; fume-tight

F.T.B. Fleet torpedo bomber

ft.b.m., fbm or **f.b.m.** feet board measure (cf. bd. ft.)

FTC or **F.T.C.** Federal Trade Commission

ft-c foot-candle

F.T.C.D. Fellow of Trinity College, Dublin

F.T.C.L. Fellow of Trinity College [of Music], London

F.T.D. Florists' Telegraph Delivery

fth., F., f., fath., fm. or **fthm.** fathom; fathoms

ft. haust., F.h. or **f.h.** (fiat haustus)(Lat.) let a draft be made (Pharm.)

fthm., F., f., fath., fm. or **fth.** fathom; fathoms

F.T.I. Fellow of the Textile Institute (Brit.)

ft-L foot-lambert

Ft. lb., ft-lb, fp., F.P., or **f.p.** foot-pound or pounds

Ft. mas. div. in pil. (fiat massa dividenda in pilulae)(Lat.) let a mass be made and divided into pills

ft.mist., F.M., f.m. (fiat misture)(Lat.), **M.ft.** or **m.ft.** (mistura fiat)(Lat.) make a mixture

F Tn Field train

ftnt., Anm. (Anmerkung)(Ger.) or **f.n.** footnote (cf. annot.; schol.)

ftnts., Anm. (Anmerkungen)(Ger.), **f.n.** or **ftnt.** footnotes (cf. annot.; schol.)

F.T.O. Fleet torpedo officer

Ft.pil. or **f.pil.** (fiat pilula)(Lat.) let a pill be made

Ft. pulv. (fiat pulvis)(Lat.) let a powder be made

ftr. fitter

ft/s, fps or **f.p.s.** foot (feet) per second

ft-sec, F.S., fs. or **f.s.** foot-second or seconds

ft-tn foot-ton; foot-tons

F.T.W. free trade wharf

FTZB or **F.T.Z.B.** Foreign Trade Zones Board

F.up or **f.up** follow up

fu-p., fnp or **fn.p.** fusion point

f.up or **F.up** follow up

fur., F. or **f.** furlong; furlongs

fur. or **furn.** furnish; furnished; furniture

fur., furr. or **fur**[r] further
furn. or **fur.** furnish; furnished; furniture
furn. or **furng.** furnishing
furng. or **furn.** furnishing
furr, fur. or **fur**[r] further
fus. fusilier; fusiliers
F.u.S.f. (Fortsetzung und Schluss folgen) (Ger.) to be continued and concluded
fut. future; futures (Exchange)
f.v. (folio verso)(Lat.) on the back of the page (cf. vo.)
F. vs. (fiat venaesectio)(Lat.) let the patient be bled
FW fog whistle
F.W. Focke-Wulf (Airplane)
f.w. fresh water
FWA or **F.W.A.** Federal Works Agency
F.W.B. four-wheel brake; Free Will Baptist (cf F.B.)
F.W.D. four-wheel drive
fwd. or **for'd.** forward
f.w.d. fresh water damage (Insurance)
fwdd. forwarded
Fwd Ech Forward echelon
F.W.O. Fleet wireless officer
FWS or **F. & W.L.S.** Fish and Wild Life Service
FX, F.X., Fx., fx or **f.x.** foreign exchange
Fx, FX, F.X., fx or **f.x.** foreign exchange
f.x., FX, F.X., Fx or **fx** foreign exchange
fxle. forecastle
fy.pd., F.p., f.p. or **f.pd.** fully paid
Fz. Franz
fz. (forzando)(Ital.), **sf., sforz.** or **sfz.** (sforzando, sforzato)(Ital.) accented; with emphasis (Music)
F.Z.A. Fellow of the Zoological Academy
F.Z.S. or **F.Z.S.L.** Fellow of the Zoological Society, London
F.Z.S.L. or **F.Z.S.** Fellow of the Zoological Society, London
F.Z.S. Scot. Fellow of the Zoological Society of Scotland

G

G Gravel (Mil.)
G., allg. (allegemein)(Ger.), **g., gen.** or **genl.** general; generally
G., Au (Chem.), **Au, au., aur.** (aurum) (Lat.) or **g.** gold
G., Cond. or **g.** conductance (Elec.)
G., g, g. or **gr.** gravity
G. or **g.** gauge; gelding; gingival; guide; gulf
G., g. or **gd.** good
G., g., gen. or **genit.** genitive
G., g., gm., gr. or **grm.** gram; grams
G., g. or **Gn** (Mil.) gun
G., g., gn., gns., gs. or **gu.** guineas
G., g., gn. or **grn.** green
G., g., gn. or **gu.** guinea
G., g. or **gr.** grain; grand
G., g., gr. or **grs.** grains
G., Gen (Mil.), **Gen.** or **Genl.** General (Army)
G., Ger. or **Germ.** German; Germany
G., Goth. or **goth.** Gothic (cf. G.L.)
G., S.G., s.g. or **sp.gr.** [specific] gravity
g [acceleration of] gravity; general intelligence (Psychology); gilbert (Elec.)
g, G., g. or **gr.** gravity
g. gloomy (Naut.); (geheim)(Ger.) secret
g., allg. (allegemein)(Ger.), **G., gen.** or **genl.** general; generally
g., Au (Chem), **Au., au., aur.** (aurum)(Lat.) or **G.** gold
g., Cond. or **G.** conductance (Elec.)
g., G., g or **gr.** gravity
g., G. or **gd.** good
g., G., gen. or **genit.** genitive
g., G., gm., gr. or **grm.** gram; grams
g., G. or **Gn** (Mil.) gun
g., G., gn., gns., gu. or **gs.** guineas
g., G., gn. or **grn.** green
g., G., gn. or **gu.** guinea
g., G. or **gr.** grain; grand
g., G., gr. or **grs.** grains
g. or **gen.** gender
g. (gauche)(Fr.), **l.** or **s.** (sinistra)(Ital., Lat.) left (cf. M.G.; S.M.; O.S.)
G-1 or **AC of S, G-1** Assistant chief of staff for personnel (cf. A-1; S-1)
G-1, G-2, G-3, G-4 First [personnel], Second [military intelligence), Third [operations and training], Fourth [supply] Section of the General Staff
G-2 or **AC of S, G-2** Assistant chief of staff for military intelligence (cf. A-2; S-2)
G-3 or **AC of S, G-3** Assistant chief of staff for operations and training (cf. A-3; S-3)
G-4 or **AC of S, G-4** Assistant chief of staff for supply (cf. A-4; S-4)
G.A. General Agent; General Assembly; General Assignment; gingivoaxial; (Groupe d'armées)(Fr.) Group of armies
G.A., G/A or **g.a.** general average (Insurance)
G/A, G.A. or **g.a.** general average (Insurance)
Ga gallium (Chem.)
Ga. Gallic
Ga. or **Geo.** Georgia
g.a., G.A. or **G/A** general average (Insurance)
G.A.C. (Groupe d'armées du centre)(Fr.) Central Army Group
G/A con. general average contribution (Insurance)
G/A dep. general average deposit (Insurance)
Gael. Gaelic
G.A.F. German Air Force
G.A.H.S. German American Historical Society
Gal. Galatians; Galen
gal. galley
gal., C., c. or **cong.** (congius)(Lat.) or **gall.** gallon

gal., gall. or **gals.** gallons
gall., C., c., cong. (congius(Lat.) or **gal.** gallon
gall., gal. or **gals.** gallons
gals., gal. or **gall.** gallons
galv. galvanic; galvanism; galvanized
Gam. Gamaliel
gam. gamut
GAO or **G.A.O.** General Accounting Office
G.A.R. Grand Army of the Republic
Gar Garage (Mil.)
G. Arch. Graduate in Architecture
garg. or **gargar.** (gargarisma)(Lat.) gargle (Pharm.)
gargar. or **garg.** (gargarisma)(Lat.) gargle (Pharm.)
gas ftr. gas fitter
G.A.S.G.A.S.G.A.S. Gild of Ancient Suppliers of Gas Appliances, Skill, Gins, Accessories and Substances
Gas NCO Gas noncommissioned officer
Gas O Gas officer
G.A.T. Greenwich apparent time
Gaul. Gaulish
gaz. gazette; gazetted; gazetteer
G.B. Gunboat
G.B., Gr. Br., Gr. Brit., Gt. Br. or **Gt. Brit.** Great Britain
g.b. or **G.b.** gold bonds
G.B. & I. or **G.B. and I.** Great Britain and Ireland
G. B. and I. or **G.B.& I.** Great Britain and Ireland
G.B.A.R.C. Great Britain Aeronautical Research Committee
G.B.E. [Knight, Dame] Grand [Cross, Order] of the British Empire
Gbr., Geb. (Gebrüder)(Ger.), **Bros., bros., FF.** (fratres)(Lat.), (Frères)(Fr.) or **Hnos.** (Hermanos)(Span.) brothers
G.B.S. George Bernard Shaw
G.C. general circular; General Consular; George Cross (Brit.); Grand Chancellor (Freemasonry); Grand Chaplain (Freemasonry); Grand Chapter (Freemasonry); Grand Conductor (Freemasonry); Grand Council (Freemasonry); Grand Cross; Gun control
G.C., G.Capt., Gp C or **Gp Capt** Group captain
G.C. or **G. Com.** Grand Commander (Freemasonry); Grand commandery
G.C.A. General Claim Agent
g-cal, g-cal. or **g.-cal.** gram calorie or calories
G.Capt., G.C., Gp C or **Gp Capt.** Group captain
G.C.A.U.S. & M. General Claims Arbitration, United States and Mexico
G.C.B. or **K.G.C.B.** [Knight] Grand Cross [of the Order] of the Bath
G.C.C. Gonville and Caius College (Cambridge)
G.C.D., gcd or g.c.d. greatest common divisor (cf. G.C.F.)
gcd, G.C.D. or **g.c.d.** greatest common divisor (cf. G.C.F.)
G.C.F., gcf, g.c.f., H.C.F., hcf or **h.c.f.** greatest or highest common factor. (cf. G.C.D.)
gcf, G.C.F., g.c.f., H.C.F., hcf or **h.c.f.** greatest of highest common factor (cf. G.C.D.
G.C.G. Grand Captain General; Grand Captain Guard
G.C.H. [Knight] Grand Cross of Hanover
G. ch., g. ch. (gothici characteres)(Lat.), **G.L.** or **g.l.** Gothic or black letters (cf. bf)
G.C.I.E. [Knight] Grand Commander [of the Order] of the Indian Empire
G.C.L.H. [Knight] Grand Cross of the Legion of Honor
G.C.M., gcm or g.c.m. greatest common measure
G.C.M. or **g.c.m.** general court-martial
gcm, G.C.M. or **g.c.m.** greatest common measure
G.C.M.G. [Knight of the] Grand Cross [of the Order] of St. Michael and St. George
GCMO (Mil.) or **G.C.M.O.** General Court-Martial Orders
G.Com. or **G.C.** Grand Commander (Freemasonry); Grand commandery
G. Cp. Graduate in Chiropody
G.C.S. Game Conservation Society
G.C.S.G. [Knight] Grand Cross of St. Gregory the Great
G.C.S.I. [Knight] Grand Commander [of the Order] of the Star of India
G.C.S.S. [Knight] Grand Cross of St. Silvester
G.C.T. Greenwich civil time
G.C.V.O. [Knight] Grand Cross[of Royal] Victorian Order
G.D. Graduate in Divinity; Grand Duchy
G.D., g.d., Grdau. or **grdau.** granddaughter
G.D. or **Gr. D.** Grand Duchess or Duke
Gd gadolinium (Chem.)
Gd (Mil.) or **gd.** guard
gd., G. or **g.** good
gd. or **Gd** (Mil.) guard
g.d. good delivery; gravimetric density
g.d., G.D., Grdau. or **grdau.** granddaughter
G.D.C. Government Defense Council
gdn. garden
gdns. gardens
gds. goods; guards
gdsm. guardsman
G.E. or **G.E.C.** General Electric Company
Ge germanium (Chem.)
g.e. gilt edges (Bookbinding)
G.E.B. General Education Board (Rockefeller Foundation)
Geb., Gbr. (Gebrüder)(Ger.), **Bros., bros., FF.** (fratres)(Lat.), (Frères)(Fr.) or **Hnos.** (Hermanos)(Span.) brothers
geb. (geboren)(Ger.), **B., b., f.** (född)(Swed.), (født)(Dan.) or **n.** (natus)(Lat.) born
G.E.C. or **G.E.** General Electic Company
gel. gelatinous

Gel. quav. (gelatina quavis)(Lat.) in any kind of jelly (Pharm.)
Gen (Mil.), **Gen.**, **G.** or **Genl.** General (Army)
Gen. Geneva; Genevan
Gen. or **Gn.** Genesis
gen. genera; generation; generator; generic; genus
gen., **allg.** (allgemein)(Ger.), **G.**, **g.** or **genl.** general; generally
gen., **G.**, **g.** or **genit.** genitive
gen. or **g.** gender
Geneal. or **geneal.** genealogy
geneal. genealogical
Gen Hosp (Mil.), **Gen. Hosp.** or **GH** (Mil.) General hospital
genit., **G.**, **g.** or **gen.** genitive
Genl., **G.**, **Gen** (Mil.) or **Gen.** General (Army)
genl., **allg.** (allgemein)(Ger.), **G.**, **g.** or **gen.** general; generally
Gen. Led. general ledger
genn. (gennaio)(Ital.), **eno.** (enero)(Span.), **Ja.**, **Jan.**, **janv.** (janvier)(Fr.) or **Stycz.** (Styczeń)(Pol.) January
Gen Serv (Mil.), **Gen. Serv.**, **G.S.** or **g.s.** General service
Gen Serv-Res General Service Reserve
gen. sig. general signification
Gent. or **gent.** gentleman; gentlemen (cf. Messrs.)
Geo. George
Geo. or **Ga.** Georgia
Geod. or **geod.** geodesy; geodetic
Geod. E. Geodetic Engineer
Geof. Geoffrey
Geog. or **geog.** geography
geog. geographer; geographic; geographical
Geol. or **geol.** geology
geol. geologic; geological; geologist
geol. or **Geol.** geology
Geol. E. Geologic Engineer
Geol. Surv. or **G.S.** Geological Survey
Geom. or **geom.** geometry
geom. geometer; geometric; geometrical
geom. or **Geom.** geometry
Ger., **G.** or **Germ.** German; Germany
Ger. or **Gmc.** Germanic
ger. gerund
Ger. E. Afr. German East Africa
Germ., **G.** or **Ger.** German; Germany
Gert. Gertrude
Ges. (Gesellschaft)(Ger.), **ass.**, **assn.**, **assoc.** or **assocn.** association (cf. Co., soc.; Ver.)
Ges. (Gesellschaft)(Ger.), **Cía.** (compañía)(Span.), **Cie**, **cie** (compagnie)(Fr.), **Co.**, **co.**, **comp.**, **Comp**[a], **compa.**, **Compy.**, **compy.**, **Coy.** or **coy.** company (cf. a.g.;g.m.b.H.)
Ges. (Gesellschaft)(Ger.), **S.**, **S.**, **Soc.**, **soc.**, **Socy.**, **socy.** or **Ver.** (Verein)(Ger.) society (cf. assn.)
Gesch. (Geschichte)(Ger.), **Hist.** or **hist.** history
gest. (gestorben)(Ger.), **D.**, **d.**, **des.**, **déc.** (décédé, décédée)(Fr.), **decd.** or **ś.p.** (świętej pamięci)(Pol.) deceased (cf. B.M.; L.; ob.; Q.E.P.D.; R.I.P.; sel.)
Gew. (Gewicht)(Ger.), **p.** (peso)(Span.), **W.**, **w.** or **wt.** weight
G.F. Grand Fleet; Grazing Farm (Queensland)
GFA or **G.F.A.** Grain Futures Administration
G.F.A. general freight agent
G.F.S. Girls' Friendly Society
G.F.T.U. General Federation of Trade Unions (Brit.)
G.G., **G.Gds.**, **Gren. Gds.** or **Gr. Gds.** Grenadier Guards
G.Gds., **G.G.**, **Gren. Gds.** or **Gr. Gds.** Grenadier Guards
g.gr., **Gr.Gro.** or **gr.gro.** great gross
GH, **Gen Hosp** (Mil.) or **Gen. Hosp.** General hospital
G.H. Grazing Homestead (Queensland); (Génie Hydrographique)(Fr.) Hydrographic Engineer
G.h. or **g.h.** gilt head
g.h. or **G.h.** gilt head
G.H.A. Georgia Hospital Association; Group Health Association
GHQ G.H.Q. or **G.Q.G.** (Grand quartier général)(Fr.) General Headquarters (cf. H.Q.)
GHQ AF General Headquarters, Air Force
GI or **G.I.** government issue
G.I. Government of India
gi. or **gl.** gill; gills
Gib. Gibraltar
Gilb. Gilbert
G. in N. Graduate in Nursing (cf. G.N.)
gir. or **gir** (Mil.) girder
G.J.C. Grand Junction Canal (Brit.)
Gk. or **Gr.** Greek
G.L. Graduate in Law; Grand Lodge (Freemasonry)
G.L., **g.l.**, **G. ch.** or **g. ch.** (gothici characteres)(Lat.) Gothic or black letters (cf. bf)
Gl glucinum; glucinium (Chem.)
gl. glass; glory; gloss
gl. or **gi.** gill; gills
gl. or **gloss.** glossary
gl. (gammel)(Dan.), **O.** or **o.** old (cf. aet.; anc.)
g.l., **G.ch.**, **g.ch.** (gothici characteres)(Lat.) or **G.L.** gothic letters; black letters (cf. bf)
G.L.A. gingivolinguoaxial
Glam. Glamorganshire
gld. guilder
Glos. or **Gloucs.** Gloucestershire
gloss. or **gl.** glossary
Glo'ster. Gloucester
Gloucs. or **Glos.** Gloucestershire
glt. or **gt.** gilt
GM gristmill (Mil.)

G.M. general manager; General Motors; George Medal (Brit.); Gold Medal; Grand Master (Freemasonry); Grand Medallist (Brit.); Gunner's mate
G.M. or **g.m.** general mortgage
gm., G., g., gr. or **grm.** gram; grams
g.m. general merchandise
g.m. or **G.M.** general mortgage
G.M.B. Great Master [of the Order] of the Bath
G.M.B. or **g.m.b.** good merchantable brand
g.m.b. or **G.M.B.** good merchantable brand
G.m.b.H. (Gesellschaft mit beschränkter Haftung), **Co. Ltd., n v** (naamlooze vennootschap)(Dutch), **S. en C.** (sociedad en Comandita)(Span.) or **Soc. an**[e] (Société anonyme)(Fr.) limited company (cf. A.G.; cie; S.A.)
G.M.C. General Medical Council (Brit.)
Gmc. or **Ger.** Germanic
G.m.e. or **g.m.e.** gilt marbled edges (Bookbinding)
G.M.I.E. Grand Master [of the Order] of the Indian Empire
G.M.K.P. Grand Master of the Knights of [the Order of] St. Patrick
G.M.L. Gold Mining Lease (Queensland)
G.M.M.G. Grand Master of [the Order of] St. Michael and St. George
G.M.P. Military Governor of Paris
G.M.P. (Groupe motopropulseur)(Fr.), **MTS** (Mil.) or **M.T.S.** Motor Transport Service
G.M.Q., G.m.q. or **g.m.q.** good merchantable quality
G.M.S.I. Grand Master [of the Order] of the Star of India
G.M.T. or **G.m.t.** Greenwich mean time
g.m.v. gram-molecular volume
G.N. Graduate Nurse (cf. G. in N.)
Gn (Mil.), **G.** or **g.** gun
Gn. or **Gen.** Genesis
gn., G., g., gns., gs, or **gu.** guineas
gn., G., g. or **grn.** green
gn., G., g. or **gu.** guinea
G.N.C. General Nursing Council (Brit.)
G-NP Chemical agent, non-persistent (Mil.)
Gnr (Mil.), **Gr.** or **Gun.** gunner
gns., G., g., gn., gs. or **gu.** guineas
GO (Mil.), **G. O.** or **g.o.** General order or orders
G.O. General officer
G.O. or **g.o.** general office; grand or great organ
Go., Goth. or **goth.** Gothic (cf. G.L.)
G.O.B. or **g.o.b.** good ordinary bonds; good ordinary brand
g.o.b. or **G.O.B.** good ordinary bonds; good ordinary brand
G.O.C. General Officer Commanding
G.O.C. in C. or **G.O.C.-in-C.** General Officer Commanding in Chief
G.O.M. Grand Old Man (William E. Gladstone)
G.O.P. General orders post; Grand Old Party (Republican)
Goth., Go. or **goth.** Gothic (cf. G.L.)
goth., Go., or **Goth.** Gothic (cf. G.L.)
Gov. or **gov.** governor
Gov., gov., Govt. or **govt.** government; governmental
Gov. Gen. or **Gov.-Gen.** Governor General
Govt., govt., Gov. or **gov.** government; governmental
Govt. Ptg. Off., GPO or **G.P.O.** Government Printing Office
G.P. general paresis (Med.); general pause (Music); (Gloria Patri)(Lat.) Glory to the Father
G.P. or **g.p.** General Practitioner (Med.)
G.P., G. Ph., Ph. G., Phar. G. or **Phm. G.** Graduate in Pharmacy
G.P. or **G.P.I.** general paralysis [of the insane] (Med.)
G-P Chemical agent, persistent (Mil.)
Gp (Mil.) or **gr.** group
gp. groups
g.p. great primer (Typog.)
G.P.A. General Passenger Agent
Gp C, G.C., G.Capt. or **Gp Capt** Group captain
Gp Capt, G.C., G.Capt. or **Gp C** Group captain
Gp Comdr Group commander
G.P.D. General Passenger Department
G.P.D., gpd or **g.p.d.** gallons per day
gpd, G.P.D. or **g.p.d.** gallons per day
G-PF Gasproof [building or dugout] (Mil.)
G. Ph., G.P., Ph.G., Phar.G., or **Phm.G.** Graduate in Pharmacy
G.P.I. or **G.P.** general paralysis of the insane (Med.)
G.P.K.T. Grand Priory of the Knights of the Temple (Freemasonry)
G.P.M. Grand Past Master (Freemasonry)
G.P.M., gpm or **g.p.m.** gallons per minute
G.P.M. (Grand prévôt militaire)(Fr.), **PM** (Mil.) or **P.M.** Provost marshal
gpm, G.P.M. or **g.p.m.** gallons per minute
Gpmt Groupment (Mil.)
GPO, G.P.O. or **Govt. Ptg. Off.** Government Printing Office
G.P.O. General Post Office
G.P.O. or **G.P.U.** (Gay-Pay-Oo)(Gosudarstvennoe Politicheskoe Upravlenie) (Rus.) Government Political Administration; Soviet secret police (cf. O.G.P.U.)
G.P.R. (genio populi Romani)(Lat.) to the genius of the Roman people
G.P.S., gps or **g.p.s.** gallons per second
gps, G.P.S. or **g.p.s** gallons per second
G.P.U. or **G.P.O** (Gay-Pay-Oo) (Gosudarstvennoe Politicheskoe Upravlenie) (Rus.) Government Political Administration; Soviet secret police (cf. O.G.P.U.)
G.Q.G. (Grand quartier général)(Fr.), **GHQ** or **G. H. Q.** General Headquarters (cf. H.Q.)

G.R. General Reserve; Grand Recorder (Freemasonry); (Georgius Rex)(Lat.) King George
G.R. or **W. R.** (Gulielmus or William Rex) (Lat.) King William
Gr (Mil.) or **gr.** grade
Gr. Grecian; Greece
Gr. or **Gk.** Greek
Gr., Gnr (Mil.) or **Gun.** gunner
gr. groschen
gr., G., g or **g.** gravity
gr., G. or **g.** grain; grand
gr., G., g., gm. or **grm.** gram; grams
gr., G., g. or **grs.** grains
gr. or **Gp** (Mil.) group
gr. or **gram.** grammar; grammarian; grammatical; grammatically
gr. or **gro.** gross
gr. or **gt.** great
gr. or **gy** (Mil.) gray
g.r. gold rubles
grad. graduate; graduated
Grad.I.A.E. Graduate Institution of Automobile Engineers
gram. or **gr.** grammar; grammarian; grammatical; grammatically
gram.sch. grammar school
Gr. Br., G.B., Gr. Brit., Gt. Br., or **Gt. Brit.** Great Britain
Gr. Brit., G.B., Gr. Br., Gt. Br. or **Gt. Brit.** Great Britain
Gr. Ch. Greek Church
G.R.C.M. Graduate of the Royal College of Music
Gr. D. or **G.D.** Grand Duchess or Duke
grd. ground
grd., gtd., gu. or **guar.** guaranteed
Grdau., G.D., g.d. or **grdau.** granddaughter
Greg. Gregoire; Gregory
Gren. Gds., G.G., G.Gds. or **Gr. Gds.** Grenadier Guards
G.R. et I. or **G.R.I.** (Georgius Rex et Imperator)(Lat.) George, King and Emperor
Gr. Gds., G.G., G.Gds. or **Gren. Gds.** Grenadier Guards
Gr.Gro., g.gr. or **gr.gro.** great gross
gr.gro., g.gr. or **Gr. Gro.** great gross
G.R.I. or **G. R. et I.** (Georgius Rex et Imperator)(Lat.) George, King and Emperor
g.r.i. guaranteed retirement income (Insurance)
Gr.-L. Graeco-Latin
grm., G., g., gm. or **gr.** gram; grams
grn., G., g. or **gn.** green
G.R.O. general routine order or orders
gro. or **gr.** gross
Gr Reg Graves registration (Mil.)
Gr Reg Bn Graves registration battalion
Gr Reg Co Graves registration company
Grs., grs., G.S. or **gs.** grandson
grs., G., g. or **gr.** grains
grs. Grs. G.S. or **g.s.** grandson
G.R.S.C.T.C. General Railway Signal Centralized Traffic Control
G.R.S.M. Graduate of the Royal School of Music (Royal Academy and Royal College)
gr.t.m. gross ton mile
Grudz. (Grudzień)(Pol.), **D., dbre.** (diciembre)(Span.), **Dec., déc.** (décembre) (Fr.), **des.** (desember)(Norw.), **Dez.** (Dezember)(Ger., Hung.), **dez.** (dezembro)(Port.) or **dic.** (dicembre)(Ital.) December
gr. wt. gross weight
GS general store (Mil.); German silver
GS (Mil.), **E.M.G.** (État-major général) (Fr.), **G.S.** or **g.s.** general staff
G.S. Grand Scribe (Freemasonry); Grand Secretary (Freemasonry); Grand Sentinel (Freemasonry); Grand Sentry (Freemasonry); Grand Steward (Freemasonry)
G.S., E.M.G. (État-major général)(Fr.), **GS** (Mil.) or **g.s.** general staff
G.S., Gen Serv (Mil.), **Gen.Serv.** or **g.s.** general service
G.S. or **Geol. Surv.** Geological Survey
G.S. or **g.s.** general secretary
G.S. or **G.S.A.** Girl Scouts; Girl Scouts of America
gs., G., g., gn., gns. or **gu.** guineas
g.s. ground speed
g.s., E.M.G. (État-major général)(Fr.), **GS** (Mil.) or **G.S.** general staff
g.s., Gen Serv (Mil.), **Gen. Serv.** or **G.S.** general service
g.s., Grs., grs. or **G.S.** grandson
g.s. or **G.S.** general secretary
G.S.A. Geological Society of America
G.S.A. or **G.S.** Girl Scouts of America; Girl Scouts
GSC (Mil.) or **G.S.C.** General Staff Corps
G.S.D. Grand Senior Deacon (Freemasonry)
G.S.M. Gold Star Mothers; Guildhall School of Music
g.s.m. good sound marketable
G.S.O. General staff officer
G.S.P. good service pension
Gsp. Gasparo
GSS General Service School (Mil.)
Gst. Gustav; Gustave; Gustavus
G.S.U. general signals use (Navy)
G.S.W. gunshot wound; Grand Senior Warden (Freemasonry)
G.T. Good Templar; Grand Tiler or Tyler (Freemasonry)
G.T. or **g.t.** gross ton
Gt., gt. or **gutt.** (gutta)(Lat.) drop (cf. gtt.; min.)
G.t., g.t., g.t.e. or **t.e.g.** gilt top [edge]; top edge gilt (Bookbinding)
gt gun turret
gt. or **glt.** gilt
gt. or **gr.** great
gt., Gt. or **gutt.** (gutta)(Lat.) drop (cf. gtt.; min.)
g.t. gas tight

g.t. or **G.T.** gross ton

g.t., G.t., g.t.e. or **t.e.g.** gilt top; gilt top edge; top edge gilt (Bookbinding) (cf. g.e.)

Gt. Br., G.B., Gr. Br., Gr. Brit. or **Gt. Brit.** Great Britain

Gt. Brit., G.B., Gr. Br., Gr. Brit. or **Gt. Br.** Great Britain

G.T.C. or **g.t.c.** good till cancelled or countermanded

g.t.c. or **G.T.C.** good till cancelled or countermanded

gtd., grd., gu. or **guar.** guaranteed

g.t.e., G.t., g.t. or **t.e.g.** gilt top edge; top edge gilt (Bookbinding)

gt.f. great folio

Gth. Gunther

G.T.M. general traffic manager

G.T.M. or **g.t.m.** good this month

g.t.m. or **G.T.M.** good this month

Gtt., gtt. or **gutt.** (guttae)(Lat.) drops (cf. gt.; min.)

gtt., Gtt. or **gutt.** (guttae)(Lat.) drops (cf. gt.; min.)

G.T.W. or **g.t.w.** good this week (becomes void on Saturday)

g.t.w. or **G.T.W.** good this week (becomes void on Saturday)

gty Gritty (Mil.)

gu. gules

gu., G., g. or **gn.** guinea

gu., G., g., gn., gns. or **gs.** guineas

gu., grd., gtd. or **guar.** guaranteed

gu., guar. or **guart.** guarantee

guar. guarantor

guar., grd., gtd. or **gu.** guaranteed

guar., gu. or **guart.** guarantee

guart., gu. or **guar.** guarantee

Guat. Guatemala; Guatemalian

Gun., Gnr (Mil.) or **Gr.** gunner

gun. gunnery

gutt., Gt. or **gt.** (gutta)(Lat.) drop (cf. gtt.; min.)

gutt., Gtt. or **gtt.** (guttae)(Lat.) drops (cf. gt.; min.)

guttat. (guttatim)(Lat.) drop by drop (Pharm.)

g.v. gravimetric volume

G.W.U. George Washington University

G.W.V.A. Great War Veterans' Association (Can.)

gy (Mil.) or **gr.** gray

gym. gymnasium; gymnastic; gymnastics

gyn. or **gynecol.** gynecological; gynecology

gynecol. or **gyn.** gynecological; gynecology

gyr. gyration

ΓΑ (Gamma Alpha) Graduate fraternity (Science)

ΓΑΧ (Gamma Alpha Chi) Professional sorority (Advertising)

ΓΒΑ (Gamma Beta Alpha) National undergraduate fraternity (Radio Broadcasting)

ΓΕΠ (Gamma Epsilon Pi) Honorary sorority (Commerce)

ΓΗΓ (Gamma Eta Gamma) Professional fraternity (Law)

ΓΦΒ (Gamma Phi Beta) National undergraduate sorority

ΓΣΔ (Gamma Sigma Delta) Honor society (Agriculture)

ΓΣΕ (Gamma Sigma Epsilon) Honorary fraternity (Chemistry)

H

H henry (elec.); horizontal [component of the earth's magnetism] (Physics); Horse (Mil.); hydrogen (Chem.); intensity of magnetic field (Physics)

H or **P^1** Law of Holiness (Bib.)

H. hypermetropia; (Hommes)(Fr.) men

H. (Höhe)(Ger.) or **alt.** altitude (cf. ht.)

H. or **h.** harbor; hardness; have (Wig-wagging); hence; high; hoy (Shipping register); husband

H., h., h (hecto-)(Greek), **C., c., cent., ct.** (centum)(Lat.), **hun.** or **hund.** hundred

H., h., hgt. or **ht.** height (cf. alt.)

H., h. or **Hon.** honor

H., h. or **hr.** hour

H., h., hr. or **hrs.** hours

H., h. or **hrd** (Mil.) hard

H., h., or **hydt.** hydrant

H., Hdqrs., hdqrs., H.Q., Hq., h.q. or **Q.G.** (Quartier général)(Fr.) headquarters (cf. G.H.Q.)

H. or **her.** (heres, heredes)(Lat.) heir; heirs

H. or **Hft.** (Heft, Hefte)(Ger.) number; part; volume (cf. no.; pt.; vol.)

H., Hft. (Heft)(Ger.), **Abt.** (Abteilung)(Ger.), **Lfg.** (Lieferung)(Ger.), **liv.** (livraison)(Fr.), **p., pt., T.** or **Th.** (Teil, Theil)(Ger.) part (cf. inst.; no.; sec.)

H., Hft. (Heft)(Ger.), **inst., Lfg.** (Lieferung)(Ger.), **liv.** (livraison)(Fr.), **T.** or **Th.** (Teil, Theil)(Ger.) installment (cf. Abt.; pt.)

H. or **hor.** horizon

h Plank's constant (Physics)

h (hecto-)(Greek), **C., c., cent., ct.** (centum)(Lat.), **H., h., hun.** or **hund.** hundred

h. hail (Naut.); hall

h. or **H.** harbor; hardness; have (Wig-wagging); hence; high; hoy (Shipping); husband

h., H., h (hecto-)(Greek), **C., c., cent.** (centum)(Lat.), **hun.** or **hund.** hundred

h., H., hgt. or **ht.** height (cf. alt.)

h., H. or **hon.** honor

h., H. or **hr.** hour

h., H., hr. or **hrs.** hours

h., H. or **hrd** (Mil.) hard

h., H. or **hydt.** hydrant

h., ho. or **mn** (maison)(Fr.) hous[illegible]

h. or **hund.** hundreds

H.A. Horse Artillery

H.A., A.L. (Artillerie lourde)(Fr.) or **Hv. Arty.** Heavy artillery
H.A. or **h.a.** high-angle (Gun)
ha. or **hect.** hectare (Metric land measure)
h.a. (hoc anno)(Lat.), **a.c.** (année courante) (Fr.), d.A. (dette Aar)(Dan.), d.J. (dieses Jahres)(Ger.) or f.é. (folyó évi) (Hung.) this year; the current year
h.a. (hoc anno)(Lat.), **a.p.** or **a. pr.** (anni praesentis)(Lat.) in this year
h.a. (huius anno)(Lat.) or **d.j.** (dieses Jahres)(Ger.) of this year; this year's
H.A.A. Heavy antiaircraft
H.A. & M., A. & M. or **A. and M.** Hymns, Ancient and Modern
H.A.B. High-altitude bombing
Hab. Habakkuk
Hab. or **hab.** habitat
Hab. Corp. or **hab. corp.** (habeas corpus) (Lat.) you have the body (Law)
hab. fa. poss. or **hab. fac. poss.** (habere facias possessionem)(Lat.) that you cause [him] to have possession
habt. (habeat)(Lat.) let him have (Pharm.)
H.A.C. Honourable Artillery Company (Brit.)
Hag. Haggai
hairdrsr. hairdresser
Hal halogen (Chem.)
Hal. Halifax (Airplane)
Hamp. Hampden (Airplane)
H.& C., h.& c., H. and C., h.and c. or **h.c.** hot and cold (Water)
H & E hematoxylin and eosin stain
H & Hq Btry Headquarters and headquarters battery
H & Mecz Horse and mechanized (Mil.)
H & RP Holding and reconsignment point
H & S Btry or **Hq & Serv Btry** Headquarters and service battery
H & S Co or **Hq & Serv Co.** Headquarters and service company
H & S Tr or **Hq & Serv Tr** Headquarters and service troop
Han. Hanover; Hanoverian
H.and C., h.and c., H.& C., h.& c. or **h.c.** hot and cold (Water)
Hants. Hampshire
H.A. or D. Havre, Antwerp or Dunkerque (Shipping)
Har. Harold
Harv. Harvard [University]
haust. (haustus)(Lat.)(Pharm.), **Dft.** or **dft.** draft
hav haversine (Math. and Navig.)
Haw. Hawaiian
H.B. Heavy bomber; (Haubitzbatterie) (Ger.) Howitzer battery
Hb, hb or **Hg.** hemoglobin
H.B.C. Hudson's Bay Company
H.B.M. His or Her Britannic Majesty
H.C. Heralds' College; High Church; Holy Communion; Hospital Corps; House of Commons
H.C. or H.Com. High Commissioner
h.c. held (hold) covered (Insurance)

h.c., H.& C., h.& c., H.and C. or **h.and c.** hot and cold (Water)
h.c. (honoris causa)(Lat.), **Hon.** or **hon.** honorary
hcap. or **hcp.** handicap
H.C.F. Honorary Chaplain to the Forces
H.C.F., hcf, h.c.f., G.C.F., gcf or **g.c.f.** highest or greatest common factor (cf. G.C.D.)
hcf, H.C.F., h.c.f., G.C.F., gcf or **g.c.f.** highest or greatest common factor (cf. G.C.D.)
h.c.l. high cost of living (Colloq.)
H.C.M. or **S.M.C.** (Su Majestad Catolíca) (Span.) His or Her Catholic Majesty
H.Com. or **H.C.** High Commissioner
H.Con.Res. House concurrent resolution
hcp. or **hcap.** handicap
H.C.S. Home Civil Service (Brit.)
HD Harbor Defense; hydrodrome
HD or **H.D.** hard-drawn; hearing distance
H.D. Hawaiian Department; Home Defense
H.D. or **HD** hard-drawn; hearing distance
H.D. or **H-Dr** (Mil.) horse-drawn
H.d., hor.decub. (hora decubitus)(Lat.) or **h.s.** (hora somni)(Lat.) at bedtime
hd., C., c. or **cap.** (caput)(Lat.) head
h.d. high density (cotton)
hdbk. handbook
HDC or **H.D.C.** Hawaiian Defense Command
hdkf. or **hkf.** handkerchief
hdlg. handling
H.D.L.W. distance at which a watch is heard with the left ear
H.Doc. House document
Hdqrs., H., hdqrs., H.Q., Hq., h.q. or **Q.G.** (Quartier général)(Fr.) headquarters (cf. G.H.Q.)
H-Dr (Mil.) or **H.D.** horse-drawn
H.D.R.W. distance at which a watch is heard with the right ear
Hds. M., Hs.M. (Hendes Majestæt)(Dan.), **H.M., H. Maj:t** (Hans Majestät) (Swed.) or **S.M.** (Sa Majesté)(Fr.), (Su Majestad)(Span.) His or Her Majesty
HE (Mil.), **H.E.** or **h.e.** high explosive
H.E. His Eminence; Hydraulic Engineer
H.E., HE (Mil.) or **h.e.** high explosive
H.E. or **h.e.** horizontal equivalent
H.E., S.E. (Su Excelencia)(Span.), **S. Exc.** (Son Excellence)(Fr.) or **S. Excia.** (Sua Excelência)(Port.) His Excellency
He helium (Chem.)
He. Heinkel (Airplane)
h.e. (hoc or hic est)(Lat.), **c.-à-d.** (c'est-à-dire)(Fr.), **d.ä.** (det är)(Swed.), **d.h.** (das heisst)(Ger.), **d.i.** (das ist)(Ger.), **d.v.s.** (det vil sige)(Dan.) (det vill saga) (Swed.), **i.e.** (id est)(Lat.) or **t.i.** (tudni illik)(Hung.) that is; that is to say (cf. viz.)
h.e., HE (Mil.) or **H.E.** high explosive
h.e. or **H.E.** horizontal equivalent
H.E.A. Hospital Exhibitors' Association

Heb. or **Hebr.** Hebrew; Hebrews
Hebr. or **Heb.** Hebrew; Hebrews
Hect. Hector
hect. or **ha.** hectare
hectog., hg. h.g. or **hgm.** hectogram
hectol., hl. or **h.l.** hectoliter
hectom., Hm. or **hm.** hectometer
H.E.D. (Haut Einheits Dosis)(Ger.) unit skin dose (X-ray)
H.E.H. His or Her Exalted Highness (Brit. India)
H.E.I.C. Honourable East India Company
H.E.I.C.S. Honourable East India Company's Service
heir app. heir apparent
heir pres. heir presumptive
Hel. Helvetia
Hel. or **Hellen.** Hellenic; Hellenistic
Hellen. or **Hel.** Hellenic; Hellenistic
Hen. or **Hy.** Henry
H.E.P.C. Hydro-Electric Power Commission
Her. or **her.** herald; heraldry
her. heraldic
her. (heres, heredes)(Lat.) or **H.** heir; heirs
Herb. Herbert
herb. recent. (herbarum recentium)(Lat.) of fresh herbs (Pharm.)
Heref. Herefordshire
herp. or **herpet.** herpetology
herpet. or **herp.** herpetology
Herts. Hertfordshire
Herz. Herzegovina
H.E.U. or **h.e.u.** hydroelectric units
h.e.u. or **H.E.U.** hydroelectric units
Hex. Hexateuch
hex. hexachord; hexagon
HF, H.F., h.f. or **h-f** high-frequency
H.F. Home Forces
H.F., HF, h.f. or **h-f** high-frequency
Hf hafnium (Chem.)
hf., S., s., SS, Ss. or **ss.** (semi)(Fr.), (semis)(Lat.) half (cf. dim.)
h.f., HF, H.F. or **h-f** high frequency
h-f, HF, H.F. or **h.f.** high frequency
HFA (Mil.), **H.F.A.** or **Hv Fld Arty** (Mil.) heavy field artillery
H.F.A., HFA (Mil.) or **Hv Fld Arty** (Mil.) heavy field artillery
H.F.A.R.A. Honorary Foreign Associate of the Royal Academy
hfbd. or **hf. bd.** half-bound (Bookbinding)
hf.bd. or **hfbd.** half-bound (Bookbinding)
H.F.C., h.f.c. or **h-f.c.** high frequency current
h-f.c., H.F.C. or **h.f.c.** high frequency current
hfcf. or **hf.cf.** half-calf (Bookbinding)
hfcl. or **hf.cl.** half-cloth (Bookbinding)
H.F.M. hold for money
hfmor or **hf. mor.** half-morocco (Bookbinding)
hf. mor. ex. half-morocco extra (Bookbinding)
H.F.R.A. Honorary Fellow of the Royal Academy [of Arts, London]
Hft. or **H.** (Heft, Hefte)(Ger.) number; numbers; part; parts (cf. no.; pt.; vol.)
Hft., H. (Heft)(Ger.), **Abt.** (Abteilung)(Ger.), **Lfg.** (Lieferung)(Ger.), **liv.** (livraison) (Fr.), **p., pt., T.** or **Th.** (Teil, Theil)(Ger.) part (cf. inst.; no.; sec.)
Hft., H. (Heft)(Ger.), **inst., Lfg.** (Lieferung)(Ger.), **liv.** (livraison)(Fr.), **T.** or **Th.** (Teil, Theil)(Ger.) installment (cf. Abt.; pt.)
HG or **H.G.** High German
H.G. His or Her Grace; Holy Ghost; Home Guard; Horse Guards (Brit.)
H.G. or **HG** High German
Hg (hydrargyrum)(Lat.) mercury (Chem.)
Hg., Hb or **hb** hemoglobin
Hg. or **Hu.** Hugo
hg. heliogram
hg., h.g. hectog. or **hgm.** hectogram
H.G.D.H. His or Her Grand Ducal Highness
hgm., hectog., hg. or **h.g.** hectogram
H.G.S.S.S. Henry George School of Social Science
hgt., h. or **ht.** height (cf. alt.)
HH half hard (Metallurgy)
HH. (Herren)(Ger.), **Messrs., MM.** (Messieurs)(Fr.), **Sig., sig.** (signori)(Ital.), **Sres.** or **Srs.** (Señores)(Span.) Sirs; gentlemen (cf. gent.)
H.H. or **S.A.** (Son Altesse)(Fr.), (Su Alteza)(Span.) His or Her Highness
H.H. or **S.S.** (Sa Sainteté)(Fr.) His Holiness
H/H Harve and Hamburg (Shipping)
hh. (hojas)(Span.), **Fol.** (Folia)(Ital., Lat.), **L., l., LL.** or **ll.** leaves (cf. ff.; f°)
HH.D. or **L.H.D.** (Litterarum Humaniorum Doctor, or In Litteris Humanioribus Doctor)(Lat.) Doctor of Humanities (cf. D.Litt.)
hhd. hogshead
H.H.J.N.A. Heavy Hardware Jobbers National Association
H.I. Hawaiian Islands (cf. H.T.)
H.I., h.i., H.J., h.j. (hic iacet or jacet)(Lat.), **H.S.** or **h.s.** (hic situs)(Lat.) here lies (cf. H.I.S.; H.S.E.; i.h.)
Hi. (Hieronymus)(Lat.) or **Jer.** Jerome
h.i., H.I., H.J., h.j. (hic iacet or jacet) (Lat.), **H.S.** or **h.s.** (hic situs)(Lat.) here lies (cf. H.I.S.; H.S.E.; i.h.)
H.I.A. Horological Institute of America
HIAS Hebrew Immigrant Aid Society
Hier. (Hierosolyma)(Lat.) Jerusalem
H.I.H., or **S.A.I.** (Son Altesse Imperiale) (Fr.),(Su Alteza Imperial)(Span.) His or Her Imperial Highness
H.I.J.M.S. His Imperial Japanese Majesty's Ship
Hil. Hilary
H.I.M. or **S.M.I.** (Sa Majesté Impériale) (Fr.), (Su Majestad Imperial)(Span.) His or Her Imperial Majesty

Hind. Hindu; Hinduism; Hindustan; Hindustani

Hip. Hippolyte; Hippolytus

H.I.S., H.J.S. (hic iacet or jacet sepultus) (Lat.), **H.S.E.** or **h.s.e.** (hic situs or sepultus est)(Lat.) here lies buried (cf. H.I.; H.J.; H.S.; i.h.)

Hist., hist. or **Gesch.** (Geschichte)(Ger.) history

hist. histology; historian; historical

hist., Hist. or **Gesch.** (Geschichte)(Ger). history

H.J., H.I., h.i., h.j. (hic jacet or iacet) (Lat.), **H.S.** or **h.s.** (hic situs)(Lat.) here lies (cf. H.J.S.; H.S.E.; i.h.)

h.j., H.I., h.i., H.J. (hic jacet or iacet)(Lat.), **H.S.** or **h.s.** (hic situs)(Lat.) here lies (cf. H.I.S.; H.S.E.; i.h.)

H.J.Res. House joint resolution

H.J.S., H.I.S. (hic jacet or iacet sepultus) (Lat.), **H.S.E.** or **h.s.e.** (hic situs or sepultus est)(Lat.) here lies buried (cf. H.I.; H.J.; H.S.; i.h.)

H.K. House of Keys (Isle of Man)

H.K.A. Hotel Keepers Association

hkf. or **hdkf.** handkerchief

hk.tls. haikwan taels (Chinese weight)

H.L. Homestead Lease (Australia)

H.L., Dom. Proc. or **D.P.** (Domus Procerum)(Lat.) House of Lords

Hl. latent hypermetropia

hl., h.l. or **hectol.** hectoliter

hl. (heilig)(Ger.), **P.** (pius)(Lat.) or **S.** holy; sacred

h.l. (hoc loco)(Lat.) in this place (cf. in loc.; ad loc.)

HLBS or **H.L.B.S.** Home Loan Bank system

H.L.I. Highland Light Infantry

H.M. hallelujah meter (cf. H.P.M.); Home Missions

H.M., Hds. M., Hs.M. (Hendes Majestæt) (Dan.), **H. Maj:t** (Hans Majestät) (Swed) or **S.M.** (Sa Majesté)(Fr.), (Su Majestad)(Span.) His or Her Majesty

H.M. or **M.H.** Master of Humanities

Hm. manifest hypermetropia

Hm., hm. or **hectom.** hectometer

Hm. or **Hrm.** Herman; Hermann

hm., Hm. or **hectom.** hectometer

h.m. handmade; (hoc mense)(Lat.) in this month

h.m. (huius mensis)(Lat.) or **l. M.** (laufenden Monats)(Ger.) of the current month (cf. inst.)

hm.^{2} square hectometer

hm.^{3} cubic hectometer

H.M.A. (Hauptmeldeamt)(Ger.) District Recruiting Office; Head Masters' Association (Brit.); His or Her Majesty's Airship

H.M.A.A. Horse & Mule Association of America

H. Maj:t (Hans Majestät)(Swed.), **Hds. M., Hs. M.** (Hendes Majestæt)(Dan.), **H.M.** or **S.M.** (Sa Majeste)(Fr.), (Su Majestad)(Span.) His or Her Majesty

H.M.A.S. His or Her Majesty's Australian Ship

H.M.C. Head Masters' Conference (Brit.); His of Her Majesty's Customs

H.M.C.S. His or Her Majesty's Canadian Ship

H.M.D. Homeopathic Doctor of Medicine

H.M.F. or **H.M.Forces** His or Her Majesty's Forces

H.M.I. Hall-Moody Institute; His or Her Majesty's Inspector

H.M.I.S. His or Her Majesty's Inspector of Schools; His or Her Majesty's Indian Ship

H.M.O.W. His or Her Majesty's Office of Works

H.M.P. (hoc monuentum posuit)(Lat.) he or she erected this monument

H.M.P. or **h.m.p.** handmade paper

H.M.R.T. His or Her Majesty's Rescue Tug

H.M.S. His or Her Majesty's Service; His of Her Majesty's Ship or Steamer

H.M.S.O. His or Her Majesty's Stationery Office

Hnos. (Hermanos)(Span.), **Bros., bros., FF.** (fratres)(Lat.), (Frères)(Fr.), **Geb.** or **Gbr.** (Gebrüder)(Ger.) brothers

H.O. head office; home office

H.O. (Heeresordnung)(Ger.) or **AR** Army Regulations

Ho holmium (Chem.)

ho., h. or **mn** (maison)(Fr.) house

HOLC or **H.O.L.C.** Home Owners' Loan Corporation

Holl. Holland

holl. (hollandais, hollandaise)(Fr.), **D.** or **Du.** Dutch; Hollander

Hom. Homer

Hom. or **Homer.** Homeric

homeo. Homeopathic

Homer. or **Hom.** Homeric

Hon., H. or **h.** honor

Hon., hon. or **h.c.** (honoris causa)(Lat.) honorary

Hon. or **Honble.** Honorable (cf. Excma.)

hon. or **Honbly** (Mil.) honorably

Honble. or **Hon.** Honorable (cf. Excma.)

Honbly (Mil.) or **hon.** honorably

Hond. Honduras; honored

Hon.M.I.A.E. Honorary Member of the Institution of Automobile Engineers

Hon. Sec. Honorary Secretary

Hor. Horace

Hor., hor., Horol. or **horol.** horology

hor. or **H.** horizon

hor. or **horiz.** horizontal

hor. decub., H.d. (hora decubitus)(Lat.) or **h.s.** (hora somni)(Lat.) at bedtime

hor. intermed. (horis intermediis)(Lat.) at intermediate hours

horiz. or **hor.** horizontal

Horol., horol., Hor. or **hor.** horology

horol. horologica

hort. or **hortic.** horticultural; horticulture

hortic. or **hort.** horticultural; horticulture

Hos. Hosea

hosp. hospital

Hosp Co Hospital company
Hosp Sgt Hospital Sargeant
Hosp Tn Hospital train (Mil.)
How (Mil.) or **how.** Howitzer
HP, hp, H.P. or **h.p.** horsepower
HP, H.P., h.p. or **h.-p.** high frequency
H.P. Houses of Parliament
H.P. or **h.p.** high power; high pressure; house physician
H.P., h.p., P. or **p.** (pontifex)(Lat.) high priest
h.p. half pay; hot-pressed [paper]
h.p. or **H.P.** high power; high pressure; house physician
h.p., H.P., P. or **p.** (pontifex)(Lat.) high priest
h.p.cyl. high pressure cylinder
hp-hr, h.p.hr. or **h.p.-hr.** horsepower hour
h.p.hr., hp-hr or **h.p.-hr.** horsepower hour
H.P.M. hallelujah particular meter (cf. H.M.)
H.P.N., hp.n. or **h.p.n.** horsepower nominal (Obsolete. See r.h.p.)
H.p.n. (haustus purgans noster)(Lat.) our own purgative draft
H.-p. n. horsepower normal
h.p.n., H.P.N. or **h.p.n.** horsepower nominal (Obsolete. See r.h.p.)
H.Q., H., Hdqrs., hdqrs., Hq., h.q. or **Q.G.** (Quartier général)(Fr.) headquarters (cf. G.H.Q.)
Hq., H., Hdqrs., hdqrs., H.Q., h.q. or **Q.G.** (Quartier général)(Fr.) headquarters (cf. G.H.Q.)
h.q. (hoc quaere)(Lat.) see this; look for this
h.q., H., Hdqrs., hdqrs., H.Q., Hq. or **Q.G.** (Quartier général)(Fr.) headquarters (cf. G.H.Q.)
Hq & Hq Btry Headquarters and headquarters battery
Hq & Hq Co Headquarters and headquarters company
Hq & Hq Tr Headquarters and headquarters troop
Hq & MP Co Headquarters and military police company
Hq & Serv Btry or **H & S Btry** Headquarters and service battery
Hq & Serv Co or **H & S Co** Headquarters and service company
Hq & Serv Tr or **H & S Tr** Headquarters and service troop
H.Q.B.A. Headquarters base area
Hq Bty Headquarters battery
Hq Co Headquarters company
Hq Comdt Headquarters commandant
Hq Plat Headquarters platoon
Hq Sec Headquarters section
Hq Tr Headquarters troop
H.R. Home Rule; Home Ruler; House of Representatives; House record
Hr. (Herr)(Dan., Ger.) or **hr.** (herr) (Swed.) equivalent of Mr.
hr., H. or **h.** hour
hr., H., h. or **hrs.** hours
hr. (herr)(Swed.) or **Hr.** (Herr)(Dan., Ger.) equivalent of Mr.
H.R.A. Honorary Royal Academician
H.R.C.A. Honorary Member of the Royal Cambrian Academy; Honorary Royal Cambrian Academician
hrd (Mil.), **H.** or **h.** hard
H.R.E. Holy Roman Emperor
H.R.E. or **S.R.I.** (Sacrum Romanum Imperium)(Lat.) Holy Roman Empire
H.Rept. House Report
H.Res. House Resolution
H.R.H. or **S.A.R.** (Son Altesse Royale) (Fr.) His or Her Royal Highness
H.R.H.A. Honorary Member of the Royal Hibernian Academy
H.R.I. Honorary Member of the Royal Institute of Painters in Water Colours
H.R.I.P. (hic requiescit in pace)(Lat.) here he or she rests in peace (cf. B.Q.; H.I.S.; R.I.P.)
Hrm. or **Hm.** Herman; Hermann
HRS hot-rolled steel
Hrs. or **Huss.** Hussars
hrs., H., h. or **hr.** hours
H.R.S.A. Honorary Member of the Royal Scottish Academy
hrsg. (herausgegeben)(Ger.), **ed.** (editus) (Lat.), **pub., pubd.** or **publ.** published
HS or **H.S.** horizontal stripes (Hydrog.)
H.S. Home Secretary; Homestead Selection (Australia); Hospital ship
H.S. or **HS** horizontal stripes (Hydrog.)
H.S. or **h.s.** (hic sepultus)(Lat.) here is buried (cf. H.I.; H.I.S., H.S.E.; i.h.); house surgeon
H.S., h.s. (hic situs)(Lat.), **H.I., h.i., H.J.** or **h.j.** (hic iacet or jacet)(Lat.) here lies (cf. H.I.S.; H.S.E.; i.h.)
Hs Horseshoe (Mil.)
Hs. (Handschrift)(Ger.), **Ms.** or **ms.** manuscript
h.s. hemstitched; high school; (hoc sensu) (Lat.) in this sense
h.s. (hora somni)(Lat.), **H.d.** or **hor. decub.** (hora decubitus)(Lat.) at bedtime
h.s., H.S. (hic sepultus)(Lat.) here is buried (cf. H.I.; H.I.S.; H.S.E.; i.h.); house surgeon
h.s., H.S. (hic situs)(Lat.), **H.I., h.i., H.J.** or **hj.** (hic iacet, hic jacet)(Lat.) here lies (cf. H.I.S.; H.S.E.; i.h.)
H.S.A. Huguenot Society of America
H.S.E., h.s.e. (hic sepultus or situs est) (Lat.), **H.I.S.** or **H.J.S.** (hic iacet or jacet sepultus)(Lat.) here lies buried (cf. H.S.; H.I.; H.J.; i.h.)
hsg. housing (Mach.)
H.S.H. His or Her Serene Highness
H.S.M. His or Her Serene Majesty
Hs. M., Hds. M. (Hendes Majestæt)(Dan.), **H.M., H.Maj:t** (Hans Majestät)(Swed.) or **S. M.** (Sa Majesté)(Fr.), (Su Majestad)(Span.) His or Her Majesty
H.S.S. (Historiae Societatis Socius)(Lat.), **F.Hist.S., F.H.S.** or **S.H.S.** (Societatis Historiae Socius)(Lat.) Fellow of the Historical Society
Hss. (Handschriften)(Ger.), **MSS.** or **mss.** manuscripts
H.T. half-time [survey] (Shipping)
H.T., H.Ty. or **T.H.** Hawaiian Territory; Territory of Hawaii (cf. H.I.)
Ht. Harriet
ht. heat

ht., H., h. or **hgt.** height (cf. alt.)
h.t. (hoc tempore)(Lat.) at this time; high tension; (hoc titulo)(Lat.) under this title
Htm. Hartmann
h. to h. heel to heel
HTS high tensile steel
Hts. or **hts.** heights
Htw. Hartwig
ht. wt. or **h.w.** hit wicket (Cricket)
H.Ty., H.T. or **T.H.** Hawaiian Territory; Territory of Hawaii (cf. H.I.)
Hu. Hugh; Hugues
Hu. or **Hg.** Hugo
Hub. Hubert
Hud. Lockheed Hudson (Airplane)
Hum. human; humanitarian; humanities (cf. Lit. Hum.); Humphrey
hum. humerous
Hun. or **Hung.** Hungary
Hun., Hung. or **ung.** (ungarisch)(Ger.) Hungarian
hun., C., c., cent., ct. (centum)(Lat.), **h** (hecto-)(Greek), **H.** or **h.,** or **hund.** hundred
hund., C., c., cent., ct. (centum)(Lat.), **h** (hecto-)(Greek), **H., h.** or **hun.** hundred
hund. or **h.** hundreds
Hung. or **Hun.** Hungary
Hung., Hun. or **ung.** (ungarisch)(Ger.) Hungarian
hunth. hundred thousand
Hunts. Huntingdonshire
Hur. Hurricane (Airplane)
Huss. or **Hrs.** Hussars
H.V. or **h.v.** high velocity; high voltage (Elec.)
Hv (Mil.) or **hy.** heavy
h.v. or **H.V.** high velocity; high voltage (Elec.)
Hv. Arty., A.L. (Artillerie lourde)(Fr.) or **H.A.** Heavy artillery
Hv Fld Arty (Mil.), **HFA** (Mil.) or **H.F.A.** heavy field artillery
Hv Pon Heavy ponton
HvW or **Hv Wpn** (Mil.) heavy weapons
Hv Wpn or **HvW** (Mil.) heavy weapons
Hv Wpn Co Heavy weapons company
Hv Wpn Sec Heavy weapons section
H.W. or **h.w.** high water
h.w. or **ht. wt.** hit wicket (Cricket)
h.w. or **H.W.** high water
Hwb. (Handwörterbuch)(Ger.) handy dictionary
H.W.M. or **h.w.m.** high-water mark
h.w.m. or **H.W.M.** high water mark
Hwy Highway (Mil.)
Hy. hypermetropia
Hy. or **Hen.** Henry
hy. or **Hv** (Mil.) heavy
Hyd., hyd., hydr., hydros. or **hydrostat.** hydrostatic; hydrostatics
hyd., Hyd., hydr., hydros. or **hydrostat.** hydrostatic; hydrostatics
hyd., Hydr., hydr. or **hydraul.** hydraulic; hydraulics
Hydr., hyd., hydr. or **hydraul.** hydraulic; hydraulics
hydr., Hyd., hyd., hydros. or **hydrostat.** hydrostatic; hydrostatics
hydr., hyd., Hydr. or **hydraul.** hydraulic; hydraulics
hydraul., hyd., Hydr. or **hydr.** hydraulic; hydraulics
hydro. hydropathic
hydrog. hydrograpic; hydrography
hydros., Hyd., hyd., hydr. or **hydrostat.** hydrostatic; hydrostatics
hydrostat., Hyd., hyd. hydr. or **hydros.** hydrostatic; hydrostatics
hydt., H. or **h.** hydrant
Hyg. or **hyg.** hygiene
hyg. hygroscopic
H.Y.M.A. Hebrew Young Men's Association
hyp. or **hypoth.** hypothesis; hypothetical
hypoth. or **hyp.** hypothesis; hypothetical
Hzg. (Herzog)(Ger.), **D.** or **Du.** Duke
Hzgin. (Herzogin)(Ger.) or **D.** Duchess
Hzk. Hezekiah

I

I inclination [of an orbit to the ecliptic] (Astron.); [moment of] inertia (Mech.); Interceptor (Mil.); iodine (Chem.)
I. or **i.** immortal; infidel
I., i., Imp. (Imperator)(Lat.) or **Emp.** Emperor
I., i., Imp., Impx. (Imperatrix)(Lat.) or **Emp.** Empress
I., i., Is., is., Isl. or **isl.** island; isle
I., Ia. or **Io.** Iowa
I., Id. or **Ida.** Idaho
I., Imp., imp., k. or **kais.** (kaiserlich) (Ger.) imperial
I., Ind. or **ind.** independent
I., Inf (Mil.), **Inf.** or **inf.** Infantry
I. or **inst.** instantaneous
I., Int (Mil.) or **Intell.** intelligence
I. or **Ir.** Irish
I., Ir. or **Ire.** Ireland
i. incisor (Dentistry); optically inactive; (id)(Lat.) that
i., Fe (Chem.) or **fe.** (ferrum)(Lat.) iron
i. or **I.** immortal; infidel
i., I., Imp. (Imperator)(Lat.) or **Emp.** Emperor
i., I., Imp., Impx. (Imperatrix)(Lat.) or **Emp.** Empress
i., I., Is., is., Isl. or **isl.** island; isle
i., imp. (imperium)(Lat.), **Emp.** or **emp.** empire
i. or **ind.** indicated
i., Int (Mil.), **Int.** or **int.** interest
i., int., intr. or **intrans.** intransitive

I.A. impedance angle; Incorporated Accountant (Brit.); Indian Army (cf. I.S.C.); infected area

Ia., I. or **Io.** Iowa

i. A. (im Auftrage)(Ger.) by order or authority of

i.a. (im allgemeinen)(Ger.) in general

I.A.A. International Association of Advocates

I.A.A.A.A. or **I.C.A.A.A.A.** Intercollegiate Association of Amateur Athletes in America

I.A.A.C.C. Inter-Allied Aeronautical Commission of Control

I.A.A.F. International Amateur Athletic Federation

I.A.A.M. Incorporated Association of Assistant Masters (Brit.)

IAB or **I.A.B.** Industrial Advisory Board

I.A.B. International Agrarian Bureau

I.A.B. or **IAB** Industrial Advisory Board

I.A.B. & S.I.W. International Association of Bridge & Structural Iron Workers

I.A.B.F. International Amateur Boxing Federation

I.A.B.S. International Association of Blind Students

I.A.B.S.E. International Association for Bridge and Structural Engineering

I.A.C. International Aerological Commission; International Air Convention

I.A.C.L. International Academy of Comparative Law; International Association of Criminal Law

I.A.C.P. International Association of Chiefs of Police

I.A.C.W. Inter-American Commission of Women

IADB or **I.A.D.B.** Inter-American Defense Board

I.A.D.M. International Association of Display Men

I.A.E. Institution of Automobile Engineers (Brit.)

I.A.E.I. International Association of Electrical Inspectors

I. Ae. S. Institute of the Aeronautical Sciences

I.A.F. Indian Air Force; International Aeronautic Federation

I.A.F.E. International Association of Fairs and Expositions

I.A.H.M. Incorporated Association of Head Masters (Brit.)

I.A.I. International Anthropological Institute

I.A.I.C.M. International Association of Ice Cream Manufacturers

I.A.I.I. Illinois Association of Ice Industries

I.A.I.P.C. Inter-American Industrial Property Commission

I.A.J.C. Inter-American Jewish Congress

I.A.L. Irish Academy of Letters

IALA or **I.A.L.A.** International Auxiliary Language Association

I.A.L.L. International Association for Labor Legislation

i-Am isoamyl (Chem.)

I.A.M.D. International Association of Milk Dealers

I.A.M.M. International Association of Medical Museums

I.A.M.P. Institute of American Meat Packers

I & I Report Inventory and Inspection Report

I.A.M.S. International Association of Milk Sanitarians

I. and R. initiative and referendum

I.A.O.S. Irish Agricultural Organization Society

I.A.P. International Aero Press

I.A.P.C.W. International Association for the Promotion of Child Welfare

I.A.R. Industria Aeronautica Romana

I.A.R.O. Indian Army Reserve of Officers

I.A.R.S. International Anesthesia Research Society

I.A.R.U. International Amateur Radio Union

I.A.S. indicated air speed; Institute of Aeronautical Sciences

I.A.S.F. International Amateur Swimming Federation

IATA or **I.A.T.A.** International Air Traffic Association; International Air Transport Authority

I.A.T.M.B. Inter-American Trade-Mark Bureau

I.A.T.S.E. International Association of Theatrical Stage Employees

I.A.U. International Academic Union; International Astronomical Union

I.B. in bond; inbound; incendiary bomb; inner bottom (Shipbuilding); Intelligence Branch; invoice book

I.B. or **Inf Brig** (Mil.) Infantry brigade

ib., ibid. (ibidem)(Lat.), **eod. loc.** (eodem loco)(Lat.) or **id. loc.** (idem loco)(Lat.) in the same place (cf. ad loc.; in loc.; loc. cit.)

I.B.A. Institute of British Architects; International Bar Association

I.B.A.A. Investment Bankers Association of America

I.B.B.A. Inland Bird Banding Association

I.B.B.U. International Bookbinders' Union

I.B.C. International Boundary Commission (United States, Alaska and Canada; United States and Mexico)

I.B.C.S. International Bureau of Commercial Statistics

I.B.E. Institute of British Engineers; International Bureau of Education

I.B.E.N. Incendiary bomb with explosive nose

I.B.I. International Bureau of Musicians; invoice book, inwards

ibid., ib. (ibidem)(Lat.), **eod. loc.** (eodem loco)(Lat.) or **id.loc.** (idem loco)(Lat.) in the same place (cf. ad loc.; in loc.; loc. cit.)

I.B.M International Brotherhood of Magicians

I.B.O. invoice book, outwards

I.B.P. Institute of British Photographers (cf. P.P.A.)

ibp or **i.b.p.** initial boiling point (cf. bp)

i.b.p. or **ibp** initial boiling point (cf. bp)

I.B.P.C.S. International Bureau for Physico-Chemical Standards

I.B.S. International Bible Students

I.B.T.L. Institut Badán Technicznych Lotnictwa

I.B.U. International Boxing Union; International Broadcasting Union

i-Bu isobutyl (Chem)

i.bu. or **imp.bu.** imperial bushel or bushels

I.B.U.P.U. International Bureau of the Universal Postal Union

I.B.W.M. International Bureau of Weights and Measures

IC index correction [of a sextant]

IC or **I.C.** Interceptor command

IC (Mil.) or **i.c.** inspected and condemned

I.C. (Institutum Fratrum Instructionis Christianae)(Lat.) Brothers of Christian Instruction; La Mennais Brothers; Missionary Sisters of the Immaculate Conception

I.C. or **IC** Interceptor command

I.C. or **I.-C.** Indo-China

I.C. or **Inst. Char.** (Institutum Charitatis)(Lat.) Institute of Charity; Fathers of the Institute of Charity; Rosminians

I.C. (Iesus Christus)(Lat.), **IX, I.X.** (Iēsous Christos)(Greek), **J.C.** or **J.-C.** (Jésus-Christ)(Fr.) Jesus Christ

I.C., J.C., j.c. or **J. Ctus.** (Iuris or Juris Consultus)(Lat.) counsellor-at-law; jurisconsult

ic. (icon)(Greek, Lat.) engraving; figure (cf. engr.; fig.)

i.c. or **IC** (Mil.) inspected and condemned

i.c. or **i/c** (Mil.) in charge of

i/c (Mil.) or **i.c.** in charge of

I.C.A. International Confederation of Agriculture

I.C.A.A. International College Athletic Association; Invalid Children's Aid Association

I.C.A.A.A.A. or **I.A.A.A.A.** Intercollegiate Association of Amateur Athletes in America

I.C.A.C.S. International Confederation of Authors' and Composers' Societies

I.C.A.N. International Commission for Air Navigation

ICAO International Civil Aviation Organization

ICC or **I.C.C.** Interstate Commerce Commission

I.C.C. International Chamber of Commerce

ICCP or **I.C.C.P.** Interdepartmental Committee on Commercial Policy

I.C.D. International College of Dentists; International Congress of Druggists; (Iesu Christo duce)(Lat.) with Jesus Christ as leader

I.C.E. or **Inst. C.E.** Institution of Civil Engineers (Brit.)

Ice. or **Icel.** Iceland; Icelandic

Icel. or **Ice.** Iceland; Icelandic

I.C.F. Italian Catholic Federation

I.C.G. Institute for Child Guidance

ich., Ichth. or **ichth.** ichthyology

Ichth., ichth. or **ich.** ichthyology

ICI or **I.C.I.** Imperial Chemical Industries

I.C.I.A. International Credit Insurance Association; International Crop Improvement Association

I.C.I.A.C.L. International Committee for the Improvement of the Amenities of Country Life

I.C.N. International Council of Nurses

I.C.N. (in Christi nomine)(Lat.) or **I.N.C.** (in nomine Christi)(Lat.) in the name of Christ (cf. I.N.J.)

Icon. or **icon.** iconography

icon. iconographic; iconographical

Icon. Ency. Iconographic Encyclopædia

I.C.O.R.A. International Catholic Office for Refugee Affairs

I.C.P. International Congress of Photography

I.C.P.C. International Criminal Police Commission

ICR Individual clothing record (Mil.)

I.C.R.E. International Council of Religious Education

I.C.R.H. International Congress on Religious History

I.C.R.S. International Commission on Radium Standards

I.C.S. Imperial College of Science (London) (now Royal College of Science); Indian Civil Service; International Confederation of Students; International Correspondence School

I.C.S.A. International Council for Scientific Agriculture

I.C.T. inflammation of connective tissue

I.C.Th.U.S. (Iēsous Christos, Theou Evios, Soter)(Greek) Jesus Christ, the Son of God, the Savior

I.C.U. Industrial and Commercial [Workers'] Union [of South Africa]

ICW or **icw** interrupted continuous waves (Radio)

I.C.W. International Council of Women

icw or **ICW** interrupted continuous waves (Radio)

I.C.W.F. International Clothing Workers' Federation

I.C.W.G. International Cooperative Women's Guild

I.C.Z. or **C.Z.** Isthmian [or Panama] Canal Zone

ID or **i.d.** inside diameter

I.D. Intelligence Department

I.D. or **Inf Div** (Mil.) Infantry division

Id., I. or **Ida.** Idaho

Id., id. (idem)(Lat.), **do.** (ditto)(Ital.), **d:o** (dito)(Swed.), **ead.** (eadem)(Lat.) or **íd.** (ídem)(Span.) ditto; the same

id., Id. (idem)(Lat.), **do.** (ditto)(Ital.), **d:o** (dito)(Swed.) **ead.** (eadem) (Lat.) or **íd.** (ídem)(Span.) ditto; the same

i.d. or **ID** inside diameter

I.D.A. Irish Drug Association; (Immortalis Dei auspicio or auxilio)(Lat.) with the guidance or help of Immortal God

Ida., I. or **Id.** Idaho

I.D.B. or **i.d.b.** illicit diamond buyer or buying (So.Afr.)

I.D.C. Imperial Defence College

i.d.c. [completed a course at, or served a year on the staff of the] Imperial Defence College (Brit.)

I.D.E.S. (Irmandade do Divino Espirito Santo)(Port.) Brotherhood of the Divine Ghost

I.D.E.S.T. (Irmandade do Divino Espirito Santo e da Trinidade)(Port.) Brotherhood of the Divine Ghost and Trinity

I.D.F. International Dairy Federation

I.D.N. (in Dei nomine)(Lat.) or **I.N.D.** (in nomine Dei)(Lat.) in the name of God

I.D.O. International Dental Organization

I.D.P.A. Inland Daily Press Association

I.D.R., Ex.R.f.d.I. (Exerzier-Reglement für die Infantrie)(Ger.) or **I.E.R.** (Infantrie-Exerzier-Reglement)(Ger.) Infantry Drill Regulations

IE index error [of a sextant]

I.E. Indian Empire; Individual equipment; Infantry equipment; Initial equipment

I.E., Ind-Eur or **Indo-Eur.** Indo-European

i.e. (id est)(Lat.), **c.-à-d.** (c'est-à-dire)(Fr.), **d.ä.** (det är)(Swed.), **d.h.** (das heisst)(Ger.), **d.i.** (das ist)(Ger.), **d.v.s.** (det vil sige)(Dan.), (det vill säga)(Swed.), **h.e.** (hoc or hic est)(Lat.) or **t.i.** (tudni illik)(Hung.) that is; that is to say (cf. viz.)

I.E.A. International Entomological Association

IEC or **I.E.C.** Industrial Emergency Council

I.E.C. International Electrotechnical Commission; International Exchange Committee

I.E.E. or **Inst. E.E.** Institution of Electrical Engineers (Brit.)

IER Individual equipment record (Mil.)

I.E.R. (Infantrie - Exerzier - Reglement) (Ger.), **I.D.R.** or **Ex. R. f. d. I.** (Exerzier-Reglement für die Infantrie)(Ger.) Infantry Drill Regulations

I.E.S. Illuminating Engineering Society; Indian Educational Service; International Exchange Service

IHΣ, IHC, IHS, JHC, JHS (Iesous)(Greek) or **Jes.** Jesus (Incorrectly regarded as the abbreviation for the Latin phrases Jesus Hominum Salvator, Jesus the Savior of Mankind, and In Hoc Signo, In this sign [thou shalt conquer])

if. (ifølge)(Dan.), **acc., ap.** (apud)(Lat.) or **sec.** (secundum)(Lat.) according to

i.f. (ipse fecit)(Lat.) he or she did it himself or herself

i.f. or **i-f** intermediate frequency

I.F.A.L.S. International Federation of Arts, Letters and Sciences

I.F.A.P. International Federation of the Agricultural Press

I.F.B.P.W. International Federation of Business and Professional Women

I.F.C. International Federation of Calvinists; International Finance Commission; International Fisheries Commission (U.S. and Canada); International Freighting Corporation

I.F.C.E. International Federation of Consulting Engineers

I.F.E.O. International Federation of Eugenic Organizations

I.F.J. International Federation of Journalists

I.F.L.A. International Federation of Library Associations

i.fol. or **imp.fol.** imperial folio

I.F.R. International Fellowship of Reconciliation

I.F.R.G. International Federation of Retail Grocers

I.F.S. International Faculty of Sciences; Irish Free State

I.F.T.A. International Federation of Teachers' Associations

I.F.T.U. International Federation of Trade Unions

I.F.U.W. International Federation of University Women

IG (Mil.), **I.G., I.-G., Insp. Gen.** or **Insp.-Gen.** Inspector General

I.G. Inner Guard; Inside Guard or Guardian; (Interessengemeinschaft)(Ger.) amalgamation

I.G. or **Indo-Ger.** Indo-Germanic

I.-G., IG (Mil.), **I.G., Insp.Gen.** or **Insp.-Gen.** Inspector General

i.gal. or **imp.gal.** imperial gallon or gallons

I.G.B. or **i.g.b.** illicit gold buyer or buying (So.Afr.)

i.g.b. or **I.G.B.** illicit gold buyer or buying (So.Afr.)

I.G.C. Inspector General of Communications

IGD (Mil.) or **I.G.D.** Inspector General's Department

I.G.M.A. International Garage & Maintenance Association

I.G.M.A.A. International Gas Model Airplane Association

ign. ignites; ignition

ign. (ignotus)(Lat.) or **unk.** unknown (cf. anon.; incog.; n.u.)

IGO Inspector General's Office

IG-Res Inspector General's Department Reserve

I.G.S. International Gutenberg Society

I.G.U. International Geographical Union

I.H., i.h., J.H. or **j.h.** (iacet or jacet hic) (Lat.) lies here (cf. H.I.; H.I.S.; H.S.; H.S.E.)

i.h. inside height

i.h., I.H., J.H. or **j.h.** (iacet or jacet hic) (Lat.) lies here (cf. H.I.; H.I.S.; H.S.; H.S.E.)

I.H.A. Illinois Hospital Association; Indiana Hospital Association; Iowa Hospital Association; International Hospital Association; International Hotel Alliance; International Hotelmen's Association

I.H.B. International Health Board (Rockefeller Foundation); International Hydrographic Bureau

IHC, IHΣ, IHS, JHC, JHS (Iesous) (Greek) or **Jes.** Jesus (Incorrectly regarded as the abbreviation for the Latin phrases Jesus Hominum Salvator, Jesus the Savior of Mankind, and In Hoc Signo, In this sign [thou shalt conquer])

I.H.F. International Hockey Federation

I.H.N. In His Name (King's Daughters)

IHP, I.H.P., ihp, i.hp. or **i.h.p.** indicated horsepower

I.H.P., IHP, ihp, i.hp. or **i.h.p.** indicated horsepower

ihp, IHP, I.H.P., i.hp. or **i.h.p.** indicated horsepower

i.hp., IHP, I.H.P., ihp or **i.h.p.** indicated horsepower

i.h.p., IHP, I.H.P., ihp or **i.hp.** indicated horsepower

ihp-hr indicated horsepower hour or hours

I.H.R. Institute of Human Relations

IHS, IHΣ, IHC, JHC, JHS (Iesous) (Greek) or **Jes.** Jesus (Incorrectly regarded as the abbreviation for the Latin phrases Jesus Hominum Salvator, Jesus the Savior of Mankind, and In Hoc Signo, In this sign [thou shalt conquer])

I/I indorsement irregular (Banking)

I.I.A. International Institute of Agriculture

I.I.A.S. International Institute of Administrative Sciences

I.I.C. International Institute of Commerce

I.I.L. Institute of International Law

I.I.R. International Institute of Refrigeration

I.I.R.I. International Industrial Relations Institute

I.I.S. International Institute of Sociology

i.J. (im Jahre)(Ger.), **a., an.** (anno)(Lat.) or **a.d.J.** (aus dem Jahre)(Ger.) in the year

I.J.C. International Joint Commission (U.S. and Canada)

i.J.d.W. (im Jahre der Welt)(Ger.) or **A.M.** (anno mundi)(Lat.) in the year of the world (i.e., when the creation is assumed to have been 4004 B.C.)

I.K. inner keel

I.L. Independence League

Il illinium (Chem.)

il. illustrator

il., Abb. (Abbildung, Abbildungen)(Ger.), **eff.** (effigies)(Lat.), **ill(s).**, **illus.** or **illust.** illustration; illustrations

il., ill., illus. or **illust.** illustrated

il. or **ils.** illustrators

i.l. inside length

I.L.A. Internationale Luftfahrt Austellung; International Leprosy Association

I.L.G.W.U. International Ladies' Garment Workers' Union

I.L.I. International Legal Institute

Ill. Illinois

ill., Abb. (Abbildung)(Ger.), **eff.** (effigies) (Lat.), **il., illus.** or **illust.** illustration

ill., il., illus. or **illust.** illustrated

ill. (illustrissimus)(Lat.), **Illmo.** (Illustrissimo)(Ital.), **Il(l)mo.** (Il(l)ustríssimo) (Port.) or **Ilmo.** (Ilustrísimo)(Span.) Most Illustrious; Most Distinguished

illit. illiterate

Illmo. (Illustrissimo) (Ital.), **ill.** (illustrissimus)(Lat.), **Il(l)mo.** (Il(l)ustríssimo) (Port.) or **Ilmo.** (Ilustrísimo)(Span.) Most Illustrious; Most Distinguished

ills., Abb. (Abbildungen)(Ger.), **eff.** (effigies)(Lat.), **il., ill., illus.** or **illust.** illustrations

illus., Abb. (Abbildung, Abbildungen) (Ger.), **eff.** (effigies)(Lat.), **il., ill(s).** or **illust.** illustration; illustrations

illus., il., ill. or **illust.** illustrated

illust., Abb. (Abbildung, Abbildungen) (Ger.), **eff.** (effigies)(Lat.), **il., ill(s).** or **illus.** illustration; illustrations

illust., il., ill. or **illus.** illustrated

Ilmo. (Ilustrísimo)(Span.), **ill.** (illustrissimus)(Lat.), **Illmo.** (Illustrissimo)(Ital.) or **Il(l)mo.** (Il(l)ustrísimo)(Port.) Most Illustrious; Most Distinguished

ILO or **I.L.O.** International Labor Office or Organization

i.l.o. in lieu of

I.L.P. Independent Labour Party (Brit.)

I.L.P.N.R. International League for the Protection of Native Races (Colored races)

ils. or **il.** illustrators

I.L.U. International Legal Union

I.L.U.S. Inventors League of the United States

I.M. (Ihre Majestät)(Ger.) your majesty; (Inscription maritime)(Fr.) Naval Reserve

I.M., I. of M., I.O.M. or **I.o.M.** Isle of Man

I.M.C. International Maritime Committee; International Missionary Council

I.M.D. Indian Medical Department

I.M.E. Institute of Makers of Explosives

I.M.E. or **I. Mech. E.** Institution of Mechanical Engineers (Brit.)

I.M.E. or **Inst. M.E.** Institution of Marine Engineers

I. Mech. E. or **I.M.E.** Institute of Mechanical Engineers (Brit.)

I.Meth. or **Ind. Meth.** Independent Methodists

I.M.I. International Metaphysical Institute

imit. imitation; imitative; imitatively

immun. immunology

immy. or **stat.** (statim)(Lat.) immediately

I.M.N.S. Imperial Military Nursing Service

I.M.O. International Meteorological Organization

Imp., I., i. (Imperator)(Lat.) or **Emp.** Emperor

Imp., I., i., Impx. (Imperatrix)(Lat.) or **Emp.** Empress

Imp., I., imp., k. or **kais.** (kaiserlich)(Ger.) imperial

imp. imparted; implement; import; imported; imports; (imprimis)(Lat.) first in order (Geneal.)(cf. prem.); imprimatur)(Lat.) let it be printed

imp. or **Aufdr.** (Aufdruck)(Ger.) imprint

imp., I., Imp., k. or **kais.** (kaiserlich)(Ger.) imperial

imp., i. (imperium)(Lat.), **Emp.** or **emp.** empire

imp., imper., imperat. or **impv.** imperative

imp., imper. or **impf.** imperfect

imp. or **impers.** impersonal

imp., impr. or **improv.** improvement

imp., impr. or **verb.** (verbesserte)(Ger.) improved
imp. or **improp.** improper
imp. or **impt.** important
imp. or **imptr.** importer
imp.bu. or **i.bu.** imperial bushel or bushels
imper., imp., imperat. or **impv.** imperative
imperat., imp., imper. or **impv.** imperative
imperf. imperforate (Philately)
imperf., imp. or **impf.** imperfect
impers. or **imp.** impersonal
impf., imp. or **imperf.** imperfect
imp.fol. or **i.fol.** imperial folio
imp.gal. or **i.gal.** imperial gallon or gallons
impr., imp. or **improv.** improvement
impr., imp. or **verb.** (verbesserte)(Ger.) improved
Impreg Impregnating (Mil.)
impreg. impregnated
improp. or **imp.** improper
improv., imp. or **impr.** improvement
impt. or **imp.** important
imptr. or **imp.** importer
impv., imp., imper. or **imperat.** imperative
Impx., I., i., Imp. (Imperatrix)(Lat.) or **Emp.** Empress
I.M.R.C. International Maritime Radio Committee
I.M.S. Indian Medical Service
I.M.U.N.A. International Molders Union of North America
I.M.W.F. International Metalworkers' Federation
In indium (Chem.)
in (Mil.), **in.** or **Z.** (Zoll)(Ger.) inch
in., ins. or **Z.** (Zolle)(Ger.) inches
in.^{2} or **sq. in.** square inch or inches
in.^{3} or **cu. in.**. cubic inch or inches
I.N.A. Indian National Airways
I.N.A. or **Inst. N.A.** Institution of Naval Architects (Brit.)
in ball. in ballast (Shipping)
inbd. inboard
I.N.C. (in nomine Christi)(Lat.) or **I.C.N.** (in Christi nomine)(Lat.) in the name of Christ (cf. I.N.J.)
inc. income; incumbent
inc., incis. (incisus)(Lat.), **eng., engr.** or **sculpt.** (sculptus)(Lat.) engraved
inc., Incl (Mil.), **Incl.** or **incl.** inclusive
inc., Incl., incl., Incls (Mil.) or **incls.** inclosure
inc. or **incl.** including
inc., incl., Incld (Mil.) or **inclus.** (inclusus) (Lat.) included
inc., incor. or **incorp.** incorporated
inc. or **incr.** increase
incept. inception; inceptive
inch. or **incho.** inchoative
incis., inc. (incisus)(Lat.), **eng., engr.** or **sculpt.** (sculptus)(Lat.) engraved
Incl (Mil.), **Incl., incl.** or **inc.** inclusive
Incl., incl., inc., Incls (Mil.) or **incls.** inclosure
incl. or **inc.** including
incl., inc., Incld (Mil.) or **inclus.** (inclusus)(Lat.) included
Incld (Mil.), **inc., incl.** or **inclus.** (inclusus) (Lat.) included
Incls (Mil.), **incls., inc., Incl.** or **incl.** inclosure
inclus. (inclusus)(Lat.), **inc., incl.** or **Incld** (Mil.) included
incog. incognito (cf. anon.; ign.)
incor., inc. or **incorp.** incorporated
incorp., inc. or **incor.** incorporated
incorr. incorrect
incr. increased; increasing
incr. or **inc.** increase
I.N.D. (in nomine Dei)(Lat.) or **I.D.N.** (in Dei nomine)(Lat.) in the name of God
Ind Indorsement (Mil.)
Ind. India; Indian; Indiana; Indies
Ind., ind. or **I.** independent
In d. or **in d.** (in dies)(Lat.) in a day; daily (cf. o.d.; p.d. q.d.)
ind. independence; index; indigo; indirect; indirectly; induline; industrial; industry
ind., I. or **Ind.** independent
ind. or **i.** indicated
ind. or **indic.** indicative
in d. or **In d.** (in dies)(Lat.) in a day; daily (cf. o.d.; p.d.; q.d.)
Ind. E. or **Ind. Engin.** Industrial Engineer
indecl. indeclinable
indef. indefinite
indemy. or **indm.** indemnity
inden. or **indent.** indention
Ind. Engin. or **Ind. E.** Industrial Engineer
indent. indenture
indent. or **inden.** indention
Ind-Eur, I.E. or **Indo-Eur.** Indo-European
indic. indicating; indicator
indic. or **ind.** indicative
individ. individual
Ind. L. Independent Liberal
indm. or **indemy.** indemnity
Ind. Meth. or **I. Meth.** Independent Methodists
Indo-Eur., I.E. or **Ind-Eur** Indo-European
Indo-Ger. or **I.G.** Indo-Germanic
Ind. T., Ind. Ter. or **I.T.** Indian Territory
Ind. Ter., Ind. T. or **I.T.** Indian Territory
induc. induction
ined. (ineditus)(Lat.) not made known; not published (cf. unpub.)
in ex. (in extenso)(Lat.) at length; (in extremis)(Lat.) in the last extremity
Inf (Mil.), **Inf., inf.** or **I.** Infantry
Inf. or **inf.** (infunde)(Lat.) infuse (Pharm.)
inf. inferior; information
inf. (infra)(Lat.) or **bel.** below
inf. or **infin.** infinitive
in f. (in fine)(Lat.) in the end; finally (cf. expl.)

Inf Armd Infantry armored
Inf Brig (Mil.) or **I.B.** Infantry brigade
Inf Div (Mil.) or **I.D.** Infantry division
infin. or **inf.** infinitive
infl. influence; influences
in-f° (in-folio)(Fr.), **F., f., fo., f°** or **fol.** folio (cf. ff.; ll.)
infra dig. (infra dignitatem)(Lat.) beneath one's dignity
Inf Regt (Mil.) or **I.R.** Infantry regiment
I.N.I. or **I.N.J.** (in nomine Iesu or Jesu) (Lat.) in the name of Jesus (cf. I.N.C.)
init. initial
init.. (initio)(Lat.), **ad init.** (ad initium) (Lat.), **in lim.** (in limine)(Lat.) or **in pr.** (in principio)(Lat.) at or in the beginning (cf. ab init.)
I.N.J. or **I.N.I.** (in nomine Jesu or Iesu) (Lat.) in the name of Jesus (cf. I.N.C.)
Inj. injection
Inj. enem. (injiciatur enema)(Lat.) let an enema be injected
in-lb inch-pound(s)
in lim. (in limine)(Lat.), **ad. init.** (ad initium)(Lat.), **init.** (initio)(Lat.) or **in pr.** (in principio)(Lat.) in or at the beginning (cf. ab init.)
in loc. (in loco)(Lat.), **L., l.** or **loc.** (loco) (Lat.) in the place (cf. ad loc.; a.h.l.)
in loc. cit. (in loco citato)(Lat.), **a.a.O.** (am angeführten Orte)(Ger.), **c.l.** or **cit.loc.** (citato loco)(Lat.), **l.c.** or **loc.cit.** (loco citato)(Lat.) in the place cited (cf. loc. laud.; loc. primo cit.; op.cit.; u.s.)
in mem. (in memoriam)(Lat.) in memory of
In. O. or **I.O.** India Office
inorg. inorganic
INP or **I.N.P.** International News Photos
in pr. (in principio)(Lat.), **ad init.** (ad initium)(Lat.), **init.** (initio)(Lat.) or **in lim.** (in limine)(Lat.) at or in the beginning (cf. ab init.)
In pulm. (in pulmento)(Lat.) in gruel
in re. in regard to (cf. m.H.t.)
I.N.R.I. or **J.N.R.J.** (Jesus Nazarenus Rex Judaeorum) (Lat.) Jesus of Nazareth, King of the Jews
I.N.R.U. International News Reel Union
INS or **I.N.S.** International News Service
Ins (Mil.), **Ins., ins.** or **insur.** insurance
Ins., ins. or **insp.** inspector
ins. insulated; insulation; insulator
ins., in. or **Z.** (Zolle)(Ger.) inches
ins., Ins (Mil.), **Ins.** or **insur.** insurance
ins., Ins. or **insp.** inspector
ins. or **insc.** inscribe; inscribed [stock] (Brit.)
in s. (in situ)(Lat.) in its original situation
insc. or **ins.** inscribe; inscribed [stock] (Brit.)
insc. or **inscr.** inscription
inscrs. inscriptions
insep. inseparable
insign. typogr. (insigne typographi)(Lat.) "Printer's mark"; colophon
insol. insoluble
insp., Ins. or **ins.** inspector
Insp. Gen., Insp.-Gen., IG (Mil.), **I.G.** or **I.-G.** Inspector General
I.N.S.T. (in nomine Sanctae Trinitatis) (Lat.) in the name of the Holy Trinity
Inst. or **inst.** institute
Inst., inst., cte. (corriente)(Span.) or **d.M.** (denne Maaned)(Dan.) instant; this month; the present month (cf. curr.)
Inst., inst. or **instn.** institution
Inst., inst., Instr (Mil.) or **instr.** instrument; instruments
inst., cte. (correinte)(Span.), **d.M.** (denne Maaned)(Dan.) or **Inst.** instant; this month (cf. curr.)
inst., H., Hft. (Heft)(Ger.), **Lfg.** (Lieferung)(Ger.), **liv.** (livraison)(Fr.), **T.** or **Th.** (Teil, Theil)(Ger.) installment (cf. Abt.; pt.)
inst. or **I.** instantaneous
inst. or **Inst.** institute
inst., Inst. or **instn.** institution
inst., Inst., Instr (Mil.) or **instr.** instrument; instruments
inst. or **instr.** instrumental
Inst. Act. Institute of Actuaries (Brit.)
Inst. C.E. or **I.C.E.** Institution of Civil Engineers (Brit.)
Inst. Char. or **I.C.** (Institutum Charitatis) (Lat.) Institute of Charity; Fathers of the Institute of Charity; Rosminians
Inst. E.E. or **I.E.E.** Institution of Electrical Engineers (Brit.)
Inst.M.E. or **I.M.E.** Institution of Marine Engineers
Inst. M.E. or **Inst. Mech. E.** Institution of Mechanical Engineers (Brit.)
Inst. Mech. E. or **Inst. M.E.** Institution of Mechanical Engineers (Brit.)
Inst. M.M. Institution of Mining and Metallurgy (Brit.)
instn., Inst. or **inst.** institution
instn., instr., instrn. or **V.** (Vorschrift)(Ger) instruction
Inst. N.A. or **I.N.A.** Institution of Naval Architects (Brit.)
instns., instrns., instrs. or **V.** (Vorschriften) (Ger.) instructions
Instr (Mil.), **instr., Inst.** or **inst.** instrument; instruments
Instr. or **instr.** instructor
instr., Inst., inst. or **Instr** (Mil.) instrument; instruments
instr. or **inst.** instrumental
instr., instn., instrn. or **V.** (Vorschrift)(Ger.) instruction
instrn., instn., instr. or **V.** (Vorschrift)(Ger.) instruction
instrns., instns., instrs. or **V.** (Vorschriften) (Ger.) instructions
Instr. of M. or **I. of M.** Instructor of Musketry
instrs., instns., instrns. or **V.** (Vorschriften) (Ger.) instructions
insur., Ins (Mil.), **Ins.** or **ins.** insurance
Int (Mil.), **I.** or **Intell.** intelligence
Int (Mil.), **Int., int.** or **i.** interest
Int (Mil.) or **inter.** intermediate

int. interim; interior; internal; interval
int., i., intr. or **intrans.** intransitive
int., Int (Mil.), **Int.** or **i.** interest
int. or **interj.** interjection
int., Internat., internat. or **Intl.** international
int., interp. or **Intpr** (Mil.) interpreter
int. al. (inter alia)(Lat.), **bl. a.** (bland annat)(Swed.), **et al.** (et alii or aliae) (Lat.) or **u.a.m.** (und andere or anderes mehr)(Ger.) among other things; and other things
intcl. intercoastal
Int.Dept. Department of the Interior
Intell., I. or **Int** (Mil.) intelligence
intens. intensive
inter. or **Int** (Mil.) intermediate
inter. or **interrog.** interrogation; interrogative
Intercom. or **Intercomn.** intercommunication
Intercomn. or **Intercom.** intercommunication
interj. or **int.** interjection
Internat., internat., int. or **Intl.** international
internat. internationally
interp., int. or **Intpr** (Mil.) interpreter
interpr. (interpres)(Lat.), **tr., trad.** (traduttore)(Ital.), **trans.** or **tras.** (traslatore) (Ital.) translator
interrog. or **inter.** interrogation; interrogative
Intl., int., Internat. or **internat.** international
Int O (Mil.) or **I.O.** Intelligence officer (cf.A-2;G-2;S-2)
Intpr. (Mil.), **int.** or **interp.** interpreter
intr., i., int. or **intrans.** intransitive
intr., intro. or **introd.** introduce; introduced; introducing; introduction; introductory
intrans., i., int. or **intr.** intransitive
in trans., i.t. (in transitu)(Lat.) or **e.r.** (en route)(Fr.) in transit; en route; on the way
Int. Rev. or **I.R.** Internal Revenue
intro., intr. or **introd.** introduce; introduced; introducing; introduction; introductory
introd., intr. or **intro.** introduce; introduced; introducing; introduction; introductory
inv. invented (cf. invt.); invention; inventor; invoice
inv., inven. or **invt.** (invenit)(Lat.) he or she invented it (cf. delt.; des.; disc.)
inven., inv. or **invt.** (invenit)(Lat.) he or she invented it (cf. delt.; des.; disc.)
invert. invertebrate
invt. inventory
invt., inv. or **inven.** (invenit)(Lat.) he or she invented it (cf. delt.; des.; disc.)
I.O. Intelligence Office
I.O. or **In.O.** India Office
I.O. or **Int O** (Mil.) Intelligence officer (cf.A-2;G-2;S-2)
I/O or **i.o.** inspecting order
Io Ionium (Chem.)
Io., I. or **Ia.** Iowa
i.o. in order
i.o. or **I/O** inspecting order
I.O.B.A. Independent Order of B'rith Abraham
I.O.B.B. Independent Order of B'nai B'rith
I.O.C. International Office of Chemistry; International Ornithological Congress
I.O.D.E. Imperial Order, Daughters of the Empire (Can.)
I.O.F. Independent Order of Foresters (cf. A.O.F.; F. of A.)
I. of M., I.M., I.O.M. or **I.o.M.** Isle of Man
I. of M. or **Instr. of M.** Instructor of Musketry
I. of W., I.O.W. or **I.W.** Isle of Wight
I. of W. or **I.W.** Inspector of Works (Brit.)
I.O.G.C. International Olympic Games Committee
I.O.G.T. International Order of Good Templars
I.O.M. Indian Order of Merit
I.O.M., I.M., I. of M. or **I.o.M.** Isle of Man
I.o.M., I.M., I. of M. or **I.O.M.** Isle of Man
Ion. Ionic
I.O.O. Inspecting ordnance officer
I.O.O.F. Independent Order of Odd Fellows (cf. O.F.)
I.O.P. Institute of Oil Painters; Institute of Painters in Oil Colours
I.O.R. Independent Order of Rechabites (Brit.)
I.O.R.M. Improved Order of Red Men
I.O.S.M. Independent Order of the Sons of Malta
IOU or **I.O.U.** I owe you
I.O.U. International Oil Union
I.O.U. or **IOU** I owe you
I.O.W., I. of W. or **I.W.** Isle of Wight
IP iron pipe size
IP (Mil.) or **P.I.** Initial point
I.P. Improvement Purchase (Australia); incisoproximal; Intelligence Police
I.P. or **i.p.** intermediate pressure (Cylinder)
i.p. installment paid (Stocks)
i.p. or **I.P.** intermediate pressure (Cylinder)
IPA Inter-Professional Association [for Social Insurance]
IPA or **I.P.A.** International Phonetic Association; International Press Association
I.P.A. International Paediatric or Pediatric Association
I.P.A. or **IPA** International Phonetic Association; International Press Association
i.p.a. including particular average
I.P.A.A. International Psycho-Analytical Association
I.P.A. of A. Independent Petroleum Association of America
I-para primipara
I.P.C. International Police Conference; International Prison Commission; International Psychological Congress; International Publishers' Congress

I.P.C.R. Institute of Physical and Chemical Research (Tokyo)

I.P.D. (in praesentia Dominorum)(Lat.) in the presence of the Lords [of Session]; Individual Package Delivery

ipecac. ipecacuanha

I.P.F. International Pharmaceutical Federation; International Police Federation

I.P.H.O. International Public Health Office

I.P.I. International Printing Ink [Corporation]

I.P.I. or **i.p.i.** (in partibus infidelium)(Lat.) in the lands of unbelievers

i.p.i. or **I.P.I.** (in partibus infidelium)(Lat.) in the lands of unbelievers

I.P.L. International Protestant League

i.p.p. india paper proofs

I.P.R. Institute of Pacific Relations

IPS, I.P.S., ips or **i.p.s.** inch(es) per second

I.P.S. Incorporated Phonographic Society (Brit.)

I.P.S., IPS., ips or **i.p.s.** inch(es) per second

ips, IPS, I.P.S. or **i.p.s.** inch(es) per second

I.Q. intelligence quotient (Phychology)

I.Q. or **i.q.** (idem quod)(Lat.) the same as

i.q.e.d. (id quod erat demonstrandum)(Lat.) that which was to be proved or demonstrated (cf. Q.E.D.; Q.E.F.; Q.E.I.)

I.R. Immediate Reserve; (Infirmerie regimentaire)(Fr.) Regimental infirmary

I.R. or **Inf Regt** (Mil.) Infantry regiment

I.R. or **Int. Rev.** Internal Revenue

Ir iridium (Chem.)

Ir. or **I.** Irish

Ir., I. or **Ire.** Ireland

I.R.A. Indian Rights Association; Irish Republican Army

Iran. Iranian; Iranic

IRB or **I. R. B.** Internal Revenue Bureau

I.R.B. Irish Republican Brotherhood

I.R.C. Infantry Reserve Corps; International Red Cross; International Relations Clubs [of the Carnegie Endowment for International Peace]; irregular route carrier

I.R.C.A. International Railway Congress Association

I.R.C.C. International Red Cross Committee

I.R.E. Institute of Radio Engineers; Institute of Refrigerating Engineers (New So. Wales)

Ire., I. or **Ir.** Ireland

I.R.G.F.A. International Railway General Foremen's Association

I.R.I. Institution of the Rubber Industry (Brit.); Inter-Industrial Relations Institute

I.R.O. Inland Revenue Office or Officer; Internal Revenue Office or Officer

iron. ironical; ironically

irr. or **irred.** irredeemable

irr. or **irreg.** irregular; irregularly

irred. or **irr.** irredeemable

irreg. or **irr.** irregular

I.R.U. international radium units; International Railway Union; international rat units

I.S. Indian Scout; intercostal space; Irish Society; Isle of Skye

I.S. or **i.-S.** inter-service

Is., is., I., i., Isl. or **isl.** island; isle

Is. or **Isa.** Isaiah

is., I., i., Is., Isl. or **isl.** isle; island

I.S.A. international standard atmosphere; International Standards Association

Isa. or **Is.** Isaiah

Isab. Isabella

I.S.C. Imperial Service College (Windsor); Indian Staff Corps (now Indian Army); International Shipping Conference

I.S.C. or **i.s.c.** interstate commerce

I.S.C.C. International Society for Crippled Children

I.S.C.M. International Society for Contemporary Music

I.S.F. International Shipping Federation; International Spiritualist Federation

I.S.I. International Statistical Institute

Isl., isl., I., i., Is. or **is.** island; isle

isl., I., i., Is., is. or **Isl.** island; isle

isls. islands

I.S.M. Imperial Service Medal (Brit.); Incorporated Society of Musicians (Brit.); (Iesus Salvator Mundi)(Lat.) Jesus Savior of the World

I.S.O. [Companion of the] Imperial Service Order

iso. isotropic

isom. isometric

isoth. isothermal

I.S.R. International Society of Radiobiology

Isr. Israel

I.S.S. International Society of Surgery

iss. issue

I.S.S.B. Inter-Service Security Board (Brit.)

I.S.S.F. International Service of the Society of Friends (Quakers)

I.S.T.A. International Seed-Testing Association

i.st.f. (i stället för)(Swed.) or **i.V.** (in Vertretung)(Ger.) in place of; instead of (cf. subst.)

Isth. or **isth.** isthmus

isth. or **Isth.** isthmus

I.S.U. International Seamen's Union

I.S.W.G. imperial standard wire gauge

I.T. Inner Temple; intermediate transportation

I.T., Ind.T. or **Ind Ter.** Indian Territory

It. or **Ital.** Italian; Italic; Italy

it. or **ital.** italic; italics (Typog.)

i.t., in trans. (in transitu)(Lat.) or **e.r.** (en route)(Fr.) in transit; en route; on the way

I.T.A.C. International Telephone Advisory Committee
Ital. or **It.** Italian; Italic; Italy
ital. or **it.** italic; italics (Typog.)
IT&T or **I.T.& T.** International Telephone and Telegraph Company
I.T.B. International Time Bureau
I.T.C.A. Indian Trans-Continental Airways
i. t. d. (i tak dalej)(Pol.), **etc.** (et cetera) (Lat.), **k.t.l.** (kai ta loipa)(Greek), **m.m.** (med mera)(Swed.), (med mere) (Dan.), **o.d.** (ock dylikt or dylika) (Swed.), **o.s.v.** (och så vidare)(Swed.), (og saa videre)(Dan.), **u.drgl.** (und dergrelchen) (Ger.), **u.s.f.** (und so fort) (Ger.), **usw.** or **u.s.w.** (und so weiter)(Ger.) and so forth; and the like; and others of like kind
I.T.F. International Transportworkers' Federation; inland transit floater (Shipping)
ITI or **I.T.I.** Industries Technical Institute [Incorporated]
itin. itinerant; itinerary
I.T.U. International Typographical Union
I.U. immunizing unit (Med.)
I.U. or **i.u.** international unit
I.U.A.C. International Union Against Cancer
I.U.A.I. International Union of Aviation Insurers
I.U.B. Interstate Underwriters Board
I.U.B.S. International Union for Biological Sciences
I.U.C. International Union of Chemistry
I.U.C.W.L. International Union of Catholic Women's Leagues
I.U.F.L.N. International University Federation for the League of Nations
I.U.P.A. International Union of Press Associations
I.U.S.S. International Union for Social Studies (Mechlin Union)
I.V. or **i.v.** initial velocity
i.V. (in Vertretung)(Ger.) or **i.st.f.** (i stället för)(Swed.) in place of; instead of (cf. subst.)
i.v. increased value; invoice value
i.v. or **I.V.** initial velocity
i.v. (in verbo or voce)(Lat.), **s.h.v.** (sub hoc verbo or sub hac voce)(Lat.) or **s.v.** (sub verbo or voce)(Lat.) under the word; under this word (used in dictionaries)
I.V.A. Independent Voters' Association
I.W. Infantry works (Fortifications)
I.W. or **I. of W.** Inspector of Works (Brit.)
I.W., I. of W. or **I.O.W.** Isle of Wight
i.w. inside width
I.W.A. or **I.W.C.A.** International Woodcarvers' Association
IWC Inland Waterway Corporation; International Wireless Committee
I.W.C.A. or **I.W.A.** International Woodcarvers' Association
I.W.G.C. Imperial War Graves Commission
I.W.L.A. Izaak Walton League of America
I.W.T.D. or **I.W.T.** Inland Water Transport Department (Brit.)
I.Wts. international [atomic] weights
I.W.W. Industrial Workers of the World
IX, I.X. (Iēsous Christos)(Greek), **I.C.** (Iesus Christus)(Lat.), **J.C.** or **J.-C.** (Jésus-Christ)(Fr.) Jesus Christ
I.Y. Imperial Yoemanry
I.Y.H.A. International Youth Hostels' Association
izq.[a], **izq.**[da] (izquierda)(Span.), **L.H., l.h., M.G., m.g.** (main gauche)(Fr.), **m.s.** (mano sinistra)(Lat.), **s.** (sinistra) (Ital.) or **S.M.** (sinistra mano)(Lat.) left hand

ΙΑΠ (Iota Alpha Pi) National undergrauate sorority (Jewish)
ΙΛΣ (Iota Lambda Sigma) Professional fraternity (Vocational Education)
ΙΣ (Iota Sigma) National undergraduate fraternity
ΙΣΠ (Iota Sigma Pi) Professional sorority (Chemistry)
ΙΤΣ (Iota Tau Sigma) National undergraduate fraternity (Osteopathy)
ΙΤΤ (Iota Tau Tau) National undergraduate society (Legion of Honor)

J

J joule (Physics)
J. Jew; (juris)(Lat.) of law
J. (Jahr)(Ger.), **A., a., An., an.** (annus) (Lat.), **r.** (rok)(Pol.), **y.** or **yr.** year
J. or **j.** judge
J. or **Jew.** Jewish
J., jl., jour. or **jr.** journal (cf. Ztg.)
J., Jn., Jno., Jo., Joh. or **Js.** (Johannes)(Lat.) John
J. or **Jul.** Julius
J., Jus., jus., Just. or **just.** justice
J. (jus)(Lat.), **L.** or **l.** law
j. or **J.** judge
JA (Mil.), **J.A.** or **J.Adv.** Judge Advocate
J.A. Joint Agent
J.A., JA (Mil.) or **J.Adv.** Judge Advocate
J.A., j.a., J/A or **j/a** joint account
J/A, j/a, J.A. or **j.a.** joint account
Ja. Jacques
Ja., eno. (enero)(Span.), **genn.** (gennaio) (Ital.), **Jan., janv.** (janvier)(Fr.) or **Stycz.** (Styczeń)(Pol.) January
Ja., Jam. or **Jas.** James
j.a., J.A., J/A or **j/a** joint account
J.A.C. Junior Association of Commerce
Jac. Jacob; Jacobus
J.A.C.L. Japanese American Citizens' League
J.Adv., JA (Mil.) or **J.A.** Judge Advocate

J.Adv.Gen., JAG (Mil.) or **J.A.G.** Judge Advocate General

JAG (Mil.), **J.A.G.** or **J.Adv.Gen.** Judge Advocate General

J.A.G., JAG (Mil.) or **J.Adv. Gen.** Judge Advocate General

JAGD (Mil.) or **J.A.G.D.** Judge Advocate General's Department

JAGN or **J.A.G.N.** Judge Advocate General of the Navy

JAGO (Mil.) or **J.A.G.O.** Judge Advocate General's Office

JAG-Res Judge Advocate General's Department Reserve

J.A.J.O. January, April, July and October (Interest)

Jam. Jamaica

Jam., Ja. or **Jas.** James

J. & D. June and December (Interest)

J. & J. January and July (Interest)

j.& w.o. jettison and washing overboard (Insurance)

Jan., eno. (enero)(Span.), **genn.** (gennaio) (Ital.), **Ja., janv.** (janvier)(Fr.) or **Stycz.** (Styczeń)(Pol.) January

janv. (janvier)(Fr.), **eno.** (enero)(Span.), **genn.** (gennaio)(Ital.), **Ja., Jan.** or **Stycz.** (Styczeń)(Pol.) January

Jap. Japan; Japanese

Jas., Ja. or **Jam.** James

JA Sec Judge advocate's section

Jasp. Jasper

Jav. Javanese

JB or **J.B.** Joint Board

J.B. John Bull (Brit.); joint bonds

J.B. (Jurum Baccalaureus)(Lat.), **B.L., B.LL.** (Baccalaureus Legum)(Lat.) or **LL.B.** (Legum Baccalaureus)(Lat.) Bachelor of Laws

J.B.C.O.A. Junior Bird Club of America

J.B.I.U.A. Journeymen Barbers' International Union of America

J.C. Julius Caesar; [Lord] Justice-Clerk (Scot.)

J.C., J.-C. (Jésus-Christ)(Fr.), **I.C.** (Iesus Christus)(Lat.), **IX** or **I.X.** (Iēsous Christos)(Greek) Jesus Christ

J.C., j.c., I.C. or **J. Ctus.** (Juris or Iuris Consultus)(Lat.) counsellor-at-law; jurisconsult; jurist

J.-C. (Jésus-Christ)(Fr.), **J.C., I.C.** (Iesus Christus)(Lat.), **IX** or **I.X.** (Iēsous Christos)(Greek) Jesus Christ

Jc, jc., jct., jctn., jn., jnc., Junc., junc. or **junct.** junction

jc., Jc, jct., jctn., jn., jnc., Junc., junc. or **junct.** junction

j.c., I.C., J.C. or **J.Ctus.** (Juris or Iuris Consultus)(Lat.) counsellor-at-law; Jurisconsult; jurist

J.C.A. Jewish Colonization Association

J.C.B. (Juris Canonici Baccalaureus)(Lat.) Bachelor of Canon Law

J.C.B. (Juris Civilis Baccalaureus)(Lat.) or **B.C.L.** Bachelor of Civil Law

J.C.D. (Juris Civilis Doctor)(Lat.), **C.L.D.** or **D.C.L.** Doctor of Civil Law

J.C.D., D.C.L. or **D.Cn.L.** Doctor of Canon Law

J.C.L. (Juris Canonici Lector or Licentiatus)(Lat.) Reader or Licentiate in Canon Law

J.C.of C. Junior Chamber of Commerce

J.C.R.S. Jewish Consumptive Relief Society

jct., Jc, jc., jctn., jn., jnc., Junc., junc. or **junct.** junction

jctn., Jc, jc., jct., jn., jnc., Junc., junc. or **junct.** junction

J. Ctus., I.C., J.C. or **j.c.** (Juris or Iuris Consultus)(Lat.) counsellor-at-law; jurisconsult; jurist

J.D. Junior Deacon; Junior Dean

J.D., Jur.D. (Juris Doctor)(Lat.), **D.J., Dr.Jur.** (Doctor Juris)(Lat.) or **D.L.** Doctor of Law (cf. LL.D.; D.J.S.)

J.D., Jur. D. (Jurum Doctor)(Lat.) or **LL.D.** (Legum Doctor)(Lat.) Doctor of Laws; Doctor of Jurisprudence

Jd. joined

J.D.C. Joint Distribution Committee [of Funds for Jewish War Sufferers]

Je., Czerw. (Czerwiec)(Pol.), **Ju., Jun.** or **jun.** (junio)(Span.) June

J.E.A. joint export agent

JEB or **J.E.B.** Joint Economy Board

JEC or **J.E.C.** Joint Economic Committee (U.S. and Canada)

Jed. Jedediah

Jem. Jemima

Jer. Jeremiah; Jeremy,

Jer. or **Hi.** (Hieronymus)(Lat.) Jerome

Jes., IHΣ, IHC, IHS, JHC or **JHS** (Iēous) (Greek) Jesus (Incorrectly regarded as the abbreviation for the Latin phrases Jesus Hominum Salvator, Jesus the Savior of Men, and In Hoc Signo, In this sign [thou shalt conquer])

Jew. or **J.** Jewish

jew. jewelry

jf., jfr. (jaevnfør)(Dan.), (jämför)(Swed.), **cf., conf.** (confer)(Lat.), **comp., compar., cp., por.** (porównaj)(Pol.), **sml.** (sammenlign)(Dan.) or **vgl.** (vergleiche)(Ger.) compare

jfr., jf. (jämför)(Swed.), (jaevnfør)(Dan.), **cf., conf.** (confer)(Lat.), **comp., compar., cp., por.** (porównaj)(Pol.), **sml.** (sammenlign)(Dan.) or **vgl.** (vergleiche)(Ger.) compare

jg, jg., j.g., Jr.Gr. or **jr.gr.** junior grade

j.g., jg, jg., Jr.Gr. or **jr.gr.** junior grade

J.G.W. Junior Grand Warden

J.H., I.H., i.h. or **j.h.** (jacet or iacet hic) (Lat.) lies here (cf. H.I.; H.I.S.; H.S.; HS.E.)

j.h., I.H., i.h. or **J.H.** (jacet or iacet hic) (Lat.) lies here (cf. H.I.; H.I.S.; H.S.; H.S.E.)

JHC, IHC, IHΣ, IHS, I.H.S., JHS (Iesous) (Greek) or **Jes.** Jesus (Incorrectly regarded as the abbreviation for the Latin phrases Jesus Hominum Salvator, Jesus the Savior of Mankind, and In Hoc Signo, In this sign [thou shalt conquer])

J.H.H. Johns Hopkins Hospital

JHS, IHΣ, IHC, IHS, JHC (Iesous) (Greek) or **Jes.** Jesus (Incorrectly regarded as the abbreviation for the Latin phrases Jesus Hominum Salvator, Jesus Savior of Mankind, and In Hoc Signo, In this sign [thou shalt conquer])
J.I.C. Joint Industrial Council (Brit.)
J.I.E. Junior Institution of Engineers (Brit.)
JJ. justices
JJ., Jud., jud. or **Judg.** judges
Jl. or **Jo.** Joel
Jl., juil. (juillet)(Fr.), **Jul., jul.** (julio) (Span.), **Jy.** or **Lip.** (Lipiec)(Pol.) July
jl., J., jour. or **jr.** journal (cf. Ztg.)
Jla. Julia
Jlt. Juliet
J.M. (Justice militaire)(Fr.) Military court
J.M.J. Jesus, Mary and Joseph (Rom. Cath.)
Jn., J., Jno., Jo., Joh. or **Js.** (Johannes)(Lat.) John
jn., Jc, jc., jct., jctn., jnc., Junc., junc. or **junct.** junction
jnc., Jc, jc., jct., jctn., jn., Junc., junc. or **junct.** junction
J.N.F. Jewish National Fund [of America]
Jno., J., Jn., Jo., Joh. or **Js.** (Johannes)(Lat.) John
Jnr., jnr., d.J. (der Jungere)(Ger.), **d.y.** (den yngre)(Swed.), **Jr., jr., Jun., jun., Junr.** or **junr.** junior
J.N.R.J. or I.N.R.I. (Jesus Nazarenus Rex Judaeorum)(Lat.) Jesus of Nazareth, King of the Jews
jnt.stk. joint stock
Jo., J., Jn., Jno., Joh. or **Js.** (Johannes)(Lat.) John
Jo. or **Jl.** Joel
Jo. or **Jos.** Joseph
Jo.Bapt. John the Baptist
J.O.C. Juvenile Organization Committee
joc. jocose; jocosely; jocular; jocularly
Jo.Div. John the Divine
Jo.Evang. John the Evangelist
Joh., Js. (Johannes)(Lat.), **J., Jn., Jno.** or **Jo.** John
join. joinery
J.O.J.A. July, October, January and April (Interest)
Jon. Jonah
Jon. or **Jona.** Jonathan
Jona. or **Jon.** Jonathan
Jos. Josiah
Jos. or **Jo.** Joseph
Josa. Josepha
Jose. Josephine
Joseph. Josephus
Josh. Joshua
J.O.U.A.M. or **Jr. O.U.A.M.** Junior Order of United American Mechanics
jour. journalist; journey; journeyman
jour., J., jl. or **jr.** journal (cf. Ztg.)
J.P. or **Jus.P.** justice of the peace (cf. C.R.)
JPB or **J.P.B.** Joint Production Board (U.S. and Great Britain)(cf. JWPC)
J.P.I.C. Jewish People's Institute of Chicago
j.p.p. Japanese paper proofs
J.Prob. judge of probate
J.R. (Jacobus Rex)(Lat.) King James
Jr. juror
Jr., jr., d.J. (der Jungere)(Ger.), **d.y.** (den yngre)(Swed.), **Jnr., jnr., Jun., jun., Junr.** or **junr.** junior
jr., J., jl. or **jour.** journal (cf. Ztg.)
Jr.Gr., jg, jg., j.g. or **jr.gr.** junior grade
jr.gr., jg, jg., j.g. or **Jr.Gr.** junior grade
Jr.O.U.A.M. or **J.O.U.A.M.** Junior Order of United American Mechanics
Js., Joh. (Johannes)(Lat.), **J., Jn., Jno.** or **Jo.** John
J.S.C.A. Japanese Students' Christian Association [in North America]
J.S.D. or **Jur.Sc.D.** Doctor of Juristic Science; Doctor of Science of Law; Doctor of Science of Jurisprudence
J.S.D.M. June, September, December and March (Interest)
J.S.S.A. Jewish Social Service Association
jt. joint
JTA or **J.T.A.** Jewish Telegraphic Agency
J.T.C. Junior Training Corps
jt.ten.w.r.of surb.& not as ten. in com. joint tenants with right of survivorship and not as tenants in common
Ju. Junkers (Airplane)
Ju., Czerw. (Czerwiec)(Pol.), **Je., Jun.** or **jun.** (junio)(Span.) June
J.U.D., J.V.D. (Juris Utriusque Doctor) (Lat.), **U.J.D.** or **V.J.D.** (Utriusque Juris Doctor)(Lat.) Doctor of Both [Canon and Civil] Laws
Jud. Judith
Jud. or **jud.** judgments (Law); judicial
Jud., jud., JJ. or **Judg.** judges
Jud. or **Judg.** Judges (O.T.)
jud. or **Jud.** judgements; judicial
Judg., JJ., Jud. or **jud.** judges
Judg. or **Jud.** Judges (O.T.)
juil. (juillet)(Fr.), **Jl., Jul., jul.** (julio) (Span.), **Jy.** or **Lip.** (Lipiec)(Pol.) July
J.U.L. (Juris Utriusque Licentiatus)(Lat.) Licentiate in Both [Canon and Civil] Laws
Jul. Jules; Julian; Julius
Jul., jul. (julio)(Span.), **Jl., juil.** (juillet) (Fr.), **Jy.** or **Lip.** (Lipiec)(Pol.) July
jul. julep
jul. (julio)(Span.), **Jl., juil.** (juillet)(Fr.), **Jul., Jy.** or **Lip.** (Lipiec)(Pol.) July
Jul.Per. Julian Period
Jun. Junius
Jun., jun. (junio)(Span.), **Czerw.** (Czerwiec)(Pol.), **Je.** or **Ju.** June
Jun., jun., d.J. (der Jungere)(Ger.), **d.y.** (den yngre)(Swed.), **Jnr., jnr., Jr., jr., Junr.** or **junr.** junior

jun. (junio)(Span.), **Czerw.** (Czerwiec) (Pol.), **Je., Ju.** or **Jun.** June
jun., d.J. (der Jungere)(Ger.), **d.y.** (den yngre)(Swed.), **Jnr., jnr., Jr., jr., Jun., Junr.** or **junr.** junior
Junc., junc., Jc, jc., jct., jctn., jn., jnc. or **junct.** junction
junc., Jc., jc., jct., jctn., jn., jnc., Junc. or **junct.** junction
junct., Jc, jc., jct., jctn., jn., jnc., Junc. or **junc.** junction
Jun. Opt. Junior Optime (Cambridge)
Junr., junr., d.J. (der Jungere)(Ger.), **d.y.** (den yngre)(Swed.), **Jnr., jnr., Jr., jr., Jun.,** or **jun.** junior
Jup. Jupiter
Jur.D., J.D. (Juris Doctor)(Lat.), **D.J., Dr.Jur.** (Doctor Juris)(Lat.) or **D.L.** Doctor of Law (cf. LL.D; D.J.S.)
Jur. D., J.D. (Jurum Doctor)(Lat.) or **LL.D.** (Legum Doctor) Doctor of Jurisprudence; Doctor of Laws
jurisp. jurisprudence
Jur.Sc.D. or **J.S.D.** Doctor of Juristic Science; Doctor of Science of Law; Doctor of Science of Jurisprudence
Jus., jus., J., Just. or **just.** justice
jus., J., Jus., Just. or **just.** justice
Jus.P. or **J.P.** justice of the peace (cf. C.R.)
Just. Justin; Justinian; Justus
Just., just., J., Jus. or **jus.** justice
just., J., Jus., jus. of **Just.** justice
Juv. Juvenal
juv. juvenile; (juvenis)(Lat.) young (Zool.)
J.V.D., J.U.D. (Juris Utriusque Doctor) (Lat.) **U.J.D.** or **V.J.D.** (Utriusque Juris Doctor)(Lat.) Doctor of Both [Canon and Civil] Laws
J.W. Junior Warden
J.W.B. Jewish Welfare Board
jwlr. jeweler
JWPC Joint War Production Committee (U.S. and Can.)
J.W.V. Jewish War Veterans
J.W.V.Aux. Jewish War Veterans Auxiliary
Jy., Jl., juil. (juillet)(Fr.), **Jul., jul.** (julio) (Span.) or **Lip.** (Lipiec)(Pol.) July

K

K Centuple calorie (Physics); kalium (potassium)(Chem.); modulus of cubic compressibility (Mech.)
K or **K.** Kelvin [thermometer scale]
K, k., Const. or **const.** constant
K., c., car., ct., k. or **kt.** karat; carat
K., k., Chev. (Chevalier)(Fr.), **knt., Kt** (Chess), **Kt.** or **R.** (Ridder)(Dan.) knight
K., k., cr., kn., Kr., kr. or **krn.** crown; crowns (krona; kronar; krone; kronen; kroner) (Coins)
K., k, k. (kilo)(Greek), **M, M., m, m.** (milli) (Lat.), **thou.** or **thous.** thousand
K., k., kal. (kalendae)(Lat.), **C., c.** or **cal.** kalends; calends
K., k., kg., kgm., kilo. or **kilog.** kilogram; kilograms
K., k., Ki., R. or **r.** (rex, regis)(Lat.) king; kings
K., k. or **kop.** kopek; kopeks
k. knot
k., C., c., cal., K. or **kal.** (kalendae)(Lat.) kalends; calends
k. (Elec.), **C., c., cap.** or **cy.** capacity
k., c., car., ct., K. or **kt.** karat; carat
k., Chev. (Chevelier)(Fr.), **K., knt., Kt** (Chess), **Kt.** or **R.** (Ridder)(Ger.) knight
k., cr., K., kn., Kr., kr. or **krn.** crown; crowns (krona; kronar; krone; kronen; kroner) (Coins)
k., Cu. or **cu.** cumulus (Meteorol.)
k., K., Const. or **const.** constant
k, K., k. (kilo)(Greek), **M, M., m, m.** (milli) (Lat.), **thou.** or **thous.** thousand
k., K., kg., kgm., kilo. or **kilog.** kilogram; kilograms
k., K., Ki., R. or **r.** (rex, regis)(Lat.) king; kings
k., K. or **kop.** kopek; kopeks
k., kais. (kaiserlich)(Ger.), **I., Imp.** or **imp.** imperial
k. or **kg.** keg
k., kg. or **kgs.** kegs
k., kgl. (kongelig)(Dan.), (königlich)(Ger.), **kir.** (királyi)(Hung.), **kungl.** (kunglig) (Swed.), **R, R., r, r., Roy.** or **roy.** royal
K.A. Knight of St. Andrew (Russia)
ka., C., c., ca. or **cath.** kathode; cathode
kais., k. (kaiserlich)(Ger.), **I., Imp.** or **imp.** imperial
kal., K., k. (kalendae)(Lat.), **C., c.** or **cal.** kalends; calends
Kan., Kans. or **Kas.** Kansas
Kans., Kan. or **Kas.** Kansas
Kap. (Kapitän)(Ger.), **cap., Capt** (Mil.), **Capt.** or **Kpt.** (Kaptajn)(Dan.) Captain
Kap. (Kapitel)(Dan.), **kap.** (kapitel) (Swed.), **C., cap.** (capítulo)(Span.), **Ch., ch., Chap., chap.** or **chapt.** chapter
kap. (kapitel)(Swed.), **C., cap.** (capítulo) (Span.), **Ch., ch., Chap., chap., chapt.** or **Kap.** (Kapitel)(Dan.) chapter
K.A.R. King's African Rifles
Kas., Kan or **Kans.** Kansas
Kath. Katharine; Katherine
KB king's bishop (Chess)
K.B. Kite balloon (R.A.F.); Knight [of the Order] of the Bath
K.B. or **B.R.** (Banco Regis)(Lat.) King's Bench
K.B., Knt. Bach. or **Kt. Bach.** Knight Bachelor
K.B.A. Knight of St. Bento d'Avis (Portugal)
K.B.E. Knight of the Black Eagle (Prussia, Russia); Knight [Commander of the Order] of the British Empire

KBP king's bishop's pawn (Chess)
K.C. King's Council or Counsel; Knight Commander
K.C. or **K.C.L.** King's College [London]
K.C. or **K. of C.** Knight or Knights of Columbus
kc. kilocycle; kilocycles; kilocycles [per second]
kcal kilocalorie; kilocalories
K.C.B. Knight Commander [of the Order] of the Bath
K.C.C. Knight Commander [of the Order] of the Crown (Belgium)
K.C.C.H. Knight Commander of the Court of Honor
K.C.H. Knight Commander of the Hanoverian [Guelphic Order] (cf. K.G.H.); Knight Commander of Hanover
K.C.I.E. Knight Commander [of the Order] of the Indian Empire
K.C.L. or **K.C.** King's College, London
K.C.M.G. Knight Commander [of the Order] of St. Michael and St. George
K.C.P. Knight Commander of Pius IX (Papal)
K.C.S. Knight of Charles III of Spain
K.C.S.G. Knight Commander of St. Gregory [the Great] (Papal)
K.C.S.I. Knight Commander [of the Order] of the Star of India
K.C.S.S. Knight Commander [of the Order] of St. Sylvester (Papal)
K.C.T. Knight Commander of the Temple
K.C.V.O. Knight Commander of the [Royal] Victorian Order
K.D. knockdown; knocked down (Com.)
kd. killed
K.D.C.L. knocked down, in carloads
K.D.F. knocked down flat
K.D.G. King's Dragoon Guards
K.D.L.C.L. knocked down, in less than carloads
K.E. Knight of the Elephant (Denmark)
Keb. Coll. Keble College (Oxford)
K.E.H. King Edward's Horse
Ken. or **Ky.** Kentucky
K.F. Knight of Ferdinand (Spain)
K.F.M. Knight of St. Ferdinand and of Merit (Sicily)
K.G. Knight [of the Order] of the Garter
kg., K., k., kgm., kilo. or **kilog.** kilogram; kilograms
kg. or **k.** keg
kg., k. or **kgs.** kegs
K.G.C. Knight Grand Commander; Knight of the Golden Circle (U.S.); Knight of the Grand Cross
kg-cal kilogram-calorie; kilogram-calories; large calorie
K.G.C.B. or **G.C.B.** Knight Grand Cross [of the Order] of the Bath
K.G.F. Knight of the Golden Fleece (Austria-Hungary, Spain)
K.G.H. or **K.H.** Knight of the Guelphs of Hanover; Knight [of the Guelphic Order] of Hanover (cf. K.C.H.)
kgl., k. (kongelig)(Dan.), (königlich)(Ger.), **kir.** (királyi)(Hung.), **kungl.** (kunglig)(Swed.), **R, R., r, r., Roy.** or **roy.** royal
kgm., K., k., kg., kilo. or **kilog.** kilogram; kilograms
kg-m or **kg.-m.** kilogram-meters
kg/m³ or **kg.per cu.m.** kilograms per cubic meter
kg.per cu.m. or **kg/m³** kilograms per cubic meter
K.G.P.S., k.g.p.s., kgps or **kg/s** kilograms per second
kgps, K.G.P.S., k.g.p.s. or **kg/s** kilograms per second
kgs., k. or **kg.** kegs
kg/s, K.G.P.S., k.g.p.s. or **kgps** kilograms per second
K.G.V. Knight of Gustavus Vasa (Sweden)
K.H. or **K.G.H.** Knight [of the Guelphic Order] of Hanover; Knight of the Guelphs of Hanover (cf. K.C.H.)
K.H.A. Kansas Hospital Association; Kentucky Hospital Association
K.H.C. Honorary Chaplain to the King
K.H.P. Honorary Physician to the King
K.H.S. Honorary Surgeon to the King; Knight of the Holy Sepulchre (Papal)
Ki Kitchen (Mil.)
Ki., K., k., R. or **r.** (rex, regis)(Lat.) king; kings
K.I.A. Killed in action
K.I.C. Knight of the Iron Crown (Austria)
K.I.H. or **K.i.H.** Kaisar-i-Hind [Medal for useful service in India] (Brit.)
kil., kilo., kilom. or **km.** kilometer; kilometers
kild. kilderkin
kilo., K., k., kg., kgm. or **kilog.** kilogram; kilograms
kilo., kil., kilom. or **km.** kilometer; kilometers
kilog., K., k., kg., kgm. or **kilo.** kilogram; kilograms
kilol. or **kl.** kiloliter; kiloliters
kilom., kil., kilo. or **km.** kilomoter; kilometers
kingd. or **km.** kingdom
kir. (királyi)(Hung.), **k., kgl.** (kongelig)(Dan.), (königlich)(Ger.), **kungl.** (kunglig)(Swed.), **R, R., r, r., Roy.** or **roy.** royal
Kit. Curtiss Kittyhawk (Airplane)
kj. kilojoule
K.K. (Kaiserlich-Königlich)(Ger.) Imperial Majesty; Kabuṣhiki Kaịsha (Japanese company)
k.k. (kaiserlich-königlich)(Ger.) or **k.u.k.** (kaiserlich und königlich)(Ger.) Imperial and Royal
K.K.K. Ku Klux Klan
K Kt king's knight (Chess)
K Kt P king's knight's pawn (Chess)
K.L. or **K.L.A.** Knight of Leopold [of Austria]
K.L. or **K. of L.** Knight or Knights of Labor
Kl. (Klasse)(Dan.) or **cl.** class
Kl. (Klokken)(Dan.), **kl.** (klockan)(Swed.), **o/c** or **o'c.** o'clock

kl. or **kilol.** kiloliter; kiloliters

kl. (klockan)(Swed.), **Kl.** (Klokken)(Dan.), **o/c** or **o'c.** o'clock

K.L.A. or **K.L.** Knight of Leopold of Austria

K.L.B. Knight of Leopold of Belgium

K.L.H. Knight of the Legion of Honor (France)

K.L.I. King's Light Infantry

K.M. Knight of Malta

km., kil., kilo. or **kilom.** kilometer; kilometers

km. or **kingd.** kingdom

km.² or **sq.km.** square kilometer

km.³ or **cu.km.** cubic kilometer

K.m.D. (Katholische militärkirchliche Dienstordnung)(Ger.) Regulations for Catholic worship in the army

K.Mess. King's Messenger

K.M.H.. Knight of Merit, Holstein

K.M.J. Knight of Maximilian Joseph (Bavaria)

K.M.P.S., kmps, k.m.p.s. or **km/s** kilometers per second

kmps, K.M.P.S., k.m.p.s. or **km/s** kilometers per second

km/s, K.M.P.S., kmps or **k.m.p.s.** kilometers per second

K.M.T. Knight of Maria Theresa (Austria)

K.N. Know-Nothing

kn., cr., K., k., Kr., kr. or **krn.** crown; crowns (krona; kronar; krone; kronen; kroner)(Coins)

Knick. Knickerbocker

K.N.L. Knight of the Netherlands Lion

K.N.S. or **R.N.O.** (Riddare af Nordstjerne Orden)(Swed.) Knight [of the Royal Order] of the Pole Star or North Star (Sweden)

knt., Chev. (Chevalier)(Fr.), **K., k., Kt** (Chess), **Kt.** or **R.** (Ridder)(Dan.) knight

Knt. Bach., K.B. or **Kt. Bach.** Knight Bachelor

K.O. keep off

K.O. or **k.o.** knockout (Pugilism)

K.O.C. Knight of the Oak Crown (Luxemburg)

K. of C. or **K.C.** Knight or Knights of Columbus

K. of H. Knight of Honor

K. of L. or **K.L.** Knight or Knights of Labor

K. of P. or **K.P.** Knight or Knights of Pythias (U.S.)

kol. (koloriert)(Ger.), **Cld** (Mil.), **cld.** or **col.** colored

Komdt. (Kommandant)(Ger.), **Comdt** (Mil) or **comdt.** Commandant

Konr. Konrad

kop., K. or k. kopek; kopeks

K.O.R.R. King's Own Royal Regiment

K.O.S.B. King's Own Scottish Borderers

K.O.Y.L.I. King's Own Yorkshire Light Infantry

KP king's pawn (Chess)

K.P. keratitis punctata (Med.); kitchen police; (Königlich Preussisch)(Ger.) Royal Prussian

K.P. or **K. of P.** Knight or Knights of Pythias (U.S.)

K.P. or **K.S.P.** Knight [of the Order] of St. Patrick

Kpt. (Kaptajn)(Dan.) **cap., Capt** (Mil.), **Capt.** or **Kap.** (Kapitän)(Ger.) Captain

KR king's rook (Chess)

K.R. King's Regulations (Brit.)

Kr krypton (Chem.)

Kr., kr., cr., K., k., kn., or **krn.** crown; crowns (krona; kronar; krone; kronen; kroner) (Coins)

kr. kreutzer (Coin)

kr., cr., K., k., kn., Kr. or **krn.** crown; crowns (krona; kronar; krone; kronen; kroner) (Coins)

K.R.C. Knight of the Red Cross

K.R.E. Knight [of the Order] of the Red Eagle (Prussia)

krn., cr., K., k., kn., Kr. or **kr.** crown; crowns (krona; kronar; krone; kronen; kroner) (Coins)

KRP king's rook's pawn (Chess)

K.R.R. King's Royal Rifles

K.R.R.C. King's Royal Rifle Corps

K.S. keep [type] standing (Typog.); King's Scholar

K.S. or **K.S.S.** Knight of the Sword [of Sweden]

K.S.A. Knight of St. Anne (Russia)

K.S.C.. Knight of St. Columba

K.S.E. Knight of St. Esprit (France)

K.S.F.. Knight of St. Ferdinand (Sicily); Knight of San Fernando (Spain)

K.S.F.M. Knight of St. Ferdinand and Merit (Naples)

K.S.G. Knight of St. George (Russia); Knight of St. Gregory [the Great] (Papal)

K.S.H. Knight of St. Hubert (Bavaria)

K.S.I. Knight [of the Order] of the Star of India

K.S.J. Knight of St. Januarius (Naples)

K.S.K. ethyl-iodo-acetate (Gas)

K.S.L. Knight of the Sun and Lion (Persia)

K.S.L.I. King's Shropshire Light Infantry

K.S.M. and S.G. Knight of St. Michael and St. George

K.S.P. Knight of St. Stanislaus of Poland

K.S.P. or **K.P.** Knight [of the Order] of St. Patrick

K.S.S. Knight of St. Sylvester (Papal); Knight of the Southern Star (Brazil, Persia)

K.S.S. or **K.S.** Knight of the Sword of Sweden

K.S.V. Knight of St. Vladimir (Russia)

K.T. Knight of Tabor; Knight [of the Order] of the Thistle (Scotland); Knight or Knights Templar

Kt (Chess), **Kt., Chev.** (Chevalier)(Fr.), **K., k., knt.** or **R.** (Ridder)(Dan.) knight

kt., c., car., ct., K. or **k.** karat; carat

Kt. Bach., K.B. or **Knt. Bach.** Knight Bachelor

Kt. Ch. Knight of Christ

k.t.l. (kai ta loipa)(Greek), **etc.** (et cetera) (Lat.), **i.t.d.** (i tak dalej)(Pol.), **m.m.** (med mera)(Swed.), (med mere)(Dan.), **o.d.** (ock dylikt or dylika)(Swed.), **o.s.v.** (och så vidare)(Swed.), (og saa videre) (Dan.), **u. drgl.** (und dergrelchen) (Ger.), **u.s.f.** (und so fort)(Ger.), **usw.** or **u.s.w.** (und so weiter)(Ger.) and so forth; and the like; and others of like kind

K.T.S. Knight [of the Order] of the Tower and the Sword (Portugal)

k.u.k. (kaiserlich und königlich)(Ger.) or **k.k.** (kaiserlich-königlich)(Ger.) Imperial and Royal

kungl. (kunglig)(Swed.), **k., kgl.** (kongelig) (Dan.), (königlich)(Ger.), **kir.** (királyi) (Hung.), **R, R., r, r., Roy.,** or **roy.** royal

K.V. (Kriegsverwenungsfähig)(Ger.) Fit for active service (cf. B.A.M.)

kv. kilovolt; kilovolts

Kv-a, kva, kva. or **kva** kilovolt-ampere or amperes

kva, kva., Kv-a or kv-a kilovolt-ampere or amperes

kvar kilovar; kilovars

kvarh kilovar-hour or hours

K.W. Knight of William (Netherlands)

kw. kilowatt

kw.-an. kilowatt-year

K.W.E. Knight of the White Eagle (Poland)

K.W.H., kw-h, kwhr, kw-hr or **kw.-hr.** kilowatt-hour or hours

kw-h, K.W.H., kwhr, kw-hr or **kw.-hr.** kilowatt-hour or hours

kwhr, K.W.H., kw-h, kw-hr or **kw.-hr.** kilowatt-hour or hours

kw.-hr., K.W.H., kw-h, kwhr or **kw-hr** kilowatt-hour or hours

Kwiec. (Kwiecień)(Pol.), **A., ab., abr.** (abril)(Span., Port.), **Ap., Apl., Apr., ápr.** (április)(Hung.), or **av.** (avril) (Fr.) April

Ky. or **Ken.** Kentucky

ΚΑ (Kappa Alpha Order)(Kappa Alpha Society) National undergraduate fraternity

ΚΑΦ (Kappa Alpha Phi) National professional fraternity (Foreign and Domestic Commerce)

ΚΑΨ (Kappa Alpha Psi) National undergraduate fraternity for Negroes

ΚΑΘ (Kappa Alpha Theta) National undergraduate sorority

ΚΒΠ (Kappa Beta Pi) Professional sorority (Law)

ΚΔ (Kappa Delta) National undergraduate sorority

ΚΔΕ (Kappa Delta Epsilon) National professional sorority (Education)

ΚΔΦ (Kappa Delta Phi) National junior college fraternity

ΚΔΠ (Kappa Delta Pi) Honor fraternity (Education)

ΚΔΡ (Kappa Delta Rho) National undergraduate fraternity

ΚΕ (Kappa Epsilon) Professional sorority (Pharmacy)

ΚΗΚ (Kappa Eta Kappa) Professional fraternity (Electrical Engineering)

ΚΓΨ (Kappa Gamma Psi) Professional society (Music)

ΚΚΓ (Kappa Kappa Gamma) National undergraduate sorority

ΚΚΚ (Kappa Kappa Kappa) National undergraduate fraternity

ΚΚΨ (Kappa Kappa Psi) Honorary fraternity (Band)

ΚΜΕ (Kappa Mu Epsilon) Honor society (Mathematics)

ΚΝ (Kappa Nu) National undergraduate fraternity

ΚΟΦ (Kappa Omicron Phi) National undergraduate sorority (Home Economics)

ΚΦΚ (Kappa Phi Kappa) National professional fraternity (Education)

ΚΦΖ (Kappa Phi Zeta) National undergraduate sorority

ΚΠ (Kappa Pi) National honor society (Art)

ΚΨ (Kappa Psi) Professional fraternity (Pharmaceutics)

ΚΣ (Kappa Sigma) National undergraduate fraternity

ΚΤΑ (Kappa Tau Alpha) National undergraduate honor fraternity (Journalism)

L

L Lambert

L (Physics), **L., l.** or **lgth.** length

L or **l** coefficient of inductance (Elec.)

L (Astron., Geod.), **Lon., lon., Long.** or **long.** longitude

L (Mil.), **Lt** (Mil.) or **lt.** light

£, L. or **l.** (libra, librae)(Lat.) pound; pounds (Money)

L. kinetic potential (Dynamics); Lady; late (cf. dec.); lightning (Naut.); lodge (Frat.); (legum)(Lat.) of laws

L. (Läufer)(Ger.), **B., b.** or **bp.** bishop (Chess)(Cf. Bp.)

L., Doz. (Dozent)(Ger.), **L.^do^** or **l.^do^** (licenciado)(Span.) or **Lic.** licenciate

L., £ or **l.** (libra, librae)(Lat.) pound; pounds (Money)

L., l or **l.** lumen

L. or **l.** lake; land; launch; leaf; line; lingual; low

L., l. or **J.** (jus)(Lat.) law

L., l., Lat. or **lat.** latitude

L., l., lb. (libra)(Lat.) or **liv.** (livre)(Fr.) pound (Weight)

L., l. or **lea.** league; leagues

L., l. or **li.** (Meas.) link; links

L., l., Lib. or **lib.** liberal

L., l., lib. (liber)(Lat.), **B., b., bk., liv.** (livre)(Fr.) or **t.** (tome)(Fr.) book

L., l. or **lit.** liter; liters

L., l., LL., ll, Fol. (Folia)(Ital., Lat.) or **hh.** (hojas)(Span.) leaves (cf. ff.; f°)
L., l. or ll. lines
L., l., loc. (loco)(Lat.) or **in loc.** (in loco) (Lat.) in the place (cf. ad loc.; a.h.l.)
L., l. or lr. lira; lire
L., l. or ltr. letter (alphabet)(cf. bklr.; ep.)
L., l. (locus)(Lat.) or **pl.** place
L. or **Lat.** Latin
L. or **Ld.** Lord
L., Ldp. or **Lp.** Lordship
L. or **Linn.** Linnaeus
l or **L** coefficient of inductance (Elec.)
l, L. or **l.** lumen
l. legitimate; long
l., Fol. (Folia)(Ital.,Lat.), **hh.** (hojas) (Span.), **L., LL.** or **ll.** leaves
l., g. (gauche)(Fr.) or **s.** (sinistra)(Ital., Lat.) left (cf. M.G.; S.M.; O.S.)
l., J. (jus)(Lat.) or **L.** law
l., L (Physics), **L.** or **lgth.** length
l. or **L.** lake; land; launch; leaf; line; lingual; low
l., L. or **£** (libra, librae)(Lat.) pound; pounds (Money)
l., L. or **l** lumen
l., L., Lat. or **lat.** latitude
l., L., lb. or **liv.** (livre)(Fr.) pound (Weight)
l., L. or **lea.** leather
l., L. or **li.** link; links (Measure)
l., L., lib. (liber)(Lat.), **B., b., bk., liv.** (livre)(Fr.) or **t.** (tome)(Fr.) book
l., L., Lib. or **lib.** liberal
l., L. or **lit.** liter; liters
l., L. or **ll.** lines
l., L., loc. (loco)(Lat.) or **in loc.** (in loco) (Lat.) in the place (cf. ad loc.; a.h.l.)
l., L. or **lr.** lira; lire
l., L. or **ltr.** letter (alphabet)(cf. bklr.)
l., L. (locus)(Lat.) or **pl.** place
l. or **l-** levo- (Chem.)
L.A. labor administration; Law Agent; Leasehold Area (New So. Wales); Legislative Assembly; Library Association; Lieutenant-at-arms; Literate in Arts; Lloyd's Agent; Local Agent; Local Authority
L.A. or **L/A** lighter than air
L/A landing account (Shipping); letter of authority
L/A or **L.A.** lighter than air
La lanthanum (Chem.)
La. Louisiana
la. last (the weight)
l.a. (lettre d'avis)(Fr.) letter of advice
L.A.A. Light antiaircraft
LAB or **L.A.B.** Labor Advisory Board
L.A.B. Lloyd Aéro Boliviano
Lab. Laborite; Labrador
lab. laborer; laboratory
lab., Lbr (Mil.) or **Lbr.** labor
Lab.Stat.Bull. United States Bureau of Labor Statistics Bulletin
L.A.C. Licentiate of the Apothecaries' Company; London Athletic Club
L.A.C. or **LA/C** Leading aircraftman
LA/C or **L.A.C.** Leading aircraftman
L.A.D.A. London Alley Dwelling Authority
Ladp., Lpd. or **Lp.** Ladyship
L.Adv. of **L.A.S.** Lord Advocate of Scotland
L. Ae.F. Ligue Aéronautique de France
Lag. (Lagena)(Lat.) flask
L.A.H. Licentiate of Apothecaries' Hall (Dublin)
L.A.M. League of American Municipalities; London Academy of Music
L.A.M. (Liberalium Artium Magister) (Lat.) or **M.A.L.** Master of Liberal Arts
Lam. Lamarck; Lamentations
lam. laminated
L. & D. loans and discounts (Banking)
L.& D. or **l.& d.** loss and damage
l. & r. or **l. and r.** lake and rail
L.A.N. Linea Aerea Nacional
L.A.N.A. Lignes Aériennes Nord-Africaines
Lance-Corp., L.-Corp., L.-corp., l. corp. or **L.-Cpl.** Lance corporal
Lancs. Lancashire
l. and r. or **l. & r.** lake and rail
Lang. Languedoc
lang. language; languages
L.A.O. Licenciate in Obstetric Art
Lap. Lapland
L.A.P.E. Linas Aereas Postales Españolas
Lapp. Lappic; Lappish
L.A.R.E.S. Lignes Aériennes Roumaines Exploité par l'Etat
laryngol. laryngological; laryngology
L.A.S. or **L.Adv.** Lord Advocate of Scotland
L.A.S. or **L.S.A.** Licentiate of the Society of Apothecaries
L.A.T. Linseed Association terms; local apparent time
Lat. or **L.** Latin
Lat., lat., L. or **l.** latitude
Lat. or **Latv.** Latvia
lat., L., l. or **Lat.** latitude
lat.def. latent defect
lat. dol. (lateri dolenti)(Lat.) to the painful side (Pharm.)
Lat.Pros. Latin Prosody
Latv. or **Lat.** Latvia
L.A.U.K. Library Association of the United Kingdom
Laur. or **Lr.** Laurence
L.A.W. League of American Wheelmen
law. lawyer
Lawr. or **Lr.** Lawrence
Laz. Lazarus
L.B. Light bomber; Local Board
L.B. or **l.b.** (lectori benevolo)(Lat.) to the kind reader

L.B., Lit. B. (Literarum Baccalaureus) (Lat.) or **B.L.** (Baccalaureus Literarum)(Lat.) Bachelor of Literature
L.B., Litt. B. (Litterarum Baccalaureus) (Lat.), **B. ès L.** (Bachelier ès Lettres) (Fr.), **B.L.** or **B. Litt.** (Baccalaureus Litterarum)(Lat.) Bachelor of Letters
lb., L., l. (libra)(Lat.) or **liv.** (livre)(Fr.) pound (Weight)
lb., lbs., lib. (librae)(Lat.) or **lv.** (livres) (Fr.) pounds (Weight)
l.b. leg-bye (Cricket)
l.b. or **L.B.** (lectori benevolo)(Lat.) to the kind reader
lb. ap. apothecaries' pound
lb. av. pound avoirdupois
L.B.C. Land Banks Commissioner
L. Bdr. or **L/Bdr** Lance bombardier
lb-ft pound-foot; pound-feet (cf. ft-lb)
lb/ft² pound or pounds per square foot
lb-in pound-inch; pound-inches
lb/in² pound or pounds per square inch
Lbr (Mil.), **Lbr.** or **lab.** labor
lbr. lumber
Lbr Bn Labor battalion
Lbr Det Labor detachment
lbs., lb., lib. (librae)(Lat.) or **lv.** (livres) (Fr.) pounds (Weight)
l.b.s. (lectori benevolo salutem)(Lat.) to the kind reader, greeting
lb.t. pound troy
l.b.w. leg before wicket (Cricket)
LC deferred cable
LC, L.C. or **Lib. Cong.** Library of Congress
LC (Mil.), **L.C., L of C** (Mil.) or **L. of C.** line or lines of communication
L.C. level crossing; London cheque; London clause; Lord Chamberlain; Lord Chancellor; Lower Canada
L.C., LC or **Lib.Cong.** Library of Congress
L.C., LC (Mil.), **L of C** (Mil.) or **L. of C.** line or lines of communication
L.C. or **l.c.** left center
L/C, lc, lc., l.c. or **l/c** lower case (Typog.)
L/C, l.c., l/c, l/c., L.Cr., l.cr., l/cr. or **Lo/C** letter of credit
lc, lc., l.c., L/C or **l/c** lower case (Typog.)
l.c. label clause (Insurance)
l.c. (loco citato)(Lat.), **a.a.O.** (am angefürten Orte)(Ger.), **c.l.** (citato loco)(Lat.), **in loc cit.** (in loco citato)(Lat.) or **loc cit.** (loco citato)(Lat.) in the place cited (cf. loc. laud.; loc. primo cit.; op. cit.; u.s.)
l.c. or **L.C.** left center
lc., L/C, lc, lc. or l/c lower case (Typog.)
l.c., L/C, l/c, l/c., L.Cr., l.cr., l/cr. or **Lo/C** letter of credit
l/c, L/C, lc, lc. or **l.c.** lower case (Typog.)
l/c, L/C, l.c., l/c., L.Cr., l.cr., l/cr. or **Lo/C** letter of credit
L.C.B. Lord Chief Baron
L.C.C. London City Council; London County Council or Councilor
L.C.D., lcd or **l.c.d.** lowest common denominator
lcd, L.C.D. or **l.c.d.** lowest common denominator
l.c.d., L.C.D. or **lcd** lowest common denominator
lce. lance
L. Ch., L. Chir. (Licentiatus Chirurgiae) (Lat.) or **L.S.** Licenciate in Surgery
L. Chir., L. Ch. (Licentiatus Chirurgiae) (Lat.) or **L.S.** Licenciate in Surgery
L.C.J. Lord Chief Justice
LCL, L.C.L. or **l.c.l.** less than carload lot
L.C.L. Licentiate of Civil Law
l.c.l., LCL or **L.C.L.** less than carload lot
LCL's, L.C.L.'s or **l.c.l.'s** less than carload lots
L.C.M., lcm or **l.c.m.** least or lowest common multiple
lcm, L.C.M. or **l.c.m.** least or lowest common multiple
L.-Corp., L.-corp., l. corp., Lance-Corp. or **L.-Cpl.** Lance corporal
L.C.P. Licentiate of the College of Preceptors (London)
L.Cpl., Lance Corp., L.-Corp., L.-corp. or **l. corp.** Lance corporal
L.Cr., L/C., l.c., l/c, l/c., l.cr., l/cr. or **Lo/C** letter of credit
L.Cr., Lieut. Com., Lt. Com., Lt. Comdr. or **Lt.-Comm.** Lieutenant commander
l.cr., L/C, l.c., l/c, l/c., L.Cr., l/cr. or **Lo/C** letter of credit
L.C.T.A. London Corn Trade Association
LD Line of departure (Mil.)
LD or **L.D.** Lady Day; Line of duty; Light Dragoons; London Docks; (laus Deo) (Lat.) praise be to God
LD., L.D., LDu. or **L.Du.** Low Dutch
L.D., D. ès L. (Docteur ès Lettres)(Fr.), **D. Litt.** (Doctor Litterarum)(Lat.) or **Litt. D.** (Litterarum Doctor)(Lat.) Doctor of Letters
L.D. or **LD** Lady Day; Line of duty; Light Dragoons; London Docks; (laus Deo) (Lat.) praise be to God
L.D., LD., LDu. or **L.Du.** Low Dutch
L.D. or **L. Div.** Licentiate in Divinity (cf. L.Th.)
Ld. or **L.** Lord
Ld., ld., Lim., Ltd., ltd. or **Ltda.** (Limitada) (Span.) limited
ld. lead (printing)
ld., Ld., Lim., Ltd., ltd. or **Ltda.** (Limitada) (Span.) limited
l.d. (litera dominicalis)(Lat.) dominical letter; (lepide dictum)(Lat.) elegantly said; low door
L.D.E.G. (Laus Deo et Gloria)(Lat.) praise and glory be to God
ldg. landing; leading; loading
ldg. and dely. landing and delivery
ld.gt. land grant
L.d'H. Legion d'Honneur (France)
L.Div. or **L.D.** Licentiate in Divinity (cf. L. Th.)
ld.lmt. load limit (Shipping)
L.D.M. Licentiate of Dental Medicine
L.^{do}, l.^{do} (licenciado)(Span.), **Doz.** (Dozent) (Ger.), **L.** or **Lic.** licenciate
Ldp., L. or **Lp.** Lordship
Ldp., Ladp. or **Lp.** Ladyship

ldr., D. or **d.** (dux)(Lat.) leader
ldry. or **lndry.** laundry
L.D.S. Latter-day Saints; Licentiate in Dental Surgery; (laus Deo semper) (Lat.) praise be to God forever
L.D.S.R.C.S. Eng. Licentiate in Dental Surgery of the Royal College of Surgeons of England
LDu., L.Du., LD. or **L.D.** Low Dutch
LE Low explosive (Mil.)
£E Egyptian pounds (Com.)
L.E. (Légion étrangère)(Fr.) Foreign Legion; Labor Exchange; leading edge (Aero.); left end (Football)
lea. leather
lea., L. or **l.** league; leagues
lea., Lv (Mil.) or **lv.** leave
lect. lecture; lecturer
Lect. Glis. Phil. Lector General of Philosophy (Franciscan degree)(cf. Ph.D.)
Lect. Glis. Sac. Theol. Lector General of Sacred Theology (Franciscan degree) (cf. S.T.D.)
Lect. Glis.S.S. Lector General of Sacred Scripture (Franciscan degree)(cf. S.T. D.)
led. ledger
Leg. Legation
Leg. or **leg.** (legato)(Ital.) smoothly (Music)
Leg. or **Legis.** Legislature
leg. (legit, legunt)(Lat.) he or she reads; they read; legal; legate; legend
leg., legis. or **legisl.** legislation; legislative
legg. (leggiero)(Ital.) light; nimble; delicate (Music)
Legis. or **Leg.** Legislature
legis., leg. or **legisl.** legislation; legislative
legisl., leg. or **legis.** legislation; legislative
Leics. Leicestershire
Leip. Leipsig
L.E.L. Laureate in English Literature
Lem. Lemuel
Leon. Leonard
l.e.s. local excitatory state (Med.)
L. ès L. (Licencié ès Lettres)(Fr.) or **Litt. L.** (Litterarum Licentiatus)(Lat.) Licentiate of or in Letters
L. ès Sc. (Licencié ès Sciences)(Fr.) Licentiate in Sciences
Let. or **Lett.** Lettish
lett. or **epp.** (epistolae)(Lat.) letters; epistles
lett.hd. letterhead
Lev. or **Levit.** Leviticus
lex. lexicon
lexicog. lexicographer; lexicographical; lexicography
Lex Merc. (Lex Mercatoria)(Lat.) mercantile law
Leyd. Leyden
L.F. left field
L.F. or **l.-f.** low frequency
lf or **l.f.** light face (Typog.)
l.f. ledger folio
l.f. or **lf** light face (Typog.)
l.-f. or **L.F.** low frequency
L.F.A. local freight agent
L.F.C., l.f.c. or **l.-f.c.** low-frequency current (Radio)
l.f.c., L.F.C. or **l.-f.c.** low-frequency current (Radio)
l.-f.c., L.F.C. or **l.f.c.** low-frequency current
L.F.D. least fatal dose (Pharm.)
Lfg. (Lieferung)(Ger.), **Abt.** (Abteilung)(Ger.), **H., Hft.** (Heft)(Ger.), **liv.** (livraison)(Fr.), **p., pt., T.** or **Th.** (Teil, Theil)(Ger.) part (cf. inst.; no.; sec.)
Lfg. (Lieferung)(Ger.), **Fasc.** or **fasc.** (fasciculus)(Lat.) fascicle
Lfg. (Lieferung)(Ger.), **H., Hft.** (Heft)(Ger.), **inst., liv.** (livraison)(Fr.), **T.** or **Th.** (Teil, Theil)(Ger.) installment (cf. Abt.; pt.)
l.F.H. (leichte Feldhaubitze)(Ger.) Light field howitzer
L.F.I.R. League for Industrial Rights
L.F.M. or **F.M.Lt.** (Feldmarschall-leutnant)(Ger.) Lieutenant field marshal
L.F.P.S. or **L.R.F.P.S.** Licentiate of the [Royal] Faculty of Physicians and Surgeons
L.Fr. Law French
Lf Tk Light fast tank
LG., L.G. or **L.Ger.** Low German
L.G. Landing ground; left guard (Football); life guard
L.G., LG. or **L.Ger.** Low German
l.g. large grain
L.G.A.R. Ladies' Grand Army of the Republic
L.G.B. Local Government Board (Brit.)
lge., lrg. or **Mag.** (magnus)(Lat.) large
L.Ger., LG. or **L.G.** Low German
LGr. or **L. Gr.** Late Greek
lgth., L (Physics), **L.** or **l.** length
lg.tn. or **l.t.** long ton
Lgts (Mil.), **Lgts.** or **lts.** lights
LH Lighthouse (Mil.)
L.H., l.h., izq.[a], **izq.**[da] (izquierda)(Span.), **M.G., m.g.** (main gauche)(Fr.), **m.s.** (mano sinistra)(Lat.), **s.** (sinistra)(Ital.) or **S.M.** (sinistra mano)(Lat.) left hand
l.h., izq.[a], **izq.**[da] (izquierda)(Span.), **L.H., M.G., m.g.** (main gauche)(Fr.), **s.** (sinistra)(Ital.) or **S.M.** (sinistra mano)(Lat.) left hand
L.H.A. Lord High Admiral
L.H.A.R. London, Hull, Antwerp, or Rotterdam (Shipping)
L.H.C. Lord High Chancellor
L.H.D. (Litterarum Humaniorum Doctor, In Litteris Humanioribus Doctor)(Lat.) or **HH.D.** Doctor of Humanities; Doctor of Humane Letters
l-hr lumen-hour or hours
L.H.T. Lord High Treasurer
L.I. Licentiate of Instruction; Long Island
L.I., Lt Inf or **Lt. Inf.** Light infantry
Li lithium (Chem.)
Li. Lockheed Lightning (Airplane)

li. (Meas.), **L.** or **l.** link; links
L.I.A. Ligue Internationale des Aviateurs
Lib. Liberator (Airplane)
Lib., lib., L. or **l.** Liberal
lib. librarian
lib., Bibl., bibl. or **biblioth.** (bibliotheca) (Lat.) library
lib., L., l. (liber)(Lat.), **B., b., bk., liv.** (livre)(Fr.) or **t.** (tome)(Fr.) book
lib., L., l. or **Lib.** liberal
lib., lb., lbs. (librae)(Lat.) or **lv.** (livres) (Fr.) pounds (Weight)
Lib.Cat. or **lib.cat.** library catalog
Lib. Cong., LC or **L.C.** Library of Congress
Lic., Doz. (Dozent)(Ger.), **L., L.do** or **l.do** (licenciado)(Span.) licenciate
Lic. Med., L.M. or **M.L.** (Medicinae Licentiatus)(Lat.) Licentiate in Medicine
L.I.D. League for Industrial Democracy
Lieut., Lt (Mil.) or **Lt.** Lieutenant
Lieut. Col., Lt Col (Mil.) or **Lt. Col.** Lieutenant colonel
Lieut. Com., L.Cr., Lt. Com. (Mil.), **Lt.-Com., Lt. Comdr.** or **Lt.Comm.** Lieutenant commander
Lieut. Gen., Lt Gen (Mil.), **Lt. Gen., Lt-Gen** or **Lt.-Gen.** Lieutenant general
Lieut. Gov., Lt. Gov. or **Lt-Gov.** Lieutenant Governor
L.I.F. left iliac fossa
Lim., Ld., ld., Ltd., ltd. or **Ltda.** (Limitada) (Span.) limited
lin. lineal; linear
Linc. or **Lincs.** Lincolnshire
Lincs. or **Linc.** Lincolnshire
lin.ft. linear foot or feet
ling. linguistics
linim. liniment
Linn. Linnaean; Linnean
Linn. or **L.** Linnaeus
lino. linotype
L.I.P. life insurance policy
Lip. (Lipiec)(Pol.), **Jl., juil.** (juillet)(Fr.), **Jul., jul.** (julio)(Span.) or **Jy.** July
Liq. or **liq.** liquor
liq. liquid
liq. or **Liq.** liquor
Listop. (Listopad)(Pol.), **N., nbre.** (noviembre)(Span.) or **Nov.** November
Lit., lit. or **liter.** literature
lit., ad lit. (ad litteram)(Lat.) or **a.v.** (ad verbum)(Lat.) literal; literally
lit., L. or **l.** liter; liters
lit., Lit. or **liter.** literature
lit. or **liter.** literary
Lit. B., L.B. (Baccalaureus Literarum) (Lat.) or **B.Lit.** (Baccalaureus Literarum)(Lat.) Bachelor of Literature
Lit. D. (Literarum Doctor)(Lat.) or **D. Lit.** (Doctor Literarum)(Lat.) Doctor of Literature
liter., Lit. or **lit.** literature
liter. or **lit.** literary
Lith. Lithuania; Lithuanian
lith., litho., Lithog. or **lithog.** lithograph; lithography
litho., lith., Lithog. or **lithog.** lithograph; lithography
Lithog., lithog., lith. or **litho.** lithograph; lithography
lithog. lithographical
lithol. lithology
Lit. Hum. (literae humaniores)(Lat.) the humanities; ancient classics (cf. Hum.)
Litt. B., L. B. (Litterarum Bassalaureus) (Lat.), **B. ès L.** (Bachelier ès Lettres) (Fr.), **B.L.** or **B. Litt.** (Baccalaureus Litterarum)(Lat.) Bachelor of Letters
Litt. D. (Litterarum Doctor)(Lat.), **D. ès L.** (Docteur ès Lettres)(Fr.), **D. Litt.** (Doctor Litterarum)(Lat.) or **L.D.** Doctor of Letters
Litt. L. (Litterarum Licentiatus)(Lat.) or **L. ès L.** (Licencié ès Lettres)(Fr.) Licentiate in or of Letters
Litt. M. (Magister Litterarum)(Lat.) or **M. Litt.** (Litterarum Magister)(Lat.) Master of Letters
Liturg. or **liturg.** liturgical; liturgy
L.I.U. Long Island University
Liv. Livius
liv. (livraison)(Fr.), **Abt.** (Abteilung)(Ger.), **H., Hft.** (Heft)(Ger.), **Lfg.** (Lieferung) (Ger.), **p., pt., T.** or **Th.** (Teil, Theil) (Ger.) part (cf. inst.; no.; sec.)
liv. (livre)(Fr.), **B., b., bk., L., l., lib.** (liber) (Lat.) or **t.** (tome)(Fr.) book
liv. (livraison)(Fr.), **H., Hft.** (Heft)(Ger.), **inst., Lfg.** (Lieferung)(Ger.), **T.** or **Th.** (Teil, Theil)(Ger.) installment (cf. Abt.; pt.)
liv. (livre)(Fr.), **L., l.** or **lb.** (libra)(Lat.) pound (Weight)
L.J. Lord Justice
L.JJ. or **LL.JJ.** Lords Justices
L.J.W. League of Jewish Women
Lk. Luke
lkg.& bkg. leakage and breakage (Insurance)
L.K.Q.C.P.I. Licentiate of the King and Queen's College of Physicians, Ireland (now Royal College of Physicians and Surgeons, Ireland)
lkr. locker
LL. laws
LL., Fol. (Folia)(Ital., Lat.) **hh.** (hojas) (Span.), **L., l.** or **ll.** leaves (cf. ff.; fo.)
LL., L.L. or **L.Lat.** Late Latin; Law Latin; Low Latin
L.L. Lend-Lease; Lord Lieutenant
L.L., l.l. or **loc. laud.** (loco laudato)(Lat.) in the place cited with approval (cf. loc. cit.)
L.L., l.l. or **lsd.li.** leased line or lines
ll., Fol. (Folia)(Ital., Lat.), **hh.** (hojas) (Span.), **L., l.** or **LL.** leaves (cf. ff.; f°)
ll., L. or **l.** lines
l.l. loose leaf
l.l., L.L. or **lsd.li.** leased line or lines
L.L.A. Lady Literate in Arts (St Andrews)
LL.AA.II. (Leurs Altesses Impériales) (Fr.) or **T.I.H.** Their Imperial Highnesses

LL.AA.RR. (Leurs Altesses Royales) (Fr.) or **T.R.H.** Their Royal Highnesses
Ll. & Cos. Lloyd's and companies (Insurance)
L. Lat., LL. or **L.L.** Late Latin; Law Latin; Low Latin
LL.B (Legum Baccalaureus) (Lat.), **B.L., B.LL.** (Baccalaureus Legum) (Lat.) or **J.B.** (Jurum Baccalaureus) (Lat.) Bachelor of Laws
L.L.B. Liberty Loan Bond
L.L.C.M. Licenciate London College of Music
LL.D. (Legum Doctor) (Lat.) or **J.D.** (Jurum Doctor) (Lat.) Doctor of Laws
L.L.I. Lord Lieutenant of Ireland
LL.JJ. or **L.JJ.** Lords Justices
LL.L. (Legum Licentiatus) (Lat.) or **L.LL.** (Licentiatus Legum) (Lat.) Licentiate in Laws
LL.M. (Legum Magister) (Lat.) or **M.L.** (Magister Legum) (Lat.) Master of Laws
LL. MM. (Leurs Majestés) (Fr.), **MM.** or **SS. MM.** (Sus Majestades) (Span.) Their Majesties
L.L.T. London landed terms
LM Land mine
L.M. Lord Mayor
L.M. or **l.m.** long meter
L.M., Lic. Med. or **M.L.** (Medicinae Licentiatus) (Lat.) Licentiate in Medicine
L.M. or **M.L.** Licentiate in Midwifery
l.M. (laufenden Monats) (Ger.) or **h.m.** (huius mensis) (Lat.) of the current month (cf. inst.)
L.M.B.C. Liverpool Marine Biology Committee
LMC or **L.M.C.** Lloyd's machinery certificate
l.m.c. low middling clause (Cotton)
L.M.C.C. Licenciate of Medical Council of Canada
L.M.D. long meter double (Music)
LMG (Mil.) or **L.M.G.** Light machine gun
LMP levee mile post
L.M.R.C.P. Licenciate in Midwifery of the Royal College of Physicians
L.M.S. Licenciate in Medicine and Surgery; London Missionary Society
L.M.S.C. let me see correspondence
L.M.S.S.A. Licenciate in Medicine and Surgery of the Society of Apothecaries (London)
L.M.T. length, mass, time (Physics); local mean time
L.N. or **L. of N.** League of Nations
Ln Liaison (Mil.)
ln or **log$_e$** logarithm (natural)
ln. lien; loan
L.N.A. Laundrymen's National Association [of America]
L.Nat. Liberal Nationalist
lndry. or **ldry.** laundry
lndrym. laundryman
Ln O (Mil.) or **L.O.** Liaison officer
L.N.U. League of Nations Union
L.O. London office
L.O. or **Ln O** (Mil.) Liaison officer
loadg.& dischg. loading and discharging (Shipping)
loadg.pt. loading point
Lo/C, L/C, l.c., l/c, l/c., L.Cr., l.cr. or **l/cr.** letter of credit
loc. local
loc., L., l. (loco) (Lat.) or **in loc.** (in loco) (Lat.) in the place (cf. ad. loc.; a.h.l.)
loc. or **locn.** location
loc. cit. (loco citato) (Lat.), **a.a.O.** (am angeführten Orte) (Ger.), **c.l.,** (citato loco) (Lat.), **in. loc. cit.** (in loco citato) (Lat.) or **l.c.** (loco citato) (Lat.) in the place cited (cf. loc. laud.; loc. primo cit.; u.s.)
loc. cur. local currency
Loc. dol. (loco dolenti) (Lat.) to the painful spot
loc. laud., L.L. or **l.l.** (loco laudato) (Lat.) in the place cited with approval (cf. loc. cit.)
locn. or **loc.** location
loco. locomotive
Loco. S. or **loco. s.** location statement
loc. primo cit. (loco primo citato) (Lat.) in the place first cited (cf. loc. cit; u.s.)
L of C, LC (Mil.), **L.C.** or **L. of C.** Line of communication or communications
L.of N. or **L.N.** League of Nations
Log. or **log.** logic
log or **log.** logarithm (common)
log. of **Log.** logic
log. or **log** logarithm (common)
log$_e$ or **ln** logarithm (natural)
L.O.M.A. Life Office Management Association
Lon., L (Astron., Geod.), **lon., Long.** or **long.** longitude
Lon. or **Lond.** London
lon., L (Astron., Geod.), **Lon., Long.** or **long.** longitude
Lond. Londonderry
Lond. or **Lon.** London
Lond., Londin., London. or **Londonin.** (Londoninensis) (Lat.) London, in signature of Bishop
Londin., Lond., London. or **Londonin.** (Londoninensis) (Lat.) London, in signature of Bishop
London., Lond., Londin. or **Londonin.** (Londoninensis) (Lat.) London, in signature of Bishop
Londonin., Lond., Londin. or **London.** (Londoninensis) (Lat.) London, in signature of Bishop
Long., L (Astron., Geod.), **Lon., lon.** or **long.** longitude
long. longitudinal
long., L (Astron., Geod.), **Lon., lon.** or **Long.** longitude
Longf. Longfellow; Longford (Topog.)
L.O.O.M. Loyal Order of Moose
loq. (loquitur) (Lat.) he or she speaks
Lor. Lorenzo
Lor. or **Lr.** Lorenz
lot. or **Lot.** lotion

LOX or **L.O.X.** liquid oxygen explosive
LP Livens projector (Mil.)
L.P. Labour Party (Brit.); Lord Provost
L.P., l.p., L.-P. or **l.-p.** low pressure
Lp., L. or **Ldp.** Lordship
Lp., Ladp. or **Ldp.** Ladyship
l.p. large post; long primer (Typog.)
l.p. or **ch. m.** (charta magna)(Lat.) large paper (Printing)
l.p., L.P., L.-P. or **l.-p.** low pressure
L.P.C. Lord of the Privy Council
L.P.M. long particular meter (Hymnol.)
L Pon Light ponton
L'pool Liverpool
L.P.S. Lord Privy Seal
L.P.W., lpw, l.p.w. or **l/w** lumen or lumens per watt
lpw, L.P.W., l.p.w. or **l/w** lumen or lumens per watt
L.Q.T. Liverpool quay terms
L.R. Law Reports; Lloyd's Register
Lr. Laurent
Lr. or **Laur.** Laurence
Lr. or **Lawr.** Lawrence
Lr. or **Lor.** Lorenz
lr., L. or **l.** lira; lire
L.R.A. Law Reports Annotated
L.R.A.M. Licentiate of the Royal Academy of Music
L.R.C. Lincoln Relief Corps
L.R.C.P. Licentiate of the Royal College of Physicians
L.R.C.P. & S. Licentiate of the Royal College of Physicians and the College of Surgeons of Edinburgh and of the Faculty of Physicians and Surgeons of Glasgow (Triple qualifications of the Scottish colleges)
L.R.C.P.E. or **L.R.C.P.Ed.** Licenciate of the Royal College of Physicians, Edinburgh
L.R.C.P.Ed. or **L.R.C.P.E.** Licentiate of the Royal College of Physicians, Edinburgh
L.R.C.P.I. Licentiate of the Royal College of Physicians, Ireland (cf. L.K.Q. C.P.I.)
L.R.C.S. Licentiate of the Royal College of Surgeons
L.R.C.S.E. or **L.R.C.S.Ed.** Licentiate of the Royal College of Surgeons, Edinburgh
L.R.C.S.Ed. or **L.R.C.S.E.** Licentiate of the Royal College of Surgeons, Edinburgh
L.R.C.S.I. Licentiate of the Royal College of Surgeons, Ireland
L.R.C.V.S. Licentiate of the Royal College of Veterinary Surgeons
L.R.F.P.S. or **L.F.P.S.** Licentiate of the Royal Faculty of Physicians and Surgeons
L.R.F.P.S.G. Licentiate of the Royal Faculty of Physicians and Surgeons of Glasgow
lrg., lge. or **Mag.** (magnus)(Lat.) large
L.R.I.B.A. Licentiate of the Royal Institute of British Architects
L.R.M.C. Lloyd's refrigeration machinery certificate (Shipping)
Lrs. Lancers
LS levee station; local sunset (Radio)
L.S. Leading seaman; Linnaean Society [of New York]
L.S., L.Ch. or **L.Chir.** (Licentiatus Chirurgiae)(Lat.) Licentiate in Surgery
L.S. or **l.s.** land service; (locus segilli) (Lat.), (lugar del sello)(Span.) place of the seal
l.s. left side; letter signed; lump sum
l.s. or **L.S.** land service; (locus segilli) (Lat.),(lugar del sello)(Span.) place of the seal
L.S.A. Linguistic Society of America
L.S.A. or **L.A.S.** Licentiate of the Society of Apothecaries
L.S.A.A. Lutheran Students' Association of America
L.S.C. Lower School Certificate
Ls/C letters of credit (cf. L.Cr.)
l.s.c. (loco sub citato)(Lat.) in the place cited below
l.s.c (loco supra citato)(Lat.) or **u.s.** (ubi supra)(Lat.) in the place cited above; where mentioned above (cf. in loc. cit.; loc. cit.)
L.S.D. Lightermen, Stevedores and Dockers (Brit.)
L.S.D., L.s.d., £ s.d. or **l.s.d.** (librae, solidi, denarii)(Lat.) pounds, shillings, pence
l.s.d., L.S.D., L.s.d. or **£ s.d.** (librae, solidi, denarii)(Lat.) pounds, shillings, pence
lsd.li., L.L. or **l.l.** leased line or lines
L.Sgt. or **L/Sgt** Lance sergeant
L.S.N.R. League of Struggle for Negro Rights
LSR local sunrise (Radio)
LSS, L.S.S. or **l.s.s.** Life-saving service; Life-saving [service] station
L.T. left tackle (Football)
L.T. or **L/T** Leading Telegraphist; line telegraphy
L.T., £T. or **T.** Turkish pound or lira
L.T., L.t. or **l.t.** low tension (Elec.)
L.T. or **L.Th.** Licentiate in Theology (cf. L.D.)
Lt (Mil.), **L** (Mil.) or **lt.** light
Lt (Mil.), **Lt.** or **Lieut.** Lieutenant
lt., L (Mil.) or **Lt** (Mil.) light
l.t. landed terms
l.t. or **lg.tn.** long ton
L.T.A. Lawn Tennis Association (Brit.)
L.T.C. Lawn Tennis Club (Brit.)
L.T.C.L. Licentiate of Trinity College [of Music), London
Lt Col (Mil.), **Lt. Col.** or **Lieut.Col.** Lieutenant colonel
Lt Com, Lt. Com., L.Cr., Lieut. Com., Lt. Comdr. or **Lt-Comm.** Lieutenant commander
Lt. Comdr., L.Cr., Lieut. Com., Lt Com, Lt. Com. or **Lt.-Comm.** Lieutenant commander

Lt.-Comm., L.Cr., Lieut. Com., Lt Com, Lt. Com. or **Lt. Comdr.** Lieutenant commander
Ltd., Ld., ld., Lim., ltd. or **Ltda.** (Limitada)(Span.) limited
ltd., Ld., ld., Lim., Ltd. or **Ltda.** (Limitada)(Span.) limited
Ltda. (Limitada)(Span.), **Ld., ld., Lim., Ltd.** or **ltd.** limited
Lt (E) Lieutenant with an emergency commission
Ltge. or **ltge.** lighterage
ltge. or **Ltge.** lighterage
Lt Gen (Mil.), **Lt. Gen., Lt-Gen, Lt.-Gen.** or **Lieut. Gen.** Lieutenant general
Lt. Gov., Lt-Gov or **Lieut. Gov.** Lieutenant Governor
L.Th. or **L.T.** Licentiate in Theology (cf. L.D.)
Lt Inf, Lt. Inf. or **L.I.** Light infantry
L Tk Light tank
L.T.L. less than truckload
L.T.M. Leading torpedo man; Licentiate in Tropical Medicine
ltng.arr. lightning arrester
Ltr., ep. (epistola)(Lat.) or **ltr.** letter
Ltr. or **ltr.** lighter
ltr., ep. (epistola)(Lat.) or **Ltr.** letter
ltr., L. or **l.** letter (alphabet)(cf. bklr.)
ltr. or **Ltr.** lighter
Ltr Inst Letter of Instructions (Mil.)
Lts., Lgts (Mil.) or **Lgts.** lights
Lt.-V. light vessel (Shipping)
L.U. Liberal Unionist
Lu lutecium (Chem.)
lubric. lubricant; lubrication
Lucr. Lucretius
L.U.E. or **l.u.e.** left upper entrance (Theat.)
l.u.e. or **L.U.E.** left upper entrance (Theat.)
L.U.O.T.C. London University Officers' Training Corps
Luth. Lutheran
LV low-voltage
L.V. Lehigh Valley
L.V. or **l.v.** legal volt; licensed victualer
Lv (Mil.), **lv.** or **lea.** leave [of absence]
lv. (livres)(Fr.), **lb., lbs.** or **lib.** (librae) (Lat.) pounds (Weight)
lv., lea. or **Lv** (Mil.) leave [of absence]
l.v. or **L.V.** legal volt; licensed victualer
L.V.L. Legislative Voters' League
L.W. (Lebensmittelwagen)(Ger.) Food supply wagon; [Rules for] Land Warfare; long wave; low water
l/w, L.P.W., lpw or **l.p.w.** lumen or lumens per watt
LwB. (Leinwandband)(Ger.) cloth binding
LWD or **L.W.D.** Local Work Department
L.W.L. load water line
L.W.M. low-water mark
L.W.O.S.T. low water ordinary spring tides
L.W.P. load water plane
lyr. lyric; lyrical
Lys. Lysander (Airplane)
L.-Zug. (Luxuszug)(Ger.) train de luxe

ΛΧΑ (Lambda Chi Alpha) National undergraduate fraternity
ΛΔΛ (Lambda Delta Lambda) Honor society (Physical Science)
ΛΚΣ (Lambda Kappa Sigma) Professional sorority (Pharmaceutics)
ΛΩ (Lambda Omega) National undergraduate sorority
ΛΦΔ (Lambda Phi Delta) Professional sorority (Fine Arts)
ΛΦΜ (Lambda Phi Mu) Professional fraternity (Medicine)

M

M magnetic [strength of pole] (Magnetism); Messier's catalog of nebulas; moment (Magnetism)
M, M., m, m. (milli)(Lat.), **K., k, k.** (kilo) (Greek), **thou.** or **thous.** thousand
M, Med (Mil.), **Med.** or **med.** medical
M (mega-)(Greek) or **mil.** million
M. Magistrate; Mary; (magister)(Lat.) master; metal (Chem.); micrococcus; (mater)(Lat.) mother
M., M, m, m. (milli)(Lat.), **K., k, k.** (kilo) (Greek), **thou.** or **thous.** thousand
M. or **m.** (main)(Fr.), (mano)(Ital.), (manus)(Lat.) hand; male; mare; martyr; mass (Mech); meter; meters; modulus; molar; moon; muscle (Anat.); muster; myopia
M., m., Man. or **man.** (manipulus)(Lat.) handful (Pharm.)
M., m., Man. (Mane)(Lat.), **mg.** or **morn.** morning
M., m. or **man.** manual
M., m. or **mar.** married
M., m. or **Marq.** Marquess
M., m., Marq. or **Mis.** Marquis
M., m., mas. or **masc.** masculine
M., m. or **ma**[tie] majesty
M., m. or **meas.** measure
M., m., Med. or **med.** medicine
M., m. or **med.** medium
M., m., Mem. or **mem.** member
M., m. or **mer.** meridian
M., m. or **mi.** mile; miles; mill; mills
M., m., mi. or **min.** minute; minutes
M., m., mid. or **ms.** (meso-)(Greek) middle
M., m. or **mil.** militia
M., m., Mk. or **mk.** mark
M., m., Mk., mk., Mks. or **mks.** marks
M., m., mo. or **mth.** month
M., m. or **Mons.** Monsieur (French equivalent of Mr.)
M., m., Mt., mt. or **mtn.** mountain
M., m. (meridiem)(Lat.), **N.** or **n.** noon
M., Man. or **Manit.** Manitoba
M. or **Mar.** Maria

M., Mar., marc., marz. (marcius or marzius) (Hung.), **Mch., mço.** (março)(Port.), **Mr.** or **mzo.** (marzo)(Span.) March
M., M[e] (maitre)(Fr.) or **Mr.** master
M., Met., met. or **metrop.** metropolitan
M., Meth. or **Method.** Methodist
M., Mo., Mon. or **Mond.** Monday
m, M, M., m. (milli)(Lat.), **K., k, k.,** (kilo) (Greek), **thou.** or **thous.** thousand
m. mist (Naut.); (mortis)(Lat.) of death
m. (mit)(Ger.), **av.** (avec)(Fr.), **c.** (cum) (Lat.) or **w.** with
m., M, M., m (milli)(Lat.), **K., k, k.** (kilo) (Greek), **thou.** or **thous.** thousand
m. or **M.** (main)(Fr.), (mano)(Ital.), (manus)(Lat.) hand; male; mare; martyr; mass (Mech.); meter; meters; modulus; molar; moon; muscle (Anat.); muster; myopia
m., M., Man. or **man.** (manipulus)(Lat.) handful (Pharm.)
m., M., Man. (mane)(Lat.) **mg.** or **morn.** morning (cf. A.M.)
m., M. or **man.** manual
m., M. or **mar.** married
m., M. or **Marq.** Marquess
m., M., Marq. or **Mis.** Marquis
m., M., mas. or **masc.** masculine
m., M. or **ma**[tle] majesty
m., M. or **meas.** measure
m., M., Med. or **med.** medicine
m., M. or **med.** medium
m., M., Mem. or **mem.** member
m., M. or **mer.** meridian
m., M. or **mi.** mile; miles; mill; mills
m., M., mi. or **min.** minute; minutes
m., M., mid. or **ms.** (meso-)(Greek) middle
m., M. or **mil.** militia
m., M., Mk. or **mk.** mark
m., M., Mk., mk., Mks. or **mks.** marks
m., M., mo. or **mth.** month
m., M. or **Mons.** Monsieur (French) equivalent of Mr.
m., M., Mt., mt. or **mtn.** mountain
m., M. (meridiem)(Lat.), **N.** or **n.** noon
m. or **min.** minim; minims (cf. gtt.)
m- (meta-)(Greek), **bet., betn., betw., btwn.** or **zw.** (zwischen)(Ger.) **between**
μ, μmm, Mmm. or **mmm.** micromillimeter; micron
$m.^2$ or **sq.m.** square meter or meters
$m.^3$ or **cu.m.** cubic meter or meters
μ^2 or **sq.mu** square micron
MA mill annealed
M.A. Machine Area (Queensland); Military Academy; Mountain artillery
M.A., A.M. or **M.és A.** (Maître és Arts) (Fr.) Master of Arts
M.A., Ma. or **ma.** milliampere; milliamperes
M.A. or **M/Agric.** Ministry of Agriculture
Ma masurium (Chem.)
Ma., M.A. or **ma.** milliampere; milliamperes
mA. milliangstrom
m/A, m/a, M/C (mio Conto)(Ger.) or **m/c** (mi cuenta)(Span.) my account
ma., M.A. or **Ma.** milliampere; milliamperes
ma., magg. (maggiore)(Ital) or **maj.** major
ma., mu a or **μa** microampere; microamperes
m/a, m/A, M/C (mio conto)(Ger.) or **m/c** (mi cuenta)(Span.) my account (Bookkeeping)
μa, ma. or **mu a** microampere; microamperes
M.A.A. Master-at-arms; Mathematical Association of America
M.A.B. Metropolitan Asylums Board (Brit.); Munitions Assignment Board (Anglo-American)
M.A.B.Y.S. Metropolitan Association for Befriending Young Servants (Brit.)
M.A.C. mean aerodynamic chord; Modern Art Collector; Motor ambulance convoy
Mac. or **mac.** (macera)(Lat.) macerate
Mac. or **Macc.** Maccabees
m/a/c or **ac.** money of account
Macc. or **Mac.** Maccabees
M. Acct. Master of Accounts
Maced. Macedonia; Macedonian
mach. or **machin.** machine; machinery; machinist
Mad., Madm. or **Mdm.** Madam
Madr. Madrid
M.A.E. or **M. Aero. E.** Master of Aeronautical Engineering
Ma. E., M.A.I. (Magister in Arte Ingeniaria)(Lat.), **M.E., M. Eng.** or **M. Engrg.** Master of Engineering
M.Aero. E. or **M.A.E.** Master of Aeronautical Engineering
maes. (maestoso)(Ital.) majestic; grandiose (Music)(cf. pomp.)
M.A.F.L. Manual of Air Force Law
Mag. (magnus)(Lat.), **lge.** or **lrg.** large
mag. magazine; magnet; magnitude [stars]
mag. or **magn.** magnetic; magnetism; magneto
Magd. Magdalen [College](Oxford); Magdalene [College](Cambridge)
magg. (maggiore)(Ital.), **ma.** or **maj.** major
magg. (maggio)(Ital.), **maj.** (majus)(Hung.) or **My.** May
magn. or **mag.** magnetic; magnetism; magneto
M. Agr. or **M. Agric.** Master of Agriculture
M. Agric. or **M. Agr.** Master of Agriculture
M/Agric. or **M.A.** Ministry of Agriculture
M. Agr. Sc. Master of Agricultural Science
mah. mahogany
M.A.I. Member of the Anthropological Institute; Museum of the American Indian (New York)
M.A.I. (Magister in Arte Ingeniaria)(Lat.), **Ma. E., M.E., M. Eng.** or **M. Engrg.** Master of Engineering
M.A. in Apologetics Master of Arts in Apologetics
M.A. in Christian Ed. Master of Arts in Christian Education

M.A. in Ed. or **A.M. in Ed.** Master of Arts in Education
M.A. in Public Adm. Master of Arts in Public Administration
Maint (Mil.) or **maint.** maintenance
M.A. in Theology Master of Arts in Theology
Maint of E or **M of E** Maintenance of equipment (Mil.)
Maint of W Maintenance of way (Mil.)
Maint Py Maintanance party (Mil.)
Maint Sec Maintenance section (Mil.)
Maj (Mil.) or **Maj.** Major
maj. majority
maj., ma. or **magg.** (maggiore)(Ital.) major
maj. (majus)(Hung.), **magg.** (maggio) (Ital.) or **My.** May
Maj Gen (Mil.), **Maj. Gen., Maj.-Gen.** or **M.G.** Major general
M.A.L. Lyons Society of African Missions (cf. S.M.A.; W.F.)
Mal. Malachi; Malay
Mal. or **Malay.** Malayan
malac. malacology
Malay. or **Mal.** Malayan
M.A.L.D. Master of Arts in Law and Diplomacy
M.A.M. milliampere minutes
Mam. Mamercus
M. & A. management and administration
M. & D. Medicine and duty (Mil.)
M. & N. May and November (Interest)
M & P material and process
M & S Maintenance and supply (Mil.)
M.& S. March and September (interest)
M. Am. Soc. C. E. Member of American Society of Civil Engineers
M. Am. Soc. M. E. or **M.A.S.M.E.** Member of the American Society of Mechanical Engineers
Man. Manasses; Manchester (Airplane); manila [Paper, Twine]
Man., M., m. or **man.** (manipulus)(Lat.) handful (Pharm.)
Man. (mane)(Lat.), **M., m., mg.** or **morn.** morning
Man., M. or **Manit.** Manitoba
man. (manège)(Fr.) horsemanship
man., M. or **m.** manual
man., M., m. or **Man.** (manipulus)(Lat.) handful
man., manc. or **Mando.** (mancando)(Ital.) gradually softer (Music)(cf. mor.; perd.)
man. or **manuf.** manufactory
man., manuf., manufd. or **mfd.** manufactured
man., manuf., mf. or **mfr.** manufacture
man., manuf. or **mfr.** manufacturer
manc., man. or **Mando.** (mancando)(Ital.) gradually softer (Music)(cf. mor.; perd.)
Manch. Manchukuo; Manchuria
Mancun. (Mancunium)(Lat.) Manchester, in signature of Bishop
Mando., man. or **manc.** (mancando)(Ital.) gradually softer (Music)(cf. mor.; perd.)
Mane pr., Man.pr. or **m.pr.** (mane primo) (Lat.) early in the morning
M.A.N.F. May, August, November, February (Interest)
Manh. Manhattan
Manit., M. or **Man.** Manitoba
man. op. or **M.O.** manually operated
Man.pr., Mane pr. or **m.pr.** (mane primo) (Lat.) early in the morning
M.A.N.S. Member of the Academy of Natural Sciences [of Philadelphia]
manuf. or **man.** manufactory
manuf., man., manufd. or **mfd.** manufactured
manuf., man., mf. or **mfr.** manufacture
manuf., man. or **mfr.** manufacturer
manuf. or **mfg.** manufacturing
manufd., man., manuf. or **mfd.** manufactured
M.A.O. Master of Arts in Obstetrics; Master of Obstetric Art
m.a.O. (med andre Ord)(Dan.) or **m.a.o.** (med andra ord)(Swed.) in other words
M.A.P. Medical aid post; Ministry of Aircraft Production
M. Ar., Ar. M. (Architecturae Magister) (Lat.) or **M. Arch.** Master of Architecture
Mar. Mitchell Marauder (Airplane)
Mar. or **M.** Maria
Mar., M., marc., marz. (marcius or marzius)(Hung.), **Mch., mço.** (março) (Port.), **Mr.** or **mzo.** (marzo)(Span.) March
Mar. or **mar.** marine
mar. maritime
mar., M. or **m.** married
mar. or **Mar.** marine
marc. (marcato)(Ital.) marked; distinct (Music)
marc., marz. (marcius or marzius)(Hung.), **M., Mar., Mch., mço.** (março)(Port.), **Mr.** or **mzo.** (marzo)(Span.) March
M. Arch., Ar. M. (Architecturae Magister) (Lat.) or **M. Ar.** Master of Architecture
March. Marchioness
M. Arch. in C. P. Master of Architecture in City Planning
Mar. E. or **M.E.** Marine Engineer
Marg. Margaret; Margery
marg. margin; marginal
Marq., M. or **m.** Marquess
Marq., M., m. or **Mis.** Marquis
Mart. martyrology
M.A.S. Master of Applied Science or Sciences; Michigan Academy of Science [Arts and Letters]; milliampere seconds
mas., M., m. or **masc.** masculine
M.A.S.A. Mail Advertising Service Association
masc., M., m. or **mas.** masculine
M.A.S.M.E. or **M. Am. Soc. M. E.** Member of the American Society of Mechanical Engineers
Mas. pil. (massa pilularum)(Lat.) pill mass
Mass. Massachusetts

M.Ast.S. Member of the [Royal] Astronomical Society
Mat (Mil.), **mat., matrl.** or **mtl.** material
Mat. Matieu
Mat. or **mat.** matins
Mat. or **Matt.** Matthew
mat. matinee; maturity
mat., Mat (Mil.), **matrl.** or **mtl.** material
mat. or **Mat.** matins
Math., math., Maths. or **maths.** mathematics
math. mathematical; mathematician
math., Math., Maths. or **maths.** mathematics
Math.C. Mathematics corps
maths., Math., math. or **Maths.** mathematics
ma^{tie}, M. or **m.** majesty
matr. or **matric.** matriculate
matric. matriculation
matric. or **matr.** matriculate
matrl., Mat (Mil.), **mat.** or **mtl.** material
Matt. Matthias
Matt. or **Mat.** Matthew
Maur. Maurice
mauv. (mauvais)(Fr.) bad (cf. adv.)
Max. or **max.** maxim
Max. or **Mx.** Maximilian
max. maximum
max. or **Max.** maxim
max.cap. maximum capacity
MB (Mil.) or **M.B.** Militia Bureau
M.B. Mark of the Beast; Medical Board; Medium bomber
M.B. (Medicinae Baccalaureus)(Lat.), **B.M.** (Baccalaureus Medicinae)(Lat.) or **B. Med.** Bachelor of Medicine
M.B. or **MB** (Mil.) Militia Bureau
M.B. or **m.b.** motorboat
M.B., Mus. B., Mus. Bac. (Musicae Baccalaureus)(Lat.), **B.M.** or **B.Mus.** (Musicae Baccalaureus)(Lat.) Bachelor in or of Music
M.b. (misce bene)(Lat.) mix well (Pharm.)
m.b. or **M.B.** motorboat
M.B.A. Master in or of Business Administration
MBCC Migratory Bird Conservation Commission
M.B.C.M. (Baccalaureus Medicinae Chirurgiae Magister)(Lat.) Bachelor of Medicine, Master of Surgery
M.B.E. Member [of the Order] of the British Empire
M.B.F. et H. (Magna Britannia, Francia et Hibernia)(Lat.) or **M.B.G. & H.** (Magna Britannia, Gallia et Hibernia)(Lat.) Great Britain, France and Ireland
M. B. G. & H. (Magna Britannia, Gallia et Hibernia)(Lat.) or **M.B.F. et H.** (Magna Britannia, Francia et Hibernia)(Lat.) Great Britain, France and Ireland
M.B.L. Marine Biological Laboratory
Mbl (Mil.) or **mob.** mobile
M.B.M. thousands [of feet] board measure
M.B.M.A. Master Boiler Makers Association
M.B.O.U. Member of the British Ornithologist Union
MBS or **M.B.S.** Mutual Broadcasting System
M.B.Sc. Master of Business Science
M.B.Sc.B. Bachelor of Medicine and Bachelor of Science
M.B.S.I. Member of the Boot and Shoe Industry
MC or **M.C.** Medical Corps
MC or **mc.** millicurie (Phys. Chem.)
M.C. Maritime Commission; master of ceremonies; Master of Chemistry; Master commandant; Member of Congress; Member of Council; Military Cross (Brit.); Motor contact (Mil.); Movement control [of troops]
M.C. or **c.m.** (carat métrique)(Fr.) metric carat
M.C. or **MC** (Mil.) Medical Corps
M.C. or **m.c.** machinery certificate (Shipping)
M.C., m.c., m/c, Mtcl or **Mtrcl** (Mil.) motorcycle
M.C., M.Ch. (Magister Chirurgiae)(Lat.), **Ch. M., C.M.** (Chirurgiae Magister) (Lat.), **M.S., M. Surg.** or **M. Surgery** Master of Surgery
M/C marginal credit (Banking); metaling clause (Marine ins.)
M/C (mio Conto)(Ger.), **m/A, m/a** or **m/c** or **m/c** (mi cuenta)(Span.) my account
mc. megacycle
mc. or **MC** millicurie (Phys.Chem.)
m.c. magnetic course; marked capacity (Freight cars)
m.c. or **M.C.** machinery certificate (Shipping)
m.c., M.C., m/c, Mtcl (Mil.) or **Mtrcl** (Mil.) motorcycle
m/c (mi cuenta)(Span.), **m/A, m/a** or **M/C** (mio Conto)(Ger.) my account
m/c, M.C., m.c., Mtcl (Mil.) or **Mtrcl** (Mil.) motorcycle
M.C.A.U.S. Manufacturing Chemists Association of the United States
MCB Motor Carriers Bureau
M.C.B.A. Master Car Builders' Association
M.C.C. Member of the County Council; Mixed Claims Commission (U.S. and Germany)
M.C.D. Doctor of Comparative Medicine
M.C.E. or **M.C.Eng.** Master of Civil Engineering
M.C.Eng. or **M.C.E.** Master of Civil Engineering
MCF thousand cubic feet
M/C G. Manchester Guardian
M. Ch., M.C. (Magister Chirurgiae)(Lat.), **Ch. M., C.M.** (Chirurgiae Magister) (Lat.), **M.S., M. Surg.** or **M. Surgery** Master of Surgery
Mch., M., Mar., marc., marz. (marcius or marzius)(Hung.), **Mch., mço.** (março) (Port.), **Mr.** or **mzo.** (marzo)(Span.) March
M.Ch.D. or **M.D.S.** Master of or in Dental Surgery
M.Ch.E. or **M. Ch. Eng.** Master of Chemical Engineering

M. Ch. Eng. or **M. Ch. E.** Master of Chemical Engineering
M.Ch.Orth. Master of Orthopaedic Surgery
M.C.L. Marine Corps League; Master of Civil Law
M.C.L.Aux. Marine Corps League Auxiliary
M.Clin. Psychol. Master of Clinical Psychology
MCM Manual for Court-Martial
M.C.M.E.S. Member of the Civil and Mechanical Engineers' Society
M.C.M.P.A. Metropolitan Certified Milk Producers' Association
M.C.O. Motor contact officer; Movement control officer
mço. (março)(Port), **M., Mar., marc., marz.** (marcius or marzius)(Hung.), **Mch., Mr.** or **mzo.** (marzo)(Span.) March
M. Com. or **M. Comm.** Master of Commerce
M.C.P. Master of City Planning; Member of the College of Preceptors (Brit); Mining Conditional Purchase (Australia); Member of Colonial Parliament
M.C.S. Madras Civil Service; Malayan Civil Service; Master of Commercial Science; Military College of Science
Mcs. Marcus
M.C.U. Motor Cycle Union
MD (Mil.) or **M.D.** Medical Department
MD., M.D., MDu. or **M.Du.** Middle Dutch
M.D. mentally deficient; Message-dropping; Mine depot
M.D. (Medicinae Doctor)(Lat.), **D.M.** or **Dr. Med.** (Doctor Medicinae)(Lat.) Doctor of Medicine
M.D. or **MD** (Mil.) Medical Department
M.D., MD., MDu. or **M.Du.** Middle Dutch
M.D., M/D or **m.d.** memorandum of deposit (Banking)
M.D. (main droite)(Fr.), **m.d.** (mano destra)(Ital.), **d.** (droite)(Fr.), **dcha.** (derecha)(Span.), **D.M.** (destra mano) (Ital.), **R.H.** or **r.h.** right hand
M/D, M.D. or **m.d.** memorandum of deposit (Banking)
M/D, M/d, m/d or **m.d.** months' date; months after date (Com.)
Md. Maryland
M/d, M/D, m/d or **m.d.** months' date; months after date
m.d. (mano destra)(Ital.), **M.D.** (main droite)(Fr.), **d.** (droite)(Fr.), **dcha.** (derecha)(Span.), **D.M.** (destra mano) (Ital.), **R.H.** or **r.h.** right hand
m.d., M.D. or **M/D** memorandum of deposit (Banking)
m.d., M/D, M/d or **m/d** months' date; months after date
m/d, M/D, M/d or **m.d.** months' date; months after date
M.D.A. Missionaries of the Divine Love of Jesus; motor discriminative acuity (Med.)
M.D.A. or **A.D.M.** Master of Domestic Arts (cf. M.D.E.)
M.D.C.M. Doctor of Medicine, Master of Surgery
Mddx., Mdx., Middlx., Midx. or **Mx.** Middlesex
M.D.E. Master of Domestic Economy (cf. M.D.A.)
M. Des. Master of Design
M.D.H.B. Mersey Docks and Harbour Board
M. d. H.H. (Mitglied des Herrenhauses) (Ger.) Member of the House of Lords (Prussia)
M.Di. Master of Didactics
M.Dip. Master of Diplomacy
M. d. L. (Mitglied des Landtags)(Ger.) Member of the Landtags or lower legislative house of the German states
Mdlle, Mdlle., Mlle, Mlle. (Mademoiselle) (Fr.), **Frk.** (Frøken)(Dan.), **frk.** (fröken)(Swed.), **Frl.** (Fraulein)(Ger.), **Snrta., Srta.** (senhorita)(Port.), **Srita., Srta.** or **Sta.** (Señorita)(Span.) Miss; unmarried woman or girl
Mdm., Mad. or **Madm.** Madam
Mdme., Mme or **Mme.** (Madame)(Fr.) title of a married woman (cf. Mrs.)
mdnt. midnight
M.D.P.M.A. Manchester and District Pharmaceutical and Masonic Association
M.d.R. (Mitglied des Reichstags)(Ger.) Member of the Reichstag
m.d.R. (mit dem Rang)(Ger.) with the rank
M.D.S. Main dressing station
M.D.S. or **M. Ch. D.** Master in or of Dental Surgery (cf. M.S.D.)
M.D.Sc. Master of Dental Science (cf. M. S. Dent.)
mdse. merchandise
M.D.S.T. Mountain Daylight Saving Time
MDu., MD., M.D. or **M.Du.** Middle Dutch
M.D.W. Military defense works
Mdx., Mddx., Middlx., Midx. or **Mx.** Middlesex
ME, ME. or **M.E.** Middle English
ME., ME or **M.E.** Middle English
M.E. Master of Elements; Middle East; Middle Eastern; Military Engineer
M.E., Excma., Exc. ma, Excmo. or **Exc. mo** (Excelentísma, Excelentísmo)(Span.) Most Excellent (cf. Hon.; M. Hon.)
M.E., Ma. E., M.A.I. (Magister in Arte Ingeniaria)(Lat.), **M. Eng.** or **M. Engrg.** Master of Engineering
M.E. or **Mar. E.** Marine Engineer
M.E., ME or **ME.** Middle English
M.E. or **M.E. Ch.** Methodist Episcopal [Church]
M.E., Mech. E., Mech.Eng. or **M. Eng.** Mechanical Engineer
M.E., M. Eng., Min. E. or **Mining Eng.** Mining Engineer
Me methyl (Chem.)
Me. Maine; Messerschmitt (Airplane)
M.e or **Me** (maître)(Fr.) master (cf. M.; prop.)
m.e. marble edges (Bookbinding)
M.E.A. Motor Equipment Association
meas. measurable
meas., M. or **m.** measure

M.E.C. Master of Engineering Chemistry; Member of the Executive Council
Mec (Mil.), **Mech** (Mil.) or **mech.** mechanic
M.E.Ch. Methodist Episcopal Church
Mech (Mil.), **mech.** or **Mec** (Mil.) mechanic
Mech., mech., Mechan. or **mechan.** mechanics
mech. mechanism
mech., Mec (Mil.) or **Mech** (Mil.) mechanic
mech., Mech., Mechan. or **mechan.** mechanics
mech. or **mechan.** mechanical
mech. or **Mecz** (Mil.) mechanized
Mechan., mechan., Mech. or **mech.** mechanics
mechan. or **mech.** mechanical
Mech. E., M.E., Mech. Eng. or **M. Eng.** Mechanical Engineer
Mech. Eng., M.E., Mech. E. or **M. Eng.** Mechanical Engineer
M.E.C.L. Master or Mistress of English and Classical Literature
Mecz (Mil.) or **mech.** mechanized
M.E.D. Master of Elementary Didactics; minimal erythema dose (Pharm.)
M. Ed., Ed. M., M. in Ed. or **M. of Ed.** Master in or of Education
Med (Mil.), **Med., med.** or **M** medical
Med., M., m. or **med.** medicine
Med., M, Med (Mil.) or **med.** medical
Med. of **med.** medieval
med. medalist
med., M, Med (Mil.) or **Med.** medical
med., M. or **m.** medium
med., M., m. or **Med.** medicine
med. or **Med.** medieval
Med Adm C (Mil.) or **Med. Adm. C.** Medical Administrative Corps
Med Bn Armd Medical battalion armored
Medit. Mediterranean
Med. Jur. Medical Jurisprudence
Med. L., Med. Lat., ML. or **M.L.** Medieval Latin
Med. R.C., Med-Res (Mil.) or **M.R.C.** Medical Reserve Corps
Med-Res (Mil.), **Med.R.C.** or **M.R.C.** Medical Reserve Corps
Med Rgt (Mil.) or **Med. Rgt.** Medical regiment
Med.Sc.D., D.M.S., M.Sc.D., Sc.D.M. or **Sc.D.Med.** Doctor of Medical Science (cf.M.D.)
Med Sq Medical squadron
Med Sup Dep Medical supply depot
M.E.E. or **M. El. Eng.** Master of Electrical Engineering
M.E.F. Mediterranean Expeditionary Force (World War II) (Brit.)
Meg. megohm
M.E.G.H.P. Most Excellent Grand High Priest
M.E.I.C. Member of Engineering Institute of Canada
M.E.L. Master of English Literature
Melan. Melanesia; Melanesian
M. El. Eng. or **M. E. E.** Master of Electrical Engineering
mem. (memento)(Lat.) remember
Mem., M., m. or **mem.** member
mem. or **Mém.** (mémoire)(Fr.) memoir; memorial
mem., Memo. or **memo.** memoranda; memorandum
M.E.M.A. Motor and Equipment Manufacturers Association
Memo., memo. or **mem.** memoranda; memorandum
mén. (ménage)(Fr.) household
M. Eng., Ma. E., M.A.I. (Magister in Arte Ingeniaria)(Lat.), **M.E.** or **M. Engrg.** Master of Engineering
M. Eng., M.E., Mech. E. or **Mech. Eng.** Mechanical Engineer
M. Eng., M.E., Min.E. or **Mining Eng.** Mining Engineer
M. Engrg., Ma.E., M.A.I. (Magister in Arte Ingeniaria)(Lat.), **M.E.** or **M. Eng.** Master of Engineering
Mensur. or **mensur.** mensuration
mep or **m.e.p.** mean effective pressure
M.E.P.A. Master of Engineering and Public Administration
Mer. or **mer.** meridional
mer., M. or **m.** meridian
merc. mercantile; mercurial; mercury
Merions. Merionethshire
mer. rect. mercury rectifier
M.E.S. Methodist Episcopal [Church] South
M. ès A. (Maître ès Arts)(Fr.), **A.M.** or **M.A.** Master of Arts
Messrs., MM. (Messieurs)(Fr.), **HH.** (Herren)(Ger.), **Sig., sig.** (signori)(Ital.), **Sres.** or **Srs.** (Señores)(Span.) Sirs; gentlemen
Met., M., met. or **metrop.** metropolitan
met. metronome
met., M., Met. or **metrop.** metropolitan
met. or **metaph.** metaphor; metaphysical
met., Metaph. or **metaph.** metaphysics
met., meteor., meteorol. or **met'l** meteorological
Metal., metal. or **metall.** metallurgy
metal. metallurgical
metall., Metal. or **metal.** metallurgy
Metaph., metaph. or **met.** metaphysics
metaph. metaphorically; metaphysician
metaph. or **met.** metaphor; metaphysical
metaphor. or **metaph.** metaphorical
metath. metathesis; metathetic
Met Co Meteorological company
Met. E. Metalurgical Engineer
Meteor., meteor. or **meteorol.** meteorology
meteor., met., meteorol. or **met'l.** meteorological
meteorol., Meteor. or **meteor.** meteorology
meteorol., met., meteor. or **met'l.** meteorological
Meth., M. or **Method.** Methodist
meth. method; methylated

Method., M. or **Meth.** Methodist
met'l., met., meteor. or **meteorol.** meteorological
m. et n. (mane et nocte)(Lat.) morning and night
Met O (Mil.) or **Met. O.** Meteorological officer
meton. metonomy
metrol. metrological; metrology
metrop., M., Met. or **met.** metropolitan
Met Sec Meteorological section
M. et sig. (misce et signa)(Lat.) mix and write a label (Pharm.)
M.E.W. Ministry of Economic Warfare
Mex. Mexican
Mex. or **Méx.** (México)(Span.) Mexico
Mex. Sp. Mexican Spanish
M.E.Z. (mitteleuropäische Zeit)(Ger.) mean European time
M.F. Master of Forestry
M.F. or **m.f.** machine finish; machine finished; mill finish; mill finished
M.F. or **M. of F.** Ministry of Food
Mf. microfilaria (Med.)
mf or **mf.** millifarad; (mezzo forte)(Ital.) moderately loud (Music)
mf, mf., μf, mfd. or **mu f** microfarad
mf, mf., μf, mfds. or **mu f** microfarads
mf., man., manuf. or **mfr.** manufacture
mf. or **M.F.** machine finish; machine finished; mill finish; mill finished
mf. or **mf** millifarad; (mezzo forte)(Ital.) moderately loud (Music)
mf., mf, μf, mfd. or **mu f** microfarad
mf., mf, μf, mfds. or **mu f** microfarads
m.f. motor freight
μf, mf, mf., mfd. or **mu f** microfarad
μf, mf, mf., mfds. or **mu f** microfarads
M.F.A. Master of Fine Arts
M.F.A. Art and Arch. Master of Fine Arts in Art and Archaeology
M.F.A. in Arch. Master of Fine Arts in Architecture
M.F.A. in Mus. Master of Fine Arts in Music
mfd., man., manuf. or **manufd.** manufactured
mfd., mf, mf., μf or **mu f** microfarad
mfds., mf, mf., μf or **mu f** microfarads
mfg. or **manuf.** manufacturing
M.F.G.B. Miners' Federation of Great Britain
M.F.H. Master of Fox Hounds
m. fl. (med flera)(Swed.), (med flere)(Dan.), **bl.a.** (bland andra)(Swed.), (blandt andre)(Dan.), **et al.** (et alii or aliae) (Lat.) or **u.a.** (und andere)(Ger.) with others; among others; and others
M.F.N. Most Favored Nation (Brit.)
M.F.O. Military forwarding officer
M.Fr. Middle French
mfr., man. or **manuf.** manufacturer
mfr., man., manuf. or **mf.** manufacture
mfrs. manufacturers
mfs. manufactures; millifarads
M.ft., F.M., f.m., ft.mist. or **m.ft.** (mistura fiat; fiat mistura)(Lat.) make a mixture
M.ft. or **m.ft.** thousand feet (cf. M.B.M.)
m.ft., F.M., f.m., ft.mist. or **M.ft.** (mistura fiat; fiat mistura)(Lat.) make a mixture
m.ft. or **M.ft.** thousand feet (cf.M.B.M.)
MG (Mil.), **M.G.** or **m.g.** Machine gun
M.G. Graduate in Music; Master general; medical gymnast
M.G., MG (Mil.) or **m.g.** machine gun
M.G., Maj Gen (Mil.), **Maj. Gen.** or **Maj.-Gen.** Major General
M.G. or **m.g.** motor generator
M.G., m.g. (main gauche)(Fr.), **izq.**[a], **izq.**[da] (izquierda)(Span.), **L.H., l.h. m.s.** (mano sinistra)(Lat.), **s.** (sinistra) (Ital.) or **S.M.** (sinistra mano)(Lat.) left hand
M.-G., MGoth., M.Goth. or **M.-Goth.** Moeso-Gothic
Mg magnesium (Chem.)
mg. modified guaranteed (securities)
mg., M., m., Man. (mane)(Lat.) or **morn.** morning
mg., mgm., mgr. or **mgrm.** milligram; milligrams
m.g., MG (Mil.) or **M.G.** machine gun
m.g. or **M.G.** motor generator
M.G.B. Motor gunboat
M.G.C. or **MG Co** (Mil.) Machine-gun company
M.G.C. or **M.G. Corps** Machine-gun Corps
MG Co (Mil.) or **M.G.C.** Machine-gun company
M.G.Corps or **M.G.C.** Machine-gun Corps
M.G.D., mgd or **m.g.d.** million gallons per day
mgd, M.G.D. or **m.g.d.** million gallons per day
M.G.G.S. Major General, General Staff
M.G.M. or **M-G-M** Metro-Goldwyn-Mayer Picture Corporation
mgm., mg., mgr. or **mgrm.** milligram; milligrams
MGO Machine-gun officer
M.G.O. Master general of ordnance
MGoth., M.Goth., M.-Goth. or **M.-G.** Moeso-Gothic
MGr. Medieval Greek
Mgr, Mgr., Mngr., Mon., Mons. Monsig. or **Msgr.** Monseigneur; Monsignor; Monsignore
Mgr. or **mgr.** manager
mgr., mg., mgm. or **mgrm.** milligram; milligrams
Mgri. Monsignors
mgrm., mg., mgm. or **mgr.** milligram; milligrams
mgt. management
MG Tr Machine-gun troop
M.Gyn. and Obs. Master in Gynecology and Obstetrics
MH or **M.H.** Medal of Honor (cf. V.M.H.)
M.H. Master of Horticulture; Miner's Homestead (Queensland); Ministry of Health
M.H. or **H.M.** Master of Humanities
M.H. or **MH** Medal of Honor (cf. V.M.H.)

M. H. or **m.h.** main hatch
M.H. or **M.Hon.** Most Honorable (cf. Excma.)
M.H. or **M. Hy.** Master of Hygiene
mh millihenry
m.h. or **M.H.** main hatch
M.H.A. Member of the House of Assembly (New Zealand)
mhcp, m.h.cp. or **m.h.c.p.** mean horizontal candlepower
m.h.c.p., mhcp or **m.h.cp.** mean horizontal candlepower
M.H.D. minimum hemolytic dose (Pharm.)
MHG. or **M.H.G.** Middle High German
M.H.K. Member of the House of Keys (Isle of Man)
mho unit of conductivity; reciprocal of the ohm (Elec.)
M.Hon. or **M.H.** Most Honorable (cf. Excma.)
M.H.R. Member of the House of Representatives
M.H.R.A. Modern Humanities Research Association (Brit.)
M.H.S. Massachusetts Historical Society; Ministry of Home Security
m.H.t. (med Hensyn til)(Dan.) with regard to (cf. in re.)
M.H.W.S. mean high water springs (ocean tides)
M.Hy. or **M.H.** Master of Hygiene
MI (Mil.) or **M.I.** Military intelligence
MI or **m.i.** malleable iron
M.I. Medical inspection; Mounted infantry
M.I., Min. Inf., C.R.M.I. (Clerici Regulares Ministrantes Infirmis)(Lat.) or **O.S. Cam.** (Ordo Sancti Camillus)(Lat.) Ministers of the Sick; Clerks Regular Attendant on the Sick; Clerks Regular Ministering to the Infirm; Order of St. Camillus; Camillian Fathers; Camillians
mi., M. or **m.** mile; miles; mill; mills
mi., M., m. or **min.** minute; minutes
mi. (Music) or **min.** minor
m.i. or **MI** malleable iron
mi.², **sq.m.** or **sq.mi.** square mile or miles
M.I.A.E. Member of the Institution of Automobile Engineers (Brit.)
M.I.Ae.E. Member of the Institute of Aeronautical Engineers (Brit.)
M.I.B.E. or **M.Inst.B.E.** Member of the Institute of British Engineers
M.I.C. (Congregatio Fratrum Marianorum Immaculate Conceptionis Mariae)(Lat.) Society of Mary of the Immaculate Conception; Marian Fathers; Marianists
Mic. Micah
M.I.C.E. or **M. Inst. C.E.** Member of the Institution of Civil Engineers (Brit.)
Mich. Michael; Michigan
Mich. or **Michs.** Michelmas
M.I.Chem.E. Member of the Institution of Chemical Engineers (Brit.)
Michs. or **Mich.** Michelmas
Mic. pan. (mica panis)(Lat.) bread crumb
micrometal. micrometallurgy
micros. microscope; microscopic; microscopical; microscopist; microscopy
M.I.C.U.M. (Mission Interallié de Contrôle d'Usines et Mines)(Fr.) Interallied Commission for the Control of [German] Factories and Mines (World War I)
M.I.D. minimum infective dose (Pharm.)
Mid., mid. or **Mid'n** Midshipman
mid., M., m. or **ms.** (meso-)(Greek) middle
mid., Mid. or **Mid'n** Midshipman
Middlx., Mddx., Mdx., Midx. or **Mx.** Middlesex
Mid'n, Mid. or **mid.** Midshipman
Midx., Mddx., Mdx., Middlx. or **Mx.** Middlesex
M.I.E.A. Member of the Institution of Engineers, Australia
M.I.E.E. or **M. Inst. E.E.** Member of the Institution of Electrical Engineers (Brit.)
M.I.E.I. or **M. Inst. E.I.** Member of the Institution of Engineering Inspection (Brit.)
M.I.F. Milk Industry Foundation
M.I.Fire E. or **M. Inst. Fire E.** Member of the Institute of Fire Engineers
M.I.G.E. or **M. Inst. Gas E.** Member of the Institution of Gas Engineers (Brit.)
m.i.h. Miles in the hour (average convoy speed) (cf m.p.h.)
M.I.I.R. Mellon Institute of Industrial Research
M.I.J. or **M.J.I.** Member of the Institute of Journalists
Mil., mil. or **milit.** military
mil. milage
mil. or **M** (mega-)(Greek) million
mil., M. or **m.** militia
Mil Att (Mil.) or **Mil. Att.** Military attaché
milit., Mil. or **mil.** military
mil.min. military mining
M.I.Loco. E. or **M. Inst. Loco. E.** Member of the Institution of Locomotive Engineers (Brit.)
Mil. Sec. or **M.S.** Military secretary
Milt. Milton
mim. or **mimeo.** mimeograph; mimeographed
M.I.Mar.E. or **M. Inst. Mar. E.** Member of the Institute of Marine Engineers (Brit.)
M.I.M.C.E. Member of the Institution of Municipal and County Engineers (Brit.)
M.I.M.E., M.I.Mech.E. or **M.Inst.Mech. E.** Member of the Institution of Mechanical Engineers (Brit.)
M.I.M.E. or **M.I.Min.E.** Member of the Institution of Mining Engineers (Brit.)
M.I.Mech.E., M.I.M.E. or **M.Inst.Mech.E.** Member of the Institution of Mechanical Engineers (Brit.)
mimeo. or **mim.** mimeograph; mimeographed
M.I.Min.E. or **M.I.M.E.** Member of the Institution of Mining Engineers (Brit.)
M.I.M.M. or **M. Inst. M.M.** Member of the Institution of Mining and Metallurgy (Brit.)
Min. or **min.** minister; ministry

Min., min. or **mineral.** mineralogy
min. mineral; minima; minimum; mining
min., M., m. or **mi.** minute; minutes
min. or **m.** minim; minims (cf. gtt.)
min. or **mi.** (Music) minor
min. or **Min.** minister; ministry
min., Min. or **mineral.** mineralogy
min. or **mineral.** mineralogical
M.I.N.A. Member of the Institution of Naval Architects (Brit.)
Min.B/L minimum bill of lading
Min.E., M.E., M.Eng. or **Mining Eng.** Mining Engineer
M. in Ed., Ed. M., M. Ed. or **M. of Ed.** Master in or of Education
mineral., Min. or **min.** mineralogy
mineral. or **min.** mineralogical
Min. Inf., M.I., C.R.M.I. (Clerici Regulares Ministrantes Infirmis)(Lat.) or **O.S. Cam.** (Ordo Sancti Camilli)(Lat.) Ministers of the Sick; Clerks Regular Attendant on the Sick; Clerks Regular Ministering to the Sick; Order of St. Camillus; Camillian Fathers; Camillians
Mining Eng., M.E., M.Eng. or **Min.E.** Mining Engineer
Minn. Minnesota
Min. Plen., Min. Plenip. or **M.P.** Minister Plenipotentiary
Min. Plenip., Min. Plen. or **M.P.** Minister Plenipotentiary
min. prem. minimum premium (insurance)
Min. Res., M.R. or **M.-R.** Minister Resident or Residentiary
M.Inst. A.E. or **M.I.A.E.** Member of the Institution of Automobile Engineers (Brit.)
M. Inst.B.E. or **M.I.B.E.** Member of the Institute of British Engineers
M.Inst. C.E. or **M.I.C.E.** Member of the Institution of Civil Engineers (Brit.)
M. Inst. E. E. or **M.I.E.E.** Member of the Institution of Electrical Engineers (Brit.)
M.Inst.E.I. or **M.I.E.I.** Member of the Institution of Engineering Inspection (Brit.)
M.Inst. Fire E. or **M.I.Fire E.** Member of the Institute of Fire Engineers
M. Inst. Gas E. or **M.I.G.E.** Member of the Institution of Gas Engineers (Brit.)
M.Inst.Loco.E. or **M.I.Loco.E.** Member of the Institution of Locomotive Engineers
M. Inst. Mar. E. or **M.I.M.E.** Member of the Institute of Marine Engineers (Brit.)
M.Inst.Mech.E., M.I.M.E. or **M.I.Mech.E.** Member of the Institution of Mechanical Engineers (Brit.)
M. Inst. Met. Member of the Institute of Metals (Brit.)
M. Inst. Min E. or **M.I.M.E.** Member of the Institution of Mining Engineers (Brit.)
M. Inst. M.M. or **M.I.M.M.** Member of the Institution of Mining and Metallurgy (Brit.)
M.Inst.P.E. or **M.I.P.E.** Member of the Institution of Production Engineers (Brit.)
M. Inst. Pet. Member of the Institute of Petroleum (Brit.)
M.Inst.P.T. or **M.I.P.T.** Member of the Institute of Petroleum Technology
M. Instr. Musketry Instructor
M.Inst.R.A. or **M.I.R.A.** Member of the Institute of Registered Architects
M.Inst.Struct.E., M.I.S.E. or **M.I.Struct.E.** Member of the Institution of Structural Engineers (Brit.)
M. Inst. T. Member of the Institute of Transport (Brit.)
M. Inst. W. E. or **M.I.W.E.** Member of the Institution of Water Engineers (Brit.)
M.Inst.W.T. or **M.I.W.T.** Member of the Institute of Wireless Technology (Brit.)
M. Int. Med. Master in Internal Medicine
M.I.O. minimal identifiable odor
M.I.O.B. Member of the Institute of Builders
M.I.P. or **m.i.p.** marine insurance policy
m.i.p. mean indicated pressure
m.i.p. or **M.I.P.** marine insurance policy
M.I.P.E. or **M. Inst. P.E.** Member of the Institution of Production Engineers (Brit.)
M.I.P.T. or **M.Inst.P.T.** Member of the Institution of Petroleum Technology
MIr. or **M.Ir.** Middle Irish
M.I.R.A. or **M.Inst.R.A.** Member of the Institute of Registered Architects
MI-Res Military Intelligence Reserve
Mis., M., m., or **Marq.** Marquis
Mis. or **Mo.** Missouri
misc. or **miscl.** miscellaneous
misc. or **msc.** miscellany
Misc.Doc. miscellaneous document
miscl. or **misc.** miscellaneous
M.I.S.E., M.Inst.Struct.E. or **M.I.Struct.E.** Member of the Institution of Structural Engineers (Brit.)
Mise. Marquise
M.I.S.I. Member of the Iron and Steel Institute (Brit.)
Miss. Mississippi
Miss. or **miss.** mission; missionary
Mist., mist. (mistura)(Lat.) or **mixt.** mixture
mistrans. mistranslation
M.I. Struct. E., M. Inst. Struct. E. or **M.I.S.E.** Member of the Institution of Structural Engineers (Brit.)
M.I.T. Massachusetts Institute of Technology
MIt. or **M. It.** Middle Italian
Mit. or **mit.** (mitte)(Lat.) send (Pharm.)
m.i.t. milled or milling in transit
Mitt. sang. (mitte sanguinem)(Lat.) bleed
M.I.W.E. or **M.Inst.W.E.** Member of the Institution of Water Engineers (Brit.)
M.I.W.T. or **M.Inst.W.T.** Member of the Institute of Wireless Technology (Brit.)
mix. mixing
mix. or **mxd.** mixed
mixt., Mist. or **mist.** (mistura)(Lat.) mixture
M.J.I. or **M.I.J.** Member of the Institute of Journalists
M.J.S. Member of the Japan Society

M.J.S.D. March, June, September and December (Interest)
Mk. Mark
Mk., M., m. or **mk.** mark (cf. RM)
Mk., M., m., mk., Mks. or **mks.** marks (cf. RM)
mk., M., m. or **Mk.** mark (cf. RM)
mk., M., m., Mk., Mks. or **mks.** marks (cf. RM)
mkd. marked
m-kg. meter-kilogram
Mks., M., m., Mk., mk. or **mks.** marks (cf. RM)
mks., M., m., Mk., mk. or **Mks.** marks (cf. RM)
mkt. market
ML., Med.L., Med.Lat. or **M.L.** Medieval or Middle Latin
M.L. midline; Mineral Lease (Queensland); muzzle-loader; muzzle-loading
M.L. (Magister Legum)(Lat.) or **LL. M.** (Legum Magister)(Lat.) Master of Laws
M.L. or **L.M.** Licentiate in Midwifery
M.L. (Medicinae Licentiatus)(Lat.), **L.M.** or **Lic. Med.** Licentiate in Medicine
M.L., Med. L., Med. Lat or **ML.** Medieval or Middle Latin
M.L. or **M/L** Mine-layer
mL millilambert
ml. mail; milliliter; milliliters
M.L.A. Member of Legislative Assembly; Mercantile Library Association; Modern Language Association
M.L.A. or **L.A.M.** (Liberalium Artium Magister)(Lat.) Master or Mistress of Liberal Arts
M.L.A. or **M.L. Arch.** Master in or of Landscape Architecture
M.L.A.A. Modern Language Association of America
M.L. Arch. or **M.L.A.** Master in or of Landscape Architecture
M.L.C. Member of the Legislative Council (New Zealand)
M.L.D. Master of Landscape Design
M.L.D. or **m.l.d.** minimum lethal dose (Pharm.)
mld. molded
mldr. molder
MLG. or **M.L.G.** Middle Low German
M.L.G. Most Loyal Gander (Order of the Blue Goose)
m.l.h.c.p. mean lower hemispherical candle power
M. Lit. (Magister Literarum)(Lat.) Master of Literature
M. Litt. (Magister Litterarum)(Lat.) or **Litt. M.** (Litterarum Magister)(Lat.) Master of Letters
Mlle, Mlle., Mdlle, Mdlle. (Mademoiselle) (Fr.), **Frk.** (Frøken)(Dan.), **fkr.** (fröken)(Swed.), **Frl.** (Fräulein)(Ger.), **Snrta., Srta.** (senhorita)(Port.), **Srita., Srta.** or **Sta.** (Señorita)(Span.) Miss; unmarried woman or girl
Mlles. (mesdemoiselles)(Fr.) Misses; unmarried women
mlnr. milliner
M.L.N.S. Ministry of Labour and National Service
MLR Main line of resistance (Mil.)
m.l.r. muzzle-loading rifle
M.L.R.G. muzzle-loading rifled gun
M.L.S. Master of Library Science
mLs millilamberts
M.L.U. Mobile laundry unit
M.L.W.S. mean low water springs (ocean tides)
MM. martyrs; (magistri)(Lat.) masters; (meritissimus)(Lat.) Most Deserving
MM., LL. MM. (Leurs Majestés)(Fr.) or **SS. MM.** (Sus Majestades)(Span.) Their Majesties
MM., Messrs. (Messieurs)(Fr.), **HH.** (Herren)(Ger.), **Sig., sig.** (signori) (Ital.), **Sres.** or **Srs.** (Señores)(Span.) sirs; gentlemen
M.M. Maelzel's metronome (Music); (Societas de Maryknoll pro Missionibus) (Lat.) Maryknoll Missioners; Catholic Foreign Missionary Society of America; Foreign Mission Brothers of St. Michael; Michaelites; Master Mason (Freemasonry); Master Mechanic; Military Medal (Brit.); Minister of Mines; mucous membrane
M.M. or **m.m.** Machinist's mate; mercantile marine; motor mechanics
M.M., M. Mus. or **Mus. M.** (Musicae Magister)(Lat.) Master of Music
Mm Marksman (Mil.)
mM millimole
mm. (matrimonium)(Lat.) matrimony; (millia)(Lat.) thousands; millimeter; millimeters
mm.^{2} or **sq.mm.** square millimeter or millimeters
mm.^{3} or **cmm.** cubic millimeter or millimeters
m.m. made merchantable; motor mechanics; (mutatis mutandis)(Lat.) the necessary changes having been made
m. m. (med mera)(Swed.), (med mere) (Dan.), **etc.** (et cetera)(Lat.), **i.t.d.** (i tak dalej)(Pol.), **k.t.l.** (kai ta loipa) (Greek), **o.d.** (ock dylikt or dylika) (Swed.), **o.s.v.** (och så vidare)(Swed.), (og saa videre)(Dan.), **u.drgl.** (und dergrelchen)(Ger.), **u.s.f.** (und so fort) (Ger.), **usw.** or **u.s.w.** (und so weiter) (Ger.) and so forth; and the like; and others of like kind
mμ or **m mu** millimicron; millimicrons
$\mu\mu$ or **mu mu** micromicron
M.M.A. Merchandise Marks Act
M.M.A. or **A.M.M.** Master of Mechanic Arts
M Maint Medium maintenance (Mil.)
M.M.E., M. Mech. E. or **M. Mech. Eng.** Master of Mechanical Engineering
M.M.E. or **M.Min.E.** Master of Mining Engineering
Mme, Mme. or **Mdme.** (Madame)(Fr.) married woman (cf. Mrs.)
M. Mech. E., M.M.E. or **M.Mech. Eng.** Master of Mechanical Engineering

M.Mech. Eng., M.M.E. or **M.Mech. E.** Master of Mechanical Engineering

Mmes (mesdames)(Fr.) ladies

M. Met. E. Master of Metallurgical Engineering

mmf., M.M.F. or **m.m.f.** magnetomotive force (Elec.)

M.Min.E. or **M.M.E.** Master of Mining Engineering

Mmm., mmm., μ or **μmm** micromillimeter; micron

mmm., Mmm., μ or **μmm** micromillimeter; micron

μmm, μ, Mmm. or **mmm.** micromillimeter; micron

M.M.P. Military mounted police

M.M.S. Moravian Missionary Society

M.M.S.A. Master of Midwifery, Society of Apothecaries; Mining and Metallurgical Society of America

M.Mus., M.M. or **Mus. M.** (Musicae Magister)(Lat.) Master of Music

M. Mus. Ed. Master of Music Education

MN magnetic north

M.N. Master of Nursing; Merchant Navy

Mn manganese (Chem.)

mn (maison)(Fr.), **h.** or **ho.** house

m.n. (mutato nomine)(Lat.) the name being changed; under a changed name

m/n (moneda nacional)(Span.) national currency

M.N.A.S. Member of the National Academy of Sciences

Mngr., Mgr, Mgr., Mon., Mons., Monsig. or **Msgr.** Monseigneur; Monsignor; Monsignore

M.N.S. Member of the Numismatic Society

MNT or **M.N.T.** mononitrotoluene

M.O. Master of Obstetrics; Master of Oratory; Medical officer; (modus operandi)(Lat.) method of working

M.O. or **man. op.** manually operated

M.O. or **m.o.** mail order; money order; municipal ownership

Mo molybdenum (Chem.)

Mo., M., Mon. or **Mond.** Monday

Mo. or **Mis.** Missouri

mo. monthly

mo., M., m. or **mth.** month

m.o. or **M.O.** mail order; money order; municipal ownership

M.O.A. or **A.O.M.** Master of Obstetric Art

M.O.B. money-order business

mob. mobilization; mobilized

mob. or **Mbl.** (Mil.) mobile

Mob. Vet. Sec. Mobile veterinary section

M.O.C. Military Order of Cooties

M.O.D. mail order department

Mod. Modification (Ordnance); modulator

Mod. or **mod.** modern

mod. moderate; (moderato)(Ital.) moderately fast (Music); modified

Mod. praesc., M.P. (modo praescripto) (Lat.), **E.M.P.** (ex modo praescripto) (Lat.) or **Mor. dict.** (more dicto)(Lat.) in the manner or way prescribed or directed (Pharm.)(cf. Ut dict.)

Mods. Moderations (Brit.)

M.O.D. Sales Mail Order Department Sales

M.O.F.A.P. Ministry of Fuel and Power

M of E or **Maint of E** Maintenance of equipment (Mil.)

M. of Ed., Ed. M., M. Ed. or **M. in Ed.** Master of or in Education

M. of F. or **M.F.** Ministry of Food

M. of M. Minister or Ministry of Munitions

Mog. Scr. mogul screw (Radio)

M.O.H. Master of Otter Hounds; Medical Officer of Health; Ministry of Health

Moh. or **Moham.** Mohammedan; Mohammedanism

M.O.I. Military operations and intelligence; Ministry of Information

mol. molecular; molecule

mold. molding

Mol. wt. or **mol. wt.** molecular weight

m.o.m. middle of the month

Mon., M., Mo. or **Mond.** Monday

Mon., Mgr, Mgr., Mngr., Mons., Monsig. or **Msgr.** Monseigneur; Monsignor; Monsignore;

Mon. or **Mons.** Monmouthshire

Mon. or **Mont.** Montana

mon. monastery; monetary

Mond., M., Mo. or **Mon.** Monday

Mong. or **Mongol.** Mongolian

Mongol. or **Mong.** Mongolian

monog. or **monogr.** monograph

monogr. or **monog.** monograph

Mons., M. or **m.** Monsieur (French equivalent of Mr.)

Mons., Mgr, Mgr., Mngr., Mon., Monsig., or **Msgr.** Monseigneur; Monsignor; Monsignore

Mons. or **Mon.** Monmouthshire

Monsig., Mgr, Mgr., Mngr., Mon., Mons. or **Msgr.** Monseigneur; Monsignor; Monsignore

Mont. or **Mon.** Montana

M.O.O. Money Order Office (Brit.)

m.o.p. mother of pearl

M.O.P.A. master oscillator, power amplifier (Radio)

Mor. Moroccan; Morocco; Morris

mor. (morendo)(Ital.) dying away (Music) (cf. manc.; perd.); morocco (leather)

M.O.R.C. Medical Officers Reserve Corps

Mor. dict. (more dicto)(Lat.), **E.M.P.** (ex modo praescripto)(Lat.), **Mod. praesc.** or **M.P.** (modo praescripto)(Lat.) in the way or manner directed or prescribed (Pharm.)(cf. Ut dict.)

morn., M., m., Man. (mane)(Lat.) or **mg.** morning

Morph., morph., Morphol. or **morphol.** morphology

morph. or **morphol.** morphological

Morphol., morphol., Morph. or **morph.** morphology
morphol. or **morph.** morphological
Mor. sol. (more solito)(Lat.) in the usual way
Mort or **Mrtr** Mortar (Mil.)
mort. mortuary
M.O.S. Mounted orderly section
M.O.S., M.S. or **M/Supp.** Ministry of Supply
mos (Mil.) or **mos.** months
mot. or **Mtr** (Mil.) motor
mot. or **Mtz** (Mil.) motorized
mot.op. motor operated
MP multipole
MP (Mil.) or **M.P.** Marine police; Military police
MP or **M Pon** Medium ponton
M.P. Master of Painting; Meeting point (Mil.); Member of Parliament; Member of Police; mesiopulpal; Methodist Protestant; Metropolitan Police; Mounted Police; Municipal Police
M.P., Min. Plen. or **Min. Plenip.** Minister Plenipotentiary
M.P., Mod. praesc. (modo praescripto) (Lat.), **E.M.P.** (ex modo praescripto) (Lat.) or **Mor. dict.** (more dicto)(Lat.) in the manner or way prescribed or directed (Pharm.) (cf. Ut dict.)
M.P. or **MP** (Mil.) Marine police; Military police
M.P., mp, m.p. or **M.Pt.** melting point
M/P mail payment; memorandum of partnership
mp, M.P., m.p. or **M.Pt.** melting point
mp. (mezzo piano)(Ital.) moderately soft (Music)
M.P.A. Master of Public Administration
MP Bn Military police battalion
M.P.C. Member of Parliament, Canada
MP Co Military police company
M.P.D. miles per dollar
M.Pd., M.Pe., M.Ped., M.Pg. (Magister Pedagogiae)(Lat.), **Pd.M., Pe.M., Ped. M., Pg.M.** (Pedagogiae Magister) (Lat.), **M.Py.** or **Py.M.** Master of Pedagogy
M.P.E. Master of Physical Education
M.Pe., M.Pd., M.Ped., M.Pg. (Magister Pedagogiae)(Lat.), **Pd.M., Pe.M., Ped. M., Pg.M.** (Pedagogiae Magister) (Lat.), **M.Py.** or **Py.M.** Master of Pedagogy
M.Ped., M.Pd., M.Pe., M.Pg. (Magister Pedagogiae)(Lat.), **Pd.M., Pe.M., Ped. M., Pg.M.** (Pedagogiae Magister) (Lat.), **M.Py.** or **Py.M.** Master of Pedagogy
M.P.F.A. Master Photo Finishers of America
M.Pg., M.Pd., M.Pe., M.Ped. (Magister Pedagogiae)(Lat.), **Pd.M., Pe.M., Ped. M., Pg.M.** (Pedagogiae Magister) (Lat.), **M.Py.** or **Py.M.** Master of Pedagogy
mpg or **m.p.g.** miles per gallon
M.P.H. Master of Public Health
M.P.H., Mph, M.p.h., mph, or **m.p.h.** miles per hour (cf. m.i.h.)
M.Ph., M.Phar., Phar.M. or **Pharm.M.** (Pharmaciae Magister)(Lat.) Master of Pharmacy
M.Ph. or **Ph. M.** (Philosophiae Magister) (Lat.) Master of Philosophy
Mph, mph (Mil.), **M.P.H., M.p.h.** or **m.p.h.** miles per hour (cf. m.i.h.)
m.p.h., M.P.H., Mph or **mph** miles per hour (cf. m.i.h.)
M.Phar., M.Ph., Phar.M. or **Pharm.M.** (Pharmaciae Magister)(Lat.) Master of Pharmacy
mphps miles per hour per second
M.P.I. or **m.p.i.** mean point of impact
M.P.L. Master of Patent Law; Master of Polite Literature
M Pon or **MP** Medium ponton
M.P.P. Member of the Provincial Parliament
MPPA Music Publishers Protective Association
m.pr., Man.pr. or **Mane pr.** (mane primo) (Lat.) early in the morning
Mp. Rdg. or **mp. rdg.** map reading
M.P.S. Member of the Pharmaceutical Society (Brit.); Member of the Philological Society (Brit.); Member of the Physical Society (Brit.); Ministry of Public Security
M.P.S.C. Military Provost Staff Corps
M.Pt., M.P., mp or **m.p.** melting point
M.P.U. Medical Practitioner's Union (Brit.); Message picking-up (Air force)
M.Py., M.Pd., M.Pe., M.Ped., M.Pg. (Magister Pedagogiae)(Lat.), **Pd.M., Pe.M., Ped.M., Pg.M.** (Pedagogiae Magister) (Lat.) or **Py.M.** Master of Pedagogy
MR Mobilization Regulations
M.R. Master of the Rolls (Brit.); Missionary Rector; Municipal Reform Party (Brit.)
M.R. or **M/R** mate's receipt (Shipping)
M.R., M.-R. or **Min. Res.** Minister Resident or Residentiary
M.R. or **m.r.** mill run; mine run (cf. r.o.m.; tal.qual.)
M/R memorandum receipt; morning report
M/R or **M.R.** mate's receipt (Shipping)
Mr, Mr., Hr. (Herr)(Dan., Ger.), **hr.** (herr) (Swed.), **M., m., Mons.** (Monsieur) (Fr.), **p.** (pan.)(Pol.), **S., Sig., sig.** (signor)(Ital.), **Snr., Sr.** (senhor) (Port.), **Sor.** or **Sr.** (Señor)(Span.) Mister; title of courtesy
Mr., M., Mar., marc., marz. (marcius or marzius)(Hung.), **Mch., mço.** (março) (Port.), or **mzo.** (marzo)(Span.) March
mr. (millier)(Fr.), **M.T.** or **t.** (tonneau)(Fr.) metric ton
m.r. or **M.R.** mill run; mine run (cf. r.o.m.; tal qual.)
M.R.A. or **M.R.A.S.** Member of the Royal Asiatic Society [of Great Britain and Ireland]
M.R.A.C. Member of the Royal Agricultural College
M.R.Ae.S. Member of the Royal Aeronautical Society (London)

M.R.A.S. Member of the Royal Academy of Science

M.R.A.S. or **M.R.A.** Member of the Royal Asiatic Society [of Great Britain and Ireland]

MRC or **M.R.C.** Metals Reserve Company

M.R.C. Medical Research Council (Brit.)

M.R.C., Med. R.C. or **Med-Res** (Mil.) Medical Reserve Corps

M.R.C.C. Member of the Royal College of Chemistry

M.R.C.O. Member of the Royal College of Organists

M.R.C.P. Member of the Royal College of Physicians (London)

M.R.C.P.E. Member of the Royal College of Physicians of Edinburgh

M.R.C.P.I. Member of the Royal College of Physicians of Ireland

M.R.C.S. Member of the Royal College of Surgeons

M.R.C.S.E. Member of the Royal College of Surgeons of Edinburgh

M.R.C.S.I. Member of the Royal College of Surgeons of Ireland

M.R.C.V.S. Member of the Royal College of Veterinary Surgeons

M.R.D. minimum reacting dose (Pharm.)

M.R.E. or **M.R. Ed.** Master of Religious Education

M.R.G.S. Member of the Royal Geographical Society

M.R.H. Member of the Royal Household

M.R.I. Member of the Royal Institution [of Great Britain]

M.R.I.A. Member of the Royal Irish Academy

M.R.I.B.A. Member of the Royal Institute of British Architects

M.R.N.S. Member of the Royal Numismatic Society

M.R.P. Master in Regional Planning

M.R.S. Medical receiving station

Mrs., D. (dona)(Port.), **d.** (donna)(Ital.), **D.^{a}, Dña.** (Doña)(Span.), **Fr.** (Frau) (Ger.), **Mdme., Mme.** (Madame)(Fr.), **p.** (pani)(Pol.), **S.^{a}, Snra.** or **Sra.** (senhora)(Port.), (señora)(Span.) Mistress; married woman; title of courtesy

M.R.S.A. Member of the Royal Society of Architects; Member of the Royal Society of Arts (London) (cf. M.S.A.)

M.R. San.I. Member of the Royal Sanitary Institute (London) (cf. M.S.I.)

M.R.S.L. Member of the Royal Society of Literature [of the United Kingdom]

M.R.S.T. Member of the Royal Society of Teachers

M.R.T. Medical Round Table [of Chicago]

Mrtr or **Mort** Mortar (Mil.)

M.R.U.S.I. Member of the Royal United Service Institution (London)

MS medium steel

MS. mailsteamer

MS., ms. or **Hs.** (Handschrift)(Ger.) manuscript

M.S. margin of safety; mess sergeant; mine sweeper; (Congregatio Missioniorum "De la Salette")(Lat.) Missionaries of Our Lady of La Salette (France); Missionary Fathers of La Salette; (memoria sacrum)(Lat.) sacred to the memory of

M.S., Ch. M., C.M. (Chirurgiae Magister) (Lat.), **M.C., M. Ch.** (Magister Chirurgiae)(Lat.), **M. Surg.** or **M. Surgery** Master of Surgery

M.S. or **Mil. Sec.** Military secretary

M.S., M.O.S. or **M/Supp.** Ministry of Supply

M.S. or **M/S** motor ship

M.S., M/S, M/s, ms., m.s. or **m/s** month's sight; months after sight (Com.)

M.S. or **m.s.** machinery survey (shipping)

M.S., M.Sc., Sc. M. or **S.M.** Scientiae Magister)(Lat.) Master of Science

M.S. or **M/Shipping** Ministry of Shipping (now Ministry of Wartime Communications)

M/S or **M.S.** motor ship

M/S, M.S., M/s, ms. or **m.s.** month's sight; months after sight (Com.)

ms. (meso-)(Greek), **M., m.** or **mid.** middle

ms., MS. or **Hs.** (Handschrift)(Ger.) manuscript

ms., M.S., m.s., M/S, M/s or **m/s** month's sight; months after sight (Com.)

m.s. mean square

m.s. (mano sinistra)(Lat.), **izq.^{a}, izq.^{da}** (izquierda)(Span.), **L.H., l.h., M.G., m.g.** (main gauche)(Fr.), **s.** (sinistra)(Ital.) or **S. M.** (sinistra mano)(Lat.) left hand

m.s. or **M.S.** machinery survey (shipping)

m.s., M.S., M/S, M/s, m/s or **ms.** month's sight; months after sight (Com.)

m/s meters per second

m/s, M.S., M/S, M/s, ms. or **m.s.** month's sight; months after sight (Com.)

M.S.A. Master of Science and Art; Member of the Society of Architects (Brit.); Member of the Society of Arts (London) (now Royal Society of Arts); Merchant Shipping Act; Military Service Act; Mineralogical Society of America; Mine Safety Appliance [Company]

M.S.A. or **M.S.Agr.** Master of Science in Agriculture; Master of Scientific Agriculture

M.S.A.E. or **M.S.Aut.E.** Member of the Society of Automotive Engineers

M.S.Agr. or **M.S.A.** Master of Science in Agriculture; Master of Scientific Agriculture

M.S. Arch. Master of Science in Architecture

M.S.Aut.E. or **M.S.A.E.** Member of the Society of Automotive Engineers

MSB Medicine and Surgery Bureau

M.S.C. Madras Staff Corps; Medical Staff Corps; (Missionarii Sacratissimi Cordis) (Lat.) Missionaries of the Most Sacred Heart

M.S.C. (Missionarii Sancti Caroli)(Lat.), **C.S.C.B.** (Congregatio Missionarii Sancti Caroli Borromeo)(Lat.) or **P.S.S.C.** Missionaries of St. Charles [Borromeo]; Pious Society of Missionaries of St. Charles Borromeo

M.Sc., M.S., Sc. M. or **S.M.** (Scientiae Magister)(Lat.) Master of Science
M sc machine screw
msc. or **misc.** miscellany
m.s.c. moved, seconded and carried
M.S.C.C. Missionary Society of the Canadian Church
M.Sc.D., D.M.S., Med.Sc.D., Sc.D.M. or **Sc.D.Med.** Doctor of Medical Science (cf.M.D.)
M.S.C.E. or **M.S. in C.E.** Master of Science in Civil Engineering
M.S.(Cer.E.) Master of Science in Ceramic Engineering
M.S.Ch.E. or **M.S. in Ch.E.** Master of Science in Chemical Engineering
M.S.Chem. or **M.S. in Chem.** Master of Science in Chemistry
M.Sc. in Agr. Eng. Master of Science in Agricultural Engineering
M.Sc. in Ed., M.S. in Ed. or **M.S. in Educ.** Master of Science in Education
M.Sc. in E.E., M.S.E.E. or **M.S. in E.E.** Master of Science in Electrical Engineering
M.Sc. in M.E. or **M.S. in M.E.** Master of Science in Mechanical Engineering
M.Sc. in Soc W. or **M.S. in S.W.** Master of Science in Social Work
M.Sc.Med. Master of Medical Science
mscp, M.S.C.P., m.s.cp. or **m.s.c.p.** mean spherical candlepower
M.Sc. Tech. Master of Science of Technology; (Magister Scientiae Technicae) (Lat.) Master of Technical Science
M.S.D. Master of Scientific Didactics; Master Surgeon Dentist (cf. M.D.S.)
M.S. Dent. Master of Science in Dentistry (cf. M.D.Sc.)
M.S.E., M.S. in Eng., M.S. in Eng'g. or **S.M. in Engin.** Master of Science in Engineering
M.S.E.E., M.Sc. in E.E. or **M.S. in E.E.** Master of Science in Electrical Engineering
M.S.F. (Congregatio Missionariorum Sanctae Familiae)(Lat.) Congregation of the Missionaries of the Holy Family; Master of Science in Forestry; Missionaries of the Holy Family
M.S.F.U. Merchant Service Fighter Unit (Air force)
Msg (Mil.) or **msg.** message
msg. or **Msg** (Mil.) message
Msg Cen Message center (Mil.)
Msg DPU Message dropping and pick-up ground (Mil.)
Msgr (Mil.) or **msngr.** messenger
Msgr., Mgr, Mgr., Mngr., Mon., Mons. or **Monsig.** Monseigneur; Monsignor; Monsignore
Msgr Sec Messenger section (Mil.)
M.Sgt. Master Sergeant
M.S.H. Master of Staghounds
M.S.H. Ec. or **M.S. in Home Ec.** Master of Science in Home Economics
M/Shipping or **M.S.** Ministry of Shipping (now Ministry of Wartime Communications)
M.S.Hyg. Master of Science in Hygiene
M.S.I. Member of the Sanitary Institute (now Royal Sanitary Institute); Member of the [Chartered] Surveyors' Institution (Brit); Museum of Science and Industry (Chicago)
M.S. in B.A. Master of Science in Business Administration
M.S. in C.E. or **M.S.C.E.** Master of Science in Civil Engineering
M.S. in Ch. E. or **M.S. Ch.E.** Master of Science in Chemical Engineering
M.S. in Chem. or **M.S. Chem.** Master of Science in Chemistry
M.S. in Com. Master of Science in Commerce
M.S. Ind. E. Master of Science in Industrial Engineering
M.S. in Ed., M.Sc. in Ed. or **M.S. in Educ.** Master of Science in Education
M.S. in Educ., M.Sc. in Ed. or **M.S. in Ed.** Master of Science in Education
M.S. in E.E., M.S.E.E. or **M.Sc. in E.E.** Master of Science in Electrical Engineering
M.S. in E.M. Master of Science in Engineering Mechanics
M.S. in Eng., M.S.E., M.S. in Eng'g. or **S.M. in Engin.** Master of Science in Engineering
M.S. in Eng'g., M.S.E., M.S. in Eng. or **S.M. in Engin.** Master of Science in Engineering
M.S. in Govt. Management Master of Science in Government Management
M.S. in Group Work Ed. Master of Science in Group Work Education
M.S. in Home Ec. or **M.S.H.Ec.** Master of Science in Home Economics
M.S. in Hyg. and Phys. Ed. or **M.S. in Hyg. and Phys. Educ.** Master of Science in Hygiene and Physical Education
M.S. in J. Master of Science in Journalism
M.S. in L.S. Master of Science in Library Science
M.S. in M.E. or **M.Sc. in M.E.** Master of Science in Mechanical Engineering
M.S. in Mus. or **M.S. in Music** Master of Science in Music
M.S. in N.E. Master of Science in Nursing Education
M.S. in Nurs. Master of Science in Nursing
M.S. in Phy.Ed. or **M.S.P.E.** Master of Science in Physical Education
M.S. in P.S.M. Master of Science in Public School Music
M.S. in Public Adm. Master of Science in Public Administration
M.S. in Ret. Master of Science in Retailing
M.S. in S.E. Master of Science in Sanitary Engineering
M.S. in Social Adm. Master of Science in Social Administration
M.S. in S.S. Master of Science in Social Service (cf. M.S. in S.W.)
M.S. in S.W. or **M.Sc. in Soc. W.** Master of Science in Social Work (cf. M.S. in S.S.; M.S.S.; M.S.W.)
M.S. in Trans. Master of Science in Transportation
M.S. in Trans. E. Master of Science in Transportation Engineering

M.S.I.U.S. Military Service Institution of the United States
M.S.L. midsternal line
M.S.L. or **m.s.l.** mean sea level
m.s.l. or **M.S.L.** mean sea level
M.S.M. Meritorious Service Medal
msngr. or **Msgr** (Mil.) messenger
M. Soc. Wk. or **M.S.W.** Master of Social Work (cf. M.S. in S.W.; M.S.S.)
m.-sopr. mezzo-soprano
M.S.P.E. or **M.S. in Phy. Ed.** Master of Science in Physical Education
M.S.P.H. Master of Science in Public Health
M.S. Phar. Master of Science in Pharmacy
M.S.P.H.E. Master of Science in Public Health Engineering
MSR Main supply road (Mil.)
M.S.R. Member of the Society of Radiographers (Brit.)
MSS., mss. or **Hss.** (Handschriften)(Ger.) (cf.) MS.) manuscripts
M.S.S. Master of Social Science; Master of Social Service (cf. M.S. in S.S.); Member of the Statistical Society
M.S.SS.T. (Missioni Servi Sanctissimae Trinitatis)(Lat.) Missionary Servants of the Most Holy Trinity; Discalced Trinitarians; Redemptionists (cf. O.Ss.T.; C.SS.R.)
M.S.T. Mountain Standard Time
M.S.T. or **S.T.M.** (Sacrae Theologiae Magister)(Lat.) Master of Sacred Theology
mst. measurement
Ms-Th mesothorium (Chem.)
mstr.mech. master mechanic
M/Supp., M.O.S. or **M.S.** Ministry of Supply
M. Surg., Ch. M., C.M. (Chirurgiae Magister)(Lat.), **M.C., M. Ch.** (Magister Chirurgiae)(Lat.), **M.S.** or **M. Surgery** Master of Surgery
M.S.W. or **M. Soc. Wk.** Master of Social Work (cf. M.S. in S.S; M.S.S.)
M.T. Masoretic Text (Old Testament); mean time; mechanical transport; Medical Technologist; Ministry of Transport; motor transport; Mountain time
M.T., mr. (millier)(Fr.) or **t.** (tonneau) (Fr.) metric ton
M.T. or **Mt.** membrana tympani
M.T. or **mt.** empty (on trucks, vans, etc.)
Mt., M., m., mt. or **mtn.** mountain
Mt. or **M.T.** membrana tympani
Mt. or **mt.** mount
mt., M., m., Mt. or **mtn.** mountain
mt. or **M.T.** empty (on trucks, vans, etc.)
mt. or **Mt.** mount
M.T.A. Motor Traders' Association [of New South Wales]
M.T. & S. Mechanized transport and supply
M.T.B. Motor torpedo boat
M.T.C. Mechanical Transport Corps
Mtcl (Mil.), **M.C., m.c., m/c** or **Mtrcl** (Mil.) motorcycle
Mtcl Co or **Mtrcl Co** Motorcycle company
mt.ct.cp. mortgage certificate coupon (securities)
Mtd (Mil.) or **mtd.** mounted
M'ter. Manchester
mtg. meeting
mtg. or **mtge.** mortgage
mtgd. mortgaged
mtge. or **mtg.** mortgage
mtgee. mortgagee
mtgor. mortgagor
M. Th., S.T.M. (Scientiae Theologicae Magister)(Lat.) or **Th. M.** (Theologiae Magister)(Lat.) Master of Theology
mth., M., m. or **mo.** month
M Tk Medium tank
mtl., Mat (Mil.), or **mat.** material
m.t.l. mean tidal level
mtn., M., m., Mt. or **mt.** mountain
M.T.O. Motor transport officer
MTP Mobilization Training Program
M.T.P.I. Member of the Town Planning Institute (Brit.)
Mtr (Mil.) or **mot.** motor
Mtrcl (Mil.), **M.C., m.c., m/c** or **Mtcl** (Mil.) motorcycle
Mtrcl Co or **Mtcl Co** Motorcycle company
Mt.Rev. or **Mt.Revd.** Most Reverend
Mtricl Motor-tricycle (Mil.)
MTS (Mil.), **M.T.S.** or **G.M.P.** (Groupe motopropulseur)(Fr.) Motor Transport Service
mts. mountains
M.T.V. Motor Transport Volunteers
Mtz (Mil.) or **mot.** motorized
M.U. Mobile unit
Mu murium (Chem.)
M.u. Mache unit (measure of radium emanation)
mu or μ micron; (micro-)(Greek) one millionth
muc. mucilage
mu f, mf, mf., μ**f** or **mfd.** microfarad
mu f, mf, mf., μ**f** or **mfds.** microfarads
mult. multiple
M.U.M. Magic, Unity, Might
mu mu or $\mu\mu$ micromicron
Mun Munitions
mun. municipal
Mun O Munitions officer
mus. museum; music; musical; musician
Mus. B., M.B., Mus. Bac. (Musicae Baccalaureus)(Lat.), **B.M.** (Baccalaureus Musicae)(Lat.) or **B. Mus.** Bachelor in or of Music
Mus. Bac., M.B., Mus. B. (Musicae Baccalaureus)(Lat.), **B.M.** (Baccalaureus Musicae)(Lat.) or **B. Mus.** Bachelor in or of Music
Mus. D., Mus. Doc., Mus. Doct., Mus. Dr. (Musicae Doctor)(Lat.), **D.M.** or **D. Mus.** Doctor of Music
Mus. Doc., Mus. D., Mus. Doct., Mus. Dr. (Musicae Doctor)(Lat.), **D. M.** or **D. Mus.** Doctor of Music

Mus. Dr., Mus. D., Mus. Doc., Mus. Doct. (Musicae Doctor)(Lat.), **D.M.** or **D. Mus.** Doctor of Music

musl. muslin

Mus. M. (Musicae Magister)(Lat.), **M.M.** or **M.Mus.** Master of Music

mut. mutilated; mutual

mu w or **μw** microwatt; microwatts

M.V. Motor vessel; (Medicus Veterinarius) (Lat.) Veterinary Physician

M.V. or **m.v.** muzzle velocity; (mezza voce)(Ital.) with medium fullness of tone (Music)

mv millivolt

m.v. market value; mean variation

M.V.D., D.V.M. or **V.M.D.** (Veterinariae Medicinae Doctor)(Lat.) Doctor of Veterinary Medicine

M.V.O. Member of the [Royal] Victorian Order

M.V.Sc. Master of Veterinary Science

MW. Middle Welsh

M.W. Most Worshipful; Most Worthy

μw or **mu w** microwatt; microwatts

M.W.A. Modern Woodmen of America

M.W.B. Metropolitan Water Board (Brit.)

MWC or **M.W.C.** Mary Washington College

M.W.C. Ministry of War Communications (cf. M.W.T.C.)

MWG or **M.W.G.** music-wire gauge

M.W.G.C.P. Most Worthy or Worshipful Grand Chief Patriarch (Freemasonry)

M.W.G.M. Most Worshipful or Worthy Grand Master (Freemasonry)

M.W.N.A. Medical Women's National Association (now American Medical Women's Association)

M.W.P. Most Worthy Patriarch (Freemasonry)

M.W.S. Most Worshipful Scribe (Freemasonry)

M.W.T. Mountain War Time

M.W.T.C. Ministry of Wartime Communications (cf. M.S.; M.T.; M.W.C.)

M.W.V. Mexican War Veteran

Mx. or **Max.** Maximilian

Mx., Mddx., Mdx., Middlx. or **Midx.** Middlesex

mxd. or **mix.** mixed

My. myopia

My., magg. (maggio)(Ital.) or **maj.** (majus) (Hung.) May

mycol. mycological; mycology

myg. myriagram

myl. myrialiter

Mym. or **mym.** myriameter

myst. mysteries; mystery

myth. or **mythol.** mythological; mythology

mythol. or **myth.** mythological; mythology

mzo. (marzo)(Span.), **M., Mar., marc., marz.** (marcius or marzius)(Hung.), **Mch., mço.** (março)(Port.) or **Mr.** March

ΜΙΣ (Mu Iota Sigma) National honorary professional fraternity (Teachers of the Blind)

ΜΟΧ (Mu Omega Xi) National honor scholastic fraternity

ΜΦΕ (Mu Phi Epsilon) National professional fraternity (Medicine)

N

N nitrogen (Chem.); not [hot-pressed](paper); [Avogadro] number (Chem.)

N, N., n., No. Nor. or **nor.** north

N, N., n., No., nor., north. or **nthn.** northern

N. nasal; Norse; northerly; Numerius

N., Listop. (Listopad)(Pol.), **nbre.** (noviembre)(Span.) or **Nov.** November

N., M., m. (meridiem)(Lat.) or **n.** noon

N. or **n.** navy; new; normal [strength solution] (Chem.); noun

N., n. or **nav.** navagating

N., n., Nav., nav. or **navig.** navigation

N., n. or **Nb.** nimbus (Meteorol.)

N., n. or **nom.** (nomen)(Lat.) name (cf. NN)

N., n. or **non.** (nonae)(Lat.) nones (Rom. calendar)

N. or **Nat.** Nationalist

N. or **Nov.** (Novellae [Constitutiones]) (Lat.) Novels, of the Corpus Juris Civilis (Rom. Law)

n refractive index

n. nephew; net; not (Nav. Wigwagging); numbered; [principal quantum] number

n. or **Anm.** (Anmerkung, Anmerkungen) (Ger.) note; notes (cf. annot.; ftnt.; schol.)

n. (natus)(Lat.), **B., b., f.** (född)(Swed.), (født)(Dan.) or **geb.** (geboren)(Ger.) born

n., M., m. (meridiem)(Lat.) or **N.** noon

n., N, N., No., Nor. or **nor.** north

n., N, N., No., nor., north., or **nthn.** northern

n. or **N.** navy; new; normal strength solution (Chem.); noun

n., N., Nav. or **nav.** navigation

n., N. or **nav.** navigating

n., N. or **nb.** nimbus

n., N. or **nom.** (nomen)(Lat.) name (cf. NN)

n., N. or **non.** (nonae)(Lat.) nones (Roman calendar)

n. or **na.** nail; nails

n. or **neut.** neuter

n., NN, NN. or **nom.** (nomina)(Lat.) names

n., No., N.º, núm. (número)(Span.), **no., n:o, nr** (numro, nummer)(Swed.), **Nr.** (Nummer)(Dan.), **Nr., Nro.** (Numero) (Ger.), **num.** or **sz.** (szám)(Hung.) number (cf. Hft.; pt.)

n., Noct. (nocte)(Lat.) or **Nt.** night

n., nom. or **nomin.** nominative

N.A. National Academician; National Army; Nautical Almanac; Naval accounts; Naval Auxiliary

N.A. or **n.a.** numerical aperature (Microscope)

N.A. or **N.A.D.** National Academy [of Design]
N.A. or **N.Afr.** North Africa; North African
N.A. or **N.Am.** North America; North American
N.A., N.Arch. or **Nav. Arch.** Naval Architect
N.A. or **N.A.S.** Nursing Auxiliary [Service](Brit.)
N/A no advice (Banking)
N/A, n.a. or **n/a** no account (Banking) nonacceptance (Banking)
Na natrium [sodium](Chem.)
na. or **n.** nail; nails
n.a. (nota del autor)(Span.) author's note
n.a. or **N.A.** numerical aperature (Microscope)
n.a., N/A or **n/a** no account (Banking); nonacceptance (Banking)
n/a, N/A or **n.a.** no account (Banking); nonacceptance (Banking)
N.A.A. National Aeronautic Association; National Artillery Association; National Automobile Association
n.a.a. not always afloat (Shipping)
N.A.A.C.P. National Association for the Advancement of Colored People
N.A.A.C.S. National Association of Accredited Commercial Schools
NAAFI, Naafi or **N.A.A.F.I.** Naval, Army and Air Force Institutes (Brit.)
N.A.A.P.P.B. National Association of Amusement Parks, Pools and Beaches
N.A.A.S. National Association of Audubon Societies
NAB or **N.A.B.** National Association of Broadcasters
N.A.B.A.I.V. National Association of Bureau of Animal Industry Veterinarians
N.A.B.M. National Association of Bedding Manufacturers
N.A.B.P. National Association of Boards of Pharmacy
N.A.C. National Archives Council; National Arts Club (New York); National Association of Chiropodists; Naval aircraftsman
NACA or **N.A.C.A.** National Advisory Committee for Aeronautics
N.A.C.A. National Association of Chemists Assistants
N.A.C.D. National Association for Civil Defense
N.A.C.G.N. National Association of Colored Graduate Nurses
Nachf. (Nachfolger)(Ger), **Suc.** or **succ.** successor
Nachm., Nm. (Nachmittag)(Ger.), **a., aft., aftn., Em.** (Eftermiddag)(Dan.) or **e.m.** (eftermiddagen)(Swed.) afternoon (cf. P.M.)
N.A.C.L. National Association of Letter Carriers
N.A.C.M. National Association of Cotton Manufacturers; National Association of Credit Men
N.A.C.U. National Association of Life Underwriters
NACW National Association of Colored Women
N.A.D. Naval air division; no appreciable disease (Med.)
N.A.D. or **N.A.** National Academy of Design
N.A.D.A. National Automobile Dealers Association
N.A.D.C. National Association of Dyers and Cleaners
N.A.D.E. National Association of Dental Examiners
N.A.D.F. National Association of Dental Faculties
N.A.E.A. Newspapers Advertising Executives Association
N.A.F. Naval Aircraft Factory
N.A.F.M. National Association of Fan Manufacturers
N.Afr. or **N.A.** North Africa; North African
Nah. Nahum
N.A.I.A. National Association of Insurance Agents
N.A.I.C. National Association of Insurance Commissioners
N.A.I.I. National Association of Ice Industries
N.A.I.T.D. National Association of Independent Tire Dealers
N.A.L.G.O. National Association of Local Government Officers (Brit.)
N.A.M. National Association of Manufacturers
N.Am. or **N.A.** North America; North American
N.A.M.B.O. National Association of Motor Bus Operators
näml. (nämligen)(Swed.), **sc., scil., SS., ss.** (scilicet)(Lat.) or **viz.** (videlicet)(Lat.) namely; to wit (cf.i.e.)
N. & M. November and May (Interest)
N. & Q. Notes and Queries (Brit.)
N.A.M.W. National Air Mail Week
NANA or **N.A.N.A.** North American Newspaper Alliance
N. and Q. Nostrums and Quackery
N.A.O. National Association of Opticians
N.A. of P.T. National Association of Piano Tuners
Nap. Napoleon (Cards)
NAPA National Association of Performing Artists
N.A.P.A. National Air Pilots Association
N.A.P.R.E. National Association of Practical Refrigerating Engineers
N.A.R.C. National Association of Retail Clothiers
N. Arch., N.A. or **Nav. Arch.** Naval Architect
N.A.R.D. National Association of Retail Druggists
N.A.R.E.B. National Association of Real Estate Boards
Narr. (narratio)(Lat.) a declaration of complaint (Law)
N.A.S. National Academy of Sciences; Naval Air Station; North American Sangerbund
N.A.S. or **N.A.** Nursing Auxiliary Service (Brit.)
N.A.S.A.O. National Association of State Aviation Officials
N.A.S.C. North America Supply Council

N.A.S.E. National Academy of Stationary Engineers
N.A.S.M. National Association of Silo Manufacturers
N.A.T. National Air Transport [Incorporated]
Nat. Natal (S. Afr.); Nathan
Nat. or **N.** Nationalist
Nat. or **nat.** natural
Nat., nat., Natl. or **natl.** national
Nat. or **Nath.** Nathanael; Nathaniel
nat. native; naturalist
nat. or **Nat.** natural
nat., Nat., Natl. or **natl.** national
N.A.T.A. National Association of Tax Administrators
Nat. Absten. National Abstentionalist
Nath. or **Nat.** Nathanael; Nathaniel
Nat. Hist. or **nat. hist.** natural history
Natl., Nat., nat. or **natl.** national
natl., Nat., nat. or **Natl.** national
Natl.Bk. national bank
N.A.T.M.A. National Association of Teachers of Marketing and Advertising (now American Marketing Association)
N.A.T.O. National Association of Taxicab Owners
Nat. Ord., nat. ord. or **N.O.** natural order (Bot.)
Nat. Phil. or **nat. phil.** natural philosophy
Nats. Nationalists
nat. sc. natural science
Nat. Sc. D. Doctor of Natural Science
N. Att. Naval attaché
Naut. or **naut.** nautical
naut.m., N.M. or **n.m.** nautical mile (cf. nauts.)
Nauts., N.M. or **n.m.** nautical miles
Nav., N., n., nav. or **navig.** navigation
nav. naval; navigable
nav., N. or n. navigating
nav., N., n., Nav. or **navig.** navigation
Nav. Arch., N.A. or **N.Arch.** Naval Architect
Nav. Const. or **Nav. Constr.** Naval Constructor
Nav. Constr. or **Nav. Const.** Naval Constructor
navig. navigator
navig., N., n., Nav. or **nav.** navigation
Nav O (Mil.) or **N.O.** Navigation officer
N.A.W.G.A. National American Wholesale Grocers Association
N.A.W.J. National Association of Woodwork Jobbers [Incorporated]
N.A.W.M. National Association of Wool Manufacturers
N.A.W.P. National Association of Women Pharmacists (Brit.)
N.A.W.S.A. National American Woman Suffrage Association
NB new bonds
NB, N.B. or **n.b.** (nota bene)(Lat.) note well; take notice
NB or **n.b.** north bound
N.B. New Brunswick; North Britain or British
N.B., NB or **n.b.** (nota bene)(Lat.) note well; take notice
Nb niobium (Chem.)
Nb., N. or **n.** nimbus (Meteorol.)
n.b. new boilers
n.b. or **NB** north bound
n.b., NB or **N.B.** (nota bene)(Lat.) note well; take notice
NBA or **N.B.A.** National Boxing Association; North British Academy
N.B.A.P.C. National Business Advisory and Planning Council
NBC or **N.C.B** National Broadcasting Company
N.B.C. Noncombatant Corps
N.B.C. or **NBC** National Broadcasting Company
NBCC or **N.B.C.C.** National Bituminous Coal Commission
NbE north by east
N.B.E.R. National Bureau of Economic Research [Incorporated]
N.B.F.U. National Board of Fire Underwriters
N.B.M.A. National Broom Manufacturers Association
NBPRP or **N.B.P.R.P.** National Board for the Promotion of Rifle Practice [in the U.S.]
nbre. (noviembre)(Span.), **Listop.** (Listopad)(Pol.), **N.** or **Nov.** November
NBS, Bur.Stds. or **N.B.S.** National Bureau of Standards
N.B.S., Bur. Stds. or **NBS** National Bureau of Standards
NbW north by west
NC Navy-Curtiss (Seaplane)
N.C. Navy Cross; New Church; North Carolina; Nurses' Corps
N.C. or **n.c.** nitro-cellulose
N/C or **n/c** new charter; new crop
n.c. or **N.C.** nitro-cellulose
n/c or **N/C** new charter; new crop
N.C.A. National Canners Association; National Coal Association; neurocirculatory asthenia
N.C.A.A. National Collegiate Athletic Association
N.C.A.C.S.S. North Central Association of Colleges and Secondary Schools
NCB or **N.C.B.** National Compliance Board
N.C.C.C. National Conference of Charities and Correction (now National Conference of Social Work)
N.C.C.I. National Council of Compensation Insurance
N.C.C.J. National Conference of Christians and Jews
N.C.C.M. National Council of Catholic Men
N.C.C.S. National Catholic Community Service
N.C.C.V.D. National Council for Combating Venereal Disease (Brit.)
N.C.C.W. National Council of Catholic Women; National Council of Church Women
N.C.F. National Civic Federation

N.C.G.W. Native Daughters of the Golden West

n. Ch., n. Chr. (nach Christo)(Ger.), **n. Chr. G.** (nach Christi Geburt)(Ger.), **A.D., a.d.** (anno Domini)(Lat.), **A.P.C.N.** (anno post Christum natum)(Lat.) or **d.C.** (dopo Cristo)(Ital.) after Christ; after the birth of Christ; in the year of our Lord

n. Chr. G. (nach Christi Geburt)(Ger.), **A.D., a.d.** (anno Domini)(Lat.), **A.P.C.N.** (anno post Christum natum) (Lat.), **d.C.** (dopo Cristo)(Ital.), **n.Ch.** or **n. Chr.** (nach Christo)(Ger.) after the birth of Christ; after Christ; in the year of our Lord

N.C.M.H. National Committee for Mental Hygiene

N.C.M.P.F. National Cooperative Milk Producers Federation

NCO (Mil.), **N.C.O., non-com.** or **noncom.** Noncommissioned officer

N.C.P.A. National Cottonseed Products Association

N.C.P.P.C. National Capital Park and Planning Commission

NCS Net control station (Mil.)

N.C.S. Noncommissioned staff

N.C.S.A. National Crushed Stone Association

N.C.S.B.E.E. National Council of State Boards of Engineering Examiners

N.C.S.W. National Conference of Social Work (cf. N.C.C.C.)

N.C.T.F. National Commercial Teachers' Federation

N.C.U. National Cyclists' Union (Brit.)

n.c.v. no commercial value

N.C.W. National Council of Women

N.C.W.C. National Catholic Welfare Conference

N.C.Y.C. National Catholic Youth Council

N.D. or **N.-D.** (Notre Dame)(Fr., Lat.) Our Lady

N.D., n.d., o.J. (ohne Jahr)(Ger.) or **s.a.** (sine anno)(Lat.) no date; not dated; without year [of publication] (cf. und.)

N.D. or **N. Dak.** North Dakota

N.-D. or **N.D.** (Notre Dame)(Fr., Lat) Our Lady

Nd neodymium (Chem.)

n.d., N.D., o.J. (ohne Jahr)(Ger.) or **s.a.** (sine anno)(Lat.) no date; not dated; without year [of publication] (cf. und.)

N.D.A. National Dairy Association; National Defense Act; National Dental Association (now American Dental Association); National Diploma in Agriculture

NDAC or **N.D.A.C.** National Defense Advisory Commission

N. Dak. or **N.D.** North Dakota

N.D.A.N.Z. National Dairy Association of New Zealand

NDC or **N.D.C.** National Defense Council

N.D.C. National Dairy Council

N.D.D. National Diploma in Dairying

NDFCA National Dairy and Food Commissioners' Association

N.D.H.A. North Dakota Hospital Association

N.D.L. (Nord-deutscher Lloyd)(Ger.) North German Lloyd [Steamship Company]

NDMB or **N.D.M.B.** National Defense Mediation Board

NE, N.E. or **n.e.** northeast; northeastern; northeasterly

N.E. Naval Engineer; Northeastern [Postal District, London]

N.E. or **N/E** no effects (Banking)

N.E., N.ed. or **n.ed.** new edition

N.E. or **N.Eng.** New England

Ne neon (Chem.)

n/e not exceeding; not to exceed

NEA or **N.E.A.** National Educational Association (U.S.A.); Newspaper Enterprise Association

N.E.A. National Editorial Association; National Erector's Association

N.E.A. or **NEA** National Educational Association (U.S.A.); Newspaper Enterprise Association

N E & B. new engines and boilers

N.E.B. National Employment Board

Neb. or **Nebr.** Nebraska

NEBA or **N.E.B.A.** National Emergency Banking Administration

NEbE northeast by east

NEbN northeast by north

Nebr. or **Neb.** Nebraska

NEC or **N.E.C.** National Emergency Council

NEC, N.E.C. or **N.E.Code** National Electric Code (cf. N.E.S.C.)

N.E.C. or **NEC** National Emergency Council

N.E.C., NEC or **N.E.Code** National Electric Code (cf. N.E.S.C.)

N.E.C.A. National Electrical Contractors Association

N.E.C. Inst. North-East Coast Institution [of Engineers and Shipbuilders]

N.E.Code, NEC or **N.E.C.** National Electric Code (cf. N.E.S.C.)

N.E.D. Naval Equipment Department; New English Dictionary (displaced by O.E.D.)

N. ed., n. ed. or **N.E.** new edition

neg. negation; negative; negatively

Neg. Ins. or **neg. ins.** negotiable instrument

neg. ins. or **Neg. Ins.** negotiable instrument

Neh. Nehemiah

N.E.H.A. New England Hospital Association

N.E.I. Netherlands East Indies (cf. Neth. Ind.)

n.e.i. (non est inventus)(Lat.) he, she or it has not been found (Law.); not elsewhere indicated (cf. N.O.E.; N.O.P.; N.O.S.)

N.E.L.A. National Electric Light Association (superseded by Edison Electric Institute)

N.E.M.A. National Eclectic Medical Association; National Electrical Manufacturers Association

nem. con. (nemine contradicente)(Lat.), **nem. dis.** or **nem. diss.** (nemine dissentiente)(Lat.) unanimous; no one contradicting; no one dissenting
nem. dis., nem. diss. (nemine dissentiente) (Lat.) or **nem. con.** (nemine contradicente)(Lat.) no one dissenting; no one contradicting; unanimous
N. Eng. or **N.E.** New England
neol. neologism
N.E.P. New Economic Policy (Russia)
Nep. or **Nept.** Neptune
Nept. or **Nep.** Neptune
NERA or **N.E.R.A.** National Emergency Relief Administration
N.E.S. or **n.e.s.** not elsewhere specified or stated (cf. n.e.i.)
n.e.s. or **N.E.S.** not elsewhere specified or stated (cf. n.e.i.)
N.E.S.C. National Electric Safety Code (cf. N.E.C.)
Neth. Netherlands
Neth. Ind. Netherlands Indies (cf. N.E.I.)
neut. neutral
neut. or **n.** neuter
Nev. Nevada
Newf., NF., N.F., Nfd. or **Nfld.** Newfoundland
New M., N.M. or **N. Mex.** New Mexico
New Test., NT. or **N.T.** New Testament
NF or **n.f.** nonfundable
NF, N.F., N/F or **n/f** no funds (Banking)
NF. or **N.F.** New French
NF., N.F., Newf., Nfd. or **Nfld.** Newfoundland
N.F. National Formulary (Pharm.)
N.F., Newf., NF., Nfd. or **Nfld.** Newfoundland
N.F., NF, N/F or **n/f** no funds (Banking)
N.F. or **NF.** New French
N.F., N. Fr., Nor. Fr. or **Norm. Fr.** Norman-French
N/F, NF, N.F. or **n/f** no funds (Banking)
nf (Mil.) or **nf.** nonfordable
n.f. noun feminine
n.f. or **NF** nonfundable
n.f. (neue folge)(Ger.), **N.S., n.s.** or **n/s** new series
n/f, NF, N.F. or **N/F** no funds (Banking)
N.F.A. National Fertilizer Association; National Founders' Association
N.F.B.A. National Food Brokers Association
N.F.B.P.W.C. National Federation of Business and Professional Women's Clubs
N.F.C.T. National Federation of Class Teachers
Nfd., Newf., NF., N.F. or **Nfld.** Newfoundland
Nfld., Newf., NF., N.F. or **Nfd.** Newfoundland
N.F.M.A. November, February, May and August (Interest)
N.F.P.A. National Fire Protection Association
N.F.P.W. National Federation of Professional Workers
N.Fr., N.F., Nor. Fr. or **Norm. Fr.** Norman-French
N.F.T. National Federation of Textiles (cf. S.A.A.)
NG or **N.G.** National Guard or Guardsmen
N.G. New Granada; New Guinea; Noble Grand
N.G. or **NG** National Guard or Guardsman
N.G. or **n.g.** no good (Slang); not good (Banking)
Ng., Nor. or **Norw.** Norwegian
n.g. or **N.G.** no good (Slang); not good (Banking)
NGA or **N.G.A.** National Gallery of Art
N.G.A. National Glider Association
N.G.A. or **NGA** National Gallery of Art
N.G.C. New General Catalog of Stars
n. gen. new genus (Bot.)
N.G.N.Y. National Guard of New York
NGR National Guard Regulations
NGr. or **N. Gr.** New Greek
N.G.S. National Geographic Society
N. H. New Hampshire
NHA or **N.H.A.** National Housing Agency (cf. FHA)
N.H.A. Nebraska Hospital Association
N.H.C. National Health Council
NHeb. or **N. Heb.** New Hebrew
N.Heb. New Hebrides
NHG. or **N.H.G.** New High German
N.H.H.S. New Hampshire Historical Society
N.H.I. National Health Insurance
N.H.P. or **n.h.p.** nominal horsepower (cf. r.h.p.)
n.h.p. or **N.H.P.** nominal horsepower (cf. r.h.p.)
N.H.P.C. National Historical Publications Commission
N.H.R. or **N. H. Rules** National Hunt Rules (Brit.)
N.H.R.U. National Home Reading Union (Brit.)
N.H. Rules or **N.H.R.** National Hunt Rules (Brit.)
N.I. Native Infantry (India); Northern Ireland
N.I. or **N.I.D.** Naval Intelligence [Department or Division] (Brit.)
Ni nickel (Chem.)
ni. (numeri)(Lat.), **Nos.** or **nos.** numbers (cf. Num.)
N.I.A. Newspaper Institute of America
NIC National Inventors Council
Nic. or **Nicar.** Nicaragua
NICB or **N.I.C.B.** National Industrial Conference Board
N.I.D. or **N.I.** Naval Intelligence Department or Division (Brit.)
N.I.F.C. National Intercollegiate Flying Club
Nig. Nigeria; Nigerian
N.I.I.P. National Institute of Industrial Psychology (Brit.)
N.I.L.C.A. National Industrial Launderers and Cleaners Association

N.I.M.D. National Institute of Manufacturers and Distributers
N.I.M.R. National Institute of Medical Research
ninupl. ninuplicate
ni. pr. or **ni. pri.** (nisi prius)(Lat.) unless before (Law)
ni. pri. or **ni. pr.** (nisi prius)(Lat.) unless before (Law)
NIRA or **N.I.R.A.** National Industrial Recovery Act
NIRA, N.I.R.A., NRA or **N.R.A.** National Industrial Recovery Administration
NIRB or **N.I.R.B.** National Industrial Recovery Board
N.I.T.L. National Industrial Traffic League
N.I.T.P.A. National Institutional Teacher Placement Association
N.J. New Jersey
N.J.F.D.A. Notices of Judgment [under the] Food and Drug Act
N.J.H. National Jewish Hospital
N.J.H.A. New Jersey Hospital Association
NL night letter
NL. or **N.L.** New Latin
N.L. National Liberal; Navy League
N.L. or **n.l.** (non liquet)(Lat.) not clear; not proven (Law); (non longe) (Lat.) not far; (non licet)(Lat.) not permitted
N.L., n.l., N.Lat. or **n. lat.** north latitude
n.l. new line (Printing)
n.l. or **N.L.** (non liguet)(Lat.) not clear; not proven (Law); (non longe)(Lat.) not far; (non licet)(Lat.) not permitted
n.l., N.L., N.Lat. or **n.lat.** north latitude
N.Lab. National Labor [Party]
N. Lat., n. lat., N.L. or **n.l.** north latitude
NLB, N.L.B., NLRB or **N.L.R.B.** National Labor [Relations] Board
N.L.C. National Liberal Club (Brit.)
NLD Not in line of duty (Mil.)
N.L.F. National Liberal Federation (Brit.)
N.L.G.I. National Lubricating Grease Institute
N.L.I. National Lifeboat Institution (Brit.)
N.L.M.A. National Lumber Manufacturers' Association
N.L.N.E. National League of Nursing Education
N.L.P.S.A. National League to Promote School Attendance
NLRB, N.L.R.B., NLB or **N.L.B.** National Labor Relations Board
NLSE National Live Stock Exchange
N.L.S.M.A. National Live Stock Marketing Association
NLSP National Live Stock Producer
NLT night letter cable
NM night message
N.M. new measure; National Museum
N.M., New M. or **N. Mex.** New Mexico
N.M., n.m. or **naut. m.** nautical mile
N.M., n.m. or **Nauts.** nautical miles
Nm. nutmeg
Nm., Nachm. (Nachmittag)(Ger.), **a., aft., aftn., Em.** (Eftermiddag)(Dan.) or **e.m.** (eftermiddagen)(Swed.) afternoon (cf. P.M.)
N/m or **n/m** no mark; not marked
nm. (nachmittags)(Ger.) in the afternoon (cf. Nm.)
n.m. noun masculine
n.m., N.M. or **naut.m.** nautical mile
n.m., N.M. or **Nauts.** nautical miles
n/m or **N/m** no mark; not marked
NMB or **N.M.B.** National Mediation Board
NMCB or **N.M.C.B.** National Munitions Control Board
N. Mex., New M. or **N.M.** New Mexico
N.M.F.C. National Motor Freight Classification
N.M.L. National Municipal League
N.M.S. National Missionary Society
N.M.T.A. National Metal Trades Association
N.M.T.B.A. National Machine Tool Builders Association
N.M.U. National Maritime Union [of America]
NN, n., NN. or **nom.** (nomina)(Lat.) names
NN., n., NN or **nom.** (nomina)(Lat.) names
N/N not to be noted (Banking)
n.n. (nomen nescio)(Lat.) or **n.u.** name unknown (cf. incog.)
NNE, N.N.E. or **n.n.e.** north-northeast
N.N.R. new and nonofficial remedies (Pharm.)
N.N.V. National Naval Volunteers
NNW, N.N.W. or **n.n.w.** north-northwest
No norium (Chem.)
N.O. Naval Officer; New Orleans
N.O., Nat. Ord. or **nat. ord.** natural order (Bot.)
N.O. or **Nav O** (Mil.) Navigation officer
N/O no orders (Banking)
No. Noah
No., N, N., n., Nor. or **nor.** north
No., N, N., n., nor., north. or **nthn.** northern
No., no., n., N.°, núm. (número)(Span.), **no., n:o, nr** (numro, nummer)(Swed.), **Nr.** (Nummer)(Dan.), **Nr., Nro.** (Numero)(Ger.), **num.** or **sz.** (szám)(Hung.) number (cf. Hft.; pt.)
n:o, nr (numro, nummer)(Swed.), **n., No., N.°, núm.** (número)(Span.), **no., Nr.** (Nummer)(Dan.), **Nr., Nro.** (Numero)(Ger.), **num.** or **sz.** (szám)(Hung.) number (cf. Hft.; pt.)
Noct. (nocte)(Lat.), **n.** or **Nt.** night
N.O.D. Naval Ordnance Department
N.O.E. or **n.o.e.** not otherwise enumerated (cf. n.e.s.)
n.o.e. or **N.O.E.** not otherwise enumerated (cf. N.E.S.)
N.O.H.P. not otherwise herein provided
N.O.I.B.N. or **n.o.i.b.n.** not otherwise indexed by name
n.o.i.b.n. or **N.O.I.B.N.** not otherwise indexed by name

nol. pros. (nolle prosequi) (Lat.) unwilling to prosecute; stay of procedure (Law)
nom. nomenclature; nominal
nom., N. or **n.** (nomen) (Lat.) name (cf. NN)
nom., n. or **nomin.** nominative
nom., NN, NN. (nomina) (Lat.) or **n.** names
N.O.M.A. National Oil Marketers Association
Nom.Cap. nominal capital
nomin., n. or **nom.** nominative
nom. nov. (nomen novum) (Lat.) new name; (Bot., Zool.)
nom. nud. (nomen nudum) (Lat.) a mere name without proper description (Biol.)
nom.std. nominal standard
non., N. or **n.** (nonae) (Lat.) nones (Rom. calendar)
Non-Coll. or **Non Coll.** Non-Collegiate
noncom., non-com., NCO (Mil.) or **N.C.O.** Noncommissioned officer
Noncon. Nonconformist
non. cul. (non culpabilis) (Lat.) not guilty (Law)
noncum. noncumulative (Stocks)
non obst. (non obstante) (Lat.) or **notwg.** notwithstanding
non pros. (non prosequitur) (Lat.) he or she does not prosecute; a judgement in which the plaintiff does not appear (Law)
non seq. (non sequitur) (Lat.) it does not follow
nonsoc. nonsociety
N.O.P., N.o.p. or **n.o.p.** not otherwise provided for (cf. n.e.i.; n.o.e.; n.o.s.; n.s.p.f.)
n.o.p., N.O.P. or **N.o.p.** not otherwise provided for (cf. n.e.i. n.o.e.; n.o.s.; n.s.p.f.)
N.O.P.H.N. National Organization for Public Health Nursing
Nor., N, N., n., No., no. or **nor.** north
Nor., Ng. or **Norw.** Norwegian
Nor. or **Norm.** Norman
Nor. or **Norw.** Norway
nor., N, N., n., No., no. or **Nor.** north
nor., N, N., n., No., north. or **nthn.** northern
Norf. Norfolk
Nor. Fr., N.F., N. Fr. or **Norm. Fr.** Norman-French
Norm. or **Nor.** Norman
norm. normal
Norm. Fr., N.F., N. Fr. or **Nor. Fr.** Norman-French
north., N, N., n., no., nor. or **nthn.** northern
Northants. Northamptonshire
Northum. or **Northumb.** Northumberland
Norvic. Norwich, in signature of Bishop
Norw., Ng. or **Nor.** Norwegian
Norw. or **Nor.** Norway
N.O.S. or **n.o.s.** not otherwise stated or specified (cf. n.e.s.; n.o.e.; n.o.i.)
Nos., nos. or **ni.** (numeri) (Lat.) numbers (cf. Num.)
nos., ni. (numeri) (Lat.) or **Nos.** numbers (cf. Num.)
n.o.s. or **N.O.S.** not otherwise stated or specified (cf. n.e.s.; n.o.e.; n.o.i.)
N.O.T.B. National Ophthalmic Treatment Board (Brit.)
Notts. Nottinghamshire
notwg. or **non obst.** (non obstante) notwithstanding
Nov., Listop. (Listopad) (Pol.), **N.** or **nbre.** (noviembre) (Span.) November
Nov. or **N.** (Novellae [constitutiones]) (Lat.) Novels, of the Corpus Juris Civilis (Rom. law)
nov. novelist
Nov. Sc. or **N.S.** Nova Scotia
NP nickel plated
N.P. no protest (Banking) (cf. N.P.N.A.); Notary Public
N.P. or **n.p.** new paragraph (Printing)
np nonparticipating (Stocks)
np. neap (Navig.)
n.p. no paging [of books so printed] (Printing) (cf. unp.)
n. p. (na przykład) (Pol.), **e.c.** (exempli cause) (Nat.), **e.g., ex. gr.** (exempli gratia) (Lat.), **f.e., f. Eks.** (for Eksempel) (Dan.), **f.i., p. ex.** (par exemple) (Fr.), **t. ex.** (till exempel) (Swed.), **v.g.** (verbi gratia) (Lat.) or **z.B.** (zum Beispeil) (Ger.) for example; for instance
n.p. or **N.P.** new paragraph
n.p. or **n/p** net proceeds
n.p., o.O. (ohne Ort) (Ger.), **S.L.** or **s.l.** (sine loco) (Lat.) without place; no place [of publication]
n/p or **n.p.** net proceeds
N.P.A. National Parks Association; National Petroleum Association; National Probation Association
NPB or **N.P.B.** National Planning Board
N.P.B.A. National Paving Brick Association; National Pig Breeders Association (Brit.)
N.P.B.E.A. National Poultry, Butter and Egg Association
N.P.C. Nisi prius cases; Nisi prius court
N.P.D. north-polar distance (Astron.)
N.P.F. National Philatelic Federation
N.P.F. or **n.p.f.** not provided for
n.p.f. or **N.P.F.** not provided for
N.Ph.D. or **D.N.Ph.** Doctor of Natural Philosophy
N.P.L. National Physical Laboratory (Brit.)
n.pl. noun plural
N.P.N. nonprotein nitrogen
N.P.N.A. no protest for non-acceptance (Banking) (cf. N.P.)
n.p.or d., o.O. u. J. (ohne Ort und Jahr) (Ger.) or **s.l.et a.** (sine loco et anno) (Lat.) no place or date; without place and year [of publication]
NPPC or **N.P.P.C.** National Power Policy Committee
NPS or **N.P.S.** National Park Service
N.P.S. National Philatelic Society
n.p.t., N.T.P. or **n.t.p.** normal [blood] pressure and temperature; normal temperature and [blood] pressure
N.P.T.F.B. National Park Trust Fund Board
N.P.U. National Pharmaceutical Union (Brit.)

N.R. Navy Regulations

Nr. or **nr.** near

Nr., Nro. (Numero)(Ger.), **n., No., N.°, núm.** (número)(Span.), **no., n:o, nr** (numro, nummer)(Swed.), **Nr.** (Nummer)(Dan.), **num.** or **sz.** (szám)(Hung.) number (cf. Hft.; pt.)

n.r. net register (Shipping); no risk (Insurance); (non repetatur)(Lat.) not to be repeated

NRA, N.R.A., NIRA, or **N.I.R.A.** National [Industrial] Recovery Administration

N.R.A. National Restaurant Association; National Rifle Association [of America]

N.R.A.A. National Railway Appliance Association

NRAB or **N.R.A.B.** National Railroad Adjustment Board

n.r.a.d. no risk after discharge (Shipping)

NRB or **N.R.B.** National Resources Board (cf. N.R.C.; N.R.P.B.)

NRC or **N.R.C.** National Research Council; National Resources Committee (cf. NRB)

N.R.C.P. Nonresidential Conditional Purchase (Australia)

N.R.D. National Registered Designer; Naval Recruiting Department

N.R.D.G.A. National Retail Dry Goods Association

Nro., Nr. (Numero)(Ger.), **n., No., N.°, núm.** (número)(Span.), **no., n:o, nr** (numro, nummer)(Swed.), **Nr.** (Nummer)(Dan.), **num.** or **sz.** (szám)(Hung.) number (cf. Hft.; pt.)

NROTC or **N.R.O.T.C.** Naval Reserve Officers Training Corps

NRPB or **N.R.P.B.** National Resources Planning Board (cf. NRB)

NRRB or **N.R.R.B.** National Recovery Review Board

NRS or **N.R.S.** National Reemployment Service; Naval Radio Station

N.R.S. National Refugee Service

N.S. National Society; New School (Eccl.); New Side (Eccl.); North Sea; Numismatic Society

N.S. or **Nov. Sc.** Nova Scotia

N.S., N.-S. (Notre-Seigneur)(Fr.) or **D.N.** (Dominus Noster)(Lat.) Our Lord

N.S. or **n.s.** nickel steel; not specified

N.S., n.s., n/s or **n.f.** (neue folge)(Ger.) new series

N.S., n.s., n/s or **n.St.** (neuen Stils)(Ger.) New Style [of dating, since 1752]

N.-S., N.S. (Notre Seigneur)(Fr.) or **D.N.** (Dominus Noster)(Lat.) Our Lord

N/S, n/s or **N.S.F.** not sufficient [funds] (Banking)

n.s. near side (Shipping)

n.s., n.f. (neue folge)(Ger.), **N.S.** or **n/s** new series

n.s. or **N.S.** nickel steel; not specified

n.s., N.S., n/s or **n.St.** (neuen Stils)(Ger.) New Style (calendar)

n/s, n.f. (neue folge)(Ger.), **N.S.** or **n.s.** new series

n/s. N.S., n.s. or **n.St.** (neuen Stils)(Ger.) New Style (calendar)

n/s, N/S or **N.S.F.** not sufficient funds (Banking)

N.S.A. National Service Act; National Skating Association; National Stationers' Association

N.S.A.A. National Ski Association of America

N.S.A.G. National Society for the Advancement of Gastroenterology

N.S.C. National Safety Council

N.S.D.P. National Society of Denture Prosthetists

N.S.F., N/S or **n/s** not sufficient funds (Banking)(cf. NF)

N.S.G.W. Native Sons of the Golden West

N.S.I.C. or **N.S.J.C.** (Noster Salvator Iesus or Jesus Christus)(Lat.) Our Saviour Jesus Christ

n.sing. noun singular

N.S.J.C. or **N.S.I.C.** (Noster Salvator Jesus or Iesus Christus)(Lat.) Our Saviour Jesus Christ

N.S.L. National Service League (Brit.); National Sunday League (Brit.)

NSLRB or **N.S.L.R.B.** National Steel Labor Relations Board

N.S.M. National Selected Morticians

N.S.O. Naval staff officer

N.S.P.B. National Society for the Prevention of Blindness

N.S.P.C.A. National Society for the Prevention of Cruelty to Animals

N.S.P.C.C. National Society for the Prevention of Cruelty to Children

N.S.P.F. or **n.s.p.f.** not specifically provided for (cf. N.O.P.)

N.S.S.E. National Society for the Study of Education

n. St. (neuen Stils)(Ger.), **N.S., n.s.** or **n/s** New Style [of dating, since 1752]

N.S.T.A. National Salesmen's Training Association

Nstd. or **nstd.** nested

nstd. or **Nstd.** nested

N.S. Trip. Natural Science Tripos (Cambridge)

N.S.W. New South Wales

NT night telegram

NT., N. T. or **New Test.** New Testament

N.T. New Translation; Northern Territory (Australia)

N.T., NT. or **New Test.** New Testament

Nt niton (Chem.)

Nt., n. or **Noct.** (nocte)(Lat.) night

N.t., N/t or **n.t.** new terms (Grain trade)

N/t, N.t. or **n.t.** new terms (Grain trade)

n.t. net ton; non watertight

n.t., N.t. or **N/t** new terms (Grain trade)

N.T.A. National Tuberculosis Association

N.T.A.M.A. National Tent and Awning Manufacturers Association

N.T. & S.A. National Trust & Savings Association

n/30 net in 30 days (Com.)

nthn., N, N., n., No., nor. or **north.** northern

n.Tit. (neuer Titel)(Ger.) new title

n.t.m. net ton mile

N.T.O. Naval transport officer; not taken out
N.T.O.M.D.A. National Typewriter and Office Machine Dealers Association
N.T.P. or **n.t.p.** normal temperature and pulse
N.T.P., n.t.p. or **n.p.t.** normal temperature and [blood] pressure; normal [blood] pressure and temperature
n.t.p. or **s.t.** (sans titre)(Fr.) no title page; without title (cf. t.p.w.)
NTS not to scale
N.T.S. Naval Transport Service
nt.wt., n.wt. or **p.° nto.** (peso neto)(Span.) net weight
n.typ. (nomen typographi)(Lat.) name of the printer
n.u. or **n.n.** (nomen nescio)(Lat.) name unknown (cf. anon.; incog.; ign.)
N.U.I. National University of Ireland
N.U.J. National Union of Journalists (Brit.)
Num. or **Numb.** Numbers (Bib.)
num. numeral; numerals
num., n., No., N.°, núm (número)(Span.), **n., n:o, nr** (numro, nummer)(Swed.), **Nr.** (Nummer)(Dan.), **Nr., Nro.** (Numero) (Ger.) or **sz.** (szám)(Hung.) number (cf. Hft.; pt.)
Numb. or **Num.** Numbers (Bib.)
numis. or **numism.** numismatic; numismatics; numismatology
N.U.R. National Union of Railwaymen (Brit.)
Nurs.R. nursery rhymes
N.U.S.E.C. National Union of Societies for Equal Citizenship (Brit.)
N.U.T. National Union of Teachers (Brit.)
N.U.T.N. National Union of Trained Nurses
N.U.W.S.S. National Union of Women's Suffrage Societies (Brit.)
N.U.W.T. National Union of Women Teachers (Brit.)
N.U.W.W. National Union of Women Workers (Brit.)
N.V. New Version
N.V., nv (naamlooze vennootschap)(Dutch), **Co.Ltd., G.m.b.H.** (Gesellschaft mit beschränkter Haftung)(Ger.), **S.en C.** (Sociedad en Comandita)(Span.) or **Soc. an^e** (Société anonyme)(Fr.) limited company (cf. A.G.; cie; S.A.)
Nv. naked vision
nv nonvoting (Stock)
nv, N.V. (naamlooze vennootschap)(Dutch), **Co.Ltd., G.m.b.H** (Gesellschaft mit beschränkter Haftung) (Ger.), **S. en C.** (Sociedad en Comandita)(Span.) or **Soc. en^e** (Société anonyme)(Fr.) limited company (cf. A.G.; cie; S.A.)
N.V.M. Nativity of the Virgin Mary
NW, N.W. or **n.w.** northwest; northwesterly; northwestern
N.W. North Wales; Northwestern [Postal District, London]
N.W.A.H. and A.C.A. National Warm Air Heating and Air Conditioning Association
NWbN northwest by north
NWbW northwest by west
N.W.C.T.U. National Woman's Christian Temperance Union
N.W.D.A. National Wholesale Druggists' Association
N.W.F.P. Northwest Frontier Province (India)
NWG National wire gauge
N.W.H.A. National Wholesale Hardware Association
NWLB, N.W.L.B., WLB or **W.L.B.** National War Labor Board
N.W.M.P. Northwest Mounted Police (now Royal Canadian Mounted Police)
N.W.P. or **N.W. Prov.** Northwest Provinces (India)
N.W.Prov. or **N.W.P.** Northwest Provinces (India)
N.W.P.W.A. National Wall Paper Wholesale Association
N.W.R.C. National Water Resources Committee
N.W.T. Northwestern Territories (Canada)
n.wt., nt.wt. or **p.° nto.** (peso neto)(Span.) net weight
N.W.T.D. non water-tight door (Shipbuilding)
N.Y. New York
NYA or **N.Y.A.** National Youth Administration
N.Y.A.M. New York Academy of Medicine
N.Y.A.S. New York Academy of Sciences
N.Y.D. or **n.y.d.** not yet diagnosed (Med.)
N.Y.H.S. New York Historical Society
N.Y.K. Nippon Yusen Kaisha (Japanese steamship line)
N.Y.M.S. New York Medical Society
n.y.p. not yet published
N.Y.P.L. New York Public Library
N.Y.S.A.A. New York State Aviation Association
N.Z. or **N.Zeal.** New Zealand
N.Zeal. or **N.Z.** New Zealand

ΝΣΝ (Nu Sigma Nu) National professional fraternity (Medicine)
ΝΣΦ (Nu Sigma Phi) National professional sorority (Medicine)

O

O oxygen (Chem.)
O. (occulus)(Lat.) eye; Ohio; opening; overcast (Naut.)
O. (Osten)(Ger.), **E, E.,** or **e.** east
O., gl. (gammel)(Dan.) or **o.** old (cf. aet.; anc.)
O. or **o.** (os)(Lat.) bone (Anat.)
O., o., Occ. or **occ.** occident; occidental
O., o., oct. 8vo. or **8vo** octavo

O., o., Or. or **or.** oriental
O., o. or **ord.** order
O., obre. (octubre)(Span.), **obro.** (outubro) (Port.), **Oct., Okt.** (Oktober)(Dan., Ger.), **okt.** (oktober)(Norw., Swed.), **ott.** (ottobre)(Ital.) or Paźdz. (Październik)(Pol.) October
O., Oc. or **oc.** ocean
O., Off., off. or **Offr.** officer
O. or **Ont.** Ontario
O., Or., Ore. or **Oreg.** Oregon
o ohm
o. off; only; over
o., gl. (gammel)(Dan.) or **O.** old (cf. aet.; anc.)
o. or **O.** (os)(Lat.) bone
o., O., Occ. or **occ.** occident; occidental
o., O., oct., 8vo or **8vo** octavo
o., O., Or. or **or.** oriental
o., O. or **ord.** order
o., op. or **opt.** (optimus, optime)(Lat.) best
o. (octarius)(Lat.), **p.** or **pt.** pint
ö. (östlich)(Ger.) eastward
O.A. Ordnance artificer
O/a, o.a. or **o/a** over all
O/a, o.a., o/a, O/Ac or **on a/c** on account;
O/a or **o/a** our account
o.a., O/a or **o/a** over all
o.a., O/a, o.a., O/Ac or **on a/c** on account; on account of
on account of
o/a or **O/a** our account
o/a, O/a or **o.a.** over all
o/a, O/a, o.a., O/Ac or **on a/c** on account; on account of
OAA or **O.A.A.** Old Age Administration
O/Ac, o.a., O/a, o/a or **on a/c** on account; on account of
OADR or **O.A.D.R.** Office of Agricultural Defense Relations
o.a.f.m. on or after full moon
O.A.G. (Ouvrier des arsenaux de la guerre) (Fr.) Army munitions worker
O.A.M. (Ouvrier des arsenaux de la marine)(Fr.) Naval munitions worker
o.a.m. (og andet mere)(Dan.) or **u.a.m.** (und anderes mehr)(Ger.) and others besides (cf. m.m.; u.s.f.)
O. & A. October and April (Interest)
o.& r. or **o.and r.** ocean and rail (cf. r.& o.)
o. and r. or **o.& r.** ocean and rail (cf. r. and o.)
o.a.n.m. on or after new moon
O.A.O.O. Oregon Academy of Ophthalmology and Otolaryngology
OAPC or **O.A.P.C.** Office of Alien Property Custodian
O.A.S. On active service
O.A.T. or **o.a.t.** one at a time
OATI or **O.A.T.I.** Office of Air Transport Information
OAWR or **O.A.W.R.** Office for Agricultural War Relations
O.B. ordered back (Banking); outside broadcast
O.B. or **O/B** opening of books
O/B or **O.B.** opening of books
Ob. or **Obad.** Obadiah
ob. oboe; obolus
ob. (obiter)(Lat.) or **e.p.** (en passant)(Fr.) incidentally; by the way
ob., obt. (obiit)(Lat.) or **d.** he or she died (cf. dec.)
Obad. or **Ob.** Obadiah
obb. obbligato (Music)
OBCCC or **O.B.C.C.C.** Office of the Bituminous Coal Consumers' Counsel
obdt. or **obt.** obedient
O.B.E. Officer [of the Order] of the British Empire
O.B.E. or **B.E.** Order of the British Empire
o.b.f.m. on or before full moon
obit. obituary
obj. object; objective
objn. or **obj.** objection
O.B/L order bill of lading
obl. oblique; oblong
o.b.n.m. on or before new moon
Ob. Ph. or **ob. ph.** Oblique photograph or photography (Air force)
obre. (octubre)(Span.), **O., obro.** (outubro) (Port.), **Oct., Okt.** (Oktober)(Dan., Ger), **okt** (oktober)(Norw., Swed), **ott.** (ottobre)(Ital.) or **Paźdz.** (Październik) (Pol.) October
obro. (outubro)(Port.), **O., obre.** (octubre) (Span.), **Oct., Okt.** (Oktober)(Dan., Ger.), **okt.** (oktober)(Norw., Swed.), **ott.** (ottobre)(Ital.) or **Paźdz.** (Październik)(Pol.) October
Obs. or **obs.** observatory
Obs., obs., Anm. (Anmaerkning)(Dan.), **anm.** (anmärkning)(Swed.), **Obsn** (Mil.) or **Obsn.** observation
obs. observe; obsolete
obs. or **Obs.** observatory
obsc. obscure
Obsn (Mil.), **Obsn., Anm.** (Anmaerkning) (Dan.), **anm.** (anmarkning)(Swed.), **Obs.** or **obs.** observation
Obsn Bn Observation battalion
Obsn Fl Observation flash
Obsn Gp Observation group
Obsn Sq Observation squadron
Obsn Sq Atchd Observation squadron attached
obsol., obsoles. or **obsolesc.** obsolescent
obsolesc., obsoles. or **obsol.** obsolescent
ob.s.p., o.s.p. (obiit sine prole)(Lat.) or **d.s.p.** (decessit sine prole)(Lat.) he or she died without issue (cf. s.l.p.; s.m.p.; s.p.; s.p.s.)
Obsr (Mil.) or **obsr.** observer
obsr. or **Obsr** (Mil.) observer
obstet. obstetrical; obstetrician; obstetrics
obt., ob. (obiit)(Lat.) or **d.** he or she died (cf. dec.)
obt. or **obdt.** obedient
O.B.U. Oklahoma Baptist University; One Big Union
OBulg. or **O.Bulg.** Old Bulgarian
obv. obverse

OC office copy
OC, O.C., OOC or **O.O.C.** Office of Censorship
OC (Mil.) or **O. i/c.** Officer in charge
O.C. (Ordo Charitatis)(Lat.) Fathers of the Order of Charity; Officer commanding; official classification (Com.); Old Carthusian; Old Catholic; open cover (Shipping)
O.C., O.Carm. (Ordo Fratrum Carmelitarum)(Lat.) or **O.C.C.** (Ordo Fratrum Carmelitarum Calceatarum)(Lat.) Order of the Calced Carmelites; Order of Our Lady of Mt. Carmel; Carmelite Fathers; Carmelites of the Ancient Observance
O.C. or **O. Cart.** (Ordo Cartusiensis)(Lat.) Carthusian Order; Carthusians
O.C., O.Cist., S.O.C., S.O.Cist. or **S.Ord. Cist.** (Sacre Ordo Cisterciensis)(Lat.) Order of Citeaux; Cistercian Order; Cistercians (cf. O.C.R.)
O/C open charter
O/C or **o/c** old charter
Oc., oc. or **O.** ocean
oc. or **o/c** overcharge
o.c. on center
o.c. or **o/c** only child (Geneal.)
o.c. or **op. cit.** (opere citato)(Lat.) in the work cited (cf. loc. cit.); (opus citatum) (Lat.) the work cited
o/c old crop
o/c, Kl. (Klokken)(Dan.), **kl.** (klockan) (Swed.) or **o'c** o'clock
o/c or **O/c** old charter
o/c or **oc.** overcharge
o/c or **o.c.** only child (Geneal.)
o'c., o/c, Kl. (Klokken)(Dan.) or **kl.** (klockan)(Swed.) o'clock
O.C.A.C. Office of Chief of Air Corps
O. Camald. (Ordo Camaldulensium)(Lat.) Camaldolese Order (Benedictine) (cf. O.S.B.)
O.Carm., O.C. (Ordo Fratrum Carmelitarum)(Lat.) or **O.C.C.** (Ordo Fratrum Carmelitarum Calceatarum)(Lat.) Order of the Calced Carmelites; Order of Our Lady of Mt. Carmel; Carmelite Fathers; Carmelites of the Ancient Observance
O.Carm., O.C.D. or **O.D.C.** (Ordo Fratrum Carmelitarum Discalceatarum)(Lat.) Order of Discalced Carmelites; Barefoot Carmelites (cf. O.C.C.)
O. Cart. or **O.C.** (Ordo Cartusiensis)(Lat.) Carthusian Order; Carthusians
O.C.C. (Ordo Fratrum Carmelitarum Calceatarum)(Lat.), **O.C.** or **O. Carm.** (Ordo Fratrum Carmelitarum)(Lat.) Order of the Calced Carmelites; Order of Our Lady of Mt. Carmel; Carmelite Fathers; Carmelites of the Ancient Observance
Occ., O., o. or **occ.** occident; occidental
occ. occasional
occ., O., o. or **Occ.** occident; occidental
occ. or **occas.** occasionally
occ. or **occn.** occasion
occas. or **occ.** occasionally
OCCCA or **O.C.C.C.A.** Office of Civilian Conservation Corps Activities
occn. or **occ.** occasion
occult. occultism
OCD or **O.C.D.** Office of Civilian Defense
O.C.D. O.D.C. or **O.Carm.** (Ordo [Fratrum] Carmelitarum Discalceatarum) (Lat.) Order of the Discalced Carmelites; Barefoot Carmelites (cf. O.C.C.)
Oceanog. or **oceanog.** oceanography
OCI or **O.C.I.** Office of Coordinator of Information
OCIA or **O.C.I.A.** Office of Coordinator of International Affairs
OCIAA or **O.C.I.A.A.** Office of Coordinator of Inter-American Affairs
O.Cist., O.C., S.O.C., S.O.Cist. or **S. Ord. Cist.** (Sacre Ordo Cisterciensis)(Lat.) Order of Citeaux; Holy Order of Citeaux; Cistercian Order; Cistercians (cf. O.C.R.)
OCNGA or **O.C.N.G.A.** Office in Charge of National Guard Affairs
OCR or **O.C.R.** Office of Civilian Requirements
O.C.R. (Ordo Cisterciensis Reformatorum (Lat.) or **O.C.S.O.** Order of Reformed Cistercians; Order of Cistercians of the Strict Observance; Reformed Cistercians; Trappists (cf. O.Cist.)
O.C.S.O. or **O.C.R.** (Ordo Cicterciensis Reformatorum) Order of Cistercians of the Strict Observance; Order of Reformed Cistercians; Trappists (cf. O.Cist.)
Oct. Octavius
Oct., O., obre. (octubre)(Span.), **obro.** (outubro)(Port.), **Okt.** (Oktober)(Dan., Ger.), **okt.** (oktober)(Norw., Swed.), **ott.** (ottobre)(Ital.) or **Paźdz.** (Październik)(Pol.) October
oct., O., o., 8vo or **8vo** octavo
Octa. Octavia
octupl. octuplicate
OD (Mil.) or **O.D.** Officer of the day
OD, O.D. or **o.d.** outside diameter
OD (Mil.), **O.D.** or **Ord Dept** (Mil.) Ordnance Department
OD. or **O.D.** Old Dutch
O.D. Operations division (Navy); Ordnance Data (Navy); Ordnance depot; overdrawn (Banking); (oculus dexter) (Lat.) right eye
O.D. or **OD** Officer of the day
O.D., OD or **o.d.** outside diameter
O.D., OD (Mil.) or **Ord Dept** (Mil.) Ordnance department
O.D. or **OD.** Old Dutch
O.D. or **O/D** overdraft (Banking)
O.D., od (Mil.) or **o.d.** olive drab
O.D. or **Opt. D.** Doctor of Optometry
O.D., O.S. or **o.s.** ordinary seaman
O/D or **O.D.** overdraft (Banking)
O/D, o.d., o/d or **o/d.** on demand
O.d., o.d. (omni die)(Lat.), **q.d.** (quaque die)(Lat.) or **Quotid.** (quotidie)(Lat.) every day; daily (cf.p.d.; s.i.d.)
od (Mil.), **O.D.** or **o.d.** olive drab

o. d. (och dylikt (dylika))(Swed.), **etc.** (et cetera)(Lat.), **i.t.d.** (i tak dalej)(Pol.), **k.t.l.** (kai ta loipa)(Greek), **m.m.** (med mera)(Swed.), (med mere)(Dan.), **o.s.v.** (och så vidare)(Swed.), (og saa videre)(Dan.), **u.drgl.** (und dergrelchen) (Ger.), **u.s.f.** (und so fort)(Ger.), **usw** or **u.s.w.** (und so weiter)(Ger.) and so forth; and the like; and others of like kind

o.d., OD or **O.D.** outside diameter

o.d., O.D. or **od** (Mil.) olive drab

o.d., O/D, o/d or **o/d.** on demand

o.d., O.d. (omni die)(Lat.), **q.d.** (quaque die)(Lat.) or **Quotid.** (quotidie)(Lat.) every day; daily (cf. p.d.; s.i.d)

o/d, o.d., O/D or **o/d.** on demand

ODa., ODan. or **O.Dan.** Old Danish

OD&RD Overseas discharge and replacement depot

ODan., ODa. or **O.Dan.** Old Danish

O.Dan., ODa. or **ODan.** Old Danish

O.D.C., O.Carm. or **O.C.D.** (Ordo Carmelitarum Discalceatarum)(Lat.) Order of the Discalced Carmelites; Discalced or Barefoot Carmelites (cf. O.C.C.)

O. de M., O.D.M. or **O.Merced.** (Ordo Beatae Mariae de Mercede Redemptionis Captivorum)(Lat.) Order of Our Lady of Mercy; Order of Mary for the Redemption of Captives; Order of Mercy; Mercedarians; Mercedarian Fathers; Mercedarian Nuns; Brothers of Mercy; Sisters of Mercy (cf. M.S.SS.T.; O.SS.T.)

O.d.H.S. (Orden der Hermann-Söhne)(Ger.) Order of Hermann Sons

ODHWS or **O.D.H.W.S.** Office of Defense Health and Welfare Services

Odly or **Ordl** Orderly (Mil.)

O.D.M., O. de M. or **O. Merced.** (Ordo Beatae Mariae de Mercede Redemptionis Captivorum)(Lat.) Order of Our Lady of Mercy; Order of Mary for the Redemption of Captives; Order of Mercy; Mercedarians; Mercedarian Brothers; Mercedarian Sisters; Brothers of Mercy; Sisters of Mercy; Redemptionists (cf. M.S.SS.T.; O.SS.T.)

O.D.P. or **F.D.P.** (Filii Divinae Providentiae)(Lat.) Order of Divine Providence; Sons of Divine Providence

ODT or **O.D.T.** Office of Defense Transportation

OE. or **O.E.** Old English

O.E. Old Etonian; (ouvrier d'état)(Fr.) government employee

O.E. or **OE.** Old English

O.E. or **o.e.** omissions excepted

OEC or **O.E.C.** Office of Economic Coordination

OED or **O.E.D.** Oxford English Dictionary (cf.N.E.D.)

O.E.L.L. Oriental Esoteric Library League

OEM or **O.E.M.** Office for Emergency Management

O.E.M. (Officier d'état-major)(Fr.) or **S.O.** Staff officer

O.E.R. Officers' Emergency Reserve

O.E.R.S.A., O.R.S.A. (Ordo Ermemitarum Recollectorum Sancti Augustini)(Lat.) or **A.R.** Order of Recollects of St. Augustine; Augustinian Recollects; Recollect Augustinian Friars or Hermits (cf. O.S.A.)

OES or **O.E.S.** Office of Economic Stabilization

O.E.S. Order of the Eastern Star

OETA or **O.E.T.A.** Occupied Enemy Territory Administration (cf. A.M.G.)

OEW or **O.E.W.** Office of Economic Warfare (formerly BAE or BEW)

OF., O. F. or **O. Fr.** Old French

O.F. Odd Fellows (cf. I.O.O.F.)

Of., off. or **offic.** official

o.F. (ohne Fortsetzung)(Ger.) no more

o.f. old face (Typog.); oxidizing flame

OFAR or **O.F.A.R.** Office of Foreign Agricultural Relations

OFC or **O.F.C.** Office of Fishery Coordination

O.F.d'I. in A. Order Sons of Italy in America

OFEC or **O.F.E.C.** Office of Foreign Economic Coordination

OFF or **O.F.F.** Office of Facts and Figures

Off. or **off.** office

Off., off., O. or **Offr.** officer

off. offer; offered; officinal

off., Of. or **offic.** official

offg. officiating

offic., Of. or **off.** official

off. nom. official nomenclature

Off. of Educ. or **O. of E.** Office of Education

Offr., O., Off. or **off.** officer

O.F.M. (Ordo Fratrum Minorum)(Lat.) Observant Franciscans; Order of Friars Minor, Franciscans; Franciscan Fathers; Franciscan Friars (cf. O.F.M.Cap.; O.F.M. Conv.)

O.F.M.Cap., O.F.M. (Ordo Fratrum Minorum Capuccinorum)(Lat.), **O.M.C., O.M.Cap.** (Ordo Minorum Capuccinorum)(Lat.) or **O.S.F.C.** (Ordo Sancti Francisci Capuccinorum)(Lat.) Order of Friars Minor, Capuchin; Order of St. Francis, Capuchin; Capuchin Franciscans; Capuchin Fathers; Capuchins (cf. O.S.F.)

O.F.M.Conv. (Ordo Fratrum Minorum Conventualium)(Lat.) or **O.M.C.** (Ordo Minorum Conventualium)(Lat.) Order of Friars Minor, Conventual; Conventual Franciscans

O. Fr., OF. or **O.F.** Old French

OFris. or **O.Fris.** Old Friesic; Old Frisian

OFRR, O.F.R.R., FRR, F.R.R., OFRRO or **O.F.R.R.O.** Office of Foreign Relief and Rehabilitation [Operations] (cf. UNRRA)

OFRRO, O.F.R.R.O., FRR, F.R.R. OFRR or **O.F.R.R.** Office of Foreign Relief and Rehabilitation Operations (cf. UNRRA)

O.F.S. Orange Free State (cf. O.R.C.)

OFT or **O.F.T.** Office of Foreign Territories

O.F.T.C. Overland Freight Transfer Co.

OG or **O. G.** ogee

O.G. Officer of the Guard; original gum (Philately); Outer Guard; Outside Guard; Outside Guardian

O.G. or **OG.** ogee

o.g. original gum (Stamps)

OGael. or **O.Gael.** Old Gaelic

O.G.P.U. (ogpu)(from the initials of the Russian words) Special Government Political Administration; Soviet secret police (cf. G.P.U.)

OGR or **O.G.R.** Office of Government Reports (absorbed by OWI)

OH or **O.H.** open hearth (Steel)

O.H.B.M.S. On His or Her Britannic Majesty's Service

OHG. or **O.H.G.** Old High German

O.H.H.S. On His or Her Highness's Service (Philately)

O.H.L. Oxford Higher Local [examination]

ohm-cm. ohm-centimeters

O.H.M.S. On His or Her Majesty's Service

OIA or **O.I.A.** Office of Indian Affairs

O.I.C. Oil Industry Commission

O. i/c. or **OC** (Mil.) Officer in charge

OIr. or **O.Ir.** Old Irish

OISC oil-insulated self-cooling

OIt. or **O.It.** Old Italian

OIWC oil-insulated water-cooled

o.J. (ohne Jahr)(Gar.), **N.D., n.d.** or **s.a.** (sine anno)(Lat.) without year [of publication]; no date (cf. und.)

O.J.A.J. October, January, April, July (Interest)

O.J.D. Order of Job's Daughters

OK or **O.K.** (orl k'rect) all correct (cf. approv.; cor.)

O.K. outer keel

OK'd or **O.K.'d** approved (cf. approv.)

Okla. Oklahoma

Okt. (Oktober)(Dan., Ger.), **okt.** (oktober) (Norw., Swed.), **O., obre.** (octubre) (Span.), **obro.** (outubro)(Port.), **Oct., ott.** (ottobre)(Ital.) or **Paźdz.** (Październik)(Pol.) October

OL or **O.L.** overload (Elec.)

OL. or **O.L.** Old Latin

O.L. Occupation License (Queensland); Officer [of the Order] of Leopold; Ordnance lieutenant

O.L. or **OL** overload (Elec.)

O.L. (oculus laevus)(Lat.), **O.S.** or **o.s.** (oculus sinister)(Lat.) left eye

Ol. Oliver

Ol. or **ol.** (oleum)(Lat.) oil

Ol. or **Olym.** Olympiad

O.L.& T. owners, landlords and tenants (Insurance)

O.L.Cr. Ordnance lieutenant commander

Old Test., A.T. (Altes Testament)(Ger.), **O.T.** or **V. T.** (Vetus Testamentum) (Lat.) Old Testament

oleo or **oleo.** oleomargarin

OLG. or **O.L.G.** Old Low German

OLLA or **O.L.L.A.** Office of Lend-Lease Administration

Ol. lini s.i. (oleum lini sine igne)(Lat.) cold drawn linseed oil

Ol. oliv. olive oil

Ol. res. oleoresin

Olym. or **Ol.** Olympiad

O.M. Order of Merit (Brit.); (Ordo [Fratrum] Minorum)(Lat.) Order of Minims of St. Francis of Paola; Minims of St. Francis de Paul; Order of Minims; Minims

O.M. or **o.m.** old measurement

O.M., o.m. (omni mane)(Lat.) or **q.m.** (quaque mane)(Lat.) every morning

om., omn. (omni)(Lat.) or **evy.** every

o.m., O.M. (omni mane)(Lat.) or **q.m.** (quaque mane)(Lat.) every morning

O.M.C., O.F.M.Cap. or **O.M.Cap.** (Ordo Fratrum Minorum Capuccinorum)(Lat.) Order of Friars Minor, Capuchin; Capuchin Fathers or Friars; Capuchin Franciscans

O.M.C. or **O.F.M.Conv.** (Ordo Fratrum Minorum Conventualium)(Lat.) Order of Friars Minor, Conventual; Conventual Franciscan Fathers or Friars

O.M.Cap., O.M.C. (Ordo Minorum Capuccinorum)(Lat.), **O.F.M.Cap., O.F.M.** (Ordo Fratrum Minorum Capuccinorum)(Lat.) or **O.S.F.C.** (Ordo Sancti Francisci Capuccinorum) Order of Friars Minor, Capuchin; Order of St. Francis, Capuchin; Capuchin Franciscans; Capuchin Fathers; Capuchins (cf. O.S.F.)

O.M.E. Ordnance mechanical engineer

O. Merced., O.D.M. or **O. de M.** (Ordo Beatae Mariae de Mercede Redemptionis Captivorum)(Lat.) Order of Our Lady of Mercy; Order of Blessed Mary for the Redemption of Captives; Order of Mercy; Mercedarians; Mercedarian Fathers; Mercedarian Nuns; Brothers of Mercy; Sisters of Mercy; Redemptionists (cf. M. S. Ss. T.)

O.M.I. (Oblati Mariae Immaculateae)(Lat.) Oblate Fathers of Mary Immaculate

omn., om. (omni)(Lat.) or **evy.** every

Omn. bih. or **omn. bih.** (omni bihora)(Lat.) every two hours (cf. q2 h.)

Omn. hor., omn. hor. (omni hora)(Lat.), **q.h., Qq.hor.** or **qq.hor.** (quaque hora) (Lat.) every hour

OMP or **O.M.P.** Office of Management Production

Om. quar. hor. (omni quadrante hora) (Lat.) every quarter of an hour

O.M.S. Organization for the Maintenance of Supplies (Brit.)

O.M.V. Master of Obstetrics of Vienna

ON. or **O.N.** Old Norse

O/N order notify

O.n., o.n. (omni noctė)(Lat.) or **q.n.** (quaque nocte)(Lat.) every night

on a/c, o.a., O/a, o/a or **O/Ac** on account; on account of

ONF, ONF. or **O.N.F.** Old Norman French; Old North French

onomat. onomatopoeia; onomatopoeic

ONOP or **O.N.O.P.** Office of Naval Officer Procurement

ONorth. Old Northumberland

O.N.R. Official Naval Reporter

Ont. or **O.** Ontario

OO (Mil.) or **O.O.** Ordnance officer

O.O. Observation officer; Operation order

O.O. or **OO**(Mil.) Ordnance Officer

O.O., O.Offr. or **Ord. Offr.** Orderly officer

O/o or **o/o** order of

o. O., Dr. u. J. (ohne Ort, Druckernamen und Jahr)(Ger.) or **s.l.a.n.** (sine loco, anno, vel nomine)(Lat.), without place, publisher or year; without place, date or name [of publisher]

o.O. (ohne Ort)(Ger.), **n.p., S.L.** or **s.l.** (sine loco)(Lat.) no place [of publication]; without place

o.o. or order

o/o or **O/o** order of

OOC, O.O.C., OC or **O.C.** Office of Censorship

O. of E. or **Off. of Educ.** Office of Education

O.Offr., O.O. or **Ord. Offr.** Orderly officer

O.O.G Officer of the guard

O.O.Q. Officer of the quarters

o.O.u.J. (ohne Ort und Jahr)(Ger.), **n.p. or d.** or **s.l. et a.** (sine loce et anno) (Lat.) without place and date [of publication]; no place or date

O.O.W Officer of the watch

OP (Mil.), **O.P.** or **o.p.** observation post or posts

O.P. official phone (Radio); Old Playgoers' [Club](Brit.); old prices (Theat.)

O.P., OP (Mil.) or **o.p.** observation post

O.P., op. or **o.p.** overproof (alcohol)

O.P. or **o.p.** open policy; opposite prompt [side]; opposite prompter (Theat.)

O.P., o.p., o/p or **vergr.** (vergriffen)(Ger.) out of print

O.P., O.Pr. or **Ord. Fratr. Praed.** (Ordo Fratrum Praedicatorum)(Lat.) Order of Preachers, Dominican Fathers (cf. O.S.D.)

op. opera

op., o. or **opt.** (optimus, optime)(Lat.) best

op., O.P. or **o.p.** overproof (alcohol)

op. or **Opn** (Mil.) operation

op. or **opp.** opposite

op. (opus)(Lat.), **W., w.** or **wk.** work

o.p. OP (Mil.) or **O.P.** observation post

o.p. or **O.P.** open policy; opposite prompt side (Theat.); opposite prompter

o.p., O.P. or **op.** overproof (alcohol)

o.p. O.P. o/p or **vergr.** (vergriffen)(Ger.) out of print

o/p, O.P., o.p. or **vergr.** (vergriffen)(Ger.) out of print

OPA or **O.P.A.** Office of Price Administration (cf. OPACS)

O.P.A. Original Purchase Address

OPACS or **O.P.A.C.S.** Office of Price Administration and Civilian Supply (now OPA)

OPC or **O.P.C.** Office of Petroleum Coordinator (now PAW)

op. cit. or **o.c.** (opere citato)(Lat.) in the work cited (cf. loc. cit.); (opus citatum) (Lat.) the work cited

OPCW or **O.P.C.W.** Office of the Petroleum Coordinator for War (cf. PAW)

O.P.H. Order of the Purple Heart

ophthal. ophthalmology

OPICND or **O.P.I.C.N.D.** Office of Petroleum Industry Coordinator for National Defense (cf. PAW)

OPL Outpost line (Mil.)

OPLR Outpost line of resistance (Mil.)

OPM or **O.P.M.** Office of Production Management (absorbed by WPB)

Opn (Mil.) or **op.** operation

opn. opinion

o.p.n. (ora pro nobis)(Lat.) pray for us

o.p.o. one price only

opp. oppose; opposed

opp. or **op.** opposite

op. posth. (opus posthumum)(Lat.) posthumous work

oppy. opportunity

O.Pr., Ord. Fratr. Praed. or **O.P.** (Ordo Praedicatorum or Ordo Fratrum Praedicatorum)(Lat.) Order of Preachers, Dominican Fathers (cf. O.S.D.)

Opr (Mil.) or **opr.** operator

opr. or **Opr** (Mil.) operator

O.Praem., O.Prem. or **Ord.Praem.** (Ordo Praemonstratensium)(Lat.) Premonstratensian Order; Premonstratensians; Norbertines (cf. C.R.P.)

OPRD or **O.P.R.D.** Office of Production Research and Development

O.Prem., O.Praem. or **Ord.Praem.** (Ordo Praemonstratensium)(Lat.) Premonstratensian Order; Premonstratensians; Norbertines (cf. C.R.P.)

Ops Opinions (Mil.)

Ops (Mil.), **ops.** or **optns.** operations

opt. optative; optical; optician; optics; option; optional

opt., o. or **opp.** (optimus, optime)(Lat.) best

Opt. D or **O.D.** Doctor of Optometry

optg. operating

opt. mineral. optical mineralogy

optns., Ops (Mil.) or **ops.** operations

O.Q.M.G. Office of the Quartermaster General

OR (Mil.), **O.R.** or **Org. Res.** Organized Reserves

O.R. Official Receiver; Official Referee; Orderly room; Other ranks (Mil.)

O.R. or **o.r.** owner's risk (Transp.)

Or. Orient

Or., O., o. or **or.** oriental

Or., O., Ore. or **Oreg.** Oregon

or., O., o. or **Or.** oriental

or. or **o^r^.** other

o.r. or **O.R.** owner's risk

o^r^. or **or.** other

ora. oratorio

orat. orator; oratorical; oratory

O.R.B. or **o.r.b.** owner's risk of breakage (Transp.)
ORC or **O.R.C.** Officers' Reserve Corps
O.R.C. Orange River Colony (now Orange Free State); Order of Railway Conductors [of America]; Order of the Red Cross
O.R.C. or **o.r.c.** owner's risk of chafing (Transp.)
orch. orchestra; orchestral
O.R.D. or **o.r.d.** owner's risk of damage
Ord (Mil.), **Ord.**, **ord.**, **Ordn.** or **ordn.** Ordnance
ord. ordained; ordinal; ordinance; ordinances; ordinarily; ordinary
ord., **O.** or **o.** order
ord. (ordo, ordines)(Lat.), **s.** or **ser.** series
o.r.d. or **O.R.D.** owner's risk of damage
Ord Bn Armd Ordnance battalion armored
Ord Co Ordnance company
Ord Co (M Maint) Ordnance company, medium maintenance
Ord Dept, OD (Mil.) or **O.D.** Ordnance Department
o.r.det. owner's risk of deterioration (Transp.)
Ord. Fratr. Praed., **O.P.** or **O. Pr.** (Ordo Praedicatorum or Ordo Fratrum Praedicatorum)(Lat.) Order of Preachers, Dominican Fathers (cf. O.S.D.)
Ordly or **Odly** Orderly (Mil.)
Ordn., **ordn.**, **Ord** (Mil.), **Ord.** or **ord.** Ordnance
Ord. Offr., **O.O.** or **O. Offr.** Orderly officer
Ord. Praem., **O.Praem.** or **O.Prem.** (Ordo Praemonstratensium)(Lat.) Premonstratensian Order; Premonstratensians; Norbertines (cf. C.R.P.)
Ord. Sgt. Ordnance Sergeant
Ore., **O.**, **Or.** or **Oreg.** Oregon
Oreg., **O.**, **Or.** or **Ore.** Oregon
O.R.F. or **o.r.f.** owner's risk of fire; owner's risk of freezing (Transp.)
org. organ; organism; organized
org. or **organ.** organic
org., **organ.** or **Orgn** (Mil.) organization
organ. or **org.** organic
organ., **org.** or **Orgn** (Mil.) organization
org.chem. organic chemistry
Orgn (Mil.), **org.** or **organ.** organization
Org. Res., **OR** (Mil.) or **O.R.** Organized Reserves
orig. origin; original; originally
Ork. Orkney [Islands]
O.R.L. or **o.r.l.** owner's risk of leakage
Orl. Orlando
o.r.l. or **O.R.L.** owner's risk of leakage
Orn. ornamental; ornamentation
Orn., **orn.**, **Ornith.**, **ornith.**, **Ornithol.** or **ornithol.** ornothologist; onrothology
orn., **ornith.** or **ornithol.** ornithological
Ornith., **ornith.**, **Orn.**, **orn.**, **Ornithol.** or **ornithol.** ornothologist; ornothology
ornith., **orn.** or **ornithol.** ornithological
Ornithol., **ornithol.**, **Orn.**, **orn.**, **Ornith.** or **ornith.** ornithologist; ornithology
ornithol., **orn.** or **ornith.** ornithological
O.R.R. or **o.r.r.** owner's risk rates (Transp.)
O.R.S. official relay station (Radio)
O.R.S. or **o.r.s.** owner's risk of shifting (Transp.)
ors. others
O.R.S.A., (Ordo Recollectorum Sancti Augustini)(Lat.), **A.R.** or **O.E.R.S.A.** (Ordo Ermemitarum Recollectorum Sancti Augustini)(Lat.) Order of Recollects of St. Augustine; Augustinian Recollects; Recollect Augustinian Friars or Hermits (cf. O.S.A.)
Orse. or **orse.** otherwise (Law)
Orth. or **orth.** orthopedic; orthopedy
O.R.W. or **o.r.w.** owner's risk of becoming wet (Transp.)
OS., **O.S.**, **OSax.** or **O.Sax.** Old Saxon
O.S. Old School (Eccl.); old series; Old Side (Eccl.); Ordnance survey; Organization Society (Brit.) Outside Sentinel
O.S., **OS.**, **OSax.** or **O.Sax.** Old Saxon
O.S., **O/S**, **O/s** or **o/s** Old Style
O.S., **o.s.** or **O.D.** ordinary seaman
O.S., **o.s.** (oculus sinister)(Lat.) or **O.L.** (oculus laevus)(Lat.) left eye
O.S. or **O.S.M.** (Ordo Servorum Mariae) (Lat.) Order of the Servants of Mary; Servite Fathers; Servites
O/S, **O.S.**, **O/s** or **o/s** Old Style
Os osmium (Chem.)
O/s, **O.S.**, **O/S** or **o/s** Old Style
O/s, **o/s** or **o/sg** outstanding (Banking)
o.s. only son (Geneal.); on spot (Com.)
o.s., **O.D.** or **O.S.** ordinary seaman
o.s, **O.S.** (oculus sinister)(Lat.) or **O.L.** (oculus laevus)(Lat.) left eye
o/s out of stock; (ore sellado)(Span.) gold peso
o/s, **O.S.**, **O/S** or **O/s** Old Style
o/s, **O/s** or **o/sg** outstanding (Banking)
O.S.A. Optical Society of America; Oratorio Society of America; (Ordo [Eremitarum] Sancti Augustini)(Lat.) Order of St. Augustine; Augustinian Fathers; Order of the Hermits of St. Augustine; Hermits of St. Augustine (cf. A.A.; O.R.S.A.)
o.s.a. (om svar anhålles)(Swed.), **R.S.V.P.**, **r.s.v.p.** (répondez s'il vous plaît)(Fr.), **S.u.** (Svar udbedes)(Dan.), **u.A.w.g.** (um Antwort wird gebeten)(Ger.) or **u. gefl. A. w.g.** (um gefällige Antwort wird gebeten)(Ger.) an answer is requested; please reply
O.S. & D., **o.s. & d.** or **o.s. and d.** over, short and damaged (Transp.)
O S & D Report Over, Short and Damaged Report (Mil.)
o.s. and d., **O.S. & D.** or **o.s. & d.** over, short and damaged (Transp.)
OSax., **OS.**, **O.S.** or **O.Sax.** Old Saxon
O.Sax., **OS.**, **O.S.** or **OSax.** Old Saxon
O.S.B. (Ordo Sancti Benedicti)(Lat.) Order of St. Benedict; Benedictine Fathers; Benedictines

O.S.B.M. (Ordo Sancti Basilii Magni) (Lat.) Order of St. Basil the Great; Basilian Fathers (Ukraine)

O.S.C. (Oblati Sancti Caroli)(Lat.) Oblates of St. Charles; Order of the Scottish Clan

O.S.C., O.S.Cr. (Ordo Sanctae Crucis) (Lat.) or **C.S.C.** (Congregatio Sanctae Crucis)(Lat.) Order of the Sacred Cross; Congregation of the Sacred Cross; Crosier Fathers; Crosiers (cf. O.S.C.R.)

Osc. Oscar

osc. oscillating; oscillator

O.S.Cam. (Ordo Sancti Camilli)(Lat.), **C.R.M.I.** Clerici Regulares Ministrantes Infirmis)(Lat.), **M.I.** or **Min. Inf.** Order of St. Camillus; Clerks Regular Ministering to the Infirm; Clerks Regular Attendant on the Sick; Ministers of the Sick; Camillian Fathers; Camillians

OScand. or **O. Scand.** Old Scandinavian

O.S.C.R. Canons Regular of the Order of the Holy Cross; Crosier Fathers; Crosiers (cf. O.S.Cr.)

O.S.Cr., O.S.C. (Ordo Sanctae Crucis)(Lat.) or **C.S.C.** (Congregatio Sanctae Crucis) (Lat.) Order of the Holy Cross; Congregation of the Holy Cross; Crozier Fathers; Croziers (cf. O.S.C.R.)

O.S.D. (Ordo Sancti Dominici)(Lat.) Order of St. Dominic; Dominicans (generally used of the Third order)(cf. O.Pr.; T.O.S.D.); Ordnance Survey Department

O.S.F. (Ordo Sancti Francisci)(Lat.) Order of St. Francis; Missionary Brothers of St. Francis (now generally used for the third order. cf. T.O.R.; T.O.S.F.)

O.S.F.C. (Ordo Sancti Francisci Capuccinorum)(Lat.), **O.F.M., O.F.M.Cap.** (Ordo Fratrum Minorum Capuccinorum)(Lat.), **O.M.C.** or **O.M.Cap.** (Ordo Minorum Capuccinorum)(Lat.) Order of St. Francis, Capuchin; Order of Friars Minor, Capuchin; Capuchin Franciscans; Capuchin Fathers; Capuchins (cf. O.S.F.)

OSFCW or **O.S.F.C.W.** Office of Solid Fuels Coordinator for War

O.S.F.S. (Oblati Sancti Francisci Salesii) (Lat.) Oblate Fathers of St. Francis de Sales (cf. S.S.)

o/sg, O/s or **o/s** outstanding (Banking)

O.S.H. (Ordo [Eremitarum] Sancti Hieronymi)(Lat.) Order of St. Jerome; Hermits or Friars of St. Jerome; Hieronymites

O.S.I.A. Order of Sons of Italy in America

O.S.J. (Congregatio Oblatorum Sancti Josephi)(Lat.) Oblates of St. Joseph

O.S.J.D. or **O.S.J. de D.** (Ordo Hospitalarius Sancti Joannis de Deo)(Lat.) Order of Hospitalers of St. John of God; Brothers of Mercy; Ignorantine Brothers; Ignorantines

OSl., O.Sl., OSLav. or **O. Slav.** Old Slavic

OSlav., OSl., O.Sl. or **O.Slav.** Old Slavic

O.S.M. or **O.S.** (Ordo Servorum Mariae) (Lat.) Order of the Servants of Mary; Servite Fathers; Servites

o.s.p., ob.s.p. (obiit sine prole)(Lat.) or **d.s.p.** (decessit sine)(Lat.) he or she died without issue (cf. s.l.p., s.m.p.; s.p.; s.p.s.)

OSRD or **O.S.R.D.** Office of Scientific Research and Development

OSS or **O.S.S.** Office of Strategic Services (Combined Chiefs of Staff)

O.SS.C. Oblati Sanctissimi Cordate)(Lat.) Oblate Fathers of Most Sacred Heart

O.SS.T., O.Ss.T. or **O.Trinit.** (Ordo Sanctissimae Trinitatis Redemptionis Captivorum)(Lat.) Order of the Most Holy Trinity; Trinitarian Fathers; Trinitarians; Redemptorists (cf. M.S.SS.T.; C.SS.R.)

o.s.t. ordinary spring tides

osteo. osteopath

O.S.U. Order of St. Ursula; Ursulines

o. s. v. (och så vidare)(Swed.), (og saa videre)(Dan.), **etc.** (et cetera)(Lat.), **i.t.d.** (i tak dalej)(Pol.), **k.t.l.** (kai ta loipa) (Greek). **m.m.** (med mera)(Swed.), (med mere)(Dan.), **o.d.** ock dylikt or dylika)(Swed.), **u.drgl.** (und dergrelchen)(Ger.), **u.s.f.** (und so fort) (Ger.), **usw.** or **u.s.w.** (und so weiter) (Ger.) and so forth; and the like; and others of like kind

OSw., O.Sw., OSwed. or **O.Swed.** Old Swedish

Osw. Oswald

OSwed., O.Swed., OSw. or **O.Sw.** Old Swedish

OT old term (Anatomy)(cf. BNA)

O.T. occupational therapy

O.T., A.T. (Altes Testament)(Ger.), **Old Test.** or **V.T.** (Vetus Testamentum) (Lat.) Old Testament

O.T. or **o.t.** oil-tight; on track; on truck; overtime

O/t old terms (grain trade)

ot. ought

o.t. or **O.T.** oil-tight; on track; on truck; overtime

otbd. outboard

O.T.C. Officers' Training Camp or Corps

O.T.C.A. Officers' Training Camp Association

OTeut. or O.Teut. Old Teutonic

otol. otology

O.Trinit. or **O. Ss. T.** (Ordo Sanctissimae Trinitatis)(Lat.) Order of the Most Holy Trinity; Trinitarians

O.T.S. Officers' Training School

ott.. (ottava)(Ital.) octave (Music)

ott. (ottobre)(Ital.), **O., obre.** (octubre) (Span.), **obro.** (outubro)(Port.), **Oct. Okt.** (Oktober)(Dan., Ger.), **okt.** (oktober)(Norw., Swed.) or **Paźdz.** (Październik)(Pol.) October

O.T.U. Officers' Training Unit

O.U. (oculus uterque)(Lat.) each eye

O.U.A. Order of United Americans

O.U.A.M. Order of United American Mechanics

O.V. or **o.v.** over voltage (Electricity)

Ov. (ovum)(Lat.) egg

o.v. oil of vitriol
o.v. or **O.V.** over voltage (Electricity)
overt. overture (Music)
ow. one way fare
OWI or **O.W.I.** Office of War Information (cf. COI; OGR; USIS)
OWM or **O.W.M.** Office of War Mobilization
Ox., Oxf. or **Oxon.** (Oxonia)(Lat.) Oxford; Oxfordshire
Oxf., Ox. or **Oxon.** (Oxonia)(Lat.) Oxford; Oxfordshire
Oxon. (Oxonia)(Lat.), **Ox.** or **Oxf.** Oxford; Oxfordshire
Oxon. or **Oxonien.** (Oxoniensis)(Lat.) of Oxford
Oxonien. or **Oxon.** (Oxoniensis)(Lat.) of Oxford
oz. ounce
oz. or **ozs.** ounces
oz. ap. apothecaries' ounce
oz. av. ounce, avoirdupois
oz-ft. ounce-foot or feet
oz-in. ounce-inch or inches
ozs. or **oz.** ounces
oz.t. ounce, troy

ΩΔΦ (Omega Delta Phi) National undergraduate fraternity
ΩΕΦ (Omega Epsilon Phi) National undergraduate fraternity (Optometry)
ΩΙΠ (Omega Iota Pi) National undergraduate fraternity
ΩΨΦ (Omega Psi Phi) National undergraduate fraternity (Negroes)
ΩΤΣ (Omega Tau Sigma) National undergraduate fraternity (Veterinary Medicine)
ΟΒΠ (Omicron Beta Pi) National undergraduate fraternity (Pre-medical)
ΟΔΓ (Omicron Delta Gamma) National undergraduate honorary sorority (Home Economics)
ΟΔΚ (Omicron Delta Kappa) National undergraduate honor fraternity (Student leadership)
ΟΚΥ (Omicron Kappa Upsilon) National undergraduate honor fraternity (Dentistry)
ΟΝ (Omicron Nu) National honorary sorority (Home Economics)

P

P pass; phosphorus (Chem.); Priestly Code (Bib.)
P or **p.** pawn (Chess)
P (Elec.), **p., pow., pr.** or **pwr.** power
P (Physics), **p.** or **press.** pressure
P (Logic) or **pred.** predicate
P. (Papa)(Lat.) Pope; pupil; presbyopia; position; pulse
P. (pius)(Lat.), **hl.** (heilig)(Ger.) or **S.** holy; sacred
P. or **p.** past; pastor; peso (coin) (cf. wt.); pie(s)(Coin); probate [court]; proconsul; prompter (Theat.)
P., p. (post)(Lat.), **a.** or **aft.** after
P., p. (padre)(Span.), (pater)(Lat.), (père) (Fr.), **F., f.** or **Fr.** father
P., p. (pontifex)(Lat.), **H.P.** or **h.p.** high priest
P., p. or **peo.** people
P. p. or **Pond.** (pondere)(Lat.) by weight
P., p., Pr. or **pr.** priest; prince
P., p., Pres., pres. or **Prest.** president
P., Pas. (Pasch)(Lat.), **E.** or **East.** Easter
P., Pas. (Pasch)(Lat.), **E., East., E.T.** or **Pas. T.** (Terminus Paschae)(Lat.) Easter or Paschal Term
P., Pt. or **pt.** port
P[1] or **H.** Law of Holiness (Bib.)
p or **p.** (piano)(Ital.) soft; softly
p. (per)(Lat.) by; (pro)(Lat.) for; (partim)(Lat.) in part; party; pectoral; perch; percussion [fuse]; perishable; pier (Mil.); pipe; (perpetuus)(Lat.) uninterrupted
p., Abt. (Abteilung)(Ger.), **H., Hft.** (Heft) (Ger.), **Lfg.** (Lieferung)(Ger.), **liv.** (livraison)(Fr.) **pt., T.** or **Th.** (Teil, Theil)(Ger.) part (cf. inst.; no.; sec.)
p., D., d., dy, or **dy.** (denarius, denarii)(Lat.) penny; pence
p. (peso)(Span.), **Gew.** (Gewicht)(Ger.), **W., w.** or **wt.** weight
p., o. (octarius)(Lat.) or **pt.** pint
p. or **P** pawn (Chess)
p. or **P.** past; pastor; peso (Coin) (cf. wt.); pie(s)(Coin); probate court; proconsul; prompter (Theat.)
p., P. (post.)(Lat.), **a.** or **aft.** after
p., P. (padre)(Span.), (pater)(Lat.), (père) (Fr.), **F., f.,** or **Fr.** father
p., P. (pontifex)(Lat.) **H.P.** or **h.p.** high priest
p., P. or **peo.** people
p., P. or **Pond.** (pondere)(Lat.) by weight
p., P (Elec.), **pow., pr** or **pwr.** power
p., P., Pr. or **pr.** priest; prince
p., P., Pres., pres. or **Prest.** president
p., P (Physics) or **press.** pressure
p. or **p** (piano)(Ital.) soft; softly
p., pág. (página)(Port., Span.), **S.** (Seite) (Ger.), (Side)(Dan.) or **s.** (sida) (Swed.) page
p., part. or **ppl.** participle
p. or **per.** period
p. or **pes.** peseta
p., pl. or **plt.** plate
p. or **pm.** premolar (Dentistry)
p. or **po.** pole
p. or **pop.** population
p., pp., S. (Sider)(Dan.), **sid.** (sidor) (Swed.) or **SS.** (Seiten)(Ger.) pages
p. (primus)(Lat.) or **prem.** (premier, première)(Fr.) first (cf. imp.)
p., Pro. or **pro.** professional
p., pt. or **pts.** pints
p- para- (Chem.)
PA Position approximate
PA or **P.A.** Petroleum Administration

P.A. (Parc d'artillerie)(Fr.) Artillery park; Passenger Agent; Post adjutant; press agent; press association; Purchasing Agent; Pulpoaxial

P.A. or **P/A** power of attorney

P.A., P/A, p.a. or **P/Av.** particular average (Marine ins.)

P.A. or **Prot. Ap.** Prothonotary Apostolic

P/A private account (Bookkeeping)

P/A or **P.A.** power of attorney

P/A, P.A., p.a. or **P/Av.** particular average (Marine insurance)

Pa protoactinium (Chem.)

Pa., Penn. or **Penna.** Pennsylvania

pa. or **pap.** paper

p.a. (par amitié)(Fr.) by favor; (pro anno) (Lat.) for the year

p.a., P.A., P/A or **P/Av.** particular average (Marine insurance)

p.a., part. adj. or **ppl. adj.** participial adjective

p.a., per an. or **per ann.** (per annum)(Lat.) annually; by the year

P.A.A. Pan American Airways

PAB or **P.A.B.** Petroleum Administrative Board

P.A.C. Pan American Congress; Public Assistance Committee

P.a.C. or **P. & C.** put and call (Stocks)

Pac. or **Pacif.** Pacific

p.a.c. Passed advanced class [Military College of Science] (Brit.)

Pacif. or **Pac.** Pacific

Pac. Oc. Pacific Ocean

P.A.D.A. Past Arch Druidess' Association

p.ae., part. aeq., p.e. (partes aequales)(Lat.), **Ā, ā, ĀĀ** or **āā** (ana)(Greek) in equal parts or quantities

P.A.F. Pan American Fisheries [Incorporated]

pág. (página)(Port., Span.), **p., S.** (Seite) (Ger.), (Side)(Dan) or **s.** (sida)(Swed.) page

P.A.G.B.I. Publishers' Association of Great Britain and Ireland

paint. painting

PAIS Public Affairs Information Service

Pal. Palestine

Pal., pal., paleon., paleont. or **paleontol.** paleontology

pal. or **paleog.** paleography

paleethnol. paleethnology

paleob. or **paleobot.** paleobotany

paleog. or **pal.** paleography

paleon., Pal., pal., paleont. or **paleontol.** paleontology

paleontol., Pal., pal., paleon. or **paleont.** paleontology

palm. palmistry

Palsgr. Palsgrave

P.A.M. Phone Activities Manager (Radio)

pam., Pamph, pamph., pm. or **pph.** pamphlet

P.A.M.A. Pan American Medical Association

P. & C. or **P.a.C.** put and call (Stocks)

P & D Sec Pioneer and demolition section

P.& F. plumber and fitter

p. & i. or **pandi** protection and indemnity (Insurance)

P. & L., P. and L., p. and l. or **p/l** profit and loss

P. & M. Packeting and Marketing [Incorporated]

P. & O. or **P. and O.** Peninsular and Oriental [Steamship Company]

p. & s. port and starboard

Pamph., pamph., pam., pm. or **pph.** pamphlet

Pan. Panama

pandi or **p. & i.** protection and indemnity (insurance)

P. and L., p. and l., P. & L. or **p/l** profit and loss

P. and S. or **phys. & surg.** physicians and surgeons

pap. or **pa.** paper

pa. p., pa. ppl., pp., P.P. or **p.p.** past participle

pa. ppl., pa. p., pp., P.P. or **p.p.** past participle

Par., par., Abs., Abschn. (Abschnitt)(Ger.) or **pár.** (párrafo)(Span.) paragraph

par. parallel; parish

pár. (párrafo)(Span.), **Abs., Abschn.** (Abschnitt)(Ger.), **Par.** or **par.** paragraph

par. or **paren.** parenthesis

Para. Paraguay

parchm. parchment

paren. or **par.** parenthesis

parens. parentheses

Parl. or **parl.** parliament; parliamentary

Parl. Agt. Parliamentary Agent

pars. paragraphs

Part Partial (Mil.)

part. participating (Securities); participial; particular; particularly

part., p. or **ppl.** participle

part. adj., p.a. or **ppl. adj.** participial adjective

part. aeq., p.ae., p.e. (partes aequales)(Lat.), **Ā, ā, ĀĀ** or **āā** (ana)(Greek) in equal parts or quantities

Pas., P. (Pasch)(Lat.), **E.** or **East.** Easter

Pas., P. (Pasch)(Lat.), **E., East., E.T.** or **Pas. T.** (Terminus Paschae)(Lat.) Easter or Paschal Term

P.A.S.B. Pan American Sanitary Bureau

P.A.S.I. Professional Associate of the Chartered Surveyors' Institution (Brit.)

pass. (passim)(Lat.) everywhere; passage; passenger; passive

Pas. T. (Terminus Paschae)(Lat.), **E., East., E.T., P.** or **Pas.** (Pasch)(Lat.) Easter or Paschal Term

Pat. or **Patr.** Patrick

pat. patent; patrol; pattern

pat. or **patd.** patented

pa. t. past tense

P.A.T.A. Proprietary Articles Trade Association (Brit.)

patd. or **pat.** patented

path. or **pathol.** pathological; pathology

patmkg. patternmaking

Pat. Off. Patent Office

Patr. or **Pat.** Patrick

PAU or **P.A.U.** Pan American Union

P/Av., P.A., p.a. or **P/A** particular average (Marine ins.)

PAW or **P.A.W.** Petroleum Administration for War (cf. OPC)

P.A.Y.E. pay as you enter (Transp.)

Paym., Paymtr., Payr., PM. or **P.M.** Paymaster

Paym.-Gen. or **P.M.G.** Paymaster General

Paymtr., Paym., Payr., PM. or **P.M.** Paymaster

Payr., Paym., Paymtr., PM. or **P.M.** Paymaster

payt., Pmt (Mil.), **pt.** or **pymt.** payment

Paźdz. (Październik)(Pol.), **O., obre.** (octubre)(Span.), **obro.** (outubro)(Port.), **Oct., Okt.** (Oktober)(Dan., Ger.), **okt.** (oktober)(Norw., Swed.) or **ott.** (ottobre)(Ital.) October

P.B. passbook; permanent bunkers; Plymouth Brethren; Primitive Baptist or Baptists

P.B., Ph.B. (Pharmacopoeia Britannica) (Lat.), **B.P., B.Ph.** or **Brit. Pharm.** British Pharmacopoeia

P.B., Ph.B. (Philosophiae Baccalaureus) (Lat.), **B.P., B.Ph.** or **B.Phil.** (Baccalaureus Philosophiae)(Lat.) Bachelor of Philosophy

P.B., Pr.Bk. or **B.C.P.** Prayer Book; Book of Common Prayer

Pb (plumbum)(Lat.) lead (Chem.)

p.b. (piso bajo)(Span.) ground floor

PBA or **P.B.A.** Public Buildings Administration

P.B.A. Patrolmen's Benevolent Association

P.Bor. (Pharmacopoeia Borussica)(Lat.) Prussian Pharmacopoeia

PC or **P.C.** Panama Canal

P.C. Parish Council or Councilor; Past Commander; Peace Commissioner (Irish Free State); (Pax Christi)(Lat.) Peace of Christ; Perpetual Curate; Philippines Constabulary; Point of contact; police constable; Post of command; Practical Chemist; Principal Chaplain or Conductor; private contract (Tea); Privy Council or Councilor

P.C. (pondus civile)(Lat.) **av., avdp.** or **avoir.** avoirdupois

P.C., P.C., p.c., P/C, p/c, pct., pe.cen., per cent, per cent., percent., per ct. (per centum)(Lat.) or **v.H.** (von Hundert) (Ger.) by the hundred

P.C. or **P. Comdr.** Post Commander

P.C. or **PP.C.** (Patres Conscripti)(Lat.) Conscript Fathers; the Roman senators; the supreme authority

P/C, p.c. or **p/c** petty cash; price current

P.c. or **p.c.** (post cibum)(Lat.) after meals

pc. piece

pc., pr. or **pret.** (pretium, pretii)(Lat.) price; prices

p.c. post card

p.c., P/C or **p/c** petty cash; price current

p.c. or **P.c.** (post cibum)(Lat.) after meals

p/c, p.c. or **P/C** petty cash; price current

P.C.A. (Parc de corps d'armée)(Fr.) Army corps park; Permanent Court of Arbitration; Physicians Casualty Association; Production Credit Association; Public Charities Association

P.C.B. or **p.c.b.** petty cash book

PCC or **P.C.C.** Production Credit Corporation

P.C.C. Parochial Church Council; Privy Council Cases

P.Cc. periscopic concave

PCD or **P.C.D.** Public Contracts Division [of the Department of Labor]

P.C.D. or **P.C. Dept.** Panama Canal Department

P.C.D.I. (Poste de commandement de division d'infanterie)(Fr.) Infantry division headquarters

PCES or **P.C.E.S.** President's Committee on Economic Security

P.C.F.B. Pacific Coast Freight Bureau

PCFEP or **P.C.F.E.P.** President's Committee on Fair Employment Practice

pchs. purchase

P.C.L. People's Commissariat of Labour

pcl. parcel

P.Clk. pay clerk

P.C.M.O. Principal Colonial Medical Officer (Brit.)

P. Comdr. or **P.C.** Post Commander

P.C.P. Past Chief Patriarch (Freemasonry)

P.C.R.C. Poor Clergy Relief Corporation

P.C.R.S. Poor Clergy Relief Society (Brit.)

P.C.S. Principal Clerk of Session

Pcs. preconscious

pcs. or **ps.** pieces

pct., P.C., P.c., p.c., P/C, p/c, pe.cen., per cent, per cent., percent., per ct. (per centum)(Lat) or **v.H.** (von Hundert) (Ger.) by the hundred

P.C.W. Press Congress of the World

PD Position doubtful

PD, P.D. or **p.d.** pitch diameter

P.D. interpupillary distance; (Pharmacopoeia Dublinensis)(Lat.) Dublin Pharmacopoeia; police department; postal district

P.D., d.p. or **p.d.** potential difference (Elec.)

P.D., PD or **p.d.** pitch diameter

P.D. or **p.d.** (per diem)(Lat.) by the day; daily (cf. o.d.; d.d. in d.; quotid.)

P.D., Ph.D. (Philosophiae Doctor)(Lat.), **D.P., D. Ph., D. Phil.** or **Dr. Phil** (Doctor Philosophiae)(Lat.) Doctor of Philosophy

Pd palladium (Chem.)

Pd. or **pd.** paid

pd. passed

pd. or **Pd.** paid

p.d. interpapillary distance; papilla diameter; port dues; prism diopter

pd., d.p. or **P.D.** potential difference (Elec.)

p.d., PD or **P.D.** pitch diameter

p.d. or **P.D.** (per diem)(Lat.) by the day; daily (cf. d.d. in d.; o.d.; quotid.)

p.d.a. (pour dire adieu)(Fr.), **P.F.S.A.**, **p.f.s.a.** (pour faire ses adieux)(Fr), **P.P.C.**, **p.p.c.** (pour prendre congé) (Fr.), **T.T.L. or t.t.l.** to say good-bye; to take leave

P.D.A.D. Probate, Divorce and Admiralty Division (Brit.)

Pd. B., **Pe. B.**, **Ped. B.**, **Pg. B.** (Pedagogiae (Baccalaureus)(Lat.), **B. Pd.**, **B. Pe.**, **B.Pg.** (Baccalaureus Pedagogiae)(Lat.), **B.Py.** or **Py. B.** Bachelor of Pedagogy

Pd.D., **Pe.D.**, **Ped.D.**, **Pg.D.** (Pedagogiae Doctor)(Lat.), **D.Pd.**, **D.Pe.**, **D.Ped.**, **D.Pg.** (Doctor Pedagogiae) (Lat.), **D.Py.** or **Py.D.** Doctor of Pedagogy

P. Dept. Philippine Department

P. Div. Philippine Division

Pd.M., **Pe.M.**, **Ped.M.**, **Pg.M.** (Pedagogiae Magister)(Lat.), **M.Pd.**, **M.Pe.**, **M.Ped.**, **M.Pg.** (Magister Pedagogiae) (Lat.), **M.Py.** or **Py.M.** Master of Pedagogy

pdr. or **pr.** pounder (as 12-pdr. or 12-pr.)

P.D.S.T. Pacific Daylight Saving Time (cf. P.W.T.)

PE or **p.e.** pinion end; pulley end

P.E. (Pharmacopoeia Edinburgensis)(Lat.) Edinburgh Pharmacopoeia; (Poste d'écoute)(Fr.) Listening post; Petroleum Engineer; Presiding Elder; probable error (Statistics); Protestant Episcopal

P.E., **P Ex** (Mil.) or **P.X.** Post exchange

p.e., **p.ae.**, **part. aeq.** (partes aequales)(Lat.), **Ā**, **ā**, **ĀĀ** or **āā** (ana)(Greek) in equal parts or quantities

p.e. or **PE** pinion end; pulley end

P.E.A. Progressive Education Association

Pe.B. (Pediatriae Baccalaureus)(Lat.) Bachelor of Pediatrics

Pe. B., **Pd. B.**, **Ped. B.**, **Pg. B.** (Pedagogiae Baccalaureus)(Lat.), **B. Pd.**, **B. Pe.**, **B. Pg.** (Baccalaureus Pedagogiae)(Lat.), **B. Py.** or **Py. B** Bachelor of Pedagogy

PEC photoelectric cell

PEC or **P.E.C.** President's Emergency Council

pe.cen., **P.C.**, **P.c.**, **p.c.**, **P/C**, **p/c**, **pct.**, **per cent**, **per cent.**, **percent.**, **per ct.** (per centum)(Lat.) or **v.H.** (von Hundert) (Ger.) by the hundred

PED Pistol expert, dismounted

Pe.D., **Pd.D.**, **Ped.D.**, **Pg.D.** (Pedagogiae Doctor)(Lat.), **D.Pd.**, **D.Pe.**, **D.Ped.**, **D.Pg.** (Doctor Pedagogiae)(Lat.), **D.Py.** or **Py.D.** Doctor of Pedagogy

ped. pedal; pedestal; pedestrian

Ped. B., **Pd. B.**, **Pe. B.**, **Pg. B.** (Pedagogiae Baccalaureus)(Lat.), **B. Pd.**, **B. Pe.**, **B. Pg.** (Baccalaureus Pedagogiae) (Lat.), **B. Py.** or **Py. B.** Bachelor of Pedagogy

Ped.D., **Pd.D.**, **Pe.D.**, **Pg.D.** (Pedagogiae Doctor)(Lat.), **D.Pd.**, **D.Pe.**, **D.Ped.**, **D.Pg.** (Doctor Pedagogiae)(Lat.), **D.Py.** or **Py.D.** Doctor of Pedagogy

Ped.M., **Pd.M.**, **Pe.M.**, **Pg.M.** (Pedagogiae Magister)(Lat.), **M.Pd.**, **M.Pe.**, **M.Ped.**, **M.Pg.** (Magister Pedagogiae)(Lat.), **M.Py.** or **Py.M.** Master of Pedagogy

PEF or **P.E.F.** Palestine Exploration Fund (Brit.)

P.E.I. Porcelain Enamel Institute; Prince Edward Island

Pek. Pekinese

Pe.M., **Pd.M.**, **Ped.M.**, **Pg.M.** (Pedagogiae Magister)(Lat.), **M.Pd.**, **M.Pe.**, **M.Ped.**, **M.Pg.** (Magister Pedagogiae)(Lat.), **M.Py.** or **Py.M.** Master of Pedagogy

P.E.N. [International Association of] Poets, Playwrights, Editors, Essayists and Novelists [Club]

Pen. or **pen.** penitent; penitentiary

Pen., **pen.** or **penin.** peninsula

pen. or **Pen.** penitent; penitentiary

penin., **Pen.** or **pen.** peninsula

Penn., **Pa.** or **Penna.** Pennsylvania

Penna., **Pa.** or **Penn.** Pennsylvania

penol. penology

Pent. Pentateuch; Pentecost

peo., **P.** or **p.** people

P.E.P. Political and Economic Planning (Brit.)

Pe.P. Principal of Pedagogics

Per., **per.** or **pers.** person

Per. or **Pers.** Persia; Persian

per. or **p.** period

per., **Per.** or **pers.** person

per., **perd.** or **perden.** (perdendo, perdendosi)(Ital.) dying away; growing fainter and slackening speed (Music) (cf. cal.; manc.; smorz.)

per Adr. (per Adresse)(Ger.), **adr.** (adress)(Swed.), **Adrs.** (Adresse)(Dan.), **C/o**, **c.o.** or **c/o** in care of

per an., **p.a.** or **per ann.** (per annum)(Lat.), annually; by the year

per ann., **p.a.** or **per an.** (per annum)(Lat.) annually; by the year

per cap. (per capita)(Lat.) for each individual

per cent, **per cent.**, **percent.**, **P.C.**, **P.c.**, **p.c.**, **P/C**, **p/c**, **pct.**, **pe. cen.**, **per ct.** (per centum)(Lat.) or **v.H.** (von Hundert) (Ger.) by the hundred

per ct., **P.C.**, **P.c.**, **p.c.**, **P/C**, **p/c**, **pct.**, **pe.cen.**, **per cent**, **per cent.**, **percent.** (per centum)(Lat.) or **v.H.** (von Hundert) (Ger.) by the hundred

perd., **per.** or **perden.** (perdendo, perdendosi) (Ital.) dying away; growing fainter and slackening speed (Music) (cf. cal.; manc.; smorz.)

perden., **per.** or **perd.** (perdendo, perdendosi)(Ital.) dying away; growing fainter and slackening speed (Music) (cf. cal.; manc.; smorg.)

perf. perforated; performer

perf., **Pf.** or **pf.** perfect

perh. perhaps

peri. or **perig.** perigee (Astron.)

per M by the thousand

Per. op. emet. (peracta operatione emeticus)(Lat.) when the action of the emetic is over

perp. perpendicular; perpetual (Bonds)

Per Pro., **per pro.**, **per proc.**, **P.P.**, **p.p** or **p.pro.** (per procurationem)(Lat.) by proxy; by authorized agency (cf. v.n.)

per proc., Per Pro., per pro., P.P., p.p. or **p.pro.** (per procurationem)(Lat.) by proxy; by authorized agency (cf. v.n.)
Pers Personnel (Mil.)
Pers. or **Per.** Persia; Persian
pers. personal; personally
pers., Per. or **per.** person
Pers Car Personnel carrier
Pers O Personnel officer
Per Sec Personnel section
persp. perspective
pert. pertaining
Peruv. Peruvian
PES or **P.E.S.** Production Engineering Service [of the War Production Board]
pes. or **p.** peseta
Pesh. Peshitta (Syriac bible)
Pet. Peter
pet. petroleum
petn. petition
Petriburg. (Petriburgensis)(Lat.) of Petersburg
petrog. petrography
petrol. petrology
P Ex (Mil.), **P.E.** or **P.X.** Post exchange
P.Ex. or **P.X.** please exchange
p.ex. (par exemple)(Fr.), **e.c.** (exempli causa)(Lat.), **e.g., ex. gr.** (exempli gratia)(Lat), **f.e., f. Eks.** (for Eksempel) (Dan.), **f.i., n.p.** (na przykład)(Pol.), **t. ex.** (till exempel)(Swed.), **v.g.** (verbi gratia)(Lat.) or **z.B.** (zum Beispiel) (Ger.) for example; for instance
P.F. Procurator Fiscal (Law)
Pf., pf. or **perf.** perfect
Pf., pf. or **pfg.** pfennig
pf, pf. or **pfte.** (piano forte)(Ital.) soft, then loud
pf., perf. or **Pf.** perfect
pf., Pf. or **pfg.** pfennig
pf., pfd., Pr., pr. or **pref.** preferred
p.f. (più forte)(Ital.) louder (Music); power factor
P.F.A. Pastoral Finance Association [Ltd.] (Australia); Private Fliers Association
P.F.C., Pfc., Pvt 1 cl or **Pvt. (1st cl.)** Private, first class
pfd., pf., Pr., pr. or **pref.** preferred
P.F.E. Pacific Fruit Express
pfg., Pf. or **pf.** pfennig
P.F.S.A., p.f.s.a. (pour faire ses adieux) (Fr.), **p.d.a.** (pour dire adieu)(Fr.), **P.P.C., p.p.c.** (pour prendre congé) (Fr.), **T.T.L.** or **t.t.l.** to take leave; to say good-bye
pfte., pf or **pf.** (piano forte)(Ital.) soft, then loud
P.F.V. or **p.f.v.** (pour faire visite)(Fr.) to make a call
p.f.v. or **P.F.V.** (pour faire visite)(Fr.) to make a call
pfx. or **pref.** prefix
PG general public-service [radio station]
P.G. Paris granite (Ceram.); Past Grand (Freemasonry); paying guest
P.G. or **Ph.G.** German Pharmacopeia
Pg., Port. or **Ptg.** Portugal; Portuguese
P.G.A. Professional Golfers' Association (Brit.)
P.G.A.A. Professional Golfers Association of America
P.G.A.D. Past Grand Arch Druidess
Pg. B., Pd. B., Pe. B., Ped. B. (Pedagogiae Baccalaureus)(Lat.), **B. Pd., B. Pe., B. Pg.** (Baccalaureus Pedagogiae) (Lat.), **B. Py.** or **Py. B.** Bachelor of Pedagogy
P.G.D. Past Grand Deacon (Freemasonry)
Pg.D., Pd.D., Pe.D., Ped.D. (Pedagogiae Doctor)(Lat.), **D.Pd., D.Pe., D.Ped., D.Pg.** (Doctor Pedagogiae)(Lat.), **D.Py.** or **Py.D.** Doctor of Pedagogy
P.G.M. Past Grand Master (Freemasonry)
Pg.M., Pd.M., Pe.M., Ped.M. (Pedagogiae Magister)(Lat.), **M.Pd., M.Pe., M.Ped., M.Pg.** (Magister Pedagogiae)(Lat.), **M.Py.** or **Py.M.** Master of Pedagogy
Pgn Co Pigeon company (Mil.)
p.g.t. per gross ton
P.H. Post hospital; public health
Ph phenyl (Chem.)
Ph. pharmacopeia
Ph. or **Phil.** Philip
Ph., Phil. or **Phila.** Philadelphia
ph. phase; phone
P.H.A. Physicians Health Association
Phar., phar., Pharm. or **pharm.** pharmaceutical; pharmacist; pharmacopoeia; pharmacy
Phar., phar., Pharm., pharm., Pharmacol. or **pharmacol.** pharmacology
phar., Phar., Pharm. or **pharm.** pharmaceutical; pharmacist; pharmacopoeia; pharmacy
Phar. B., Ph. B., Phm. B. (Pharmaciae Baccalaureus)(Lat.), **B. of Pharm.** or **B.P.** (Baccalaureus Pharmaciae)(Lat.) Bachelor of Pharmacy
Phar. C. or **Ph.C.** Pharmaceutical Chemist
Phar. D., Pharm. D., Ph.D. (Pharmaciae Doctor)(Lat.) or **D.P.** Doctor of Pharmacy
Phar. G., G.P., G.Ph. Ph.G. or **Phm.G.** Graduate in Pharmacy
Phar. M., Pharm. M. (Pharmaciae Magister)(Lat.), **M.Ph.** or **M.Pharm.** Master of Pharmacy
Pharm., pharm., Phar. or **phar.** pharmaceutical; pharmacist; pharmacopoeia; pharmacy
Pharm., pharm., Phar., phar., Pharmacol. or **pharmacol.** pharmacology
pharm., Phar., phar. or **Pharm.** pharmaceutical; pharmacist; pharmacopoeia; pharmacy
pharm., Phar., phar., Pharm., Pharmacol. or **pharmacol.** pharmacology
Pharmacol., pharmocal., Phar., phar., Pharm. or **pharm.** pharmacology
Pharm. D., Phar. D., Ph. D. (Pharmaciae Doctor)(Lat.) or **D.P.** Doctor of Pharmacy
Pharm. M., Phar. M. (Pharmaciae Magister)(Lat.) **M.Ph.** or **M.Pharm.** Master of Pharmacy

Ph.B., P.B. (Philosophiae Baccalaureus) (Lat.), **B.P., B.Ph.** or **B.Phil.** (Baccalaureus Philosophiae)(Lat.) Bachelor of Philosophy
Ph.B., P.B. (Pharmacopoeia Britannica) (Lat.), **B.P., B.Ph.** or **Brit.Pharm.** British Pharmacopoeia
Ph. B., Phar. B., Phm. B. (Pharmaciae Baccalaureus)(Lat.), **B. of Pharm.** or **B.P.** (Baccalaureus Pharmaciae)(Lat.) Bachelor of Pharmacy
Ph.B. in B.A. Bachelor of Philosophy in Business Administration
Ph.B. in J. Bachelor of Philosophy in Journalism
Ph.B. in Sp. Bachelor of Philosophy in Speech
ph. bz. phosphor bronze
Ph.C. Philosopher of Chiropractic
Ph.C. or **Phar.C.** Pharmaceutical Chemist
P.H.D., D.P.H. or **Dr.P.H.** Doctor of Public Health
Ph. D., P.D. (Philosophiae Doctor)(Lat.), **D.P., D. Ph., D. Phil.** or **Dr. Phil.** (Doctor Philosophiae)(Lat) Doctor of Philosophy
Ph.D., Phar.D., Pharm. D. (Pharmaciae Doctor)(Lat.) or **D.P.** Doctor of Pharmacy
Ph.D. in Ed. Doctor of Philosophy in Education
Ph.G., G.P., G.Ph., Phar. G. or **Phm. G.** Graduate in Pharmacy
Ph.G. or **P.G.** German Pharmacopeia
P.H.I. Public Health Institute
Phil. Philippians (New Testament); Philippine; Philippines
Phil. or Ph. Philip
Phil., Ph. or **Phila.** Philadelphia
Phil., phil., Philos. or **philos.** philosopher; philosophical; philosophy
Phil. or **Philem.** Philemon
phil., Phil., Philos. or **philos.** philosopher; philosophical; philosophy
phil. or **philol.** philological; philologist; philology
Phila., Ph. or **Phil.** Philadelphia
Philem. or **Phil.** Philemon
Phil.L.D. (Philologiae Lituanicae Doctor) (Lat.) Doctor of Lithuanian Philology
philol. or **phil.** philological; philologist; philology
Philos., Phil., phil. or **philos.** philosopher; philosophical; philosophy
philos., Phil., phil. or **Philos.** philosopher; philosophical; philosophy
Phil. Soc. Philosophical Society
Phil. Soc. or **Ph. Soc.** Philological Society
Ph.L. Licentiate of Pharmacy; Licenciate in Philosophy
Ph.M. (Philosophiae Magister)(Lat.) or **M. Ph.** Master of Philosophy
Phm. B., Phar. B., Ph. B. (Pharmaciae Baccalaureus)(Lat.), **B. of Pharm.** or **B. P.** (Baccalaureus Pharmaciae) (Lat.) Bachelor of Pharmacy
Phm. G., G.P., G.Ph., Ph.G. or **Phar.G.** Graduate in Pharmacy
Phoen. Phoenician
phon. or **phonet.** phonetic; phonetics
phon. or **phonol.** phonology
phonet. or **phon.** phonetic; phonetics
phonog. phonography
phonol. or **phon.** phonology
phot. photogravure; photogravures
phot., photo. or **photog.** photograph; photographic; photographs; photography
photog., phot. or **photo.** photograph; photographic; photographs; photography
photom. photometrical; photometry
Photo Sec Photographic section
Photo Sq Photographic squadron
p.h.p. packing house products
Phr. or **phr.** phrase
phr. phraseology
phr. or **Phr.** phrase
phren. or **phrenol.** phrenological; phrenology
phrenol. or **phren.** phrenological; phrenology
PHS or **P.H.S.** Public Health Service
P.H.S. Pennsylvania Historical Society; Presbyterian Historical Society
Ph. Soc. or **Phil. Soc.** Philological Society
Phys., phys. or **physiol.** physiological; physiology
phys. physical; physician; physicist; physics
phys. & surg. or **P. and S.** physicians and surgeons
phys. chem. physical chemistry
phys. chem. or **physiol. chem.** physiological chemistry
physiog. physiography
physiol. physiologist
physiol., Phys. or **phys.** physiological; physiology
physiol. chem. or **phys. chem.** physiological chemistry
phys. sci. physical sciences
phytogeog. phytogeography
P. I. Philippine Islands; Phonographic Institute; Photographic Institute; protamine insulin
P.I. (point initial)(Fr.) or **IP** (Mil.) Initial point
Pi. or **pias.** piaster; piasters
P.I.A. Pine Institute of America
P.I.A.N.C. Permanent International Association of Navigation Congresses
P.I.A.R.C. Permanent International Association of Road Congresses
pias. or **Pi.** piaster; piasters
PIAT or **piat** projector infantry antitank
PIB or **P.I.B.** Plant Industry Bureau
P.I.B.A.C. Permanent International Bureau of Analytical Chemistry
P.I.C.I.M. Permanent International Commission on Industrial Medicine
pict. pictorial
Pil., pil. (pilula, pilulae)(Lat.) or **Bol.** (bolus, boli)(Lat.) pill; pills
pinx., pinxt., pnxt. or **pxt.** (pinxit)(Lat.) he or she painted it (cf. del.; fec.)
Pion (Mil.) or **pion.** pioneer
P.I.R.A. Prison Industries Reorganization Administration

pizz. (pizzicato)(Ital.) plucked by the fingers instead of being played with the bow; also, a passage so played (Music)
P.J. police justice; presiding judge; probate judge
PJBD or **P.J.B.D.** Permanent Joint Board on Defense (U.S. and Can.)
pk (Mil.) or **pk.** pack
pk. peak, peck
pk. or **pk** (Mil.) pack
pk. or **Prk** (Mil.) park
pkg. or **pkge.** package
pkg. or **pkgs.** packages
pkge. or **pkg.** package
pkgs. or **pkg.** packages
Pkmr Packmaster (Mil.)
Pkr (Mil.) or **pkr.** packer
pkr. or **Pkr** (Mil.) packer
pks. packs; parks; pecks
pkt. packet
Pk Tn Pack train (Mil.)
Pk Tr Pack troop
pkts. packets
PKV peak kilovolts
PL Post laundry
P.L. (Pharmacopoeia Londinensis)(Lat.) London Pharmacopoeia; Poet Laureate; Primrose League (Brit.)
P.L. or **p.l.** perception of light
Pl. Paul
pl., L. or **l.** (locus)(Lat.) place
pl., p. or **plt.** plate
pl., pla. (placitum, placita)(Lat.), **D.** or **d.** decree, decrees; decision; decisions (Law)
pl., pll., pls. or **plts.** plates
pl., plu. or **plur.** plural
p.l. pamphlet laws; partial loss (Ins.); preliminary leaf or leaves; proportional logarithm; public laws; public liability
p.l. or **P.L.** perception of light
p/l, P. and L., p. and l. or **P. & L.** profit and loss
P.L.A. Port of London Authority
pla., pl. (placitum, placita)(Lat.), **D.** or **d.** decree; decrees; decision; decisions (Law)
p.l. & p.d. public liability and property damage (Insurance)
P.L. & R. Postal Laws and Regulations
Plat (Mil.) or **plat.** platoon
plat. platform
plat. or **Plat** (Mil.) platoon
Plat Comdr Platoon commander
Plat Hq Platoon headquarters
P.L.B. Poor Law Board
plbg. plumbing
plbr. plumber
P.L.C. Poor Law Commissioner or Commissioners
plen. plenipotentiary
plff., plf. or **pltff.** plaintiff
pll., pl., pls. or **plts.** plates
Pl.-N. place name
PLPB or **P.L.P.B.** Petroleum Labor Policy Board
pls., pl., pll. or **plts.** plates
Pl.Sgt. Platoon Sergeant
plstr. plasterer
plt., p. or **pl.** plate
pltff., plf. or **plff.** plaintiff
pltffs. plaintiffs
plts., pl., pll. or **pls.** plates
plu., pl. or **plur.** plural
plup. or **plupf.** pluperfect
plur. plurality
plur., pl. or **plu.** plural
PM (Mil.) **P.M.** or **G.P.M.** (Grand prévôt militaire)(Fr.) Provost marshal
PM., Paym., Paymtr., Payr. or **P.M.** Paymaster
PM. or **P.M.** Postmaster
P.M. Pacific Mail; Past Master (Freemasonry); Past midshipman; Police Magistrate; Prime Minister
P.M., Paym., Paymtr., Payr. or **PM.** Paymaster
P.M., PM (Mil.) or **G.P.M.** (Grand prévôt militaire)(Fr.) Provost marshal
P.M. or **PM.** Postmaster
P.M., P-M or **p-m** phase modulation (Radio)
P.M. or **p.m.** (post mortem)(Lat.) after death; (post meridiem)(Lat.) after midday (cf. aftn.)
P.M., Pon. Max. or **Pont. Max.** Pontifex Maximus
P/M or **P/m** put of more (Stock Exchange)
P-M, P.M. or **p-m** phrase modulation (Radio)
Pm., pm. or **prem.** premium
P/m or **P/M** put of more (Stock Exchange)
pm. or **p.** premolar (Dentistry)
pm., pam., Pamph., pamph. or **pph.** pamphlet
pm., Pm. or **prem.** premium
p.m. or **P.M.** (post mortem)(Lat.) after death; (post meridiem)(Lat.) after noon (cf. aftn.)
p-m, P.M. or **P-M** phrase modulation (Radio)
P.M.A. Pure Milk Association
P.M.B polymorphonuclear basophil leucocytes
P.M.C. Pennsylvania Military College
P.M.E. polymorphonuclear eosinophil leukocytes
PMG Provost Marshal General
P.M.G. Postmaster General
P.M.G. or **Paym.-Gen.** Paymaster General
P.M.G.D. Provost Marshal General's Department
P.M.I. point of maximal impulse
pmk. postmark
pmkd. postmarked
P. mks. Polish marks
P.M.N. polymorphonuclear neutrophil leukocytes
P.M.O. Principal medical officer (Brit.)
p.m.r. point of minimum radius [of a curve]

P.M.S. President Miniature Society
P.M.S. & T. Professor of Military Science and Tactics
Pmt (Mil.), **payt., pt.** or **pymt.** payment
P.N. percussion note
P/N or **p.n.** promissory note
p.n. or **P/N** promissory note
P.N.C.S. Post noncommissioned staff
P.N.E.U. Parents' National Education Union (Brit.)
pneum. pneumatic; pneumatics
p.n.g. (persona non grata)(Lat.) unacceptable person
pntr. painter
pnxt., pinx., pinxt. or **pxt.** (pinxit)(Lat.) he or she painted it (cf. del.; fec.)
P.O. (Professor Ordinarius)(Lat.) Ordinary Professor; Province of Ontario
P.O. (Presbyteri Oratorii)(Lat.), **Cong. Orat., Congr. Orat.** or **C. Orat.** (Congregatio Oratorii)(Lat.) Congregation of the Oratory of St. Philip Neri; Fathers of the Oratory; Oratorians
P.O. or **p.o.** personnel officer; petty officer; postal order; post office; public office or officer
Po polonium (Chem.)
po. put out (Baseball)
po. or **p.** pole
po., Pt (Mil.) or **pt.** point
p.o. or **P.O.** personnel officer; petty officer; postal order; post office; public office or officer
p.o.a.s. printed on ass's skin
P.O.B. or **p.o.b.** post-office box
p.o.c. port of call (Com.)
Pocil. (pocillum)(Lat.) small cup
Pocul. (poculum)(Lat.) cup
P.O.D. Post Office Department
P.O.D. or **p.o.d.** pay on delivery
poet. poetic; poetical; poetry
P. of H. Patrons of Husbandry
P. of L. Port of London
Pol. Poland; Polish
pol. polish; polished
pol. or **polit.** political; politics
Pol.Econ., pol.econ., Polit.Econ. or **polit. econ.** political economy
pol.econ., Pol.Econ., Polit.Econ. or **polit. econ.** political economy
polit. or **pol.** political; politics
Polit.Econ., Pol.Econ., pol.econ. or **polit. econ.** political economy
polit.econ., Pol.Econ., pol.econ. or **Polit. Econ.** political economy
poly. polytechnic
pom. or **pomol.** pomological
P.O.M.O. post-office money order
pomol. or **pom.** pomological
pomp. (pomposo)(Ital.) grandiose; pompous (Music) (cf. maes.)
Pon (Mil.) or **pont.** pontoon
Pond., P. or **p.** (pondere)(Lat.) by weight
Pon. Max., P.M. or **Pont. Max.** Pontifex Maximus
pont. or **Pon** (Mil.) pontoon
Pont. Max., P.M. or **Pon. Max.** Pontifex Maximus
p.° nto. (peso neto)(Span.), **nt.wt.** or **n.wt.** net weight
P.O.O. Principal Ordnance Officer
P.O.O. or **p.o.o.** post-office order (Brit.)
p.o.o. or **P.O.O.** post-office order (Brit.) (cf. P.O.M.O.)
P.O.P. printing-out paper (Photog.)
pop. popular; popularly
pop. or **p.** population
pop. ed. popular edition
P.O.R. or **p.o.r.** payable on receipt; pay on return (Express)
por. (porównaj)(Pol.), **cf., comp., compar., conf.** (confer)(Lat.), **cp., jf., jfr.** (jaevnør)(Dan.), (jämför)(Swed.), **sml.** (sammenlign)(Dan.) or **vgl.** (vergleiche) (Ger.) compare
por., eff. (effigies)(Lat.) or **port.** portrait; portraits
p.o.r. or **P.O.R.** payable on receipt; pay on return (Express)
p.o.r.p. Printed on rice paper
Port., Pg. or **Ptg.** Portugal; Portuguese
port., eff. (effigies)(Lat.) or **por.** portrait; portraits
Port. E. Af. Portuguese East Africa
Port. W. Af. Portuguese West Africa
pos. or **posit.** positive
pos., posn. or **posit.** position
pos. or **poss.** possession
pos., poss. or **possess.** possessive
P.O.S.B. Post-Office Savings Bank
posit. or **pos.** positive
posit., pos. or **posn.** position
posn., pos. or **posit.** position
poss. possible; possibly
poss. or **pos.** possession
poss., pos. or **possess.** possessive
possess., pos. or **poss.** possessive
post. postal
post.rcts. postal receipts
Post Sec Postal section
pot. potential; potter; pottery (cf. fict.)
pow., P (Elec.), **p., pr.** or **pwr.** power
pow. or **pulv.** (pulvis)(Lat.) powder
PP. (Patres)(Lat.) Fathers (Eccl.)
PP., P.P. (Piissimus)(Lat.), **SS.** or **S.S.** (Sanctissimus)(Lat.) Most Holy
P.P. (Pater Patriae)(Lat.) Father of His Country; past president; (Pastor Pastorum)(Lat.) Shepard of the Shepards (Papal title)
P.P., C.P. or **C.S.P.** (Congregatio Sancti Pauli) Congregation of St. Paul the Apostle; Missionary Society of St. Paul the Apostle; Society of St. Paul; Paulist Fathers; Paulists
P.P., Per Pro., per pro., per proc., p.p. or **p.pro.** (per procurationem)(Lat.) by proxy; by authorized agency (cf. v.n.)
P.P., PP. (Piissimus)(Lat.), **SS.** or **S.S.** (Sanctissimus)(Lat.) Most Holy

P.P. or **p.p.** parcel post; parish priest; play or pay; percussion primer
P.P., p.p., fco., fr. (franco)(Ital.), (franko) (Ger.) or **ppd.** postpaid
P-P pallagra-preventive factor
P.p. (punctum proximum)(Lat.) near point
pp. (pianissimo)(Ital.) very softly (Music)
pp., p., S. (Sider)(Dan.), **sid,** (sidor)(Swed.) or **SS.** (Seiten)(Ger.) pages
pp., P.P., p.p., pa. p. or **pa. ppl.** past participle
pp. or **priv. pr.** privately printed
p.p. (praemissis praemittendis)(Lat.) omitting preliminaries; part paid; personal property; picked ports
p.p., Per Pro., per pro., per proc., P.P. or **p.pro.** (per procurationem)(Lat.) by proxy; by authorized agency (cf. v.n.)
p.p., pres.part. or **pr.p.** present participle
P.P.A. Professional Photographers' Association [of Great Britain and Ireland] (now Institute of British Photographers); Professional Pilots Association
P.p.a. (phiala prius agitata)(Lat.) the bottle having first been shaken (Pharm.)
p.p.a. per power of attorney
PP.C. or **P.C.** (Patres Conscripti)(Lat.) Conscript Fathers
P.P.C., p.p.c. (pour prendre congé)(Fr.), **p.d.a.** (pour dire adieu)(Fr.), **P.F.S.A., p.f.s.a.** (pour faire ses adieux)(Fr.), **T.T.L.** or **t.t.l.** to take leave; to say good-bye
p.p.c. picture post card
p.p.c., P.P.C. (pour prendre conge)(Fr.), **p.d.a** (pour dire adieu)(Fr.), **P.F.S.A., p.f.s.a.** (pour faire ses adieux)(Fr.), **T.T.L.** or **t.t.l.** to take leave; to say goodbye
P.P.D. purified protein derivative
ppd. prepaid
ppd., fco., fr. (franco)(Ital.), (franko)(Ger.) **P.P,** or **p.p.** postpaid
pp.[do] (próximo pasado)(Span.), **utl., ulto.** (ultimo)(Lat.) or **v.M.** (vorigen Monats)(Ger.) last month
pph., pam., Pamph., pamph. or **pm.** pamphlet
P.P.I. or **p.p.i.** parcel post insured; policy proof of interest (Marine Ins.)
p.p.i. or **P.P.I.** parcel post insured; policy proof of interest (Marine Ins.)
ppl., p. or **part.** participle
ppl. adj., p.a. or **part. adj.** participial adjective
ppm or **p.p.m.** parts per million
ppp. (pianississimo)(Ital.) as soft as possible (Music)
P.P.R.I. Pan Pacific Research Institution
p.pro., Per Pro., per pro., per proc., P.P. or **p.p.** (per procurationem)(Lat.) by proxy; by authorized agency (cf. v.n.)
P.P.S. or **p.p.s.** (post postscriptum)(Lat.) additional postscript; Prickly Pear Selection (Queensland)
p.p.s. or **P.P.S.** (post postscriptum)(Lat.) additional postscript; Prickly Pear Selection (Queensland)
ppt. precipitate; prompt
ppt. (praeparatus)(Lat.) or **prep.** prepared
P.P.U. Pan-Pacific Union
P.P.W. Public Watering Place (Australia)
P.Q. permeability quotient
P.Q., Q or **Que.** Province of Quebec
p.q. previous question
PR or **P/R** payroll
P.R. Paradise Regained; Parliamentary Reports; press release; proportional representation; Porto or Puerto Rico; (populus Romanus)(Lat.) Roman people
P.R. or **p.r.** prize ring
P/R or **PR** payroll
Pr praseodymium (Chem.); propyl (Chem.)
Pr. presbyopia
Pr., P., p. or **pr.** priest; prince
Pr., pf., pfd., pr. or **pref.** preferred
Pr. or **pr.** prism
Pr. or **prim.** primitive
Pr., Prov. or **Provenç.** Provençal
P.r. (punctum remotum)(Lat.) far point
pr. pair; printing paper; prior
pr., P (Elec.), **p., pow.** or **pwr.** power
pr., P., p. or **Pr.** priest; prince
pr., pc. or **pret.** (pretium, pretii)(Lat.) price; prices
pr. or **pdr.** pounder (as 12-pr. or 12-pdr.)
pr., pf., pfd., Pr. or **pref.** preferred
pr. or **Pr.** prism
pr. or **prep.** preposition
pr. or **pres.** present
pr., print. or **ptr.** printer
pr. or **pron.** pronoun; pronounced; pronunciation
pr. or **prop.** proposition
pr., Prov. or **prov.** province
pr. or **prs.** pairs
pr. or **prtd.** printed
p.r. (pro rata)(Lat.) in proportion
p.r. or **P.R.** prize ring
PRA or **P.R.A.** President's Reemployment Agreement; Public Roads Administration
P.R.A. President of the Royal Academy
P. rat. aetat. (pro ratione aetatis)(Lat.) in proportion to age
P.R.B. Pre-Raphaelite Brotherhood (Brit.)
Pr.Bk., P.B. or **B.C.P.** Prayer Book; Book of Common Prayer
P.R.C. (post Roman conditam)(Lat.) or **P.U.C.** (post urbem conditam)(Lat.) after the founding of Rome; after the founding of the city [of Rome] (cf. A.P.R.C.)
P.R.C.A. President of the Royal Cambrian Academy
Prcht (Mil.) Parachute
preb. prebend; prebendary
prec. preceding; precentor
pred. predication; predicative; predicatively; prediction
pred. or **P** (Logic) predicate

pref. preface; prefaced; prefatory; preference; prefixed
pref., pf., pfd., Pr. or **pr.** preferred
pref. or **pfx.** prefix
Pref. Ap. Prefect Apostolic
prehist. or **pre-hist.** prehistoric
prelim. preliminary
Prem. Premier (Govt.)
prem. (premier, première)(Fr.) or **p.** (primus)(Lat.) first (cf. imp.)
prem., Pm. or **pm.** premium
prep. preparation; preparatory; prepare (cf. ppt.)
prep. or **ppt.** (Praeparatus)(Lat.) prepared
prep. or **pr.** preposition
Pres. or **pres.** Presumptive
Pres., pres., P., p. or **Prest.** President
pres. presidency.
pres., P., p., Pres. or **Prest.** president
pres. or **pr.** present
pres. or **Pres.** presumptive
pres., Presdl. or **presdl.** presidential
Presb. Presbyter
Presbyt. or **Presb.** Presbyterian
Presdl., pres. or **presdl.** presidential
presdl., pres. or **Presdl.** presidential
pres.part., p.p. or **pr.p.** present participle
press., P (Physics) or **p.** pressure
Prest., P., p., Pres. or **pres.** President
pret. preterit
pret. (pretium, pretii)(Lat.), **pc.** or **pr.** price; prices
pre-Teut. pre-Teutonic
prev. previous; previously
P.R.F. Personnel Research Federation
P.R.H.A. President of the Royal Hibernian Academy
P.R.I. President of the Royal Institute [of Painters in Water Colours]
P.R.I.B.A. President of the Royal Institute of British Architects
prim. primary; primate
prim. or **Pr.** primitive
prin. principal; principals; principally; principle; principles
print., pr. or **ptr.** printer
print., prtg. or **ptg.** printing (cf. Aufl.)
Priv., priv., Pte., pte., Pvt (Mil.), **Pvt.** or **pvt.** private
priv. privately; privative
priv. pr. or **pp.** privately printed
Prk (Mil.) or **pk.** park
P.R.N. or **p.r.n.** (pro re nata)(Lat.) as circumstances may require (Pharm.)
Pro., p. or **pro.** professional
pro., p. or **Pro.** professional
pro., Prog. or **prog.** progressive
Prob. probate; probation
prob. probable; probably; problem
Proc. or **proc.** proclamation
proc. proceedings; process; proctor
proc. or **Proc.** proclamation
prod. produce; produced; producer; product
Prof. or **prof.** professor
prof. profession
prof. or **Prof.** professor
Prof. Eng. Professional Engineer
Prog., prog. or **pro.** progressive
prog. progress
prog., pro. or **Prog.** progressive
prom. promenade; promontory
pron. or **pr.** pronoun; pronounced; pronunciation
pron. or **pronom.** pronominal
pro. no. progressive number
pronom. or **pron.** pronominal
prop. proper; properly; property
prop. or **pr.** proposition
prop., propr. or **Pty.** proprietary
propr. proprietor
propr., prop. or **Pty.** proprietary
pros. prosody
Pros. Atty. prosecuting attorney
Prot. Protestant
Prot. Ap. or **P.A.** Prothonotary Apostolic
pro tem. or **p.t.** (pro tempore)(Lat.) for the time being; temporarily (cf. ad int.)
Prov. Provence; Proverbs (Bib.)
Prov., Pr. or **Provenç.** Provençal
Prov., pr. or **prov.** province
Prov. or **prov.** Provost
prov. proverbial; provident; provision; provisional
prov., pr. or **Prov.** province
prov. or **Prov.** Provost
prov. or **provinc.** provincial
prov. aws. provided always
Provenç., Pr. or **Prov.** Provençal
Prov. G.M. Provincial Grand Master (Freemasonry)
provinc. or **prov.** provincial
prox. (proximo)(Lat.) next; next month
prox. acc. (proxime accessit or accesserunt)(Lat.) he (she, they) came next [in a prize contest]
pr.p., p.p. or **pres.part.** present participle (cf. p.pr.)
pr.pf. prior preferred (Stocks)
P.R.R.I. Puerto or Porto Rico Regiment of Infantry
P.R.S. Pedic Research Society; President of the Royal Society (London); Protestant Reformation Society
prs. or **pr.** pairs
P.R.S.A. President of the Royal Scottish Academy
P.R.S.E. President of the Royal Society of Edinburgh
prsfdr. pressfeeder
prsmn. pressman
Pr.Spec. process specification
Pr. St. Private Statute
prtd. or **pr.** printed
prtg., print. or **ptg.** printing (cf. Aufl.)
Prus. or **Pruss.** Prussia; Prussian

P.R.V. or **p.r.v.** (pour rendre visite) (Fr.) to return a call

p.r.v. or **P.R.V.** (pour rendre visite) (Fr.) to return a call

PS (Mil.) or **P.S.** Philippine Scouts

P.S. Pastel Society; Police Sergeant; Privy Seal

P.S., P/S or **p.s.** public sale

P.S., P.s. (Postskriptum) (Dan.) or **p.s.** postscript

P.S. or **p.s.** Passed School [of Instruction] (Brit.); passenger steamer; permanent secretary; prompt side (Theat.)

P/S, P.S. or **p.s.** public sale

Ps. or **Psa.** Psalm

Ps., Psa. or **Pss.** Psalms

ps. or **pcs.** pieces

ps. or **pseud.** pseudonym; pseudonymous

ps- pseudo- (Chem.)

p.s., P.S. or **P/S** public sale

P.S.A. Photographic Society of America; Pleasant Sunday Afternoons [Society] (Brit); Poultry Science Association

P.S.A. or **p.s.a.** Passed the Royal Air Force Staff College (Brit.)

Psa. or **Ps.** Psalm

Psa., Ps. or **Pss.** Psalms

P.S.A.C. [Non-Member] Preferred Stock Advisory Committee

PSC or **P.S.C.** Public Service Commission

P.S.C. or **p.s.c.** Passed [the examination and scrutiny of the Military or Naval] Staff College (Brit.)

P.S.C.J. Society of the Priests of the Sacred Heart of Jesus

PSD Pistol sharpshooter, dismounted

P.S.E.A. Pacific Service Employees' Association

pseud. or **ps.** pseudonum; pseudonymous

psf pound or pounds per square foot

P.S.I. Pharmaceutical Society of Ireland

psi pound or pounds per square inch

psia pound or pounds per square inch absolute

P.S.M. (Pia Societas Missionum) (Lat.) Pious Society of Missions; Fathers of the Pious Society of Missions; Pallottine Fathers; Pallottini

P.S.P. (Poste sémaphorique) (Fr.) Signal station

P.S.P., Sch.P. (Patres Scholarum Piarum) (Lat.) or **C.R.S.P.** (Clericai Regulares Pauperum Matris Dei Scholarum Piarum) (Lat.) Clerks Regular of the Poor Men of the Mother of God for Pious Schools; Fathers of the Religious Schools; Piarists

PSS Postal Savings System

P.SS. or **p.ss.** postscripts

P.S.S. or **S.S.** (Presbyteri Sancti Sulpicii) (Lat.) Priests of the Society of St. Sulpice; Society of St. Sulpice; Fathers of St. Sulpice; Sulpicians

Pss., Ps. or **Psa.** Psalms

p.ss. or **P.SS.** postscripts

P.S.S.C., C.S.C.B. (Congregatio Missionarii Sancti Caroli Borromeo) (Lat.) or **M.S.C.** (Missionarii Sancti Caroli) Pious Society of St. Charles; Pious Society of Missionaries of St. Charles Borromeo; Missionaries of St. Charles; Society of Missionaries of St. Charles [Borromeo]

P.S.T. Pacific Standard Time; Provincial Standard Time (Can.)

psych. psychic; psychical

psychol. or **psych.** psychological; psychologist; psychology

P.T. Pacific Time; paying teller; physical training; pupil teacher; (Poste télégraphique) (Fr.) telegraph station

P.T. or **p.t.** post town; postal telegraph

Pt platinum (Chem.)

Pt (Mil.), **pt.** or **po.** point

Pt., P. or **pt.** port

pt., o. (octarius) (Lat.) or **p.** pint

pt., P. or **Pt.** port

pt., p., Abt. (Abteilung) (Ger.), **H., Hft.** (Heft) (Ger.), **Lfg.** (Lieferung) (Ger.), **liv.** (livraison) (Fr.), **T.** or **Th.** (Teil, Theil) (Ger.) part (cf. inst.; no.; sec.)

pt., p. or **pts.** pints

pt., payt., Pmt (Mil.) or **pymt.** payment

pt., po. or **Pt** (Mil.) point

p.t. private terms (Grain trade); privilege ticket

p.t. or **pro tem.** (pro tempore) (Lat.) for the time being; temporarily (cf. ad int.)

p.t. or **P.T.** post town; postal telegraph

P.T.A. (Poste téléphonique d'artillerie) (Fr.) Artillery telephone station; Parent-Teachers' Association

ptas. pesetas

ptbl. portable

P.T.C. postal telegraph cable

pt/disch port of discharge (Shipping)

pt/dstin port of destination (Shipping)

Pte., pte., Priv., priv., Pvt (Mil.), **Pvt.** or **pte.** private

Ptg., Pg. or **Port.** Portugal; Portuguese

ptg., print. or **prtg.** printing (cf. Aufl.)

Ptg.Std. Petrograd Standard (Timber)

P.T.I. (Poste téléphonique d'infantrie) (Fr.) Infantry telephone station

P.T.O., p.t.o., T.S.V.P., t.s.v.p. (tournez s'il vous plaît) (Fr.), **W.S.g.u.** or **w.S.g.u.** (weden Sie gefälligst um) (Ger.) turn over please (cf. T.O., v.s.)

pt.pf. participating preferred (Stocks)

ptr., pr. or **print.** printer

ptrnmkr. patternmaker

ptrs. printers

pts. parts

pts., p. or **pt.** pints

Pty., prop. or **propr.** proprietary

pub. public-house (Brit.)

pub., ed. (editus) (Lat.), **pubd., publ.** or **hrsg.** (herausgegeben) (Ger.) published

pub., éd. (éditeur) (Fr.), **publ., V.A.** (Verlags anstalt) (Ger.) or **V.B.** (Velagsbuchhandlung) (Ger.) publisher

pub. or **publ.** public; publication; publishing

pubd., ed. (editus)(Lat.), **pub., publ.** or **hrsg.** (herausgegeben)(Ger.) published

Pub. Doc. Public Document or Documents

publ., ed. (editus)(Lat.) **pub., pubd.** or **hrsg.** (herausgegeben)(Ger.) published

publ., éd. (éditeur)(Fr.), **pub., V.A.** (Verlagsanstalt)(Ger.) or **V.B.** (Verlagsbuchhandlung)(Ger.) publisher

publ. or **pub.** public; publication; publishing

PUC or **P.U.C.** Public Utilities Commission

P.U.C. (post urbem conditam)(Lat.) or **P.R.C.** (post Roman conditam)(Lat.) after the founding of the city [of Rome]; after the founding of Rome (cf. A.P.R.C.)

P.U.C. or **PUC** Public Utilities Commission

P.U.D. pick-up and delivery (Transportation)

Pulm. (pulmentum)(Lat.) gruel

pulv. pulverized

pulv. (pulvis)(Lat.) or **pow.** powder

pun. puncheon (Wine meas.)

punct. punctuation

P.U.R. Public Utilities Report

Pur Pursuit (Mil.)

pur. or **purch.** purchaser; purchasing

Purch.Clk. purchasing clerk

Pur Gp Pursuit group

pur.m. purchase money (Bonds)

Pur Sq Pursuit squadron

P.U.S., U.S.P. or **U.S. Pharm.** Pharmacopoeia of the United States

P.V. or **p.v.** priest-vicar

p.v. par value; post village (cf. p.t.); (papier vélin)(Fr.) vellum paper

p.v. or **P.V.** priest-vicar

Pvt (Mil.), **Pvt., pvt., Priv., priv., Pte.** or **pte.** private

Pvt 1 cl (Mil.), **Pfc., P.F.C.** or **Pvt. (1st cl.)** Private, first class

Pvt. (1st cl.), Pfc., P.F.C. or **Pvt 1 cl.** (Mil.) Private, first class

PW Prisoners of war

P.w. or **p.w.** packed weight (Transp.)

PWA or **P.W.A.** Public Works Administration (cf. FEAPW; WPA)

PWAHD or **P.W.A.H.D.** Public Works Administration Housing Division

PWAP or **P.W.A.P.** Public Works Art Projects

PWD or **P.W.D.** Public Works Department

PWEHC or **P.W.E.H.C.** Public Works Emergency Housing Corporation

PWELC or **P.W.E.L.C.** Public Works Emergency Leasing Corporation

P.W.P. Past Worthy Patriarch (Freemasonry); Past Worthy President

P.W.R. Police War Reserve

pwr., P (Elec.), **p., pow.** or **pr.** power

PWRCB or **P.W.R.C.B.** President's War Relief Control Board

P.W.T. Pacific War Time (cf. P.D.S.T.)

pwt. or **dwt.** (denarius weight) pennyweight

P.X., P.E. or **PEx** (Mil.) Post exchange

P.X. or **P.Ex.** please exchange

pxt., pinx., pinxt. or **pnxt.** (pinxit)(Lat.) he or she painted it (cf. del.; fec.)

Py Party (Mil.); pyridine; pyridyl (Chem.)

Py. B., B. Pd., B. Pe., B. Pg. (Baccalaureus Pedagogiae)(Lat.) **B. Py., Pd. B., Pe. B., Ped B. or Pg. B.** (Pedagogiae Baccalaureus)(Lat.) Bachelor of Pedagogy

Py.D., D.Pd., D.Pe., D.Ped., D.Pg. (Doctor Pedagogiae)(Lat.), **D.Py., Pd.D., Pe.D., Ped.D.** or **Pg.D.** (Pedagogiae Doctor) (Lat.) Doctor of Pedagogy

Py.M., M.Pd., M.Pe., M.Ped., M.Pg. (Magister Pedagogiae)(Lat.), **M.Py., Pd.M., Pe.M., Ped.M.** or **Pg.M.** (Pedagogiae Magister)(Lat.) Master of Pedagogy

pymt., payt., Pmt (Mil.) or **pt.** payment

pyro. or **pyrotech.** pyrotechnics

pyroelec. pyroelectricity

pyrotech. or **pyro.** pyrotechnics

ΦΑ (Phi Alpha) National undergraduate fraternity

ΦΑΔ (Phi Alpha Delta) Professional fraternity (Law)

ΦΑΓ (Phi Alpha Gamma) Professional fraternity (Medicine)

ΦΑΣ (Phi Alpha Sigma) Professional fraternity (Medicine)

ΦΑΤ (Phi Alpha Tau) National undergraduate fraternity (Public Speakers and Actors)

ΦΑΘ (Phi Alpha Theta) Honor society (History)

ΦΑΖ (Phi Alpha Zeta) National undergraduate fraternity

ΦΒ (Phi Beta) Professional sorority (Music and Drama)

ΦΒΔ (Phi Beta Delta) National undergraduate fraternity

ΦΒΓ (Phi Beta Gamma) Professional fraternity (Law)

ΦΒΚ (Phi Beta Kappa) Honor society (General)

ΦΒΠ (Phi Beta Pi) National fraternity (Medicine)

ΦΒΣ (Phi Beta Sigma) National undergraduate fraternity (Negroes)

ΦΧ (Phi Chi) Professional fraternity (Medicine)

ΦΧΘ (Phi Chi Theta) Professional sorority (Business Women)

ΦΔ (Phi Delta) National undergraduate sorority;

ΦΔΧ (Phi Delta Chi) Professional fraternity (Pharmaceutical Chemistry)

ΦΔΔ (Phi Delta Delta) Professional sorority (Law)

ΦΔΕ (Phi Delta Epsilon) National fraternity (Medicine)

ΦΔΓ (Phi Delta Gamma) National fraternity (Forensics)

ΦΔΚ (Phi Delta Kappa) National fraternity (Education)

ΦΔΜ (Phi Delta Mu) National undergraduate fraternity

ΦΔΦ (Phi Delta Phi) Professional fraternity (Law)
ΦΔΠ (Phi Delta Pi) Professional sorority (Physical Education)
ΦΔΘ (Phi Delta Theta) National undergraduate fraternity
ΦΕΚ (Phi Epsilon Kappa) Professional fraternity (Physical Education)
ΦΕΠ (Phi Epsilon Pi) National undergraduate fraternity
ΦΗ (Phi Eta) National graduate fraternity
ΦΗΣ (Phi Eta Sigma) Freshman honorary society
ΦΓΔ (Phi Gamma Delta) National undergraduate fraternity
ΦΓΝ (Phi Gamma Nu) Professional sorority (Commerce)
ΦΚ (Phi Kappa) National undergraduate fraternity
ΦΚΛ (Phi Kappa Lambda) Honor fraternity (Music)
ΦΚΝ (Phi Kappa Nu) National undergraduate fraternity
ΦΚΦ (Phi Kappa Phi) Honorary scholarship society
ΦΚΨ (Phi Kappa Psi) National undergraduate fraternity
ΦΚΣ (Phi Kappa Sigma) National undergraduate fraternity
ΦΚΤ (Phi Kappa Tau) National undergraduate fraternity
ΦΛΚ (Phi Lambda Kappa) Professional fraternity (Medicine)
ΦΛΘ (Phi Lambda Theta) National undergraduate fraternity
ΦΛΥ (Phi Lambda Upsilon) Honorary fraternity (Chemistry)
ΦΜ (Phi Mu) National undergraduate sorority
ΦΜΑ (Phi Mu Alpha) Professional fraternity (Music)
ΦΜΔ (Phi Mu Delta) National undergraduate fraternity
ΦΜΓ (Phi Mu Gamma) Professional sorority (Fine Arts)
ΦΩΠ (Phi Omega Pi) National undergraduate sorority
ΦΠΦ (Phi Pi Phi) National undergraduate fraternity
ΦΨ (Phi Psi) Professional fraternity (Textile Arts)
ΦΡΠ (Phi Rho Pi) National honor society (Forensics)(Junior Colleges)
ΦΡΣ (Phi Rho Sigma) National fraternity (Medicine)
ΦΣ (Phi Sigma) Professional society (Biology)
ΦΣΔ (Phi Sigma Delta) National undergraduate fraternity
ΦΣΕ (Phi Sigma Epsilon) Professional fraternity (Education)
ΦΣΓ (Phi Sigma Gamma) Professional fraternity (Osteopathy)
ΦΣΙ (Phi Sigma Iota) Honorary society (Romance Languages)
ΦΣΚ (Phi Sigma Kappa) National undergraduate fraternity
ΦΣΜ (Phi Sigma Mu) Professional and honorary fraternity (Public School Music)
ΦΣΝ (Phi Sigma Nu) National fraternity (Junior Colleges)
ΦΣΠ (Phi Sigma Pi) Professional fraternity (Education)
ΦΣΣ (Phi Sigma Sigma) Non-sectarian undergraduate society for women
ΦΘΚ (Phi Theta Kappa) Junior college sorority
ΦΘΨ (Phi Theta Psi) National undergraduate fraternity
ΦΘΥ (Phi Theta Upsilon) Professional fraternity (Optometry)
ΦΥΟ (Phi Upsilon Omicron) Professional sorority (Home Economics)

ΠΒΦ (Pi Beta Phi) National undergraduate sorority
ΠΔΕ (Pi Delta Epsilon) Honor society (College Journalism)
ΠΔΝ (Pi Delta Nu) Professional sorority (Chemistry)
ΠΔΦ (Pi Delta Phi) National undergraduate fraternity (French)
ΠΔΘ (Pi Delta Theta) Professional sorority (Education)
ΠΓΜ (Pi Gamma Mu) National honor society (Social Science)
ΠΚΑ (Pi Kappa Alpha) National undergraduate fraternity
ΠΚΔ (Pi Kappa Delta) Honor society (Forensics)
ΠΚΛ (Pi Kappa Lambda) Honorary society (Music)
ΠΚΦ (Pi Kappa Phi) National undergraduate fraternity
ΠΚΣ (Pi Kappa Sigma) Professional sorority (Education)
ΠΛΦ (Pi Lambda Phi) National undergraduate fraternity
ΠΛΘ (Pi Lambda Theta) National sorority (Education)
ΠΜΕ (Pi Mu Epsilon) Honor society (Mathematics)
ΠΩΠ (Pi Omega Pi) Honor society (Business Education)
ΠΣΑ (Pi Sigma Alpha) Honor society (Political Science)
ΠΣΓ (Pi Sigma Gamma) National undergraduate sorority
ΠΤΣ (Pi Tau Sigma) Honor fraternity (Mechanical Engineering))
ΠΥΡ (Pi Upsilon Rho) Professional fraternity (Homeopathy)

ΨΧ (Psi Chi) Honor society (Psychology)
ΨΩ (Psi Omega) Professional fraternity (Dentistry)
ΨΥ (Psi Upsilon) National undergraduate fraternity

Q

Q queen (Chess)
Q., P.Q. or **Que.** Quebec [Province]; Province of Quebec
Q., q., qn., Qu., qu. or **ques.** question
Q., q., Q°, qto., 4°, 4to. or **4to** quarto (folded) in 4)
Q., q., Qr., qr., qrtly., qu., quar. or **quart.** quarterly

Q., q., Qu., qu., Qy. or **qy.** query
Q., q., Qu., qu., R., r., Reg. or **reg.** (regina) (Lat.) Queen
q. squall
q., Q., qn., Qu., qu. or **ques.** question
q., Q., Q°, qto., 4°, 4to. or **4to** quarto
q., Q., Qr., qr., qrtly., qu., quar. or **quart.** quarterly
q., Q., Qu., qu., Qy. or **qy.** query
q., Q., Qu., qu., R., r., Reg. or **reg.** (regina) (Lat) Queen
q. or **ql.** quintal (cf. cwt.)
q., Qr. or **qr.** quire
q., Qr., qr., qt., qtr., qu., quar. or **quart.** quarter
q., qt., qu. or **quar.** quart
q. or **qu.** quasi
q., qua., qr. (quadrans)(Lat.), **F., f.** or **far.** farthing
Q.A.B. Queen Anne's Bounty
Q.A.I.M.N.S. Queen Alexandra's Imperial Military Nursing Service
Q.A.L.A.S. Qualified Associate, Land Agents' Society (Brit.)
Q.A.R.N.N.S. Queen Alexandra's Royal Naval Nursing Service
QB queen's bishop (chess)
QB or **q.b.** quick break
Q.B. Queen's Bays (2nd Dragoon Guards)
Q.B. or **B.R.** (Banco Reginae)(Lat.) Queen's Bench
q.b. or **QB** quick break
Q.B.D. Queen's Bench Division (Law)
QBP queen's bishop's pawn (Chess)
Q.B.S.M. or **q.b.s.m.** (que besa su mano) (Span.) who kisses your hand; respectfully yours (to a man)
Q.B.S.P. or **q.b.s.p.** (que besa sus pies) (Span.) who kisses your feet; yours respectfully (to a lady)
QC, Q.C., QMC or **Q.M.C.** Quartermaster Corps
Q.C. Queen's College (Oxford); Queen's Council or Counsel
Q.C., QC, QMC or **Q.M.C.** Quartermaster Corps
Q.d., q.d. or **q.i.d.** (quater die, quater in die) (Lat.) four times a day (cf. q.d.s.)
q.d. (quasi dicat)(Lat.) as if he should say; (quasi dixisset)(Lat.) as if he had said
q.d. (quaque die)(Lat.), **O.d., o.d.** (omni die)(Lat.) or **Quotid.** (quotidie)(Lat.) every day; daily (cf. p.d.; s.i.d.)
q.d., Q.d. or **q.i.d.** (quater die, quater in die) (Lat.) four times a day (cf. q.d.s.)
q.d.a. quantity discount agreement
Q.D.D.G. (que de Dios goce)(Span.) may he be in God's keeping (cf. Q.D.G.; Q.E.G.E.; Q.E.P.D.)
Q.D.G. (que Dios guarde)(Span.) may God keep him (cf. Q.D.D.G.; Q.E.G.E.; Q.E.P.D.)
q.d.s. (quater die sumendum)(Lat) to be taken four times a day (cf.q.i.d.)
q.e. (quod est)(Lat.) which is
Q.E.D. or **q.e.d.** (quod erat demonstrandum) (Lat.) which was to be demonstrated (cf. i.q.e.d.; Q.E.F.; Q.E.I.)
q.e.d. or **Q.E.D.** (quod erat demonstrandum) (Lat.) which was to be demonstrated (cf. Q.E.F.; i.q.e.d.)
Q.E.F. or **q.e.f.** (quod erat faciendum)(Lat.) which was to be done (cf. I.Q.E.D.; Q.E.F.; Q.E.I.)
q.e.f. or **Q.E.F.** (Quod erat faciendum)(Lat.) which was to be done (cf. Q.E.D.)
Q.E.G.E. (que en Gloria esté)(Span.) may he be in Glory (cf. Q.D.D.G.; Q.D.G.; QE.P.D.)
Q.E.I. or **q.e.i.** (quod erat inveniendum) (Lat.) which was to be found out (cf. Q.E.D.; Q.E.F.)
Q.E.P.D. (que en paz descanse)(Span.), **E.P.D.** (en paz descanse)(Span.) or **R.I.P.** may he rest in peace (cf. B.Q.; H.R.I.P.; Q.D.D.G.; Q.D.G.; Q.E.G.E.)
Q.F. quick fire; quick-firing [gun] (cf. R.F.)
q.4h., Q.Q.H., Q.q.h. or **q.q.h.** (quaque quatra hora)(Lat.) every fourth hour
Q.G. (Quartier général)(Fr.), **H., Hdqrs., hdqrs., H.Q., Hq.** or **h.q.** headquarters (cf. G.H.Q.)
Q.G.A. (Quartier général d'armée)(Fr.), **AHQ** (Mil.), **A. H. Q.** or **A. O.** (Armee Obercommando)(Ger.) Army headquarters
Q.G.B. (Quartier général de brigade)(Fr.) Brigade headquarters
Q.G.C. (Quartier général de corps d'armée) (Fr.) Army corps headquarters
Q.G.D. (Quartier Général de division)(Fr.), **DHQ** (Mil.), **D.H.Q.** or **Div Hq** (Mil.) Division headquarters
Q.h., q.h., Qq.hor., qq.hor. (quaque hora) (Lat.), **Omn.hor.** or **omn.hor.** (omni hora)(Lat.) every hour
Q.H.P. Queen's Honorary Physician
q.i.d., Q.d. or **q.d.** (quater in die, quater die)(Lat.) four times a day (cf.q.d.s.)
QKt. queen's knight (Chess)
QKtP queen's knight's pawn (Chess)
Q.l., q.l., q.lib. (quantum libet)(Lat.), **Q.p., q.p., q.pl.** (quantum placeat)(Lat.), **Q.v.** or **q.v.** (quantum vis)(Lat.) as much as you please; as much as you will (cf. ad.lib.; Q.s.)
ql. or **q.** quintal (cf. cwt.)
q.l., Q.l., q.lib. (quantum libet)(Lat.), **Q.p., q.p., q.pl.** (quantum placeat)(Lat.), **Q.v.** or **q.v.** (quantum vis)(Lat.) as much as you please; as much as you will (cf. ad lib.; Q.s.)
q. lib., Q.l., q.l. (quantum libet)(Lat.), **Q.p., q.p., q. pl.** (quantum placeat)(Lat.), **Q.v.** or **q.v.** (quantum vis)(Lat.) as much as you please; as much as you will (cf. ad lib.; Q.s.)
qlty. quality
QM (Mil.), **Q.M.** or **Qmr.** Quartermaster
qm. (quomodo)(Lat.) how; by what means
qm. (quondam)(Lat.) or **f.d.** (för detta) (Swed.) formerly
qm. (quondam)(Lat.) or **fhv.** (forhenvaerende)(Dan.) former; late (cf. dec.)
q.m. (quaque mane)(Lat.), **O.m.** or **o.m.** (omni mane)(Lat.) every morning
Q.M.A.A.C. Queen Mary's Army Auxiliary Corps (Women's Army Auxiliary Corps) (cf. W.A.C.)
QM Bn Armd Quartermaster battalion armored
QMC, QC, Q.C. or **Q.M.C.** Quartermaster Corps

Q.M.C., QC, Q.C. or **QMC** Quartermaster Corps
Q.M.C.R. or **QM-Res** (Mil.) Quartermaster Corps Reserve
QMG (Mil.), **Q.M.G.** or **Q.M. Gen.** Quartermaster General
Q.M.Gen., QMG (Mil.) or **Q.M.G.** Quartermaster General
QMGO Quartermaster General's Office
Q.M.O.R.C. Quartermaster Officers' Reserve Corps
Qmr., QM (Mil.) or **Q.M.** Quartermaster
Q.M.R.C. Quartermaster Reserve Corps (cf. Q.M.C.R.)
QM-Res (Mil.) or **Q.M.C.R.** Quartermaster [Corps] Reserve
Q.M.S. or **Q.M. Sgt.** Quartermaster sergeant
QM Sec Quartermaster section
Q.M.Sgt. or **Q. M. S.** Quartermaster sergeant
QMSO Quartermaster supply officer
QM Sq Quartermaster squadron
qn., Q., q., Qu., qu. or **ques.** question (cf. Qy.)
q.n. (quaque nocte)(Lat.), **O.n.** or **o.n.** (omni nocte)(Lat.) every night
QP queen's pawn (Chess)
Q.p., q.p., q. pl. (quantum placeat)(Lat.), **Q.l., q.l., q.lib.** (quantum libet)(Lat.), **Q.v.** or **q.v.** (quantum vis)(Lat.) as much as you please; as much as you will (Pharm.) (cf. ad lib.; Q.s.)
q.pl., Q.p., q.p. (quantum placeat)(Lat.), **Q. l., q.l., q. lib.** (quantum libet)(Lat.), **Q.v.** or **q.v.** (quantum vis)(Lat.) as much as you please; as much as you will (Pharm.) (cf. ad lib.; Q.s.)
QQ. or **qq.** questions
Qq or qq quartos (cf. Qto.)
qq. or **QQ.** questions
qqf. (quelquefois)(Fr.) sometimes
Q.Q.H., q.q.h. or **q.4 h.** (quaque quarta hora)(Lat.) every fourth hour
Qq. hor., qq.hor., Q.h., q.h. (quaque hora) (Lat.), **Omn.hor.** or **omn. hor.** (omni hora)(Lat.) every hour
qq.v. (quae vide)(Lat.) which [things] see
QR queen's rook (Chess)
Qr Quartering (Mil.)
Qr., Q., q., qr., qrtly., qu., quar. or **quart.** quarterly
Qr., q. or **qr.** quire
Qr., q., qr., qt., qtr., qu, quar. or **quart.** quarter
qr., Q., q., Qr., qrtly., qu., quar. or **quart.** quarterly
qr., q. or **Qr.** quire
qr., q., Qr., qt., qtr., qu., quar. or **quart.** quarter
qr., q., qua. (quadrans)(Lat.), **F., f.** or **far.** farthing
Qr Det Quartering detachment
Qr O Quartering officer
QRP queen's rook's pawn (Chess)
Qrs (Mil.) or **qrs.** quarters
qrs. quires
qrtly., Q., q., Qr., qr., qu., quar. or **quart.** quarterly
Q.S. Quarter Sessions (Law)
Q.S., q.s. or **quant.suff.** (quantum sufficit) (Lat.) as much as suffices; in sufficient quantity (Pharm.) (cf. ad lib.; q. lib.; q. pl.; q. v.)
q.s. (quid or quae supra)(Lat.) the thing[s] noted above (cf. loc. cit.; l.s.c); quarter section
Q.T. quiet (Slang)
qt. quantity
qt., q., Qr., qr., qtr., qu., quar. or **quart.** quarter
qt., q., qu. or **quar.** quart
qt. or **qts.** quarts
qt. or **qty.** quantity
q.3 h. (quaque tertia hora)(Lat.) every third hour
qto., Q., q., Q°, 4°, 4to. or **4to** quarto
qtr., q., Qr., qr., qt., qu., quar. or **quart.** quarter
qts. or **qt.** quarts
q.2 h. (quaque secunda hora)(Lat.) every second hour (cf. omn. bih.)
qty. or **qt.** quantity
Qu. Quintius; Quintus
Qu., Q., q., qn., qu. or **ques.** question (cf. Qy.)
Qu., Q., q., qu., Qy. or **qy.** query (cf. ques.)
Qu., Q., q., qu., R., r., Reg. or **reg.** (regina) (Lat.) Queen
qu., Q., q., qn., Qu. or **ques.** question (cf. Qy.)
qu., Q., q., Qr., qr., qrtly., quar. or **quart.** quarterly
qu., Q., q., Qu., Qy. or **qy.** query
qu., Q., q., Qu., R., r., Reg. or **reg.** (regina) (Lat.) Queen
qu. or **q.** quasi
qu., q., Qr., qr., qt., qtr., quar. or **quart.** quarter
qu., q., qt. or **quar.** quart
qua., q., qr. (quadrans)(Lat.), **F., f.** or **far.** farthing
quad. quadrangle; quadrant; quadrat; quadrilateral; quadruple
quadrupl. quadruplicate
Qual Qualified (Mil.)
quant. suff., Q.S. or **q.s.** (quantum sufficit) (Lat.) as much as suffices; in sufficient quantity (Pharm.) (cf. ad lib., q. lib.; q.v.)
quar., Q., q., Qr., qr., qrtly., qu. or **quart.** quarterly
quar., q., Qr., qr., qt., qtr., qu. or **quart.** quarter
quar., q., qt. or **qu.** quart
quart., Q., q., Qr., qr., qrtly., qu. or **quar.** quarterly
quart., q., Qr., qr., qt., qtr., qu. or **quar.** quarter
quat. (quattuor)(Lat.) four
Q.U.B. Queen's University, Belfast
Que., P.Q. or **Q.** Quebec [Province]; Province of Quebec
Queensl. Queensland
ques., Q., q., qn., Qu. or **qu.** question (cf. Qy.)
Q.U.I. Queen's University of Ireland
quin. or **quint.** quintuple; quintuplet
Quint. (quintus)(Lat.) fifth
quint. or **quin.** quintuple; quintuplet
quintupl. quintuplicate

quor. quorum
quot. quotation; quoted
Quotid. (quotidie)(Lat.), **O.d., o.d.** (omni die)(Lat.) or **q.d.** (quaque die)(Lat.) every day; daily (cf. p.d.)
q.v. (quod vide)(Lat.) which see
q.v., Q.v. (quantum vis)(Lat.), **Q.l., q.l., q. lib.** (quantum libet)(Lat.), **Q.p., q.p.** or **q.pl.** (quantum placeat)(Lat.) as much as you will; as much as you please (Pharm.)(cf. ad lib.; Q.s.)
Qy., qy., Q., q., Qu. or **qu.** query (cf. ques.)

R

R gas constant (Phys. chem.); rank (Math.); ratio (Math.); red; Regulating (Mil.); rogue (branded on rogues in old times
R (Mil.) or **R.** rifle
R, R., r, or **Re** rupee (cf. Rx)
R, R., r, r., k., kgl. (kongelig)(Dan.), (königlich)(Ger.), **kir.** (királyi)(Hung.), **kungl.** (kunglig)(Swed.), **Roy** or **roy.** royal
R, R., r, Rs, rs or **Rs.** rupees (cf. Rx)
R, R., r. or **T.** (Thurm)(Ger.) rook or castle (Chess)
R, r, r., rb. or **Ro.** ruble
R, r (Elec., ohm), **res.** or **Resist.** resistance
R or **rad.** radical
R. (remotum)(Lat.) far or remote point [of vision]; respond; response (Church service); runic
R. (Ridder)(Dan.), **Chev.** (Chevalier)(Fr.), **K., k., knt., Kt** (Chess) or **Kt.** knight
R. or R (Mil.) rifle
R., R, r or **Re** rupee (cf. Rx)
R., R, r, Rs, Rs. or **rs** rupees (cf. Rx)
R. or **r.** rabbi
R., r., ch. de f. (chemin de fer)(Fr.), **rly., R.W., rw., Rwy.** or **Ry.** railway (cf. R.R.)
R., r., d. (droit)(Fr.), (destra)(Ital.) or **rt.** right
R., r. (rex, regis)(Lat.), **K., k.** or **Ki.** king; kings
R., r. or **rad.** radius
R., r., Rd. or **rd.** road
R, r., Rec., rec., rp. or **Rx** recipe; take (Pharm.)
R., r., Rect. or **rect.** rector
R., r., Red. (Redaktør)(Dan.), **red.** (redaktör)(Swed.), **réd.** (rédacteur)(Fr.), **ed.** or **edit.** editor; redactor
R., r., Reg., reg. (regina)(Lat.), **Q., q., Qu.** or **qu.** queen
R., r., Res (Mil.) or **res.** reserve
R., r. or **Rg** (Mil.) range
R., r. or **riv.** river
R., r., Ro., ro. (recto)(Lat.), **f.r.** or **fo.ro.** (folio recto)(Lat.) right hand page
R., r., RR or **R.R.** railroad (cf. Rwy.)
R., Ré. or **Réaum.** Réaumur scale (Temperature)
R., Red. (Redaktør)(Dan.), **r., red.** (redaktör)(Swed.), **réd.** (rédacteur)(Fr.), **ed.** or **edit.** editor
R., reg. or **regd.** registered
R., Rep., rep., Repub., repub., RP., R.P. or **r.p.** (res publica)(Lat.) republic
R., Rep. or **Repub.** Republican
R. (Med.) or **resp.** respiration
R., Ro., ro. (recto)(Lat.), **f.r.** or **fo.ro.** (folio recto)(Lat.) right-hand page
r, R, R. or **Re** rupee (cf. Rx)
r, R, R., Rs, Rs. or **rs** rupees (cf. Rx)
r, R, r., rb. or **Ro.** ruble
r, R (Elec., ohm), **res.** or **Resist.** resistance
r. racemic (Chem.); rare; reddish (Dyeing); rises; rubber; rule (Law); run (deserted)(Navy); runs (Cricket), (Baseball)
r. (rok)(Pol.), **A., a., An., an.** (annus)(Lat.), **J.** (Jahr)(Ger.), **y.** or **yr.** year
r., a.D. (ausser Dienst)(Ger.), **Ret** (Mil.), **ret.** or **retd.** retired
r., ch. de f. (chemin de fer)(Fr.), **R., rly., R.W., rw., Rwy.** or **Ry.** railway (cf. R.R.)
r., d. (droit)(Fr.),(destra)(Ital.), **R.** or **rt.** right
r. or **R.** rabbi
r., R. (rex, regis)(Lat.), **K., k.** or **Ki.** king; kings
r., R, r, rb. or **Ro.** ruble
r., R. or **rad.** radius
r., R., Rd. or **rd.** road
r., R., Rec., rec., rp. or **Rx** recipe; take (Pharm.)
r., R., Rect. or **rect.** rector
r., R., Res (Mil.) or **res.** reserve
r., R. or **Rg** (Mil.) range
r., R. or **riv.** river
r., R., Ro., ro. (recto)(Lat.), **fo.ro.** or **f.r.** (folio recto)(Lat.) right hand page
r., R., RR or **R.R.** railroad (cf. Rwy.)
r., rcd., rec. or **recd.** received
r., Rd. or **ro.** rood
r., Rd. or **rd.** rod
r. or **Rds.** rods
r., red. (redaktör)(Swed.), **R., Red.** (redaktør)(Dan.), **réd.** (rédacteur)(Fr.), **ed.** or **edit.** editor
r. or **res.** residence; resident; resides
R A Railroad Administration
RA (Mil.) or **R.A.** Regular Army; Resettlement Administration
R.A. Residence Area (Queensland); right ascension (Astron.); Road Association; Royal Academician; Royal Arcanum; Royal Arch (Freemasonry); Royal Art; Royal Artillery
R. A. (República Argentina)(Span.) or **Arg. Rep.** Argentine Republic
R.A. or **R.A.A.** Royal Academy [of Arts, London]
R.A., R.-Adm., Rear Adm. or **Rear-Adm.** Rear Admiral
R.A. (Reverendus admodum)(Lat.) or **V. Rev.** Very Reverend
R/A refer to acceptor (Com.)
Ra or **Rd** radium (Chem.)
Ra. Rachel

R.A.A. or **R.A.** Royal Academy of Arts [London]
Ra-A, Ra-B, etc. radium-A, radium-B, etc. (Chem.)
Ra-Ac, Ra-Act or **Rd-Ac** radioactinium (Chem.)
R.A.A.F. Royal Australian Air Force
rabb. rabbinical
R.A.C. Royal Agricultural College; Royal Arch Captain (Freemasonry); Royal Automobile Club
R.A.C. or **R. A. Chap.** Royal Arch Chapter (Freemasonry)
RACC or **R.A.C.C.** Regional Agricultural Credit Corporations
R. A. Chap. or **R. A. C.** Royal Arch Chapter (Freemasonry)
R.A.Ch.D. Royal Army Chaplains Department
Rad (Mil.) or **rad.** radio
Rad. or **rad.** (radix)(Lat.) root
rad. radiant
rad. or **R** radical
rad., R. or **r.** radius
rad. or **Rad** (Mil.) radio
rad. or **Rad.** (radix)(Lat.) root
Radar radio direction and ranging
Rad Co (Mil.) or **Rad. Co.** Radio company
raddol. (raddolcendo)(Ital.) becoming softer (Music)(cf. cal.)
Rad Int Radio intelligence (Mil.)
Rad Int Co Radio intelligence company (Mil.)
R.-Adm., R.A., Rear Adm. or **Rear-Adm.** Rear Admiral
Rad Sec (Mil.) or **Rad. Sec.** Radio section
R.A.E. Royal Air Force Establishment
R.Ae. S. Royal Aeronaurical Society (London)
RAF or **R.A.F.** Royal Air Force
R.A.F. Royal Aircraft Factory
R.A.F. or **RAF** Royal Air Force
R.A.F.S.R. Royal Air Force Volunteer Reserve
R.A.G.C. Royal and Ancient Golf Club [St. Andrews]
R.A.I.C. Russian-American Industrial Corporation
ral., rall. or **rallo.** (rallentando)(Ital.) slackening; gradually slower (Music) (cf. perd.; rit.; slent.; smorz.)
rall., ral. or **rallo.** (rallentando)(Ital.) slackening; gradually slower (Music)(cf. perd. rit.; slent.; smorz.)
R.A.M. Royal Academy of Music; Royal Arch Mason (Freemasonry)
R.A.M.C. Royal Army Medical Corps (cf. A.M.C.)
ramp rampion
r. & c. or **r. and c.** rail and canal (Transp.)
r. & c.c. riot and civil commotions (Insurance)
r. & l. or **r. and l.** rail and lake (Transp.)
r. & o. or **r. and o.** rail and ocean (Transp.)
R & P Sec Radio and panel section
R. & R.U. Reformatory and Refuge Union (Brit.)
R. & S.M. Royal and Select Masters
r. & t. or **r. and t.** rail and truck
r. & w. or **r. and w.** rail and water (Transp.)
R.A.N. Royal Australian Navy
r. and c. or **r. & c.** rail and canal (Transp.)
r. and l. or **r. & l.** rail and lake (Transp.)
r. and o. or **r. & o.** rail and ocean (Transp.)
r. and t. or **r. & t.** rail and truck
r. and w. or **r. & w.** rail and water (Transp.)
R.A.O.A. Railway Accounting Officers Association
R.A.O.B. Royal Antediluvian Order of Buffaloes
R.A.O.C. Royal Army Ordnance Corps
R.A.P. rupees, annas, pies
R.A.P.C. Royal Army Pay Corps
R.A.S. Research Advisory Service; Royal Agricultural Society [of England]; Royal Asiatic Society [of Great Britain and Ireland]; Royal Astronomical Society
Ras. (rasurae)(Lat.) shavings
R.A.S.C. Royal Army Service Corps
R.A.T. (Reserve de l'armée territorial)(Fr.) Territorial Reserves; Rapeseed Association terms
Ra-Th or **Rd-Th** radiothorium (Chem.)
R.A.V.C. Royal Army Veterinary Corps
RB Road bend (Mil.)
R.B. Rifle brigade
Rb rubidium (Chem.)
rb., R, r, r. or **Ro.** ruble
R.B.A. Railway Business Association; Royal [Society of] British Artists
R.B.S. Royal [Society of] British Sculptors
R.C. Red Cross (cf. A.N.R.C.); Reserve Corps
R.C. or **r.c.** right center
R.C. or **Rom. Cath.** Roman Catholic
R/C reconsigned
r.c. release clause; relief claim
r.c. or **R.C.** right center
RCA or **R.C.A.** Radio Corporation of America; Reformed Church in America
R.C.A. Radio Club of America; Railway Clerks' Association (Brit.); Royal Cambrian Academician or Academy; Royal Canadian Academy; Royal College of Arts
RCAF or **R.C.A.F.** Royal Canadian Air Force
r.c. & l. or **r.c. and l.** rail, canal, and lake (Transp.)
r.c. and l. or **r.c. & l.** rail, canal, and lake (Transp.)
RCC Rag Chewers' Club (Radio)
r.c.c. & s. riots, civil commotions, and strikes (Insurance)
R.C.Ch. Roman Catholic Church (cf.S.R.E.)
Rcd (Mil.), **Rec.** or **rec.** record
rcd., r., rec. or **recd.** received
RCDC Royal College of Dental Surgeons
R.C.I. Royal Colonial Institute (London) (now Royal Empire Society)
R.C.L. Ruling Case Law
R.C.M. Royal College of Music
R.C.M. or **r.c.m.** regimental court martial

r.c.m. or **R.C.M.** regimental court martial
R.C.M.P. Royal Canadian Mounted Police (cf. N.W.M.P.)
R.C.N. Royal Canadian Navy
Rcn Reconnaissance (Mil.)
Rcn Bn Reconnaissance battalion
Rcn LR Reconnaissance long range
Rcn MR Reconnaissance medium range
Rcn O Reconnaissance officer
R.C.N.R. Royal Canadian Naval Reserve
Rcn Sq Reconnaissance squadron
Rcn Tr Reconnaissance troop
R.C.O. Royal College of Organists
R Co Rifle company
R. Comm. Royal Commission
R.C.P. Royal College of Physicians (London); Royal College of Preceptors (London)
Rcpt., rcpt., rct., rec., Rect., rect., rec't., Rept. or **rept.** receipt
rcpt., Rcpt., rct., rec., Rect., rect., rec't., Rept. or **rept.** receipt
R.C.S. Revenue Cutter Service; Royal College of Science (London)(cf. I.C.S.; R.S.M.); Royal College of Surgeons
R.C.S. or **R. Signals** Royal Corps of Signals
Rct Recruit **(Mil.)**
rct., Rcpt., rcpt., rec., Rect., rect., rec't., Rept. or **rept.** receipt
Rctg (Mil.), **Rctg.** or **rtcg.** recruiting
rctg., Rctg (Mil.) or **Rctg.** recruiting
rcts. receipts
R.C.V.S. Royal College of Veterinary Surgeons
R.D. Dominican Republic; Regional Director; Royal [Naval Reserve] Decoration; Royal [Naval Reserve Officers'] Decoration; Royal [Volunteer Reserve] Decoration; Royal Dragoons; Rural Dean (Eccl.)
R.D., De R., DR or **Ea.R.** (Entartungs-Reaktion)(Ger.) reaction of degeneration
R.D. or **R/D** refer to drawer (Banking)
R.D. or **R.D.S.** Rural Delivery [Service] (cf. RFD)
R/D or **R.D.** refer to drawer
Rd or **Ra** radium (Chem.)
Rd (Mil.), **Rd.** or **red.** reduce; reduced
Rd., r. or **rd.** rod
Rd., r. or **ro.** rood
Rd., Rd (Mil.) or **red.** reduce; reduced
Rd. or **rd.** rix-dollar
Rd., rd., R. or **r.** road
rd. round
rd., R., r. or **Rd.** road
rd., r. or **Rd.** rod
rd. or **Rd.** rix-dollar (cf. Rds.)
rd.^{2} or **sq.rd.** square rod or rods
r.d. running days (Shipping)
Rd-Ac, Ra-Ac or **Ra-Act** radioactinium (Chem.)
R.D.C. Royal Defence Corps; Rural District Council (Brit.)
R.D.C. or **r.d.c.** running down clause
r.d.c. or **R.D.C.** running down clause
R.D.F. radio direction finder
Rdg Reducing (Mil.)
RDP Ration distributing point (Mil.)
R.D.S. Royal Drawing Society; Royal Dublin Society
R.D.S. or **R.D.** Rural Delivery Service (cf. RFD)
Rds., r. or **rds.** rods
Rds. or **rds.** rix-dollars
rds., r. or **Rds.** rods
Rd-Th or **Ra-Th** radiothorium (Chem.)
R.D.Y. Royal Dockyard
R.E. real estate; Right Excellent; Royal [Society of Painter-Etchers and] Engravers; Royal Exchange
R.E. or **Ref.E.** Reformed Episcopal (cf. R.P.E.)
R.E. or **R. Eng.** Royal Engineers
R/E repayable to either (Banking)
Re rhenium (Chem.)
Re., R, R. or **r** rupee (cf. Rs; Rx)
Ré., R. or **Réaum.** Réaumur [scale] (Temperature)
r.e. red edges (Bookbinding)
REA or **R.E.A.** Rural Electrification Administration
react. or **x** reactance (Elec.)
Reaptd (Mil.) or **reaptd.** reappointed
reaptd. or **Reaptd** (Mil.) reappointed
Rear Adm., R.A., R.-Adm. or **Rear-Adm.** Rear Admiral
Réaum., R. or **Ré.** Réaumur [scale] (Temperature)
Rec Recreation (Mil.)
Rec. or **rec.** recorded; recorder; recording
Rec., rec., R, r., rp. or **Rx** recipe; take (Pharm.)
Rec., rec. or **Rcd** (Mil.) record
rec. receptacle; reclamation
rec., R., r., Rec., rp. or **Rx** recipe; take (Pharm.)
rec., r., rcd. or **recd.** received
rec., Rcd (Mil.) or **Rec.** record
rec., rct., Rcpt., rcpt., Rect., rect., rec't., Rept. or **rept.** receipt
rec. or **Rec.** recorded; recorder; recording
recap. recapitulation
recd., r., rcd. or **rec.** received
recip. reciprocal; reciprocity
recit. recitative
recogns. or **recogs.** recognizances
recogs. or **recogns.** recognizances
Recons Reconstruction (Mil.)
Recons Prk Reconstruction park
Recp Reception (Mil.)
Recp Cen Reception center (Mil.)
Recr. or **recr.** receiver
recr. or **Recr.** receiver
Rec. Sec., rec. sec. or **R. S.** recording secretary
Rect., R., r. or **rect.** rector
Rect., rct., Rcpt., rcpt., rec., rect., rec't., Rept. or **rept.** receipt
Rect. or **rect.** rectified; rectory

rect., R., r. or **Rect.** rector
rect., rct., Rcpt., rcpt., rec., Rect., rec't., Rept. or **rept.** receipt
rect. or **Rect.** rectified; rectory
rec't., rct., Rcpt., rcpt., rec., Rect., rect., Rept. or **rept.** receipt
Red., R. (Redaktør)(Dan.), **red.** (redaktör) (Swed.), **r., réd.** (rédacteur)(Fr.), **ed.** or **edit.** editor; redactor
red. reduction
red., Rd (Mil.) or **Rd.** reduce; reduced
réd. (rédacteur), **R., Red.** (Redaktør) (Dan.), **r., red.** (redaktör)(Swed.), **ed.** or **edit.** editor; redactor
redisc. rediscount
redup. or **redupl.** reduplicated; reduplication
redupl. or **redup.** reduplicated; reduplication
Reenl Reenlist
Reenlmt Reenlistment
Ref (Mil.), **refg.** or **refrig.** refrigeration
Ref. or **ref.** referee; reference; reformation
Ref., ref. or **refd.** referred; reformed
ref. refining; reformer; refunding
ref. or **Ref.** referee; reference; reformation
ref., Ref. or **refd.** referred; reformed
refash. refashioned
Ref. Ch. Reformed Church
refd., Ref. or **ref.** referred; reformed
Ref.E. or **R.E.** Reformed Episcopal (cf. R.P.E.)
refg., Ref (Mil.) or **refrig.** refrigeration
refg. or **refrig.** refrigerating
refl. reflection; reflective; reflectively; reflex
refl. or **reflex.** reflexive; reflexively
reflex. or **refl.** reflexive; reflexively
Ref Plt Refrigerating plant (Mil.)
Ref.Pres. or **R.P.** Reformed Presbyterian
refrig., Ref (Mil.) or **refg.** refrigeration
refrig. or **refg.** refrigerating
Ref. Sp. or **R.S.** Reformed Spelling
Reg. Reginald
Reg. or **reg.** register; regular
Reg., reg., R., r. (regina)(Lat.), **Q., q., Qu.** or **qu.** queen
Reg., reg., Regr. or **regr.** registrar
Reg., reg., Regt (Mil.), **Regt., regt., RGT, Rgt** or **Rgt.** Regiment
reg. region; registry; regularly; regulation; regulator
reg., R., r., Reg. (regina)(Lat.), **Q., q., Qu.** or **qu.** queen
reg., R. or **regd.** registered
reg. or **Reg.** register; regular
reg., Reg., Regr. or **regr.** registrar
reg., Reg., Regt (Mil.), **Regt., regt., Rgt** (Mil.) or **Rgt.** regiment
reg., Regt. or **regt.** regent
regd., R. or **reg.** registered
Reg.Gen. or **Reg.-Gen.** Registrar General
Reg. Prof. or **R.P.** Regius Professor
Regr., Reg., reg. or **regr.** registrar
regr., Reg., reg. or **Regr.** registrar
Regt (Mil.), **Regt., regt., Reg., reg., RGT, Rgt** (Mil.) or **Rgt.** Regiment
Regt., reg. or **regt.** regent
regt., Reg., reg., Regt (Mil.), **Regt., RGT, Rgt** (Mil.) or **Rgt.** regiment
regt., reg. or **Regt.** regent
Regtl (Mil.), **Regtl.** or **Rgtl** (Mil.) Regimental
Reg. umb. (regio umbilici)(Lat.) region of the navel
Reg. U.S. Pat Off. All Rts. Res. registered at United States Patent Office, all rights reserved
Reinf Reinforced (Mil.)
Rejd Rejoined (Mil.)
rel. relating; relative; relatively; released; religious
rel. or **relig.** religion
rel., Reliq. or **reliq.** (reliqua, reliquiae)(Lat.) relics
Reld Relieved (Mil.)
relig. or **rel.** religion
Reliq., reliq. or **rel.** (reliqua, religuiae)(Lat.) relics
rel. pron. relative pronoun
rem. remittance
rem., Anm. (anmaerkning)(Dan.) or **anm.** (anmärkning)(Swed.) remark
R. Eng. or **R.E.** Royal Engineers
R.E.N.P.A. Railroad Employes' National Pension Association
Rep (Mil.), **Rep., rep.** or **repr.** repair
Rep., R. or **Repub.** Republican
Rep. or **rep.** reporter
Rep., rep., R., Repub., repub., RP., R.P. or **r.p.** (res publica)(Lat.) republic
Rep., rep. or **repet.** (repetatur)(Lat.) repeat
Rep., rep. or **repr.** representative
Rep., rep., rept. or **rpt.** report; reported
rep., Rep. or **repet.** (repetatur)(Lat.) repeat
rep., Rep. or **repr.** representative
rep., Rep., rept. or **rpt.** report; reported
repet. (repetatur)(Lat.), **Rep.** or **rep.** repeat
Repl Replacement (Mil.)
Repr (Mil.), **Repro** (Mil.) or **repro.** reproduction
repr. represent; representing
repr., R/P, r.p. or **r-p.** reprint; reprinted; reprinting
repr., Rep (Mil.), **Rep.** or **rep.** repair
repr., Rep. or **rep.** representative
Repro (Mil.), **repro.** or **Repr** (Mil.) reproduction
Rep Sec Repair section
Rept., Rcpt., rcpt., rct., rec., Rect., rect., rec't. or **rept.** receipt
rept., Rcpt., rcpt., rct., rec., Rect., rect., rec't. or **Rept.** receipt
rept., Rep., rep. or **rpt.** report; reported
Repub., R. or **Rep.** Republican
Repub., repub., R., Rep., rep., RP., R.P. or **r.p.** (res publica)(Lat.) republic
Req (Mil.) or **req.** requisition
req. require; required
Requal Requalified (Mil.)

RES reticulo-endothelial system

R.E.S. Royal Empire Society (London) (cf. R.C.I.)

Res (Mil.), **R.**, **r.** or **res.** reserve

Res. or **res.** resolution

res. research; residue; resistor; resort

res., **R.**, **r.** or **Res** (Mil.) reserve

res., **R**, **r** (Elec., ohm) or **Resist.** resistance

res. or **r.** residence; resident; resides

res. or **Res.** resolution

res. or **Resgd** (Mil.) resigned

Resgd (Mil.) or **res.** resigned

Resist., **R**, **r** (Elec., ohm) or **res.** resistance

R E S M A Railway Electrical Supply Manufacturers Association

resp. respective; respondent

resp., **bez.**, **bezgw.** or **bezw.** (beziehungsweise)(Ger.) respectively

resp. or **R.** (Med.) respiration

Res.Phys. resident physician (cf. H.P.)

Res.Surg. resident surgeon (cf. H.S.)

restr. restaurant

Resurr. Resurrection

Ret (Mil.), **a.D.** (ausser Dienst)(Ger.), **r.**, **ret.** or **retd.** retired

ret. retain; return

ret., **a.D.** (ausser Dienst)(Ger.), **r.**, **Ret** (Mil.) or **retd.** retired

ret., **retd.** or **rtd.** returned

retd. retained

retd., **a.D.** (ausser Dienst)(Ger.) **r.**, **Ret** (Mil.) or **ret.** retired

retd., **ret.** or **rtd.** returned

retel. referring to telegram

R. et I. (Regina et Imperatrix)(Lat.) Queen and Empress; (Rex et Imperator)(Lat.) King and Emperor (cf. R.I.)

retnr. or **Retr.** retainer (Law)

Retr. or **retnr.** retainer (Law)

retrog. retrogressive

Rets Returns (Mil.)

Rev. Revelation [of St. John]

Rév. révue

Rev. or **rev.** review

Rev. or **Revd.** Reverend

rev. revenue; reverse (cf. f.v., vo.); reversed; revise; revision; revolving

rev. or **Rev.** review

rev. or **revol.** revolution

rev., **umgearb.** (umgearbeitet)(Ger.) **ver.** or **veränd.** (verändert)(Ger.) revised

Rev. A/c or **rev A/C** revenue account (Bookkeeping)

Revd. or **Rev.** Reverend

revol. or **rev.** revolution

revol. or **revs.** revolutions

Revs. Reverends

revs. or **revol.** revolutions

revs per min., **RPM**, **R.P.M.**, **rpm** or **r.p.m.** revolutions per minute

revs.per sec., **RPS**, **R.P.S.**, **rps** or **r.p.s** revolutions per second

Rev. Stat., **RS** (Mil.) or **R.S.** Revised Statutes

Rev. Ver. or **R.V.** Revised Version [of the Bible]

R.F. (République française)(Fr.) French Republic; representative fraction; Reserve Force; Rockefeller Foundation

R.F. or **r.f.** range finder; reducing flame; right field

R.F., **r.f.** or **r-f** radio frequency

R, F., **r.f.** or **T.R.** (Tiré rapide)(Fr.) rapid fire; rapid firing (cf. Q.F.)

R.F. or **R. Fus.** Royal Fusiliers

rf. rough finish (Paper)

rf. or **rfg.** refunding

rf., **rfz.** or **rinf.** (rinforzando)(Ital.) reinforcing; imparting additional stress (Music)

r.f. or **R.F.** range finder; reducing flame right field

r.f., **R.F.** or **r-f** radio frequency

r.f., **R.F.** or **T.R.** (Tiré rapide)(Fr.) rapid fire; rapid firing (cf. Q.F.)

r-f, **R.F.** or **r.f.** radio frequency

R.F.A. Rockefeller Family Association; Royal Field Artillery

RFC or **R.F.C.** Reconstruction Finance Corporation

R.F.C. Royal Flying Corps (superseded by R.A.F.)

R.F.C. or **RFC** Reconstruction Finance Corporation

RFCMC or **R.F.C.M.C.** Reconstruction Finance Corporation Mortgage Company

RFD or **R.F.D.**. Rural Free Delivery (cf. R.D.)

R.F.G. rapid-fire gun

rfg. or **rf.** refunding

R.F.T.E.A. Railway Fuel and Traveling Engineers' Association

R.Fus. or **R.F.** Royal Fusiliers

rfz., **rf.** or **rinf.** (rinforzando)(Ital.) reinforcing; imparting additional stress (Music)

R.G.. Royal Grenadier Guards

R.G. or **r.g.** right guard

Rg (Mil.), **R.** or **r.** range

r.g. or **R.G.** right guard

R.G.A. Royal Garrison Artillery

Rg O Range officer

R.G.S. Royal Geographical Society

RGT, **Reg.**, **reg.**, **Regt** (Mil.), **Regt.**, **regt.**, **Rgt** (Mil.) or **Rgt.** regiment

Rgt (Mil.), **Reg.**, **reg.**, **Regt** (Mil.), **Regt.**, **regt.**, **RGT** or **Rgt.** regiment

Rgtl, **Regtl** (Mil.) or **Regtl.** Regimental

RH Roundhouse

RH, **R.H.**, **r.h.**, **d.** (droit)(Fr.), **dcha.** (derecha)(Span.), **D.M.** (destra mano) (Ital.), **M.D.** or **m.d.** (main droit)(Fr.), (mano destra)(Ital.) right hand

R.H. Royal Highlanders; Royal Highness

Rh rhodium (Chem.)

R.H.A. Royal Hibernian Academician or Academy; Royal Horse Artillery

rhap. rhapsody (Music)

R.H.B. or **r.h.b.** right half back (Football)

R.H.D. relative hepatic dullness

Rhd (Mil.) or **rhd.** railhead
Rhd Det Railhead detachment (Mil.)
rheo. rheostat; rheostats
rhet. rhetoric; rhetorical
R.H.G. Royal Horse Guards
rhinol. rhinology
R.Hist.S. or **R.H.S.** Royal Historical Society (London)
RH O Railhead officer
r.h.p. rated horsepower
RHQ Regimental headquarters
R.H.S. Royal Horticultural Society (London); Royal Humane Society (London)
R.H.S. or **R. Hist. S.** Royal Historical Society (London)
R.I. (Rex or Regina Imperator)(Lat.) King Emperor or Queen Empress (cf. R. et I.); Rhode Island; Royal Institute [of Painters in Water-Colours]; Royal Institution [of Great Britain]
R.I.A. Royal Irish Academy
R.I.A.S.C. Royal Indian Army Service Corps
R.I.B.A. Royal Institution of British Architects
R.I.C. Royal Irish Constabulary
Rich. or **Richd.** Richard
Richd. or **Rich.** Richard
R.I.E. Royal Indian Engineers
r.i.e. retirement income endowment (Insurance)
R.I.E.C. Royal Indian Engineering College
R.I.F. right iliac fossa
R.I.L.U. Red International of Labor Unions
R.I.M. Royal Indian Marines
R.I.M.R. Rockefeller Institute of Medical Research
R.I.N. Royal Indian Navy
rinf., **rf.** or **rfz.** (rinforzando)(Ital.) reinforcing; imparting additional stress (Music)
R.I.P. (requiescat in pace)(Lat.), **E.P.D.** (en paz descanse)(Span.) or **Q.E.P.D.** (que en paz descanse)(Span.) may he or she rest in peace (cf. B.Q.; H.R.I.P.; Q.D.D.G.; Q.D.G.; Q.E.G.E.)
rip. (ripieno)(Ital.) additional; supplementary (Music)
R.I.P.H.H. Royal Institute of Public Health and Hygiene (London)
rit. (ritardando, ritenuto)(Ital.), **ritard.** (ritardando)(Ital.) or **ritten.** (ritenuto) (Ital.) retarded; held back; becoming gradually slower (Music)(cf. perd.; rall.; slent.; smorz.)
r.i.t. refining in transit
ritard. (ritardando)(Ital.), **rit** (ritardando, ritenuto)(Ital.) or **ritten.** (ritenuto) (Ital.) retarded; held back; becoming gradually slower (Music)(cf. perd.; rall.; slent.; smorz.)
ritten. (ritenuto)(Ital.), **rit.** (ritardano, ritenuto)(Ital.) or **ritard.** (ritardando) (Ital.) retarded; held back; becoming gradually slower (Music)(cf. perd.; rall.; slent.; smorz.)
riv., **R.** or **r.** river
RJ Road junction (Mil.)
rkva reactive kilowatt-ampere
rky. rocky
RL right line (Math.)
r.l. & r. or **r.l. and r.** rail, lake and rail
r.l. and r. or **r.l. & r.** rail, lake and rail
R.L.O. Returned Letter Office (Brit.)
R.L.S. Robert Louis Stevenson
rly., **ch. de f.** (chemin de fer)(Fr.), **R.**, **r.**, **R.W.**, **rw.**, **Rwy.** or **Ry.** railway (cf. R.R.)
RM, R.M. or **r.m.** reichsmark
R.M. (Réquisitions militaires)(Fr.) Military requisitions; Resident Magistrate; Royal Mail; Royal Marines
R.M., RM or **r.m.** reichsmark
rm. ream; room
r.m. ring micrometer
r.m., RM or **R.M.** reichsmark
R.M.A. Radio Manufacturers' Association; Royal Marine Artillery; Royal Military Academy (Woolwich); Royal Military or Marine Asylum
RMB or **R.M.B.** Regional Mediation Board
R.M.C. Royal Military College (Sandhurst)
R. Met. S. or **R.M.S.** Royal Meteorological Society (London)
R.M.L.I. Royal Marine Light Infantry
R.M.M. or **C.M.Mh.** (Congregatio Missionariorum de Mariannhill)(Lat.) Religious Missionaries of Mariannhill; Congregation of Missionaries of Mariannhill; Mariannhill Fathers
RMS, rms, R.M.S., r.m.s. or **r-m-s** root mean square
R.M.S. Railway Mail Service; Royal Mail Service or Steamship; Royal Microscopical Society (London); Royal Society of Miniature Painters
R.M.S. or **R. Met. S.** Royal Meteorological Society (London)
rms, RMS, R.M.S., r.m.s. or **r-m-s** root mean square
rms. reams; rooms
r-m-s, RMS, R.M.S., rms or **r.m.s.** root mean square
Rmt Remount
Rmt Dep Remount depot
Rmt O Remount officer
Rmt Serv Remount Service
R.N. registered nurse; Royal Navy
Rn radon (Chem.)
R.N.A.F. Royal Naval Air Force (now R.A.F.); Royal Norwegian Air Force
R.N.A.S. Royal Naval Air Service (now R.A.F.)
R.N.A.V. Royal Naval Artillery Volunteers
R.N.D. Royal Naval Division
R.N.O. (Riddare af Nordstjerne Orden) (Swed.) or **K.N.S.** Knight of the [Royal] Order of the Pole or North Star (Sweden)
R.N. of A. Royal Neighbors of America
R.N.R. Royal Naval Reserve
R.N.V. Royal Naval Volunteer
R.N.V.R. Royal Naval Volunteer Reserve

R.N.V.S.R. Royal Naval Volunteer Supplementary Reserve
RNZAF or **R.N.Z.A.F.** Royal New Zealand Air Force
RO Regulating officer
RO (Mil.) or **R.O.** Regimental orders
R.O. Receiving Office or Officer; Receiving Order (Law); Recruiting officer; Relieving officer; Returning officer; Royal Observatory (Greenwich)
R.O. or **RO** (Mil.) Regimental Orders
R.O., roy. 8vo or **roy. 8vo** royal octavo
Ro., R, r, r. or **rb.** ruble
Ro., R., r., ro. (recto)(Lat.), **f.r.** or **fo.ro.** (folio recto)(Lat.) right hand page
ro., R., r., Ro. (recto)(Lat.), **f.r.** or **fo.ro.** (folio recto)(Lat.) right hand page
ro., rd. or **Rd.** rood
Rob. or **Robt.** Robert
r.o.b. remain or remaining on board
Robt. or **Rob.** Robert
R.O.D. refused on delivery
Roentgenol. roentgenological; roentgenology
Roffen. Rochester, in the signature of Bishop
R. of O. Reserve of Officers (Brit.)
R.O.G. or **r.o.g.** receipt of goods
Rog. Roger
r.o.g. or **R.O.G.** receipt of goods
R.O.I. Royal [Institute of] Oil Painters
Rol. Roland
Rom. Roman; Romance; Romans
Rom. or **rom.** roman (Typog.)
r.o.m. run of mine (Coal)(cf. M.R.; tal. qual.); run of mill
Rom. Cath. or **R.C.** Roman Catholic
R.o.p. or **r.o.p.** run of paper (advertising)
R.O.S. Royal Order of Scotland
R.O.S.C. Reserve Officers Sanitary Corps
rot. rotating; rotten
rot. or **rotn.** rotation
R.O.T.C. Reserve Officers' Training Camp or Corps
rotn. or **rot.** rotation
rotn.no. rotation number
Roum. or **Rum.** Roumania or Rumania; Roumanian or Rumanian
Roxb., Rxb. or **rxb.** Roxburgh (Bookbinding)
Roy., k., kgl. (kongelig)(Dan.), (königlich) (Ger.), **kir.** (királyi)(Hung.), **kungl.** (kunglig)(Swed.), **R. R., r, r.** or **roy.** royal
roy., k., kgl. (kongelig)(Dan.), (königlich) (Ger.), **kir.** (királyi)(Hung.), **kungl.** (kunglig)(Swed.), **R, R., r, r.** or **Roy.** royal
roy. 8vo., roy 8vo, or **R.O.** royal octavo
roy. 4to or **roy. qto.** royal quarto
RP Refilling point; Regulating point
RP or **R.P.** reply paid
RP., Rep., rep., Repub., repub., R.P. or **r.p.** (res publica)(Lat.) republic
R.P. (Reverendus Pater)(Lat.) Reverend Father; Royal Society of Portrait Painters
R.P. or **Ref.Pres.** Reformed Presbyterian
R.P. or **Reg. Prof.** Regius Professor
R.P., Rep., rep., Repub., repub., RP. or **r.p.** (res publica)(Lat.) republic
R.P. or **RP** reply paid
R/P, repr., r.p. or **r-p.** reprint; reprinted; reprinting
R/p return of post [for orders] (grain trade)
rp., R, r., Rec., rec. or **Rx** recipe; take (Pharm.)
r.p. return premium (Insurance)
r.p., Rep., rep., Repub., repub., RP. or **R.P.** (res publica)(Lat.) republic
r.p., repr., R/P or **r-p.** reprint; reprinted; reprinting
r-p, repr., R/P or **r.p.** reprint; reprinted; reprinting
R.P.D. (Rerum Politicarum Doctor)(Lat.) Doctor of Political Science; Regius Professor of Divinity; Royal Purple Degree
R.P.E. Reformed Protestant Episcopal
rpf. reichspfennig
R Plat Rifle platoon
RPM, R.P.M., rpm, r.p.m. or **revs.per min.** revolutions per minute
rpm, RPM, R.P.M., r.p.m. or **revs.per min.** revolutions per minute
R.P.N.Y. Regional Plan of New York
R.P.O. Railway Post Office
RPPA Republican Postwar Policy Association
RPS, R.P.S., rps, r.p.s. or **revs.per sec.** revolutions per second
R.P.S. Royal Photographic Society [of Great Britain]
rps, RPS, R.P.S., r.p.s. or **revs.per sec.** revolutions per second
rpt., Rep., rep. or **rept.** report; reported
R.Q. (Ravitaillement quotidiens)(Fr.) Daily replenishment of supplies
R.Q. or **r.q.** respiratory quotient
r.q. or **R.Q.** respiratory quotient
RR, R.R., R. or **r.** railroad (cf. Rwy.)
RR. (reverendissimus)(Lat.) Most Reverend
R.R. Railway Reserve (Australia); rural route
R.R., RR, R. or **r.** railroad (cf. Rwy.)
R.R. or **Rt. Rev.** Right Reverend
Rr (Mil.) or **Rr.** Rear
Rr. or **Rr** (Mil.) Rear
RRA or **R.R.A.** Rural Resettlement Administration
RRB or **R.R.B.** Railroad Retirement Board
RRC Rubber Reserve Company
R.R.C. regular route carrier; Royal Red Cross; Lady of the Royal Red Cross
Rr Ech Rear echelon
Rr Gd Rear guard
RRL Regimental reserve line
RS Road space (Mil.)
RS (Mil.) or **R.S.** Regular supplies

RS (Mil.), **R.S.** or **Rev. Stat.** Revised Statutes
R.S. Receiving ship; Recruiting Service
R.S., Rec. Sec. or **rec. sec.** recording secretary
R.S. or **Ref. Sp.** Reformed Spelling
R.S., Rev-Stat. or **RS** (Mil.) Revised Statutes
R.S. or **RS** (Mil.) regular supplies
R.S. or **r.s.** right side
R.S. or **R.S.L.** Royal Society [of London]
R/S Report of Survey (Mil.)
Rs, R, R., r, Rs. or **rs** rupees (cf. Rx)
rs, R, R., r, Rs or **Rs.** rupees (cf. Rx)
r.s. or R.S. right side
R.S.A. Railway Signal Association; Royal Scottish Academician or Academy
R.S.A. or **R.S.A.I.** Royal Society of Antiquaries of Ireland
R.S.A. or **R. S. Arts** Royal Society of Arts (London)(cf. S.A.)
R.S.A.I. or **R.S.A.** Royal Society of Antiquaries of Ireland
R.S. Arts or **R.S.A.** Royal Society of Arts (London)(cf) S.A.)
R.S.B. Regimental stretcher bearer (Brit.)
R.S.C.J. (Religiosa Sacratissimi Cordis Jesu)(Lat.) Religious of the Most Sacred Heart of Jesus (cf. R.S.H.)
R.S.D. Royal Society of Dublin
R.S.E. Royal Society of Edinburgh
R.S.E.S. Refrigeration Service Engineers' Society
RSFSR or **R.S.F.S.R.** Russian Socialist Federated Soviet Republics (cf. U.S.S.R.)
R.S.Fus. Royal Scots Fusiliers
R.S.H. Religious of the Sacred Heart (cf. R.S.C.J.)
R.Signals or **R.C.S.** Royal Corps of Signals
R.S.L. Royal Society of Literature [of the United Kingdom]
R.S.L. or **R.S.** Royal Society of London
R.S.M. Regimental sergeant major; Royal School of Mines (London)(now Royal College of Science); Royal Society of Medicine (London)
R.S.N.A. Radiological Society of North America; Royal Society of Northern Antiquaries or Antiquities
RSO Regimental supply officer (cf. S-4)
R.S.O. Railway Sorting Office; Railway Station Office or Suboffice (Brit.)
R.S.P.B. Royal Society for the Protection of Birds (London)
R.S.P.C.A. Royal (now National) Society for the Prevention of Cruelty to Animals
R.S.P.M.A. Refrigeration Supplies and Parts Manufacturers Association
R Sqd Rifle squad
R.S.S. Royal Statistical Society (London) (cf. S.S.)
R.S.S. (Regiae Societatis Sodalís)(Lat.), **F.R.S.** or **S.R.S.** (Societatis Regiae Socius)(Lat.) Fellow of the Royal Society [of London]
R Sta Regulating station
R.S.V.P., r.s.v.p. (répondez s'il vous plaît) (Fr.), **o.s.a** (om svar anhålles)(Swed.), **S.u.** (Svar udbedes)(Dan.), **u.A.w.g.** (um Antwort wird gebeten)(Ger.) or **u. gefl. A. w. g.** (umgefällige Antwort wird gebeten)(Ger.) a reply is requested; please reply
R.S.W. Royal Scottish Water Colour Society
R.S.W. or **R.W.S.** Royal Society of [Painters in] Watercolours
R.S.W.C. right side up with care
R.T. reading test
R.T. or **r.t.** right tackle
R/T radio-telegraphy
rt. round trip
rt., d. (destra)(Ital.), (droit)(Fr.), **R.** or **r.** right (cf. m.d.; ro.)
r.t. or **R.T.** right tackle
RTC Replacement Training Center
R.T.C. Royal Tank Corps
rtd., ret. or **retd.** returned
rte. route
Rt. Hon. Right Honorable
RTO (Mil.) or **R.T.O.** Railroad transportation officer; Railway transport officer
R Traf O Railway traffic officer
Rt. Rev. or **R.R.** Right Reverend
R.T.S. Religious Tract Society (Brit.)(now United Society for Christian Literature); Royal Toxophilite Society
Rts. (stocks) or **rts.** rights
Rt.W., Rt.Wpfl., Rt.Wpful. or **R.W.** Right Worshipful (Freemasonry)
Rt.W. or **R.W.** Right Worthy (Freemasonry)
Rt.Wpfl., Rt.Wpful., Rt.W. or **R.W.** Right Worshipful (Freemasonry)
R.U. rat unit or units; Rugby Union
Ru ruthenium (Chem)
Rud. Rudolf
R.U.E. or **r.u.e.** right upper entrance (Theat.)
R.U.I. Royal University, Ireland
Rum. or **Roum.** Rumania or Roumania; Rumanian or Roumanian
R.U.R. or **R.U.Rif.** Royal Ulster Rifles
R.U. Rif. or **R.U.R.** Royal Ulster Rifles
Rus. or **Russ.** Russia; Russian
R.U.S.I. Royal United Service Institution (London)(cf. U.S.I.)
R.U.S.Mus Royal United Service Museum
Russ. or **Rus.** Russia; Russian
russ. russia (Leather)
Rutd. or **Rutl.** Rutlandshire
Rutl. or **Rutd.** Rutlandshire
R.V. Reformed Version; Rifle Volunteers
R.V. or **Rev. Ver.** Revised Version [of the Bible]
RVA or **rva** reactive volt-ampere
R.V.A. Regular Veterans Association
rva or **RVA** reactive volt-ampere
R.V.C. Rifle Volunteer Corps (Brit.); Royal Veterinary College
R.V.O. or **V.O.** Royal Victorian Order

R.V.S.V.P. (répondez vite, s'il vous plaît) (Fr.) please reply at once
R.V.W.A. or **R.V.W.Assn.** Regular Veterans Women's Association
R.V.W.Assn. or **R.V.W.A.** Regular Veterans Women's Association
R.W. or **Rt.W.** Right Worthy (Freemasonry)
R.W., Rt.W., Rt.Wpfl. or **Rt.Wpful.** Right Worshipful (Freemasonry)
R.W., rw., ch. de f. (chemin de fer)(Fr.), **R., r., rly., Rwy.** or **Ry.** railway (cf. R.R.)
R.W.A. Royal West [of England] Academician or Academy
R.W.D.G.M. Right Worshipful Deputy Grand Master (Freemasonry)
R.W.G.M. Right Worshipful Grand Master (Freemasonry)
R.W.G.R. Right Worthy Grand Representative (Freemasonry)
R.W.G.S. Right Worthy Grand Secretary (Freemasonry)
R.W.G.T. Right Worthy Grand Templar (Freemasonry); Right Worthy Grand Treasurer (Freemasonry)
R.W.G.W. Right Worthy Grand Warden (Freemasonry); Right Worshipful Grand Warden (Freemasonry)
R.W.J.G.W. Right Worthy Junior Grand Warden (Freemasonry)
R.W.M. Right Worshipful Master (Freemasonry)
R.W.S. or **R.S.W.** Royal Society of [Painters in] Watercolours
R.W.S.G.W. Right Worshipful Senior Grand Warden (Freemasonry)
Rwy., ch. de f. (chemin de fer)(Fr.), **R., r., rly., R.W., rw.** or **Ry.** railway (cf. R.R.)
Rx, R, r., Rec., rec. or **rp.** recipe; take (Pharm.)
Rx, Rx. or **rx** tens of rupees (cf. rs.)
Rxb., rxb. or **Roxb.** Roxburgh (Bookbinding)
Ry., ch. de f. (chemin de fer)(Fr.), **R., r., rly., R.W., rw.** or **Rwy.** railway (cf. R.R.)
Ry Bn Railway battalion
R.Y.S. Royal Yacht Squadron
rys. railways

PX (Rho Chi) National undergraduate honor fraternity (Pharmacy)

S

S sand; scalar (Math.); sulphur (Chem.)
S, S. or **s.** (signa)(Lat.) mark [directions to the patient] (Pharm.)
S, S., s. or **So.** south
S. (sumendum)(Lat.) to be taken
S., Abs. (Abschnitt)(Ger.), **Abt.** (Abteilung) (Ger.), **s., sec.** or **sect.** section
S., Ges. (Gesellschaft)(Ger.), **s., Soc., soc., Socy., socy.** or **Ver.** (Verein)(Ger.) society (cf. assn.)
S., hl. (heilig)(Ger.) or **P.** (pius)(Lat.) sacred; holy
S. (Seite)(Ger.), (Side)(Dan.), **p., pág.** (página)(Port., Span.) or **s.** (sida) (Swed.) page
S. (Sider)(Dan.), **p., pp., sid.** (sidor)(Swed.) or **SS.** (Seiten)(Ger.) pages
S., S or **s.** (signa)(Lat.) mark [directions to the patient]
S., S, s. or **So.** south
S. or **s.** scribe; steel
S., s. (Socius, Sodalis)(Lat.) or **F.** Fellow
S., s., San, Sta. (santa)(Port., Span.), **São, Sto.** (santo)(Port.), **Skt.** (Sankt)(Ger.), **St., Ste** (sainte)(Fr.), **św.** (świety) (Pol.), **sz.** or **szt.** (szent)(Hung.) saint
S., s., Sch (Mil.) or **sch.** school
S., s. or **sec.** secondary
S., s., Sen. or **sen.** senate
S., s. or **sing.** singular
S., s., So., Sou. or **Sthn.** southern
S., s. or **Soc.** Socialist
S., s. or **sop.** soprano
S., s. (Geneal.), **suc.** or **succ.** succeeded
S., s. (siehe)(Ger.), **V.** (véase)(Span.), **v.** (voir)(Fr.), **v., vid.** (vide)(Lat.) or **voy.** (voyez)(Fr.) see (cf. attn.; obs.)
S., Sa., Sat., St. or **Stdy.** Saturday
S. or **Sab.** Sabbath
S. or **Sax.** Saxon
S., sbre. (se(p)tiembre)(Span.), **Sep., Sept., set.** (setembro)(Port.), **sett.** (settembre) (Ital.), **szept.** (szeptember)(Hung.) or **Wrzes.** (Wrzesień)(Pol.) September
S., Sc., sc., sci. or **Wiss.** (Wissenschaft) (Ger.) science
S., Sig. or **sig.** Signor (Italian equivalent of Mr.)
S. or **sigill.** (sigillum)(Lat.) seal
S., Su., Sun. or **Sund.** Sunday
S- attached to sulphur (as S-methyl-thiophenol)(Chem.)
s. (sepultus)(Lat.) buried; (saeculum) (Lat.) generation; geological age; (subito)(Ital.) quickly (Music); sacral (Anat.); set; sets; sign; sire (Pedigree); solo; sou; stem; stere; stock; sun
s., a., Ag (Chem.), **Ar., ar., arg.** (argentum) (Lat.) or **sil.** silver
s., Abs. (Abschnitt)(Ger.), **Abt.** (Abteilung) (Ger.), **S., sec.** or **sect.** section
s. (siècle)(Fr.), **C., c., cen., cent.** or **w.** (wiek)(Pol.) century
s., F. or **f.** (filius)(Lat.) son
s. (sinistra)(Ital., Lat.), **g.** (gauche)(Fr.) or **l.** left (cf. M.G.; S.M.; O.S.)
s., Ges. (Gesellschaft)(Ger.), **S., Soc., soc., Socy., socy.** or **Ver.** (Verein)(Ger.) society (cf. assn.)
s. (sinistra)(Ital.), **izq.ª, izq.ᵈᵃ** (izquierda) (Span.), **L.H., l.h., M.G., m.g.** (main gauche)(Fr.), **m.s.** (mano sinistra) (Lat.) or **S.M.** (sinistra mano)(Lat.) left hand
s. (sida)(Swed.), **p., pág.** (página)(Port., Span.) or **S.** (Seite)(Ger.), (Side) (Dan.) page
s., S, or **S.** (signa)(Lat.) mark [a prescription]
s., S, S. or **So.** south
s. or **S.** scribe; steel
s., S. (Socius, Sodalis)(Lat.) or **F.** Fellow

s., S., San, Sta. (santa)(Port., Span.), **São, Sto.** (santo)(Port.), **Skt.** (Sankt)(Ger.), **St., Ste** (sainte)(Fr.), **św.** (święty)(Pol.), **sz.** or **szt.** (szent)(Hung.) saint
s., S., Sch (Mil.) or **sch.** school
s., S. or **sec.** secondary
s., S., Sen. or **sen.** senate
s., S. or **sing.** singular
s., S., So., Sou. or **Sthn.** southern
s., S. or **Soc.** socialist
s., S. or **sop.** soprano
s., S., SS, Ss., ss. (semi)(Fr.),(semis)(Lat.) or **hf.** half
s. (Geneal.), **S., suc.** or **succ.** succeeded
s, s., sym. or **sym-** (Chem.) symmetrical
s., sb. or **subst.** substantive
s. or **sec.** second
s., sec. or **secs.** seconds
s., ser. or **ord.** (ordo, ordines)(Lat.) series
s. or **sgd.** signed
s. or **sh.** shilling; shillings
s. or **sin** sine (Math.)
s., Sn. (sine)(Lat.), **sen.** (senza)(Ital.)(Music), **w.o.** or **wt.** without
s. or **sph.** spherical
s. or **St.** stratus
s. or **str.** steamer
s. or **sur.** surplus
S-1 Personnel officer (Brigades and lower units) (cf. A-1; G-1)
S-2 Intelligence officer (Brigades and lower units)(cf. A-2; G-2)
S-3 Plans and training officer (Brigades and lower units)(cf. A-3; G-3)
S-4 Supply officer (Brigades and lower units)(cf. A-4; G-4)
SA or **S.A.** Sugar Agency
SA (Mil.) or **s.a.** Small arms
S.A. Salvation Army; Society of Apothecaries; Society of Arts (Brit.)(now Royal Society of Arts); special [temporary] authorization; (Sturm Abteilung)(Ger.) Storm Division (Nazi party army)
S.A. (Sociedad Anónima)(Span.), **A/B, a.-b.** (aktiebolag, aktiebolaget)(Swed.), **A.G.** (Aktien Gesellschaft)(Ger.) or **A/S** (Aktieselskab, Aktieselskapet)(Dan.) joint stock company (cf.Ges.; G.M.b.H.; S. en C.)
S.A. (Son Altesse)(Fr.), (Su Alteza)(Span.) or **H.H.** His or Her Highness
S.A. or **SA** Sugar Agency
S.A. or **s.a.** semiannual
S.A., S. Af. or **S. Afr.** South Africa
S.A., S. Am. or **S. Amer.** South America
S.A. or **S. Aus.** South Australia
Sa or **Sm** samarium (Chem.)
Sa. sable
Sa., S., Sat., St. or **Stdy.** Saturday
S.a. subject to approval
S.ª, Snra. or **Sra.** (senhora)(Port.), (señora)(Span.). title of courtesy, married woman; lady (cf. L.; Mrs.)
s.a. (sine arte)(Lat.) without art or rule (cf. sec. nat.)
s.a. (sine anno)(Lat.), **N.D., n.d.** or **o.J.** (ohne Jahr)(Ger.) without year [of publication]; no date
s.a. or **SA** (Mil.) small arms
s.a. or **S.A.** semiannual
s.a. or **sec. art.** (secundum artem)(Lat.) artificially; scientifically
s/a subject to approval
S.A.A. Silk Association of America (now National Federation of Textiles)
S.A.A. or **SA Am** (Mil.) small arms ammunition
SA Am (Mil.) or **S.A.A.** small arms ammunition
SAB or **S.A.B.** Science Advisory Board
S.A.B. Society of American Bacteriologists
S.A.B. or **SAB** Science Advisory Board
Sab. or **S.** Sabbath
S.A.C. Scottish Automobile Club
SACOA Southern Appalachian Coal Operators' Association
Sad Saddler (Mil.)
S.A.E. Society of Automotive Engineers
S.A.F. Society of American Foresters
S. Af., S.A. or **S. Afr.** South Africa
S.Af. or **S.Afr.** South African
S.A.F. and O.H. Society of American Florists and Ornamental Horticulturists
S. Afr., S. A. or **S. Af.** South Africa
S.Afr. or **S.Af.** South African
S.Afr.D. South African Dutch
S.A.I. (Son Altesse Impériale)(Fr.), (Su Alteza Imperial)(Span.) or **H.I.H.** His or Her Imperial Highness
S.A.I.F. South African Industrial Federation
S.A.J. Society for the Advancement of Judaism
S.A.L. Sons of the American Legion
Sales Comm Sales commissary
Sales Comm Bn Sales commissary battalion
Sales Comm Co Sales commissary company
Salop. Shropshire
S.A.L.P. South African Labor Party
Salv Salvage (Mil.)
Salv. Salvador; Salvator
Salv Bn Salvage battalion
Salv Co Salvage company
S.A.M. Society of American Magicians
S. Am., S. A. or **S. Amer.** South America
S.Am. or **S. Amer.** South American
Sam. Samaritan
Sam. or **Saml.** Samuel
S.A.M.E. Society of American Military Engineers
S.Amer., S.A. or **S.Am.** South America
S.Amer. or **S.Am.** South American
Saml. or **Sam.** Samuel
S&B Sterilization and bath (Mil.)
s. & c. or **s. and c.** shipper and carrier; sized and calendered (paper)
S & F Sound and flash (Mil.)
S. & F.A. Shipping and Forwarding Agent

S & F Bn Sound and flash battalion

S. & H. exc. Sundays and holidays excepted

s. & l.c. sue and labor clause (Insurance)

s. & s.c. or **s. and s.c.** sized and supercalendered paper

S. & T. or **S. and T.** supply and transport (Brit.)

San, Sta. (santa)(Port., Span.), **S., s., São, Sto.** (santo)(Port.), **Skt.** (Sankt)(Ger.), **St., Ste** (sainte)(Fr.), **św.** (świety)(Pol.), **sz.** or **szt.** (szent)(Hung.) saint

San. C. or **S. C.** Sanitary Corps

San.D. Doctor of Sanitation

s. and c. or **s. & c.** shipper and carrier; sized and calendered (paper)

S. and M. Sodor and Man [Diocese], in the signature of Bishop

s. and s.c. or **s. & s.c.** sized and supercalendered paper

S. and T. or **S. & T.** supply and transport (Brit.)

San Fran. or **S.F.** San Francisco

s.a.n.r. subject to approval, no risk

Sans., Sansc., Sansk., Scrt., Skr., Skrt. or **Skt.** Sanscrit; Sanskrit

Sansc., Sans., Sansk., Scrt., Skr., Skrt. or **Skt.** Sanscrit; Sanskrit

Sansk., Sans., Sansc., Scrt., Skr., Skrt. or **Skt.** Sanscrit; Sanskrit

São, Sto. (santo)(Port.), **S., s., San, Sta.** (santa)(Port., Span.), **Skt.** (Sankt)(Ger.), **St., Ste** (sainte)(Fr.), **św.** (świety)(Pol.), **sz.** or **szt.** (szent)(Hung.) saint

S.A.P. South African Party; South African Police

s. ap. scruple apothecaries' weight

s.a.p. semi-armour piercing; soon as possible

SAPFT or **S.A.P.F.T.** Special Adviser to the President on Foreign Trade

SAR Semiautomatic rifle

S.A.R. Sons of the American Revolution; South African Republic

S.A.R. (Son Altesse Royale)(Fr.) or **H.R.H.** His or Her Royal Highness

Sar. Sardinia; Sardinian

Sarum. Salisbury, in the signature of Bishop

S.A.S. (Societatis Antiquariorum Socius (Lat.) or **F.A.S.** Fellow of the Society of Antiquaries; Fellow of the Antiquarian Society

S.A.S. (Section d'automobiles sanitaires) (Fr.) or **S.S.A.** (Section sanitaire automobile)(Fr.) Automobile ambulance section (cf. Amb Sec)

Sask. Saskatchewan

SASRD Instl Subaqueous sound ranging development installation

S.A.S.S. or **S. Atto. S.S.** (su atento y seguro servidor)(Span.) your obedient and faithful servant

Sat. Saturn

Sat., S., Sa., St. or **Stdy.** Saturday

S.A.T.A. South African Teachers' Association

S.A.T.B. Soprano, alto, tenor, and bass

SATC or **S.A.T.C.** Students' Army Training Corps

sat. sol. saturated solution (Chem.)

S.Atto.S.S. or **S.A.S.S.** (su atento y seguro servidor)(Span.) your obedient and faithful servant

S. Aus. or **S.A.** South Australia

Sav. or **sav.** savings

sav. or **Sav.** savings

s.av. scruple avoirdupois

S.A.W.V. Spanish American War Veterans

Sax. Saxony

Sax. or **S.** Saxon

SB, S.B. or **s.b.** southbound

S.B. sales book; Shipping Board; short bill (Banking); simultaneous broadcast (Radio); small bonds; South Britain

S.B., SB or **s.b.** southbound

S.B. or **s.b.** steamboat

S.B., Sc.B. (Scientiae Baccalaureus)(Lat.), **B. ès S.** (Bachelier ès Sciences)(Fr.), **B.S.** or **B.Sc.** Bachelor of Science or Sciences

S/B statement of billing (Transp.)

Sb (stibium)(Lat.) antimony (Chem.)

Sb (Mil.) or **swbd.** switchboard

sb., s. or **subst.** substantive

s.b. (sur bois)(Fr.) [engraved] on wood

s.b., SB or **S.B.** southbound

s.b. or **S.B.** steamboat

SBAC Society of British Aircraft Construction

S.B.Comm., B.S.C., B.S.Comm., B.S. in C. or **B.S. in Com.** Bachelor of Science in Commerce

SbE south by east

S.B. in Chem., B.S. Chem., B.S. in Chem. or **Sc.B. in Chem.** Bachelor of Science in Chemistry

S.B. in Ed., B.Sc. Ed., B.Sc. in Ed., B.S.E., B.S.Ed., B.S. Educ., B.S. in Ed., B.S. in Edu., B.S. in Educ. or **B.S. in Educa.** Bachelor of Science in Education

S.B. in Engin., B.S.E., B.S. Engin., B.S. in E., B.S. in Engr., B.S. in Engrg. or **Sc. B. in Eng.** Bachelor of Science in Engineering

S.B. in Geol. or **B.S. in Geol.** Bachelor of Science in Geology

S.B. in Med., B.Sc. in Med., B.S. in Med. or **B.S. Med.** Bachelor of Science in Medicine

S.B. in Phar., B.Sc. in Pharm., B.S. in Ph., B.S. in Pharm., B.S. in Phcy., B.S.P., B.S. Phar. or **B.S. Pharm.** Bachelor of Science in Pharmacy

S.B.L.E. Society of Biblical Literature and Exegesis

SBPW or **S.B.P.W.** Special Board for Public Works

sbre. (se(p)tiembre)(Span.), **S., Sep., Sept., set.** (setembro)(Port.), **sett.** (settembre) (Ital.), **szept.** (szeptember)(Hung.) or **Wrzes.** (Wrzesień)(Pol.) September

SbW south by west

SC Summary Court (Mil.)

S.C. special circular; special constable; Staff Corps; Supply Corps

S.C. or **San. C.** Sanitary Corps

S.C. or **s.c.** Staff College (Brit.)

S.C., s.c. or **Sc.** (senatus consultum)(Lat.) decree of the Roman senate

S.C., Sig C or **Sig. C.** Signal Corps

S.C. or **So. Car.** South Carolina

S.C. (Salesianorum Congregatio)(Lat.) or **S.S.** (Societas Sancti Fancisci Salesii) (Lat.) Congregation of St. Francis de Sales; Salesian Fathers; Society of St. Francis de Sales; Salesians of St. John Bosco (cf.O.S.F.S.)

S.C., Sup. C. or **Sup. Ct.** Supreme Court

S/C Statement of Charges (Mil.)

Sc Sidecar (Mil.); scandium (Chem.)

Sc. Scots

Sc., S., sc., sci. or **Wiss.** (Wissenschaft) (Ger.) science

Sc., S.C. or **s.c.** (senatus consultum)(Lat.) decree of the Roman senate

Sc. or **Scot.** Scotch; Scottish

sc, s.c., s.caps., sm.c., sm. cap. or **sm. caps.** small capital letters (Printing)

sc, s.c., sm.c. or **sm. cap.** small capital letter (Printing)

sc. scale; scene; screw

sc., S., Sc., sci. or **Wiss.** (Wissenschaft) (Ger.) science

sc., scil., SS., ss. (scilicet)(Lat.), **näml.** (nämligen)(Swed.) or **viz.** (videlicet) (Lat.) namely; to wit (cf. i.e.)

sc. or **scr.** scruple (cf. s.ap.; s. av.)

sc., sculp., sculps. or **sculpt.** (sculpsit)(Lat.) he or she carved or engraved it

s.c. salvage charges; sharp cash; single column; supercalendered [paper]

s.c. or **S.C.** Staff College (Brit.)

s.c., S.C. or **Sc.** (senatus consultum)(Lat.) decree of the Roman senate

s.c., sc, s.caps., sm.c., sm.cap. or **sm. caps.** small capital letters (Printing)

s.c., sc, sm.c. or **sm.cap.** small capital letter (Printing)

s/c (son compte)(Fr.) his or her account; (su cuenta)(Span.) your account; surcharge

SCAA State Charities Aid Association

s.c. & s. or **s.c. and s.** strapped, corded, and sealed (Transp.)

Scan. or **Scand.** Scandinavia; Scandinavian

s.c. and s. or **s.c. & s.** strapped, corded, and sealed (Transp.)

Scan. Mag. or **scan. mag.** (scandalum magnatum)(Lat.) Scandal of Peerage [Act]; scandal of magnates; defamation of dignity

S.C.A.P.A. Society for Checking the Abuses of Public Advertising

s. caps., sc, s.c., sm.c., sm. cap. or **sm. caps.** small capital letters (Printing)

S Car or **Sct C** Scout car (Mil.)

S.C.A.S. Signal Corps Aviation School

Sc.B., S.B. (Scientiae Baccalaureus)(Lat.), **B. ès S.** (Bachelier ès Sciences)(Fr.), **B.S.** or **B.Sc.** Bachelor of Science or Sciences

Sc.B. in Chem., B.S.Chem., B.S. in Chem. or **S.B. in Chem.** Bachelor of Science in Chemistry

Sc.B. in Eng., B.S.E., B.S. Engin., B.S. in E., B.S. in Engr., B.S. in Engrg. or **S.B. in Engin.** Bachelor of Science in Engineering

SCC or **S.C.C.** State Corporation Commission; Surplus Commodities Corporation

S.C.C. single cotton covered wire (Elec.)

S.C.C. or **SCC** State Corporation Commission; Surplus Commodities Corporation

SCD or **S.C.D.** Surgeon's certificate of disability

S.C.D. or **D.C.S.** Doctor of Commercial Science

Sc.D., S.D. (Scientiae Doctor)(Lat.), **Dr. Sci., D. S.** or **D.Sc.** Doctor of Science

Scd Scheduled (Mil)

Sc.D.M., D.M.S., Med.Sc.D., M.Sc.D. or **Sc.D.Med.** Doctor of Medical Science

Sc.D.Med., D.M.S., Med.Sc.D., M.Sc.D. or **Sc.D.M.** Doctor of Medical Science (cf. M.D.)

S.C.E. single cotton over enamel (Elec.)

S.C.F.C. (Section des chemins de fer de campagne)(Fr.) Army railroad section

Sch (Mil.), **S., s.** or **sch.** school

sch., S., s. or **Sch** (Mil.) school

sch., schl. or **Schol.** scholar

sch. or **schol.** (scholium)(Lat.) marginal note (cf. Anm.; annot.)

sch. or **schr.** schooner

sched. schedule

schl., sch. or **Schol.** scholar

Sch.Mus.B., B.Sch.Mus., B.Sch.Music or **B.S.M.** Bachelor of School Music

Schol., sch. or **schl.** scholar

schol. scholastic

schol. or **sch.** (scholium)(Lat.) marginal note (cf. Anm.; annot.)

Sch.P., P.S.P. (Patres Scholarum Piarum) (Lat.) or **C.R.S.P.** (Clerici Regulares Pauperum Matris Dei Scholarum Piarum)(Lat.) Clerks Regular of the Poor Men of the Mother of God for Pious Schools; Fathers of the Religious Schools; Piarists

schr. or **sch.** schooner

S.C.I. Society of Chemical Industry (Brit.)

sci. scientific

sci., S., Sc., sc. or **Wiss.** (Wissenschaft) (Ger.) science

sci. fa. (scire facias)(Lat.) show cause (Law)

scil., sc., SS., ss. (scilicet)(Lat.), **näml.** (nämligen)(Swed.) or **viz.** (videlicet) (Lat.) namely; to wit (cf. i.e.)

S.C.J. (Societas Sacredotum a SS. Corde Jesu)(Lat.) Society of the Priests of the Sacred Heart of Jesus; (Societas Sacratissimi Cordis Jesu Infantis) (Lat.) Society of the Most Sacred Heart of the Infant Jesus

S.C.L. Student of the Civil Law

SCM Special court-martial

S.C.M. (Sacra Catolíca Majestad)(Span) Sacred Catholic Majesty; (Sacra Cesárea Majestad)(Span.) Sacred Imperial Majesty; State Certified Midwife; Student Christian Movement (Brit.)

Sc.M., S.M. (Scientiae Magister)(Lat.), **M.S.** or **M.Sc.** Master of Science
s.c.m. or **Sum CM** (Mil.) summary court-martial
S.Con.Res. Senate concurrent resolution
Scot. or **Sc.** Scotch; Scottish
Scot. or **Scotl.** Scotland
SCP, scp or **s.cp.** spherical candlepower
scp. or **scr.** scrip; script
s.cp., SCP or **scp** spherical candlepower
S.C.P.I. Structural Clay Products Institute
SCPL Seed and Crop Production Loans
scr. or **sc.** scruple (cf. s. ap.; s. av.)
scr. or **scp.** scrip; script
Script. Scriptural; Scripture
Scrt., Sans., Sansc., Sansk., Skr., Skrt. or **Skt.** Sanscrit; Sanskrit
SCS and **S.C.S.** Soil Conservation Service
S.C.S. Superintendent Car Service
S.C.S. or **SCS** Soil Conservation Service
scs. scales
Sct Scout (Mil.)
Sct C or **S. Car** Scout car (Mil.)
Sct C Ht Scout car, half track
sculp., sc., sculps. or **sculpt.** (sculpsit)(Lat.) he or she carved or engraved it
sculp. or **sculpt.** sculptor; sculptural; sculpture
sculps., sc., sculp. or **sculpt.** (sculpsit)(Lat.) he or she carved or engraved it
sculpt. (sculptus)(Lat.), **eng., engr., inc.** or **incis.** (incisus)(Lat.) engraved
sculpt., sc., sculp. or **sculps.** (sculpsit)(Lat.) he or she carved or engraved it
sculpt. or **sculp.** sculptor; sculptural; sculpture
S.C.V. Sons of Confederate Veterans
S.C.W. Society of Colonial Wars
SD (Mil.) or **s.d.** Special duty
SD or **Supt.Doc.** Superintendent of Documents
S.D. (salutem dicit)(Lat.) he or she sends greetings; Senior Deacon; Southern Department (Army)
S.D., Sc.D. (Scientiae Doctor)(Lat.), **Dr. Sci., D.S.** or **D.Sc.** Doctor of Science
S.D. or **s.d.** standard deviation (Math.)
S.D. or **S. Dak.** South Dakota
S/D or **s.d.** sea-damaged; sight draft
s.D. (samme Dato)(Dan.) same date
sd. said (aforesaid); sewed
s.d. several dates; short delivery; single deck; solid-drawn; (sine die)(Lat.) without a day [being set]
s. d. (samma dag)(Swed.) or **a.ds.T.** (an demselben Tage)(Ger.) the same day (cf. s.D.)
s.d. or **S.D.** standard deviation (Math.)
s.d. or **S/D** sea-damaged; sight draft
SDA specific dynamic action
S.D.A. Seventh Day Adventist
S. Dak. or **S. D.** South Dakota
S.D.B.L. sight draft, bill of lading attached
S.D.C. St. David's College; Society of the Divine Compassion
S.D.Co. Safe Deposit Company
S.D.F. Social Democratic Federation (Brit.)
sdg. siding
S.D.M.J. September, December, March, June (Interest)
S.Doc. or **Sen.Doc.** Senate Document
S.D.P. Social Democratic Party
S.D.S. (Societas Divini Salvatoris)(Lat.) Society of the Divine Savior; Salvatorians
S.D.U.K. Society for the Diffusion of Useful Knowledge (Brit.)
S.D.V. or **S.V.D.** (Societas Divini Verbi) (Lat.) Society of the Divine Word; Fathers of the Divine Word
SE, S.E. or **s.e.** southeast
S.E. Society of Engineers; southeastern
S. E. (Su Excelencia)(Span.), **H.E., S. Exc.** (Son Excellence)(Fr.) or **S. Excia.** (Sua Excel(l)ência)(Port.) His Excellency
S.E., SE or **s.e.** southeast
Se selenium (Chem.)
s.e. second entrance (Theat.); single entry (Bookkeeping)
s.e., SE or **S.E.** southeast
Sea. seaman
Sea.1c. seaman, first class
SEbE southeast by east
SEBM Society for Experimental Biology and Medicine
SEbS southeast by south
SEC or **S.E.C.** Securities and Exchange Commission
S.E.C. Supreme Economic Council
S.E.C. or **SEC** Securities and Exchange Commission
Sec., sec., Secy., secy. or **Srio.** (secretario) (Span.) secretary
sec. secant (Math.); sector; secured; security
sec., Abs. (Abschnitt)(Ger.), **Abt.** (Ab teilung)(Ger.), **S., s.** or **sect.** section
sec. (secundum)(Lat.), **ap.** (apud)(Lat.), **if.** (ifølge)(Dan) or **acc.** according to
sec., S. or **s.** secondary
sec. or **s.** second
sec., s. or **secs.** seconds
sec., Sec., Secy., secy. or **Srio.** (secretario) (Span.) secretary
sec., secs. or **ss.** sections
sec^{-1} per second
sec^{-2} per second per second
sec. art. or **s.a.** (secundum artem)(Lat.) according to art; scientifically; artificially
sec.-ft. second-foot; second-feet (cf. c.f.s.)
sech. hyperbolic secant
Sec. Leg. Secretary of Legation
sec. leg. or **S. L.** (secundum legem)(Lat.) according to law (cf. sec. reg.)
sec. nat. or **s.n.** (secundum naturam)(Lat.) according to nature; naturally (cf. s.a.)
sec. reg. (secundum regulam)(Lat.) according to rule (cf. f.l.a.; sec. leg.)
secs., s. or **sec.** seconds
secs., sec. or **ss.** sections

sect. sectional
sect., Abs. (Abschnitt)(Ger.), **Abt.** (Abteilung)(Ger.), **S., s.** or **sec.** section
sec.us. (secumdum usum)(Lat.) according to usage (cf. ad us.)
Secy., Sec., sec., secy. or **Srio.** (secretario) (Span.) secretary
secy., Sec., sec., Secy. or **Srio.** (secretario) (Span.) secretary
S.E.E.C.W.. Society to Eliminate Economic Causes of War
S.E.e.O., s.e.e.o. (salvis erroribus et omissis) (Lat.) or **E. & O.E.** errors and omissions excepted (also used in the singular)(cf. e.e.; S.E.ou O.)
S.E.F.A. Southeastern Freight Association
S.E.G. Society of Economic Geologists
seg. segment
seismol. seismological; seismology
sel. (selig)(Ger.) blessed (hence, deceased) (cf. B.M.; dec.) selection
sel. or **ausgew.** (ausgewählt)(Ger.) selected
Selw. Selwyn [College] (Cambridge)
S.E.M. (Secrétaire d'état-major)(Fr.) Staff secretary
Sem Semimobile (Mil.)
Sem. (Semel)(Lat.) once (Pharm.); Seminary; Semitic
sem. semble; semicolon
semp. (sempre)(Ital.) always; in the same manner throughout (Music)
Sen., S., s. or **sen.** senate
Sen. or **sen.** senator
Sen., sen., d. A. (der Ältere)(Ger.), **d.ä.** (den äldre)(Swed.), **Senr., senr., Sr.** or **sr.** senior
sen., S., s. or **Sen.** senate
sen. (senza)(Ital.)(Music), **s., Sn.** (sine) (Lat.), **w.o.** or **wt.** without
S. en C. (Sociedad en Comandita)(Span.), **Co. Ltd., G.m.b.H.** (Gesellschaft mit beschränkter Haftung)(Ger.), **n v** (naamloose vennootschap)(Dutch) or **Soc. an^e^** (Société anonyme)(Fr.) limited company (cf. A.G.; cie; S.A.)
sen.clk. senior clerk
Sen.Doc. or **S.Doc.** Senate Document
Sen.Opt. Senior optime
Senr., senr., d. A. (der Ältere)(Ger.), **d.ä.** (den äldre)(Swed.), **Sen., sen., Sr.** or **sr.** senior
Sent (Mil.) or **sent.** sentence
Sentd (Mil.) or **sentd.** sentenced
s.e.o.o., S.E. ou O. (sauf erreur ou omission)(Fr.), **E.O.O.E., e.o.o.e.** (erreurs ou omissions exceptées)(Fr.) or **S.E.u.O.** (salvo error u omisión) (Span.) errors or omissions excepted (singular and plural)(cf. e.e.; S.E.e.O.)
S. E. ou O., s.e.o.o. (sauf erreur ou omission)(Fr.), **E.O.O.E., e.o.o.e.** (erreurs ou omissions exceptées)(Fr.) or **S.E.u. O.** (salvo error u omisión) (Span.) errors or omissions excepted (singular and plural)(cf e.e.; S.E.e.o.)
Sep., S., sbre. (se(p)tiembre)(Span.), **Sept., set.** (setembro)(Port), **sett.** (settembre) (Ital.), **szept.** (szeptember)(Hung.) or **Wrzes.** (Wrzesień)(Pol.) September
Sep. or **Sept.** Septuagint [Version of the Old Testament]
sep. sepal; separate
Sept., S., sbre. (se(p)tiembre)(Span.), **Sep., set.** (setembro)(Port.), **sett.** (settembre)(Ital.), **szept.** (szeptember)(Hung.) or **Wrzes.** (Wrzesień)(Pol.) September
Sept. or **Sep.** Septuagint [Version of the Old Testament
septu. septuplicate
seq. sequel
seq., seqq., sq., sqq. (sequens, sequentes, sequentia)(Lat.), **F., f., ff., fol.** or **foll.** the following (cf. et seq.)
seq., sequ. or **sq.** (sequitur)(Lat.) it follows (logical inference)
seqq. (sequentibus)(Lat.) in the following places
seqq., seq., sq., sqq. (sequens, sequentes, sequentia)(Lat.), **F., f., ff., fol.** or **foll.** the following (cf. et seq.)
sequ., seq. or **sq.** (sequitur)(Lat.) it follows (logical inference)
SER serial service (telegrams)
SER or **S.E.R.** Soil Erosion Service
ser. serial; sermon
ser., s. or **ord.** (ordo, ordines)(Lat.) series
ser., Serv. (Mil.), **serv.** or **Svc** (Mil.) service
Serb. Serbia; Serbian
Serg., serg., Sergt., sergt., Serj., serj., Serjt., serjt., Sgt. or **sgt.** Sergeant or Serjeant
Sergt., sergt., Serg., serg., Serj., serj., Serjt., serjt., Sgt. or **sgt.** Sergeant or Serjeant
Serj., serj., Serg., serg., Sergt., sergt., Serjt., serjt., Sgt. or **sgt.** Serjeant or Sergeant
Serjt., serjt., Serg., serg., Sergt., sergt., Serj., serj., Sgt. or **sgt.** Serjeant or Sergeant
Serv (Mil.), **ser., serv.** or **Svc** (Mil.) service
Serv. Servia; Servian
serv. (serva)(Lat.) preserve
serv., ser., Serv (Mil.) or **Svc** (Mil.) service
serv. or **servt.** servant
Serv Bn Service battalion
Serv Btry Service battery
Serv Co Service company
servt. or **serv.** servant
Serv Tr Service troop
SESAC Society of European Stage Authors and Composers
sesquih. or **Sesquih.** (sesquihora)(Lat.) an hour and a half
sess. session
sesunc. (sesuncia)(Lat.) an ounce and a half
set. (setembro)(Port.), **S., sbre.** (se(p)tiembre)(Span.), **Sep., Sept., sett.** (settembre)(Ital.), **szept.** (szeptember)(Hung.) or **Wrzes.** (Wrzesień)(Pol.) September
sett. (settembre)(Ital.), **S., sbre.** (se(p)tiembre)(Span.), **Sep., Sept., set.** (setembro) (Port.), **szept.** (szeptember)(Hung.) or **Wrzes.** (Wrzesień)(Pol.) September

S. E. u O. (salvo error u omisión)(Span.), **E.O.O.E., e.o.o.e.** (erreurs ou omissions exceptées)(Fr), **S.E. ou O.** or **s.e.e.o.** (sauf erreur ou omission)(Fr.) errors or omissions excepted (singular and plural)(cf. E. & O.E.; e.e.)
S. Exc. (Son Excellence)(Fr.), **H.E., S.E.** (Su Excelencia)(Span.) or **S. Excia.** (Sua Excel(l)ência)(Port.) His Excellency
S. Excia. (Sua Excel(l)ência)(Port.), **H.E., S.E.** (Su Excelencia)(Span.) or **S. Exc.** (Son Excellence)(Fr.) His Excellency
sextupl. sextuplicate
SF semifinished
S.F. (Congregatio Filiorum Sanctae Familiae)(Lat.) Congregation of Sons of the Holy Family, or Sons of the Holy Family; Senior Fellow; ship fitter; sinking fund; Sinn Fein
S.F. or **San Fran.** San Francisco
S.f. (Schluss folgt)(Ger.) to be concluded [in our next]
sf., sforz., sfz. (sforzando, sforzato)(Ital.) or **fz.** (forzando)(Ital.) forced; with emphasis (Music)
s.f. (sub finem)(Lat.) near the end
s. F. H. (schwere Feldhaubitze)(Ger.) Heavy field howitzer
S.F.I.B. Southern Freight Inspection Bureau
S.F.N.D.A. Stove Founders' National Defense Association
sforz., sf., sfz. (sforzando, sforzato)(Ital.) or **fz.** (forzando)(Ital.) forced; with emphasis (Music)
S.F.S.C. (Societas Fratrum Sacri Cordis) (Lat.) or **F.S.C.** Brothers of the Sacred Heart; Society of Brothers of the Sacred Heart
S.F.S.R. Socialist Federation of Soviet Republics (cf. RSFSR; U.S.S.R.)
sfz., sf., sforz. (sforzando, sforzato)(Ital.) or **fz.** (forzando)(Ital.) forced; with emphasis (Music)
SG, S.G., s.g., G. or **sp. gr.** specific gravity
SG, S.G. or **Surg. Gen.** Surgeon General
S.G., S.-G., Sol. Gen. or **Sol.-Gen.** Solicitor General
sgd. or **s.** signed
sgl. or **sing.** single
SGO Surgeon General's Office (Mil.)
Sgt., sgt., Serg., serg., Sergt., sergt., Serj., serj., Serjt. or **serjt.** Sergeant or Serjeant
Sgt. Maj. or **S.M.** Sergeant major
S.G.W. Senior Grand Warden (Freemasonry)
SH (Mil.) or **S.H.** schoolhouse
S.H. specified hours
S.H. or **SH** school house
sh. sheep (Bookbinding); sheet; shunt
sh. or **s.** shilling
sh., Shr. or **shr.** share
Shak. or **Shaks.** Shakespeare
Shaks. or **Shak.** Shakespeare
S.H.D. Subsistence Homesteads Division
shd. should (Ms.)
shipt. or **shpt.** shipment
S.H.M. simple harmonic motion
shp, s.hp. or **s.h.p.** shaft horsepower
s.h.p., shp or **s.hp.** shaft horsepower
shpt. or **shipt.** shipment
Shr., shr. or **sh.** share
Shr., shr., shrs., shrs. or **shs.** shares
shr., sh. or **Shr.** share
shr., Shr., Shrs., shrs. or **shs.** shares
Shrs., Shr., shr., shrs. or **shs.** shares
S.H.S. Serb-Croat-Slovene (Yugoslavia)
S.H.S. (Societatis Historiae Socius)(Lat.) **F.Hist.S., F.H.S.** or **H.S.S.** (Historiae Societatis Socius)(Lat.) Fellow of the Historical Society
shs., Shr., shr., Shrs. or **shrs.** shares
shtg. shortage
sh. tn., S.t. or **s.t.** short ton
s.h.v. (sub hoc verbo, sub hac voce)(Lat.), **i.v.** (in verbo or voce)(Lat.) or **s.v.** (sub verbo or voce)(Lat.) under this word; under the word (used in dictionaries)
S.I. Sandwich Islands; Staten Island (New York)
Si silicium, silicon (Chem.)
s.i. short interest
Sib. Siberia; Siberian
SIC, S.I.C. or **s.i.c.** specific inductive capacity (Elec.)
Sic. Sicilian; Sicily
s.i.c., SIC or **S.I.C.** specific inductive capacity (Elec.)
S.I.C.P. Society for Improving the Condition of the Poor
sid. (sidor)(Swed.), **p., pp., S.** (Sider)(Dan.) or **SS.** (Seiten)(Ger.) pages
s.i.d. (semel in die)(Lat.) once a day (cf. o.d.; p.d.)
S.I.E. Society of Industrial Engineers
Sierp. (Sierpień)(Pol.), **Ag., agto.** (agosto) (Span., Port.) or **Aug.** August
Sig (Mil.) or **sig.** signal
Sig. or **sig.** signature (cf. S.S., subscr.)
Sig., sig. (signori)(Ital.), **HH.** (Herren) (Ger.), **Messrs., MM.** (Messieurs)(Fr.), **Sres.** or **Srs.** (Señores)(Span.) Sirs; gentlemen
Sig., sig. or **S.** Signor (Italian equivalent of Mr.)
sig. signifying
sig., S. or **Sig.** Signor (Italian equivalent of Mr.)
sig. or **Sig.** signature (cf. S.S.; subscr.)
sig., Sig. (signori)(Ital.), **HH.** (Herren) (Ger.), **Messrs., MM.** (Messieurs)(Fr.), **Srs.** or **Sres.** (Senores)(Span.) sirs; gentlemen
Sig Bn Signal battalion
Sig C, Sig. C. or **S.C.** Signal Corps
Sig Co Signal company
Sig Co Armd Signal company armored
Sig Dep Signal depot
sigill. or **S.** (sigillum)(Lat.) seal
sig.mis. signature missing
Sig O Signal officer

Sig-Res Signal Corps Reserve
Sig Sec Signal section
Sig Tr Signal troop
sig.unk. signature unknown
Sil. Silicia
sil., a., Ag (Chem.), **Ar., ar., arg.** (argentum)(Lat.) or **s.** silver
S.I.M. Sergeant-instructor of musketry
Sim. Simeon; Simon
sim. simile
simlr. or **sim.** similar; similarly
sin or **s.** sine (Math.)
sing. (singulorum)(Lat.) of each (cf. āā)
sing., S. or **s.** singular
sing. or **sgl.** single
Singh. Singhalese
sinh hyperbolic sine
Sino-Jap. or **Chino-Jap.** Chinese-Japanese
S.I.O. Scripps Institution of Oceanography
Si op.sit., S.op.S., S.O.S., s.o.s. (si opus sit) (Lat.) or **e.F.** (erforderlichen Falls) (Ger.) if occasion require; if necessary (Pharm.)
S.I.S.A. Scotch-Irish Society of America
sist. or **Sr.** (soror)(Lat.) sister
S.I.T. Stevens Institute of Technology
s.i.t. stopping in transit (Transp.)
S.I.U. Students International Union
S.I.W. self-inflicted wound
S.J. (Societas Jesu)(Lat.) Society of Jesuits; Jesuits
s.j. (sub judice)(Lat.) under consideration
S.J.C. Supreme Judicial Court
S.J.D. (Scientiae Juridicae Doctor)(Lat.) or **D.J.S.** Doctor of Juridical Science
S.J.Res. Senate Joint Resolution
S.K. store keeper
Sk Sick (Mil.)
sk. sack
s. k. (så kallad)(Swed.) or **sog.** (sogennant) (Ger.) so-called
Skr., Sans., Sansc., Sansk., Scrt., Skrt. or **Skt.** Sanscrit; Sanskrit
Skrt., Sans., Sansc., Sansk., Scrt., Skr. or **Skt.** Sanscrit; Sankrit
sks. or **sx.** sacks
Skt. (Sankt)(Ger.), **S., s., San, Sta.** (santa) (Port., Span.), **São, Sto.** (santo)(Port.), **St., Ste** (sainte)(Fr.), **św.** (świety) (Pol.), **sz.** or **szt.** (szent)(Hung.) saint
Skt., Sans., Sansc., Sansk., Scrt., Skr. or **Skrt.** Sanscrit; Sanskrit
SL Support line
SL, S Lt or **Slt** Searchlight (Mil.)
S.L. Settlement Lease (Australia); Special Lease (Queensland)
S.L. or **sec. leg.** (secundum legem)(Lat.) according to law (cf. sec. reg.)
S.L. or **s.l.** (suo loco)(Lat.) in its place; seditious libeler; sergeant-at-law; solicitor at law
S.L., s.l. (sine loco)(Lat.), **n.p.** or **o.O.** (ohne Ort)(Ger.) without place; no place [of publication]
S.L., s.l., S. Lat. or **S. lat.** south latitude
S.L., Sqd. Ldr., Sq. Ldr. or **Sqn. Ldr.** Squadron leader (R.A.F.)
S-L Sound locator
s.l. salvage loss
s.l. or **S.L.** (suo loco)(Lat.) in its place; seditious libeler; sergeant at law; solicitor at law
s.l., S.L. (sine loco)(Lat.), **n.p.** or **o.O.** (ohne Ort)(Ger.) without place [of publication]; no place
s.l., S.L., S.Lat. or **S.lat.** south latitude
S.L.A. Special Libraries Association
s.l. & c. or **s.l. and c.** shipper's load and count
s.l. & t. or **s.l. and t.** shipper's load and talley
s.l.a.n. (sine loco, anno, vel nomine)(Lat.) or **o. O.,Dr. u. J.** (ohne Ort, Druckernamen und Jahr)(Ger.) without place, date or name; without place, publisher, and year [of publication]
s.l. and c. or **s.l. & c.** shipper's load and count
s.l. and t. or **s.l. & t.** **shipper's load and** talley
S.Lat., S.lat., S.L. or **s.l.** south latitude
Slav. Slavic; Slavonian; Slavonic
SL Btry or **S Lt Btry** Searchlight battery
sld. sailed; sealed
slent. (slentando)(Ital.) slackening in time (Music)(cf. perd.; ritard.; ritten.)
s.l.et a. (sine loco et anno)(Lat.), **n.p.or d.** or **o.O.u.J.** (ohne Ort und Jahr)(Ger). without place and year; no place or date [of publication]
slg. sailing
SLIC or **S.L.I.C.** Savings and Loan Insurance Corporation
S.L.P. Socialist Labor Party
s.l.p. (sine legitima prole)(Lat.) without lawful issue (cf. o.s.p.; s.m.p.; s.p.; s.p.s.)
SLRB or **S.L.R.B.** Steel Labor Relations Board
slsmgr. salesmanager
slsmn. salesman
S Lt, SL or **Slt** searchlight (Mil)
Slt, SL or **S Lt** searchlight (Mil.)
S Lt Btry or **SL Btry** Searchlight battery
SM Sawmill (Mil.)
S.M. short meter; silver medallist (Bisley) (Brit.); (Societas Mariae)(Lat.) Society of Mary; Marist Fathers; Brothers of Mary; Marists (cf. F.M.S.); Soldier's Medal; Sons of Malta; State Militia; Stipendiary Magistrate
S.M. (Sa Majesté)(Fr.), (Su Majestad) (Span.), **Hds. M., Hs.M.** (Hendes Majestæt)(Dan.), **H.M.** or **H.Maj:t** (Hans Majestät)(Swed.) His or Her Majesty
S.M. (sinistra mano)(Lat.), **izq.**[a], **izq.**[da] (izquierda)(Span.), **L.H., l.h., M.G., m.g.** (main gauche)(Fr.), **m.s.** (mano sinistra)(Lat.) or **s.** (sinistra)(Ital.) left hand
S.M., Sc.M. (Scientiae Magister)(Lat.), **M.S.** or **M.Sc.** Master of Science
S.M. or **Sgt. Maj.** Sergeant major
Sm or **Sa** samarium (Chem.)

Sm. or **Smith. Inst.** Smithsonian [Institution]

sm. small

SMA or **S.M.A.** Surplus Marketing Administration (now Agricultural Marketing Administration)

S.M.A. (Section de muntions d'artillerie) (Fr.) Artillery ammunition section; School of Military Aeronautics; Society of Marine Artists (Brit.)

S.M.A. or **Afr. Miss. Soc.** Society of Missionaries to Africa; African Missionary Society (cf. W.F., M.A.L.)

S.M.C. (Su Majestad Catolíca)(Span.) or **H.C.M.** His or Her Catholic Majesty

sm. c., sc, s.c., s. caps., sm. cap. or **sm. caps.** small capital letters (Printing)

sm. cap., sc, s.c. or **sm.c.** small capital letter (Printing)

sm. cap., sm. caps., sc, s.c., s. caps. or **sm.c.** small capital letters (Printing)

S.M.C.C. Special Mexican Claims Commission

S.M.E. (Sancta Mater Ecclesia)(Lat.) Holy Mother Church; School of Military Engineering (Brit.)

SMG Submachine gun

S.M.I. (Section de munitions d'infanterie) (Fr.) Infantry ammunition section

S.M.I. (Sa Majesté Impériale)(Fr.), (Su Majestad Imperial)(Span.) or **H.I.M.** His or Her Imperial Majesty

S.M. in Engin., M.S.E., M.S. in Eng. or **M.S. in Eng'g.** Master of Science in Engineering

Smith. Inst. or **Sm.** Smithsonian Institution

sml. (sammenlign)(Dan.), **cf., conf.** (confer)(Lat.), **comp., compar., cp., jf., jfr.** (jaevnfør)(Dan.), (jämför)(Swed.), **por.** (porównaj)(Pol.) or **vgl.** (vergleiche)(Ger.) compare

S.M.Lond. Soc. (Societatis Medicae Londinensis Socius) Fellow of the London Medical Society

S.M.M. (Sancta Mater Maria)(Lat.) Holy Mother Mary; (Societas Mariae de Montford)(Lat.) Missionaries of the Company of Mary; Company of Mary, Montfort; Society of the Company of Mary; Fathers of the Company of Mary; Sail maker's mate

S.M.M.& T. Society of Motor Manufacturers and Traders

S.M.O. Senior medical officer (Brit.)

smorz. (smorzando, smorzato)(Ital.) dying away (Music) (cf. cal.; manc.; perd.)

S.M.P. Submarine mine property

s.m.p. (sine mascula prole)(Lat.) without male issue (cf. o.s.p.)

S.M.P.E. Society of Motion Picture Engineers

S.M.S., F.d'I. (Societa Mutuo Soccorso, Figli d'Italia)(Ital.) Society for Mutual Help, Sons of Italy

smstrs. seamstress

S.M.T.O. Senior mechanical transport officer (Brit.)

SN or **S/N** shipping note

S/N or **SN** shipping note

Sn (stannum)(Lat.) tin (Chem.)

Sn (Mil.) or **Sn.** sanitary

Sn., s. (sine)(Lat.), **sen.** (senza)(Ital.) (Music) **w.o.** or **wt.** without

sn sine of the amplitude (elliptic function)

s.n. (sine nomine)(Lat.) without name

s.n. or **sec. nat.** (secundum naturam)(Lat.) according to nature; naturally (cf. s.a.)

S.N.A.M.E. Society of Naval Architects and Marine Engineers

S.N.D. static no delivery (Mech.)

Snr. or **Sr.** Senhor (Portuguese equivalent of Mr.)

Snra., S.ª or **Sra.** (senhora)(Port.), (señora) (Span.) title of courtesy, married woman (cf. Mrs.)

Sn-Res Sanitary Corps Reserve

Snrta., Srta. (senhorita)(Port.), **Frk.** (Frøken)(Dan.), **frk.** (fröken)(Swed.), **Frl.** (Fräulein)(Ger.), **Mdlle., Mlle.,** (Mademoiselle)(Fr.), **Srita., Srta.** or **Sta.** (Señorita)(Span.) Miss; unmarried woman or girl

SO (Mil.) or **s.o.** special order or orders

S.O. Stationery Office (Brit.)

S.O. or **O.E.M.** (Officer d'état-major)(Fr.) Staff officer

S.O., S/O or **s.o.** seller's option

S.O. or **s.o.** sub-office

S/O, S.O. or **s.o.** seller's option

So., S, S. or **s.** south

So., S., s., Sou. or **Sthn.** southern

s.o. shipping order; ship's option

s.o. or **S.O.** sub-office

s.o., S.O. or **S/O** seller's option

s.o. (siehe oben)(Ger.) or **v.s.** (vide supra) (Lat.) see above

S.O.A. Standard Optical Appliances

SOB or **S.O.B.** Senate Office Building

S.O.C. Society for Organizing Charity

S.O.C., O.C., O.Cist., S.O.Cist. or **S. Ord. Cist.** (Sacer Ordo Cisterciensis)(Lat.) Holy Order of Citeaux; Cistercian Order; Cistercians (cf. O.C.R.)

Soc. Socrates

Soc., S. or **s.** Socialist

soc., Ges. (Gesellschaft)(Ger.), **S., s., Soc., Socy., socy.** or **Ver.** (Verein)(Ger.) society (cf. assn.)

Soc. anᵉ (Société anonyme)(Fr.), **Co. Ltd., G.m.b.H.** (Gesellschaft mit beshränkter Haftung)(Ger.), **n v** (naamloose vennootschap)(Dutch) or **S. en C.** (sociedad en Comandita)(Span.) limited company (cf. A.G.; cie; S.A.)

So. Car. or **S.C.** South Carolina

sociol. sociological; sociology

Soc. Is. or **Soc. Isl.** Society Islands

S.O.Cist., O.C., O.Cist., S.O.C. or **S.Ord. Cist.** (Sacer Ordo Cisterciensis)(Lat.) Holy Order of Citeaux; Cistercian Order; Cistercians (cf. O.C.R.)

Socy., Ges. (Geselllschaft)(Ger.), **S., s., Soc., soc., socy.** or **Ver.** (Verein)(Ger.) society (cf. assn.)

socy., Ges. (Gesellschaft)(Ger.) **S., s., Soc., soc., Socy.** or **Ver.** (Verein)(Ger.) society (cf. assn.)

S.O.D. Shorter Oxford Dictionary

s.o.d. seller's option to double

S. of Sol. Song of Solomon

S. of T. or **S.T.** Sons of Temperance

S. of V. or **S.V.** Sons of Veterans

sog. (sogennant)(Ger.) or **s.k.** (så kallad) (Swed.) so-called

SOI Signal operations instructions

Sol Soldier (Mil.)

Sol. Solomon

Sol., sol. or **soln.** solution (cf. solut.)

Sol., sol. or **solr.** solicitor

sol. soluble

sol., Sol. or **soln.** solution (cf. solut.)

sol., Sol. or **solr.** solicitor

s.o.l. ship owner's liability

Sol. Gen., Sol.-Gen., S.G. or **S-G.** Solicitor General

soln., Sol. or **sol.** solution (cf. solut.)

solr., Sol. or **sol.** solicitor

solut. (solutus)(Lat.) or **dissd.** dissolved (cf. sol.; solv.)

solv. (solve)(Lat.) dissolve (Pharm.)(cf. sol.; solut.)

Som. Somerset; Somersetshire

son. sonata (Music)

Sons of S.A.W.V. Sons of Spanish American War Veterans

SOP Standard order of procedure; Standing operating procedure

S.O.P Special orders, post

sop., S. or **s.** soprano

Soph. Sophister; Sophocles

S.op.S., Si op.sit, S.O.S., s.o.s. (si opus sit) (Lat.) or **e.F.** (erforderlichen Falls) (Ger.) in case of need; if necessary (Pharm.)

Sor. or **Sr.** Señor (Spanish equivalent of Mr. q.v.)

S.O.R.C. Signal Officers Reserve Corps

S. Ord. Cist., O.C., O.Cist, S.O.C or **S.O. Cist.** (Sacer Ordo Cisterciensis)(Lat.) Holy Order of Citeaux; Cistercian Order; Cistercians (cf. O.C.R.)

SOS international wireless code call for help (not an abbreviation) (Variously and incorrectly interpreted as "Save Our Souls!" "Save Our Ship," and the like)

S.O.S. Service or Services of Supply; suspend other service

S.O.S., Si op.sit, S.op.S., s.o.s. (si opus sit) (Lat.) or **e.F.** (erforderlichen) Falls) (Ger.) if occasion require; if necessary (Pharm.)

sos., sost., sosten. (sostenuto)(Ital.) or **ten.** (tenuto)(Ital.) sustained (Music)

s.o.s., Si op.sit, S.op.S., S.O.S. (si opus sit) (Lat.) or **e.F.** (erforderlichen Falls) (Ger.) if occasion require; if necessary (Pharm.)

S.O.S.B. (Congregatio Sylvestrini Ordo Sancti Benedicti)(Lat.) Sylvestrine Order of St. Benedict; Sylvestrine Benedictines (cf. O.S.B.)

sosten., sos., sost. (sostenuto)(Ital.) or **ten.** (tenuto)(Ital.) sustained (Music)

Sou., S., s., So. or **Sthn.** southern

Sov. or **sov.** sovereign

sovs. or **Sovs.** sovereigns

S P Shore patrol

SP or **s.p.** single pole

S.P. (Section de parc de campagne)(Fr.) Field park section; Scout patrol; small pica (Typog.); Special Purchase [of Crown Lands without competition] (Australia); stop payment; submarine patrol

S.P., Chart. or **chart.** (chartula)(Lat.) (Pharm.) small paper

S.P. or **S.p.** starting price (Betting)

S.P. or **s.p.** supra protest (Banking, Law)

Sp. Spain

Sp., sp., Spir., spir. or **Spt.** (spiritus)(Lat.) spirit; spirits (Pharm.)

Sp. or **Span.** Spaniard; Spanish

S.p. or **S.P.** starting price (Betting)

sp. specimen; spelling; spell out (Printing);

sp. or **spec.** special

sp., spec. or **specif.** specific; specifically

sp. or **spp.** species

s.p. (sub polo)(Lat.) under the pole (Astron.); (sine prole)(Lat.) without issue; without offspring (cf. o.s.p.; s.l.p.; s.m.p; s.p.s.)

ś. p. (świętej pamięci)(Pol.), **D., d., dec., déc.** (décédé, décédée)(Fr.), **decd.** or **gest.** (gestorben)(Ger.) deceased (cf. B.M.; L.; ob.; Q.E.P.D.; R.I.P.; sel.)

s.p. or **SP** single pole

s.p. or **S.P.** supra protest (Banking)

s.p. or **S-ph** single phase (Elec.)

S.P.A. (Service de la poste aux armées) (Fr.), **APS** (Mil.) or **A.P.S.** Army Postal Service

s.p.a. subject to partial average (Marine ins.)

S.P.A. & C. Society for the Promotion of Aviation and Chemistry

SPAB Supply Priorities and Allocations Board (succeeded by WPB)

Sp. Am. Spanish American

Span. or **Sp.** Spaniard; Spanish

S.P.A.S. (Societatis Philosophiae Americanae Socius)(Lat.) or **F.A.P.S.** Fellow of the American Philosophical Society

S.P.C. Society for the Prevention of Crime

S.P.C.A. Society for the Prevention of Cruelty to Animals (cf. A.S.P.C.A. and R.S.P.C.A.)

S.P.C.C. Society for the Prevention of Cruelty to Children (cf. N.S.P.C.C.)

S.P.C.K. Society for the Promotion of Christian Knowledge

s.p.d. steamer pays dues

S.P.E. Society for Pure English (Brit.)

spec. specially; specialty; specification; speculation

spec. or **sp.** special

spec., sp. or **specif.** specific; specifically

specif., sp. or **spec.** specific; specifically

Specl Specialist (Mil.)

S.P.E.E. Society for the Promotion of Engineering Education

Spens. Spenser

S.P.G. Society for the Propagation of the Gospel (Brit.)
spg. spring
sp. gr., G., SG, S.G. or **s.g.** specific gravity
spgs. springs
S-ph or **s.p.** single phase (Elec.)
sph. or **s.** spherical
sp. ht. or **c** specific heat (Physics)
Spir., spir., Sp., sp. or **Spt.** (spiritus)(Lat.) spirit; spirits (Pharm.)
spirit. spiritualism
spkr. speaker; sprinkler
SPM Self-propelled mount (Mil.)
S.P.M. short particular meter; (Societas Patrum Misericordiae)(Lat.) Society of the Fathers of Mercy; Fathers of Mercy
S.P.M.P. Society for Plant Morphology and Physiology (now Botanical Society of America)
sp. nov. (species nova)(Lat.) new species (Bot. and Zool.)
S.P.O.A. Society of Progressive Oral Advocates
spp. or **sp.** species
S.P.Q.R. (Senatus populusque Romanus) (Lat.) the Senate and the people of Rome
S.P.Q.R. or **s.p.q.r.** small profit, quick returns
S.P.R. Society for Psychical Research (Brit.)
S.P.R.C. Society for the Prevention and Relief of Cancer (Brit.)
S.P.R.L. Society for the Promotion of Religion and Learning (Brit.)
S.P.R.S.I. (Sociedade Portuguesa Raínha Santa Isabel)(Port.) Portuguese Society of Queen Saint Isabel
s.p.s. (sine prole superstite)(Lat.) without surviving issue (cf. o.s.p.)
S.P.S.P. St. Peter and St. Paul (Papal seal)
Spt., Sp., sp. Spir., or **spir.** (spiritus)(Lat.) spirit; spirits (Pharm.)
spt. seaport
Sp Tr or **Sp Trs** Special troops (Mil.)
S.P.T.T.E. Society of Proletarian Travel Tours and Excursions
S.P.V.D. Society for the Prevention of Venereal Disease (Brit.)
sp.vol.. specific volume
Sp W or **Sp Wpn** Special weapons (Mil.)
Sp Wpn Plat Special weapons platoon
Sp Wpn Tr Special weapons troop
Sq (Mil.), **Sq., sq., Sqd., sqd., Sqn.** or **sqn.** squadron
sq. sequence; square (cf. quad.)
sq., seq., seqq., sqq. (sequens, sequentes, sequentia)(Lat.), **F., f., ff., fol.** or **foll.** the following (cf. et seq.)
sq., seq. or **sequ.** (sequitur)(Lat.) it follows (logical inference)
sq., Sq (Mil.), **Sq., Sqd., sqd., Sqn.** or **sqn.** squadron
sq.ch. square chain
sq.cm., cm.² or **cmr.²** square centimeter
Sqd (Mil.) or **sqd.** squad
Sqd., sqd., Sq (Mil.) **Sq., sq., Sqn.** or **sqn.** squadron
sqd. or **Sqd.** (Mil.) squad
Sqd. Ldr., S.L., Sq. Ldr. or **Sqn. Ldr.** Squadron leader (R.A.F.)
sq. ft. or **ft.²** square foot or feet
Sq Hq Squadron headquarters
Sq Hq & Hq Det Squadron headquarters and headquarters detachment
sq. in. or **in.²** square inch or inches
sq.km. or **km.²** square kilometer
Sq. Ldr., S.L., Sqd. Ldr. or **Sqn. Ldr.** Squardon leader (R.A.F.)
sq.m. or **m.²** square meter or meters
sq.m., mi.² or **sq.mi.** square mile or miles
sq.mi., mi.² or **sq.m.** square mile or miles
sq.mm. or **mm.²** square millimeters
sq.mu or μ^2 square microns
Sqn., sqn., Sq (Mil.), **Sq., sq., Sqd.** or **sqd.** squadron
Sqn. Ldr., S.L., Sqd. Ldr. or **Sq. Ldr.** Squadron leader (R.A.F.)
sqq., seq., seqq., sq. (sequens, sequentes, sequentia)(Lat.), **F., f., ff., fol.** or **foll.** the following (cf. et seq.)
sq.rd. or **rd.²** square rod or rods
sq. yd. or **yd.²** square yard or yards
SR Sound ranging
S.R. School Reserve [Lands] (Queensland); sedimentation rate; shipping receipt; Society of Rheology; Sons of the Revolution (cf. S.A.R.); star route; state room
S/R shipping and receiving
Sr strontium (Chem.)
Sr. or **D.** (Dom)(Port.), (Don)(Span.) Sir
Sr. (Soror)(Lat.) or **sist.** sister
Sr. or **Snr.** Senhor (Portuguese equivalent of Mr.)
Sr. or **Sor.** Señor (Spanish equivalent of Mr.)
Sr., sr., d. A. (der Ältere)(Ger.), **d.ä.** (den äldre)(Swed.), **Sen., sen., Senr.** or **senr.** senior
s.r. short rate (Insurance)
Sra., S.ª or **Snra.** (senhora)(Port.), (señora) (Span.) title of courtesy, married woman (cf. Mrs.)
Sra.D.ª (Señora Dona)(Span.) title given to a married gentlewoman
S.R.C. (Sacrorum Rituum Congregatio) (Lat.) Congregation of the Sacred Rites; Signal Reserve Corps; Special Reserve Corps
s.r.c.c. strikes, riots, and civil commotions (Insurance)
Sr.D. (Señor Don)(Span.) title given to a gentleman
S.R.E. (Sancta Romana Ecclesia)(Lat.) Holy Roman Church (cf. R.C.Ch.)
S.Rept. Senate Report
S.Res. Senate Resolution
Sres., Srs. (Señores)(Span.), **HH.** (Herren)(Ger.), **Messrs., MM.** (Messieurs) (Fr.), **Sig** or **sig.** (signori)(Ital.) sirs; gentlemen (cf. gent.)
S.R.I. (Sacrum Romanum Imperium)(Lat.) or **H.R.E.** Holy Roman Empire

Srio. (secretario)(Span.), **Sec., sec., Secy.** or **secy.** secretary

Srita., Srta., Sta. (Señorita)(Span.), **Frk.** (Frøken)(Dan.), **frk.** (fröken)(Swed.), **Frl.** (Fräulein)(Ger.), **Mdlle., Mlle.** (Mademoiselle)(Fr.), **Snrta.** or **Srta.** (senhorita)(Port.) Miss; unmarried woman or girl

S.R.N. State Registered Nurse (Brit.)

S.R.O. standing room only; Supplementary Reserve of Officers

S.R.O.T. (Service des renseignements de l'observation du terrain)(Fr.) Land observation information detachment

S.R.S. (Societatis Regiae Socius)(Lat.) **F.R.S.** or **R.S.S.** (Regiae Societatis Sodalis)(Lat.) Fellow of the Royal Society [of London]

Srs., Sres. (Señores)(Span.), **HH.** (Herren) (Ger.), **Messrs., MM.** (Messieurs)(Fr.), **Sig.** or **sig.** (signori)(Ital.) Sirs; gentlemen (cf. gent.)

Srta., Snrta. (senhorita)(Port.), **Frk.**, (Frøken)(Dan.), **frk.** (fröken)(Swed.), **Frl.** (Fräulein)(Ger.), **Mdlle., Mlle.** (Mademoiselle)(Fr.), **Srta., Srita.** or **Sta.** (senorita)(Span.) Miss; unmarried woman or girl

SS, S., s., Ss., ss. (semi)(Fr.), (semis)(Lat.) or **hf.** half

SS or **S.S.** (Schutz-Staffel)(Ger.) National Sociatlist Elite Corps; Storm Troopers

SS. collar of S's (worn by Lord Chief Justice of England)

SS. (Seiten)(Ger.), **p., pp., S.** (Sider)(Dan.) or **sid** (sidor)(Swed.) pages

SS., S.S. (Sanctissimus)(Lat.), **PP.** or **P.P.** (Piissimus)(Lat.) Most Holy

SS., S.S. or **S/S** steamship

SS., ss., sc., scil. (scilicet)(Lat.), **näml.** (nämligen)(Swed.) or **viz.** (videlicet) (Lat.) namely; to wit (cf. i.e.)

SS., ss. (sancti)(Lat.) or **Sts.** saints

S. S. (Su Señoría)(Span.) His Lordship; Sabbath School; Saint Simplicius (Brit.); Secretary of State; simplified spelling; Staff Surgeon; Statistical Society [of London], (now Royal Statistical Society); Straits Settlements; Sunday School; (supra scriptum)(Lat.) superscription (cf. Sig., subscr.); Supply sergeant

S.S. (Sa Sainteté)(Fr.) or **H.H.** His Holiness

S.S. or **P.S.S.** (Presbyteri Sancti Sulpicii) (Lat.) Society of St. Sulpice; Priests of St. Sulpice; Fathers of St. Sulpice; Sulpicians

S.S. (Societas Sancti Francisci Salesii) (Lat.) or **S.C.** (Salesianorum Congregatio)(Lat.) Society of St. Francis de Sales; Congregation of St. Francis de Sales; Salesian Fathers (cf. O.S.F.S.)

S.S. or **SS** (Schutz-Staffel)(Ger.) National Socialists Elite Corps; Storm Troopers

S.S., SS. (Sanctissimus)(Lat.), **PP.** or **P.P.** (Piissimus)(Lat.) most Holy

S.S., SS. or **S/S** steamship

S.S. or **s.s.** screw steamer

S.S., s.s. (seguro servidor)(Span.), **S.S.S.** or **s.s.s.** (su seguro servidor)(Span.) your faithful servant; yours truly

S/S, SS. or **S.S.** steamship

Ss Sharpshooter (Mil.)

Ss., SS, ss., S., s. (semis)(Lat.), (semi) (Fr.) or **hf.** half

ss. (scriptores)(Lat.), **AA.** (autores)(Span.), (autori)(Ital.) or **auths.** authors

ss., S., s., SS, Ss. (semi)(Fr.), (semis)(Lat.) or **hf.** half

ss., sc., scil., SS. (scilicet)(Lat.), **näml.** (nämligen)(Swed.) or **viz.** (videlicet) (Lat.) namely; to wit (cf. i.e.)

ss., sec. or **secs.** sections

ss., SS. (sancti)(Lat.) or **Sts.** saints

s.s. soap suds

s.s. or **S.S.** screw steamer

s.s., S.S. (seguro servidor)(Span.), **S.S.S.** or **s.s.s.** (su seguro servidor) (Span.) your faithful servant; yours truly

SSA or **S.S.A.** Social Security Act

S.S.A. Seismological Society of America; Soaring Society of America

S.S.A. (Section sanitaire automobile)(Fr.) or **S.A.S.** (Section d'automobiles sanitaires)(Fr.) Automobile ambulance section (cf. Amb Sec)

S.S.A. or **SSA** Social Security Act

SS.AA. (Sus Altezas)(Span.) Their Highnesses

SSB or **S.S.B.** Social Security Board

S.S.B. (Sacrae Scripturae Baccalaureus) (Lat.) Bachelor of Sacred Scripture; Simplified Spelling Board

S.S.C. Chinese Mission Society of St. Columban; (Service de santé des troupes coloniales)(Fr.) Medical Service of the Colonial Army; Sculptors Society of Canada; Silver Citation Star; single silk covered wire (Elec.); Society of the Holy Cross (Anglican); Solicitor [before the] Supreme Courts [of Scotland]

SS.CC. or **C.SS.CC.** (Congregatio Sacratissimorum Cordium)(Lat.), (Congregatio Sacrorum Cordium Jesu et Mariae) (Lat.) Congregation of the Most Sacred Hearts of Jesus and Mary; Fathers of the Sacred Hearts

S.Sc.D. or **D.S.Sc.** Doctor of Social Science

SS.D. or **S.S.D.** (Sanctissimus Dominus) (Lat.) Most Holy Lord [the Pope] (cf. SS. D.N.)

S.S.D. (Sacrae Scripturae Doctor)(Lat.) or **D.S.S.** (Doctor Sacrae Scripturae)(Lat.) Doctor of Sacred Scripture

SS. D.N. (Sanctissimus Dominus Noster) (Lat.) Our Most Holy Lord [the Pope] (cf. SS.D.)

SSE, S.S.E. or **s.s.e.** south-southeast

S.S.E. single silk over enamel (Elec.); (Societas Sancti Edmundi)(Lat.) Society of St. Edmund

s.s.e., SSE or **S.S.E.** south-southeast

S.S.F.A. Soldiers' and Sailors' Families Association (Brit.)

S.Sgt. or **Stf.Sgt.** Staff Sergeant

S.S.J. (Societas Sancti Josephi Sanctissimi Cordis)(Lat.) St. Joseph's Society of the Most Sacred Heart; Josephite Fathers; Missionaries of Mill Hill

S.S.J.D. Sisterhood of St. John the Divine

S.S.J.E. Society of St. John the Evangelist
S.S.L. (Sacrae Scripturae Licentiatus) (Lat.) Licentiate of Sacred Scripture
S.S.M. (Service de santé de la marine) (Fr.) Naval Medical Service; Society of the Sacred Mission
SS.MM. (Sus Majestades) (Span.), **LL. MM.** (Leurs Majestes) (Fr.) or **MM.** Their Majesties
S.S.N. or **s.s.n.** (signato suo nomine) (Lat.) signed with his own name
S.S.P. (Pia Societas Sancti Pauli) (Lat.) Pious Society of St. Paul
SSR or **S.S.R.** Socialist Soviet Republic (cf. U.S.S.R.)
S.S.R.C. Social Science Research Council
SSS or **S.S.S.** Selective Service System
S.S.S. (Societas Sanctissimi Sacramenti) (Lat.) Society of the Blessed Sacrament; Fathers of the Blessed Sacrament; specific soluble substance
S.S.S., s.s.s. (su sequro servidor) (Span.), **S.S.** or **s.s.** (sequro servidor) (Span.) your faithful servant; yours truly
S.s.s. (stratum super stratum) (Lat.) layer upon layer
s.s.s. or **S.S.S.** (su sequro servidor) (Span.), **S.S.** or **s.s.** (sequro servidor) (Span.) your faithful servant
S.S.U. Sunday School Union
S.S.V. (sub signo veneni) (Lat.) under poison label
SSW, S.S.W. or **s.s.w.** south-southwest
ST single throw
S.T. Scholar in Theology; sounding tube
S.T. or **S. of T.** Sons of Temperance
S.T. or **Supt.Trans.** Superintendent of Transportation
St., S., s., San, Sta. (santa) (Port., Span.), **São, Sto.** (santo) (Port.), **Skt.** (Sankt) (Ger.), **Ste** (sainte) (Fr.), **św.** (świety) (Pol.), **sz.** or **szt.** (szent) (Hung.) saint
St., S., Sa., Sat. or **Stdy.** Saturday
St. or **s.** stratus
St. or **st.** (stet) (Lat.) let it stand (Pharm., Print.); state; street
St. or **stat.** statute; statutes
St. or **str.** strait
S.t., s.t. or **sh. tn.** short ton
st. stand; stanza; stone (Weight); strophe
s.t. shipping ticket; (senza tempo) (Ital.) without regard to time (Music)
s.t. (sans titre) (Fr.) without title (cf. n.t.p.)
s.t., sh.tn. or **S.t.** short ton
Sta (Mil.), **Sta., sta., Stn.** or **stn.** station
Sta., San (santa) (Port., Span.), **S., s., São, Sto.** (santo) (Port.), **Skt.** (Sankt) (Ger.), **St., Ste** (sainte) (Fr.), **św.** (świety) (Pol.), **sz.** or **szt.** (szent) (Hung.) saint
Sta., Srita., Srta. (señorita) (Span.), **Frk.** (Frøken) (Dan.), **frk.** (fröken) (Swed.), **Frl.** (Fräulein) (Ger.), **Mdlle., Mlle.** Mademoiselle) (Fr.), **Snrta.** or **Srta.** (senhorita) (Port.) Miss; unmarried woman or girl
Sta., Sta (Mil.), **sta., Stn.** or **stn.** station
sta. stationary; stator
sta., Sta (Mil.), **Sta., Stn.** or **stn.** station
Stab (Mil.) or **stab.** stable
stac. or **stacc.** (staccato) (Ital.) distinct; separated (Music)
stacc. or **stac.** (staccato) (Ital.) distinct; separated (Music)
sta.eng. stationary engineer
Staffs. Staffordshire
sta.mi. or **stat.** statute miles
stan. stanchion
Staph. Staphylococcus
Stat., stat. (statim) (Lat.) or **immy.** immediately
stat. static; stationary; statistics; statuary; statue
stat. or **sta. mi.** statute [miles]
stat. or **St.** statute; statutes
stat., Stat. (statim) (Lat.) or **immy.** immediately
Stat. at L. Statutes at Large
S.T.B. (Sacrae Theologiae Baccalaureus) (Lat.) or **B.S.T.** Bachelor of Sacred Theology
S.T.B. (Scientiae Theologicae Baccalaureus) (Lat.) **B.T., B.Th.** or **Th.B.** (Theologiae Baccalaureus) (Lat.) Bachelor of Theology
stbd. starboard
S.T.C. single trip container
St.Cu. or **st-cu** strato-cumulus (Meteorol.)
st-cu or **St.Cu.** strato-cumulus (Meteorol.)
S.T.D. (Sacrae Theologiae Doctor) (Lat.) or **D.S.T.** Doctor of Sacred Theology
S.T.D. (Scientiae Theologicae Doctor) (Lat.), **D.T., D. Th., D. Theol.** or **Th.D.** (Theologiae Doctor) (Lat.) Doctor of Theology
Std. or **std.** standard
std. or **Std.** standard
Stdy., S., Sa., Sat. or **St.** Saturday
Ste (sainte) (Fr.), **S., s., San, Sta.** (santa) (Port., Span.), **São, Sto.** (santo) (Port.) **Skt.** (Sankt) (Ger.), **St., św.** (świety) (Pol.), **sz.** or **szt.** (szent) (Hung.) saint
St. Edm. Saint Edmund
sten. stencil
sten., steno. or **stenog.** stenographer; stenography
steno., sten. or **stenog.** stenographer; stenography
stenog., sten. or **steno.** stenographer; stenography
ster., sterl., stg. or **stlg.** sterling
stereo. stereotype
sterl., ster., stg. or **stlg.** sterling
Stev Stevedore (Mil.)
St.Ex. or **Stk. Ex.** Stock Exchange
Stf Staff (Mil.)
Stf Gp Staff group
Stf.Sgt. or **S. Sgt.** Staff Sargeant
Stf Sq Staff squadron
S.T.F.U. Southern Tenant Farmers' Union
stg., ster., sterl. or **stlg.** sterling
stge. or **stor.** storage
Sthn., S., s., So. or **Sou.** southern
stiff. stiffener
stip. stipend; stipendiary; stipulation
S Tk Slow tank (Mil.)

stk. stock
Stk.Ex. or **St.Ex.** Stock Exchange
stk.mkt. stock market
S.T.L. (Sacrae Theologiae Licentiatus) (Lat.) Licentiate in Sacred Theology; (Sacrae Theologiae Lector)(Lat.) Reader in Sacred Theology
stlg., ster., sterl. or **stg.** sterling
S.T.M. (Sacrae Theologiae Magister)(Lat.) or **M.S.T.** Master of Sacred Theology
S.T.M. (Scientiae Theologicae Magister) (Lat.), **M. Th.** or **Th. M.** (Theologiae Magister)(Lat.) Master of Theology
stmftr. steamfitter
Stn., Sta (Mil.), **Sta., sta.** or **stn.** station
stn., Sta (Mil.), **Sta., sta.** or **Stn.** station
Sto., São (santo)(Port.), **S., s., San, Sta.** (santa)(Port., Span.), **Skt.** (Sankt) (Ger.), **St., Ste** (sainte)(Fr.), **św.** (święty)(Pol.), **sz.** or **szt.** (szent) (Hung.) saint
S'ton Southampton
stor. or **stge.** storage
S. to S. station to station
S.T.P. (Sacrae Theologiae Professor)(Lat.) Professor of Sacred Theology; Professor of Divinity (old form of D.D.)
stp. stamped
Str. strings (Music)
Str. or **str.** stroke oar
str. string
str. or **s.** steamer
str. or **St.** strait
str. or **Str.** stroke oar
Strag L Straggler line (Mil.)
Strep. streptococcus
string. (stringendo)(Ital.) in accelerated time (Music)
STS special treatment steel
S.T.S. Scottish Text Society
Sts., SS. or **ss.** (Sancti)(Lat.) Saints
stsm. statesman
St. Tr. state trials
stud. student
stwd. steward
Stycz. (Styczeń)(Pol.), **eno.** (enero)(Span.), **genn.** (gennaio)(Ital.), **Ja., Jan.,** or **janv.** (janvier)(Fr.) January
S.U. sensation unit (Radio); Siemen's unit [of resistance] (Elec.)
S.U. or **s.u.** set up (Transp.)
Su. Susan
Su., S., Sun. or **Sund.** Sunday
S.u. (Svar udbedes)(Dan.), **o.s.a.** (om svar anhålles)(Swed.), **R.S.V.P., r.s.v.p.** (répondez s'il vous plaît)(Fr.), **u.A.w.g.** (um Antwort wird gebeten)(Ger.) or **u. gefl. A. w.g.** (um gefällige Antwort wird gebeten)(Ger.) a reply is requested; please reply
s.u. (siehe unten)(Ger.) or **v.i.** (vide infra) (Lat.) see below
Sub (Mil.) or **sub.** Submarine
sub. (subaudi)(Lat.) supply [implied words]; subaltern; suburb; suburban
sub. or **subj.** subject
sub., subs., subscr. or **subscript.** subscription (cf. Sig.; S.S.)
sub. or **subst.** substitute; substitutes (cf. i st.f.)
Subaq Subaqueous (Mil.)
subd. subdivision
subj. subjective; subjectively; subjunctive
subj. or **sub.** subject
subpar. subparagraph
subrogn. subrogation
Subs Subsistence (Mil.)
subs. subsidiary
subs., sub., subscr. or **subscript.** subscription (cf. Sig.; S.S.)
subscr., sub., subs. or **subscript.** subscription (cf. Sig.; S.S.)
subscript., sub., subs. or **subscr.** subscription (cf. Sig.; S.S.)
subsec. or **subsect.** subsection
subseq. subsequent; subsequently
subst., s. or **sb.** substantive
subst. or **sub.** substitute; substitutes (cf. i st.f.)
suc. suction
suc., Nachf. (Nachfolger)(Ger.) or **succ.** successor
suc., S., s. (Geneal.) or **succ.** succeeded
succ., Nachf. (Nachfolger)(Ger.) or **suc.** successor
succ., S., s. (Geneal.) or **suc.** succeeded
S.U.C.L. set up in carloads (Transp.)
sue & l. sue and labor (Insurance)
suf. or **suff.** suffix
Suff. Suffolk
Suff. or **Suffr.** Suffragan
suff. sufficient
suff. or **suf.** suffix
Suff. B., Bp. Suff. or **B. Suff.** Bishop Suffragan; Suffragan Bishop
Suffr. or **Suff.** Suffragan
sug. or **sugg.** suggested; suggestion
S.U.L.C.L. set up in less than carloads (Transp.)
Sult. Sultan
Sum. or **sum.** (sume, sumendus)(Lat.) take; to be taken (Pharm.) (cf. cap.)
sum. (sumat)(Lat.), **Cap., cap.** or **cpt.** (capiat)(Lat.) let him take
sum. or **Sum.** (sume, sumendus)(Lat.) take; to be taken (cf. cap.)
Sum CM or **s.c.m.** Summary court-martial
Sun., S., Su. or **Sund.** Sunday
Sund., S., Su. or **Sun.** Sunday
sund. sundries
Sup (Mil.) or **sup.** supply
Sup., sup. or **supr.** supreme
sup. supine
sup. (supra)(Lat.) or **abv.** above
sup., Beibl. (Beiblatt)(Ger.), **Erg.H.** (Ergänsungsheft)(Ger.), **supp.** or **suppl.** supplement
sup. (supra)(Lat.) or **f.d.** (för detta)(Swed.) before; formerly
sup. or **Sup** (Mil.) supply
sup., Sup. or **supr.** supreme

sup. or **super.** superfine; superior
sup. or **superl.** superlative
sup., supp. or **suppl.** supplementary
Sup. C., S.C. or **Sup. Ct.** Supreme Court
Sup. C. or **Sup. Ct.** Superior Court
Sup Co Supply company
Sup. Ct., S.C. or **Sup. C.** Supreme Court
Sup. Ct. or **Sup. C.** Superior Court
super. supernumerary
super. or **sup.** superfine; superior
super., Supt. or **supt.** superintendent
superl. or **sup.** superlative
Sup O Supply officer (cf. S-4)
Supp. (Mil.) or **supp.** supplemental
supp., Beibl. (Beiblatt)(Ger.), **Erg.H.** (Ergänsungsheft)(Ger.), **sup.** or **suppl.** supplement
supp., sup. or **suppl.** supplementary
suppl., Beibl. (Beiblatt)(Ger.), **Erg.H.** (Ergänsungsheft)(Ger.), **sup.** or **supp.** supplement
suppl., sup. or **supp.** supplementary
Supp. Res. Supplementary Reserve [of Officers] (Brit.)
supps. supplements
supr., Sup., or **sup.** supreme
Sup Sec Supply section
Sup.Sgt. Supply Sergeant
Supt., supt. or **super.** superintendent
Supt. Doc. or **SD** Superintendent of Documents
Supt.Trans. or **S.T.** Superintendent of Transportation
supvr. supervisor
Sur. Surrey
sur. or **s.** surplus
Surg (Mil.) or **surg.** surgeon; surgical
surg., Ch. or **ch.** (chirurgia)(Lat.) surgery
Surg. Gen., SG or **S.G.** Surgeon General
Surg Hosp Surgical hospital
Surg.Maj. or **Surg.-Maj.** Surgeon Major
Surr. Surrogate
surr. surrender; surrendered
Surv (Mil.) or **surv.** survey; surveying; surveyor
surv. surviving
Surv.Gen. or **Surv.-Gen.** Surveyor General
Sus. Sussex
Susp Suspended (Mil.)
sus.per col. (suspensio per collum)(Lat.) literally, suspension by the neck; execution by hanging
S.V. (Sancta Virgo)(Lat.) Holy Virgin (cf. B.V.); (Sanctitas Vestra)(Lat.) Your Holiness
S.V. or **S. of V.** Sons of Veterans
S.v. or **s.v.** (spiritus vini)(Lat.) spirit of wine; alcoholic spirit (cf. alc.; S.V.R.; S.V.T.)
s.v. sailing vessel
s.v. (sub verbo or voce)(Lat.), **i.v.** (in verbe or voce)(Lat.) or **s.h.v.** (sub hoc verbo, sub hac voce)(Lat.) under the word; under this word (used in dictionaries)
s.v. or **S.v.** (spiritus vini)(Lat.) spirit of wine; alcoholic spirit (cf. Spir.; S.V.R.; S.V.T.)
Svc (Mil.), **ser., Serv** (Mil.) or **serv.** service
S.V.D. (Societas Verbii Divini)(Lat.) Society of the Divine Word
S.V.E. Society for Visual Education
S.V.F. (Service viande fraîche)(Fr.) Fresh meat supply section
S.V.P. (Societas Sancti Vincenti Pauli) (Lat.) Society of St. Vincent de Paul
S.V.P. or **s.v.p.** (s'il vous plaît)(Fr.) if you please
S.V.R., s.v.r. (spiritus vini rectificatus) (Lat.) or **alc.** rectified spirit of wine; alcohol (cf. S.V.T.)
S.V.T. or **s.v.t.** (spiritus vini tenuis)(Lat.) proof spirit of wine (Pharm.) (cf. S.V.R.)
SW, S.W. or **s.w.** southwest; southwestern
S.W. Senior Warden (Freemasonry); South Wales
Sw. Swiss
Sw. or **Swed.** Sweden; Swedish
sw. swatch; swell (Organ); switch
św. (święty)(Pol.), **S., s., San, Sta.** (santa) (Port., Span.), **São, Sto.** (Santo)(Port.), **Skt.** (Sankt)(Ger.), **St., Ste** (sainte) (Fr.), **sz.** or **szt.** (szent)(Hung.) saint
s.w. salt water; sea water; sent wrong; shipper's weights
s.w., SW or **S.W.** southwest; southwestern
S.W.A. Southwest Africa
Swab. Swabia; Swabian
swbd. or **Sb** (Mil.) switchboard
SWbS southwest by south
SWbW southwest by west
Sw C Switching central (Mil.)
swchmn. switchman
S.W.D. sliding watertight door
Swed. or **Sw.** Sweden; Swedish
SWG or **S.W.G.** standard wire gauge
swg. or **swtg.** switching
Swit. or **Swtz.** Switzerland
S.W.O.C. Steel Workers Organizing Committee (now United Steel Workers of America)
SWPC or **S.W.P.C.** Smaller War Plants Corporation
swtg. or **swg.** switching
Swtz. or **Swit.** Switzerland
sx. or **sks.** sacks
S.Y. steam yacht
syl. or **syll.** syllable
syll. or **syl.** syllable
Sym. sym., sym-, s, or **s.** symmetrical
sym. symbol; symphony (music.)
syn. synonym; synonymous; synonymy
syn. or **synch.** synchronize; synchronized; synchronizing
synch. or **syn.** synchronize; synchronized; synchronizing
Synd. or **synd.** syndicate

synd. or **Synd.** syndicate
synop. synopsis
Syr. Syria; Syriac; Syrian
syr. syrup
syst. system
s.Z. (seiner Zeit)(Ger.) at that time
sz. (szám)(Hung.), **n., No., N.°, núm.** (número)(Span.), **no., n:o. nr.** (numro, nummer)(Swed.), **Nr.** (Nummer)(Dan.), **Nr., Nro.** (Numero)(Ger.) or **num.** number (cf. Hft.; pt.)
sz., szt. (szent)(Hung.), **S., s., San, Sta.** (santa)(Port., Span.), **São, Sto.** (santo) (Port.), **Skt.** (Sankt)(Ger.), **St, Ste** (sainte)(Fr.) or **św.** (świety)(Pol.) saint
szept. (szeptember)(Hung.), **S., sbre.** (se(p)-tiembre)(Span.), **Sep., Sept., set.** (setembro)(Port.), **sett.** (settembre)(Ital.) or **Wrzes.** (Wrzesień)(Pol.) September
szt., sz. (szent)(Hung.), **S., s., San, Sta. (santa)(Port., Span.), São, Sto. (santo)** (Port.), **Skt.** (Sankt)(Ger.), **St., Ste** (sainte)(Fr.) or **św.** (świety)(Pol.) saint

ΣΑΕ (Sigma Alpha Epsilon) National undergraduate fraternity
ΣΑΙ (Sigma Alpha Iota) National undergraduate sorority (Music)
ΣΑΜ (Sigma Alpha Mu) National undergraduate fraternity
ΣΧ (Sigma Chi) National undergraduate fraternity
ΣΔΧ (Sigma Delta Chi) Professional society (Journalism)
ΣΔΚ (Sigma Delta Kappa) National fraternity (Law)
ΣΔΦ (Sigma Delta Phi) Honor sorority (Oratory)
ΣΔΨ (Sigma Delta Psi) National undergraduate society (Physical Education)
ΣΔΡ (Sigma Delta Rho) National undergraduate fraternity
ΣΔΤ (Sigma Delta Tau) National undergraduate sorority
ΣΗΧ (Sigma Eta Chi) National undergraduate sorority
ΣΓΕ (Sigma Gamma Epsilon) National undergraduate fraternity (Geology, Mining, Metallurgy)
ΣΙΧ (Sigma Iota Chi) National undergraduate sorority
ΣΚ (Sigma Kappa) National undergraduate sorority
ΣΛΠ (Sigma Lambda Pi) National undergraduate fraternity
ΣΜΣ (Sigma Mu Sigma) National undergraduate fraternity
ΣΝ (Sigma Nu) National undergraduate fraternity
ΣΝΦ (Sigma Nu Phi) National undergraduate fraternity (Law)
ΣΦ (Sigma Phi) National undergraduate fraternity
ΣΦΒ (Sigma Phi Beta) National undergraduate sorority
ΣΦΕ (Sigma Phi Epsilon) National undergraduate fraternity
ΣΦΣ (Sigma Phi Sigma) National undergraduate fraternity
ΣΠ (Sigma Pi) National undergraduate fraternity
ΣΠΣ (Sigma Pi Sigma) National honorary fraternity (Physics)
ΣΣΦ (Sigma Sigma Phi) Honor fraternity (Osteopathy)
ΣΣΣ (Sigma Sigma Sigma) Professional sorority (Education)
ΣΤ (Sigma Tau) National undergraduate honor society (Engineering)
ΣΤΔ (Sigma Tau Delta) National undergraduate fraternity (English)
ΣΤΓ (Sigma Tau Gamma) Professional society (Teachers Colleges)
ΣΤΦ (Sigma Tau Phi) National undergraduate fraternity
ΣΥ (Sigma Upsilon) National undergraduate fraternity (Literary)
ΣΞ (Sigma Xi) National undergraduate honorary society (Science)
ΣΖ (Sigma Zeta) Undergraduate honor society (Science)

T

T temperature [on the absolute scale]; [surface] tension (Physics); Transport (Mil.)
T or **t.** time
T or **Ta** tantalum (Chem.)
T. triangle (Surveying)
T. (Tome)(Ger.), **B., Bd.** (Band)(Ger.), (Bind)(Dan.), **b., bd.** (band)(Swed.), **t., tom.** (tome)(Fr.),(tomo)(Span.), (tomus)(Lat.), **v., Vol.** or **vol.** volume
T., L.T. or **£T.** Turkish pound or lira
T. (Thurm)(Ger.), **R, R.,** or **r.** rook or castle (Chess)
T., t. or **ten.** tenor
T., t., Ter., ter., terr., terr., Ty. or **ty.** territory
T., t., Tp., tp., Twp. or **twp.** township
T. or **Test.** Testament
T., Th. (Teil, Theil)(Ger.), **Abt.** (Abteilung) (Ger.), **H., Hft.** (Heft)Ger.), **Lfg.** (Lieferung)(Ger.), **liv.** (livraison)(Fr.), **p.** or **pt.** part (cf. inst.; no.; sec.)
T., Th. (Teil, Theil)(Ger.), **H., Hft.** (Heft) (Ger.), **inst., Lfg.** (Lieferung)(Ger.) or **liv.** (livraison)(Fr.) installment (cf. Abt.; pt.)
T. or **Trin.** Trinity
T. or **T.T.** Trinity [Term]
T., Tu. or **Tues.** Tuesday
T. or **Turk.** Turkish
T- triple bond (Chem.)
t. (tutti)(Ital.) all, all the performers together (Music); (tace)(Ital.) be silent (Music); taken (Betting); tempo; tense; tensor; troy; tun

t. (tome)(Fr.), **B., b., bk., L., l., lib.** (liber) (Lat.) or **liv.** (livre)(Fr.) book
t. (tomes)(Fr.), **BB, Bde.** (Bände)(Ger.), **v.** or **vols.** volumes
t. (tonneau)(Fr.), **mr.** (millier)(Fr.) or **M.T.** metric ton
t. or **T** time
t., T. or **ten.** tenor
t., T., Ter., ter., Terr., terr., Ty. or **ty.** territory
t., T., Tp., tp., Twp. or **twp.** township
t., tel., teleph. or **Tp** (Mil.) telephone
t. or **temp.** (tempore)(Lat.) in the time of; temperature; temporal
t. or **ter.** territorial
t. or **term.** terminal
t. or **tgt.** target
t. or **tn.** ton; tons; town
t., tom. (tome)(Fr.),(tomo)(Span.),(tomus) (Lat.), **B., Bd.** (Band)(Ger.),(Bind) (Dan.), **b., bd.** (band)(Swed.), **T.** (Tome)(Ger.), **v., Vol.** or **vol.** volume
t., Tr or **tr.** (trillo)(Ital.) trill (Music)
t. or **tr.** tare
t., tr. or **trans.** transitive
t. or **trans.** transit
T.A. telegraphic address; Territorial Army (Brit.); Traffic Agent; Traffic Auditor
T.A. or **T.A.T.** toxin-antitoxin
T/A (Mil.) Table of Allowances (cf. TB/A)
Ta or **T** tantalum (Chem.)
t.a. (testantibus actis)(Lat.) as the acts show
T.A.A. Territorial Army Association
T.A.B. Total Abstinence Brotherhood
Tab. Tabitha
tab. table; tables
Tac Tactical (Mil.)
T.A.F.I. Technical Association of the Fur Industry
TAG The Adjutant General (cf. A. G.)
tal. (talis)(Lat.) such a one
tal. qual., T/Q, T/q or **t/q** (tale quale, talis qualis)(Lat.) as they come; average quality (cf. r.o.m.; M.R.)
Tam. Tamil
T.A.M.C. Texas Agricultural and Mechanical College
t. & g. tongued and grooved (lumber)
t. & o. or **t. and o.** taken and offered
T. & S. or **T. and S.** Trust and Savings (Banking)
tan or **tan.** tangent
t. and o. or **t. & o.** taken and offered
T. and S. or **T. & S.** Trust and Savings (Banking)
tanh hyperbolic tangent
T.A.P.P.I. Technical Association of the Pulp and Paper Industry
tar-mac. tar-macadam
tart. tartaric
Tasm. Tasmania; Tasmanian
Tass (Telegrafnoe Agenstvo Soyusa Sovetskih Socialisticheskih)(Rus.) News Agency of U.S.S.R.
T.A.T. Transcontinental Air Transport
T.A.T. or **T.A.** toxin-antitoxin
taut. tautology
t.a.w. twice a week (Advertising)
TB, T.B., tb. or **t.b.** tubercle bacillus; tuberculosis
T.B. Tariff Bureau; Torpedo boat; Traffic Bureau
T.B., TB, tb., or **t.b.** tubercle bacillus; tuberculosis
Tb or **Tr** terbium (Chem.)
tb., TB, T.B. or **t.b.** tubercle bacillus; tuberculosis
t.b. trial balance
t.b., TB, T.B. or **tb.** tubercle bacillus; tuberculosis
TB/A or **T/BA** (Mil.) Table of Basic Allowances (cf. T/A)
T.B.D. Torpedo-boat destroyer
tbs., c.amp. coch.amp., cochl.amp. (cochleare amplum)(Lat.), **c.mag., cochl.mag., coch.mag.** (cochleare magnum)(Lat.) or **tbsp.** tablespoon; tablespoonful
tbsp., c.amp., coch.amp., cochl.amp. (cochleare amplum)(Lat.), **c.mag., coch. mag., cochl.mag.** (cochleare magnum)(Lat.) or **tbs.** tablespoon; tablespoonful
TC or **T.C.** Training Circular (Mil.)
T.C. Tank Corps; Tariff Commission; temporary constable (Brit.); Town Councillor; training camp; Turret captain
T.C. or **TC** Training Circular
tc., tcs. or **trcs.** tierces
tc. or **tier.** tierce
t.c. till countermanded
T.C.D Trinity College, Dublin
T.C.F. Touring Club de France
T.C.F.B. Transcontinental Freight Bureau
tchr. teacher
TCI or **T.C.I.** Touring Club Italiano
T Co Transport or Transportation company
tcs., tc. or **trcs.** tierces
T.C.U. Teachers Casualty Underwriters; Texas Christian University
TCUS or T.C.U.S. Tanners Council of the United States
T.C.W. & I.B. Transcontinental Weighing and Inspection Bureau
TD or **T.D.** Territorial Decoration or Decorations (Brit.)
TD or **Tk Dtyr** Tank destroyer
TD or **Tr Dr** Tractor-drawn (Mil.)
T.D. Telegraph Department; Telephone Department; Traffic Director; Treasury Decision or Decisions; Treasury Department
T.D. or **TD** Territorial Decoration or Decorations (Brit.)
T.D. or **T/D** time deposit (Banking)
T/D or **T.D.** time deposit (Banking)
T.d. or **t.i.d.** (ter in die)(Lat.) three times a day (cf. t.d.s.)
t.d.s. (ter die sumendum)(Lat.) to be taken three times a day (Pharm.)(cf. t.i.d.)
T.E. Topographical Engineer
T/E Tables of equipment (Mil.)

Te tellurium (Chem.)
TEC The Executive Council (cf. E.C.)
tech. or **techn.** technical; technically
tech., techn. or **technol.** technology
Techn Technician (Mil.)
techn. or **tech.** technical; technically
techn., tech. or **technol.** technology
technol. technological; technologically
technol., tech. or **techn.** technology
Tech.Sgt. or **T.Sgt.** Technical Sergeant
t.e.g., G.t., g.t. or **g.t.e.** top edge gilt; gilt top edge (Bookbinding)
tel., t., teleph. or **Tp** (Mil.) telephone
tel. or **teleg.** telegraphic; telegraphy
tel., teleg., telg., Tg (Mil.) or **tg.** telegram
tel., teleg. or **Tg** (Mil.) telegraph
tel. or **teleph.** telephonic; telephony
tel., Tg (Mil.), **tg.** or **teleg.** telegram
Tel. & Tel. Telephone and Telegraph
Tel.Bn. Telegraph Battalion
teleg. or **tel.** telegraphic; telegraphy
teleg., tel., telg., Tg (Mil.) or **tg.** telegram
teleg., tel. or **Tg** (Mil.) telegraph
teleph., t., tel. or **Tp** (Mil.) telephone
teleph. or **tel.** telephonic; telephony
telg., tel., teleg., Tg (Mil.) or **tg.** telegram
T.E.M. (Train des équipages militaires) (Fr.) Military train
temp. temperance; temporary (cf. pro tem.)
temp. or **t.** temperature; (tempore)(Lat.) in the time of; temporal
Temp. sinist. (tempori sinistro)(Lat.) to the left temple
ten. tenement
ten. (tenuto)(Ital.), **sos., sost.,** or **sosten.** (sostenuto)(Ital) held; sustained (Music)
ten., T. or **t.** tenor
Tenn. Tennessee; Tennyson
tens.str., T.S., ts or **t.s.** tensile strength
Ter., T., t., ter., Terr., terr., Ty. or **ty.** territory
ter., T., t., ter., Terr., terr., Ty. or **ty.** territory
ter. or **t.** territorial
ter. or **terr.** terrace
TERA or **T.E.R.A.** Temporary Emergency Relief Administration
terat. or **teratol.** teratology
term. termination; terminology
term. or **t.** terminal
Terr., T., t., Ter., ter., terr., Ty. or **ty.** territory
terr., T., t., Ter., ter., Terr., Ty. or **ty.** territory
terr. or **ter.** terrace
Test. or **T.** Testament
test. testamentary; testator
Teut. Teuton; Teutonic
Tex. Texan; Texas
t. ex. (till exempel)(Swed.), **e.c.** (exempli causa)(Lat.), **e.g., ex.gr.** (exempli gratia)(Lat.), **f.e., f. Eks.** (for Eksempel) (Dan.), **f.i., n.p.** (na pryzkład)(Pol.), **p.ex.** (par exemple)(Fr.), **v.g.** (verbi gratia)(Lat.) or **z.B.** (zum Beispiel) (Ger.) for example; for instance
Text. Rec. or **text. rec.** (textus receptus) (Lat.) received text (Bib.)
TF Training film (Mil.)
T.F. Territorial Force or Forces (Brit.)
tf. or **t.f.** till forbidden (Advtg.)
tfr., trans., transf. or **trfr.** transfer
TG Tollgate (Mil.)
Tg (Mil.), **tel.** or **teleg.** telegraph
Tg (Mil.), **tel., teleg., telg.** or **tg.** telegram
tg., tel., teleg., telg. or **Tg** (Mil.) telegram
t.g. type genus
t.g.b. tongued, grooved and beaded (Lumber)
Tgp Telegraph printer (Mil.)
Tg Sec Telegraph section
tgt. or **t.** target
T.H., H.T. or **H.Ty.** Territory of Hawaii; Hawaiian Territory (cf. H.I.)
Th thorium (Chem.)
Th., T. (Theil, Teil)(Ger.), **Abt.** (Abteilung)(Ger.), **H., Hft.** (Heft)(Ger.), **Lfg.** (Lieferung)(Ger.), **liv.** (livraison)(Fr.), **p.** or **pt.** part (cf. inst.; no.; sec.)
Th., T. (Theil, Teil)(Ger.), **H., Hft.** (Heft) (Ger.), **inst., Lfg.** (Lieferung)(Ger.) or **liv.** (livraison)(Fr.) installment (cf. Abt.; pt.)
Th., Thdr. or **Theo.** Theodor; Theodore
Th. or **Theoph.** Theophilus
Th., Tho. or **Thos.** Thomas
Th., Thur. or **Thurs.** Thursday
Th-A, Th-B, etc. thorium A, thorium B, etc.
Th.A. Theological Associate
Thad. Thaddeus
Th. B. (Theologiae Baccalaureus)(Lat.), **B.T.** (Baccalaureus Theologiae)(Lat.), **B.Th.** or **S.T.B.** (Scientiae Theologicae Baccalaureus)(Lat.) Bachelor of Theology
Thbd. Theobald
Th.D. (Theologiae Doctor)(Lat.), **D.T., D. Th., D. Theol.** or **S.T.D.** (Scientiae Theologicae Doctor) Doctor of Theology
thd. thread
Thdr., Th. or **Theo.** Theodor; Theodore
theat. theater
theatr. or **theat.** theatrical
Th-Em thorium emanation (Chem.)
Theo. Theodosia; Theodosius
Theo., Th. or **Thdr.** Theodor; Theodore
theol. theologian; theological; theology
Theoph. Theophrastus
Theoph. or **Th.** Theophilus
theor. theorem
theos. theosophical; theosophist; theosophy
therap. therapeutic; therapeutics
therm. thermometer

thermochem. thermochemistry

thermodyn. thermodynamics

Thesaur. Amer. Septent. Sigil. (Thesaurus Americae Septentrionis Sigillum)(Lat.) Seal of the Treasury of North America (U.S. Treasury)

Thess. Thessalonians; Thessaly

Th. Ill. Thrice Illustrious

thk. thick

Th.L. Licenciate in Theology (cf. S.T.L.)

Th. M. (Theologiae Magister)(Lat.), **M. Th.** or **S.T.M.** (Scientiae Theologicae Magister)(Lat.) Master of Theology

Tho., Th. or **Thos.** Thomas

Thor. thoriated (Radio)

Thos., Th. or **Tho.** Thomas

thou., K., k, k. (kilo)(Greek), **M, M., m, m.** (milli)(Lat.) or **thous.** thousand

thous., K., k, k., (kilo)(Greek), **M, M., m, m.** (milli)(Lat.) or **thou.** thousand

THQ Theater headquarters

3-P three-pole (Elec.)

Thur., Th. or **Thurs.** Thursday

T.H.W.M. Trinity high-water mark

Ti titanium (Chem.)

Ti. or **Tib.** Tiberius

t.i. (tudni illik)(Hung.), **c.-a-d.** (c'est-à-dire) (Fr.), **d.a.** (det är)(Swed.), **d.h.** (das heisst)(Ger.), **d.i.** (das ist)(Ger.), **d.v.s.** (det vil sige)(Dan.), (det vill säga) (Swed.), **h.e.** (hoc or hic est)(Lat.), or **i.e.** (id est)(Lat.) that is; that is to say (cf. viz.)

Tib. or **Ti.** Tiberius

t.i.d. or **T.d.** (ter in die)(Lat.) three times a day (cf. t.d.s.)

TIDAC, T.I.D.A.C. or **t.i.d.a.c.** (ter in die, ante cibum)(Lat.) three times a day, before meals

TIDPC, T.I.D.P.C. or **t.i.d.p.c.** (ter in die, post cibum)(Lat.) three times a day, after meals

tier. or **tc.** tierce

T.I.H. or **LL. AA. II.** (Leurs Altesses Impériales)(Fr.) Their Imperial Highnesses

Tim. Timotheus; Timothy

timp. (timpani)(Ital.) kettledrums

tinct., Tr. or **tr.** tincture

tip. (tipografía)(Span.) printing office

Tit. Titus

tit. or **tît.** (tître)(Fr.) title

Tk Tank

Tk Bn Tank battalion

Tk Co (Mil.) Tank Company

Tk Dtyr or **TD** Tank destroyer

t.k.o. technical knockout

tkr. tanker

TL time lengths

T.L. truck load

T.L. or **T/L** time loan

T/L or **T.L.** time loan

Tl thallium (Chem.)

t.l. total loss

T.L.A. Truck Line Association

Tlmkr (Mil.) or **tlmkr.** toolmaker

T.L.O. or **t.l.o.** total loss only (Marine ins.)

T.L.R. Times Law Reports

Tlr Trailer (Mil.)

TLRB or **T.L.R.B.** Textile Labor Relations Board

tls. taels

TM Technical Manual; Training Manual (Mil.)

T.M. Traffic Manager; Trainmaster

T.M. or **t.m.** true mean [value]

T.M. or **T Mort** Trench Mortar (Mil.)

Tm or **Tu** thulium (Chem.)

t.m. or **T.M.** true mean [value]

T.M.F.B. Trans-Missouri Freight Bureau

tmkpr. timekeeper

T.M.O. or **t.m.o.** telegraph money order

T Mort or **T.M.** Trench mortar (Mil.)

T Mort Btry Trench mortar battery (Mil.)

TN true North

Tn thoron (Chem.)

Tn (Mil.), **Tn., tn.** or **tr.** train

tn. or **t.** ton; tons; town

tn., Tn (Mil.), **Tn.** or **tr.** train

TNA or **T.N.A.** tetranitroaniline

TNEC or **T.N.E.C.** Temporary National Economic Committee

Tng Training (Mil.)

T.N.I.I. Tuskegee Normal and Industrial Institute

TNT or **T.N.T.** trinitrotoluene; trinitrotoluol

TNX or **T.N.X.** trinitroxylene

TO tincture of opium; Troop orders

TO (Mil.) or **T.O.** Transport officer

T.O. Telegraph Office; Telephone Office

T.O. or **TO** Transport office

T.O., t.o. or **v.** (verte)(Lat.), (volti)(Ital.) turn over (cf. P.T.O., v.s.)

T/O Tables of Organization (Mil.)

Tob. Tobiah; Tobias; Tobit

Toc H. Talbot House [Society]

T of Opns Theater of operations

togr. together

tom., t. (tome)(Fr.),(tomo)(Span.),(tomus) (Lat.), **B., Bd.** (Band)(Ger.)(Bind) (Dan.), **b., bd.** (band)(Swed.), **T.** (Tome)(Ger.) **v., Vol.** or **vol.** volume

t. o. m. (till och med)(Swed.) even

tonn. tonnage

Top or **Topo** Topographic (Mil.)

Top (Mil.) or **topog.** topographical

Topo or **Top** Topographic (Mil.)

topog. topography

topog. or **Top** (Mil.) topographical

T.O.R. (Tertius Ordo Regularis de Poenitentia)(Lat.) Third Order Regular of St. Francis (cf. O.S.F.; T.O.S.F.)

Tor. Dep. Torpedo depot

T.O.S.D. or **T.S.D.** (Tertius Ordo Sancti Dominici)(Lat.) Third Order of St. Dominic; Dominican Fathers; Dominicans (cf. O.S.D.)

T.O.S.F. Third Order of St. Francis (cf. T.O.R.; O.S.F.)
tox. or **toxicol.** toxicology
TP technical paper
T.P. (Trésor et postes)(Fr.) Postal and Paymasters Department
Tp (Mil.), **t.**, **tel.** or **teleph.** telephone
Tp., **T.**, **t.**, **tp.**, **Twp.** or **twp.** township
tp., **T.**, **t.**, **Tp.**, **Twp.** or **twp.** township
tp., **Tr** (Mil.) or **Tr.** troop
t.p. (timbres-poste)(Fr.) postage stamp; title page
T.P.A. Technical Publicity Association; Travelers' Protective Association [of America]
T Plat Transport or Transportation platoon
t.p.m. title page mutilated (Bibliog.)
Tpr. or **tpr.** trooper
t.p.r. temperature, pulse, respiration
T.P.R.F. Tropical Plant Research Foundation
T.P.S. (télégraphie par le sol)(Fr.) earth or ground telegraphy
Tps. or **tps.** townships
Tp Sec Telephone section (Mil.)
t.p.w. title page wanting (cf. n.t.p.)
T/Q, **tal.qual.**, **T/q** or **t/q** (tale quale, talis qualis)(Lat.) as they come; average quality (cf. r.o.m.; M.R.)
t/q, **tal.qual.**, **T/Q** or **T/q** (tale quale, talis qualis)(Lat.) as they come; average quality (cf. r.o.m.; M.R.)
T.Q.R.J. (Train quotidien de ravitaillement journalier)(Fr.) Daily supply train
TR Technical Regulations (Mil.); Training Regulations (Mil.)
T.R. (Train régimentaire)(Fr.) Regimental train
T.R. (Tiré rapide)(Fr.), **R.F.** or **r.f.** rapid fire; rapid firing (cf. Q.F.)
T.R. or **T/R** transportation request; trust receipt
T.R. or **t.r.** (tempore regis)(Lat.) in the time of the king; tons registered (Shipping); (teste Rege)(Lat.) witness, the King
T/R or **T.R.** transportation request; trust receipt
Tr or **Tb** terbium (Chem.)
Tr (Mil.), **Tr.** or **tp.** troop
Tr., **t.** or **tr.** trill (Music)
Tr., **tinct.** or **tr.** tincture
Tr., **tp.** or **Tr** (Mil.) troop
Tr. or **tr.** trustee
Tr., **tr.**, **Treas.**, **treas.** or **treasr.** treasurer
tr. trace; trust
tr., **Abh.** (Abhandlung, Abhandlungen) (Ger.) or **trans.** transaction; transactions
tr., **interpr.** (interpres)(Lat.), **trad.** (traduttore)(Ital.), **trans.** or **tras.** (traslatore) (Ital.) translator
tr. or **t.** tare
tr., **t.** or **Tr.** trill (Music)
tr., **t.** or **trans.** transitive
tr., **tinct.** or **Tr.** tincture
tr., **Tn** (Mil.), **Tn.**, or **tn.** train
tr. or **Tr.** trustee
tr., **Tr.**, **Treas.**, **treas.** or **treasr.** treasurer
tr., **trad.** (traduit)(Fr.), **trans.**, **transl.** or **übers.** (übersetzt)(Ger.) translated
tr., **trans.** or **transl.** translation
tr., **trans.** or **trs.** transpose
Trac Tractor (Mil.)
trad. (traduttore)(Ital.), **interpr.** (interpres) (Lat.), **tr.**, **trans.** or **tras.** (traslatore) (Ital.) translator
trad. (traduit)(Fr.), **tr.**, **trans.**, **transl.** or **übers.** (übersetzt)(Ger.) translated
Traf Traffic (Mil.)
trag. tragedy; tragic
trans. transformer (Elec.); transverse
trans., **Abh.** (Abhandlung, Abhandlungen) (Ger.) or **tr.** transaction; transactions
trans., **interpr.** (interpres)(Lat.), **tr.**, **trad.** (traduttore)(Ital.) or **tras.** (traslatore) (Ital.) translator
trans. or **t.** transit
trans., **t.** or **tr.** transitive
trans., **tfr.**, **transf.** or **trfr.** transfer
trans., **tr.**, **trad.** (traduit)(Fr.), **transl.** or **übers.** (übersetzt)(Ger.) translated
trans., **tr.** or **transl.** translation
trans., **tr.** or **trs.** transpose
trans., **transf.**, **transfd.** or **Trfd** (Mil.) transferred
trans. or **transp.** transparent; transportation
transf. transference
transf., **tfr.**, **trans.** or **trfr.** transfer
transf., **trans.**, **transfd.** or **Trfd** (Mil.) transferred
transfd., **trans.**, **transf.** or **Trfd** (Mil.) transferred
transl., **tr.**, **trad.** (traduit)(Fr.), **trans.** or **übers.** (übersetzt)(Ger.) translated
transl., **tr.** or **trans.** translation
translit. transliteration
transp. or **trans.** transparent; transportation
tras. (traslatore)(Ital.), **interpr.** (interpres) (Lat.), **tr.**, **trad.** (traduttore)(Ital.) or **trans.** translator
trav. traveler; travels
Tr. Co. Trust Company
tr. coil tripping coil
Tr. Coll. Training College
trcs., **tc.** or **tcs.** tierces
Tr Dr or **TD** Tractor-drawn (Mil.)
Treas., **Tr.**, **tr.**, **treas.** or **treasr.** treasurer
Treas. or **treas.** treasury
treas., **Tr.**, **tr.**, **Treas.** or **treasr.** treasurer
treasr., **Tr.**, **tr.**, **Treas.** or **treas.** treasurer
Trem. or **trem.** (tremando, tremolando, tremolo)(Ital.) trembling (Music)
Trep. treponema
TRF tuned radio frequency
Trf. or **trf.** tariff
trf., **trans.**, **transf.** or **trfr.** transfer
trf. or **Trf.** tariff
Trfd (Mil.), **trans.**, **transf.** or **transfd.** transferred

trfr., tfr., trans. or **transf.** transfer
T.R.H. or **LL. AA. RR.** (Leurs Altesses Royales)(Fr.) Their Royal Highnesses
Tricl Mtr Tricycle, motor (Mil.)
trig. or **trigon.** trigonometric; trigonometrical; trigonometry
Trin. or **T.** Trinity
tripl. triplicate
trit. triturate
Trk (Mil.) or **trk.** truck
trk. or **Trk** (Mil.) truck
Trk Bn Truck battalion
Trk Dr or **Trk-Dr** Truck-drawn (Mil.)
Trk hd Truck head
Trk Sec Truck section
trop. tropic; tropics; tropical
Trs Troops
Trs. or **trs.** trustees
trs., tr. or **trans.** transpose
Truron. Truro (in the signature of a bishop)
TS tool steel
T.S., ts, t.s. or **tens. str.** tensile strength
T.S. or **t.s.** (tasto solo)(Ital.) one key only (Music); test solution
ts, T.S., t.s. or **tens. str.** tensile strength
ts., coch. parv., cochl. parv., c. par., c. parv. (cochleare parvum)(Lat.) or **tsp.** teaspoon; teaspoonful
t.s. transport and supply; tub-sized (Paper)
t.s. or **T.S.** (tasto solo)(Ital.) one key only; test solution
t.s., T.S., ts or **tens.str.** tensile strength
T.S.C. Tonic Sol-fa College
T.S.D. or **T.O.S.D.** (Tertius Ordo Sancti Dominici)(Lat.) Third Order of St. Dominic; Dominican Fathers; Dominicans (cf. O.S.D.)
T.S.F. (Telegraphie sans fil)(Fr.), **W.T., W/T** or **w.t.** wireless telegraph or telegraphy
T.Sgt. or **Tech.Sgt.** Technical Sergeant
T.S.H. Their Serene Highnesses
T.S.O. town sub-office
tsp., coch. parv., cochl. parv., c. par., c. parv. (cochleare parvum)(Lat.) or **ts.** teaspoon; teaspoonful
t.s.r. traveling stock reserve
T.S.V.P., t.s.v.p. (tournez s'il vous plaît) (Fr.), **P.T.O., p.t.o., W. S. g. u.** or **w. S. g. u.** (wenden Sie gefälligst um) (Ger.) turn over please (cf. T.O.; v.s.)
T.T. Torpedo tubes
T.T. or **T.** Trinity Term
T.T. or **t.t.** telegraphic transfer (Banking)
T.T.L., t.t.l., p.d.a. (pour dire adieu)(Fr.), **P.F.S.A., p.f.s.a.** (pour faire ses adieux) (Fr.), **P.P.C.** or **p.p.c.** (pour prendre conge)(Fr.) to say good-bye; to take leave
T.U. toxic unit; transmission unit (Elec.); (tres urgent)(Fr.) very urgent [telegram]
TU. or **t.u.** Trades union
Tu or **Tm** thulium (Chem.)
Tu or **Tung.** tungsten(Chem.)
Tu., T. or **Tues.** Tuesday
TUC, T.U.C. or **t.u.c.** Trades Union Congress or Council (Brit.)
T.U.C. Transvaal University College
Tues., T. or **Tu.** Tuesday
Tung. or **Tu** tungsten (Chem.)
Turk. Turkey
Turk. or **T.** Turkish
Tus. or **tus.** (tussis)(Lat.) cough
TVA or **T.V.A.** Tennessee Valley Authority
Tw. or **Twad.** Twaddell (Hydrometer)
TWA Transcontinental and Western Airlines
TWAB Textile Work Assignment Boards
Twad. or **Tw.** Twaddell (Hydrometer)
12°, 12mo, 12mo., D. or **duo.** duodecimo (folded in 12)
TWG twist drill gauge
T.W.I.M.C. To whom it may concern
TWOC Textile Workers Organizing Committee
2-P two-pole (Elec.)
Twp., T., t., Tp., tp., or **twp.** township
twp., T., t., Tp., tp. or **Twp.** township
TWS timed wire service (Telegraph)
T.W.U. Transport Workers' Union (Brit.)
Ty. type (Med.)
Ty., T., t., Ter., ter., Terr., terr. or **ty.** territory
ty., T., t., Ter., ter., Terr., terr., or **Ty.** territory
T.Y.C. two-year[-old] course (Racing)
typ., typo., or **typog.** typographer; typographic; typographical; typography
typw. typewriter; typewritten
tx. tax; taxes
Tz. I.K. (Tzentralny Ispolnitelny Kommitet)(Rus.) or **C.E.C.** [Soviet Union] Central Executive Committee (cf. U.C.E.C; V.Tz. I. K.)

ΤΒΠ (Tau Beta Pi) National undergraduate honor society (Engineering)
ΤΔΚ (Tau Delta Kappa) Professional fraternity (Commerce)
ΤΔΦ (Tau Delta Phi) National undergraduate fraternity
ΤΕΦ (Tau Epsilon Phi) National undergraduate fraternity
ΤΕΡ (Tau Epsilon Rho) Professional fraternity (Law)
ΤΚΑ (Tau Kappa Alpha) Honorary society (Orators and Debaters)
ΤΚΕ (Tau Kappa Epsilon) National undergraduate fraternity
ΘΑΦ (Theta Alpha Phi) National undergraduate dramatic society
ΘΧ (Theta Chi) National undergraduate fraternity
ΘΧΔ (Theta Chi Delta) National honor fraternity (Chemistry)
ΘΔΧ (Theta Delta Chi) National undergraduate fraternity

ΘΚΝ (Theta Kappa Nu) National undergraduate fraternity

ΘΚΦ (Theta Kappa Phi) National undergraduate fraternity

ΘΚΨ (Theta Kappa Psi) Professional fraternity (Medicine)

ΘΝΕ (Theta Nu Epsilon) National undergraduate fraternity

ΘΦΑ (Theta Phi Alpha) National undergraduate sorority

ΘΣΦ (Theta Sigma Phi) Honorary sorority (Journalism)

ΘΣΥ (Theta Sigma Upsilon) National undergraduate sorority (Education)

ΘΤ (Theta Tau) Professional fraternity (General Engineering)

ΘΥ (Theta Upsilon) National undergraduate sorority

ΘΥΩ (Theta Upsilon Omega) National undergraduate fraternity

ΘΞ (Theta Xi) National undergraduate fraternity

U

U or **Ur** uranium (Chem.)

U. uniform; Unionist; unit

U. or **u.** uncle

U., u. Univ. or **univ.** university

U., u. or **up.** upper

U. or **Un.** Union; United

u. (und)(Ger.) and

u., U., Univ. or **univ.** university

U/A, U/a or **u/a** underwriting account (Marine ins.)

u.a. (und andere)(Ger.), **bl.a.** (bland-andra) (Swed.), (blandt andre)(Dan.), **et al.** (et alii ar aliae)(Lat.) or **m. fl.** (med flera)(Swed.), (med flere)(Dan.) and others; among others; with others

u.a.a.O. (und an andern Ort)(Ger.) or **et al.** (et alibi)(Lat.) and elsewhere

U.A.B.S. Union of American Biological Societies

u.a.m. (und andere mehr, und anderes mehr)(Ger.), **bl. a.** (bland annat) (Swed.), (blandt andet)(Dan.), **et al.** (et alii or aliae)(Lat.) or **int.al.** (inter alia)(Lat.) and other things; among other things

u.a.m. (und anders mehr)(Ger.) or **o.a.m.** (og andet mere)(Dan.) and so forth; and others besides (cf. m.m.; u.s.f.)

u. & o. use and occupancy (Insurance)

U.A.O.D. United Ancient Order of Druids

U.A.W. United Automobile Workers

u.A.w.g. (um Antwort wird gebeten)(Ger.), **o.s.a.** (om svar anhålles)(Swed.), **R.S.V.P., r.s.v.p.** (répondez s'il vous plaît)(Fr.), **S.u.** (Svar udbedes)(Dan.) or **u. gefl. A.w.g.** (um gefällige Antwort wird gebeten)(Ger.) a reply is requested; reply please

U.B. United Brethren [in Christ]; Upper Bench

UBC United Buyers Corporation

übers. (übersetzt)(Ger.), **tr., trad.** (traduit) (Fr.), **trans.** or **transl.** translated

UBIF United Brewers Industrial Foundation

U-boat (Unterseeboot)(Ger.) submarine

U.C. University College; Upper Canada

u.c. (una corda)(Ital.) with the soft pedal (Music)

u.c. (upper case), **cap.** or **caps.** capital letters; capitals

u/c or **u.c.** undercharge

UCDLG University and College Departmental Librarians Group

UCEC or **U.C.E.C.** [Soviet] Union Central Executive Committee (cf. ARCEC; CEC; Tz.I.K.)

U.C.L. University College, London

U.C.L.A. University of California in Los Angeles

U.C.R. United China Relief

U.C.T. United Commercial Travelers [of America]

U.C.V. United Confederate Veterans

Ud., V. or **Vd.** (usted)(Span.) you (sing.)

u.d., Ut dict. or **ut dict.** (ut dictum)(Lat.) as directed (cf. E.M.P., mod. praesc.; mor. dict.)

U.D.C. Union of Democratic Control (Brit.); United Daughters of the Confederacy; Urban District Council (Brit.)

U.D.F. Union Defence Forces (So. Afr.)

U.D.F.I. Union Defence Force Institute (So. Afr.)

u.drgl. (und dergrelchen)(Ger.), **etc.** (et cetera)(Lat.), **i. t. d.** (i take dalej)(Pol.), **k.t.l.** (kai ta loipa)(Greek), **m.m.** (med mera)(Swed.), (med mere)(Dan.), **o.d.** (ock dylikt or dylika)(Swed.), **o.s.v.** (och så vidare)(Swed.), (og saa videre) (Dan.), **u.s.f.** (und so fort)(Ger.), **usw.** or **u.s.w.** (und so weiter)(Ger.) and so forth; and the like; and others of like kind (cf. **et al.; u.a.m.**)

Uds., Vds. or **VV.** (ustedes)(Span.) you (pl.)

U.E.I.C. United East India Company

U.E.L. United Empire Loyalists (Can.)

U.E.S. United Engineering Society

U.F. or **U.F.C.** United Free Church of Scotland

U.F.A. United Farmers of Alberta

U.F.C. or **U.F.** United Free Church of Scotland

u. gefl. A. w.g. (um gefällige Antwort wird gebeten)(Ger.), **o.s.a.** (om svar anhålles)(Swed.), **S.R.V.P., r.s.v.p.** (répondez s'il vous plaît)(Fr.), **S.u.** (Svar udbedes)(Dan.) or **u.A.w.g.** (um Antwort wird gebeten)(Ger.) an answer is requested; please reply

U.G.S.S.S. Union of Girls' Schools for Social Service (Brit.)

UGT urgent (Telegram)

u-h-f ultra-high frequencies **(Radio)**

U.H.S. Unitarian Historical Society

u.i. or **ut inf.** (ut infra)(Lat.) as [shown or stated] below
U.I.P. United Ireland Party
U.I.W.V. United Indian War Veterans
U.J.A. United Jewish Appeal
U.J.D., V.J.D. (Utriusque Juris Doctor)(Lat.), **J.U.D.** or **J.V.D.** (Juris Utriusque Doctor)(Lat.) Doctor of Both [Canon and Civil] Laws
U.K. United Kingdom [of Great Britain and Ireland]
U.K.A. Ulster King-of-Arms; United Kingdom Alliance
U.K./Cont. United Kingdom or Continent (Shipping)
U.K./Cont (B-H) United Kingdom or Continent Bordeaux-Hamburg range (Shipping)
U.K./Cont. (G-H) United Kingdom or Continent Gibraltar-Hamburg range (Shipping)
U.K./Cont. (H-H) United Kingdom or Continent Havre-Hamburg range (Shipping)
U.K.f.o. United Kingdom for orders
U.K.H.A.D. United Kingdom, Havre, Antwerp, or Dunkerque (Shipping)
Ukr. Ukraine
ult. ultimate; ultimately
ult., ulto. (ultimo)(Lat.), **pp.**[do] (próximo pasado)(Span.) or **v.M.** (vorigen Monats)(Ger.) last month; in the month preceding the present one
ult. praes. (ultimum praescriptus)(Lat.) prescribed last time
um. or **unm.** unmarried
U.M.C.A. Universities Mission to Central Africa (Brit.)
U.M.F.C. United Methodist Free Churches (Brit.)
umgearb. (umgearbeitet)(Ger.), **rev., ver.** or **veränd.** (verändert)(Ger.). revised
UMW or **U.M.W.** United Mine Workers
Un. or **U.** Union; United
un. unified or unifying (Bonds)
unabr. unabridged
Unasgd Unassigned (Mil.)
unaufg. (unaufgeschnitten)(Ger.) or **unct.** uncut
unb., unbd. or **ungeb.** (ungebunden)(Ger.) unbound
unc. uncertain
unct. or **unaufg.** (unaufgeschnitten)(Ger.) uncut
und. (undantag)(Swed.), **ex** or **exc.** exception
und.dk. under deck (Shipping)
undsgd. undersigned
undtkr. undertaker
Ung. or **ung.** (unguentum)(Lat.) ointment
ung. (ungarisch)(Ger.), **Hun.** or **Hung.** Hungarian
ungeb. (ungebunden)(Ger.), **unb.** or **unbd.** unbound
unis. unison
Unit. Unitarian; Unitarianism
Univ. Universalist
Univ., U., u. or **univ.** university
univ. or **allg.** (allgemein)(Ger.) universal; universally
univ., U., u. or **Univ.** university
unk. or **ign.** (ignotus)(Lat.) unknown (cf. anon.; incog.; n.u.)
unl. unlimited
unm. or **um.** unmarried
unnumb. unnumbered
unof. unofficial
unp. unpaged (cf. n.p.)
unpub. or **ined.** (ineditus)(Lat.) unpublished
UNRRA or **U.N.R.R.A.** United Nations Relief and Rehabilitation Administration
Unsat Unsatisfactory (Mil.)
unsgd. unsigned
unwmkd. unwatermarked
U. of S.A., U. of S. Afr. or **U.S.A.** Union of South Africa
U.O.J.C.A. Union of Orthodox Jewish Congregations of America
UOP Universal Oil Products
U.O.T.S. United Order of True Sisters
UP or **U.P.** United Press
U.P. Union Pacific [Railroad]
U.P. or **UP** United Press
U.P., up. or **u.p.** underproof (Spirits)
U.P. or **U.P.C.** United Presbyterian [Church]
up., U. or **u.** upper
u.p., U.P. or **up.** underproof (Spirits)
U.P.C. or **U.P.** United Presbyterian Church
U.P.E.C. (União Portuguesa do Estado da California)(Port.) Portuguese Union of the State of California (cf. U.P.P.E.C.)
uphol. upholsterer; upholstering; upholstery
u.p.o. undistorted power output (Elec.)
U.P.P.E.C. (União Portuguesa Protectora do Estado da California)(Port.) Portuguese Protective Union of the State of California (cf. U.P.E.C.)
U.P.U. Universal Postal Union
U.R. Uniform Regulations
U.R. or **u.r.** (uti rogas)(Lat.) as you ask; aye (in voting)
Ur or **U** uranium (Chem.)
Ur. or **ur.** urine
urol. urology
Uru. Uruguay
US or **U.S.** Universal Service (News)
U.S. Uncle Sam; Unconditional Selection (Queensland); United Service or Services
U.S., EE.UU. or **E.U.** (Estados Unidos)(Port., Span.) or **Ver.St.** (Vereinigte Staaten)(Ger.) United States (cf. U.S.A.)
U.S. or **US** Universal Service (News)
u.s. uniform system (Photog.)
u.s. (ubi supra)(Lat.) or **l.s.c.** (loco supra citato)(Lat.) where mentioned above; in the place cited above (cf. in loc. cit.; loc. cit.)

u.s., ut sup. (ut supra)(Lat.), **co.so.** (come sopra)(Ital.) or **w.o.** (wie oben)(Ger.) as above

U.S.A. United States Army

U.S.A., EE.UU.da A., E.U.A. (Estados Unidos da América)(Port.), **EE.UU.de A., E.U.A.** (Estados Unidos de América) (Span.) or **É.U.A.** (États-Unis-Amérique)(Fr.) United States of America (cf.U.S.)

U.S.A., U. of S.A. or **U. of S.Afr.** Union of South Africa

USAAC or **U.S.A.A.C.** United States Army Air Corps

USAAF or **U.S.A.A.F.** United States Army Air Force

USAAS or **U.S.A.A.S.** United States Army Air Service; United States Army Ambulance Service

USAFFE or **U.S.A.F.F.E.** United States Armed Forces in the Far East

USAMPS or **U.S.A.M.P.S.** United States Army Motion Picture Service

USAR or **U.S.A.R.** United States Army Reserve

USBA United States Brewers' Association

USBC or **U.S.B.C.** United States Bureau of the Census

USBTA or **U.S.B.T.A.** United States Board of Tax Appeals

USC or **U.S.C.** United States Code

U.S.C. United States of Colombia

U.S.C.A. United States Cavalry Association

U.S.C. & G.S. or **USCGS** United States Coast and Geodetic Survey

U.S.C.C. or **U.S.C.Ct.** United States Circuit Court

U.S.C.C. or **U.S.Ct.Cls.** United States Court of Claims

U.S.C.C.A. United States Circuit Court of Appeals

U.S.C.C.P.A. United States Court of Customs and Patent Appeals

USCG or **U.S.C.G.** United States Coast Guard

USCGS or **U.S.C. & G.S.** United States Coast and Geodetic Survey

U.S.C.L. United Society for Christian Literature (Brit.)(cf. R.T.S.)

USCND United States Council of National Defense

USCS or **U.S.C.S.** United States Conciliation Service

USCSC or **U.S.C.S.C.** United States Civil Service Commission

U.S.Ct.Cls. or **U.S.C.C.** United States Court of Claims

USDA or **U.S.D.A.** United States Department of Agriculture

U.S.D.C. or **U.S.Dist.Ct.** United States District Court

USECC or **U.S.E.C.C.** United States Employee's Compensation Commission

USES or **U.S.E.S.** United States Employment Service

u.s.f. (und so fort)(Ger.), **etc.** (et cetera) (Lat.), **i.t.d.** (i tak dalej)(Pol.), **k.t.l.** (kai ta loipa)(Greek), **m.m.** (med mera) (Swed.),(med mere)(Dan.), **o.d.** (och dylikt or dylika)(Swed.), **o.s.v.** (och så vidare)(Swed.), (og saa videre) (Dan.), **u.drgl.** (und dergrelchen)(Ger.), **usw.** or **u.s.w.** (und so weiter)(Ger.) and so forth; and the like; and others of like kind (cf. et al; u.a.m.)

USFCACUS United States Farm Credit Administration Credit Union Section

USFPC or **U.S.F.P.C.** United States Federal Power Commission

USG, U.S.G. or **U.S.S.G.** United States standard gauge

U.S.G.A. United States Golf Association

USHA or **U.S.H.A.** United States Housing Authority or Administration

U.S.H.C. United States High Commission

U.S.H.G. United States Home Guard

U.S.I. United Service Institution (London) (now Royal United Service Institution)

USIS United States Information Service (absorbed by OWI)

USITA United States Independent Telephone Association

U.S.L. United States Legation

USLSSA United States Live Stock Sanitary Association

USLTA United States Lawn Tennis Association

USM or **U.S.M.** United States Mail; United States Marines (cf. U.S.M.C.); United States Mint (cf. USMD; USMP; USM SF)

U.S.M.A. United States Military Academy

USMC or **U.S.M.C.** United States Marine Corps (cf. U.S.M.); United States Maritime Commission

USMCR or **U.S.M.C.R.** United States Marine Corps Reserve

USM D United States Mint, Denver

U.S.M.H. United States Marine Hospital

U.S.M.H.S. United States Marine Hospital Service

U.S.Mil.Res. United States Military Reserve

USM P United States Mint, Philadelphia

USMS or **U.S.M.S.** United States Maritime Service

USM SF United States Mint, San Francisco

USN or **U.S.N.** United States Navy

U.S.N.A. United States National Army; United States Naval Academy

U.S.N.A.S. United States Navy Air Service

U.S.N.C.B. United States Navy Consulting Board

U.S.N.G. United States National Guard

U.S.N.R. United States Naval Reserve

U.S.N.R.F. United States Naval Reserve Force

USO or **U.S.O.** United Service Organizations [for National Defense]

USOE or **U.S.O.E.** United States Office of Education

USP United States Patent

U.S.P., P.U.S. or **U.S.Pharm.** United States Pharmacopoeia

USP & DO United States Property and Disbursing Officer (Mil.)

U.S.Pharm., P.U.S. or **U.S.P.** United States Pharmacopoeia

USPHS or **U.S.P.H.S.** United States Public Health Service

USPO or **U.S.P.O.** United States Patent Office; United States Post Office
USQMC or **U.S.Q.M.C.** United States Quartermaster Corps
U.S.R. United States Reserves
USRA or **U.S.R.A.** United States Resettlement Administration
USRCS or **U.S.R.C.S.** United States Revenue Cutter Service
USRS or **U.S.R.S.** United States Reclamation Service
USS United States Steel
U.S.S. United States Scouts; United States Senate; United States Ship or Steamer; United States Standard
USS & EC or **U.S.S.E.C.** United States Securities and Exchange Commission (cf. S.E.C.)
U.S.S.C. or **U.S.S.Ct.** United States Supreme Court
U.S.S.E.C. or **U.S.S. & E. C.** United States Securities and Exchange Commission (cf. S.E.C.)
USSG, USG or **U.S.G.** United States Standard Gage
USSR or **U.S.S.R.** Union of Socialist Soviet Republics
U.S.S.S. United States Steamship
USTB or **U.S.T.B.** United States Travel Bureau
USTC or **U.S.T.C.** United States Tariff Commission
USTMA United States Trade Mark Association
usu. usual; usually
U.S.V. United States Volunteers
USVA or **U.S.V.A.** United States Veterans Administration (cf. USVB; VA; VAF)
USVB or **U.S.V.B.** United States Veterans' Bureau
usw., u.s.w. (und so weiter)(Ger.), **etc.** (et cetera)(Lat.), **i.t.d.** (i tak dalej)(Pol.), **k.t.l.** (kai ta loipa)(Greek), **m.m.** (med mera)(Swed.), (med mere)(Dan.), **o.d.** (ock dylikt or dylika)(Swed.), **o.s.v.** (och så vidare)(Swed.), (og saa videre)(Dan.), **u.drgl.** (und dergrelchen)(Ger.) or **u.s.f.** (und so fort)(Ger.) and so forth; and the like; and others of like kind (cf. et al., u.a.m.)
USWA United Steel Workers of America (cf. S.W.O.C.)
USWB or **U.S.W.B.** United States Weather Bureau (cf. W.B.)
U.S.W.V. United Spanish War Veterans
Ut. Utah
ut. utility
U.T.A. United Typothetae of America
UTC United Transformer Corporation
Ut dict., ut dict. or **u.d.** (ut dictum)(Lat.) as directed (cf. E.M.P.; mod. praesc.; mor.dict.)
Utend. (utendus)(Lat.) to be used
ut inf. or **u.i.** (ut infra)(Lat.) as [shown or stated] below
ut sup., u.s. (ut supra)(Lat.), **co. so.** (come sopra)(Ital.) or **w.o.** (wie oben)(Ger.) as above
U.u.r. or **u.u.r.** under usual reserves
u.ü.V. (unter üblichem Vorbehalt)(Ger.) under the usual proviso
U.V. ultra violet
U/w underwriter
U/ws underwriters
U-X uranium X (Chem.)
ux. (uxor)(Lat.), **con.** (conjunx)(Lat.), **Fr.** (Frau)(Ger.) or **w.** wife (cf. Mrs.)
U-Y uranium Y (Chem.)

YA (Upsilon Alpha) National undergraduate sorority (Dentistry)
ΥΔΣ (Upsilon Delta Sigma) National undergraduate society (Arts and Sciences)

V

V vagabond; vector (Math.); velocity
V, V., v or **v.** volt
V or **Vd** vanadium
V. Ventske [scale] (Chem.)
V. (Vorschrift)(Ger.), **instn., instr.** or **instrn.** instruction
V. (Vorschriften)(Ger.), **instns., instrns.** or **instrs.** instructions
V. (véase)(Span.), **S., s.** (siehe)(Ger.), **v.** (voir)(Fr.), **v., vid.** (vide)(Lat.) or **voy.** (voyez)(Fr.) see (cf. attn.; obs.)
V., Ud. or **Vd.** (usted)(Span.) you (sing.)
V., V, v or **v.** volt
V. or **v.** vision (cf. Va.)
V., v. or **ver.** version
V., v., Vic. or **vic.** vicar
V., v. vs. (versus)(Lat.), **adv., advs.** (adversus)(Lat.), **Agt., agt., agst., con.** or **cont.** (contra)(Lat.) against
V. or **Va.** visual acuity
V. or **Ven.** Venerable
V. or **Virg.** Virgin
V., Vis., Visc. or **Visct.** Viscount
V., Vul. or **Vulg.** Vulgate
v, V, V. or **v.** volt
v. valve; (vena)(Lat.) vein; ventral; vice; voice; voltage
v., B., Bd. (Band)(Ger.), (Bind)(Dan.), **b., bd.** (band)(Swed.), **T.** (Tome)(Ger.), **t., tom.** (tome)(Fr.), (tomo)(Span.), (tomus)(Lat.), **Vol.** or **vol.** volume
v., BB., Bde. (Bände)(Ger.), **t.** (tomes)(Fr.) or **vols.** volumes
v. (van)(Dutch), (von)(Ger.), **fm., fr.** or **frm.** from
v. (voir)(Fr.), **S., s.** (siehe)(Ger.), **V.** (véase)(Span.), **v., vid.** (vide)(Lat.) or **voy.** (voyez)(Fr.) see (cf. attn.; obs.)
v. (verte)(Lat.), (volti)(Ital.), **T.O.** or **t.o.** turn over (cf. P.T.O.; v.s.)
v., V, V. or **v** volt
v. or **V.** vision (cf. Va.)
v., V. or **ver.** version
v., V., Vic. or **vic.** vicar
v., V., vs. (versus)(Lat.), **adv., advs.** (adversus)(Lat.), **Agt., agt., agst., con.** or **cont.** (contra)(Lat.) against
v. or **vb.** verb

v. or **ver.** verse
v., vid. (vide)(Lat.), **S., s.** (siehe)(Ger.), **V.** (véase)(Span.), **v.** (voir)(Fr.) or **voy.** (voyez)(Fr.) see (cf. attn.; obs.)
v. or **vil.** village
v., vl. or **vn.** violin
v., Vo., or **vo.** (verso)(Lat.) left hand page (cf. f.v.)
v. or **voc.** vocative
v., Vol. or **Vols** (Mil.) volunteers
v. or **vy.** very
v- vicinal (Chem.)
VA or **V.A.** Veterans Administration (cf. USVA; USVB; VAF)
V.A. [Order of] Victoria and Albert; Volunteer Artillery; (Vuestra Alteza)(Span.) Your Highness
V.A. (Verlagsanstalt)(Ger.), **éd.** (éditeur)(Fr.), **pub., publ.** or **V.B.** (Verlagsbuchhandlung)(Ger.) publisher
V.A., V.-Adm., Vice Adm. or **Vice-Adm.** Vice Admiral
V.A. or **Vic. Ap.** Vicar Apostolic
Va. or **V.** Visual acuity
Va., Vir. or **Virg.** Virginia
va or **v-a** volt-ampere or amperes
va. or **vla.** viola
v.a. verb active
v.a. (vixit . . . annos)(Lat.) **A.V.,** or **a.v.** (anno vixit)(Lat.) he or she lived [so many] years
v.a. or **vb.a.** verbal adjective
v-a or **va** volt-ampere or amperes
vac. vacuum
VAD or **V.A.D.** Volunteer Aid Detachment
V.-Adm., V.A., Vice Adm. or **Vice-Adm.** Vice Admiral
VAF or **V.A.F.** Veterans Administration Faciiities (cf. VA; VB; USVA)
Val. Valenciennes (Lace)
val. valentine; valuation; value
val.@ or **vald.at** valued at
vald.at or **val@** valued at
V. and M. Virgin and Martyr
V. and T. volume and tension [of pulse]
var reactive volt-ampere or amperes
var. variant; variation; variety; variometer; various
var. lect., v.1., vv.11. (varia lectio, variae lectiones)(Lat.) **al.l.** (alia lectio or aliae lectiones)(Lat.) or **v.r.** other or variant reading or readings
Vat. Vatican
v. aux. verb auxiliary
VB or **V.B.** Veterans' Bureau (cf. VA; VAF; USVB)
V.B. (Verlagsbuchhandlung)(Ger.), **éd.** (éditeur)(Fr.), **pub., publ.** or **V.A.** (Verlagsanstalt)(Ger.) publisher
vb. or **v.** verb
vb. or **vbl.** verbal
vb.a. or **v.a.** verbal adjective
vbl. or **vb.** verbal
vb.n. verbal noun
VC Veterinary Corps
V.C. acuity of color vision; Vice Chairman; Vice Chancellor; Vice Consul; Victoria Cross; Volunteer Corps
vc. violincello
v.c. valuation clause (Insurance)
v.Ch., v. Chr. (vor Christo)(Ger.), **A.C.** (ante Christum)(Lat.), **av. C.** (avanti Christo)(Ital.) or **B.C.** before Christ (cf. v.Chr.G.)
v. Chr. G. (vor Christi Geburt)(Ger.), **A.C.N.** (ante Christum natus)(Lat.) or **A.N.C.** (ante nativitatem Christi)(Lat.) before the birth of Christ; (cf. v.Ch.)
Vct. or **Vic.** Victor
V.D. venereal disease; Vounteer [Officers'] Decoration
Vd or **V** vanadium
Vd., Ud. or **V.** (usted)(Span.) you (sing.)
v.d. vapor density; various dates (cf. v.y.)
V.D.A. Veteran Druggists' Association; visual discriminatory acuity
V.^{da} (viuda)(Span.), **v^{e}, vve** (veuve)(Fr.), **wid.** or **Wwe.** (Witwe)(Ger.) widow
v.def. verb defective
v.dep. verb deponent
V.D.G. venereal disease—gonorrhea
V.D.H. valvular disease of the heart
V.D.M. (Verbi Dei Minister)(Lat.) Minister of the Word of God (cf. Min.; P.; R.)
V.D.S. venereal disease—syphilis
Vds., Uds. or **VV.** (ustedes)(Span.) you (pl.)
V.E. (Votre Eminence)(Fr.) Your Eminence
V. E., V. Excia (Vossa Excel(l)ência)(Port.), (Vuestra Excelencia)(Span.) Your Excellency
v^{e}, vve (veuve)(Fr.), **V.^{da}** (viuda)(Span.), **wid.** or **Wwe.** (Witwe)(Ger.) widow
vedr. (vedrørende)(Dan.), **ang.** (angaaende)(Dan.), (angående)(Swed.) or **conc.** concerning
Vehic. vehicle
vel. vellum
Ven. Venice; Venus
Ven. or **V.** Venerable
Venet. Venetian
Venez. Venezuela
vent. ventilation; ventilator; ventilating
Ver. (Verein)(Ger.), **Ges.** (Gesellschaft)(Ger.), **S., s., Soc., soc., Socy.** or **socy.** society (cf. assn.)
ver., V. or **v.** version
ver. or **v.** verse
ver., veränd. (verändert)(Ger.), **rev.** or **umgearb.** (umgearbeitet)(Ger.) revised
ver. or **vv.** verses
veränd., ver. (verändert)(Ger.), **rev.** or **umgearb.** (umgearbeitet)(Ger.) revised
verb. (verbesserte)(Ger.), **imp.** or **impr.** improved
verb. sap., verbum sap. (verbum sapienti)(Lat.), **verb. sat.** or **verbum sat.** (verbum satis [sapienti])(Lat.) a word to the wise is enough

verb. sat., verbum sat. (verbum satis [sapienti])(Lat.), **verb. sap.** or **verbum sap.** (verbum sapienti)(Lat.) a word to the wise is enough
verbum sap., verb sap. (verbum sapienti) (Lat.), **verb. sat.** or **verbum sat.**(verbum satis [sapienti])(Lat.) a word to the wise is enough
verbum sat., verb. sat. (verbum satis [sapienti])(Lat.), **verb. sap.** or **verbum sap.** (verbum sapienti)(Lat.) a word to the wise is enough
Verf. (Verfasser)(Ger.), **A.** (autor)(Span.), **aut.** (auteur)(Fr.), (autore)(Ital.), **Au., auth., förf.** (författare, or författarinna) (Swed.) or **Forf.** (Forfatter)(Dan.) author
vergr. (vergriffen)(Ger.), **O.P., o.p.** or **o/p** out of print
Verm. or **Vt.** Vermont
verm. (vermehrte)(Ger.) or **enl.** enlarged (cf. augm.; sup.)
vers or **vers.** versed sine; versine
Ver.St. (Vereinigte Staaten)(Ger.), **EE.UU., E.U.** (Estados Unidos)(Port., Span.) or **U.S.** United States (cf. U.S.A.)
vert. vertebra; vertebrata; vertebrate; vertical
ves. (vesica)(Lat.) bladder; vessel; vestry
vesic. (vesicula)(Lat.) blister
Vet (Mil.), **vet.** or **veter.** veterinarian; veterinary
vet. veteran
vet., Vet (Mil.) or **veter.** veterinarian; veterinary
Vet Co Veterinary company
veter., Vet (Mil.) or **vet.** veterinarian; veterinary
Vet Evac Hosp Veterinary evacuation hospital
Vet Serv Veterinary Service
Vet.Surg. Veterinary Surgeon
V.Excia or **V.E.** (Vossa Excel(l)ência) (Port.), (Vuestra Excelencia)(Span.) Your Excellency
V.F. Vicar Forane (R.C. Church); vocal fremitus (Med.)
V.F., F. or **V.f.** visual field; field of vision
v.f. very fair
V.F.W. Veterans of Foreign Wars [of the United States]
VG (Mil.) or **v.g.** very good
V.G. Vicar General (R.C.Church); Vice-Grand
v.g. (verbi gratia)(Lat.), **e.c.** (exempli causa)(Lat.), **e.g., ex.gr.** (exempli gratia)(Lat.), **f.e., f. Eks.** (for Eksempel) (Dan.), **f.i., n.p.** (na przykład)(Polish), **p.ex.** (par exemple)(Fr.), **t.ex.** (till exempel)(Swed.) or **z.B.** (zum Beispiel) (Ger.) for example; for instance
v.g. or **VG** (Mil.) very good
vgl. (vergleiche)(Ger.), **cf., conf.** (confer) (Lat.), **comp., compar., cp., jf., jfr.** (jaevnfør)(Dan.), (jämför)(Swed.), **por.** (porównaj)(Pol.) or **sml.** (sammenlign) (Dan). compare
v.g.u. (verlesen, genehmigt, unterschrieben) (Ger.) read, approved and signed
v. H. (von Hundert)(Ger.), **P.C., P.c., p.c., P/C, p/c, pct., pe.cen., per cent, per cent., percent.** or **per ct.** (per centum) (Lat.) by the hundred
V.H.S. Honorary Surgeon to the Viceroy of India
V.I. Virgin Islands
Vi virginium (Chem.)
v.i. verb intransitive
v.i. (vide infra)(Lat.) or **s.u.** (siehe unten) (Ger.) see below
vib. vibration
Vic., V., v. or **vic.** vicar
Vic. or **Vct.** Victor
Vic. or **vic.** vicarage
Vic. or **Vict.** Victoria; Victorian
vic., V., v. or **Vic.** vicar
vic. or **Vic.** vicarage
Vic. Ap. or **V.A.** Vicar Apostolic
Vice Adm., V.A., V.-Adm. or **Vice-Adm.** Vice Admiral
Vice Pres., V.P. or **V.Pres.** Vice President
Vict. or **Vic.** Victoria: Victorian
vid., v. (vide)(Lat.), **S., s.** (siehe)(Ger.), **V.** (véase)(Span.), **v.** (voir)(Fr.) or **voy.** (voyez)(Fr.) see (cf. attn.; obs.)
vil. or **v.** village
v. imp. verb impersonal
Vin. Vincent
Vir., Va. or **Virg.** Virginia
Virg. Virgil
Virg. or **V.** Virgin
Virg., Va. or **Vir.** Virginia
v. irr. verb irregular
Vis (Mil.) or **vis.** visibility; visual (cf. Va.; V.f.)
Vis., V., Visc. or **Visct.** Viscount
Vis., Visc. or **Visct.** Viscountess
vis. or **Vis** (Mil.) visibility; visual (cf. Va.; V.f.)
Visc., V., Vis. or **Visct.** Viscount
Visc., Vis., or **Visct.** Vicountess
Visct., V., Vis. or **Visc.** Viscount
Visct., Vis. or **Visc.** Vicountess
vitel. (vitellus)(Lat.) yolk
Vit. ov. sol. or **V.o.s.** (vitello ovi solutus) (Lat.) dissolved in egg yolk
viv. (vivace)(Ital.) lively; with spirit (Music)
viz. (videlicet)(Lat.), **näml.** (nämligen) (Swed.) **sc., scil., SS.** or **ss.** (scilicet) (Lat.) namely; to wit (cf. i.e.)
v.J. (vorigen Jahres)(Ger.) of the past year
V.J.D., U.J.D. (Utriusque Juris Doctor) (Lat.), **J.U.D.** or **J.V.D.** (Juris Utriusque Doctor)(Lat.) Doctor of Both Canon and Civil Laws
V.K. vertical keel (Shipbuilding)
V.L. Vice-lieutenant
vl., v. or **vn.** violin
v.l., var. lect., vv.ll. (varia lectio, variae lectiones)(Lat.), **al.l.** (alia lectio, aliae lectiones) or **v.r.** other or variant reading or readings
vla. or **va.** viola

V.L.O. Volunteer Land Order (Australia)
V.M. (Vuestra Majestad)(Span.) Your Majesty
V.M. or **Vm.** (Vuestra Merced)(Span.) Your Worship
V.M. or **Vmcê** (Vossa Mercê)(Port.) Your Grace
Vm. or **V.M.** (Vuestra Merced)(Span.) Your Worship
v.M. (vorigen Monats)(Ger.), **pp.^{do}** (próximo pasado)(Span.), **ult.** or **ulto.** (ultimo)(Lat.) last month
v.M., Vorm. (Vormittags)(Ger.), **Fm.** (Formiddag)(Dan.) or **f.m.** (formiddagen) (Swed.) forenoon (cf. A.M.)
vm. voltmeter
v/m volts per meter
Vmcê. or **V. M.** (Vossa Mercê)(Port.) Your Grace
V.M.D. (Veterinariae Medicinae Doctor) (Lat.), **D.V.M.** or **M.V.D.** Doctor of Veterinary Medicine
V.M.H. Victoria Medal of Honor
V.M.I. Virginia Military Institute
vn., v. or **vl.** violin
v.n. (vicario nomine)(Lat.) as representative; proxy (cf. per proc.)
v.n. or **v.neut.** verb neuter
V.N.A. Visiting Nurse Association
v.neut. or **v.n.** verb neuter
VO Verbal orders (Mil.)
V.O. or **R.V.O.** [Royal] Victorian Order
Vo., v. or **vo.** (verso)(Lat.) left hand page (cf. f.v.)
vo., v. or **Vo.** (verso)(Lat.) left hand page (cf. f.v.)
v.o. (von oben)(Ger.) from the top
V.O.A. Vasa Order of America
V.O.B.C. Verbal orders, battery commander
voc. or **v.** vocative
vocab. vocabulary
V.O.C.C. Verbal orders, company commander
VOKS, V.O.K.S (Vsesoiuznoe obshchestvo kulturnoĭ sviazi s sagranitzeĭ)(Rus.), **ARSCRFC, A.R.S.C.R.F.C., AUSCRFC** or **A.U.S.C.R.F.C.** All-Russia or All-Union Society for Cultural Relations with Foreign Countries
Vol (Mil.), **Vol.** or **vol.** volunteer
Vol., v., or **Vols** (Mil.) volunteers
Vol., Vol (Mil.) or **vol.** volunteer
vol., B., Bd. (Band)(Ger.), (Bind)(Dan.), **b., bd.** (band)(Swed.), **T.** (Tome) (Ger.), **t., tom.** (tome)(Fr.),(tomo) (Span.), (tomus)(Lat.), **v.** or **Vol.** volume
vol., Vol (Mil.) or **Vol.** volunteer
vol. or **volc.** volcanic; volcano
volc. or **vol.** volcanic; volcano
Vols (Mil.), **v.** or **Vol.** volunteers
vols., BB., Bde. (Bände)(Ger.), **t.** (tomes) (Fr.) or **v.** volumes
V.O.N. Victorian Order of Nurses (Brit.)
v.o.p. valued as in original policy (Insurance)
V.O.P.C. Verbal orders, post commander
V.O.R.C. Verbal orders, regimental commander
Vorm., v.M. (Vormittags)(Ger.), **Fm.** (Formiddag)(Dan.) or **f.m.** (formiddagen) (Swed.) forenoon (cf. A.M.)
V.o.s. or **Vit. ov. sol.** (vitello ovi solutus) (Lat.) dissolved in yolk of egg
V.O.T.C. Verbal orders, troop commander
vou. or **Vou** (Mil.) voucher
vox pop. (vox populi)(Lat.) voice of the people
voy. voyage
voy. (voyez)(Fr.), **S., s.** (siehe)(Ger.), **V.** (véase)(Span.), **v.** (voir)(Fr.), **v.** or **vid.** (vide)(Lat.) see (cf. attn.; obs.)
V.P., Vice Pres. or **V.Pres.** Vice President
v.p. various pagings; various places [of publication]; verb passive
v.p. or **vt.pl.** voting pool (Stocks)
V.P.I. Virginia Polytechnic Institute
V.Pres., Vice Pres. or **V.P.** Vice President
V. R. (Victoria Regina)(Lat.) Queen Victoria; Vicar Rural; Village Reserve (Australia); vocal resonance
v.r. verb reflexive
v.r., al.l. (alia lectio, aliae lectiones)(Lat.), **var. lect., v.l.** or **vv.ll.** (varia lectio, variae lectiones)(Lat.) variant reading or readings; other reading or readings
V.R.B. Veterans' Relief Board
V.R.C. Volunteer Rifle Corps
V.R. et I. or **V.R.I.** (Victoria Regina et Imperatrix)(Lat.) Victoria, Queen and Empress
V. Rev. or **R.A.** (Reverendus admodum) (Lat.) Very Reverend
V.R.I. or **V.R. et I.** (Victoria Regina et Imperatrix)(Lat.) Victoria, Queen and Empress
V.R.P. (Vestra Reverendissima Paternitas) (Lat.) Your Most Reverend Paternity
V. S. Veterinary Surgeon
V.S. or **v.s.** volumetric solution
Vs. (venasectio)(Lat.) venesection
vs., V., v. (versus)(Lat.), **adv., advs.** (adversus)(Lat.), **Agt., agt., agst., con.** or **cont.** (contra)(Lat.) against
v.s. (volti subito)(Ital.) turn over quickly (Music) (cf. P.T.O.; v.); vibration seconds (Sound); visible supply
v.s. (vide supra)(Lat.) or **s.o.** (siehe oben) (Ger.) see above
v.s. or **V.S.** volumetric solution
Vs.B. (venasectio brachii)(Lat.) bleeding in the arm
V.S.C. Volunteer Staff Corps
VSS. versions
v.str. verb strong
VT vacuum tube (Radio)
V.T. voice tube
V.T. (Vetus Testamentum)(Lat.), **A.T.** (Altes Testament)(Ger.), **Old Test.** or **O.T.** Old Testament
Vt. or **Verm.** Vermont
vt. voting
v.t. or **v. tr.** verb transitive

V.T.C. Volunteer Training Corps (Brit.)
V.T.C. or **v.t.c.** voting trust certificate; voting trust company
vt.pl. or **v.p.** voting pool (Stocks)
v.tr. or **v.t.** verb transitive
VTsSPS, V.Ts.S.P.S. (Vesoîuznyi Tsentralnyĭ Sovet Professionalnyph Soîuzov) (Rus.), **ARCCTU, A.R.C.C.T.U., AUCCTU** or **A.U.C.C.T.U.** All Russia or All-Union Central Council of Trade Unions
V. Tz. I.K. (Vserossiisky Tzentralny Ispolnitelny Kommitet) (Rus.), **ARCEC, A.R.C.E.C., AUCEC** or **A.U.C.E.C.** All-Russian Central Executive Committee (cf. CEC; Tz.I.K.; U.C.E.C.)
v.u. (von unten) (Ger.) from the bottom
Vul., V. or **Vulg.** Vulgate
Vulg., V. or **Vul.** Vulgate
vulg. vulgar; vulgarity; vulgarly
VV or **vv.** violins
VV., Uds. or **Vds.** (ustedes) (Span.) you (pl.)
V.V. or **v.v.** (vice versa) (Lat.) the order being changed; conversely
vv. or **ver.** verses
vv. or **VV** violins
v.v. or **V.V.** (vice versa) (Lat.) the order being changed; conversely
vve, v^{e} (veuve) (Fr.), **V.**^{da} (viuda) (Span.), **wid.** or **Wwe.** (Witwe) (Ger.) widow
vv.ll., var.lect., v.l. (vario lectio, variae lectiones) (Lat.), **al.l.** (alia lectio or aliae lectiones) (Lat.) or **v.r.** other or variant reading or readings
V.W. Very Worshipful; vessel wall (Med.)
V.Y. or **v.y.** various years (cf. v.d.)
vy. or **v.** very
v.y. or **V.Y.** various years (cf. v.d.)

W

W, W. or **w.** west
W. Welsh; Wolfram (tungsten) (Chem.)
W. or **w.** warden; warehousing; watt; western; width; won
W., w., Gew. (Gewicht) (Ger.), **p.** (peso) (Span.) or **wt.** weight
W., w., op. (opus) (Lat.) or **wk.** work
W., w. or **west.** western
W., w. or **wks.** works
W., Wash. or **Wn.** Washington
W., We. or **Wed.** Wednesday
w. wanting; wicket; wide
w., av. (avec) (Fr.), **c.** (cum) (Lat.) or **m.** (mit) (Ger.) with
w. (wiek) (Pol.), **C., c., cen., cent.** or **s.** (siècle) (Fr.) century
w., con. (conjunx) (Lat.), **Fr.** (Frau) (Ger.), or **ux.** (uxor) (Lat.) wife (cf. Mrs.)
w., Gew. (gewicht) (Ger.), **p.** (peso) (Span.) **W.** or **wt.** weight
w., W or **W.** west
w. or **W.** warden; warehousing; watt; width; won
w., W. or **west.** western
w. or **wd.** word
w. or **wk.** week
w. or **wks.** weeks
W.A. or **w.a.** with average (Insurance)
W.A. or **W.Afr.** West Africa
W.A. or **W. Aust.** West or Western Australia
Wa. Walter; Walther
w.a. or **W.A.** with average (Insurance)
WAAC or **W.A.A.C.** Women's Army Auxiliary Corps (cf. W.A.C.)
W.A.A.E. World Association for Adult Education (Brit.)
W.A.A.F. or **W.A.A.F.S.** Women's Auxiliary Air Force [Services] (Brit.)
W.A.A.F.S. or **W.A.A.F.** Women's Auxiliary Air Force Services (Brit.)
WAAM or **W.A.A.M.** Women's Auxiliary Aircraft Mechanic
WAC Women's Army Corps (formerly WAAC)
W.A.C. Club Worked All Continents Club (Radio)
Wadh. Wadham
w.a.f. with all faults
W.A.F.F. West Africa Frontier Force (Brit.)
W. Afr. or **W.A.** West Africa
W. Afr. R. West African Regiment (Brit.)
WAFS or **W.A.F.S.** Women's Auxiliary Ferrying Squadron
Wag Wagon (Mil.)
wag. or **Wagr** (Mil.) wagoner
Wag Bn Wagon battalion
Wag Co Wagon company
Wagmr or **Wag Mr** Wagonmaster (Mil.)
Wagr (Mil.) or **wag.** wagoner
Wag Sec Wagon section
Wag Tn Wagon train
Wal. Walloon
Wal. or **Walach.** Walachian
wal. walnut
w. & f. or **w. and f.** water and feed (Transp.)
w. & r. or **w. and r.** water and rail
w. and f. or **w. & f.** water and feed (Transp.)
W. and H., WH or **W.H.** Westcott and Hort's [critical text of the Greek New Testament]
W. and M. [King] William and [Queen] Mary
w. and r. or **w. & r.** water and rail
WANS or **W.A.N.S.** Women's Auxiliary National Service
War. Warwickshire
war., wrnt. or **wt.** warrant
WARF or **W.A.R.F.** Wisconsin Alumni Research Foundation
warrtd. warranted
warrty. warranty
WAS Club Worked All Stations Club (Radio)
Wash., Wn. or **W.** Washington
WASPS or **W.A.S.P.S.** Women's Auxiliary State Police School
WATC or **W.A.T.C.** Women's Ambulance and Transport Corps
watt-hr., wh., whr or **whr.** watt-hour or hours

W. Aust. or **W.A.** West or Western Australia
WAVES or **W.A.V.E.S.** Women Appointed for Volunteer Emergency Service (Women's Reserve, U.S. Naval Reserve)
WB or **w.b.** westbound
W.B. Water Board; Weather Bureau (cf. U.S.W.B.)
W.B. or **W/B** waybill
W.B. or **w.b.** warehouse book
W/B or **W.B.** way bill
w.b. water ballast
w.b. or **WB** westbound
w.b. or **W.B.** warehouse book
W.B.A. Women's Benefit Association
WBLE Wives of the Brotherhood of Locomotive Engineers
W.B.M. Women's Board of Missions
WbN west by north
WbS west by south
w.b.s. without benefit of salvage (Shipping)
WC, W.C. or **w.c.** water closet
W.C. Wesleyan Chapel; Western Central [Postal District, London]
W.C. or **w.c.** without charge
w.c., WC or **W.C.** water closet
w.c. or **W.C.** without charge
w/c, WPC or **wpc** watt or watts per candle
W.C.A. Women's Christian Association; World Calendar Association
W.C.E.U. World's Christian Endeavor Union (cf. C.E.)
W.C.O.F. Women's Catholic Order of Foresters
W.C.S.A. West Coast of South America
W.C.T.U. Women's Christian Temperance Union
WD or **W.D.** War Department
W.D. Works Department
wd. wood; would; wound
wd. or **w.** word
WDC or **W.D.C.** War Damage Corporation
W.D.C. War Department Citation
wdg. winding; wording
WDO or **W.D.O.** War Department Orders
wd.sc. wood screw
We., W. or **Wed.** Wednesday
WEA Women's Emancipation Association
W.E.A. Workers' Educational Association (Brit.)
Wea Weather (Mil.)
Wea Gp Weather group (Mil.)
Wea O Weather officer
Wea sq Weather squadron
Wed., W. or **We.** Wednesday
W.E.F. war emergency formula (Pharm.)
W.E.R.S. War Emergency Radio Service
West. or **Westm.** Westminster
west., W. or **w.** western
W.F., Afr. Miss.Soc. or **S.M.A.** (Societas Missionum ad Afros)(Lat.) African Missionary Society; White Fathers
wf or **w.f.** wrong font (Type)
w.f. or **wf** wrong font (Type)
WFA or **W.F.A.** War Food Administration
WFC or **W.F.C.** War Finance Corporation
W.F.L. Women's Freedom League (Brit.)
W.F.P.S.A. Wild Flower Preservation Society of America
WG Worthy Grand
W.G. or **w.g.** wire gauge
Wg Wing (Mil.)
w.g. weight guaranteed
w.g. or **W.G.** wire guage
Wg.Cdr. Wing Commander
W. Ger. or **W.Gmc.** West Germanic
WH, W.H. or **W. and H.** Westcott and Hort's [critical text of the Greek New Testament]
wh. which
wh., watt-hr., whr or **whr.** watt-hour or hours
W'hampton Wolverhampton
whf. wharf
whge. wharfage
W.H.M.A. Women's Home Missionary Association
whr., watt-hr., wh. or **whr.** watt-hour or hours
whr.m. watt-hour meter
whs. warehouse
whsle. wholesale
whsmn. warehouseman
Whs.Rec., whs.rec., W.R. or **w.r.** warehouse receipt
whs.rec., Whs.Rec., W.R. or **w.r** warehouse receipt
whs.stk. warehouse stock
whs.war., W.W. or **W/W** warehouse warrant
whvs. wharves
WI or **w.i..** wrought iron
wi or **w.i.** when issued (Securities)
w.i. or **WI** wrought iron
w.i. or **wi** when issued (Securities)
WIA Wounded in action
W.I.A.B. Wistar Institute of Anatomy and Biology
W.I.D. West India Dock
wid. widower
wid., V.da (viuda)(Span.), **ve, vve** (veuve) (Fr.) or **Wwe.** (Witwe)(Ger.) widow
Wigorn. Worcester, in the signature of Bishop
W.I.I.U. Workers' International Industrial Union
W.I.L.P.F. Women's International League for Peace and Freedom
Wilts. Wiltshire
w.i.m.c. whom it may concern (cf. T.W.I.M.C.)
WINS or **W.I.N.S.** Women in National Service
Winton. (Wintoniensis)(Lat.) of Winchester
W.I.R. West India Regiment (Brit.)
Wis. or **Wisc.** Wisconsin
Wisd. [Book of] Wisdom
Wiss. (Wissenschaft)(Ger.), **S., Sc., sc.** or **sci.** science

wk. weak
wk., op. (opus)(Lat.), **W.** or **w.** work
wk. or **w.** week
w.k. well known (Humorous)
wkg. working
wkly. weekly
wks., W. or **w.** works
wks. or **w.** weeks
W.L. Western Lines
W.L., W/L or **w.l.** wave length
w.l. water line (Shipbuilding)
WLA or **W.L.A.** Women's Land Army
WLB, W.L.B., NWLB or **N.W.L.B.** [National] War Labor Board
wldr. welder
W.L.F. Women's Liberal Federation
W. Long., W. long. or **W. lon.** West longitude
W.M. Western Maryland; Worshipful Master (Freemasonry)
Wm. William
Wm. or **wm.** wattmeter
wm. or **Wm.** wattmeter
w/m weight and/or measurement (Shipping)
WMB or **W.M.B.** War Meat Board
WMC or **W.M.C.** War Manpower Commission
W. Midl. West Midland (Dialect)
wmk. watermark
wmkd. watermarked
W.M.S. Wesleyan Missionary Society (Brit.)
W.M.S.I. Women's Medical Service of India (Brit.)
Wn Winch (Mil.)
Wn., W. or **Wash.** Washington
W.N.A. winter North Atlantic
WNDA or **W.N.D.A.** World Narcotic Defense Association
W.N.F.G.A. Woman's National Farm and Garden Association
W.N.L.F. Women's National Liberal Federation (Brit.)
W.N.P. or **w.n.p.** wire non-payment (Banking)
w.n.p. or **W.N.P.** wire non-payment (Banking)
WNW, W.N.W. or **w.n.w.** west-northwest
WO or **W.O.** War Office; Warrant officer
w.o. (wie oben)(Ger.), **co.so.** (come sopra) (Ital.), **u.s.** or **ut sup.** (ut supra)(Lat.) as above
w.o., s., Sn. (sine)(Lat.), **sen.** (senza)(Ital.) (Music) or **wt.** without (cf. ex)
w.o.b. washed overboard (Shipping)
W.O.C. Wilson Ornithological Club; without compensation
WO Ck or **W.O.Ck.** Warrant officers' cook
w.o.g. with other goods
WOJG Warrant Officer, junior grade
w.o.l. wharfowner's liability
Wood Tech. Wood Technologist
Wor., Wp., Wpfl. or **Wpful.** Worshipful
Worcs. Worcestershire
work. comp. workmen's compensation
workho. workhouse
WO Std or **W.O. std.** Warrant officers' steward
WOW or **W.O.W.** Women Ordnance Workers
W.O.W. Woodmen of the World
W.P. working point; Worthy Patriarch (Freemasonry); Worthy President (Freemasonry)
W.P. or **w.p.** weather permitting; wire payment
Wp., Wor., Wpfl. or **Wpful.** Worshipful
wp. worship
w.p. or **W.P.** weather permitting; wire payment
WPA or **W.P.A.** Work Projects Administration
W.P.A. or **w.p.a.** with particular average (Marine ins.)
WPB or **W.P.B.** War Production Board (cf. OPM; SPAB)
W.P.B. waste-paper basket
WPC, w/c or **wpc** watt or watts per candle
W.P.C. World Power Conference
wpc, w/c or **WPC** watt or watts per candle
Wpf., Wor., Wpfl. or **Wpful.** Worshipful
Wpfl., Wor., Wpf. or **Wpful.** Worshipful
Wpful., Wor., Wpf. or **Wpfl.** Worshipful
WPI Wall Paper Institute
Wpn Carr Weapon carrier
Wpn Plat Weapons platoon
Wpn Tr Weapons troop
WP or NP or **W.P. or N.P.** wire payment or non-payment
w.p.p. waterproof paper packing
WPRA or **W.P.R.A.** Western Petroleum Refiners Association
WPWP or **W.P.W.P.** War Public Works Program
W.R. Water Reserve (Australia); West Riding (England)
W.R. or **G.R.** (William or Gulielmus Rex) (Lat.) King William
W.R., Whs. Rec., whs.rec. or **w.r.** warehouse receipt
W.r. Wassermann reaction
wr. writing [paper]
w.r. war risk (Insurance); with rights (Securities)
w.r., Whs.Rec., whs.rec. or **W.R.** warehouse receipt
WRA or **W.R.A.** War Relocation Authority
WRAF or **W.R.A.F.** Women's Royal Air Force
wrang. wrangler
W.R.C. Women's Relief Corps
W.R.Ck. Wardroom cook
WREN or **W.R.N.S.** Women's Royal Naval Service
Wrm. wardroom
W.R.N.S. or **WREN** Women's Royal Naval Service
wrnt., war. or **wt.** warrant
w.r.o. war risk only (Insurance)
W.R. Std. Wardroom steward

Wrzes. (Wrzesień)(Pol.), **S., sbre.** (se(p)-tiembre)(Span.), **Sep., Sept., set.** (setembro)(Port.), **sett.** (settembre)(Ital.) or **szept.** (szeptember)(Hung.) September
W.S. Weather Station (Australia); West Saxon (England); Writer to the Signet
WSA or **W.S.A.** War Shipping Administration
W.S.A.P. Women's South African Party
W.S.C.F. World's Student Christian Federation
WSCID Washington State College Institute of Dairying
W.S.g.u., w. S. g. u. (Wenden Sie gefälligst um)(Ger.), **P.T.O., p.t.o., T. S. V. P.** or **t.s.v.p.** (tournez s'il vous plaît)(Fr.) turn over please (cf. T.O.; v.s.)
W.S. of J. White Shrine of Jerusalem
W.S.P.U. Women's Social and Political Union (Brit.)
WSTIB or **W.S.T.I.B.** Woolen & Silk Textiles Industries Board
W Sup Water supply (Mil.)
WSW, W.S.W. or **w.s.w.** west-southwest
WT (Mil.) or **W.T.** water tender
WT or **W Tk** Watertank (Mil.)
W.T. wireless telephone
W.T., T.S.F. (Telegraphie sans fil)(Fr.), **W/T** or **w.t.** wireless telegraph or telegraphy
W.T. or **WT** (Mil.) water tender
W.T. or **w.t.** war tax; water tight
W/T, T.S.F. (Telegraphie sans fil)(Fr.), **W.T.** or **w.t.** wireless telegraph or telegraphy
wt., Gew. (Gewicht)(Ger.), **p.** (peso) (Span.), **W.** or **w.** weight
wt., s., Sn. (sine)(Lat.), **sen.** (senza)(Ital) (Music) or **w.o.** without
wt., war. or **wrnt.** warrant
w.t., T.S.F. (Telegraphie sans fil)(Fr.), **W.T.** or **W/T** wireless telegraph or telegraphy
w.t. or **W.T.** war tax; water tight
WTB or **W.T.B.** War Trade Board
WTD watertight door
W Tk or **WT** Water tank (Mil.)
W Tk Bn Water tank battalion
W Tk Tn Water tank train
wt.prej. without prejudice
wts. weights
WTUA Women's Trade Union Association (Brit.)
W.U.S.L. Women's United Service League (Brit.)
W.Va. West Virginia
WVS or **W.V.S.** Women's Voluntary Service (Brit.)
WW Waterworks (Mil.)
W.W., whs.war. or **W/W** warehouse warrant
W/W, whs.war. or **W.W.** warehouse warrant
ww or **w.w.** with warrants (Securities)
W.W.C.T.U. World's Women's Christian Temperance Union (cf. W.C.T.U.)
w.w.d. weather working days
Wwe. (Witwe)(Ger.), **v.da** (viuda)(Span.), **ve, vve** (veuve)(Fr.) or **wid.** widow
Wy. or **Wyo.** Wyoming
W.Y.C.M. World Youth Congress Movement
Wyo. or **Wy.** Wyoming
W.Y.W.C.A. World's Young Women's Christian Association (cf. Y.W.C.A.)

X

X, Xt. (Christos)(Greek) or **Chr.** Christ
X., Chr., Xn. or **Xtian.** Christian
x an abscissa; an unknown quantity
x or **react.** reactance (Elec.)
X.C., ex coup., ex cp., ex cu., xc, x-c., xcp, xcp., x/cp. or **x-cp.** ex coupon; without coupon (Bonds)
xc, ex coup., ex cp., ex cu., X.C., x-c., xcp, xcp., x/cp. or **x-cp.** ex coupon; without coupon (Bonds)
x-c., ex coup., ex cp., ex cu., X.C., xc, xcp, xcp., x/cp. or **x-cp.** ex coupon; without coupon (Bonds)
xcp., xcp., x/cp., x-cp., ex-coup., ex-cp., ex cu., X.C., xc, or **x-c.** ex-coupon; without coupon (Bonds)
X-cut or **xcut** crosscut
X.D., xd, x.d., x-d, e.d., ex d., ex div., xdiv or **x-div.** ex dividend; without dividend (Stocks)
xdiv, x-div., e.d., ex d., ex div., X.D., xd, x.d. or **x-d** ex dividend; without dividend (Stocks)
Xe xenon (Chem.)
Xen. Xenophon
X.i., x.i., x-i., ex int., X. in., x in., x. int. or **x-int.** ex interest; without interest (Stock exchange)
Xing or XING crossing
x. int., x-int., ex int., X.i., x.i., x-i., X. in. or **x in.** ex interest; without interest (Stock exchange)
Xm. or **Xmas.** Christmas
Xmas. or **Xm.** Christmas
X-N., X-n., x-n., ex n. or **X-new** ex new; without the right to new shares (Stock exchange)
Xn., Chr., Xt. or **Xtian.** Christian
X-new, ex n., X-N., X-n. or **x-n.** ex new; without the right to new shares (Stock exchange)
Xnty. or **Xty.** Christianity
X out cross out
xpr, x pr. or **ex pr.** ex privileges; without privileges (Securities)
XQ. cross-question
Xr. (Kreuzer)(Ger.) cruiser
xr, ex r., X-rts. or **x rts.** ex rights; without rights (Stock exchange)
X rds. or **CR** (Mil.) crossroads
x-ref. or **cr. ref.** cross reference
X-rts., X rts., ex r. or **xr** ex rights; without rights (Stock exchange)
X strong extra strong
Xt., Chr. or **X** (Christos)(Greek) Christ

Xt., Chr., Xn. or **Xtian.** Christian
Xtian, Chr., Xn. or **Xt.** Christian
xtry. extraordinary
Xty. or **Xnty.** Christianity
xw or **ex w.** ex warrant; without warrants (Securities)
xyl. (xylographa)(Lat.) xylographs

ΞΨΦ (Xi Psi Phi) National undergraduate professional society (Dentistry)
ΞΣΠ (Xi Sigma Pi) National undergraduate honorary fraternity (Forestry)

Y

Y, Yb or **Yt** ytterbium (Chem.)
Y or **Y.M.C.A.** Young Men's Christian Association
y admittance (Elec.); an ordinate; an unknown quantity
y. youngest
y., A., a., An., an. (annus)(Lat.), **J.** (Jahr) (Ger.), **r.** (rok)(Pol.) or **yr.** year
y., ann. (anni)(Lat.), **yr.** or **yrs.** years
y. or **yd.** yard
y., yd. or **yds.** yards
y. or **yr.** younger; your
Y.A., Y/A or **Y./A.** York-Antwerp [Rules] (Marine ins.)
Y.B. or **yearb.** yearbook
Yb, Y or **Yt** ytterbium (Chem.)
Y.C.L. Young Communist League
Y.C.S Youth Consultation Service
yd. or **y.** yard
yd., y. or **yds.** yards
yd.² or **sq. yd.** square yard or yards
yd.³ or **cu. yd.** cubic yard or yards
yday. or **yesty.** yesterday
yds., y. or **yd.** yards
yearb. or **Y. B.** yearbook
Yeo, yeo. or **yeom.** Yeomanry
yesty. or **yday.** yesterday
Y.L.I. Young Ladies Institute; Yorkshire Light Infantry
Y.M.& Y.W.H.A. Young Men's and Young Women's Hebrew Association
Y.M.C.A. or **Y.** Young Men's Christian Association
Y.M. Cath A. Young Men's Catholic Association
Y.M.C.U. Young Men's Christian Union
Y.M.F.S. Young Men's Friendly Society
Y.M.H.A. Young Men's Hebrew Association
Y.M.I. Young Men's Institute
yn. yen
Yorks or **Yorks.** Yorkshire
Y.P.B.U. Young People's Baptist Union
yr., A., a., An., an. (annus)(Lat.), **J.** (jahr) (Ger.), **r.** (rok)(Pol.) or **y.** year
yr. or **y.** younger; your
Y.R.A. Yacht Racing Association (Brit.)
yrs. yours
yrs., ann. (anni)(Lat.), **y.** or **yr.** years
Y.P.S.C.E. or **C.E.** Young People's Society of Christian Endeavor (cf. C.E.U.)
Y.P.S.L. Young People's Socialist League
y.s. yellow spot [of the retina]
Y.T. Yukon Territory (Can.)
Yt, Y or **Yb** ytterium (Chem.)
Yuc. Yucatán
Y.W. or **Y.W.C.A.** Young Women's Christion Association (cf. W.Y.W.C.A.)
Y.W.C.A. or **Y.W.** Young Women's Christian Association (cf. W.Y.W.C.A.)
Y.W.C.T.U. Young Women's Christian Temperance Union
Y.W.H.A. Young Women's Hebrew Association

Z

Z zenith distance (Astron.)
Z (Chem.), **At. No.** or **at. no.** atomic number
Z. (Zoll)(Ger.), **in** (Mil.) or **in.** inch
Z. (Zolle)(Ger.), **in.** or **ins.** inches
Z. or **z.** zone
z an unknown quantity
z. zero
z. or **Zn** zinc
Zach. Zacharia; Zacharias; Zachary
z.B. (zum Beispiel)(Ger.), **e.c.** (exemple causa)(Lat.), **e.g., ex.gr.** (exempli gratia)(Lat.), **f.e., f. Eks.** (for Eksempel) (Dan.), **f.i., n.p.** (na przysład)(Pol.), **p.ex.** (par exemple)(Fr.), **t. ex.** (till exempel)(Swed.), or **v.g.** (verbi gratia) (Lat.) for example; for instance
z. D. (zur Disposition)(Ger.) unattached
Zeb. Zebadiah; Zebedee
Zech. Zechariah
Zeph. Zephaniah
z.F. (zu Fuss)(Ger.) by foot
Z.G. Zoological Garden or Gardens
z. H. (zu Händen)(Ger.), **att., atten.** or **attn.** attention; to the attention
Zn or **z.** zinc
Z.O.A. Zionist Organization of America
Z of I Zone of the interior (Mil.)
zoochem. zoochemical; zoochemistry
zoogeog. zoogeographical; zoogeography
zool. zoological; zoologist; zoology
zooph. zoophytological; zoophytology
Zr zirconium (Chem.)
Z.S. Zoological Society
z.S. (zur Sache)(Ger.) relating to the matter
Ztg. (Zeitung)(Ger.) newspaper; journal (cf. jour.)
Ztr. (Zentner)(Ger.), **C., c., ctl.** or **cwt.** hundredweight; cental
Z.V. (Zollverein)(Ger.) Customs Union
zw. (zwischen)(Ger.), **bet., betn., betw., btwn.** or **m-** (meta-)(Greek) between
Z.Y.C. Zionist Youth Commission
Zz. (zingiber)(Lat.) ginger
z.Z. (zur Zeit)(Ger.) at the time

ZBT (Zeta Beta Tau) National undergraduate fraternity

ZKΨ (Zeta Kappa Psi) National undergraduate honor sorority (Forensics)

ZΦH (Zeta Phi Eta) National undergraduate sorority (Oratory)

ZΦΣ (Zeta Phi Sigma) National undergraduate sorority (Negroes)

ZΨ (Zeta Psi) National undergraduate fraternity

ZTA (Zeta Tau Alpha) National undergraduate sorority